A SIGNIFICANT IRISH EDUCATIONALIST

A Significant
Irish Educationalist

The Educational Writings of P. H. Pearse

Edited by

Séamas Ó Buachalla

THE MERCIER PRESS
Dublin and Cork

Buíochas

Gabhann na foilsitheoirí buíochas le Rialtas na hÉireann a thug deontas fial dóibh le go bhféadfaí an saothar seo a fhoilsiú.

The Mercier Press Limited,
25 Lower Abbey Street, Dublin 1
4 Bridge Street, Cork

A SIGNIFICANT IRISH EDUCATIONALIST
ISBN 85342 569 8
© Introductory Essay and Selection
Séamas Ó Buachalla, 1980

Printed in the Republic of Ireland by *The Leinster Leader,* Naas.

Table of Contents

Foreword

In collecting and editing Pearse's extensive educational writings, I have been motivated by a desire that his educational work be more widely known and that his role as an educationalist be evaluated on the evidence of his own writings. In an introductory essay I have attempted to provide an historical framework outlining the comtemporary educational developments in Ireland and Europe.

I have not included all of the educational writings from *An Claidheamh Soluis* which in editorials alone reach a total of a quarter of a million words; considerations of space and of relevance have imposed a policy of selection which I trust, does not distort the pattern of his educational thought.

I wish to record my indebtedness to Donnchadh Ó Súilleabháin and Séan Mac Mathúna of Conradh na Gaeilge for their kind assistance and to the staffs of the National Library and of Trinity College, for their courtesy and assistance.

Séamas Ó Buachalla,
Trinity College,
Dublin

March 1979.

TO ALL WHO HAVE LABOURED FOR
THE REFORM OF IRISH
EDUCATION

A Significant
Irish Educationalist

When W. B. Yeats sought in 'Easter 1916' to commemorate the leaders and personalities of the Rising whom he knew, he characterised Pearse solely in terms of his poetry and of St. Enda's, the school he founded:

> This man had kept a school
> And rode our winged horse.

It may seem strange that Yeats should select the schoolmaster and the poet as typifying the life-work of Pearse; many other observers would have regarded his achievements in the Gaelic League or his later political and revolutionary activities as more characteristic of a short life-span of thirty six years. It is significant that of the many facets of Pearse's life, his educational work has received relatively little attention either from political adherents or academic historians. This lack of attention is unexpected in view of the relative prominence of his educational activities which covered almost twenty years of his life. His early involvement in the Gaelic League convinced him of the primary importance of educational reform in securing 'the intellectual independence of Ireland', which represented a major objective of the League. His membership of the Education Committee of the League offered him an opportunity to gain an understanding of the education system and generated in him a deep interest in the issues which coloured educational controversy at the turn of the century. Even while still a university student, he had begun in occasional literary reviews to draw attention to educational issues and to anomalies which he observed in the educational system. It is hardly surprising then, that, on assuming the editorship of the weekly bilingual paper of the League, *An Claidheamh Soluis*, in March 1903, he proposed to include education among the wide range of topics covered in the paper.[1] His strong conviction on the central importance of education is echoed in an early editorial wherein he states: 'Take up the Irish problem at what point you may, you inevitably find yourself in the end back at the education question'.[2] Over the six years of his editorship he devoted considerable time and attention to educational issues ranging from curricular problems in the national or elementary school to the problems and controversies associated with the reform of university education. His active membership of various central committees of the League, especially the educational bodies, during the period of his editorship, afforded him a position of influence in determining educational policy and brought him into close contact with Eoin Mac Neill, Archbishop W. J. Walsh, Dr. Séan Mac Enrí, T. P. Mac Fhionlaoich, Rev. Professor M. O'Hickey, Professor Mary Hayden and other prominent League members who had an interest in education. His editorial position provided him with a weekly opportunity to publicise and disseminate the League's policies on the educational issues of the day while systematically developing his own skill as an educational writer and extending his knowledge of education. Over the period of his editorship there is scarcely an issue of *An Claidheamh Soluis* which does not contain an article on some aspect of education. Some of these articles are concerned with the internal controversies which surrounded the League's educational policies and as such do not have a direct relevance to the development of Pearse's educational thinking. The main body of the leading articles however and the weekly editorial commentary which appeared under the title 'Gleo na gCath' on the leader page, present a regular analysis of the main educational questions of the day according to the canons of the League's cultural programme. Pearse's teaching experience at both secondary and university levels afforded a solid practical base to his writing and provided an opportunity for keeping in touch with the opinions of teachers and school authorities and with the realities of the Irish classroom. In addition to his lecturing experience in University College and in the Gaelic League, and his tutorship at his old school, C.B.S. Westland Row, he was permanent teacher of Irish at Alexandra College, Earlsfort Terrace, from 1904, where his teaching ability and enthusiasm were publicly acknowledged.[3] In 1907 he acted as Extern Examiner for the Jesuit College at Clongowes Wood, Co. Kildare[4] and he lectured in Coláiste Laighean as well as in other Gaelic League Colleges. This wide teaching experience provides the foil to the weekly writing and also explains the comprehensive range of educational topics covered in *An Claidheamh Soluis.*

His writings on the Belgian education system and its bilingual policy which appeared in *An Claidheamh Soluis* in two series from August 1905 to March 1907 are of particular significance. In their empirical character they are matched only by his writings on St. Enda's which appeared in *An Macaomh* 1909-1913. These articles, 'Belgium and its Schools' are based on his visit to Belgium in July 1905, during which, with the cooperation of the Ministry of the Interior and Public Instruction, he visited up to thirty educational institutions, both public and private, from kindergarten and elementary schools to universities. They are divided into two series; the first series offers an account of the structure and anatomy of Belgian education and of the socio-political factors which influenced it; the second series is concerned more with pedagogy and offers a detailed analysis of the teaching methods observed especially in the realm of language teaching. The two series combine to present a comprehensive analysis of the structural and process features of Belgian education and of the socio-cultural matrix surrounding the system. This latter aspect of the articles, from a perspective of seventy years later may seem a commonplace in comparative education; in the first decade of the century it would have been directly in line with the new approach in comparative writing advocated by

M. E. Sadler and consequently rather unusual and innovative.[5]

Perhaps the single most significant benefit which Pearse derived from the Belgian visit was a deepening of his knowledge of bilingualism and his understanding of the related pedagogical issues. As a result of an earlier visit to Wales in 1899, as the Gaelic League delegate to the National Eisteddfod at Cardiff, he developed an interest in the educational aspects of language policy. The close contacts between the League in Dublin and the Cymmrodorion Society in Wales generated a common interest in bilingualism and prompted some common initiatives in cultural activities and educational policy.[6]

Pearse's specific interest in the Belgian educational system was due primarily to a comparative study by T. R. Dawes of Aberystwyth University, published in Cambridge in 1903 which was reviewed by Pearse. This study, *Bilingual Teaching in Belgian Schools* described the implementation of the bilingual policy in the schools visited by Dawes in the course of a travelling studentship which he spent in Belgium.[7] While Pearse had already written extensively on Bilingual Education prior to his Belgian visit[8] and had collaborated with Dr. W. J. Walsh in the preparation of a bilingual scheme five years earlier,[9] it was his Belgian visit in the summer of 1905 which crystallised his understanding and confirmed him in the conviction that bilingualism was the appropriate and most effective policy for Irish schools.

The article 'Education in the West of Ireland' differs in style and purpose from the rest of Pearse's educational writings but in its content and analysis it is very similar to the letter to the Dublin press on 'Irish in the Schools' of February 1900. This letter was part of a campaign organised by the League in which Mac Neill, Fr. O'Hickey and Miss Borthwick also participated. The four letters were published as a booklet by the League as *Irish in the Schools*. 'Education in the West of Ireland' was published in the Edinburgh Gaelic journal *Guth na Bliadhna* in 1905, for a readership which Pearse designated as 'my Scottish Gaelic friends'. Its style is characterised by a dramatic narrative quality and at times, reads very much like a short story with a rural setting. The piece had a very specific purpose — to inform the readers of the iniquitous language policy which had been and was being implemented in the schools of the Gaeltacht, the Irish-speaking districts in Ireland. The schools, in these districts, where Irish was the home language, ignored the language as an instrument in education; there were schools 'in which while the pupils speak no English, the teacher speaks no Irish'. These educational and linguistic incongruities, as well as the broader cultural inadequacies of the national schools, Pearse contends, would have been widely publicised, if they had happened in Poland, Finland or in Alsace-Lorraine. The control by Britain of the press agencies excludes the possibility of these issues being widely publicised; Pearse's article in the Edinburgh journal was an attempt to defeat the paper wall surrounding Ireland.

In the 1900 letter to the press, 'Irish in the Schools', Pearse displays a clear understanding of the educational principles involved in choice of medium of instruction in the elementary school and of the mutual interaction of first and second languages in the educational process. The content is logically arranged and the style is rational and coherent to a degree not frequently found in undergraduates of twenty years. This item of his writings shows Pearse to have developed a very early interest in educational policy and an ability to analyse systematically the contemporary issues which arose in Irish education — an ability which he developed further in the editorial chair of *An Claidheamh Soluis*.

In turning to the section of his educational writings dealing with St. Enda's, we encounter a new phase in Pearse the educationalist, a phase characterised by writing which is more personal and school-based, which chronicles the environment with which he surrounded his pupils and in which is outlined his philosophy of education. These writings on St. Enda's are composed of the articles 'By Way of Comment' from the four issues of the school journal, *An Macaomh* (June and Christmas 1909, Christmas 1910 and May 1913) and the article 'St. Enda's' which Pearse wrote for the first number of the bilingual journal of the Belfast Gaelic League, *An Craobh Ruadh*, in May 1913. In a document which Pearse drew up prior to his execution in May 1916, containing his instructions as to his literary works, he mentions the series of articles on St. Enda's which he had written for *An Macaomh* under the title 'By Way of Comment'. He had prepared a revised edition of these suitable for publication which 'form a continuous and more or less readable narrative of the history of St. Enda's from its foundation up to May 1913'. He asked that his former pupil and friend, Desmond Ryan, would write a further chapter on the fortunes of the school since 1913 and that the whole be published as a book under his editorship. This was done, and the composite volume appeared in August 1917 as *The Story of a Success* containing also, in addition to the original articles and Ryan's retrospective chapter, the article which Pearse wrote for the Belfast journal, *An Craobh Ruadh*. The volume was edited by Ryan in Cullenswood House to which the school had returned in May 1916 for the duration of the period during which The Hermitage in Rathfarnham was occupied by the British army.

These writings on St. Enda's are highly concentrated in their field of focus; they are concerned with the philosophy, ethos and spirit of the school, with the physical and aesthetic environment of the school in its two locations at Ranelagh and Rathfarnham and principally with those pedagogical features and innovations which characterised the school and distinguished it from other intermediate or secondary schools of its time in Ireland. Unlike the writings from *An Claidheamh Soluis* these articles are not so much concerned with structural features of the educational system nor with broad policy issues but with more fundamental classroom or process issues. Indeed they form an admirable professional guide to the individual teacher; in his introduction to the 1917 volume, Desmond Ryan describing these writings says 'As a teacher's handbook, one would have to travel far to find their equal'. They also afford an autobiographical glimpse of Pearse, of his buoyant resolute spirit in pursuit of a conviction, of his dedication to a cultural and educational ideal and of his sensitive response to the noble generosity of the few steadfast friends who made St. Enda's possible initially and guaranteed its continuity. Above all, these writings throw abundant light on Pearse the master, on his attitude to and respect for boys and on his deep understanding of their ways and on how they responded to his personality. Desmond Ryan asserts that to know Pearse it was essential to have known him as a teacher. From these writings, describing St. Enda's and its headmaster, it is obvious that he would have been an unusual teacher and that his school provided an uncommon, if not a unique, educational experience.

The growing involvement of Pearse in political activity and his growing support for political separatism, both of which are observable from about

1912, are clearly reflected in his educational writings. Those of his educational writings which are included in Section V are clearly conceived and written within the context of a rapidly changing political reality, a reality which had begun to leave the realm of the constitutional politics of the Irish Party and move inexorably towards the logic of a separatism which had both cultural and political dimensions.

The four items presented in Section V, include a lecture delivered in the Mansion House in December 1912, and published in *An Claidheamh Soluis* January 4th to March 1st in 1913, two articles in the *Irish Review* (February 1913 and June 1914) and a series of three articles on Irish Education published in *Irish Freedom* for the issues of February, March and April of 1913. These four items constitute a unit in that they contain some common ideas and concepts but also, in that they represent in Pearse's educational thinking, the interaction of his St. Enda's phase with the earlier phase of educational journalist and editor. The writings in this section represent the resultant of the two earlier phases, the early emphasis upon policy and structure and the later phase, coterminous with the *Macaomh* articles which emphasised the inner workings of the educational process. These articles show Pearse groping towards a synthesis — a synthesis which identifies both the major weaknesses in the existing educational system and the essential features which should characterise a true education. Furthermore this synthesis, besides offering an analysis and critique, identifies in general terms the ideal education system which an independent Ireland should seek — a system vivified by 'the divine breath that moves through free peoples, the breath that no man in Ireland has felt in his nostrils for so many centuries'.[10] These writings in their emphasis upon Home Rule, reflect the sustained political controversy which centred on the third Home Rule Bill introduced by the Liberal government of Asquith in April 1912.

The Murder Machine, which constitutes section VI of the writings, is the item by which Pearse is most widely known as an educationalist; it also represents the apex and terminal point of his educational writings. In it are crystallised and distilled much of the educational ideals and concepts found at greater length in the earlier writings, especially those from the period after the foundation of St. Enda's. The compact and coherent structure of the work exercises a certain effect on the reader; that effect however is enhanced significantly by the dramatic quality of the writing. The reader is acutely aware that a political dimension has imparted a new compelling urgency to the educational innovations which Pearse suggests are needed to break the Murder Machine. Its murderous character resided in its weakness in regard to basic educational considerations and in its fundamental anti-national dimension. Mere reform would not be adequate; an act of creation was necessary. This creative act by which the various branches would be drawn into an organic whole and the national factor restored to the educational system would have a high priority in a free Ireland. That national factor involved much more than the restoration of a national culture: 'It has to restore manhood to a race that has been deprived of it'. According to Pearse in *The Murder Machine*, the English education system in Ireland, by eliminating the national factor, had succeeded so well in making slaves, that the slaves no longer were conscious of their slavery. To achieve the abolition of that slavery required educational reform as much as it required political independence.

The New Education Movement 1890-1920

In Europe, the decades which preceded and followed the birth of the twentieth century witnessed many developments and initiatives in education which, while having some general common features, scarcely enjoyed the cohesion or the homogeneity usually associated with a united movement. Attitudinal changes in the political, socio-cultural and economic spheres in many European countries produced a disenchantment with aspects of the nineteenth century and generated heightened expectations in relation to the new century. It was widely believed that scientific technology and the associated political enlightenment, already apparent and expected to blossom further in the new century, would enable modern man to overcome those deep social and economic problems whose emergence in the late nineteenth century characterised the fabric of European society. These general expectations were enhanced in the field of education by factors deriving from the nature of educational provision in the decaying century and from some emerging seminal ideas in pedagogy, sociology and psychology. Furthermore the rigidity in educational theory and practice, so characteristic of the Victorian age, had produced a counter-movement, a rejection of the *Instrumentary Education*, whose narrow literary curriculum and prescribed methodology, epitomised the education then available in most European countries. Developments in social legislation which promoted greater state involvement in housing, welfare and health, had an associated effect in educational systems by creating a wide expectation of greater public responsibility for educational provision. In general, social reform agencies tended to identify educational reform as a matter of high priority and the thrust of their innovations tended to reinforce the pedagogic changes contained in the New Education.

The challenge posed to the established economic and industrial orders by the rapid growth in the economies of Germany and the United States was interpreted frequently as possessing a direct educational dimension. The technological advances which fuelled the German economic miracle of the turn of the century owed as much to reform in technical and higher education as it did to native talent, application and industry. The complacency and falling capacity of the British economy of the same period was traced by many observers to an educational system in need of drastic reform.

Though the *New Education* lacked the cohesion of a regular movement, it is possible to identify some of its component parts and to chart its manifestations in different countries. It is also possible to characterise some basic pedagogic principles and concepts which permeated its institutions and inspired the work of its leading groups and individuals. In essence, while each of the groups which constituted the *New Education* had a particular reform emphasis or theoretical stance, they were united in their opposition to the instrumentary education of the last century and to the educational practices which were inevitably associated with funding systems based on examination performance such as the 'payment-by-results' system. While each group criticised the curricular restriction of the three R's and the pedagogy which placed a premium on rote memory and pupil passivity, each in turn proposed new subject areas or new approaches to existing curricular elements. The inertia found frequently in educational systems and the discontinuity between the educational process and the larger external world were both found in an aggravated form in the education of the last century. It forced the teacher to pursue a limited educational objective by methods derived from pedagogic criteria, which paid scant attention to the needs of the individual child. It should not be assumed however that the motives which inspired these various reform groups can be classified as focussing singularly on pupil welfare and educational principle; some arose from social and political ideology, others from moral principles and utilitarian considerations, others still can be traced to a desire to apply the theories of eminent pedagogues or the empirical findings of scientific research. The rise of the *New Education* should not be envisaged as a simple case of the victory of enlightenment over obscurantism; many of the educational ills of the nineteenth century in all European countries, were a function of inadequate financial resources, the low professional status of teachers and sub-standard school premises.

While some groups defy unique classification labels it is possible following Selleck's system to identify six distinct groups or sub-movements which participated in the *New Education* and contributed to its development; these were the Practical Educationalists, the Social Reformers, the Naturalists, the Herbartians, the Scientific Educationalists and the Moral Educationalists.[11]

The Practical Educationalists were concerned with introducing practical subjects or 'Hand and Eye' subjects into the curriculum of the elementary school. In some countries the inclusion of such subjects was an overt attempt to utilise the educational system to raise the national industrial and economic efficiency, on the principle 'that trade will follow the flag only if education precedes it'.[12] The educational value of such practical subjects was recognised and proclaimed by many educators to be the major consideration advocating the inclusion of drawing, woodwork, physical education, nature study and science in the normal curriculum.

The main impetus in the recognition of the educational value of these subjects came from the educational systems of Finland and Sweden and the pioneering work of Cygnaeus and Salomon respectively. Otto Cygnaeus (1810-1888), as Director of Education, introduced the Slojd system of handwork as an essential subject in the elementary school. His pedagogic approach was examined by Otto Salomon (1849-1907), a Swedish Inspector of Schools, who established at Naas a world-famous centre for teacher education in Slojd work, an institution which influenced developments in many countries.

In addition to advocating new subjects the Practical Educationalists sought also to alter the methods employed in teaching such subjects as geography, history, language and mathematics and to modify the emphasis placed on the more abstract realms of these subjects. In science teaching a new importance was attached to experimental work based on the Heuristic Method advocated by Armstrong of Edinburgh.[13] The introduction of practical subjects helped to make learning an active experience for the pupil, and liberated both him and teacher from the excessive bondage of books which characterised the old education; furthermore according to H. T. Mark, 'it directed the attention of teacher and pupil towards the world in which they lived'.[14]

In the context of instrumentary education, the typical school was concerned solely with the intellectual training of the pupil in a narrow and limited set of skills; by the second decade of this century many schools were beginning to show the impact of changes which sought to promote the 'overall development of the child' by means of a wider curriculum and a modified school environment. These modifications in the environment were

xv

designed to enable the school to cater for the physical, recreational and aesthetic, as well as the moral and cultural aspects of the child's development. The Social Reformers as a recognisable group within the *New Education* were mainly responsible for the introduction of physical education, school meals, medical inspection and special education for handicapped children, the modernisation of school buildings, fittings and furniture and especially in generating a concept of education as an agent of social change and reform. In addition they were mainly responsible for democratising the provision, administration and access to education and the extension of technical and secondary education facilities.

In many countries the innovative mechanism involved voluntary groups providing some new school feature or agitating for its introduction and eventually convincing the public authority to undertake its provision. The 'drill' of the instrumentary education, which was replaced by physical education and organised games in the *New Education,* in its content and utilitarian purpose owed more to military needs than educational considerations. The development of the Ling or Swedish system of physical exercises (1814) and its introduction into other European educational systems helped significantly to liberate the school playgrounds from the tyranny of army drill sergeants whose exercises normally were more suited to army recruits than to school children. Besides its utilitarian value, the conventional 'drill' was invested with a high moral and disciplinary value as were many of the practices of the schools of the last century.

The educational policies of the Social Reformers were grounded in the general egalitarian principles which informed the socialist and trade union movements of the period.[15] If some of the Social Reformers placed undue confidence in the schools as agents of social engineering, they can be forgiven for not recognising in the early century what is only becoming crystal clear in the closing decades — that education is not an autonomous agent and that educational reform is no substitute for social reform. The efforts of the Social Reformers were instrumental in ushering in a new era in political attitudes to education and in creating a more humane atmosphere in schools. The long-term impact of their pioneering work is best observed in the complex structural reforms which were introduced in European education after World War II.

The Naturalist movement owed its influence in the *New Education* to a re-awakening of interest in the works of Pestalozzi and Froebel and to innovative practices derived from the writings of Montessori, Dewey and Homer Lane. In the sense that it produced a universally recognisable educational unit in the kindergarten, the Naturalist movement may be seen to have exerted a fundamental influence; the progressive schools of Europe and America were the most flamboyant contribution of the Naturalists to the New Education. Johann Heinrich Pestalozzi (1746-1827) and his student Friedrich Wilhelm Froebel (1782-1852) are by no means identical in their philosophical systems, yet they have some ideas in common from which it is possible to fabricate a coherent set of pedagogic principles and practices. They proposed that the development of man should be in accord with nature and that the aim of education should be the harmonious development of the faculties and dispositions, the unfolding of the latent forces and powers and the fostering of the growth of personality. Froebel's concept of the unity of all life and the discrete nature of each individual stage of life, the recognition of childhood as a life phase with its own needs and not an imperfect form of adult life are of major significance. Such an autonomous concept of childhood posited the need for new approaches to the infant and elementary school. It is possible to identify some common principles of the Naturalists which have a direct bearing on the classrooms of the *New Education*:

(i)   The educational process was a matter of developing the powers and unfolding the latent energies of the pupil. According to Holmes 'the function of education is to foster growth'.[16]

(ii) In the educational process the pupil needs a marked degree of freedom. Montessori would regard the liberty of the pupil as a fundamental principle.[17]

(iii) The role of the teacher was not that of dominant overlord but that of servant of the learning process. The child was the real actor in the drama of school life.

(iv) The pupil is not an imperfect adult and the teacher's role is not to form pupils to his/her own image.

One of the most active British educators of the Naturalist group Margaret Macmillan, has clearly expressed the social concern which inspired their work in asserting that 'we must try to educate every child as if he were our own and just as we would educate our own'.[18] The Froebelian metaphor of the plant and the garden proved very fruitful in developing a style of teaching methodology which was highly compatible with general Naturalist principles.

Towards the end of the last century, the followers and systematic philosophic works of Johann Friedrich Herbart (1776-1841) were partly responsible for introducing a scholarly discipline into the study of educational problems. His central contribution, his theory of mental processes, in turn generated an associated systematic approach to instructional methodology popularly known as the Herbartian Steps. In Europe and America by the first decade of this century Herbartian principles and Herbartian textbooks for elementary teachers were dominant forces in training colleges. Although to Herbart, instruction as an element in the educational process was less important than the development of humane convictions and character, to many teachers seeking the assurance of a compact procedural system, his Instrumental Steps became the essence of his theory. The formalism and the inevitable sterility which later masqueraded under the banner of Herbartian methodology does less than justice to the noble ideals expressed in his *Science of Education* and his *Brief Encyclopaedia of Practical Philosophy*.

In practice, Herbartianism espoused a wide curriculum making no distinction between the humanities, the sciences and the practical subjects; by means of the formal steps in the typical lesson the quality of instruction was improved and the range of pupil activity was extended. By the 1880's Herbartianism was widely accepted and acclaimed in the United States, mainly through the work of Herbart's followers at Leipzig — Stoy, Rein, and Ziller. One of the significant outcomes of Herbartianism, mainly due to Ziller, is the concept of *concentration* in the curriculum. Ziller proposed that a special position be accorded to those subjects believed most likely to promote character formation i.e. religion, history and literature. This concept finds an echo in the modern concept of the 'core' curriculum.

The element of the *New Education* which was slowest to exert a detectable influence on the schools was that of the scientific educators who from the end of the last century sought to systematise the study of education along scientific lines. With the publication in 1879 of Bain's

Education as a Science, the movement to construct a science of education founded upon experimental procedures found a focus for action; by 1901 when the British Association for the Advancement of Science formally accepted education as a discipline, the movement's future was assured.

In the development of the scientific approach, an early and significant lead was given by some eminent scientists who applied their professional techniques to the study of their own children, as Piaget was to do some decades later with such seminal consequences. Charles Darwin's *Biographical Sketch of an Infant* (1877) and Wilhelm Preyer's *The Mind of the Child* (1881) were influential and early examples of such 'domestic' experimental studies.

The impetus in the promotion of the scientific education which switched during the nineties from Germany to America had in turn reverted to Europe during the first decade of the new century. It found expression in the work of such pioneers at Wundt at Leipzig, Hall, Cattell and Thorndike in America, Galton and Binet in Europe. The rapid development of the associated statistical techniques by Pearson, Spearman and Terman accelerated the quantitative analysis of educational problems and the emergence of standardised tests. Those early developments however were only marginally relevant to the work of the average schoolroom in the early decades of this century; it required the quantitative educational expansion of the forties and later decades to afford adequate scope to empirical analysis and provide resources for scientific educational research in many systems.

Among those associated with the movement for Moral Education were many influences and organisations, seeking a wide variety of reforms which find only a vague group identity in the term 'Moral Education'. Some were overtly religious, others were political, while others arose from the coincidence of the liberalising influence of educational reform and the loosening of the adherence of many to rigid doctrinal teaching. According to Michael Sadler, the prominent English pioneering comparative educationalist, moral education was the heart of the modern educational problem; he saw moral education as offering the only adequate protection against the changes and the weakening of established tradition so characteristic of the modern age.[19] The moral education movement was much wider in its scope than the ethical and external behavioural aspects normally associated with the term. Due to the relative rise and fall of European states in economic and prestige terms, the moral education movement frequently was seen as part of the process of nation building and national aggrandisement. Consequently it was envisaged in many countries as involving the promotion of patriotism, civic responsibility and common national ideals. While those who advocated the need to promote moral education differed as to its precise content and objectives, the schools were unanimously regarded as the natural agency by which it should be provided. In an educational issue which lacked precise specification it is not surprising that the role of the teacher should offer a focus for deep controversy. The moral educators were fundamentally divided on the relative merits of direct and indirect instruction. Those who favoured direct methods advocated explicit teaching in a systematic fashion using the conventional lesson format; the advocates of indirect instruction emphasised the general ethos and disciplinary environment of the school and relied on the incidental use of school activities and lesson material in promoting moral instruction. This difference as to methodology signalled a much deeper controversy as to the nature of the school as a social unit, its organisational structure and the individual as a member of a social entity. Thus those schools which advocated and permitted student participation in school organisation and provided various 'freedoms with responsibilities' were attempting to reduce to intelligible practice the tenets and principles of indirect moral education.

The *New Education* movement had a profound effect on the schools of many countries not in a systematic homogeneous manner but rather by playing a catalytic or innovative role. It possessed no sacred books on basic tenets or theories; nor did it have a centralised coherent structure though it did find later some international organisational links. It was characterised by some basic new approaches to the educational process which were made manifest in a number of experimental schools and in the education works of a number of individuals. Though geographically dispersed, these individuals and their schools form a significant network of innovation which merits a brief examination. Inevitably the innovative schools of the New Education, because they were challenging the ethos and philosophy of the public school system, were impelled to do so from a position outside that system. Their apparent elitism or selectivity was not always an inherent characteristic of the movement; it arose from the nature of this innovative strategy. They were most unlikely to be allowed to function within a public system whose operational tenets they rejected unquestionably.

In Germany educational reform and innovation were especially fruitful in the quarter century before the outbreak of World War I. At the University of Jena, Wilhelm Rein, through his teacher training school and his textbook *Pedagogik im Grundriss*, exercised a wide innovative influence. One of his colleagues, Hermann Lietz (1868-1919), having examined educational practice and school organisation in Germany and England founded a series of Landerziehungsheime or Country Boarding Schools of which four are still functioning. From the early Lietz schools experienced masters left to found their own schools, the most innovative of whom was Paul Geheeb (1870-1961). Geheeb, whose educational work was inspired largely by the neo-humanism of Goethe, Schiller and Fichte, introduced some new organisational features at Wickersdorf which he founded in 1906 and in Odenwald founded in 1910. These Frei Schulgemeinde were co-educational, catered for children aged 9-19, were organised in family units and held weekly assemblies of pupils and masters to discuss routine school government. Geheeb leaving Germany in 1935 founded a similar school in Switzerland, L'Ecole de l'Humanité.

These early German schools developed close links with the English reformer, Cecil Reddie (1858-1932) and the school he founded at Abbotsholme in Derbyshire. Rein's influence on Reddie when visiting Jena was matched by the significant impression made on Lietz by Reddie's school, where he taught for a year. Reddie's educational philosophy was dominated by the concept of the school as a miniature state with a specific role in the preparation of leaders of the nation. He replaced the usual contemporary emphasis on competitive games by compulsory practical farm and garden work. Since Abbotsholme never attracted more than forty pupils and inspired only one other foundation, that founded at Bedales by Badley, it seems that Reddie's main role in the *New Education* movement lay more in the field of publicising his own achievements abroad than in significantly modifying English educational practice.

The French educational system to which the Napoleonic Laws and the Guizot Scheme of 1833 had imparted a strong homogeneity and uniformity came in contact with the new schools through the sociologist Edmond Demolins. In 1897 his analysis of contemporary Europe prompted him to attribute a claimed Anglo-Saxon superiority to the excellence of the British educational system.[20] His book, on translation into English in 1898, attracted international attention and publicity to the three non-typical schools upon which Demolins has based his assessment of the English system. In 1898 he published *L'Education Nouvelle* in which he advocated radical changes in French education which would develop a generation offering initiative and leadership in contrast to the conformity and mediocrity promoted by the traditional French schools. To demonstrate that his reforms were realisable, he founded L'Ecole de Roches in Normandy, strongly modelled on Bedales, offering in splendid rural surroundings an education which sought to develop initiative and whose animating spirit was freedom. This school emphasised the individual development of students, offered a broad curriculum which included outdoor pursuits and practical subjects, promoted student involvement in school organisation and stressed those qualities of leadership and community service so characteristic of the scout movement in which it participated.

These schools in Germany, France and Britain form a homogeneous group sharing some common important features of organisation and philosophy; they were further linked later by the system developed by Ferriere for the identification of New Schools which he based entirely on the Reddie-Lietz schools.

The work of Montessori and Decroly, both of whom became involved in educational reform by means of their medical work for the physically handicapped, made a significant contribution to the *New Education* and led to the foundation of new school types. Maria Montessori (1869-1952) adopted and developed some of the earlier practices and theories of Seguin for the education of the mentally defective. The application of her method to normal children especially its application to the children of the tenements of Rome and its elaboration by means of her written works aroused world-wide interest[21]. In the Montessori system, the child is provided with a specially designed learning environment in which to develop graded skills; the teacher's role is that of kindly manager of that environment.

Ovide Decroly (1871-1932) was initially interested in the problems of the mentally maladjusted but having founded the Institute for Abnormal Children at Uccle (Brussels), he quickly saw the potential of the 'learning for living' method for the education of the normal child. In 1907, he founded his school for normal children in which a variety of workshop classrooms provided the environment by which the individual learning needs of each child were catered for according to a well designed plan based on centres of interest. Guided by Decroly's work, Edouard Claparède (1873-1940) advocated in Geneva the importance of providing an education suitable to each child's needs and aptitudes and was one of the founders in 1912 of the Institut J. J. Rouseau which has been the centre of important pedagogic research.

Developments outside of Europe were not so numerous; yet in India and in the United States schools were founded which were in many respects institutional cousins of the Rein-Lietz foundations. The Indian poet and dramatist Rabindranath Tagore, founded his sanctuary school at

Santiniketan near Calcutta in 1901. This school, based on the ashram or forest sanctuary principle offered a haven of peace and solitude to adults and children where both teachers and pupils lived together as one family. Tagore's school offered an opportunity to its pupils to learn art in the studios of artists who lived in the sanctuary; similarly with music and other practical subjects. Tagore wrote poetry and drama which the students presented. The school was initially opposed to having any link with external examining agencies but eventually affiliated with Calcutta University and its matriculation system. In 1922 an Agricultural College was added to the Sancturay school by Elmhirst who later established Darlington Hall in Devon. There are interesting links between Pearse and Tagore; W. B. Yeats, the poet, in a lecture on Tagore described his ashram school as 'the Indian St. Enda's' and Pearse's play *An Ri* was produced by the pupils of Tagore's school in 1915.

The schools of the New Education, diverse in origin and organisation displayed a common basic stance on educational reform; they were committed to the democratic concept of the individual's importance and to providing an education which allowed the student the freedom to develop his talents and personality. These schools had one further common link. They were bound together by the inspiration of the Swiss educationalist Adolf Ferrière (1879-1960) who in 1899 founded the International Bureau of New Schools. Through the Bureau, he built up a network of individuals and institutions, organised meetings and conferences and in 1926 merged his organisation with the International Bureau of Education founded in 1925 in Geneva.

Irish Education 1890-1920

The period coterminous with Pearse's active life was characterised by a growing public debate on the Irish educational system, by government concern with various aspects of expenditure and control in education and by a significant movement of cultural nationalism spearheaded by the Gaelic League which sought to replace the anti-national imperial ethos which dominated the schools by a system which was unashamedly national in tone and inspiration.

By the end of the last century, elementary education, which encompassed the educational experience of the majority, was provided in national schools established under the Stanley scheme of 1831. These were clerically managed on a denominatial basis, covered the age range 6-16 and were under the general direction of the Commissioners of National Education who exercised fiscal and curricular control. The teachers of the national schools were trained in training colleges which were government funded, clerically managed and denominationally divided.

Education beyond the elementary stage was provided, for a fortunate minority in secondary schools or colleges; these prepared students in a classical curriculum for examinations organised by the Commissioners of Intermediate Education established by an Act of 1878. Under this limited scheme, the main function of the Commissioners was to conduct annual examinations upon the results of which they paid grants to schools on the principle of 'payment-by-results' a mechanism introduced by Robert Lowe in Britain, some decades earlier. There was no provision for the establishment, accreditation or inspection of schools; examination criteria were the sole arbiters of excellence in the secondary schools. University education was available in two universities, Dublin University, whose single institution, Trinity College, was founded in 1591 and the Royal University of Ireland, a non-teaching institution founded in 1879, which assimilated the already existing Queen's Colleges in Cork, Galway and Belfast. During the first decade of this century university reorganisation was a major theme in the educational debate. Trinity College was not acceptable to the Catholic Bishops who had in 1875 legislated against Catholic students attending there; in theory the former Queen's Colleges were not favoured by episcopal approval and the only higher education available to Catholics was that provided by the remnants of Newman's Catholic University and in some colleges which prepared students for the examinations of the Royal University. Two Commissions on University education, reporting in 1903 and 1907, failed to provide an acceptable solution; it was Birrell's Bill of 1908 which, by establishing the National University of Ireland created a multi-college institution and satisfied a long-standing grievance.

Technical and scientific education was provided under the aegis of the Department of Agriculture and Technical Instruction, established in 1899 under the enlightened Horace Plunkett. This government agency, besides promoting technical education on a permanent basis, also funded the teaching of scientific and technical subjects in secondary schools and trained teachers of these subjects.

The position and status of teachers at both primary and secondary levels was a source of major and continuing controversy; primary teachers were frequently caught in cross fire between the church authorities and the Commissioners while both Churches and the state sought to have a teaching body which was subservient and docile. Secondary teachers did not have any organised body representing their interests until 1909 when the Association of Secondary Teachers of Ireland was founded; they were the casual employees of schools suffering from inadequate funding and enjoyed neither security of tenure and adequate salary nor the professional status deriving from contractual arrangements. The Irish National Teachers' Organisation founded in 1868 had by the end of the century been placed under ecclesiastical ban in two of the provinces of the country for seeking protection for its members against summary dismissal by school managers.[22] During the second decade of the century, both the primary and the secondary teachers organised strikes to secure improvements in salary and employment conditions.

Pedagogic and curricular changes of a radical nature were attempted in both primary and secondary schools at the turn of the century. These were inspired by the prevailing currents of educational thinking on the continent and by the growing disenchantment with the 'payment-by-results' system and its uniform syllabuses. The Belmore Commission (1897) which examined the role of manual and practical instruction in primary schools recommended a more balanced curriculum.[23] As a result the national schools acquired a new revised programme in 1900, which sought to liberate their pedagogy from the tyranny of books and included various 'hand and eye' subjects in a curriculum which was inspired by a Froebelian philosophy and the Slojd movement. In the secondary schools similar curricular reforms followed the recommendations of the Commission on Intermediate Education of 1898; diversification was introduced in 1902 whereby a Classical Grammar and a Modern Course were made available as alternatives and the following year this principle was extended by the inclusion of two further options, a Scientific and a Mathematical course.

Whereas English appeared as a required subject in each of the courses, the Irish language did not — an issue which was of concern to the Gaelic League. The League won a major victory in 1904 with the introduction of the Bilingual Programme in the primary schools whereby in districts where Irish was the vernacular, or in bilingual districts, both languages could be taught or used as instructional media.

Various commissions of inquiry examined aspects of the education system at the end of the last and during the opening decades of this century. Curricular matters were the main concern of the Belmore and Vice-Regal Commissions which reported in 1898 on the primary and secondary schools respectively.[24] The Robertson Commission of 1903 and the Fry Commission which reported in 1907 examined the question of higher education and the relationship of existing institutions to the proposed new university.[25] Two significant surveys of primary and secondary education were conducted by F. H. Dale, an English inspector, in 1904 and 1905; in the latter survey he was assisted by another colleague, T. A. Stephens.[26] Relations between teachers in national schools and the Inspectors was the main issue examined by the Dill Inquiry of 1913.[27] Extensive reforms of Irish education were recommended in the reports of the Killanin and Molony Commissions of 1918.[28] During the first two decades of the century, localised popular control of education was a recurring element of official policy, especially during the Liberal administrations. The Irish Devolution Bill of 1907 was one such measure which generated major controversy. Pearse was one of the small number of nationalists who openly supported the Bill because 'it gave control of Irish education to the Irish people'; his support for the bill drew sharp criticism from many quarters of the Gaelic League.[29]

The Gaelic League, although its fundamental objective was the restoration of the Irish language as a vernacular, proved to be one of the main advocates of educational reform in the period. Dr. Douglas Hyde President of the League, giving evidence before the Robertson Commission in 1902, said a major aim of the League was 'to reform all education in Ireland from the national school to the university'.[30] This identification of the League with educational reform is further evidenced in an editorial by Pearse in 1904 when he declared:

> Had the education of the country been sane and national for the last hundred years, there would never have been a necessity for the language movement.[31]

In the period from the mid-nineties to the early twenties, Irish educational issues were frequently the subject of popular controversy and were keenly discussed in the cultural and political journals of the day. The League both utilised and developed this popular interest to make educational reform a central element in its own programme of cultural renewal. It succeeded in extending the constituency in which these educatioonal topics were discussed from the restricted circle of those professionally or managerially involved to the general arena of popular interest. This it did by informing the public by means of its weekly bilingual newspaper, *An Claidheamh Soluis*, by the publication of pamphlets on various issues and by organising national campaigns on specific questions. Arising from his membership of many of the League committees, Pearse was deeply involved in the elaboration and implementation of its educational policies. As editor of *An Claidheamh Soluis* 1903-1909, he was instrumental in making educational issues matters of public interest, in moulding public opinion and in educating League members in a national philosophy whereby they would regard 'the education of its children as the most important secular problem that can engage the thoughts of a people'.[32] In his educational work in the League, he was joined by a group of fellow workers who shared his conviction on the importance of education in the national context; this group included Eoin Mac Neill who became first Minister of Education in the Irish Free State, Fr. Dineen the noted scholar and lexicographer, Mary Hayden the historian, Dr. Michael O'Hickey of Maynooth and a host of teachers in many parts of the country. In his case however his educational work was coloured by an international dimension which was lacking in many of his contemporaries who were concerned with education in Ireland. He had established a network of contacts in Wales, Scotland, Belgium, France and Denmark, in which educational questions figured predominantly. He became familiar with current educational issues in Europe and America by means of published official reports and personal visits and had a detailed knowledge of language issues in a number of European countries. His educational theories on freedom and inspiration in education, on individual differences, on nature study and school environment, on language teaching and bilingualism, and on the role and status of the teacher place him securely within the *New Education* movement. The principles on which he conducted St. Enda's, the wide curriculum on offer, his concern for the individual student's needs, the environment of self motivation and freedom which he created for his pupils render him worthy to be grouped with such European innovators as Rein, Lietz, Reddie, Demolins and Ferrière, who also opened up new pedagogic avenues by means of the pioneering work of their schools. Following his study tour of Belgian schools in 1905, he maintained close ties with Mons. Alfons Tas, a noted Belgian educator and with a number of his schools; he organised exchange schemes whereby boys from St. Enda's spent periods in Belgium and some Belgian students came to school in Dublin. His committed nationalism would seem to have been complemented by an enlightened internationalism which advocated for other cultures the acceptability and respect which he demanded for that of his own country.

It is quite obvious that education dominated Pearse's life almost from the time when he graduated from school in 1896. In a letter written in 1908, he wrote that his chief hobby had been the study of education in all its phases.[33] The range of the educational writings contained in this collection demonstrates the industry with which he applied himself to his hobby. By any criteria, his educational work was significant, original, extensive and progressive; his wider recognition as an innovative educationalist has been impeded by the manner in which his literary and political achievements have tended to obscure its significance in the popular image. The availablity of his collected writings on education may accelerate the belated recognition of his educational work in its Irish and European dimensions.

References

1. Letter to Mrs. M. Hutton, 9.9.1903.
2. *An Claidheamh Soluis,* 18.4.1904.
3. *Alexandra College Magazine,* June 1904, p. 43.
4. Letters to Pearse from Fr. P. J. Connolly, S.J., 13.3.1907, 19.3.1907.
5. Sadler, M. E., 'The School in Some of its Relations to Social Organisation and National Life' in *Sociological Society Papers.* London, 1906.
6. Southall, J. E., *Wales and her Language.* London 1893.
7. Dawes, T. R., *Bilingual Teaching in Belgian Schools.* Cambridge U.P. 1890.
8. *An Claidheamh Soluis,* 2.1.1904, 9.1.1904, 16.1.1904, 23.1.1904 etc.
9. Letters to Dr. W. J. Walsh from Pearse, 22.11.1900, 22.12.1900, 19.12.1900.
10. *The Murder Machine.* Political Writings and Speeches, p. 50.
11. Selleck, R. J. W., *The New Education,* London, 1968.
12. Magnus, L., 'Aims and Efforts' in Magnus, L. (ed.), *Educational Aims and Efforts.* London, 1910.
13. Armstrong, H. E., *The Teaching of Scientific Method.* London, 1910.
14. Mark, H. T., *The New Movement in Education,* London, 1904.
15. Simon, B., *Education and the Labour Movement,* 1870-1920, London, 1965.
16. Holmes, E. G. A., *What is and What Might Be,* London, 1912.
17. Montessori, M., *The Montessori Method,* London 1912.
18. Lowndes, G. A. N., *Margaret Macmillan,* London, 1960.
19. Sadler, M. (ed.), *Modern Instruction and Training in Schools,* London, 1908.
20. Demolins, E., *A Quoi Aient la Superiorité de Inglo-Saxons?,* Paris, 1897.
21. Montessori, M., *The Discovery of the Child,* Madras, 1963.
22. O'Connell, T. J., *One Hundred Years of Progress,* Dublin, 1968, p. 58.
23. Commission on Manual and Practical Instruction in Primary Schools (Belmore), Final Report 1898. (Cd. 8923) H.C.
24. Commission on Intermediate Education (Ireland) 1898. H.C. 1899, xxii, xxiii.
25. Royal Commission on University Education in Ireland. H.C. 1902 and 1903.
26. Report of F. H. Dale on Primary Education in Ireland (Cd. 1891) H.C. 1904. Report of F. H. Dale and T. A. Stephens on Intermediate Education in Ireland (Cd. 2546), H.C. 1905.
27. Vice-Regal Committee of Inquiry into Primary Education (Ireland) 1913. Final Report, 1914, (Cd. 7235).
28. Vice-Regal Committee of Inquiry into Primary Education (Ireland) 1918. Final Report, (Cd. 60) H.C. 1919. Vice-Regal Committee on the Conditions of Service and Remuneration of Teachers in Intermediate Schools etc., (Cd. 66) H.C. 1919.
29. *An Claidheamh Soluis,* editorials. 11.5.1907, 18.5.1907, 25.5.1907.
30. *Irish in University Education,* Gaelic League Pamphlet No. 29. Dublin, 1902.
31. *An Claidheamh Soluis,* 13.8.1904.
32. ibid., 28.5.1904.
33. Letter to P. Mac Manus, 4.3.1908, N.L.I. Ms. 18578.

An Claidheamh Soluis

THE ISSUE AT STAKE
14.3.1903

The Gaelic League stands for the intellectual independence of Ireland.
That sums up its programme in a sentence. It is well to emphasise the
point here on the eve of Language Week. On Sunday next the greatest
demonstration that the streets of Dublin have ever seen will take place in
our capital. On St. Patrick's Day practically all Ireland will unite in paying
national honours to the National Apostle. On Wednesday a great meeting
will assemble in the Rotunda to deliberate on some of the most pressing
problems which confront Irish Ireland. Throughout the week a collection
for the Language Fund will be made in every parish where the standard of
Irish Ireland has been raised. The immediate object of the demonstration
and collection is to place at the disposal of the League the funds necessary
for carrying on the work of organising the Irish-speaking areas. But, taken
in conjunction with the St. Patrick's Day Festival — the work, of course, of
the men of the League — Seachtmhain na Gaedhilge has a wider, deeper
significance. It is a symbol of the national character of the League's
propaganda. It is a sign and a token to all whom it may concern that the
language question has, once and for all, been set high on the national plane,
and placed in the very forefront of the vital questions of the hour in Ireland.

This is no mere academic movement, no mere literary cult. This is a
movement which touches the nation's life. No academic movement, no
literary cult, has ever had at its back the passion, the stark earnestness, the
brave self-sacrifice that have characterised the language movement. A
movement like ours cannot fail. There is something irresistible in sheer
conviction, in downright doggedness. We have taken the advice given by a
great Churchman to the toilers in another movement: we have set our faces
like iron against the opposition of good men and bad.

The young men who founded the League grasped primary truths, and
clung to them as shipwrecked men cling to a plank. They gripped the fact
that the language of this country enshrines the mind and soul of this
country. That was the first step. They then grasped that other primary fact,
that a language is a living energising force only so long as it is a living idiom
on the lips of living men and women. From that moment forth the
programme of the Gaelic League was shaped: it was to conserve the living

1

Irish language as the living medium for expressing the thoughts of this land.

That programme has never been lost sight of. It is only within the last twelve months, however, that the League has really succeeded in touching the heart of the question. It has been enabled to do that largely as the result of its call to the nation last Language Week. It now repeats that call. What is the nation going to do?

On the success of Seachtmhain na Gaedhilge depends the extent to which the League can operate on the Irish-speaking districts during the coming twelve months. On the organisation of the Irish-speaking districts depends the life or death of the language. On the life or death of the language depends the life or death of the nation. That is the issue at stake.

THE UNIVERSITY COMMISSION REPORT
28.3.1903

We are concerned with the Report of the Royal Commission on University Education only at the points where it touches the interests of the mere Gael. If, indeed, the Report had been a square attempt to grapple with a grave and momentous question — the gravest and most momentous that affects the secular life of men — every line and syllable of it would have been fraught with intense interest for us of the Gaelic League. But the Report fizzles out in the recommendation of a half-measure. When will those who venture to lay their hands on 'the magnificent and awful ark' of this land's destinies, come to see that half-measures are not, and cannot be, statesmanship? Why make the prostrate form of this country the eternal subject of educational and political experiments? Are we always to remain a corpse on the dissecting table?

When the University Commission met, the Gaelic League, through its President, seized the opportunity of placing its views plainly and unmistakably before the Commission. It boldly took up its stand for a National University — a University that should represent and summarise in itself the whole national life. That ideal is not yet to be realised; that it will ultimately be realised in all its largeness is as certain as that the Gael will yet rule in this land.

Premising, then, that we are discussing what is frankly a half-measure, and presuming that the legislation which is imminent will proceed along the lines here sketched out, let us see what is the Gael's outlook in the matter of University Education. It is suggestive to note in passing that at an early stage of the Report the Commissioners formally recognise the existence of Irish Ireland. At page 30 they write: 'We are, indeed, told by competent observers that there are signs of an awakening intellectual life throughout Ireland, manifesting itself in various movements, among others in the study of the Celtic language and literature, on the part of the younger generation, who, though they lack the facilities for organised study, are aware of the dignity that learning adds to national existence. If such forces are at work even within a limited circle of young men, the fact is of good augury for the growth of a new academical ideal'. That, of course, is a very imperfect appreciation of the real significance of the work of the Gaelic League, but it is about as far as one could reasonably expect the pundits forming a Royal Commission to go.

Before considering the section in which the Commission deals specifically with the future position of Irish studies, it is necessary, for the sake of clearness, that we grip the main lines of the Report as a whole. Briefly, its tenor is the reconstruction of the Royal University on federal lines, and as a teaching University, the constituent colleges to be the three Queen's Colleges, and a new Roman Catholic College which it is proposed to erect in Dublin. The individual colleges are to have a large measure of autonomy.

The following is the text of the section dealing with the Irish language: —

'We had interesting evidence from some distinguished witnesses as to the position which should be accorded in any new University system to the study of the Irish language. The evidence of two of these witnesses — Dr. Douglas Hyde, who is President of the Gaelic League, and Mr. Edward J. Gwynn, Fellow of Trinity College, Dublin, who is Todd Lecturer in the Royal Irish Academy — deals solely with this subject. We have also had evidence in point from three heads of colleges, Rev. Dr. Salmon of Trinity College; Rev. Dr. Delaney of University College, and Sir Rowland Blennerhassett of Queen's College, Cork; and among other witnesses who touched on the question should be specially mentioned the Right Hon. O'Conor Don and Dr. Michael F. Cox.

'The striking development of interest which has recently taken place in Ireland with regard to the Irish Language and Literature, Irish History, Archaeology, and Art, gives promise that the reconstituted University, which through its constituent Colleges will be brought into close touch with the national life of the country, will be able to do much for the advancement of these studies. Various questions have been discussed in the evidence; for instance, the number of Professors that should be assigned to these subjects; whether Irish should be introduced generally into the Colleges, or should merely form a special study, and whether Modern Irish should be regarded as ranking in importance with Old Irish; but these are matters whick, we think, the Colleges may properly determine for themselves. We do not think it necessary to do more than to record our concurrence with the opinion unanimously expressed by the witnesses, that an Irish University should encourage and make adequate provision for a department of Irish studies.'

Now, that declaration is satisfactory as far as it goes, but it is still in the pious opinion stage; and pious opinions — even when expressed by Royal Commissions — do not go very far. Of course, it was not the Commission's business to go into details as to the precise status of Irish on the various curricula. But it was its business to point out a way of carrying its pious opinions into effect. On this point, the Gaelic League was, as usual, very specific and plain-spoken. It bluntly said that the only satisfactory way of realising a large and enlightened national spirit in the conduct of the University, and, at the same time, of securing due recognition of native studies in its programme, was to provide for adequate popular representation on its governing body.

Now the suggested constitution of the Senate or governing body of the whole University, provides for the representation of Heads of Colleges, Professors, Graduates, and the Crown. Mere Ireland is to have no voice in its management. Of course, in a country where normal conditions prevailed, the chosen representatives of the Professors and Graduates of a National University might conceivably form an adequate representation of the nation at large. But the condition of Ireland, from whatever side you take it, is abnormal. We are no upholders of the *régime* which has given us fox-hunting squires and coal-merchants as controllers of our educational systems; but neither, at the present moment, would we willingly see higher education in Ireland solely in the hands of University Dons and Crown nominees. Surely the people ought to have a look in.

Coming to the outlined constitution of the new Catholic College, we find that it provides for representatives of the Professors, the Graduates, the Roman Catholic Hierarchy, and — *slán an comhartha* — the Dublin Corporation! The last-mentioned item is apparently intended to meet the demand of the League for popular representation. Really, the proposal is of the comic-opera order. Why not have suggested two members of the Licensed Vintners' Committee straight off? On the governing body of a College which is admittedly to be an all-Ireland one, and which, in practice, will be the new University, mere Ireland is to be represented by two members of Dublin Corporation, as against fifteen academicals. Of course, the nominees of the Hierarchy will, in a sense, represent popular opinion, and will certainly enjoy popular confidence; but their specific function on the Board will be to safeguard the interests of the Church.

On the whole, then, whilst the Commission has expressed itself as in sympathy with the aspirations of Irish Ireland, it has indicated no way of giving effect to those aspirations. Following recent precedents, it has thrown the programme of studies on the controlling bodies of the individual Colleges. If those bodies are constituted on the lines suggested by the Commission, it looks as if it will be the duty of Irish Ireland to fight them as soon as they are called into existence.

MAYNOOTH
18.4.1903

Take up the Irish problem at what point you may, you inevitably find yourself in the end back at the education question. The prostitution of education in this land has led to many other prostitutions. Poisoned at its source, the whole stream of national life has stagnated and grown foul.

The divorce of education from the soil has extended from the tiniest national school on a Kerry mountainside up to the high academic places of the land. It has been part of the history of Maynooth. Maynooth, too, has reacted on the countrysides, and helped to widen the divorce. The very zealousness of its alumni, their devotion, self-abnegation, have made their influence in favour of anglicisation all the more telling.

The saving of Maynooth, in a measure, demanded the life-blood of one of its bravest and gentlest sons. But Maynooth is saved. Yea, and has become the hearthstone, not of a famishing and despairing Ireland, but of a buoyant Ireland, hopefully realising itself. Maynooth is, in many senses, the hub of this new, strenuous, pulsating entity which we call Irish Ireland.

Manful, zealous, the new race of young Maynooth priests are the strongest hope of the Gael. If they be true, the look-out is cheery. And true they are, to the heart's core; true as befits the pupils of the strong earnest men — Father Eugene and Father Michael — who have spent themselves that these young priests might be worthy of themselves and of Ireland; worthy of the work for Ireland that lies before them.

In Maynooth, the best of the young men came together a few years ago, and banded themselves in a League for national work. That League is now the dominant force in Maynooth life. The Columban League is, in point of fact, the Gaelic League on a small scale: like the Gaelic League, it touches the national life at all points — intellectual, social, industrial. We were present the other evening when Father O'Doherty, President of the League, addressed his fellow-students on the work that has been done, and the work that is still to do. His address showed that all the phenomena which have followed in the track of the Gaelic League are reproducing themselves in Maynooth in the wake of the League of St. Columba: the students, like so many more of us, are re-entering into their inheritance.

After the President's address came a sprightly Irish play, written by one of the students, and delightfully staged and acted by them. Then the Vice-President of the College, Dr. O'Dea, announced the results of the competitions — in Irish prose, poetry, and archaeology — promoted by the League; it was, in fact, a Feis on a small scale. And all through one felt that a new purpose, a new dignity, had come into the lives of these young men; the calling of a priest is sacred and awful, but even it gains a new solemnity from the superaddition of a spirit of nationalism, reasoning and energising.

Maynooth is the hub. If the hub works true the whole machine will, with ordinary vigilance, pull along gallantly.

THE NEW COISDE GNÓTHA: ITS WORK
9.5.1903

A few months ago 'Conán Maol' urged, in the *Gaelic Journal*, the necessity of establishing an Irish School in some Irish-speaking county, and Father Dinneen, in endorsing the proposal, suggested that the school should be founded and maintained by the subscriptions of Irish Irelanders. This single school is, of course, intended to be the commencement of a great scheme for establishing similar ones wherever Irish is the vernacular speech. In suggesting the establishment of such an extensive system of bilingual education by voluntary endowment, they evidently consider it useless to expect that those who control the Primary Education System will give genuine co-operation, nor do they ask anything from the Gaelic League as an organisation except the blessing of the Ard-Fheis. These schools will, if they succeed, necessarily withdraw the pupils from the existing 'National' Schools, and they will, of course, be under the exclusive control of Irish Irelanders appointed by the subscribers. The scheme, therefore, proposes to dig a grave for the Commissioners, the managers, and most of the teachers, of the existing schools in the Irish-speaking districts. It is a project that would gladden the heart of every Irish Irelander if it could be accomplished in time to save the living language. By all means let as many schools of this kind as possible be established, but I would suggest, at the same time, that, if the spoken tongue is to be saved, we must not relax our efforts to get hold of, and Gaelicise, the existing State schools.

The obstacles in the way of Gaelicising the 'National' schools are the Commissioners, the managers, and the teachers. As the Commissioners can only act as a body, a minority of them may, for all we know, be disposed to establish a proper bilingual system, voted down, however by the hostile majority. But the managers, as well as the teachers, can act individually. Besides, the managers, with their absolute powers of appointment and dismissal of teachers, and their increased authority for controlling the course of instruction under the New Regulations, could ere now, were they competent and disposed to do so, have established a bilingual system little short of the requirements of the Gaelic League. This they could have done

5

individually as is shown by what Father Anderson has done in the heart of Dublin. By acting in combination they could either have compelled the Board to give way, or else, by bringing the system to a deadlock, hound the bigots from office. But not one has been found to support Colonel Moore. This shows that the managers are certainly indifferent to *National* Education. I know, indeed, one instance where the manager has refused permission for the teaching of Irish within school hours, although all the children, except a few in one school, are Irish speakers. And several instances have been given, from time to time in the 'Claidheamh', of the appointment of teachers who know no Irish to schools where pupils know no English; and this has been done within the last few years even by managers who pose as zealous Irish Irelanders. Coming to the teachers, there are many of them in the Irish-speaking districts who cannot speak the native tongue, and are, consequently, incapable of teaching an Irish school. If the Irish people valued their Nationality those teachers would not, of course, be tolerated a week in such positions. Amongst those of them who, in the Irish-speaking districts, have vernacular use of Irish, there are few genuine Irish Irelanders. Because where managers are not hostile, the teachers can, if they choose, establish anything, short of a thoroughly satisfactory bilingual system. If the teachers in the Irish-speaking districts combined they could, in this matter, dictate any terms they pleased to the Board. But it seems as hopeless to expect this of them as to expect it of the managers. Amongst the whole number there is not a single Irish school and no serious attempt at making such.

But, with a majority of the Commissioners hostile, and the managers and teachers either incompetent, or indifferent to National Education and actively engaged in killing the language, how can the schools be Gaelicised? There is £185,000 a year due to Ireland for Primary Education, and the Chief Secretary has stated that an Education Bill is to follow the Land Bill. Two years ago he supported the principle of bilingual education in the House of Commons but complained, as he did a few days ago again, that he had no power over the Board. Whatever Mr. Wyndham's real views may be, the least observant Gaelic Leaguer cannot have failed to see that Dr. Starkie is a fearless supporter of a bilingual system, and it is highly probable that, through his influence, the Bill will be satisfactory in this respect. There can be no doubt also that the present Board of Commissioners is doomed, and there seems to be better authority than the ordinary newspaper report for the statement that two experts, a Catholic and a Protestant, will take their place. But no matter how well-disposed the new Commissioners may be, their efforts can be nullified by the inaction, or obstruction, of the local managers and the teachers. It is, however, stated on fairly reliable authority that the present managerial system, as well as the position of the teachers as servants of the State, will be radically altered. Under the new scheme the Commissioners are to have authority to transfer a teacher, according to his fitness, from one school to another. This, of course, involves the transference of the powers of appointing and dismissing teachers from the school managers to the Commissioners. Such authority as this in the hands of Irish Ireland Commissioners would, in twelve months, revolutionise the whole system of education in the Irish-speaking districts. The schools in those places would be manned by teachers competent to conduct a thorough bilingual system, the present teachers who are incompetent in this respect being transferred to English-speaking localities. This direct control of the teachers would make it

6

inevitable also that the Commissioners should have increased authority over the Training Colleges. But, though the managers' direct authority over the teachers be abolished, it is probable that that portion of the New Regulations which enables them to draw up programmes suited to local needs, as well as to generally superintend the course of instruction, and to make recommendations to the Commissioners, will be continued in force. Then there is the further question — Who are to be the future local managers? With the Technical Education System under the control of popularly-elected bodies, as well as judging from some passages in Dr. Starkie's Belfast address, it does not seem likely that the Primary Schools will be left under the exclusive control of the parish clergy.

And now, having indicated some important points in which the Education Bill is likely to differ from the present system, it remains to be considered what attitude the Gaelic League should adopt towards it. Much will depend on who the new Commissioners will be. If they be anti-Irish it would be a doubtful advantage to transfer to them so much authority from the local managers, even though the latter are mainly responsible for the Anglicisation of the country. But of the two experts mentioned, we may reasonably expect that Dr. Starkie will be one. We know likewise that the projected scheme is being prepared by him, that he is a supporter of bilingual education, and that he has the courage to initiate reforms, when it might be more to his own advantage to let things drift.

THE BRITISH UNIVERSITY
31.10.1903

The Vice-Provost of Trinity College has written a letter to the *Irish Times*, claiming for his university the credit of being 'the only successful British institution in Ireland'. His letter has been followed up by a string of other letters from fellows, senators and graduates of the University, not one of whom dissents in the least from the Vice-Provost's description. That Trinity was a 'British institution' we knew all along, but it is useful to have an authentic avowal up to date. The same people are no doubt among those who are bewildered and pained to learn that the University of Dublin is obnoxious to the majority of the Irish people.

The University is not successful but quite the contrary. It is steadily going down the hill, and the fact is as plain to its champions as to the outsider, and plainer. Its social prestige is gone. 'Nobody who is anybody' nowadays will allow his sons to go to Trinity. The reason is obvious. It is just as easy to send them to really successful British institutions in England. So the *élite* go to Oxford and Cambridge, and Dublin gets the leavings. There is no getting over this fact. In abandoning their nationality, the Anglo-Irish gentry shifted their social centre of gravity from Ireland to England. It was an inevitable sequel to the sale of the Irish constitution. The Act of Union sealed the doom of Dublin University, and all the king's horses and the all the king's men cannot set Humpty Dumpty up again. The University is now going scraping and begging and engineering for funds. But funds won't alter nature. The wealth of Andrew Carnegie could not mend an egg of the value of one penny, once it is smashed. The exodus of the great gentry after the Union ruined Dublin and its University socially. The fresh exodus that will follow the land settlement will level the ruins. The only successful British institution has been quite successful in

7

Anglicising its alumni, and it cannot complain if they put a logical interpretation on its teaching, and prefer the real British thing to a provincial understudy.

There is only one way in which Dublin University can be saved and that is by becoming heartily and sincerely a successful Irish institution. But Seaghan Buidhe, or rather Seoinín Buidhe, cannot change his skin. Nothing short of a miracle can purge the shoneen University of its shoneens in high places. The devil has no interest in working this prodigy, and it is not likely to come from any other source. Meanwhile, the University being what it is, the Irish people should not allow themselves to be blandished into any manner of softness for it. Let it be left, as in the past, to enjoy its Britishism and its success, and much good may they do it.

Irishmen are often prone to think that the hand of God has been heavy upon them. They should recognise in the history of Dublin University the existence of a healthy Nemesis even in this world. One by one the triumphs founded on murder, rapine, and oppression in the past have come to a miserable and ignoble end. We read in Joyce's *Social History of Ancient Ireland* that Trinity's first great luminary, Archbishop Ussher, signed the death warrant of a brilliant Irish school in Galway. Such has been the spirit of learning and freedom cultivated in the successful British institution. His own college will need no death warrant. Truly 'Is mairg a bhíos go holc agus go bocht 'n-a dhiaidh'. The true criterion of a university's success is the culture it propagates and the public spirit it creates. Despite the scientific vanity of the age, these things are greater than science, and even in science Dublin ranks about tenth rate. But where in Ireland is the evidence of its work for culture and public spirit? In music, in literature, in the arts, in the professions, compare Dublin of today with Dublin before the Union, when she responded in some degree to the claims of nationality. Whatever there is of inspiration in present-day West Britain arises, as everybody knows, from the very sources that the successful British institution has done its utmost to dry up or to pollute.

Now that the question of granting the Irish people their right to University education is again to the fore, it is the duty of Irishmen to secure that they shall not be smitten with the success of another British institution. Such an institution will of necessity degrade them, not raise them, will narrow their culture, not broaden it. West Britishism can do the Irish people no good either in this world or in the next. A university national without reserve, as every university should be, is certain to succeed and to bring untold blessings to the nation. Any other kind will defeat the best intentions and falsify the brightest hopes. We do not want to compete or associate on even or any other terms with British institutions. We want to go our own way.

AN EDUCATIONAL PROGRAMME
7.11.03

Through all the leading articles which have recently appeared in *An Claidheamh Soluis* there has run, as we hope our readers have observed, a certain sequence of thought. We do not write leading articles at haphazard, selecting whatever topic happens to be uppermost in our mind at the moment. Rather, we aim at leading the thought of the movement by developing from week to week a policy always consistent with itself, and

8

always possessing a certain continuity of purpose, however much it may be affected on the surface by the currents of the hour. We are convinced that progress can be made in this, as in any other movement, only as the result of hard, thorough work on definite profitable lines. We must understand precisely what we want, and precisely how best and quickest to get what we want. Hence the necessity to keep hammering away at the same old questions, the necessity to keep the main issues daily and weekly before the country, even at the risk of growing tedious and platitudinous.

We have managed, we think, during the last few weeks, to give definiteness to certain aspects of the League's programme. At the outset of the autumn session we sketched out in general terms a forward policy, both for the organisation as a whole and for its local bodies. Since then we have been engaged in filling in the details of the sketch. We have dealt with the more important phases of the duty of the members of the organisation (in the term 'members' we include both bodies and individuals) to the organisation at large. We have also dealt with two important phases of the public work of the League, mapping out in considerable detail a line of action for the movement, (1) as regards its relations with elective public bodies, and (2) as regards its duties and limitations in the matter of Irishising popular politics.

There remains a phase which, in final resort, is of much more moment than either of these, a phase which is, beyond all question, the most important of the secular life of men. We refer, of course, to education. In no department of the League's work is a clearly understood programme on what we have called definite and profitable lines so essential as here. Of course, we all know in a general way what we want; we have got to Irishise education in this country from the smallest National School on a western mountainside, through all the stages of primary, intermediate, and university education, religious and secular, literary, scientific, professional and technical up to the highest educational institutions in the land.

Whilst it is essential that this large programme be kept in full view, our efforts can be fruitful only if conducted on certain definite lines, and in accordance with a well thought-out plan. Let us attempt to map out an educational programme to be followed by local members of the organisation (bodies and individuals). For the present, we can omit the phase of University Education, as one with which local League bodies are not, as a rule, likely to come into immediate contact.

In dealing with the two remaining branches of education, the following are the main objectives to be worked for: —

(1) The complete Irishising of education in the Irish-speaking districts; in other words, the employment of Irish *as the medium of instruction* in every district in which Irish is the home language (including districts where it is constantly spoken only by grown people).

(2) The *introduction of Irish* as a subject *into every day and boarding school in Ireland.*

(3) The teaching of Irish as a *living spoken tongue*; and with this end —

(4) The employment of *competent Irish-speaking teachers*; and

(5) The drawing up of *proper programmes* in Irish, so that the schools may turn out speakers, readers, and writers of the language.

(6) The increased use of the facilities afforded by the National Board for the employment of *extern teachers*.

(7) The *improvement of teaching methods* in schools as well as in League classes, and the encouragement of oral teaching.

9

(8) The use of Irish in *school devotions* and in *religious instruction*; also in calling the roll, in giving drill and manual training; and the encouragement of its use in the playground. These points apply to schools in anglicised districts as well to those in the Irish-speaking districts.

(9) The extended utilisation of *Evening Schools* under the National Board under the Department of Agriculture and Technical Instruction for the purpose of teaching Irish.

(10) The *Irishising of Colleges*, viz., Maynooth, the Seminaries, the Training Colleges, the Intermediate Colleges.

(11) The *introduction of Irish History* into every school and college in Ireland.

During the coming few weeks we hope to deal, point by point, with the various lines of work here indicated. For the present, let each coisde ceanntair, craobh, and individual member of the League set about thinking how best our educational programme may be carried out in its or his own district.

SHAM TEACHING AND REAL TEACHING
14.11.1903

Irish is now being taught under one form or another in something like 3,000 National Schools. In how many of these is a working knowledge of the living language being imparted? In how many of them is a serious effort being made to impart such a knowledge? In how many of them have even the preliminary steps towards making such an effort been taken?

The essentials appear to us to be (1) competent Irish-speaking teachers; (2) oral instruction; and (3) profitable and attractive programmes.

To take the last first. There is no reason on the face of the earth why teachers should continue to torture children by inflicting 'Mac-Ghníomhartha Fhinn', or Part II of 'Foras Feasa ar Éirinn' on them; the National Board allows the manager and teacher practically a free hand in framing their programme. In the Commissioners' own words, 'The programme as specified for each extra subject is not obligatory, but is merely an indication of the aims and desires of the Commissioners. The Commissioners will consider other programmes which managers may bring under their notice. But such programmes must be arranged in the first instance in conference with the Inspector of the district'.

Now, the specimen programme of the Commissioners includes such antiquated and unsuitable texts as 'Forus Feasa' and 'Diarmuid agus Gráinne' for the Third Year's Course, and the 1st and 2nd Books of the Society for the Preservation of the Irish Language for the First Year's Course; but, as is made clear in the extract quoted, there is no obligation whatever on teachers to adopt any of these recommendations, which are intended solely as an indication of the quantity of matter the Commissioners will expect the pupils of each year to prepare. By the selection of attractive books — say 'An Prímhleabhar', 'An Chéad Léightheóir', 'Ceachta Beaga Gaedhilge', and such simple texts as 'Tadhg Gabha', 'Taidhbhse an Chrainn', 'Seaghan an Díomais', and the like — teachers, provided they can superadd an interesting method of imparting instruction, may make the half-hour or hour spent at Irish the most enjoyable of the whole day. Well-given 'Object Lessons' in Irish will contribute still further towards the same end. We have repeatedly printed specimen programmes

10

for schools both in Irish-speaking and in English-speaking districts; now that there is a wider field of selection in the matter of texts, teachers will appreciate some further specimens which we hope to publish during the next few weeks.

But the teaching of Irish need not necessarily be confined within the half-hour or hour laid down in the programme. Both in Irish-speaking and in English-speaking areas, the most valuable part of the Irish teaching is that which can be introduced incidentally throughout the entire course of the day. Teachers can, in fact, make the school atmosphere as Irish or as un-Irish as they please; they can do much to impart a speaking knowledge of Irish without ever setting it down as a subject on their programme; on the other hand, they may wear themselves out in the effort to teach it as a specific subject, without accomplishing anything of national or educational value. It is all a question of spirit, adaptability to circumstances, and method.

There is no reason why the teacher should not (even in English-speaking districts) employ Irish freely as a medium of communication with the children throughout the day; why he should not always address them by their Irish names; call the roll in Irish; teach the prayers in Irish; teach Irish songs and hymns; give the ordinary words of command in Irish; use a certain amount of Irish in giving instructions in physical drill and hand-and-eye training; seize the countless opportunities presented by geography, history, and reading lessons for the explanation of an Irish personal or place name, or a reference to an incident in Irish history or story; actively encourage the use of Irish in the playground; and so on. In fact, every moment and incident of the school life may be made to contribute its quota towards fostering Irish nationality. Irish self-respect, and Irish culture. The lessons which count for most are not those extracted from text-books but those which the pupils unconsciously draw from the precept and example, the personality and habits, the daily life and conversation of the teacher.

THE FUNCTION OF NATIONALISM IN EDUCATION
5.12.1903

Mr. T. P. Gill delivered a very striking address on the occasion of the formal opening of the Kilkenny Technical Schools on Thursday last. The whole address was singularly thoughtful and suggestive but there is one passage which had a very special interest for us. We quote it at length: —

'It cannot be too often repeated that we must look upon education as a whole and that Technical Education is only a part of the whole. I hope to see eventually in our evening Technical Schools which, remember, are only at their beginnings, some elements of broader culture, of humane culture, introduced besides the teaching of purely Technical subjects. This, for the sake of the Technical teaching itself, as well as for the sake of the general welfare of the individual and the community, for it is a fact everywhere recognised, and now thoroughly proved from experience — and nowhere have I seen it more emphatically insisted on than in the most up-to-date Technical colleges of America — that you will not get the best from Technical training unless it is founded upon or accompanied by a training which humanises the man, which broadens his sympathies, strengthens his will and nourishes his heart, his imagination and his soul. I hope to see in these evening schools, or in connection somehow with this movement, which is the only way of reaching young men whose day-school life is over, opportunities given to young men to learn something of literature, of history, of economics; above all of the history, the literature, and the language of their own country. Frankly, I am all for the Gaelic movement in this matter. I believe its educational influence will be inestimable — It will be the chief means of putting a soul into a soulless, lifeless, educational system. The funds of our Department, under existing circumstances, are not available for teaching of this kind, unless in very special circumstances when a case can be made out that gives the teaching another object, that is, a purely technical object, than that which should be its true intention. And, as a matter of fact, our Technical Instruction funds, now all hypothecated, are not equal to the calls upon them for the needs of strictly technical teaching. But by some means — revision of the evening continuation codes, or voluntary means — and pray do not let the value of voluntary means be overlooked in this matter, the best things in education have derived their origin from efforts for which no public funds were available — by some means, I trust aid will yet be forthcoming for this broader teaching in evening schools, which will help to give the thinking workers whom we are going to train, a clearer outlook both upon their own country and upon the other countries with which she has to compete.'

The Technical Schools

Now this utterance is important in the first place as a frank recognition by the Secretary of the Department of the educational worth of the language movement; and in the second place as embodying what may be regarded as an official intimation that, at present, the funds of the Department are not available for the teaching of Irish except in very special circumstances. This leads us to introduce a subject into which we have for some time back been inquiring with a view to entering on it in detail in the columns of *An Claidheamh Soluis*, — viz., the extent to which the Technical Schools may be utilised for the propagation of Irishism, and how best the Technical Schools may be approached.

Technical schemes are of two classes according as they apply to urban or to county areas. In urban areas provision is made for the teaching of languages, and in two instances — viz., in Clonmel and in Limerick — the Department has recognised Irish as a language which may be taught. In county areas no provision is made for the teaching of languages as such; the only instance in which the study of Irish as a specific subject is being promoted under a county Technical Scheme is in Kerry, where, with the sanction of the Department, the County Technical Committee has offered three sums of £5 as prizes for essays in Irish on technical and agricultural subjects. Now the local Technical Committee — Urban or County — must draw up at the commencement of each session a programme for submission to the Department, and through the Department to Parliament. Subjects for which provision is not made in this programme cannot afterwards be introduced. Therefore, in no district — whether urban or county — where the current scheme makes no provision for the teaching of Irish can the language be introduced before next autumn. The only schemes, as far as we are aware, which have made such provision are those of Clonmel and Limerick. Elsewhere, then, the first step must be to commence a vigorous agitation for the inclusion of Irish in next year's scheme. As the schemes are submitted to Parliament early in the year, and will therefore be shortly in the melting pot, agitation should be commenced at once.

In the rural areas — the main thing is to secure that Irish be made the medium of instruction in places where it is the ordinary spoken language, and with this end to agitate for the appointment by the Department of qualified, Irish-speaking instructors. As the Department has no jurisdiction in the Congested Districts, which include the chief Irish-speaking areas, the Irish-speaking districts which come within its sphere of operations are comparatively few, and could be staffed with little difficulty. The districts in question are chiefly Waterford, the Irish-speaking parts of Cork, and portion of Kerry. The minimum demand should be that every instructor sent by the Department into any of these districts be fully competent to lecture in Irish. We are glad to notice that one such instructor, Miss Doyle, has been using Irish to good effect in giving practical and theoretical demonstrations in butter-making in the Brosna district, Co. Kerry. We read that in a course of demonstrations at Cordal, Miss Doyle lectured fluently in Irish as well as in English, and that in her concluding lecture she strongly appealed to her audience to study the Irish language and to revive and propagate it until it became universal. We trust that the Department will appoint more Irish-speaking instructors in all the branches, fishery, dairying, agriculture, and so on. Meanwhile we would ask League Craobhacha to draw our attention, and the attention of the public, to cases in which instructors under the Department are helping to anglicise Irish-speaking localities by carrying on a purely English propaganda.

The Situation in the Secondary Schools

Under the new regulations of the Intermediate Board, in accordance with which only the numbers (and not the names or schools) of successful students are published, there is no means of ascertaining in what secondary schools Irish is being taught, and in what secondary schools it is being boycotted: elsewhere on this page we outline a plan by which this information can be collected by the local Coisdí Ceanntair and Craobhacha of the Gaelic League. We have before us, however, the definite and discreditable fact that only 39 per cent of the Irish boys, and only 28 per cent of the Irish girls who went through an Intermediate course this year, were taught Irish. How far is this state of affairs chargeable to the heads of colleges., and how far to the Intermediate Board? Next year's results lists will furnish a very valuable criterion of the sincerity of the heads of colleges: those who have been teaching Irish under protest will seize the opportunity afforded by the unfavourable new rules to drop Irish; those who are sincere in the matter of Irish teaching will stick to it in spite of the pains and penalities imposed by the Board.

Meanwhile, however, the programme for 1905 is on the stocks, and will be issued to the public early in the new year. It is the business of Irish Ireland to see that in the 1905 programme Irish be placed on a footing of full equality with every modern language, in every course, in every grade; and that Irish History be restored to the Senior Grade course. As a preliminary to the agitation of this question a survey of the present status of Irish will be enlightening. Speaking generally, the Intermediate system makes provision for the teaching of English, of Experimental and Practical Science, of Mathematics, of Classics, and of Modern Languages. Of Modern Languages *five* are recognised, viz., French, German, Irish, Italian and Spanish. Italian and Spanish, however, are only 'pass' subjects — their teaching is tolerated but not encouraged, and in the fierce struggle for existence these two languages are practically crushed out. It is only under exceptional circumstances that we should expect to find them taught in Intermediate schools. The inclusion of Irish amongst 'Honours Subjects' places it, so far, on the same footing as French and German; but the treatment accorded the language in other respects is very different, and the result is that teachers and students are unwilling to take up Irish, they find it more profitable to take French and German. Let us briefly examine this matter.

The Intermediate system provides for *four* distinct 'Courses' – a Classical Course, a Modern Literary Course, a Mathematical Course, and an Experimental Science Course; and each 'Course' has a number of sub-heads, generally five, and distinguished as A, B, C, D. E. A student *must* pass in each of these sub-heads. In 1903 the 'Experimental Science Course' has as one of its sub-heads, – Sub-head D, – 'French or German'; so that every student following this course, – whether in Junior, Middle, or Senior Grade, – had to take French or German. Irish was not named. This, of course, placed Irish at a disadvantage. The friends of Irish hoped that the revised 1904- programme would place Irish on the same level as French and German; but when the 1904 programme was issued it was found that Irish was still left out in the cold. 'French or German' is still the sub-head. Why not 'French, or German, or Irish'?

In 1903 the 'Mathematical Course' had no obligatory *language* except English, which, as a separate sub-head, is obligatory for every course and for every grade. For 1904 a new sub-head has been added to the Mathematical Course and in future every student who follows this 'Course' must pass in 'Latin, French, or German'. Here, again, Irish is treated with marked disfavour. Why not make the sub-head 'Latin, or French, or German, or Irish'? In 1903, while 'Exhibitions' were given in money, 'Prizes' were given in books. For 1904 valuable 'Money Prizes' have been added (£10, £7, and £5), but these Money Prizes are only for Greek and for *German*. Here, again, Irish is placed at a disadvantage compared with German. It is quite plain, therefore, that German is, on the whole, more favoured by the Intermediate system than French; and that German and French are, very markedly more favoured than Irish.

For 1905 things look even worse. In that year 'Experimental Science' will be obligatory for all courses except the 'Classical Course'. Making any subject obligatory ensures its being taught, but renders it more difficult for a subject like Irish, which is not obligatory, to find a place. In view, therefore, of the prospect for 1905, it becomes the duty of every League body, of every public Board that is pledged to the League programme, and of every educationalist in Ireland, to take steps to checkmate the designs of the anti-Irsh Intermediate Board; and as the programme for 1905 is probably under consideration already, this is the moment for action.

AN EDUCATIONAL POLICY
12.12.1903

Six weeks ago we outlined an educational programme for the winter campaign. Ever since we have been hammering away at the details of that programme, taking the primary, the secondary, and the technical schools in turn. We have still much to say on these heads, and much also on other heads, – as, for instance, the seminaries and the training colleges. At present, however, it seems to us that the most useful work we can do is to

14

keep on hammering away at certain details connected with the teaching of Irish in the primary schools. We are aware that the public loathes details, and would probably prefer us to agitate this question in the orthodox Irish way, — to talk generalities and to thunder against the 'National' Board, the Managers, and the teachers. This would possibly prove more entertaining than the discussion of dry-as-dust details. But we do not publish this paper so much for the amusement of the public as for its instruction; and the public — Managers, teachers, Gaelic Leaguers and all — sadly wants instruction on the details and possibilities of the various educational systems that are in force in our midst.

The Primary Schools

It should be unnecessary to re-affirm that the educational policy of the Gaelic League demands (1) that Irish be made the medium of instruction in every district in which it is the home language; and (2) that Irish and Irish History be taught as specific subjects to every child in every class in every school in the country. In an early issue we propose to enter in detail on the first part of this programme; meanwhile we continue to concentrate attention on ways and means for ensuring the effective teaching of Irish as a specific subject, whether in Irish-speaking or in English-speaking areas.

Now the essentials seem to us to be (1) competent Irish-speaking teachers; (2) oral instruction; (3) attractive and profitable programmes; and we may add (4) the arrangement of the time-table in such a manner as shall ensure a full attendance at the Irish lesson. On Head (3) — the importance of attractive and profitable progammes — we have strongly insisted for weeks past, and feel it necessary to insist further. Teachers are pre-eminently men who move in grooves and are governed by traditions, — a fact which probably accounts for the difficulty which many of them continue to exhibit in realising that the official programme of the Commissioners is no longer a compulsory one. Nothwithstanding our repeated insistence on this point and the explicitness — for once — of the Commissioners themselves we have, within the last few weeks, received a number of long letters roundly abusing the Commissioners' programme. Once more, the Commissioners' programme is a specimen, and nothing more; it is no more obligatory than the specimen programmes which have from time to time appeared in our own columns. The Commissioners' words are: 'The Programme as specified for each Extra Subject *is not obligatory, but is merely an indication of the aims and desires of the Commissioners. The Commissioners will consider other Programmes which managers may bring under their notice.* But such Programmes must be arranged in the first instance in conference with the Inspector of the district.'

We hope to print next week a further alternative programme based on the O'Growney books, and carefully drawn up in consultation with practical teachers. We have received a letter from a Southern teacher from which we gather that he considers some of our specimen programmes difficult. Any teacher who agrees with him can, of course, modify our programmes as he thinks best: they are merely intended as *helps* towards the drawing up of suitable programmes, carefully framed in accordance with the capacity of the children, their state of development, the extent to which they already know Irish, and so on. As we have already written, the programmes we have been publishing are primarily intended for Irish-speaking districts: for use in anglicised areas they might usefully be

15

rendered somewhat less difficult. One thing teachers may take from us: it is unlikely that the Inspectors of the Board will accept *a less amount of matter* than we have suggested in these specimen programmes. From our inquiries amongst teachers in all parts of the country we are enabled to say that the Inspectors are unwilling to accept less than some 16 or 20 pages of literary matter in the Second Year's Course, and some 60 pages in the Third Year's Course. The Inspectors seem to be insisting on a considerable share of book-work; a programme which struck us as otherwise an admirable one has recently been rejected because it did not provide for a sufficient amount of literary work in the Second and Third Years' Courses.

Our recommendation is that Irish be taught as an extra to all children from Third Standard up, and that it be taught as an ordinary subject within 'school hours' to the lower standards, using 'Aibghitir na Gaedhilge', the Reading Tablets of the Gaelic League and the 'Prímhleabhar' as a basis. We also recommend that *Object Lessons* in Irish be given to the whole school; that the Catechism and Prayers be taught in Irish; that Irish songs and hymns be taught; that physical drill be conducted in Irish (the technical terms will be found in Mr. Concannon's 'Mion-Chomhrádh'; and, finally, that the teacher constantly use Irish in his intercourse with the children. In addition, the teacher should be quick to seize the countless opportunities presented during the day — as by reading, geography and history lessons — of explaining an Irish place or personal name, illustrating a point in Irish History, or inculcating Irishism in any form.

Good Teaching and Bad Teaching

In this matter of effective Irish teaching much necessarily depends on the personality, attainments and methods of the teacher. These things are far more important than time-tables or programmes. A teacher worth his salt can make the Irish lesson the most fascinating part of the day's work; a teacher who either does not know the language, or who, knowing the language, does not know how to teach it, can succeed in making the Irish lesson wholly repulsive and unpopular, — and this in spite of the fact that Irish is the one subject of the school programme which makes an appeal to the child's imagination and heart. In point of fact, we frequently come across statements to the effect that the children largely absent themselves from school on the day on which Irish is appointed to be taught; such a statement was made the other day by a School Manager at the meeting of a Northern Coisde Ceanntair. This state of affairs infallibly points, not to a low ebb of patriotism in the district, but to inefficient and uninteresting teaching. When the teacher has the right spirit and the faculty of making his teaching interesting, our experience is that the children invariably respond. Witness the recent statement in a report from Seaghán Mac Enri that throughout the Killala Diocese Irish is the most popular subject on the programme. In several western parishes with which we are acquainted Irish is actually the attraction which draws the young men to the evening schools.

This brings us to a discussion as to the ways and means by which the deficiencies of the present teachers may be best supplemented. There are two alternative plans, either of which may be adopted according as local circumstances suggest. The first is the systematic employment of extern teachers, the second the scheme which is at present in operation in Killala, or some modification of it. In connection with the former plan, the work of the Wexford Coside Ceanntair is deserving of close study. The first step in

16

Wexford was to appoint a sub-committee of the Coisde Ceanntair for the purpose of approaching the school managers throughout the county. The sub-committee did its work so well that within a short time it held signed pledges from every school manager in the county (with three exceptions), by which the managers bound themselves, from January 1st, 1905, to appoint only teachers who, being otherwise satisfactory, are capable and willing to teach Irish. Pending the coming into force of this pledge the travelling teachers of the Coisde Ceanntair are, in addition to their organising and teaching work within the League itself, acting (1) as extern teachers in the schools and (2) teaching the teachers. One of the secrets of the success of the Wexford plan is that, instead of passing resolutions in general terms, the Coisde Ceanntair in the first instance approached the Managers personally in a friendly and business-like spirit.

The Killala Scheme

In this connection, a glance at the fortunes of the Killala scheme cannot but be helpful. It will be recollected that the essential feature of the scheme consists in the joint action of all the Managers of the Diocese under the sanction and with the active co-operation of the Bishop. Every teacher in the Diocese is required by his Manager to teach Irish, and in order that the teachers may qualify themselves to teach the language efficiently they are required to attend a course of training at an appointed centre. The teacher is Seaghán Mac Enri, the League Timthire for the district, whose expenses are borne jointly by the Coisde Gnótha and the district. The Timthire is, of course, free to undertake a large amount of general organising work. Readers will be interested to know to what extent the teachers are availing of the advantages offered by the scheme. To save ourselves from the invidious task of pointing out what parishes are failing, and what parishes are doing their duty, we print a return prepared by Mr. Fitzhenry showing (*a*) the number of teachers on roll from each parish in the Diocese; and (*b*) *their average attendance during the month of November. The list speaks for itself:* —

	No. of Teachers	Average weekly attendance for November
Ballina	35	29
Crossmolina	15	13
Backs	14	9
Ballycastle	11	6
Castleconnor	5	4
Kilglass	7	3
Ardagh	5	3
Lahardane	5	2
Moygownagh	4	4
Ballysokeery	3	3
Killala	4	3
Lacken	4	$2\frac{1}{4}$
Kilfian	4	$\frac{1}{2}$
Easkey	11	3
Skreen and Dromard	5	2
Templeboy	5	4
Dromore West	4	0

Mr. Fitzhenry explains that having been notified of the illness of a teacher in each of the parishes of Backs, Ballycastle, Ballina, and Kilglas, he has included them as 'present' in the above average. In Lahardane appointments have just been made to some of the schools, and the teachers may be expected to attend as soon as they have settled down to their duties. There is also a teacher in this parish — at Glenhest — from whom, owing to the situation of his school, a regular attendance can hardly be expected. In Ballycastle parish some of the teachers were on vacation during the month. It will be seen that, whilst there is decided room for improvement in some of the parishes, the average attendance is, on the whole, fairly creditable — indeed highly so in the case of two or three parishes. Mr. Fitzhenry adds that the parishes which show best in the foregoing average would also do so in any other month that might be selected. We hope that the publication of these figures will cause the teachers who have been remiss in attendance to bestir themselves.

When the scheme was first launched we asked what Diocese would be the first to follow the lead of Killala in taking up the school question on business-like lines. We have since many times repeated the query in one form or another. So far, there has been no reply. Outside Killala and Wexford, and some forty small areas where there are local travelling teachers under Coisdí Ceanntair and Craobhacha, the efforts to introduce effective Irish teaching in the schools have been sporadic and spasmodic.

THE 'STILL SMALL VOICE' ANSWERED
19.12.1903

The query asked by Dr. Henebry's 'still small voice' at Kilkenny has been effectively answered. The query, it will be recollected, was as to the status of Irish teaching in the schools of Kilkenny. The implied suggestion that all was not precisely as it should be immediately called forth indignant protests: Father W. Delany, C.C., took the field against Dr. Henebry in the local press, and the *Kilkenny People* treated him to a leading article couched in a style which one had hoped was obsolete in Irish journalism. Dr. Henebry replied in the columns of the *Kilkenny Journal*. Meanwhile the Kilkenny Craobh went quietly and systematically to work: a Schools' Committee was appointed and charged with the specific task of collecting detailed statistics as to the actual status of the Irish language in all the Kilkenny schools. The total number of children on the rolls was officially procured from the Kilkenny School Attendance Committee. Except in five instances, the number learning Irish in each school was elicited either from the teacher, or from the Superior or Manager of the school in question. In the five exceptional cases the facts were within the personal knowledge of members of the Committee. The statistics thus collected vouched for, in most instances, by the responsible authorities of the schools — are before us as we write. They are published in full on page 3 of this issue of *An Claidheamh Soluis*.

Now, we shall address ourselves exclusively to the hard facts and figures revealed in this return. Our readers have the return under their eyes, and they can check us if we stray outside its four corners. The first fact which stands out in relief is that Irish is being taught in only fourteen out of every twenty-nine schools comprised in the return. The second fact is that of the

3,498 children on the rolls in these 29 schools, only 1,022, or 29.2 per cent, are being taught Irish. The third fact is that of all the 'National' schools in the four parishes in only one is any portion of the ordinary school hours being devoted to Irish. The fourth fact is that no Irish whatever is being taught in St. Kieran's Diocesan College.

The schools which show up best are those of the Christian Brothers, in which Irish is taught to 278 boys out of the 300 on the rolls; St. John's Male, Female and Infant National Schools, in which it is taught to 265 out of 338; and St. Joseph's Industrial School, in which it is taught to 90 out of 102. In only two instances does the number of hours devoted to Irish per week exceed two-and-a-half; in two instances it is only one, and in five only one and a fraction. In the Presentation Convent — whose attitude towards Irish was specifically criticised by Dr. Henebry, and defended by Father Delany — out of the immense number of 727 children on the rolls, only 58 are being taught Irish, the average attendance at the Irish classes being as low as 38.

The situation, it will be seen, stands thus: Dr. Henebry pointedly asked what was the status of the Irish Language in the schools of Kilkenny; it was interpreted that the mere asking of the question was an implied slander on the schools of the district, and a cowardly attack on Superiors, Managers and teachers. Thanks to the business-like action of the Kilkenny Craobh the public is now in possession of detailed statistics bearing on the situation.

The action of the Kilkenny Craobh has, however, had a sequel which calls for reference at our hands. The Craobh has just adopted its Annual Report. In the course of the report the statistics which we print this week are summarised and commented upon. A copy was forwarded to the *Kilkenny Journal* for publication. The *Kilkenny Journal* suppressed it and devoted a leader to justifying the suppression. We quote the major part of the leader: —

> Coercion is a bad spur by which to work reform, and so far as the Irish people are concerned coercion is the worst whip that a rider ever laid upon a willing horse. The Gaelic League is doing excellent work, not only in Kilkenny but throughout Ireland, but when the Gaelic League catches on to some of the theories of American faddists there is danger ahead for the safety of that most excellent organisation. We have this week declined to publish an official report of the Kilkenny Branch of the Gaelic League, which report was ordered to be printed and circulated. We shall probably be challenged for our reasons. Well, our reasons are these. The report is practically an attack upon the Catholic Schools of Kilkenny. There are innuendoes and insinuations in the report which are not only suggestive of insult but are absolutely insulting. If the Irish Language movement is to progress, and if the programme of the Gaelic League is to find favour generally it will not be by the tone of report which we understand is to be now promulgated. If the Gaelic League is going to run on these lines, let it declare itself so at once — if it wants the support of the Bishops and priests let it stop its covert attacks upon their colleges and convents, and drop their sneers about 'clerical managers'. Ireland is not yet ripe for a policy of this kind, nor, bad as we are, can we be bulldosed into Americanisms of the free shooter, 'you must' policy . . . . The cultivation of the Irish Language is not the only item in the

Gaelic League programme, and should they fasten upon this particular detail only to possibly alienate support without which the Irish Language Revival would be impossible, and alienate support, moreover, which is at present practically given? The Convents and the Colleges and the Clerical Masters are doing much; would that some of those who preach the Gaelic League propaganda did half as much. Cheap sentiment used to be at a premium in Ireland some years ago; cheap sentiment now is at a terribly low discount.

The portion of the article which we have not quoted is a solemn defence of the Bishops and priests of Ireland against the 'innuendoes and insinuations' of the Kilkenny Branch of the Gaelic League. Indeed, passing from the particular to the general, our contemporary appears to accuse the Gaelic League at large of 'covert attacks' on colleges and convents and of 'sneers' at clerical managers. Now, we shall not waste time in endeavouring to convince the *Kilkenny Journal* that the cultivation of the Irish language is a little more than a mere 'detail' in the programme of the Gaelic League; nor shall we so far take this absurd article seriously as to ask our contemporary to justify *its* innuendoes by specifying when and where the Gaelic League, either as a corporate body, or through any accredited branch, organ or representative, has made 'covert attacks' on colleges and convents, or indulged in 'sneers about clerical managers'. In the document before us the Report of the Kilkenny Craobh — we find neither 'covert attacks' nor 'sneers' and only one paragraph which we would not have written ourselves. The spirit which has produced and which animates our movement is essentially opposed to wanton antagonism towards any class of Irishmen, as a class, — still more so to wanton antagonism towards the clerical managers of Ireland, from whose ranks the League draws some of its staunchest supporters. However, lest anyone might detect 'innuendoes and insinuations', 'covert attacks' or 'sneers' in our own columns on the present occasion, we have decided not to set off by a single observation the story told by the Kilkenny returns; we trust that not even the *Kilkenny Journal* will succeed in mistaking a table of statistics for a 'covert attack' or 'sneers' lurking beneath cold figures vouched for, in nearly every instance, by the Head Masters, Managers and Teachers concerned themselves.

Wanted — More Statistics
    The question arises how far is the state of affairs revealed in Kilkenny typical of the state of affairs throughout the country? As yet we are without the data on which to found an answer to this question, inasmuch as there is nothing like a detailed and reliable set of statistics showing the status of Irish in all the schools in the country. We know, indeed that only 39 per cent of the boys and only 28 per cent of the girls who passed the Intermediate Examinations this year passed in Irish; but we do not know — nor are there any official returns to show — in which of the Intermediate schools Irish is being taught, and in which it is being boycotted; nor do we know to what extent, and with what success, Irish is being taught to the thousands of non-Intermediate pupils who attend the secondary schools and the primary schools attached to them, — as, for instance, those of the Christian Brothers. We can deduce from the returns supplied to the Gaelic League each year by the 'National' Board that *some* Irish is being taught (as an 'Extra') in about one-third of the primary schools, but there is no adequate means of determining either the extent or the character of this

teaching, and there is no means whatever of gauging the extent and success with which Irish is being taught as an ordinary subject within school hours. Obviously, therefore, we are not in possession of all the conditions of the problem we are attempting to solve.

This brings us back to the point we were agitating a fortnight ago, — the urgent necessity for the collection of accurate and detailed statistics showing the present status of Irish in the schools. The League Timthirí are at present actively engaged in doing this work for the Irish-Speaking districts; throughout the rest of the country it must be done by the Coisdí Ceanntair. The sooner the work is vigorously and systematically taken in hand the better.

A word as to the character of the returns which are required. As we wrote a fortnight ago, they must be both accurate and detailed. It does not help to know that forty children in a given school are being taught Irish, if we are left in the dark as to how many children in the school are *not* being taught Irish. As Dr. Henebry put it in referring to the Kilkenny schools, it is all a question of fractions: what it is essential to know is the ratio of Irishism to foreignism in a given school, a given parish, a given diocese. To report, as is often reported when information as to the status of Irish in a district is asked for, that 'Irish is being taught in every school in this parish', is simply to throw dust in the eyes of the public, if, as is very often the case, Irish is being taught (and perhaps badly taught) to only about one-fourth of the total number of the children on the rolls.

Now in order to determine the ratio of Irishism to foreignism in the instruction conveyed in a given school it is necessary to be in the possession of information as to (1) the total number of pupils on the rolls; (2) the number under instruction in Irish; (3) the number of hours per week devoted to Irish; (4) the competence of the teacher; and (5) the status of Irish History in the curriculum. Additional information — as to, for instance, the general tone and spirit of the school, the methods employed by the teacher, the extent to which he uses Irish in addressing the children, etc., — is also of the utmost value. Now the Coisde Gnótha has carefully prepared two sets of forms, one for secondary, and one for primary schools, which allow space for the recording of all these and other particulars. These forms will be sent by the Ard-Rúnaidhe to any Coisde Ceanntair or Craobh on application. We trust that they will be largely availed of, and that in a few months we shall be in possession of a reliable and detailed body of statistics bearing on the position of Irish in all the primary and secondary schools of the country.

Different modes of procedure may be adopted in different localities as circumstances suggest. The best plan will probably be found to be that followed in Kilkenny, — viz., the appointment of a special Schools' Committee, charged with the specific purpose of preparing and publishing these returns. The first step of such a committee would be to write to the Ard-Rúnaidhe of the League for a supply of the forms. A form should then be forwarded to every Manager and Principal of a school in the district, with a courteous covering letter explaining its purpose, and requesting that the form be filled up and signed by the Manager or Principal as the case may be. In order to ensure accuracy it should always be the objective to get

21

each form signed by the Manager or Principal responsible for the schools enumerated in it. We imagine that few Managers or Principals would refuse to supply the information asked for: should any do so, other sources of information are always available and should be utilised. As soon as the forms are complete, they should be summarised, the copies of the summary forwarded to the Ard-Rúnaidhe of the League, to *An Claidheamh Soluis,* to the local press, to the Bishop of the Diocese, and to all the Managers or Principals interested; also to the local Association of School Managers and to the Central Committee of Clerical Managers, or the Headmasters' Association, according as the schools involved be primary or secondary. We cannot promise to publish all such returns in our own columns, at least until we have concluded the series of detailed returns dealing with the Irish-speaking districts which we are now giving from week to week; but we propose to preserve all the returns sent to us, and as soon as we have sufficient material collected, to compile a general table showing the status of the Irish language in all the schools of Ireland. We ask Coisdí Ceanntair and Craobhacha of the League to facilitate this scheme by at once taking steps for the collection of statistics in their respective districts.

THE PRIMARY SCHOOLS
26.12.1903

In this issue we publish a very carefully constructed Irish programme for primary schools. It will be seen that it covers the full school course of six Standards, and that it provides for the teaching of Irish as part of the ordinary day's work (within 'School Hours') to Infants and to the First, Second and Third Standards, and for its teaching as an 'Extra' (for special fees) to the Fourth, Fifth and Sixth Standards. For Infants and the early Standards we recommend that the basis of instruction be 'Treóir an Pháisde' and that, *from the outset*, the class language be Irish. One cannot too strongly dwell on the importance of commencing to teach Irish from the moment of the child's first entry to school, and on the necessity — above all, at this early stage — of teaching it *orally*, just as a mother teaches her child. We are convinced that if the children be commenced with at a sufficiently early age, and if attractive oral methods be employed from the start, the results will be astonishingly successful. By catching the children young, the schools in spite of crude methods have succeeded and are still succeeding in turning Irish speakers into English speakers; catching them young, and employing intelligent methods, the schools ought surely to succeed in making English-speaking children Irish-speaking, — especially when it is rememebered that in the latter case they will be working with the grain, whereas in the former case they were and are working against it. The task of a teacher who takes a very young child in hand for the purpose of teaching him Irish is immensely facilitated not merely by the fact that the child is naturally quicker in acquiring new sounds than an adult, but also by the more important fact that the child (granting it to be of Irish parentage) was *meant* to speak Irish: his vocals organs have, as the result of heredity working through generations, got — in Father O'Leary's phrase the Irish 'twist' to begin with. The English 'twist', which makes the acquisition of Irish by an adult a matter of such comparative difficulty, is acquired, and is not native to any child born of Irish parents. Teachers and parents should recognise that the earlier they begin to teach Irish to a child, the easier will the task be; and if they commence at the cradle it will actually be easier to teach Irish than to teach English.

Our Three Years' specimen course for Irish as an 'Extra' will give an idea of what we mean by an 'attractive and profitable programme'. Teachers may take it from us that this programme — or its equivalent as regards quantity and proportion of matter — will be accepted by the Commissioners. It will be observed that for First Year we recommend 'Ceachta Beaga', I and II, with either 'An Prímhleabhar' or O'Growney, I: and that for Second Year we recommend either 'An Céad Léightheóir' and 'Tadhg Gabha' or O'Growney II and 'Tadhg Gabha' (of course, 'Taidhbhse an Chrainn', 'Greann na Gaedhilge' or any book of similar length might be substituted for 'Tadhg Gabha'). Throughout the course conversation and the memorising of Irish poetry hold prominent places. On the importance of the former it should be unnecessary to dwell further. The latter is a most useful exercise which we would wish to see introduced into every school in Ireland. The Ossianic lays are the very best poetry that could be selected for memorising.

Whilst we suggest that the teaching of Irish as an 'Extra' (i.e., for special fees) should be confined mainly to the Fourth, Fifth and Sixth Standards, and that the Infants and early Standards should be taught the language as a part of the ordinary programme during 'School Hours', we by no means advocate that the Irish teaching of the upper Standards should be tied down by the exigencies of a set programme for Irish as an 'Extra', or that it should all be conducted outside 'School Hours'. Object Lessons and other forms of instruction might usefully be given to the whole school within 'School Hours'. But the Irish teaching should not stop even here. As we have so often insisted, the most important teaching of all is that which is conveyed informally and, as it were, incidentally, throughout the whole course of the day; and, in this sense, Irish can be, and should be, taught all day long to every child on the rolls, no matter what his standing. In the first place, the teacher should himself talk Irish constantly, not only for the purpose of accustoming the children to the sound of the language, but with the object of encouraging them to regard Irish not merely as a desirable literary acquirement, but as a living instrument of thought to be used always and for all purposes, as a mere matter of course. Thus, the teacher should call the roll in Irish; should address each child by his Irish name and encourage the children themselves to make use of the Irish forms of their names when addressing one another, — as also to invariably use their Irish signatures. Again prayers should be taught and recited in Irish, and as much of the religious instruction as is feasible should be given in that language. Irish songs and hymns should be taught; physical drill should be conducted in Irish, or, at least, bilingually; the song or rhyme which the children in many schools sing when moving from class to class should invariably be in Irish. Then, the innumerable words of command, of praise, of reproof spoken by the teacher during the day should be in Irish, exclusively so in Irish-speaking districts, and as far as practicable in English-speaking districts; and answers in Irish should, as far as possible, be insisted upon. Also the teacher should systematically encourage the children to use Irish amongst themselves in school, at play, and on their way to and from school; and children whose parents are Irish-speaking should be individually and personally asked to endeavour to get their parents to speak Irish to them at home. We are here advocating no Utopian scheme: we are keeping strictly within the four corners of the

23

Commissioners' rules, and have recommended nothing which is not at present being done in some primary school or other of our acquaintance. The Organiser's notes on the methods of Mr. Ward, the teacher of Ardaghy Male School in the parish of Omeath, which are appended to the table of returns on page 3, show how far a teacher, even in a district which is practically an anglicised one, can travel in the direction we suggest.

BILINGUAL EDUCATION
2.1.1904

In last week's issue we said what shall be our last word for the present on the subject of attractive and profitable programmes for the teaching of Irish as a set subject in primary schools. It is high time that the full attention of the organisation be directed to a matter of still more vital importance, — the necessity for adapting school programmes in the Irish-speaking districts to the special conditions of those districts. Of course, all that we have been writing on the subject applies to the Irish-speaking and the bilingual areas equally with the English-speaking ones; but over and above the necessity for the efficient teaching of Irish, as a language, in the schools of the Irish-speaking districts, there is the very urgent necessity for re-modelling the whole school programme in those schools, — or rather for sweeping away all existing programmes, and substituting for them programmes based on the postulate that the children for whom they cater are Irish-speaking and not English-speaking. Irish is being taught with considerable efficiency in many scores of schools in the Irish-speaking districts; but in almost all of these the programme proceeds from the start on the supposition that the children are English-speaking to commence with. We know of only six schools in all Ireland in which the programme consistently proceeds on the contrary supposition.

It thus appears that whilst the Gaelic League's general educational policy is slowly but surely forcing its way into the schools, practically no advance has been made in the matter of bilingual education in the Irish-speaking areas. It is now four years since the famous Memorial signed by the Managers of upwards of a thousand schools in Irish-speaking districts declared that the defects of the existing educational system in those districts could be removed only 'by teaching the children to read and write, and utilise to the fullest capacity, the language in common use among the grown people in these districts'. It is four years since the New Programme of the Commissioners came into force, — and that Programme, in the opinion of the Archbishop of Dublin, removed every obstacle to the introduction of the great reform asked for by the school managers. It is over three years since His Grace delivered his notable address on Bilingual Education at Baggot Street Training College, which he afterwards edited and gave to the public through the Publication Committee of the Gaelic League. It is nearly three years since His Grace announced the result of his competition for the best Programmes for the working of a school on bilingual lines, and published the four best Programmes, also through the medium of the Publication Committee. The Managers have demanded Bilingual Education; the Commissioners have practically sanctioned its introduction, — throwing the onus of introducing it, however, on the Managers; the Archbishop of Dublin has given the public four detailed Programmes carefully constructed to meet the special needs of a bilingual system; the

24

Gaelic League has published a Primer, a First Reader, and an admirable set of Reading Charts; all this has been accomplished history for the last three years and yet Bilingual Education is apparently as far off as ever.

Fifty years ago Sir Patrick Keenan wrote: 'The real policy of the educationalist would, in my opinion, be to teach Irish grammatically and soundly to the Irish-speaking people, and then to teach them English through the medium of their national language'. What the Gaelic League presses for at the present moment is just this, the teaching of Irish grammatically and soundly to Irish-speaking children, and the teaching of English (and other useful subjects) through the medium of Irish. The question at once arises how best and most efficiently may this be done? That question has been faced and solved by a number of continental countries, and to a certain extent by Wales. The solution they have found has invariably been in some form or other of Bilingual Education.

What is Bilingual Education?

Bilingual Education is a system which obtains in most of those continental countries in which, as in Ireland, there are two vernaculars, or spoken languages, in use side by side. It admits of countless modifications, and is probably alike in all its details in no two countries. The essential feature of the system is the teaching of two languages side by side, and, so to say, *pari passu*, all through the school course, the pupil's knowledge of the one language being constantly utilised to help him in the acquisition of the other. It is a matter of option as to whether all the books used should be bilingual, or whether two sets of books should be used concurrently.

Now, there are a great many schools in Ireland in which Irish is the only language spoken by the children when they first come to school; there is a considerably larger number in which, whilst a proportion of the children speak Irish only, the majority of them speak Irish and English with equal or practically equal facility; and there is a still larger number in which, whilst all or nearly all the children *understand* Irish, most of them habitually speak English. In all these three classes of schools — in other words, in the schools over nearly one third of the total area of Ireland — 'the real policy of the educationalist' would be to introduce some form of the system we have described in outline; that is what the Gaelic League means when it says that the desideratum in the Irish-speaking districts is the introduction of a system frankly and fully bilingual. The managers of upwards of a thousand schools were four years ago convinced of the soundness of this view. But we have it on the authority of the Archbishop of Dublin that there is nothing whatever in the existing rules of the Board to prevent the introduction of a Bilingual System into the schools in the Irish-speaking areas to-morrow morning. Referring to the reform demanded in the Managers' Memorial, His Grace's words are:—

'Now, so far as the Commissioners of National Education are concerned, there is, as you know, no longer any obstacle in the way of the introduction of this great reform. In the words of the New Programme: —

"Irish . . . may be taught in all National Schools, and may be taught in these schools during the ordinary schools hours, provided the adequacy of the course of instruction in the usual day school subjects is not impaired or hampered thereby.'

'As to the effect on the course of instruction, and upon the instruction itself, of basing the whole work of the school upon the teaching of Irish as the medium of instruction, — I am speaking of course, of the schools in

Irish-speaking districts, those districts in which Irish is the vernacular language of the children, as much as English is of the children here in Dublin — we shall see, as we proceed that, so far from there being any question of "impairing" or of "hampering" the work of the school by such a change, the effect will be the very opposite. For it will enormously facilitate the work of those schools in all their branches. I may indeed go farther. It will give such schools the one chance they can have of doing real educational work at all.'

These words were spoken by His Grace whilst he was yet a member of the National Board. They have been standing in cold print for three years. Yet the schools in which a bona fide effort has been since made in the direction of introducing a system of any sort which, without doing violence to language, could be called a bilingual one, could probably be counted on the fingers of the two hands. Whose is the fault? It is certainly not the National Board's. Is it the Managers', is it the Teachers', or is it — the Gaelic League's?

BILINGUAL EDUCATION
9.1.1904

As we insisted last week, the educational programme of the Gaelic League demands not only that the language and history of Ireland be taught to every child in every class in every school in Ireland, but that, in all districts where Irish is the home language, or one of the home languages, the whole educational system be re-modelled in accordance with the special linguistic conditions of the locality. We also pointed out that the experience of the continental countries which have had to face and solve a similar problem shows that the only adequate, or rather the only possible solution, is one along the lines of Bilingual Education. We further pointed out that in the opinion of the Archbishop of Dublin, the New Programme of the Commissioners has rendered such a solution in Ireland absolutely feasible, and that, as a matter of fact, 'so far as the Commissioners of National Education are concerned, there is . . . no longer any obstacle in the way of the introduction of this great reform (Bilingual Education)'.

It will be remembered that we divided the districts in which the special linguistic conditions call for the introduction of some form of Bilingual Education into three classes: (*a*) those in which Irish is the only vernacular of the children when they first come to school; (*b*) those in which, whilst a proportion of the children speak Irish only, the majority of them speak Irish and English with equal or practically equal facility; and (*c*) those in which, whilst all or nearly all of the children *understand* Irish, most of them habitually speak English. In all these three classes of schools, the educational policy of the Gaelic League demands the introduction of some form or other of Bilingual Education. The precise form must be determined by the local conditions. Bilingual Education is not a rigid cast-iron 'method': it allows of as many modifications as there are conceivable variations in the relative prevalence of each of the two vernaculars; it admits both of oral and of book teaching; it scorns neither Gouin nor Berlitz, nor yet Bizeray; it permits either of the employment of bilingual readers or of the concurrent use of two sets of books, one in each language; its one essential requirement is that the two languages be taught side by side as spoken tongues throughout the whole school course, the pupil's knowledge of the one language being systematically utilised at every stage in the acquisition of the second, and *vice versa*.

So much for the general principles of bilingual teaching. Let us discuss in some detail its application to an Irish-speaking district. The teaching both of Irish and English should be commenced during the first year the child attends school. It does not, however, follow that the teaching of both must necessarily commence at one and the same moment. It will usually be found that the children of a district, even though they may be fluent in both Irish and English, are more at home in one or other of them, which they habitually speak from choice. In such cases, a month or two may be devoted to instruction in the more familiar vernacular — be it Irish or English — as a start; but, *at the earliest possible moment*, instruction in the two languages should be proceeded with, and systematically carried out through all the standards, until the child emerges from school an educated speaker, reader and writer of both Irish and English.

The two alphabets should be taught concurrently, — or practically so, subject to the reservation indicated in the preceding paragraph. Personally, we are strongly in favour of the traditional Irish names* of the Irish letters being taught from the outset, or else the phonetic names suggested in the Gaelic League's Infant Primer; this, however, is a matter which we would willingly leave to the teacher's option, and, provided c be pronounced 'cé', e 'ay', and g 'gé' we should not, for the present, object to the other letters of the Irish alphabet being called by the current English names. All the explanation as to the function and formation of the letters, the distinction between vowels and consonants, etc., should be given bilingually, — first in the more familiar vernacular and immediately afterwards in the other.

When the First Reader is put into the hands of the pupils a similar course should be followed. As has already been stated, it is optional whether bilingual readers be employed concurrently. In either case, the children have Irish primers in their hands. To test whether they understand what they are reading the teacher asks them to give in Irish, in their own words, a résumé of a lesson, or even the sense of a particular sentence or phrase. He then asks them to give a résumé of the lesson or passage in English, or the English equivalent of the sentence or phrase. A direct and word-for-word translation from either language into the other should not be insisted on or even encouraged. The first and primary object is to see that the child thoroughly understands the Irish which he is reading; the second to see that he can express the same ideas in idiomatic English. The child should be able to turn instantly from one language to the other *without confusing the idioms:* if he is taught intelligently on bilingual lines he will, without any conscious effort, learn to do this; if he is taught on no system, if knowledge be simply *shovelled into him*, without reference to his capability of receiving it, above all, if it is attempted to instruct him through a medium which he only imperfectly comprehends, he will as often as not use English idiom when he attempts to speak in Irish, and Irish idiom when he attempts to

* We do not of course, refer to the fancy names Ailm, Beith, Coll, etc., which we cannot imagine were ever used in *spelling*, but to the names á, bé, cé, dé, etc., still used by many old Irish speakers, who were taught to read and write Irish upwards of half-a-century ago.

27

speak in English. Bilingual Education in the Irish-speaking districts would not only mean the saving of the Irish language as a spoken tongue, but it would also mean that the children would be taught English and other useful subjects properly; in other words, it would admit the possibility of their being educated, a possibility which is at present entirely precluded.

So far we have been dealing with the teaching only of Irish and English, — i.e., the two languages themselves which are the basis of our bilingual system. It need hardly be added that all other subjects on the school programme — Arithmetic, Geography, Object Lessons, Drawing, Needlework, Manual Training, Physical Drill, and the rest, — can equally be taught on bilingual lines, and in bilingual districts should be so taught. As before, the more familiar of the two vernaculars should be employed first; our own experience is that where children speak both Irish and English, their Irish vocabulary is generally the larger of the two, and their command of Irish expression greater than their command of English expression; in such cases it goes without saying that all explanations and instruction will be more efficiently given if given in the first instance in Irish, and afterwards in English.

There are many other points which will suggest themselves to the common sense of every practical teacher. Thus, from a very early stage children should be got to write down from dictation on their slates the difficult words both in the Irish and English readers. For the juniors, a headline should be written on the blackboard — in Irish and English on alternate days to be copied neatly on slates or paper. From the second standard up either Bilingual Copybooks or separate Irish and English Copybooks on alternate days should be used for writing-lessons. The ordinary transcription and dictation lessons should be divided into two periods, one for each language, or else Irish and English transcription and dictation lessons set on alternate days. Composition in the two languages should be attempted as soon as the pupils have made sufficent progress in spelling: for original composition the translation of continuous passages from one language to the other may be occasionally — but only occasionally — substituted.

It may be commented that this system makes large demands on the capacity and energies of the teacher: all effective teaching does. And let us not forget that the mind and soul of Ireland cannot be saved without large, very large, demands on the capacity and energies of teachers and others.

BILINGUAL EDUCATION
16.1.1904

We trust that it will not be imagined that the science of Bilingual Education which we outlined in our last issue is a mere fanciful and academic scheme evolved out of our inner consciousness, and having no reference to the actual state of affairs in Ireland here and now. On the contrary, it is essentially a scheme based on the possibilities of the existing programme and rules of the Commissioners of 'National' Education, and we have been at pains to make no single recommendation which could not be put in practice to-morrow morning in any and every school in an Irish-speaking part of Ireland. We are not theorising, or writing in the air: we are simply laying before our readers the results of our inquiries into the subject of Bilingual Education, as understood and practised in other lands, and pointing out how the system may be applied to the existing condition of affairs in the Irish-speaking districts, *under the existing rules and regulations of the 'National' Board*. For the suggestions we have made and shall make we are indebted mainly to four sources: (*a*) our inquiries into the systems of Bilingual Teaching in vogue on the Continent, notably in Belgium; (*b*) our personal observations of the actual working of a bilingual system in some Welsh primary schools which we visited in 1899; (*c*) our personal observations in a number of schools in Irish-speaking districts in which, whilst there can scarcely be said to be a regularly thought-out bilingual mode of instruction in vogue, yet both Irish and English are taught side by side more or less on bilingual lines; and (*d*) for a number of valuable suggestions we are indebted to the programme drawn up by Micheál Ó Máille, of Cornamona, which was awarded first prize in the Archbishop of Dublin's competition for the best programme for the working of a school bilingually. Mr. O'Malley's own school is probably the nearest approach to a bilingually-worked school which there is in Ireland.

It may be well to make it clear that we have not been giving an exposition of any particular 'teaching method'. Some of our recommendations, in point of fact, drive a coach and horses through the cardinal principles of some of the most approved continental 'methods'. What we have been keeping in view all along is the existing state of affairs in the Irish-speaking districts and the existing rules of the 'National' Board; and, granted that state of affairs and those rules, our object has been to show how best Irish and English may be soundly and grammatically taught as living tongues to children who, to begin with, are already bilingualists, more or less. Personally, of course, we are not particularly anxious that Irish children should be taught English at all; but under the rules of the 'National' Board, the teaching of English is at present compulsory in every primary school, and, keeping strictly within the four corners of the Commissioners' rules, we are, in the spirit of the Archbishop of Dublin's Baggot Street address, endeavouring to secure that the most be made of those rules.

Sham Teaching
The justness of the criticism we have been levelling against the *sham* teaching — the word is not a bit too strong — of Irish in many primary and secondary schools is daily borne testimony to by correspondents who write us from all parts of the country. Not merely the Organisers' reports, but the many letters on the subject which reach us from all quarters, go to show that in most even of those schools which have the name of being favourable to the movement, Irish is being taught only to a minority of the children on the rolls, and that to these it is, as often as not, being taught indifferently. Thus, a Connacht priest — who is one of the closest observers and most effective workers which the League has in the West — writes us as to the schools in his district: 'It is very difficult to get definite information from the teachers around here as to what number of their pupils are being taught Irish. Irish is being taught in the Convent Schools and in the Christian Brothers' Schools, in two others, male and female, and in two more, one male and one female, — in all some eight or nine our of twenty-four or

29

twenty-six schools in my immediate neighbourhood. In each of these schools there are not, at most, any more than the two senior classes — and, as you know, in rural districts these are by far the smallest — learning Irish. The numbers are bad enough, but the manner of teaching the language is infinitely worse. — *e.g.*, rod and bod are the conventional way for pronouncing ród and bád in a large local school; and if these things happen in the dry wood what about the green? In a large number of schools Irish is taken up in the mere hope of pecuniary gain and, the system of marking in that subject being what it is, there is no probability of Irish being properly taught until the rules are changed. As long as the First Year's Examination is held by written cards and by inspectors who know no Irish things can't improve. The majority of the Inspectors, too, are constantly sneering at the language and have, in an indirect way, given the teachers to understand that the teaching of Irish gives a low tone to a school. The whole system is unsound, and until it is kicked out of the country, I fear we are but knocking our heads against a stone wall. Things may be different in the cities, but in the country . . . '.

Now, we believe with our correspondent that the 'National' Board, as at present constituted, must go before a really Irish system of education is possible in the primary schools of this country; but the case for the abolition of the 'National' Board is hopelessly weak as long as such facilities as it has given remain unavailed of to the full. And this is why we have recently devoted so much space to pointing out how the existing rules of the Board, such as they are, may be made the most of. We believe our correspondent is quite correct in saddling the Inspectors with a large share of the responsibility for the unsatisfactory status of the language in many schools of which the Managers and teachers are, apparently, sympathetic. This is a point on which we may have more to say in the near future.

Sham Tests
One way in which the Board has directly encouraged what we have called 'sham teaching' is by their persistent adherence to the absurd method of examination by means only of printed cards. The Munster Provincial Clerical Managers' Association, meeting at Mallow under the presidency of Right Rev. Mgr. Keller, has done a public service by prominently drawing attention to this out-of-date mode of testing language-teaching. The resolution adopted by the Managers puts the objections admirably: 'That we have heard with regret that the proficiency of the pupils in Irish has been in some instances judged by means of written examination alone; that we consider that such examination is but a partial and unsatisfactory test of the knowledge of pupils in any language; that the accurate pronunciation and reading of a language should receive due consideration from the Inspector, and that any system of examination which excludes these is unfair both to pupils and teacher'; — and we may add, to the language. It is characteristic of the 'National' Board that whilst its rules allow the fullest liberty for the teaching of Irish both as an extra and as an ordinary and permit even of the employment of the language as the medium of instruction in the case of Irish-speaking children, yet the Board, partly by its unsatisfactory system of examination, and partly through the medium of its Inspectors, is still actively discouraging the teaching of Irish as far as it dares.

Since we wrote the foregoing we have received a copy of the new 'Programmes of Instruction for National Schools' which the Commissioners are about to issue, and which will come into operation on 1st April, 1904. These programmes are, the Commissioners state, 'based on the Revised Programme of 1900, with such modifications as the experience of the past three years has shown to be desirable'. The chief modifications of a general character are three in number: Geography and Grammar have been restored to the rank of 'ordinary subjects'; much less prominence is given to Manual Instruction, which the Commissioners will not henceforward require to be taught beyond the Second Standard; and provision has been made for an additional or Seventh Standard. With regard to the teaching of Languages (including Irish) there is a new and valuable provision: —

'The examination in languages will be *both oral and written. Fairly correct pronunciation will be essential for a pass.*'

This provision, if universally and effectively carried out, will remove the grievance to which attention has been drawn by the Munster Managers.

BILINGUAL EDUCATION
23.1.1904

Last week we sought to make it clear that everything we have hitherto written on the subject of Bilingual Education has been written in full view of all the existing circumstances in the primary schools of the Irish-speaking districts. Our recommendations have been conditioned by those circumstances and by the exigencies of the existing 'Rules and Regulations' of the Commissioners of 'National' Education. We have not been suggesting an alternative set of 'Rules and Regulations', but have rather been endeavouring to point out to what extent the 'Rules and Regulations', actually in force permit of the introduction of a bilingual system, and by what ways and means full advantage may be taken of the undoubtedly large facilities which they allow. Whilst we have drawn hints from what we have read of the methods in use in the bilingual countries of the Continent and from our personal observations in bilingual Wales, we have throughout been at pains to make no recommendation which could not be put in practice at the present moment in any school in an Irish-speaking or bilingual part of Ireland. The time will come when Irish Ireland will be strong enough to march forward and require those responsible for the government of the country to introduce a bilingual system as the established and recognised order; at present the most profitable line of action is to see that the existing system, such as it is, be made the most of. And we think we have shown that a great deal can be made of it.

The Example of Belgium

Meanwhile, however, an examination in some detail of what other lands have actually accomplished in the field of Bilingual Education cannot but be illuminating. We shall take Belgium, in many respects a typical bilingual nation. We have before us a little work on *Bilingual Teaching in the Belgian Schools*, recently issued by the Cambridge University Press. The genesis of the book is as follows: In 1899, Mr. T. R. Dawes, M.A.,

Headmaster of the Pembroke Dock County School, spent thirteen weeks in Belgium as Gilchrist Travelling Student of the University of Wales, for the purpose of inquiring into the subject of bilingual teaching as understood and practised in the primary and secondary schools of Belgium. The book before us is the Report presented by Mr. Dawes on his return to the Court of the University of Wales. In passing, we may note the suggestive point that this inquiry was undertaken under the aegis and at the expense of the popular Welsh University, — an institution which is in close touch with Welsh national life, and which is, indeed, the direct outcome of the Welsh Language Movement. (The Society of Cymmrodorion, which corresponds to the Gaelic League, was chiefly instrumental in wresting the charter of the University of Wales from Government). If Ireland had anything approximating to a National University, such things might be thought of here.

Through the good offices of the Belgian Minister of Education, Mr. Dawes was enabled to visit educational institutions of every order, from the primary school to the University. He gives a highly interesting description of language-lessons heard by him, extracts from directors' instructions to teachers, records of conversations with experts, and many incidental details which throw light upon the general state of education in Belgium. Every page of the books is full of instruction, of illumination, of suggestion.

Belgium and Ireland

First as to the mutual relations of the two languages in Belgium. We shall let Mr. Dawes speak: 'Two races having widely different characteristics are united under the name Belgian. The Flemings, who are the most numerous, are a race of German extraction, brothers to the Dutch of the neighbouring kingdom of Holland, speaking the Low German language Flemish, which is practically identical with Dutch, and inhabiting the North-Western portion of Belgium, north of a line drawn through Courtraie and Louvain, and a small portion of Flanders now forming part of France. The Walloons, south of this line, are French alike in race and language, and while the sympahty of the Flemings lean to Holland and Germany, those of the Walloons turn rather to France. French and Flemish are thus the languages of Belgium. It is true that a French patois is spoken by many Walloons in the South, but this has no literature, and is merely a corrupt form of French. German is also spoken by many Belgians near the frontier of Germany — but when Belgium is termed a bilingual country the languages referred to are French and Flemish.' Now, though the majority of Belgians are Flemings, the official language of Belgium was for many years French, and is so to a certain extent at the present time; 'but', writes Mr. Dawes, 'the progress of the Flemish movement which has for its object the maintenance of the Flemish`tongue in Flanders (the Flemish portion of Belgium), and indeed the spread of the language throughout Belgium, has brought about great changes, and tends to make the Belgians more and more a bilingual people'. A glance at the stormy history of Belgium during the past three centuries accounts for the dominant position that French has held. In the seventeenth century Belgium was part of the Spanish dominions; it then passed into Austrian, and subsequently into French hands. After Waterloo it was united to Holland and the two countries constituted the monarchy of Holland and Belgium which lasted till 1830. Numerous grievances, such as the favouritism shown to Hollanders in all official positions, created disaffection amongst the Belgians, and this feeling culminated in the revolution of 1830, when Belgium became an independent kingdom. 'During these centuries,' continues Mr. Dawes, 'Flemish remained the language of the great majority of people, but the language of the government, of administration, of the law courts, of the schools, and generally of the upper classes was French'. How, *mutatis mutandis*, we seem to be reading of 18th and 19th century Ireland! And again: 'The upper and middle classes, educated in schools in which the language was French, discarded Flemish and learned to despise it. The 'masses' retained their native tongue; but their children for the most part received no education; the national schools charged fees they could not pay, and the teaching was in a language they did not understand.' All the arguments against the native speech with which we are familiar in Ireland were levelled against Flemish by the French faction, and in time came to be adopted by degenerate Flemings. Flemish was an insignificant and moribund idiom, spoken only by a few thousand over a portion of a small country; it had no literature; it could not express the ideas of modern life; it was bound to give way before French, a world-tongue, spoken by millions, and with a rich literature. Thus, French became the language of administration, of commerce, of education, of the press, of the 'daoine móra': only the peasants in the backwoods and the poor folk in the smaller provincial towns went on speaking Flemish.

'In Flanders Flemish'

So far, the parallel with Ireland is very close. But the parallel ceases with 1830. The Flemish language movement came sixty years sooner than the Irish language movement. Signs on it, during the last three-quarters of a century, whilst Ireland has been growing less Irish, Belgium has been growing more Flemish; whilst Ireland has been listless, Belgium has been strenuous; whilst Ireland has been retrograding morally, intellectually, industrially, Belgium has been marching forward in all three respects. Let us hear Mr. Dawes on the achievements of the language movement in Belgium: 'Since 1830 a great popular movement in favour of the use of Flemish in Flanders has sprung up and achieved numerous reforms. The motto of this Flemish movement is 'In Flanders Flemish', and Flemish has in later years become more and more the language of the Law Courts and of Government officials. No judge or advocate can now be appointed in Flanders unless he has a knowledge of Flemish. 'We object', say the Flemings, 'to be judged by men whom we hear but do not understand'. In the Communes (local government bodies), in the primary and secondary schools, and in the army, Flemish has to some extent taken the place of French. The streets throughout Belgium are named in both languages, and all official documents, including the official *Monitor*, are published in both languages, generally in parallel columns. The Flemish tongue is spoken by greater numbers now than at the beginning of the century; the Flemish papers, such as the *Handelblad* of Antwerp, have a very large circulation; important works in all branches of literature and science are written in Flemish, and Flemish plays are played in the theatres. Especially remarkable is the progress of Flemish in the secondary schools of the Walloon district, and the desire shown by the directing classes that their children shall acquire a good knowledge of Flemish in the schools. The prejudice formerly felt against Flemish dies away as its utility in a country which is becoming more and more bilingual manifests iitself. The Walloons are taunted today with their quickness in learning Flemish when an official position is at stake. It would now be impossible for an official to protest against the teaching of Flemish in the public schools of Brussels lest 'the learning of this patois should spoil the French accent of the children'; neither would a Burgomaster of Brussels assert, 'there are no Flemings in Brussels'. A general conference held each year of those interested in preserving for Flemish Belgium its native language has had great influence in promoting this object; and one striking proof of the conviction held by the Government that this national feeling must be conciliated was the appointment of the great Flemish novelist Conscience as teacher of Flemish to the royal princes'. All this, it should be observed, has taken three-quarters of a century in the accomplishment: a fact which should be noted by those who fret and fume because the Gaelic League has not in ten years saved the Irish language. Enduring national revivals have always been slow.

Bilingualism in the Belgian Schools

To come to the schools. Elementary Education in Belgium is now free but not compulsory. 'The programme of the instruction varies greatly in different localities, each Commune making its own programme. The Belgians prize the great communal liberty which they enjoy and do not share in the French love of centralisation and unity in education. In the country districts of Flanders the only language taught in the elementary school is Flemish, and little is done for French, it being felt that with the time at the disposal of the school no serious progress can be made with a second language.' These districts would correspond with the exclusively Irish-speaking districts in Ireland. 'In some village schools, however, I found French lessons given after school hours, and for these a charge was made'; (French as our familiar 'extra'); 'in other villages again, where the population was considerably mixed, the second language was part of the ordinary school work. In Brussels, which provides the best instances of bilingual elementary schools, I found that pupils leaving the elementary schools had a good knowledge of both French and Flemish.'

THE UNIVERSITY QUESTION
30.1.1904

The University question is one in which the Gaelic League has, and must necessarily have, a very real interest. The absence of provision for University training of a kind acceptable to the great body of the people of Ireland is not merely a Catholic grievance, but a national grievance; the whole nation suffers, and must necessarily suffer, from the fact that three-quarters of the inhabitants of the island are practically debarred from any form of University training. The ghastly failure of the primary and secondary educational systems is largely due to the non-existence, for all practical purposes, of a thinking and cultured class, informed with a national spirit and with its eyes fixed on the realities of Irish life. Most of those amongst us who have been 'educated' have been 'educated' foreignwards; those who are in contact with Irish traditions are, for the most part, not educated at all. This fact tells every day and at all points against the work of the Gaelic League; and for that reason, if for no other, all the force of the Gaelic League should be thrown into the struggle for the immediate settlement of the University question.

The League's Policy

The League, as a corporate body, has already outlined its policy on the subject. It remains for the members of the organisation, by collective and individual action, to see that this policy be carried out, whatever form of solution be arrived at. That the agitation may be kept within the proper lines, it is as well that we should reiterate the League's position. That position was authoritatively and luminously stated by our President before the late University Commission. It is not a mere question of professorships, courses, or scholarships; it is a matter of the atmosphere, the spirit of the institution. These must be frankly Irish; otherwise our last state will be worse than our first. We do not want another 'British institution', as Trinity College is now admitted to be by its own dignitaries; we want an *Irish University*.

'We press now,' said Dr. Hyde before the Commission, 'for a University that shall be Irish in the fullest and broadest sense of the word. It must be Irish in the same sense that Oxford and Cambridge are English. It must not be an English educational institution, constituted with more or less regard for local conditions. It must not be in any sense a local University, like Birmingham or Manchester. It must recognise that Ireland is a separate entity in just the same sense as Wales is, with a separate national life, language, literature, and history. We have plenty of so-called Universities in this country, but we have none that meets our wants, none in which the atmosphere is national and Irish . . . We believe that the only hope of a new University doing good to Ireland will be to have it frankly and robustly national, in a spiritual and intellectual sense, from the very outset. If not, it will never grip the Irish mind, or be popular in any deep sense with the bulk of the Irish people. We want an intellectual headquarters for Irish Ireland.

Now, the Gaelic League does not, and it is not necessary that it should, declare itself in favour of any one solution of the University question as against another. Any form of solution which commends itself to the general Catholic body-hierarchy, clergy and laity — will commend itself to the Gaelic League, provided that the interests of Irish Ireland be secured. It is obvious that the safeguarding of those interests depends not so much on external form as on internal organisation; in other words, whether the solution take the form of a new National University, of a new Catholic University, or of a new College within Dublin University, is a matter of indifference to the League, as long as it be secured that the new University institution itself, whatsoever its form, provide organic means for the due representation of Irish national sentiment in its governing body. On this point the League through its President was perfectly explicit and definite: —

'The League desires that the popular element, either through itself or the County Councils, or some other medium, be allowed to nominate a certain proportion of the Senate of any new University that may come into existence as the outcome of this Commission; thus, in all probability, securing that a certain proportion of the men

35

nominated on the Senate be men of recognised scholarship in Irish. If the Senate has not the confidence of the rank and file of the Irish nation, if it only represents what we call the 'shoneens', then we would just as soon have no University at all. We want broadminded men upon the Senate, and men who understand us, and know how to make us respond to the education that they offer us. We do not want wealthy dignitaries and country gentlemen, nominated by the Castle out of mere compliment to themselves.'

The first essential, therefore, is that the new University or University body should be in close touch with Ireland; should be not only in Ireland, but of Ireland. And the means for effecting this is clearly pointed out, — the due representation of the popular element in the governing body. The President of the League suggests two mediums through which the popular element might have a due voice in shaping the destinies of the University; a third would be the adequate representation of the general body of graduates on the Senate or other governing body. In Wales the national University has been brought into touch with Welsh popular life by just such means.

What Wales has done

Now, Wales, as Dr. Hyde has said, 'really seems to have solved, as perhaps no other part of the Three Kingdoms has done, the problem of University teaching for the masses;' and as University teaching for the masses is precisely what we want in Ireland, and as, moreover, the situation in Wales, linguistically, intellectually and educationally, presents many parallels with that in Ireland, it will be helpful to discuss, in the first place, the movement which led up to the establishment of the Welsh University, and in the second, the constitution and fortunes of that body since its foundation in 1893.

Now, the secret of the success of the University of Wales is that, in the words of Dr. Isambard Owen, its Senior Deputy Chancellor, 'it originated by a thoroughly popular movement, one that sprang from the very heart of Welsh popular life'. The story of its foundation was sketched by Dr. Owen before the University Commission. The University consists of three residential Colleges, — Aberystwyth, Cardiff and Bangor. Aberystwyth dates from 1873, and the other two arose out of a Departmental Committee on Welsh Education which was appointed in 1880. This Departmental Committee framed a recommendation in general terms that it would be desirable to establish a University in Wales. Nothing further was done until 1887, except that the late Principal Jones of Cardiff never omitted an opportunity of impressing on the Government and the public that the whole state of education in Wales logically led up to the foundation of a University. In 1887 the matter was taken up by the Cymmrodorion Society, which to a certain extent corresponds to the Gaelic League. In that year the Society held a series of meetings in connection with the National Eisteddfod, in which the whole subject of education in Wales was considered, and a series of resolutions framed, including one which called for the establishment of a University in Wales in connection with the existing Colleges. In the following January the same Society called a second conference, to which the men representing the academic life of Wales were alone summoned. This conference re-affirmed the necessity for the establishment of a Welsh University. The Conference

36

then met the Welsh Members of Parliament and a number of peers connected with Wales and obtained their acquiescence in its demands. In the following summer, 1888, the same Society called a further Conference in connection with the National Eisteddfod to consider the question of establishing a University. The desirability of doing so was again unanimously affirmed. 'The next step', Dr. Owen goes on, 'was a meeting of representatives of the three University Colleges at present associated in the University, who went as a deputation to Lord Cranbrook, then President of the Council. Lord Cranbrook invited the three Colleges to prepare a scheme and submit it to him. In the year 1891, a Conference was formed of representatives of Intermediate Education Committees . . . This Conference met in 1891, and laid down the general principles upon which they believed the University ought to be founded. The Conference also appointed a Committee to draw up details . . . The Committee reported a complete scheme to the Conference in the early part of 1893. The Conference adopted this scheme, and at once ordered it to be issued to every member of every County Council in Wales, to every member of every authority of the constituent Colleges, to all the members of the joint Intermediate Education Conference, and to the public both by post and through the press. For five months the scheme was laid before the whole country in this way for consideration. At the end of five months the Conference met again, made some alterations of detail that appeared to be required, and submitted it in the form of a draft charter to the Privy Council. That Charter, with only some trivial changes, was approved by the Privy Council, and received the royal assent in November, 1893. The University was constituted in the early part of the succeeding year, it framed its statutes during 1894, it commenced operations in the summer of 1895, and September 1895 may be said to have begun our first academic year.'

A number of significant facts detach themselves from this narrative: (1) The impetus came, in the first instance, from the Welsh language movement. (2) In the agitation which culminated in the foundation of the University, the language leaders, the academic bodies, the politicians and the County Councils worked side by side. (3) The movement practically took shape, developed and come to a head within six years — from 1887 to 1893. (4) The British Government yielded to the demands of the Weslh people almost as soon as those demands found authentic and concrete expression. (5) The system of University teaching accorded was that system which the Welsh people themselves thought best, not that which the British Government thought best. There are here several very obvious morals for us.

THE UNIVERSITY QUESTION
6.2.1904

The stock plea of those who, in pursuance of the benign British policy of 'state-aided ignorance' in Ireland, are bitterly opposed to the planning of facilities for higher education to the people of this country, has always been that the demand for those facilities is, and from the start has been, a Bishops' demand. In order to bolster up that plea, Dr. Mahaffy some two years ago made an excursion, probably for the first time, into the field of

Irish history; and as a result was able to inform the astonished University Commission that the very earliest demand for an Irish University — which was made by no less a person than Hugh O'Neill — was a Bishops' demand. 'Anyone who reads history,' said Dr. Mahaffy, 'knows that Tyrone spoke as the mouthpiece, not of the Irish Roman Catholic people, but of the Roman Catholic Ecclesiastics; and that that, which was the earliest demand made for a Roman Catholic University, was not the demand of the people, but the demand of the ecclesiastics, whose desire was, and is, to dominate the whole situation.' Now, anyone who reads history knows that if man ever spoke in the name of the Irish people, that man was Hugh O'Neill; if political movement in Ireland were ever national that movement was the movement of Hugh O'Neill. And anyone who reads history knows that if there be one question on which there is a consensus of opinion in Ireland, that question is the University question. The great meeting of last week was merely a reaffirmation of this fact. The demand for adequate provision for University training of a kind acceptable to the majority of the people is not, and never was, a demand put forward by the Bishops and clergy for their own purposes: it is the demand of the Catholic laity of Ireland, it is the demand of every Protestant who sincerely wishes well to Ireland; it is a demand in which Irishmen who agree on no other public question are in absolute unanimity: and whilst backed by Irishmen of every sect, party and class, it is backed also by bodies like the Gaelic League, which, whilst knowing no distinction of sect, party or class, stands simply for Ireland and her interests.

The absolute unanimity of the National demand for equality in University education was, then, the first thing demonstrated by last week's meeting; the second was the fact that the nation is in no temper to brook further delay. The meeting was, we trust, but the commencement of an agitation which will end only when its object has been attained. In that agitation the Gaelic League has a very important part to play.

One of the speakers at the Mansion House meeting said that, in answer to Ireland's demands for bread, England had always given her stones. Ireland must take care that no more stones are foisted upon her. She must summon up the moral courage to firmly reject anything which she cannot accept with a clear conscience. Fifty years ago she rejected the godless colleges thrust upon her by the British Government: should that Government now or in any time seek to thrust on her a nationless college, she must equally reject it. Within the walls of any University or University College that may be established as the result of the present agitation, Ireland must rule supreme.

As we pointed out last week, the extent to which a University body is really national is less a matter of external form than of internal organisation: call it a University, call it a College, — be it autonomous and practically independent, or be it closely bound up with and dependent on a larger institution, — but let its internal organisation supply a means through which Irish public opinion shall have the major part in the shaping of its destinies, and we will have it; make its senate a preserve for the hangers-on of Dublin Castle, for the alumni of the 'only successful British institution in Ireland', for all those, whatsoever their class or creed, whose faces are turned Britainwards, and Ireland will have none of it.

There are several means by which Irish popular opinion might find expression on the governing body of the new institution. A very obvious one would be through the representatives of the Catholic Hierarchy. Another would be through representatives nominated by the County Councils and County Boroughs. A third would be through nominees of the general body of graduates. No scheme which did not provide means for this third form of popular representation could, in our opinion, be regarded as satisfactory. It is of the very essence of University life that the alumni of the University itself should have an adequate part in the moulding of its character and policy. And, moreover, — to look at the matter from the Gaelic League's own peculiar standpoint — it may be taken for granted that the rank-and-file graduates of any possible University body acceptable to the majority of Irishmen would be strongly imbued with Irish-Ireland principles; for they would be drawn just from that class which forms the backbone of the League itself. In this connection it is interesting to note that the young University of Wales has been brought into close touch with Welsh popular life by just such means as we suggest: indeed, the extent to which the distinctively popular element is represented on its governing body is in very suggestive contrast with the proposals of the late University Commission as to the representation of mere Ireland on the governing body of the proposed Catholic College. The popular element, it will be recollected, was to be represented by one member of the Dublin Corporation!

University Education in Wales

The University of Wales is a federal University, its constituent Colleges being Aberystwyth, Bangor, and Cardiff. Wales is at present without any recognised capital, — though Cardiff's pretensions to the dignity are coming to be generally admitted, — and the University has, therefore, no particular 'seat'. Meetings of the court — which is the supreme governing body of the University — are held partly at the constituent Colleges, taking each of them in turn, and partly at any other centres that the court itself may determine on. There would, of course, be no necessity for a similar arrangement in Ireland: but, apart from this, there is a close parallel between the situation which the Welsh University was created to meet, and that which any new Irish University or University body would be required to meet. In Wales, as in Ireland, there was a Celtic people, which for generations had been deprived of all education of a national or rational kind: in Wales the vast majority were Non-conformist, as in Ireland the vast majority are Catholic; in Wales in 1893 there already existed three independent academic seats — north, centre, and south — corresponding respectively to Belfast, Dublin, and Cork. This parallelism alone suggests that the mode in which the problem was solved in Wales is deserving of close study in any discussion of the possible modes of solution in Ireland.

MR. DALE ON THE IRISH LANGUAGE
26.3.1904

The attidude of the 'National' Board towards the national language has now been categorically condemned by the teachers, by the managers, by the leading members of the Irish Hierarchy, by the majority of the elective public bodies in Ireland, by the Vice-President of the Department of Agriculture and Technical Instruction, by the Board's own Resident

Commissioner, by the Chief Secretary for Ireland, by the English House of Commons. Amidst this chorus of condemnation, one condemnation by implication is particularly interesting. It is that of Mr. Dale, the eminent English expert imported by the Board for the purpose of reporting on the situation in the primary schools. Mr. Dale's rebuke to the Commissioners is the more valuable as it is rather incidental and implied than deliberate and express. He bears witness to the value of the Irish language in interesting not merely the children but the parents in school-work. The most vital defect in Irish education, as he sees it, is the lack of any local interest in the conduct of education, except amongst the clergy; and he writes: 'There is so far as I can ascertain no step, *except perhaps the revival of the Irish language,* which has done so much to arouse the interest of the parents in the education of their children in the primary schools as the introduction of Cookery into the curriculum. On this ground alone — even were the instruction less useful than it is — measures for its extension deserve, I think, the most earnest attention of the Central Office.' Mr. Dale, it is to be presumed, has no motive for seeking 'to bolster up the hopeless pretence of Ireland as a Nation'; so that his witness to the educational worth of the Irish language, and its value in evoking the intelligent interest of the parents, may be fairly taken as unprejudiced. Yet, almost simultaneously with the issue of this report, which thus bears striking testimony, from a purely educational standpoint, to the value of the Irish language, the Commissioners fulminate their 'Instructions to Inspectors' practically forbidding the teaching of the language in the schools!

A NATIONAL EDUCATION
16.4.1904

Within the past fortnight there have been published two remarkable volumes on the educational systems of the United States. One is the collected reports of the members of the Mosely Educational Commission which visited the United States last year for the purpose of studying American ideals and methods in education, and more particularly of investigating the extent to which the industrial greatness of America is to be attributed to her educational systems. The other volume is a report covering practically the same ground from Commissioners sent out by the Department of Agriculture and Technical Instruction in Ireland.

A word as to the genesis of the Mosely Commission. It owes its origin to Mr. Alfred Mosely, an English business man, whose study of America and American industrial methods had convinced him that the astonishing success of that nation in the industrial arena was in a large measure due to the form of education imparted in American schools. In order to test the soundness of his conclusions, he conceived the idea of organising two Commissions of experts, one industrial, the other educational, for the purpose of inquiring into the subject on the spot. He asked his Industrial Commission to find an answer to the question, 'How is it that the United States can afford to pay half a dollar in wages where we pay a shilling, and yet compete with us in the markets of the world?' The reply of the Commission is to be found in the volume of its reports published some time ago. The Educational Commission was asked to investigate especially the following subjects: — (1) the development of individuality in the primary schools: (2) the social and intellectual effects of the wide distribution of secondary education; (3) the effect of specific education given (*a*) in business methods, (*b*) in applied science; (4) the present state of opinion as to the value of professional and technical instruction of University rank designed with special reference to the tasks of business life.

These headings will suggest the absorbing interest of this volume of reports to the educationalist in Ireland, for the points examined are precisely the points in which our educational systems utterly fail. It is neither possible for us, nor would it be quite our province, to follow the various members of the Commission in their discussion of the matters submitted to them for investigation. But we have carried away from the perusal of the volume a few large facts, bearing on our own work, which we should like to blazon far and wide through Ireland.

The first fact that stands out is that education in America is frankly national. Its function is understood to be to train the children of America to be good citizens of the United States. In the large cities, where a large proportion of the scholars are the children of alien immigrants, there is, of course, a special need for this; but the principle is recognised and carried out all through the country, in the rural as well as in the town schools, in the case of American-born as of foreign-born children, that one of the chief aims of education, as well as one of the chief factors in it, if it is to be successful, is the systematic inculcation of patriotism. 'Great importance,' writes one of the Commissioners (Mr. Anderton, p. 2), 'is attached to the teaching of the duties of citizenship, and this is emphasised in the schools by the parade of the national flag, which is saluted by the children as they pass out of the Assembly Hall. National songs are sung in the schools, so that very early in life not only the native-born American children, but also the children of foreign immigrants, having had put before them the greatness and possibilities of the nation, soon become imbued with national instincts and aspirations.' In Ireland to teach nationality in a 'national' school is to introduce politics!

In the large city schools the magic lantern is largely utilised for the purpose of familiarising the children with the history of the Republic, as well as with its natural features, scenery, and industrial resources. The greatness of America, the dignity of American citizenship, the duties of the individual to the state are constantly inculcated. The American teacher does not regard the children under his care as so many ignoramuses, into whom he must ram a prescribed amount of information: he regards them as future citizens whom it is his privilege to form and train.

One of the most interesting of the movements having for their object the fostering of patriotism is the nature-study carried on in many places, notably throughout New York State, where it forms part of the invaluable work being done by the College of Agriculture at Cornell University. The study is promoted by the formal organisation of junior naturalist clubs in schools all over the State. This Department is under the direction of Mr. John W. Spencer, who is known to the children as 'Uncle John'. 'The object of such clubs is the study of nature to the end that every member thereof shall love the country better and be content to live therein. Each member is expected to tell Uncle John at least once a month by letter or by drawings what he or she has seen or thought on some topic in nature-study suggested by the teacher or by the Bureau of Nature-Study. These letters are duly registered and read. On the receipt of the fourth, a badge-pin is sent to be worn as a testimony that the owner is entitled to all the honours due to a young naturalist. At intervals, Uncle John writes a letter to his young friends. These letters are full of charm' (Dr. Armstrong, p. 23).

41

Attendance at school is compulsory up to 14 years of age, but so strong is the public sentiment in favour of education that attendance officers are few and have little to do. The fact that the school life directly appeals to the child's finer instincts no doubt largely accounts for the circumstance that there is little necessity for the use of official pressure in inducing attendance. The American school is not a place of punishment, but, in the words of a memeber of the Commission, holds in the child's life a place similar to that held by the club in the life of the adult citizen.

Education is free to all classes. The school system generally consists of primary and grammar schools, these schools combined being equivalent to our elementary schools; and high schools, representing nothing exactly that we have in Ireland, but giving a course corresponding roughly to that covered by our higher Intermediate Grades. The organisation is perfect, the various grades of education being correlated in such a way that a student passes automatically from an elementary to a high school, and thence to a University, — all at the expense of the State. The Universities, indeed, are not nominally free, but are in practice rendered so in the case of many students by the existence of bursaries and scholarships.

There are, of course, private schools supported by individuals or by religious communities, but the free public schools are largely availed of by all classes. The children of the President of the United States sit side by side with the children of his coachman or his greengrocer. 'In Washington,' writes one of the Commissioners, 'we saw the son of the President of the United States, two grandsons of the late President Garfield, and many children of members of Congress sitting and working in the same classes as the children of coachmen, gardeners, labourers, etc. Not the slightest difference is observed in regard to these children; they mix in the classes and playgrounds on terms of practical equality.' Fancy this in an Irish country town with its half-score of water-tight social compartments!

Amongst the most interesting passages in the reports are those which deal with the relations subsisting between teacher and pupil. On this subject, Professor Rhys, whose report is one of the most suggestive in the book, writes: — '. . . the gulf between the teacher and the pupil is usually much narrower there, if it exists at all. This is to be noticed throughout from the kindergarten up to the college and the university. In the younger classes the intimacy between teacher and taught is facilitated by the circumstance that the teacher is usually a woman, whose better understanding of infant life and readier sympathy with its troubles tend to render the relation between them closer and friendlier than where the teacher belongs to the other sex. However, I have not been able to detect that the distance is any greater between the teacher and pupil in the higher classes of secondary schools; and as for college, there it becomes merged readily into the *seminar* method of teaching. In one case which I have in my mind, the professor was a man well-known both in America and Europe as one of the foremost representatives of the philosophy which he has made his own. On the occasion to which I refer he conducted himself not so much as a professor teaching his pupils in any direct way as a *primus inter pares* directing a subtle discussion in which the members of his class took part by asking questions criticising the views of their fellows, and otherwise expressing themselves with the utmost freedom. This I felt to be in part at least the working out of the democratic axiom that 'one man is as good as another', and my enjoyment of the half-hour I spent in that class would have been perfect had not the subtleness of some of the questions asked kept prompting my Celtic mind on the lines of a well-known story regardless of logic, to add to that axiom just the words 'and better, too'. Needless to say, the method here in question is not relied on alone, but allowed to alternate with more formal teaching. It is excellent and thoroughly to be recommended.'

An outstanding fact of American life which is mentioned by all the Commissioners, is partially the cause and partially the consequence of the educational system in vogue. We refer to the splendid enthusiasm for education which exists amongst every class. The expenditure of money on education is generous, — 'to the verge of extravagance,' Father Finlay thinks. Millionaires found universities, states and municipalities sometimes devote as much as one-third of their revenue to educational purposes. Everywhere there is keen interest in educational topics. The Americans, in short, have recognised that education is far and away the most important secular subject that can engage the attention of a people; and they have further recognised that education, to be really effective from the moral, as well as from the industrial standpoint, must be chiefly directed towards the building up of character.

BILINGUAL EDUCATION!
23.4.1904

Some twelve months ago we set ourselves the task of educating public opinion, within the Gaelic League and without it, on the problems of Irish education. In order to qualify ourselves for that task we felt that it was necessary in the first instance to make ourselves thoroughly acquainted with the nature, limitations and possibilities of our existing educational systems; and an examination of those systems revealed the fact that, in spite of radical defects, they were capable of being largely utilised for the forwarding of the educational ideals of the Gaelic League. Accordingly, our first care was to endeavour to convert those of the managers, head masters and teachers of the country who were more or less favourably disposed towards the movement, to the view that the fuller utilisation of the existing facilities, such as they were, of the systems in vogue, was a condition precedent to the extortion of further concessions from the unsympathetic education boards. It will be recollected that during some months this was the main burden of all that we wrote on the subject of Irish in the schools.

So successful was our teaching in this respect that by the beginning of the year the number of primary schools in which Irish was taught had increased to such an extent that the National Board found it necessary to appoint a special staff of Inspectors to deal with Irish. This necessity, however, added to the growing expenditure on special fees for Irish, aroused the Board to a consciousness of the fact that the Irish tide was, in deadly earnest, rushing into the schools and the Board conceived it to be its duty to make an effort to stem that tide. This was confessedly the aim and object of the now famous 'Circular to Inspectors' of January last. Fortunately, we got wind of the Circular almost as soon as it had left the Education Office, and we immediately entered on a campaign having for its object the enlightenment of public opinion as to the disastrous consequences likely to ensure from the enforcement of the new Circular. What followed has passed into history. Within a few weeks, the Gaelic League, without asking or receiving the aid of any external body or organ, had evoked such a volume of public opinion against the Circular that the very existence of the National Board was threatened. Led by the Bishop and clergy of Killala, the Catholic managers of the country rallied round the League to a man; the teachers followed suit; the public boards throughout the country fell into line; the Irish Parliamentary Party loyally cooperated; and the agitation culminated in the dramatic defeat of the Government in the House of Commons on the afternoon of March 15th. The substantive withdrawal of the obnoxious Circular thus became a certainty. It was the greatest victory the Gaelic League had yet achieved; but it was only the prelude to the greater victory which we chronicle today.

Before referring to this later and greater victory let us make clear the existing situation with regard to Irish as an extra. We gave last week a summary of the contents of the new or explanatory Circular of March 21st, which at the time we had not seen. A copy of the Circular has since come into our hands, and we find that our anticipatory summary was wholly accurate. The new Circular (1) makes it clear that the rule as to the non-ability of the teachers of schools which fail to secure the award 'Good' to earn special fees for extras, does not affect the position of extern teachers; externs can still earn special fees irrespective of the proficiency of the school as a whole, or of the competence of the ordinary teacher. (2) At the discretion of the Inspector, *even the teacher* of a school which fails to obtain 'Good' can henceforth earn results for the teaching of Irish and other extras, — apparently, even though his award be as low as 'Middling' or 'Bad'. At first sight, it would appear that this leaves the teacher altogether at the mercy of the Inspector. But the Board informs the Inspectors that, in arriving at a decision as to whether the proficiency in a given school is such as to warrant the introduction of extras, they are to take into consideration *all the local circumstances*, — the class of children attending, the length they remain at school, the nature of the locality, the occupations of the people, etc., etc. This clearly means that the teaching of Irish as an extra will be permitted as a matter of course in all schools in the Irish-speaking districts. (3) The Inspectors are pointedly reminded that Irish and other extras can be taught as ordinary subjects within school hours, provided their teaching does not militate against the general efficiency of the school; and (4) the Commissioners announce that they have in preparation a Bilingual Programme intended for adoption in Irish-speaking and semi-Irish-speaking districts.

This brings us to the announcement of a new departure, which marks the beginning of the end of the fight for the primary schools. A few months ago we devoted much space to the subject of Bilingual Education, drawing particular attention to the example of Belgium, and showing in considerable detail how the system might be applied to the Irish-speaking and bilingual districts of Ireland. Well, — to put the matter in a nut-shell, — our policy and substantially our programme have been adopted by the Commissioners of National Education! Bilingualism in education is at long last, officially established in Ireland! We write 'at long last' because the struggle has seemed long in the waging, but in reality we have moved very much faster than any other language revivalists in Europe. The Flemish movement was sixty years old before it advanced so far!

We print elsewhere the 'Bilingual Programme for National Schools', which has just been issued by the Commissioners of National Education. 'It is intended,' the Commissioners write, 'to apply to Irish-speaking districts and to districts where Irish and English are both commonly spoken, and will be approved for use in schools where specially sanctioned by the Board'. We have no hesitation in describing the programme as an admirable one: indeed, we have read it with a glow of something akin to paternal pride, for not merely do we find the majority of the principles for which we have contended carried into practice, but the Irish side of the programme is almost bodily lifted from our own columns!

The adoption of the programme in a given school will mean henceforward, so far from Irish being *tabu*, it will be taught side by side with English as part of the compulsory school course, and that from the lowest standard up to the highest. However, 'it is contemplated that both courses should be taught concurrently to *infants*. Teacher may teach whichever course he prefers first, and when one course is taught, the other course may be commenced'. Readers of articles on Bilingual Education will recollect our insistence on the principle that during the first few months the teaching should be confined to the more familiar vernacular.

But the adoption of the programme in a school will mean not only that Irish will be taught as a matter of course to every child in every standard, but that in the case of Irish-speaking children Irish will be made the medium of instruction. With regard to the teaching of subjects other than Irish and English, the Commissioners write: '. . . Instruction and progress in Arithmetic, Singing, Drawing, Drill, Needlework, Elementary Science, and Object Lessons, and Manual Instruction and Kindergarten, etc., should be beneficially rather than detrimentally affected by instruction in Irish in Bilingual and Irish-speaking Districts . . . . Irish and English may be used in instructing pupils in these subjects'. Again: 'Independent Object Lessons may be given in English and in Irish, or, Object Lessons in the same subject may be given in both languages and each lesson whether in English or in Irish, will count as a distinct Object Lesson. These Object Lessons can be utilised in teaching the names of common objects, of articles and implements used in trade or art, of agricultural and household articles etc., to pupils of all standards, both in Irish and in English'. And yet again: 'Songs in Irish and English may be taught. Irish songs, set to music both in the Tonic sol-fa and in the staff notations, are now procurable'. And so on. The revolt commenced by the Gaelic League ten years ago has verily swelled into a revolution.

No indication is given of the machinery by which the adoption of the Programme is to be enforced. Yet another Circular is in preparation, but, whilst it will contain further provisions of a highly satisfactory nature, we do not gather that it will touch on this important point. Apparently, the onus of putting the Programme into operation in their respective districts will be thrown on the managers. But it may be assumed that in establishing Bilingualism the managers and teachers may henceforth count on the active co-operation of the Board and its Inspectors instead of, as heretofore, having to reckon with their unyielding opposition; whilst the moral effect of the recognition of Bilingualism by the Commissioners need not be insisted on. We are sanguine that, now that the principle of Bilingual Education has received official sanction of the most formal kind, the education problem in the Irish-speaking districts will, granted friendly co-operation on the part of the managers, the teachers and the Gaelic League, move steadily, if not (at first) rapidly, towards its solution.

THE BILINGUAL PROGRAMME
30.4.1904

The education problem in the Irish-speaking and bilingual districts has now resolved itself into a question of getting the Bilingual Programme of the Board generally adopted by the managers and teachers. We are not, however, by any means done with the Board yet. It remains to be seen how far its conversion to the principle of bilingual education is sincere. It remains to be seen how far the adoption of the Bilingual Programme will be facilitated by the Inspectors. And it remains to be seen what steps will be taken towards ensuring the effective inspection of bilingual schools. That the examination of such schools cannot be left to the ordinary inspectoral staff seems quite clear, for the ordinary inspectoral staff is almost exclusively composed of men ignorant of Irish. Neither would it appear that, what with its duties in connection with Evening Schools and its duties in connection with the examination of Irish as an extra, the existing staff of Irish Inspectors could possibly undertake the inspection of such schools as may adopt the Bilingual Programme. It will obviously be necessary either to strengthen Mr. O'Lehane's staff, or to appoint special Irish-speaking Inspectors to take charge of the Irish-speaking and bilingual districts. The Board might do worse than promote half a dozen teachers who have had practical experience of school-work in Irish-speaking and bilingual areas, and constitute them a special staff for the purpose not merely of inspecting bilingual schools, but of educating the teachers in the working of the scheme.

This brings us to the chief obstacle in the way of the scheme, — the utter lack of training amongst teachers, the utter unfitness of so many of the present teaching staff in Irish-speaking districts to undertake the working of anything so complicated as a bilingual system. The teachers are now brought face to face with a system of which they had no previous experience, and of the elementary principles of which the vast majority of them have not even the haziest notions. This state of affairs can be met only in one way: facilities must be supplied for the training of the teachers in the theory and practice of bilingual education as worked in Belgium and the other continental countries which have adopted the system. In an early issue we shall discuss ways and means by which this may best be done.

Experience may show that the Board's Programme itself may require a certain amount of modification, but its main lines are unquestionably admirable. It proceeds on the principle that the vernacular is to be the sole basis of education in the very early stages, but that the second language is to be introduced as soon as feasible, and to be thenceforth taught side by side with the vernacular. The English course for bilingual schools is reduced by one-half, at least as regards reading and spelling. It does not appear that the English course in Writing, Grammar and Composition is reduced, — a strange anomaly. This, if our reading of the Programme is correct, will assuredly require modification. It is grossly unfair to require children who have to get up Irish Grammar and to exhibit a certain amount of Irish writing and composition exercises, to prepare exactly as much English Grammar, writing and composition as children who have no Irish at all to prepare. The rest of the Programme is conceived in so reasonable a spirit, and with such apparent knowledge of the difficulties of both teachers and pupils, that this would appear to be an oversight rather than a deliberately-framed requirement. Whatever it be, it will have to be modified.

46

THE BILINGUAL PROGRAMME
7.5.1904

The very great importance of the Bilingual Programme is our justification for again bringing it before the notice of our readers. On the educational side it is unquestionably the most pregnant event that has yet taken place in the movement. In this particular matter the Board has, to a large extent, met our demands, and the responsibility is shifted. It now lies with the country, the schools and the various Gaelic League bodies throughout Ireland to rise to the occasion and take the fullest advantage out of the situation. We would earnestly impress on all concerned, especially Branches of the League and Coisdí Ceanntair in the Irish-speaking counties, the urgent necessity for immediate action in the matter. We would point out that there is now nothing whatever to prevent the introduction of a thoroughgoing bilingual system into at least 1,000 National Schools. The whole thing is entirely in the hands of the teachers and managers in the Irish-speaking districts, on whom the responsibility now rests and not on the National Board. Heretofore it was the Board that was on its trial; now it is the country.

The country, we hope, will not be found wanting. It will be remembered that in February, 1900, nearly 200 managers, representing 1,007 schools in districts where Irish is commonly spoken, presented a memorial demanding that a system of education on bilingual lines be immediately established for such districts. Now the desired concession has been made. And it is not in purely Irish-speaking districts alone that the system can be introduced, as it is made clear that it applies to districts where Irish and English are commonly spoken.

We now see nothing to prevent the signatories to the memorial referred to from having their schools conducted on real bilingual lines as they themselves have demanded. We strongly urge on the various League bodies throughout the country to cooperate in the most cordial and strenuous manner with teachers and managers in this matter. We shall view developments with interest and confidence. And we expect the Training Colleges to do their share of the work by making Irish compulsory in the entrance examinations, and thus providing proper teaching machinery to carry the programme into effect.

WAYS AND MEANS
14.5.1904

During the next few years all the energies of the organisation must be bent to the task of establishing bilingual education, in fact as well as in form, in the Irish-speaking and semi-Irish-speaking districts. As we wrote when the Bilingual Programme of the Commissioners first appeared, the chief obstacle in the way of its wide and immediate adoption is the utter lack of training amongst the teachers. If one fact stood out more clearly than another in the series of articles on the bilingual methods of Belgium, which recently appeared in *An Claidheamh,* it was that the administration of a bilingual system demands, above all things, an intelligent, zealous and highly-trained teaching staff. Now, granting to the teachers of the Irish-speaking and bilingual parts of Ireland the maximum of zeal and intelligence, it must be admitted that they are woefully deficient in the sort of training which is absolutely essential to the efficient working of a bilingual system. Some of them have, at best, but crude notions of teaching of any sort; and it is not to be wondered at that in presence of a thing so utterly new to them, and, at first sight, so complicated in itself as a Bilingual Programme, many are simply dismayed.

Obviously, then, a condition precedent to the general adoption of the Bilingual Programme is the training of the teachers in bilingual methods. Who is going to train them? We submit that it is the business of the Board. The Board is mistaken if it imagines that it has undone the work of three-quarters of a century by simply flinging a Bilingual Programme at the head of the country. Unless it provides ways and means for the carrying out of its Programme, the Programme will remain a mere curiosity.

It is to be assumed that the Commissioners are now really desirous to see bilingual education introduced into the Irish-speaking districts. It is also to be assumed that they are well aware of the fact that, perhaps, nine-tenths of the teachers in those districts have as hazy ideas on the subject of bilingual education as they had four years ago on the subjects of Hand-and-Eye Training and Physical Drill. We hope it may further be assumed that the Commissioners who, four years ago, went to much trouble and expense for the purpose of training teachers in the subjects of the New Programme will now take similar steps to train them for the administration of the bilingual scheme. We think the first essential is that itinerant instructors should be sent to conduct courses at suitable centres in the districts concerned. In addition to conducting teachers' classes the instructors should visit the schools and actively promote the introduction of the system. The work of these itinerant instructors might be supplemented by special courses at the Training Colleges, to which relays of teachers might be summoned during the summer and autumn months. The object of all such courses should be not to so much to teach teachers Irish as to train them in the theory and practice of bilingual teaching. It goes without saying that the instructors should be thoroughly acquainted with the methods in vogue in Belgium and elsewhere, and that they should be practical teachers, and that they should be Irish speakers.

Some such steps as these are absolutely necessary to fit the actual teaching staff in the Irish-speaking districts for the administration of the Bilingual Programme. There remains, of course, the further necessity to make permanent provision for the regular supply, for service in the Irish-speaking and bilingual counties, of an adequate and efficient staff of Irish-speaking teachers trained in the most approved bilingual methods. Both these questions must be tackled by the Board at once; and the Gaelic League would do well, following the lead of the Coisde Gnotha, to keep them well to the front until a satisfactory solution is forthcoming.

IRISH EDUCATION
28.5.1904

We do not know under whose auspices last week's meeting on the education question was held, or on whose initiative it was summoned. But the holding of such a meeting is a sign altogether healthy. The Gaelic League has for ten years been preaching that the education of its children is far and away the most important secular problem that can engage the thought of a people; for good education is at the root of all national progress, and bad education is at the root of all national decadence. But the Gaelic League has been as the voice of one crying in the wilderness. The one question which up to quite recently our people and their leaders have refused to interest themselves in, or in which, at best, their interest has been a thing of fits and starts, is this one which ought to have been the subject of their unwearied thought and well-organised action. The Catholic Hierarchy, indeed, have never lost sight of the importance of the question; and the teachers have from time to time agitated a number of subsidiary issues, mainly of professional interest. But the Irish public has gone on regarding the removal of chains which merely shackled the body as a paramount urgency to the removal of chains which shackled the mind. There is no reason why the Nation's activities should not be exercised in both directions; but it were a fatal policy to concentrate all our energies on the less vital phases of the combat, and yield up, without a murmur, the very citadel of our national life to the domination of the foreigner.

We have been so much preoccupied with other Irish matters this week that we have neither time nor space to discuss the suggestive address of Dr. MacNamara. But, as the impetus to whatsoever thought has recently been forthcoming on the problem of the Irish education has undoubtedly come from the Gaelic League, it may be well to indicate how far exactly the Gaelic League is prepared to go in its demands for reform. We have only to refer to our previous utterances on the point. The Gaelic League has directed, and will continue to direct, well-deserved criticism at the ideals, methods and personnel of the existing education boards, but the substitution for those boards of an English department, under the control of an English Minister, and responsible to the English Parliament, is no part of the League's policy. The League would fain see Irish educational authorities responsible not to British public opinion, but to Irish public opinion; and it believes that, in fact, if not in form, the existing educating boards could be brought into touch with Irish public opinion by a mere change in their personnel. It does not matter in the least how unrepresentative and irresponsible a board may be in theory, if, in fact its members are in communion with the heart of the nation, know its needs, and possess its confidence. After all we have written on the subject during the past year, it is unnecessary to insist that it is perfectly feasible to bring about the desired change, without any radical alteration in the form of the existing system, and without imperilling a single interest, save and except the interest of the West Briton.

THE TRAINING COLLEGES
18.6.1904

As we briefly announced in our last issue, the Commissioners of National Education have included an optional course in Irish in the programme for what is called 'The King's Scholarship Examination' for 1905. This examination must be passed by Monitors and Pupil-Teachers at the end of their periods of service, and also by candidates seeking admission to a Training College. Monitors and Pupil-Teachers, on completing their terms of service and having passed the examination on this programme, are eligible for appointment as Assistants in National Schools. Candidates for entrance to a Training College, who are not Monitors or Pupil-Teachers, are required to pass this examination prior to being placed on the list of candidates eligible for training. From this rule persons who are already certificated National Teachers are exempt, these latter being eligible for admission to a course of training without undergoing any examination. Except in the case of certificated teachers, therefore, this examination is the ordinary door through which students enter the Training Colleges.

The course is a long one, and embraces the following subjects: — English (including Reading, Writing, Spelling , Grammar, English Literature and Composition); Geography, Arithmetic and Mensuration, Algebra (Men), Geometry (Men), Book-keeping, Practice of Teaching, etc., History, Drawing, Needlework (Women), Domestic Economy and Hygiene, Vocal Music *(Theory)*, Vocal Music *(Practical Test)*, and General Information. All these subjects are obligatory. Irish has now been added as an optional subject, — we print the course (a very easy one) on page 4.

The inclusion of Irish in this programme will be of indirect rather than of direct value. Not only is the subject purely optional, but the marks scored in it will not be taken into account in determining the priority of students. Candidates other than Monitors and Pupil-Teachers 'will be examined on all the obligatory subjects of the Programme except Practice of Teaching. Their position on the Lists prepared for the Training Colleges *will be determined solely by the result of this Examination*'. Marks scored in Irish, therefore, do not count towards the general aggregate on which a candidate's position in the list is determined.

However the placing of Irish on this programme will be of service in pointing a way for the Training Colleges themselves. We understand that in practice the Training Colleges (with the exception of Marlborough Street) do not call up students for training in the exact order determined by the Board's examination. Only those who have passed the examination are eligible, but the Colleges take extraneous circumstances into consideration in determining priority. One College only has made a knowledge of Irish a factor in determining this priority. This is the De La Salle College, Waterford, whose optional programme in Irish appears in our advertisement columns on page 11. In selecting candidates to fill its places it is the practice of the College to give a preference to candidates who pass an examination in Irish on this course.

Our suggestion is that the other Training Colleges adopt a similar practice. There would thus be a strong inducement — amounting almost to a compulsion — to candidates to take up Irish. The Training Colleges themselves could not fail to benefit. It is the laudable ambition of the Colleges to secure positions as principals or assistants for as many as possible of their pupils. The demand for teachers able to teach Irish is already greater than the supply, and it is bound to rapidly increase. Obviously, the College which can turn out the greatest number of teachers thoroughly competent to teach Irish will have a considerable pull over its rivals.

The adoption of the De La Salle plan by the other Colleges would entail this further advantage. At present, the course of studies within the Training College is so long that no student who does not already know Irish can well afford to take it up. Those who do take it up for the first time within the College cannot hope, during the short period of training, to obtain any real knowledge of the language; moreover, their presence within a class of students who are already speakers or advanced learners, is found to be a clog, rather than otherwise, on the general progress. By giving an

50

inducement to students to commence Irish *before entering the College*, the authorities would ensure a constant stream of incoming students already grounded in the elements of the language, and capable of benefiting by the Irish course provided within the College.

THE EDUCATION QUESTION
13.8.1904

The Ard-Fheis concerned itself with so many different phases of League activity that one desirous of evaluating its work or underlining its decisions must necessarily take up its Agenda Paper section by section and point by point. We prefer to commence with what appears to us to have been infinitely the most important part of the programme of the Ard-Fheis, as it is infinitely the most important part of the programme of the Gaelic League itself. We refer, of course, to the vital, ever-pressing, many-sided education problem.

When all is said, the task which the language movement has set itself largely resolves itself into the recasting of Irish education along Irish lines. Had the education of the country been sane and national for the last hundred years there would never have been a necessity for the language movement: when it is thoroughly sane and national again in all its branches the necessity for the language movement will have ceased.

The League ideal in education is, or should be, sufficiently well known. It is that education in this Irish land must be Irish. It must be Irish right through, and all along the line. It must take as its standpoint 'This is Ireland', not 'This is No-Man's Land', and still less 'This is West Britain'. It must be based on a primary system, national not merely in name, but in fact and essence; it must include a secondary system; and it must culminate in a University which, whatever its form — and that, to us, is a matter of supreme indifference — shall in spirit and complexion, be Irish and national.

This is an ambitious programme. But the Gaelic League must carry out every line of it. To fail in a single tittle would be to fail in the League's primary object. And the failure of the League in its primary object would be for Ireland — the Irish Ireland of our ancestors, for there is no other Ireland — the end of all things. Let us beware, then, lest we fail.

We have not gone into details this week. We prefer to once again put our educational programme before the organisation in all its largeness. During the next few weeks we shall go over in detail the lines of agitation and organisation marked out by the Ard-Fheis. In doing so we shall be largely repeating ourselves. That is a consideration which does not trouble us. The League has had from the outset clear ideas as to what it wants, and clear ideas as to how best to attain what it wants. Its work for ten years has chiefly consisted in hammering away at precisely the same propositions with which it started. And vast as is the programme which remains to be realised it has hammered, we think, to some little effect. Let us keep 'trusting in God and hammering away' for yet a little longer.

THE PRIMARY SCHOOLS
20.8.1904

The education problem is the vastest and most momentous that con-

51

fronts Ireland to-day. Of the education problem itself the most pressing and, at the same time, the most intrinsically important phase, is the problem of the primary school. The primary school, as an institution, is still a pillar of foreignism in Ireland. Individual schools, individual teachers, individual managers, to the number of hundreds are amongst the most vigorous propagants of Irishism in the country; yet the broad statement remains true that the system, as a system, is still in ideal and practice a system which spells anglicisation.

But the Gaelic League has got its foot well within the school door. Its grip of its position is strong, and it may not be dislodged. The complete capture of the schools is now only a question of time. The essential is that the League should not relax its efforts for one moment, that it should not pause even for an instant on the threshold, but, knowing its own mind, and having its programme thought out clearly and in detail, that it should march boldly in.

We wrote much some months ago on the advisability of conducting the campaign for the schools along certain definite and fruitful lines. The burden of the Ard-Fheis's resolutions on the primary school question was to a similar purport. The Ard-Fheis simply restated the programme that has time and again been put before the organisation by the Coisde Gnótha and by *An Claidheamh*. The needs of the moment will be better understood after a glance at the actual status of the national language and history in the primary schools as affected by all the recent legislation and counter-legislation of the National Board. As things stand, (1) Irish may be taught as a part of the Ordinary school programme to children of all stages in every school in Ireland; (2) Irish may be taught as an extra Subject (for special fees) to children from Standard IV, upwards, whatever be the proficiency of the school, provided that in the case of a school marked 'Fair', ' 'Middling', or 'Bad' the Inspector is of opinion that Irish may usefully be taught as an Extra; (3) where the teacher is unable to teach Irish an Extern Teacher (who must be certified) may be employed, and may earn special fees; (4) in Irish-speaking and bilingual districts, the whole school work may be conducted on bilingual lines, in accordance with the new Bilingual Programme; (5) the introduction of the Bilingual Programme in a given school *does not* prevent the teaching of Irish as an Extra Subject for special fees in that school; (6) Irish History may be taught as a part of the Ordinary school programme in every school in Ireland.

A mere recital of these concessions is sufficient to show that we have marched fast and far within the past few years. It is obvious that, *if the existing facilities were fully availed of by managers and teachers,* the question of Irish in the primary schools would be on the high road towards solution. In this connection, a remark dropped by Pádraig Ó Séaghdha, himself a teacher, in his Oireachtas Oration will bear repitition: if, in any school in Ireland, Irish and Irish History are not yet taught, and Irishism systematically inculcated, the fault is no longer the fault of the National Board, but that of the teacher, the manager, or the parents.

This does not imply that we are yet done with the National Board. On the contrary, the national language still labours under glaring disabilities. Apart from the absence of due provision for the training of teachers — a phase of the question with which we shall deal later on — the foregoing recital of concessions suggests several pertinent queries. Why, for instance,, should the teaching of Irish as an Extra be confined to the higher standards? Why should so large a discretion be given to inspectors in the

52

case of schools which fail to secure the award 'Good'? When will the course in Irish as an Extra be spread over a period of four years, as has been so constantly urged in these columns? When will an ascending scale of fees, according as the pass is on a First, a Second, a third, or a fourth Year's Course, be adopted? When will the Ordinary course be co-ordinated with the Extra course, and both with the course of the Bilingual Programme? When, finally, will steps be taken to actively facilitate the introduction of the Bilingual system into the districts for which it is intended? These queries indicate lines of agitation which are emphatically definite and which will, we think, prove decidedly fruitful.

THE BILINGUAL PROGRAMME
24.9.1904

At its latest meeting the Coisde Gnótha again drew the attention of the organisation to the capital importance of the Bilingual Programme. The Coisde has in substance resolved that, during the autumn and winter campaign, the main objective to be held in view by the officers at headquarters and by the organisers in the country shall be the inducing of the managers and teachers in the Irish-speaking and bilingual areas to put the Programme into operation in their schools.

Enquiries which we have been making during the past month reveal the fact that some half-dozen schools have already formally adopted the Bilingual Programme. A large number of schools are preparing to do so, and await only the termination of the current school-year before making a start. Other schools are adopting certain features of the Bilingual Programme whilst continuing to carry on the major part of the school work on the same lines as heretofore.

Our enquiries go to show that almost everywhere the Bilingual Programme is regarded by the teachers with a certain amount of timidity. The impression prevails that the Programme will prove immensely more cumbrous and taxing than the existing unilingual programme. We have admitted from the start that the adequate working of a bilingual scheme will at first make larger demands on the thought and energies of a teacher than any scheme at present in operation in a national school. The teacher will require to devote more time to thinking out his day's work, to preparing his lessons beforehand, to organising his classes. But increased trouble is incidental to increased efficiency: all good teaching, as we have so often pointed out, makes large demands on the time and thought and energy and patience of the teacher. Modern teaching methods, whilst they tend to reduce the drudgery of the pupil to a minimum, do not at all tend in the same degree to reduce the labour of the master; rather the contrary. But, whilst we see that the successful handling of the Bilingual Programme will at first call for special exertions on the part of the teacher, we are convinced that in the long run it will vastly lighten the burden of work both for teachers and pupils. Though it seem paradoxical, it is a profound truth that it is easier to teach two languages than to teach one. If we had the direction of education in this country we should make all education bilingual, and should require the teaching of at least two languages to every child in every school in the country. The Belgians are doing this, the Germans are doing it, and, to a lesser extent, so are the French. It would be as easy to work the Commissioners' Bilingual Programme in a Dublin or a Belfast school as it is to work the present unilingual programme.

But, apart from this, it seems so self-evident as to need no urging that the adoption of the new Bilingual Programme, be its faults what they may (and we have allowed from the first that it is not without fauts) will immensely facilitate the work of education in the Irish-speaking and bilingual districts. Consider the present incredibly and amazingly absurd system, — the system under which the child's whole mental history is ignored, the system under which instruction is from the first hour conveyed in a language utterly unknown to the child, the system under which there is absolutely no communion of thought between pupil and teacher. Grant that the Bilingual Programme errs on the side of length and difficulty, it cannot fail, even if imperfectly grasped and indifferently worked, to produce better results than the system which at the end of six years' schooling turned out a mere atrophied intelligence. Under the old system the teacher was expected, through the medium of English (or practically so), to make the Irish-speaking child of Ring or Rosmuck or Tory as proficient in English and general knowledge as a child in Dublin or Belfast or Cork! Under the Bilingual Programme such a child is required to know only half as much English as the Dublin or Belfast child, whilst general subjects such as Geography, History, Arithmetic, Geometry, Object Lessons, Drill can be taught through the medium of "Irish *and* English." In the former case, the teacher was attempting the morally and physically impossible; in the latter, be his initial difficulties and perplexities what they may, he will be working with nature, and he will have the whole instinct, intelligence and sympathy of the child with him.

Last week we revisited a school of our acquaintance in which, for a few years past, the instruction has been given on lines which are essentially bilingual. We found Arithmetic taught through the medium of Irish; Geography and History taught largely in Irish; Object Lessons given chiefly in Irish; Physical Drill taught in Irish. The reading and writing and spelling of Irish were taught solely through the medium of Irish. English was taught mainly through the medium of English, but the teacher never hesitated to give the meaning of a word or to explain the sense of a paragraph in Irish. We do not know what is the character of the report furnished by the non-Irish-speaking Inspector in whose circuit the district is included on the work which is being carried on in this school. But this we do know: that the boys who are being taught as we have described are being *educated* in a large and full sense; and further that, whilst they are being taught to read and write the language which they already speak, they are at the same time gaining a better knowledge of English than the children in hundreds of schools inside the doors of which it is *tabu* to utter a syllable of Irish.

THE BILINGUAL PROGRAMME IN PRACTICE
1.10.1904

The Bilingual Programme is intended to apply to Irish-speaking districts and to districts where Irish and English are both commonly spoken. It seems to us that, with regard to certain details, the Programme will require to be differently handled according as it is sought to apply it to one or other of these two classes of district. In broad principle, of course, a bilingual system of instruction is equally applicable to an Irish-speaking, a bilingual, or an English-speaking area; but it is obvious that the details of the system would require to be modified according as the relations of the two vernaculars to each other vary. We hold that the very early stages of a child's education — the first timid steps — should be conducted in the language which is the more familiar to him, — in Irish if his vernacular be Irish, in English if his vernacular be English; but we hold just as strongly that the teaching of the second language should commence at the earliest possible moment, — certainly within the second school year, and before the Infants' Class is left. It is within the capacity of every normal infant to learn two languages, and within the capacity of many to learn three or four; and, as we wrote last week, it will generally be found easier to teach a child two languages concurrently than to teach him one. Hence, the earlier the teaching of the second language is commenced the better.

At this stage it may be well to iterate that the object at which the bilingual system aims is the education of the child in two languages. The system does not, as many seem to imagine, merely contemplate that Irish should be utilised in the teaching of English. Its object is the teaching of Irish just as much as the teaching of English, and the teaching of English just as much as the teaching of Irish; or, to be more accurate, its object is not so much the teaching either of Irish or of English, as the education of the child through the medium of both Irish and English. This, of course, implies the adequate teaching of the two languages both as spoken and written tongues; and it also implies that by the time a child has finished his school course he should be able to discuss problems in Arithmetic, Algebra, Geometry, History, Geography, and whatever other subjects are taught in the school, *equally well in Irish and in English.*

Having clarified his ideas as to the object of a bilingual programme, it behoves the teacher to conscientiously think out the lines on which the Programme may, with the maximum of good, be applied to the particular set of circumstances existent in his own school. There are probably no two schools in the country in which all the circumstances are exactly alike, and it follows that there are no two schools to which the same programme will apply in all its details. But from the point of view of the Bilingual Programme, all the schools affected may roughly be divided into two classes, — those in Irish-speaking and those in bilingual areas. We propose to devote our leading articles for the next few weeks to a discussion of the general principles which should be held in view by a teacher in his efforts to adapt the Bilingual Programme to the special conditions of his own district, be it Irish-speaking or bilingual; always premising that what we write is intended to be merely *suggestive*, and that, in final resort, the teacher who desires to make a success of the Bilingual or of any other programme must do his own thinking, and, in every step he takes, be guided by all the facts and circumstances of his own particular situation. We take this opportunity of inviting the criticism and suggestions of teachers, especially of those who are actually facing the problem of administering the Bilingual Programme in their own schools.

THE BILINGUAL PROGRAMME IN AN IRISH-SPEAKING DISTRICT
8.10.1904

The districts to which the Bilingual Programme is intended to apply are of two kinds — 'Irish-speaking' and 'bilingual'. By an 'Irish-speaking' district in the present context we understand a district in which Irish is the ordinary language of the young as well as the old and the middle-aged. Such districts are more numerous and extensive than is commonly imagined. The Ring district in Waterford; certain localities in West Cork and the adjoining part of Kerry; Corca Dhuibhne (the Dingle Promontory); a large part of County Galway, including Aran, the whole of Iar-Connacht, practically all Connemara, the Joyce Country, and large tracts east and south of Lough Corrib; the portions of Mayo immediately bordering on Galway; the Erris district, together with numerous isolated spots in Tirawley; a great part of the country comprised in the rural districts of Glenties, Dunfanaghy and Donegal in Tir Chonaill; — all these areas come within the category of districts which are, for practical purposes, exclusively Irish-speaking. The towns, where such exist, have, of course, to be excepted.

Now, in these areas, the school programme should proceed from the start on the postulate that when the children first come to school they are Irish-speaking, and not English-speaking. The object of the teacher is to educate them, — in other words, to draw out their faculties, to train their intelligence, to prepare them for the duties of citizenship; and the instrument which is placed in his hands for effecting this object is the Bilingual Programme. That Programme, as we have seen, contemplated the education of the child through the medium of two languages, and incidentally, of course, the imparting of a sound oral and literary knowledge of those two languages. The two languages on which, for some time to come, Ireland's bilingual system must be based are Irish and English.

Let us place ourselves in the position of a teacher in a purely Irish-speaking district who is desirous of introducing the Bilingual Programme. Hitherto, his school work has been carried out on unilingual lines; he has taught, or attempted to teach, solely through the medium of English, his use of Irish never going beyond the explaining the sense of a pasage or the giving the meaning of a word in the vernacular; he may or may not have taught Irish as an extra to the more advanced classes, — and his teaching, even of Irish, has been done mainly through the medium of English. This is an accurate description of the *status quo* in the average school in an Irish-speaking district.

It is possible that in such a school there would be found a certain amount of difficulty in applying the Bilingual Programme in its entirety straight off, especially in the higher standards. In our view, the Programme may be most usefully introduced *upwards*, commencing with the Infants' classes. First-class results cannot be expected, even under the Bilingual Programme, in the case of children who have stumbled through the standards as far as Fifth or Sixth under the hideous system which has hitherto prevailed. These children are for the most part mere wrecked intelligences who within a year or two after leaving school will lapse back into illiteracy, will forget the 'English' they have spent six years acquiring, and will have lost a large part of their mental nimbleness in and native mastery over Irish. Yet, whilst absolutely satisfactory results can be expected only in the case of children whose education has from the start been conducted on bilingual lines, the application of the Bilingual Programme even in the upper forms cannot but be followed by increased efficiency in the school-work and increased interest on the the part of the children.

In the earlier standards the Programme in its entirety should be put in operation at the earliest possible moment. Let us see how things will work out. Take the Infants' Class. The children, to start with, are, in the case we are supposing, all Irish-speaking. For their first school year we should give them nothing but Irish. We should not teach them as much as the letters of the alphabet, or the meanings of the most elementary words in English. Our first step would be to give them some very simple object-lessons in Irish. We should then set them to learn the Irish alphabet, and to copy it from the blackboard on slates. Next we should proceed to teach them to read, spell and understand words of two and three letters as in, say, the first eight lessons of 'An Prímhleabhar'. With regard to Arithmetic, we should give lessons in elementary counting on the Ball-frame, teach them to set down the numerals up to 10, to add pairs of numbers, the sum not exceeding 10, mentally and on slates, — all in Irish. Similarly, we should conduct such Kindergarten work, Drawing, Drill, etc., as is apportioned to the Infants' Class altogether in Irish; and, of course, Prayers, Christian Doctrine, Singing, etc., would be conducted exclusively in Irish. All this is expressly allowed under the Bilingual Programme. The Commissioners state: 'It is not contemplated that both courses (Irish and English) should be taught concurrently to Infants. Teacher may teach whichever course he prefers first, and when one course is taught, the other course may be commenced. As Infants usually spend two years in the Infants' Class, both courses ought to be gone over by the time they are about to be promoted to the first or highest section of Standard I.'

Having devoted the first school year solely to instruction in and through the medium of Irish, we should in the second school year (whilst the child is still in the Infants' Class) commence the teaching of English. We should impart it by attractive oral methods and chiefly through the medium of English; but — *pace* theorists on language teaching — we should never hesitate to use Irish for the purpose of explaining a new English word or idea. The second school year would not, of course, be devoted solely or mainly to the teaching of English. The reading and writing of Irish would continue to be taught through Irish only; and all lessons in Arithmetic, Kindergarten, etc., would be given *first in Irish*, and then in English.

This system would be logically continued throughout the higher standards. The reading, writing, recitation, singing, etc., of Irish would be taught exclusively in Irish; the reading, writing, etc., of English, would be taught mainly in English; mathematical, geographical and historical lessons would be given first in Irish and then in English; object lessons would be given, and composition exercises set, in both languages. All the ordinary school commands would be given in Irish only. A child taught on these lines would in his advance from class to class acquire a real education in Irish, and at the same time a sound acquaintance, spoken and written, with English. At the end of his course he would be an educated bilingualist. Primarily an Irish speaker, his mastery of English would be complete.

The foregoing paragraphs do not embody a single recommendation which is not practicable under the Bilingual Programme. Teachers, however, may ask: 'What about the Inspectors? The system you describe is an ideal one from every point of view; and, in theory, everything you recommend may be feasible under the Bilingual Programme. But can we safely put all your recommendations in force whilst we are at the mercy of the existing staff of Inspectors?' The query raises a side of the question which we reserve for discussion in a future article.

THE BILINGUAL PROGRAMME IN OPERATION
15.10.1904

Last week we embodied in a leader our personal views as to the lines on which the Bilingual Programme may be applied to a school in an Irish-speaking district with the maximum of result. The convictions we hold on the subject are based on a personal study of the actual working of schools in Irish-speaking districts together with an enquiry, as complete as our opportunities would allow, into the scope and characteristics of Bilingual Education as understood and practised in Wales and on the continent. Whilst we have borne large general principles in mind, we have endeavoured always to write with full advertence to the actual conditions which exist in a national school in a rural part of Ireland, and with the text of the Bilingual Programme of the Commissioners firmly fixed in view. We have not been so much outlining an ideal scheme as showing how the most can be made of the scheme which the Commissioners have provided. Our recommendations throughout have been conditioned by the possibilities of the Bilingual Programme.

Whilst we are convinced of the practicability of every suggestion we have thrown out, we realise that we are liable to be told by teachers who in their own district and in their own schools have to face the problem of actually administering the Programme, that it is very much easier to sit at a desk in Dublin and make suggestion than to carry out those suggestions in Connemara or Corca Dhuibhne. It was to guard against a possible retort of this sort that we a fortnight ago invited the criticism and suggestion of teachers actually face-to-face with the handling of the Programme in an Irish-speaking or a bilingual district.

The communications we have received in answer to this invitation have satisfied us that we have not been writing in the air. Every teacher who has adopted the Programme has already felt the benefit. Suggestions whose feasibility we have heard doubted have already been reduced to practice with the happiest results. In every respect, the experience of such teachers as have communicated with us bear out the soundness of the principles we have been inculcating and the practicability of the advice we have been giving.

We select for publication the following record of the experience of a teacher whose work lies in a locality which comes within our category of 'Irish-speaking' as distinguished from 'bilingual' districts. The writer is Domhnall Ua Duibhne of Spiddal Male National School: —

'Having proposed a resolution which was unanimously passed at the Ard-Fheis calling upon the Organisers of the League to arrange parish conferences as soon as possible between managers and teachers with a view to the general introduction of the Bilingual Programme I, on my return home, decided to set the example myself.

Although the pupils in this school without exception have for years been taught Irish, and the course of instruction has necessarily been to a certain extent bilingual, owing to the fact that the majority of children speak little or no English at home, yet I always felt that much more was needed. Hence I hailed with delight the issue of a Bilingual Programme by the Commissioners themselves.

I sought my manager's permission to introduce it, which was at once cheerfully granted. Indeed, he expressed himself as highly pleased, and said it was the right and proper thing to do. He wrote immediately to the Education Office stating that the Programme would be followed in this school, pointed out the books we had selected, and requested the sanction of the Board, — which by the way, has not as yet been granted, though, of course, it cannot be withheld, as the staff consists of three certificated Irish teachers, and two monitors.

I prepared a suitable Time Table, which I have followed since; and I now in all sincerity declare, limited as is my experience of its operation, that I should feel very sorry were I obliged to revert to the old Programme and Time Table again. School work is now more pleasant, for we feel, and the pupils appear to realize too, that we are educating in the proper use of the word, imparting real rational instruction.

The difficulty of inducing children to practice home reading was one which teachers generally experienced, and still experience, under the old programme in Irish-speaking localities. Little wonder! The language of their English readers is so foreign to them that reading aloud at home would be as trying on the children as it would be dull and uninteresting to the parents.

With the Irish readers it is quite different: the language is their own: they understand what they read, and the reading, instead of being mechanical and painful, is entertaining and pleasant. A taste for reading is thus promoted, and this once accomplished, the key which unlocks the storehouse of erudition has been secured. As the Board does not, I think wisely, contemplate that for Infant and First Class children instruction in English and Irish should proceed concurrently, I have decided to get them over the latter first, at which they are at present employed.

For the other classes, provision for concurrent instruction in Irish and English is made on my Time Table, a certain number of hours each week being devoted to the requirements for both in Reading, Writing, Spelling, Grammar and Composition, while instruction in the other subjects — Arithmetic, Science, Geography, History, Drawing, etc., — is given through the medium of Irish, which is also used in all explanations and directions. I use Father Murphy's *History of Ireland* (edited by Father Finlay), with Keating's *Foras Feasa ar Éirinn* (edited by Dr. Joyce) for reference and elucidation.

The pupils are required to be able to write down and spell correctly sentences from their Irish readers at the commencement of each lesson (apart from the ordinary dictation exercises). This also applies to Catechism lessons. Special blackboard lessons are given in Irish grammar. For some time the exercises in Composition for the Second, Third and Fourth Standards will consist of formation of sentences which shall contain words dictated. The Fifth, Sixth and Seventh Standards write letters and descriptive essays. The principle initial difficulty is the preparation of a suitable Time Table; but this once done, the work goes on smoothly and pleasantly.

We have not, of course, as yet Readers which can be regarded as quite suitable, but a fair selection can be made from the Gaelic League catalogue.'

This narrative of the actual experience of a practical teacher is of the utmost value as bearing witness alike to the practicability and to the soundness of the principles and methods we advocate. We trust, too, that it will go towards removing any possible impression that what we write on the subject of Bilingual Education is mere impertinent theorising.

THE PROGRAMME IN A BILINGUAL DISTRICT
22.10.1904

During the past few weeks we have been endeavouring to throw into relief certain principles which must be borne in mind in applying the Bilingual Programme to a school in an Irish-speaking district. We have also been submitting for the consideration of those whose task it will be to administer the Programme our views as to how, in such a district, a bilingual scheme of education may most smoothly and profitably be worked. Those views are tendered simply for what they are worth, and we have little doubt but that their chief value will lie in the fact that they are likely to stimulate the thought of teachers and thus induce them to face for themselves the problems discussed.

It remains for us to see how far it may be necessary to modify our maxims and methods when we come to apply the Programme to a district which is not Irish-speaking, but bilingual. In a bilingual district the problem is considerably complicated. The typical school of such a district will probably contain children whose vernacular is Irish, side-by-side with children whose vernacular is English. Most of the English speakers will, indeed, know some Irish, and nearly all the Irish speakers will know some English. But, as a rule, a child has only one vernacular: there is one language which he speaks by choice, or, perhaps we should say, by instinct, one language only which is entirely indigenous to him, however excellent may be his mastery over a second. It is a common experience in the class of district now under discussion to find a household in which the vernacular of the children is English, and next door to it a household in which the vernacular is Irish. So much depends on the spirit of the parents, the degree to which they have themselves been educated or de-educated, their wealth and social standing, the length of time the mother has spent in America, the frequency with which the father goes to Scotland or England, and a hundred other considerations. In a typical 'bilingual' district it is never safe to generalise as to the language which is really the vernacular of the youngest generation.

Now, as we have said, the average school in such a district will probably contain children whose vernacular is Irish and children whose vernacular is English. Which language is to be the basis of instruction in the early standards? We must once more bear in mind our old maxim that the first stages of a child's education ought to be conducted in the child's vernacular. The carrying out of this principle, the soundness of which is so self-evident that we need not insist on it, will, in the class of school we are considering, involve the division of the Infants and First Class children — these at least — into two groups, — those whose vernacular is Irish and those whose vernacular is English. For the first year the instruction of the former group should be confined to Irish, and that of the latter group to English. During the second year, and before the Infants' Class is left, instruction in the second vernacular ought to be commenced. By the time the children have reached Second or Third Standard, the Irish speakers will have

60

learnt enough English, and the English speakers enough Irish, to permit of the amalgamation of the two groups. From this point forward all should be taught in common on the plan already developed — the teaching of Irish being conducted in Irish, that of English in English, and that of Arithmetic, Geography, etc., in both Irish and English.

This is the only system which seems to us to be rational. It will, of course, entail double work in the lower classes, — the teaching of two groups of children instead of one; and in small schools the inconvenience of dividing already small classes in two will be considerable. But we see no way out of it, if the spirit of the Programme is to be carried out, and if entirely satisfactory results are to be looked for from its adoption.

It is interesting to note that the very same problem has been dealt with in Belgium, and dealt with precisely in the way which we suggest. There are in Belgium Flemish districts, Walloon districts, and districts in which Flemings and Walloons are found in fairly equal proportions. In some of the quarters of Brussels the schools are attended by children both from Flemish-speaking and from French-speaking homes. In such schools the Flemings and the Walloons are instructed apart for the first four years of the school course. They are then grouped together and instructed in common until they leave school. The system works admirably: there is no reason, in the nature of things, why it should not work admirably in Ireland.

THE TRAINING COLLEGES
22.10.1904

It will be recollected that the recent Ard-Fheis instructed the Coisde Gnótha to approach the authorities of the various Training Colleges in Ireland with a request that the latter should receive a deputation from the Gaelic League in reference to the position of Irish on their curricula. We publish elsewhere the replies which have been received from the Training Colleges. Of the six Colleges approached, two have not as yet sent any answer. These are the Marlboro' Street Training College, Dublin, and St. Mary's Training College, Carysfort, Blackrock, (formerly Baggot Street). The College of Mary Immaculate, Limerick, courteously replies that it will receive a deputation at the convenience of the League. The principal of the Church of Ireland Training College, Kildare Street, explains that as the introduction of a new subject would involve financial considerations, the matter is not one for him, but for the Board of the College: the Coisde Gnótha will, of course, approach the Board. Father Byrne, C.M., the principal of St. Patrick's Training College, Drumcondra, declines to receive a deputation on the ground that he does 'not see what good results would follow from such an interview, bearing in mind the fact that the course of studies in our College must, in the main, be governed by the rules and regulations of the National Board'. It is, no doubt, quite true that the course of studies in a Training College must in the main, be governed by the rules and regulations of the National Board; but, whilst in no iota contravening those rules, the De La Salle College has found a means of promoting the study of the Irish language by making it a 'preferential' subject at entrance. One of the objects of the proposed deputation was to suggest that a similar plan should be adopted by the other Training Colleges. We regret that Father Byrne has not seen his way to give the League an opportunity of discussing this and other points with him. There

61

may be reasons of which we know nothing which make what is possible in De La Salle impossible in Drumcondra; but granted that there are, it seems strange that the League should not be allowed at least to state its case. The superioress of St. Mary's Training College, Belfast, writing in Irish, requests further information as to the objects of the proposed deputation before consenting to receive it. The correspondence, on the whole, does not indicate a very sympathetic attitude on the part of those responsible for the management of the Training Colleges. Needless to say, the matter will not rest here.

THE INSPECTION OF BILINGUAL SCHOOLS
29.10.1904

It may be profitable at this stage to consider, from the point of view of the practical teacher, some of the difficulties which have to be reckoned with in any attempt to apply the principles and methods of bilingual teaching to an Irish school. The teachers with whom we have discussed the subject are unanimous in placing the Inspector in the forefront of these difficulties. It is a strange commentary on the past history of the 'National' system that teachers should instinctively feel that amongst the enemies of the reform now being introduced under the auspices of the Board itself must be reckoned the majority of the Board's own officers! Not that it is likely that the Inspectors will actively oppose the introduction of the Programme, — they dare not, even should they be so inclined. The difficulty with regard to the Inspectors is less a matter of their hostility, overt or covert, than of their utter incapacity to test the efficiency of such schools as may adopt the Bilingual Programme. The five Inspectors whose knowledge of Irish and whose sympathy with the movement are well known have for some time past been removed from the general inspectoral staff, and form a special staff with the duties of examining in Irish as an extra subject and looking after the night schools. The formation of this special staff was in itself a very good thing, but it has left the general staff of inspectors, which has charge of the supervision and examination of all the day-schools in the country, without, so far as we are aware, a single man capable of testing the efficiency of a school conducted on bilingual lines.

It is obvious that it is the merest farce to send a non-Irish-speaking Inspector to examine a school which has adopted the Bilingual Programme. However anxious he may be to do justice to all concerned, he is quite unable. The Bilingual Programme expressly sanctions an arrangement under which Infants may be taught only Irish for the first year of their school course. How are Inspectors ignorant of Irish to test the proficiency of such Infants? A few weeks ago we heard of an Inspector who declared that a class of Infants 'knew nothing', though they were able to understand, read and spell half of 'Primhleabhar'. The Inspectors do not seem to realise that even the National Board itself has outgrown the stage in which 'knowledge' was equated with 'knowledge of English', and in which the definition of 'reading and writing' was 'the reading and writing of English'.

Again, Arithmetic can be taught in both Irish and English. A child who is purely Irish-speaking to start with cannot possibly have learned enough English by the time he reaches, say, Third Standard to be able to fully understand and answer arithmetical questions in English. The same is true of Geography, Elementary Science, Manual Instruction, etc. How can an

Inspector ignorant of Irish test the knowledge in these subjects of a class of Third Standard Irish-speaking children? How can an Inspector ignorant of Irish report on the general intelligence of the children in a bilingual school or on the efficiency of the teacher?

Plainly, unless the Bilingual Programme is intended for ornament rather than for use, the Board must send Irish-speaking Inspectors to all schools which adopt it, and that not merely for the purpose of examining them in the Irish part of their work, but for the purpose of testing their general proficiency and progress. At the present moment Inspectors wholly ignorant of Irish — Englishmen in some cases — are patrolling the Irish-speaking districtrs, and gravely going through the pretence of examining schools which have actually adopted the Programme. Some of these gentlemen, to our personal knowledge, are insisting on as much English matter from children taught under the Programme as from children taught under unilingual lines. In doing so they are simply acting outside their authority, and we advise the teachers not to allow themselves to be bullied by them. The Gaelic League is now strong enough in the land to make it impossible that any Irish teacher should suffer at the hands of an Inspector or anyone else for his devotion to the national language. If we are communicated with in every case in which an Inspector shows or hints hostility to the teaching of Irish or throws obstacles in the way of its adequate treatment, we shall know how to act, without in any way compromising the interests of the teacher.

Meanwhile the following communication from the Secretary of the National Board is of interest. It has been received in answer to a communication of the Ard-Rúnaidhe of the League drawing attention to the attitude of certain Inspectors towards the teaching of Irish, and to the fact that in reporting on the general proficiency and progress of schools Inspectors are wont to leave wholly out of sight the excellent educational work accomplished in so many schools through the medium of Irish teaching. The document will serve as an encouragement to teachers and as a warning to such Inspectors as may need it: —

'Sir, — In reply to your letter of the 13th instant, I am directed to inform you that it has not come under the notice of the Commissioners that some of their Inspectors are hostile to the teaching of the Irish language in the National Schools, and they would be much surprised if any of their officers assumed such an attitude.

I am to add that Inspectors when forming an opinion of a school are bound to take all the circumstances of the school into consideration.'

TEXT-BOOKS
5.11.1904

We do not regard the absence of a complete series of school text-books in Irish as a serious obstacle in the way of the immediate introduction of the Bilingual Programme. In fact, we should like to see teachers dispensing as far as possible with the use of text-books, and depending more and more on *viva-voce* teaching, with constant recourse to the assistance of the blackboard. We fear that the possiblities of the blackboard in teaching

63

languages, composition, arithmetic, geography, elementary science, and so on, are not adequately realised. A blackboard in the hands of a teacher who knows how to use it is worth a cartload of wall charts and a trainload of text-books.

Certain text-books are, of course, indispensable. Amongst these the most important are Literary Readers. The first two of a series of Literary Readers have already been published by the Gaelic League, and others are in active preparation. Except in Standard I., for which 'An Prímhleabhar' and 'Ceachta Beaga' are named as alternatives, the Commissioners do not specify any particular Readers. With regard to the other standards, 'Managers and teachers may submit Readers which they consider suitable, for approval. During the first year in which the Bilingual Course is taught, Standards II and III may use a common reader, and Standards IV, V, and VI may use a common reader. In submitting books for approval it should be borne in mind that no mere phrase book having English and Irish translations can be sanctioned. For 3rd and higher standards texts containing short stories or other suitable continuous Irish reading matter would be accepted.'

This means, in substance, that teachers are practically free to select their own reading-books for the present, — a very valuable liberty. For Standards II and III matter of the style of 'Greann na Gaedhilge', 'Aesop,' etc., would, we have no doubt be sanctioned; and for Standards IV, V and VI such texts as 'An Buaiceas', 'Cathair Conroí,' and 'Eochaidh Mac Rí'nÉirinn' would be suitable. We understand that the same texts as are used within school hours, whether as readers under the Bilingual Programme or in teaching Irish as an 'ordinary' subject, may also be selected as the course in Irish as an 'extra' taught outside school hours. Thus, — granting that Irish is retained as an 'extra' subject, — a teacher who adopts the Bilingual Programme and who also teaches Irish as an 'extra' will not need to have two sets of Irish reading-books. The work done inside school hours will count towards the earning of fees, as long as the required time is given to the subject outside school hours as well.

Grammar and Geography have now gone out of fashion as set subjects taught from formal text-books. 'Má's maith é, is mithid'. Grammar is best taught incidentally during the course of the reading and other lessons. The dry-as-dust geography-books of our youth have been replaced by several series of (more or less) attractive and interesting Geographical Readers. An Irish Geographical Reader has been prepared for the Publication Committee by Seaghán Mac a'Bháird and will be published as early as possible. But the greater part of the geographical teaching in a school should be done orally by the teacher, with constant reference to the map, the chart, and the indispensable blackboard. The last-named is the most valuable of all three. The teacher who knows his business will be able to draw in chalk on the blackboard a plan of the school, a rough map of the playground, of the townland, of the parish; and to illustrate by outline sketches the meaning of 'oileán,' 'loch,' 'abhainn,' 'cnoc,' 'sliabh,' and so on. *Local* instances of the various natural divisions of land and water should invariably be given: it is grotesque to teach a child living on the shores of a Connemara loch that 'a lake is a sheet of fresh water entirely surrounded by land, as Lake Tchad in Nigritia, Lake Sir-i-Kol on the table-land of Pamir'.

History, like Geography, is now taught mainly through special Readers. An Irish Historical Reader has been prepared for the Publication

Committee by Eoghan Ó Neachtain, and its publication is being proceeded with; Mícheál Breathnach's *Child's History of Ireland* will also be issued as soon as possible, and will form a capital school book. Moreover, the series of historical studies which 'Conán Maol' commences in this issue of *An Claidheamh* will, when re-issued in book form, as is contemplated, provide admirable reading matter for the higher standards in schools, and will prove most suggestive to teachers. In a short time, therefore, there will be no lack of Historical Readers in Irish. As in the case of Geography, however, much of the history-teaching should be done *viva-voce*. In particular, the teacher should never fail to tell the children, as spiritedly and as vividly as he can, the story of any local dún or ecclesiastical site or battlefield, or of any local saint or hero. Such tales might afterwards supply themes for composition exercises.

A text-book on Arithmetic would be useful, but is hardly a crying desideratum. Arithmetic should be taught from the blackboard, and in more than one Western school we have seen it admirably taught from the blackboard in Irish. Most of the technical terms required will be found in *Eolas ar Áireamh*. Teachers should *not* use or tolerate such words as 'subtractáil', 'divideáil'. The correct Irish terms are part of the vocabulary of every Irish speaker.

Objects which should hang on the walls not merely of every bilingual school, but of every school in which Irish is taught, are the League's Irish Reading Tablets ('Treoir an Pháisde,), and the Banba Charts. A Map of Ireland, with the names marked in Irish, is in preparation.

THE PHILOSOPHY OF EDUCATION
12.11.1904

In bringing to a conclusion the series of leading articles which we have devoted to the Bilingual Programme, we may with advantage dwell on certain maxims and methods of modern educationists which are, indeed, applicable to unilingual equally with bilingual teaching, but which in our opinion are especially deserving of the study of every teacher who would make a success of the Bilingual Programme. Educational reform in Ireland has hitherto followed the language movement; it would be only in the nature of things that the introduction of the Bilingual Programme should be accompanied by the growth of truer educational ideals and the employment of saner educational methods amongst Irish educators generally. At all events we desire in connection with the Bilingual Programme to put forward, not indeed for the first time in these columns, the following suggestions for the consideration of Irish teachers. Though the subject is tempting, we shall compress what we have to say within the limit of two articles.

Now, the aim of education is not the imparting of knowledge but the training of the child to be a perfect man or woman — 'to prepare for complete living,' said Herbert Spencer. Neither is the chief *means* of education the imparting of knowledge; the imparting of knowledge is, indeed, only an incident of the process of education. The real education consists in the forming of the child's character, the drawing out of his faculties, the disciplining of his intellect. These are truisms, but they are truisms whose truth is not yet recognised in Ireland except in so far as the Gaelic League has been able to impress its ideas on our educators. We wish we were sure that every teacher in Ireland realised the dignity and responsibility and possibilities of his position. To have confided to one's care the moulding for good or evil of the most beautiful thing that God has made — the soul and the mind of a child — is surely a high dignity and a high responsibility.

Now, we conceive that in educating a child the inculcation of truth, manliness, purity, and reverence, is more important than the teaching of vulgar fractions and Latin roots. Under the National School system instruction in dogmatic religion is rigidly restricted to a single half-hour each day; but there is no hour of the day during which the teacher cannot, by precept and example, enkindle in his pupils' minds a love of truth and goodness and a hatred of falsehood and baseness. The whole life of a teacher should, indeed, be a sermon to his pupils. There is one virtue the inculcation of which is one of the special duties of a teacher — the virtue of Patriotism. We owe it to our children that they should be taught to know and love their country. If we hide that knowledge from them we commit a crime. *A fortiori,* if actively or by acquiescence, we teach them to be ashamed of their country, to despise her speech, her song, her music, her traditions, we are morally as guilty as if we poisoned their minds against their own parents, and taught them to cast costumely on them; nay, we are, if anything, more guilty, for duty to country is paramount to duty to parents.

Every Irish child has, then a fundamental right to be taught that Ireland is his mother — the duty to know her, the duty to love her, the duty to work for her. This, of course, implies his right to be taught her language and her history, and to be shown how to study and appreciate her literature and lore. The systematic inculcation of patriotism is part of the school *régime* of every enlightened country. Its necessity is understood on the Continent, in America, and partially in Britain. In Denmark old Danish folksongs are sung in the schools, in Belgium the children are taught that the Battle of Waterloo was a Flemish victory, and that Wellington and the British were mere items in the army that crushed Napoleon; in America school-children salute the American flag as they pass to their desks.

Far more effective than the mere didactic preaching of patriotism would be well-directed efforts to bring the children into some direct relation with the country they inhabit — its natural beauty, its wild living things, its rocks, its rivers, its ruins. Saturday excursions should be made to the scenes of famous fights, the sites of famous dúns or churches. The story of the spot should be told in simple language by the teacher, to form afterwards the theme for a composition exercise. The lives of the children should be brought into touch with the beautiful and mysterious life around them. Love of nature should be instilled, and minute and intelligent observation of the ways of nature encouraged. The children might be asked to bring to school each week some new wild flower or plant, together with its Irish name, gleaned from the old people. The specimens so collected should be preserved, and would form the nucleus of a botanical collection which would grow constantly until it was fully representative of the flora of the district. In places near the sea-coast the children might be asked to bring specimens of the various species of shell and sea-weed to be found on the shore, with the Irish name of each. Thus would be formed another treasure-house to be drawn on in future object-lessons. Again, the children should be taught to know and to love every wild thing that flies in the air or creeps in the grass — to know their names, their haunts, their habits, to recognise their forms and cries. They should, above all, be taught that the lives of animals are sacred, and that wantonly to kill or hurt a beast or bird or insect is a wicked and a mean thing. The children again might be asked to note the first appearance in the locality of migratory birds — to bring the teacher word of the first swallow seen, the first cuckoo heard in spring or the last to leave in autumn. The appearance of rare birds and insects in the locality should also be noted. Every child ought to keep his own record, and the more interesting items could be transferred to a common school list kept by the teacher or a senior pupil.

Work of this sort forms part of the school programme in many Continental countries and in America. In America, indeed, the idea has of late years been immensely developed. There are school libraries, formed by the children, school museums, collected by them, school gardens, cultivated by them. Nay, children are taught at school to cultivate orchards, to grow corn, to rear chickens and pigs. To the youngsters it is all play, but in reality they are being trained to habits of observation, of method, of cleanliness, of economy. 'In Illinois children are raising corn and oats, sweet peas and lilies, trying experiments with clover and alfalfa. In their arithmetic lessons they keep their accounts, do the book-keeping of their tiny farms; in their composition exercises they describe what they have done. Girls and boys, big and little, plan their home gardens, their school-gardens, and send samples of their results to the State University. Interested fathers are benefiting by the instruction colleges and teachers give their children. An estimate based on the actual results of school experiments credits one county in the next few years with hundreds of thousands of dollars' financial increase in agricultural business. A boy or a girl in a corner of Wisconsin owns hens, or a pair of pigs, a present from a father or an uncle. Close to his public school is a county agricultural school. He asks the director how to feed, how to house and care for his stock. With the right care his animals thrive better than his father's. In his school composition there often figures the child's account of the father's amused scepticism, and the father's conversion to new ways of farming. Interest in grain-growing, interest in the dairy, a love of the farm, are born that way. And the girl or boy bringing the discoverer's zeal to old tasks becomes a woman, not a drudge; a man, not a bumpkin'.*

In Ireland we are, under the aegis of the National Board, and facilitated by the absence of a National University, assiduously and successfully raising not women, but drudges; not men, but bumpkins.

THE NATIONAL LANGUAGE IN MAYNOOTH
12.11.1904

We have deferred discussion of the recent changes in the curriculum of Maynooth College until we should be in a position clearly to understand and explain their exact bearing on the status of the national language in the College. That status, we fear, has been disastrously affected by the changes. In order that we may be able accurately to realise the drift of what has been done, some reference to the recent history of Irish in Maynooth is necessary.

From the appointment of Father O'Growney to the Irish Chair up to a

---

* Adele Mary Shaw in *The World's Work*.

few years ago, Irish was a compulsory subject during the first three years of the College course. During the remaining years it was not compulsory, but large facilities for its voluntary study were given. Two or three years ago, as part of a general scheme, Irish and several other subjects were made optional merely; but the programme was so arranged that Irish was taken up, almost as a matter of course, by practically all the students. In the first year, for instance, students had to take English, Latin, and French, and in addition any one or more from the group, Irish, Italian, German. It goes without saying that of these alternatives Irish was selected by the vast body of the students, some adding one or both of the other two languages. Similarly, in the second year, there was given an alternative between Latin, Greek, Irish, French, Italian, and German; and students who had already taken Irish in their first year, naturally retained it in the second.

The Trustees of the College have now adopted as the College course in Arts the programme of the Royal University. Students must henceforward have matriculated before going to Maynooth; during their first year in College they will study for the 1st Arts, during their second year for the 2nd Arts, during their third year for the B.A. Examination; and unless the University examination be passed at the end of the year, the student will lose his year. This is, in itself, a departure which has a good deal to recommend it; but, the Programme of the Royal University being what it is, and the curricula of the Diocesan Seminaries what they are, there is incidentally entailed a serious blow to the study of Irish both within the College and in the Seminaries. The course for Matriculation is (1) Latin; (2) any one of the following languages: — Greek, French, German, Italian, Spanish, "Celtic," Sanskrit, Hebrew, Arabic; (3) English; (4) Mathematics; (5) Natural Philosophy. Now, Greek is taught in all the seminaries, and French in nearly all; Irish, for practical purposes, is not taught in the seminaries at all. Moreover, Greek carries 1,200 marks, as against 800 for Irish. Almost inevitably, every student must take Greek, or if not, French. Again, having entered Maynooth, the student will, of course, continue Greek or French in the First Arts, and so on with the Second Arts and the B.A. Not more than 5 per cent of the students who enter Maynooth know any Irish; the remainder, if they commence at all within the College, must commence at the elements. Everyone who knows anything about Royal University work will be aware that no student can in one year get up, in addition to his other subjects, enough Irish to pass the First Arts. In other words, it is next to impossible for 95 per cent of the students in Maynooth to select Irish for their University course; they may study it as an extra and purely voluntary subject, but they will do so at a sacrifice.

All this would be remedied if (1) Irish were made a compulsory subject of study within the College — i.e., if every College student were required by the College rules to select Irish as one of his University subjects; or if (2) Irish were made a compulsory subject for entrance to Maynooth. Now, the Ard-Fheis of 1903 respectfully requested the Board of Trustees to make Irish a compulsory subject for entrance, but the Board did not accede to the request. This year's Ard-Fheis renewed the request. In response the Board has decided that Irish shall be a subject at the Entrance Examination in and after 1906, but the right is reserved to each Bishop dispensing his students from presenting themselves in Irish. The concession is valuable as establishing the principle that a knowledge of the national language is, in the ordinary course, required of every candidate for the Irish priesthood. If the power reserved to the Bishops simply meant that a Bishop could, for reason shown, dispense an individual student from presenting himself in Irish, there could be no reasonable objection to the clause; but we understand that a Bishop is empowered to dispense the whole body of his diocesan students from presenting themselves in Irish. Assuming, as we think it may be assumed, that the Bishops are not likely to exercise this power in a wholesale manner, the situation is still unsatisfactory. Irish does not become a subject for entrance until 1906, and in the meantime the University Programme has been adopted and an immediate desertion of the Irish classes in Maynooth may be anticipated.

We do not imagine that the bearing of the new obligations on the position of Irish in the College can have been adverted to by the Trustees when framing the scheme; and we rest confident that as soon as that bearing is clearly realised, a remedy will be found in the directions we have indicated.

THE CHILDREN
26.11.1904

We are not sure that the Gaelic League is sufficiently mindful of the interests of its young folk, sufficiently alive to their great importance in the movement. This is perhaps part of a general national tendency. Modern Ireland, this strangely blind, strangely unthinking, strangely topsy-turvy land, does not seem to interest itself as it should in the well-being, the happiness, the thoughts and doings of its children. One cannot help feeling that the life of the ordinary Irish child, town or country, might easily be made brighter and blither than it is. True, there is always the spaciousness of the bogland, the mystery of the woods, the life and colour of the meadows, the music of the running stream, the freedom of country roads. Children love these things, but they also love other things more human and sociable. They love pleasant gatherings, with the telling of tales and singing of songs; they love the wonderland of the stage; they love toys; they love tea-cakes, apples, nuts, sweets and so forth. We really think that Irish children do not get enough of these things. Social evenings for children are rare things in our towns, and all but unknown in our villages and hamlets. Toys are not often seen in an humble or even in a middle-class Irish home. Why, one wonders? The average Irish parent will tell you that he cannot afford to buy toys for his children — that he finds it hard enough to buy boots. Yet he manages to keep himself in tobacco and drink!

In other countries things are not so. In philistine England, the children of all classes, save perhaps those of the submerged tenth in the great cities, are thoughtfully looked after. In America it is the same. In France and Germany the catering for child wants, the brightening of child life, is carried almost to a mania. Nor are there wanting evidences that the old Gael, with his true and genial outlook on life, fully appreciated the importance of the child. No passages in our older literature are more interesting that those which give us glimpses of boy and girl life whether in the dúns of kings, in the homesteads of farmers, or in the cloisters of saints. More than one Irish saga, more than one Irish life of saint or sage, embodies records of the thoughts and doings of very winsome and lovable Irish children. But the sympathies of the old Gael, especially the Gael of early Christian Ireland, extended even to the wild things of the air and the meadows and the woodland — 'the little ones of God,' as he called them — and it were strange if those sympathies did not also embrace the most mysterious and beautiful of all God's little ones — the children of whom He has said, 'Suffer them to come unto Me, and forbid them not'.

In brief, we make a plea for the recognition of the importance of Young Ireland. The League, as a whole, has as yet done little to make Irish Ireland a reality for the children. Our London friends have, indeed, made special arrangements to cater for children in several of their local schools. In Dublin, too, a little has been done by 'Ingheana na hÉireann'. Elsewhere, and especially in the country, the problem of the child has for the most part not been attacked at all, save indirectly through the National School. This is not as it should be. The League must try to capture the children for Ireland. In doing so it will incidentally be making them better, happier, brighter, quicker.

To come to our immediate purpose in writing this article, we suggest that every Craobh of the League should hold a Christmas party or entertainment of the Irish Ireland children of its district. In most places it would be quite easy to raise a special fund of a few pounds for the purpose. Should this not be possible, the branch funds might be called upon. We can conceive no more fruitful mode of expenditure.

The form of the entertainment would depend on circumstances. In some places it might take the shape of an impromptu Children's Feis, in which prizes of Irish-made toys would be given to the best children. Now that Ireland has taken to manufacturing beautiful and distinctive toys, the giving of toys as prizes to very young children ought to be encouraged. Dolls from Dublin and wooden things from the Antrim Glens would form attractive alternatives to the books usually given, which are too often of the dry-as-dust order. Where feasible, a play should form a part of the Christmas entertainment, and it would, of course, be all the better if the children themselves were the actors. Most of the Irish plays that have been written have already been performed by child players in schools and colleges. An Craoibhin's Nativity Play would constitute a very appropriate piece for a Christmastide entertainment, and would have an especial appeal for children. In non-Irish-speaking districts 'Cuairt na Bainrioghna' would serve. Music, song, and dance should, of course, follow the play or Feis, and the children themselves should be the main performers. A magic lantern display, or, if possible, a cinematograph display, would also prove a popular feature. The pictures shown should, for the most part, be of an Irish interest, but no one but a prig would object to the inclusion of humorous pictures not distinctively Irish, as long, of course, as they were not vulgar. A short and simple address on the duties of Irish children to their country — what they should do and what they should not do — might usefully be added.

A certain social character should be given to the gathering. The children should be entertained to tea and cakes and fruit, and these should be of good quality and attractively presented. The average organiser of 'school treats' seems to imagine that a stale bun and a tin mug of ginger-beer represent the heart's-desire of the average child. This is a mistake.

Games of various sorts might precede or follow the tea.

It should be understood that to such an entertainment as we suggest only the 'good' children would be invited — *i.e.*, clean, well-conducted boys and girls who have been steady and fairly punctual attendants at an Irish class whether in a school or at a League Craobh. No grown-up people should receive tickets except those whose help would be required in amusing the children or otherwise carrying out the arrangements.

May we hope that the approaching Christmastide will see the commencement of a genuine and widespread effort to popularise the language movement amongst the young folk?

THE UNIVERSITY QUESTION
17.12.1904

Mr. Dillon's address to the Catholic Graduates' and Under-Graduates' Association was at once encouraging and disappointing. It was encouraging in its full recognition that what Ireland requires is a University Irish and National, the natural outgrowth of the soil of Ireland, drawing the sap of its life from the traditional life of Ireland, managed exclusively by Irishmen in accordance with Irish ideas. It was disappointing in that it suggested no way in which the realisation of such a University might be brought about, outlined no bold and statesmanlike policy to which the whole country might rally.

It is highly satisfactory, we repeat, that the ideas of so earnest an Irishman and so prominent a politician as Mr. Dillon are so sound and definite as to the kind of University that is needed. His statement of the essentials of the case for a National University was admirable. Our University must be 'genuinely national'; it must be 'extremely democratic'; it must be 'given from the start the priceless gift of a free academic life and self-government, ensuring that it will be a genuine expression of national intellect and national ideals'; it must be absolutely independent of Castle control; it must borrow its traditions and prestige from no pre-existing institution, for, — and this is, perhaps the most valuable passage of the whole address, — 'the real traditions we have to look to for inspiration are the traditions of the wandering and outlawed scholars and poets of our race, the traditions of the Hedge Schools and unnamed and unrenowned men who through ages of persecution and suffering carried on the high tradition of devotion to learning and to all the 'things of the mind' in the midst of poverty and privation and at the risk of life itself, and back through them to the ages when Ireland had a civilisation of her own and was admitted to be the chief seat of learning in Europe. And as for prestige, we must create it for ourselves, and not seek to beg or borrow it from Trinity College'.

All this is excellently put, if it embodies nothing new. It is, of course, a re-statement of what the Gaelic League, through its President, demanded before the Royal Commission, and of what has again and again been urged in the columns of *An Claidheamh Soluis*. In a word, we are in agreement with Mr. Dillon, at least in broad outline, as to the kind of University which Ireland requires. We differ from him as to how that University may be obtained. Mr. Dillon, if we understand him aright, has no more luminous suggestion to offer than that we continue to call on the British Government to give us the sort of University we desire. With the Archbishop of Tuam, we are convinced that the British Government will never, unless a miracle supervenes, do anything of the kind. We are amazed that Mr. Dillon should think that, by insisting on the *National* rather that on the Catholic character of the University which we desiderate, we shall induce the British Government to listen more favourably to us. Is it likely that England will

71

ever give to Ireland a University which will satisfy the lofty ideal of Mr. Dillon and of us all, — a University which shall be Irish and National through and through, a centre and rallying point for Irish nationality, an intellectual headquarters of our race? We cannot think so.

Far more statesmanlike is the suggestion of Father Finlay, so lightly, not to say contemptuously brushed aside by Mr. Dillon. Ireland must create her own National University. 'But,' says Mr. Dillon, 'we tried before and failed, losing £200,000 in the effort'. Is this quite true? The University erected half-a-century ago was not a National, but a Catholic University, and for a Catholic University no one now calls. Moreover, given the internal organisation of the Catholic University, and given the woeful state of public opinion at the time — it was in the dark days which immediately followed the Famine, when even political nationalism was at a low ebb, and Irish Ireland was in the misty future — failure was inevitable. As we wrote last week, neither the internal nor the external causes which wrecked the Catholic University are likely to re-occur in our day. And because an effort on (more or less) right lines failed fifty years ago from causes which are no longer likely to act, are we to lose faith in the policy of self-help, and continue to the end of the chapter to beseech a foreign State to do for us what it is neither its desire nor, perhaps, its interest to do?

In advocating the view here expressed, we bind neither the Gaelic League as a whole nor Gaelic Leaguers as individuals to adopt it; neither do we preclude ourselves from welcoming hereafter any proposed solution of the University Question, which, whilst not going the full length we would desire, yet sufficiently safeguards the interests which we believe to be vital.

WHAT IS A NATIONAL LANGUAGE?
28.1.1905

A language is evolved by a nation for the purpose of expressing its thought. Thus a nation's speech is in a real sense the creation of that nation. Now, anything created by me is what it is because I, its creator, am what I am. I am what I am because of my history, personal and ancestral. Applying this commonplace of psychology, a nation's language is what it is because the nation is what it is. The nation is what it is by reason of its past history, immediate and remote.

Thus the Irish language is, so to speak, the logical and inevitable outcome of Irish history. The Gael being what he is, his language is what it is. Its sounds have been fashioned precisely so, and not otherwise, because the vocal organs of the Gael are of a particular conformation, and because his ear likes or dislikes particular sounds. Similarly, its grammar and idioms are the inevitable outcome of the Gael's way of looking at things. They reflect his personality, and express it. It is because the Gael thinks in a particular way, and not otherwise, that there is in the Irish language a particular idiom which is not in other languages; it is because of this that there are certain grammatical forms in the language which are not in other languages; and it is because a particular point of view has never presented itself to the Gael that a particular idiom or grammatical form occurring in other languages may be absent in Irish.

If we admit all this, and admit it we must, we see how inadequate is the notion of those who tell us that a language is a mere set of labels, a mere collection of declensions and conjugations. Even regarded as a mere set of labels a language is to a certain extent biographical. It is the result of the physical and mental conformation of the nation which produced it, and for all time will be a witness to that conformation. But even when arranged in parallel columns in a dictionary a language is very much more than a mere collection of labels. In actual practice there is no such thing as a word apart from its connotation and associations. One cannot turn over the pages of a dictionary without coming into contact with the mind of the race which fashioned the language whose vocabulary is there recorded.

So far, we have been speaking of a language proper, apart from its literature and folklore. When we go on to consider the literature of a language, the argument becomes infinitely more compelling. A literature is the expression in literary form of the mind of a race. Races also express themselves in art, in industry, in political institutions, and in other ways, but language and literature must always remain the most important channels for national self-expression, a nation's language and literature must always remain the fullest and most understandable record of its thought. Thus if we want to get at the mind of Ireland we must go to her language and literature. For practical purposes Ireland's mind has not been expressed otherwise than in language and literature. Ireland has not yet expressed herself to any great extent in art — her ancient art, distinctive as it was, was but a very imperfect expression of her personality, — expressed, in fact, only one aspect of a very complex national character; and it stopped short at a very early stage. Nor can Ireland be said to have adequately expressed herself in industry or in political institutions. Emphatically, then, the mind of Ireland has been expressed in her language, with its literature and folklore. If we do not find the Irish mind here we can find it nowhere.

Seeing that the language of a nation, as to its sounds, its idioms, its grammatical forms, and still more, as to its literature and folklore, it indelibly stamped with the personality of the nation, it is obvious that by coming into touch with the language, we come into touch with that personality. We cannot come into touch with the language without coming into touch with the mind of the nation, nor can we come into touch with the mind of the nation otherwise than through its language, — except, in so far as we can do so through its art, industry, political institutions, and so on. Thus, to get at the real Ireland, we must go to the Irish language. The language sums up what the Gaelic race has been thinking ever since there was a Gaelic race. It contains Ireland's message to her children and to the world. In it Ireland's temperament is expressed, its point of view is Ireland's. Moreover, it imposes the Irish point of view and Irish modes of thought on those who use it.

All this is next to self-evident, and people who speak of a language as a 'mere set of sounds', are either incapable of thinking or else are saying something which they do not believe. In point of fact, is the only difference between the Irish-speaking and English-speaking Irishman (strange contradiction!) this, that the two make use of different 'sets of sounds', of different declensional and conjugational systems? The merest casual observer can see that there is another and a profounder difference. It is that one is in contact with the Irish mind, and the other in contact with the English mind, that one is in line with Irish history, Irish tradition, the other with English history, English tradition, that one has the Irishman's standpoint, the other the Englishman's.

73

Remembering this, we come to see that the question of retaining the Irish language is not a mere question of retaining a set of sounds developed by ourselves for the mere pleasure of being unlike other men; it is a question of remaining in communion with the past of our race.

THE UNIVERSITY QUESTION: MR. GWYNN'S PROPOSALS
28.1.1905

Mr. Stephen Gwynn's address on 'The Irish University Question considered from a National Point of View' surprised everyone by turning out to be a plea for Trinity College. Mr. Gwynn made a sincere but, as we think, an unsuccessful attempt to understand and to state the point of view of the majority of the Irish people. If we understand aright the attitude of the Catholic Hierarchy, then Mr. Gwynn misunderstands it; if we understand aright the attitude of the general body of Catholic laymen, Mr. Gwynn misunderstands it also. But what concerns us more nearly, and what surprises us much more than his failures in other respects, is that Mr. Gwynn scarcely seems to recognise that there are profound objections to Trinity College from the national as well as from the Catholic standpoint. We should like to emphasise the fact that if there were no religious considerations involved at all there would still be an Irish University Question. The crying grievance of Ireland is, not merely that there exists no genuine University institution which Catholics can conscientiously enter, but that there exists no Irish University at all, — no University drawing the sap of its life from the soil of Ireland, animated by the traditional spirit of Ireland, and having for its aim the 'making of Irishmen and Irishwomen'. If Trinity were as Catholic as it is Protestant, it is conceivable — not, indeed, likely, but certainly conceivable — that it might be quite as un-Irish as it is to-day.

We come to Mr. Gwynn's concrete queries and proposals. It is, of course, for Catholics, *qua* Catholics, to deal with them from the Catholic standpoint, — here we deal with them only from the national standpoint. To the query, Is it possible so to re-organise Trinity College as to render it an institution which nationalists may enter with a view to subsequently 'dominating' it? we answer, Yes, certainly. There is nothing inherently impossible in the problem. But to the query, Would the adoption of the measures which have been suggested by the Board of Trinity College, by Mr. Gwynn, and by others, render Trinity such an institution? we answer, No, it certainly would not.

What, in fact, are the actual proposals which have been made? They are (1) that a Catholic Chapel should be built within the walls of Trinity; (2) that the Chair of Philosophy should be duplicated; (3) 'that Irish should be recognised as an honour subject for degrees, and, if possible, a new Chair of Irish founded, or else the existing Chair put on a different foundation from that on which it stands at present;' and (4), that the governing faculty should be separated from the occupancy of paid posts, the government of the institution to be given to an elective body holding office for a limited term of years, on which Catholics would have a representation proportionate to their numbers in the University. It is for the Catholic body to say whether the granting of these 'concessions' would remove their conscientious objections to Trinity. We unhesitatingly say that, in our judgement, modifications far more profound will have to be proposed and carried out before Trinity becomes even a potential National University.

One suggestion of Mr. Gwynn's we welcome, because it is in harmony with our fixed view that Irishmen ought to settle this question for themselves. A round-table conference, representative of the various interests concerned, supposing the difficulty as to the authorisation of the Catholic representatives got over, could do no harm and might do some good. On the whole, we believe that the University Question has marched further towards a solution within the past few months than it had during the preceding three decades. Not, indeed, that there is at present any more prospect of legislation at Westminster than there has been at any previous point, but that is a fact which does not trouble us. What does interest us is that the people of Ireland are really commencing to wake up to the capital importance of the question, and that the volume of public opinion in favour of the policy of self-help is a constantly growing quantity. Within the last three months three concrete proposals have been put before the Irish people — Mr. Dillon's proposal that we should ask the English Parliament to establish and endow a new National University; Mr. Gwynn's proposal that it would meet what he conceives to be the needs of the case; and Father Finlay's proposal that, turning our backs on the English Parliament and on Trinity, we should erect for ourselves a National University of the precise kind that we desire. On all three proposals we have expressed our opinion; and, whilst we do not preclude ourselves from accepting a solution from any direction whatsoever, nothing that has been said or written has shaken our conviction that Father Finlay's suggestion is the most statesmanlike and the most practicable that has yet been put forward.

LANGUAGE AND NATIONALITY
4.2.1905

It will be evident from what we have written in our last two leading articles that a nation's language — fashioned as it is by the nation itself for the purpose of expressing its thought, conditioned by the nation's peculiarities, mental and physical, which, in turn, are conditioned by the nation's past history, expressive of the nation's point of view, working by methods peculiar to the nation, and imposing that point of view and those methods on whomsoever uses it — it will be evident, we say, that this language is an essential part of the nation's nationality. Nationality we have defined as the sum total of the characteristics which mark off a people as a distinct entity, and we think the definition is both accurate and adequate. Of such characteristics there are many: some are physical, others mental; some are of great, others of minor importance.

It is sufficient for our purpose to predicate that language is one of these characteristics, — that is, that it is an element in the compound, nationality. Every element in a compound is an essential part of the compound: if one element be withdrawn, the compound is not what it was, but something else. Were the Irish language to disappear, then, the people which we should have in Ireland, whatever else it might be, would not be the Irish Nation.

But, from what we have said it is plain that the national language is not merely an element — that is, an essential — of nationality, but that it is the largest and most important of all the elements which go to make up a nationality. It is this partly in virtue of what it is itself — the main expression and record of the nation's thought — and partly in that it is a preservative of most of the other characteristics of nationality which are not merely physical. For instance, it is a preservative not merely of the literature and the folklore of the nation, but of the nation's habits of thought, the nation's popular beliefs, the nation's manifold bents, prepossessions, idiosyncrasies of various sorts. It is a preservative also of nationalism in art, in industry, in pastimes, in social and civic customs. It is further, partly through its function in keeping the nation in touch with its past, partly through the fact of its enshrining the national literature and lore, the well-spring from which artists and industrialists and publicists draw imspiration.

What is meant by saying that the national language is a *preservative* of many of the other elements of nationality will be grasped at once by remembering how far those amongst us who have retained the national speech have retained the other notes of Irishism in comparison with those who have become English-speaking. How much of Irishism in mind, in manner, in lore, in music, in song, in pastimes, in dress, in customs social and civic, does one not see in comparing a Donegal or a Galway or a Kerry countryside with a rural district in Meath or Kildare or Dublin? Wherever the language has been lost, all or nearly all of such characteristics — purely physical ones excepted — have disappeared, or are disappearing. And the extent to which they have disappeared is measured by the length of time which has elapsed since the language disappeared.

It has sometimes been said 'language is nationality'. That dictum we take to be merely a forcible way of stating the truth that language is, so to speak, the determining factor in nationality, — the largest and most important element in the compound. If it be meant that the terms 'language' and 'nationality' are co-extensive, — that they connote exactly the same things — we must dissent. Nationality, in our view, is a complex thing, and language, whilst the largest and most important of its factors, is still only a part of the whole. We imagine that this is all the dictum means. Language is at once an important element itself, and a safeguard of other important elements, at once a test and a symbol, of nationality; so that, if the statement 'language is nationality' be true only when regarded as a figure of speech, the statement 'there is no nationality independent of language' is true absolutely and universally.

'What about the United States?' says someone. We shall say somewhat about the United States next week.

THE BRITISH TREASURY AND IRELAND
25.2.1905

At the suggestion of the Coisde Gnótha the Dublin Coisde Ceanntair has invited the citizens to a public meeting of protest against the starvation policy of the British Treasury with regard to Irish primary education. The meeting will also consider various other important questions in reference to the primary and secondary schools, but its main purpose will be to call the attention of the country to the attempt of the British Government to ruin the future of Irish primary education *by the degradation of the teachers*.

The official excuse for all such attempts is 'the need for economy'. Seaghán Buidhe undertakes a 'picnic to Pretoria', a 'peaceful mission to Tibet', or some other 'Imperial' enterprise with which Ireland at all events has little concern and less sympathy. Having 'muddled through somehow' — the phrase has become appropriated to John Bull's method of carrying

76

out his 'Imperial' mission — the worthy Seaghán has to pay the bill, or preferably get someone else to pay it for him; and the first and most obvious expedient is to mulct Ireland. This is not precisely the explanation we should give of the starvation policy of the Treasury with regard to Irish education, but it is a fair statement of the Treasury's own explanation, shorn indeed of the graceful and conciliatory phraseology with which it would be invested by Mr. Balfour or Mr. Wyndham.

Taking that explanation for what it is worth, it is for Ireland to say clearly and with one voice that her primary teachers shall not be mulcted, that her poverty-stricken people shall not be taxed twice or thrice over the upkeep and repair of schoolhouses, and that her language shall not be crushed out of the schools, merely because it has pleased Seaghán Buidhe to go on a picnic to Pretoria or to undertake a 'peaceful' mission to Tibet. Ireland at least had no part in these enterprises, and Ireland is not going to pay for them.

The facts with regard to the remuneration of teachers have already been stated in *An Claidheamh*. The initial salary of an Irish male primary teacher of the Third Class is £56 a year; his maximum possible salary (exclusive of capitation grants and special fees, both of which may be non-existent) is £77 a year, a figure at which he arrives, continued good service supposed, at the end of nine years; and this even though he be the principal of a school, responsible in a large measure for the moral and intellectual welfare to the children of a whole parish. In the case of a female teacher of similar rank, the minimum salary is £45, and the maximum £66. The scheme for retiring pensions is on a correspondingly munificent scale. The magnitude of the scandal will be appreciated when it is remembered that Third Class teachers constitute over 66 per cent (roughly, some 8,000 out of 12,000) of the entire body of primary teachers.

The results of this policy have already become apparent. The teaching profession is no longer attracting as many or as capable young men and women as it did before the new régime came into force. This year only one of the Training Colleges was able to find candidates to fill all its vacant places, — in former years there had always been more candidates than vacancies. Moreover, a fact of still gloomier significance, the Training College authorities are already complaining of a deterioration in the quality of the young men and women who are coming up for training. Again, an alarming proportion of recently-trained teachers — teachers, remember, whose training is charged to the account of Ireland — are seeking and obtaining posts in Scotland and England. Even the Training Colleges are educating for export.

There can be only one outcome of all this, if it is allowed to continue. As the older teachers retire — and the Board is 'retiring' them as fast as it can in order to make room for fifty-six pounders — a new generation of less capable and cultured men and women will take their places; the quality of the education — which, in final resort, depends almost entirely on the character and capacity of the teachers — given in our primary schools will steadily deteriorate; and all the League's work in reforming Irish education along Irish lines will go for nothing.

The Treasury, with the apparent acquiescence of the 'National' Board, is also seeking to 'economise' by docking the special fees for instruction in Irish and other special subjects. Thus, no fees will be allowed for the teaching of Irish in any standard under Fourth; no fees at all will be allowed to the teacher of any school which, according to the Inspector's report,

77

does not show 'merit' — a very elastic term which the Inspector can interpret just as he chooses; and the Board is enforcing a drastic rule for the calculation of attendances at Irish to the effect that, however many lessons may be given, only two per week count towards the earning of fees. Again, still owing to the necessity for 'economy', the Board will not, or cannot, appoint organisers to pioneer the introduction of the Bilingual Programme, whilst it has dismissed its organisers in music and other subjects.

The 'National' Board is supposed to look after the welfare of primary education in this country. If the Board were really concerned for the true educational interests of the land, nay, if it had the slightest spark of honourable ambition or even the ordinary regard for its own dignity which one expects from an administrative body, it would put itself at the head of a national protest against the tactics of the British Treasury, and thus go far towards wiping out the memory of its unhappy past. The Board has not chosen to do this: it is content, on the contrary, to become the submissive slave of the British Treasury, and its chief function nowadays appears to be the carrying into effect of the autocratic behests of 'My Lords'. Where the 'National' Board has failed, the Gaelic League once more steps forward. And it calls on the country to follow it in its attack on this new conspiracy of Gall and Gall-Ghaedheal, be its explanation the need for 'economy' or the old traditional desire of British and West-British administrators to keep Ireland ignorant and ineffective for the benefit of England. The League will put its case before the nation at the great meeting which will assemble in the Round Room on this (Saturday) evening.

THE TRAINING COLLEGES
8.4.1905

A fortnight ago we published figures which afford a rough criterion of the present position of Irish in the various Training Colleges. It appears from a return supplied to the Ard-Rúnaidhe of the League by the Commissioners of National Education that last year 91 'King's Scholars' qualified to teach Irish. These were divided as follows amongst the Training Colleges: — St. Mary's, Belfast, 33; De La Salle, Waterford, 22; St. Patrick's, Drumcondra, 19; Our Lady of Mercy, Blackrock (formerly Baggot Street), 10; Mary Immaculate, Limerick, 4; Marlboro' Street, 3.

These figures are sufficient to show that the Colleges, with one or two notable exceptions, are making no effort to supply the large and growing demand for teachers qualified to teach Irish. But matters are even less satisfactory than would appear at first sight. The obtaining of the Board's certificate is after all a not very reassuring guarantee of ability to teach Irish. The question is: Are the Training Colleges actually turning out teachers capable of giving instruction in Irish, and in what number? What is the actual status of Irish in these institutions, and what is the provision for training in methods of teaching Irish?

The study of Irish by future national teachers is directly penalised by the facts (1) that it in no way helps students to pass the entrance examination of the College, and (2) that it in no way helps students to obtain a certificate of training.

In spite of these penalties, the great bulk of the students, in perhaps a majority of the Colleges, are eager to take up Irish. But here again the position of the language as a mere extra operates in a hostile sense. We

78

shall make matters clear by a reference to the actual state of affairs in the most important of the Male Training Colleges in Ireland.

At the commencement of the present session over 100 out of 166 students entered the Irish classes. Of these classes, which are purely voluntary, there are two, — one for beginners, and the other in the regular programme. Each class meets twice a week for 45 minutes — say, 40 minutes, allowance having been made for changing from study hall to class hall, marking roll, etc.

Now, the time for the Irish classes is taken from the ordinary time for evening study. It follows at once that students attend the Irish classes at what appears to them to be a personal sacrifice. They feel for the most part that all the time at their disposal is required to ensure a satisfactory result at their final examination in the subjects made compulsory by the Board, and of which Irish is not one. Hence the very hours fixed for the Irish classes are calculated to deter students from taking up Irish. A further consequence of the present arrangement is that many of the students are tempted to rely entirely on class work — scanty as it is — for their advancement in Irish. There is no inducement for them, under the Board regulations, to make any effort to help themselves, whether by devoting part of the regular study time to Irish or otherwise.

About 80 per cent of the students who take up Irish in this particular College — and it is probably typical — have had no appreciable previous knowledge of it. Accordingly, all the students in one class have to commence the course with the very elements of pronunciation, spelling, etc. It is obvious that such beginners, being allowed only two very short classes per week during the academical year, cannot as a rule become even moderately proficient in Irish by the end of the second year. Thus, unless the student knows Irish on entering the College, it is almost a physical impossibility to train him to teach it during his college course.

The first thing to insist on is, therefore, that a knowledge of Irish be required as a part qualification for admittance to training. In the present state of public opinion it would perhaps be a mistake to demand that Irish should be made compulsory on every student for training. We simply ask that those who know Irish should be allowed credit for that knowledge in competition with others. If even this can be secured the position of Irish in the Colleges will be enormously strengthened. Monitors, teachers, etc., who mean to become candidates for training, will be induced to take up Irish, and persons who already know Irish will be encouraged to present themselves as candidates.

This reform secured, a large proportion of the students entering College would already be instructed in the elements of Irish. Rudimentary instruction, we submit, should be given outside and not inside the Colleges. The business of a Training College is to train teachers to teach and to give instruction of an advanced nature. That Training Colleges should have to spend time in giving rudimentary instruction in a primary subject is an anomaly and a scandal. What would the public think of engaging an extra professor to teach the mulplication table in a Training College as an extra subject during extra hours? Irish is now a primary subject in the National Schools, taught to infants, and at an earlier stage than the multiplication table.

In the second place, it must be insisted that the position of Irish *within the College* be put on a satisfactory basis. It would of necessity have to be made a subject carrying merit at the final or leaving examination. No doubt

79

any demand for reform will be met — nay, the Gaelic League's recent demands, following on the resolutions of the Ard-Fheis have been met — with the objection that room cannot be made for Irish on a par with other necessary subjects without detriment to the general scheme of training. The answer is that within the last few years room has been found for several new introductions in the ordinary curriculum, and that the room so found has been since evacuated.

The two chief demands touching the Training Colleges are, therefore: —

1. Recognition of Irish as a subject qualifying for admittance to training.
2. Recognition of Irish as a subject carrying merit in any examination for status as a teacher.

THE BOARD, THE TRAINING COLLEGES AND THE NATIONAL LANGUAGE
15.4.1905

It is not to be assumed that the Board alone is responsible for the unsatisfactory position of Irish in the Training Colleges. Neither is it to be assumed that the College authorities are alone responsible. Both the Board and the Colleges are guilty, and neither is absolved by the guilt of the other. In speaking of the Colleges as 'guilty' we must not, of course, be taken as including them all in the same category: two Colleges — St. Mary's, Belfast, and De La Salle, Waterford — seem to be doing as much, or nearly as much, as they are free to do under the regulations of the Commissioners. The fact that *notwithstanding those regulations* two Colleges, one Male and the other Female, find it possible to do so much, takes away all force from the excuse of the others, that they are prevented from doing more for Irish by the exigencies of the programme imposed on them by the Commissioners.

The Commissioners' rules, as we have seen, operate against the position of Irish at two different points. First, Irish is not recognised as a subject qualifying for entrance to training; secondly, it is not recognised as a subject carrying merit at the final examination for status as a teacher. The Commissioners must be allowed no rest until they satisfactorily amend their programme in both of these respects. But in the meantime the Colleges can themselves to a large extent remedy the state of affairs created by the Commissioners. They can meet the first difficulty by establishing a College entrance examination in Irish, as has been done by the De La Salle College, and giving the candidates who pass it priority over all others. And, with regard to the second, the fact that Irish is not a subject carrying merit at the final examination does not, as far as we can see, prevent the College authorities from making adequate provision for its proper treatment during the College course. It does not prevent them from allotting a reasonable amount of time per week to Irish; it does not prevent them from fixing for the Irish class an hour at which the students can attend without an apparent self-sacrifice; it does not prevent them from actively encouraging the study of Irish and the propagation of an Irish spirit generally.

'But,' object the Colleges, 'the Board's compulsory course is so long and so exacting that we have no room for subjects such as Irish, which do not form part of that course'. One answer is, as we pointed out last week, that within the past few years room has actually been found for new introductions, and that that room has *since been vacated*. Another answer

80

is that two of the Training Colleges, working under exactly the same conditions as the other five, have found it possible to make very fair provision for the teaching of Irish. Where there's a will there's a way.

If the Training Colleges are in earnest let them, instead of falling back on the Board's rules as a justification for their own unsatisfactory attitude, make common cause with Irish Ireland in demanding the alteration of those rules. Are they in earnest?

THE TRAINING COLLEGES AND IRISH
22.4.1905

In 1903 Irish was taught either as an extra or as an ordinary subject, or as both, in 2,018 National Schools, and to as many as 92,619 pupils. We may be quite sure that during the fifteen months which have elapsed since December 31st, 1903, — the date to which these returns refer — the number both of the schools in which Irish is taught and of the pupils to whom it is taught has been largely increased. In 1904, as much as £12,069 was paid in the form of special fees for instruction in Irish as an extra, representing at 10 shillings a head some 6,000 pupils who satisfied the examiners. Irish is therefore an important subject of study in Irish National Schools. As an extra it is taught to perhaps forty times as many pupils as French, the next most popular extra language. It is, moreover, taught as a *primary* subject within ordinary school hours to probably 100,000 children. Futhermore, over one-third of the total area of the country, Irish may be used as a medium of instruction in imparting the other subjects of the school programme, and may be employed by teachers in conducting the general business of the school.

Thus, in the National School system, Irish now stands on a totally different footing from French, Latin, or any other merely extra branch. It is taught widely as an ordinary subject in all classes from the Infants' up; it is taught widely as an extra subject; and it is made the basis of the whole school-work in a considerable and increasing number of schools.

All this being so, it is nothing short of amazing to find the Training Colleges making such scant provision for the training of their students in Irish. The Colleges in this connection do not seem to be mindful even of their own interests. Leaving out of consideration the claims of the National Language, as such, on the attention of those responsible for the training of our future teachers, here is a subject which is taught in several thousand schools to some 100,000 children; which is taught widely as an ordinary subject, and is imcomparably the most popular of the extras; which may be made the basis of instruction in nearly one-third of the schools of the country; — and yet the Training Colleges make less provision for its teaching than they do for the teaching of Latin or algebra.

But this does not complete the picture. Such instruction in Irish as the Training Colleges do provide is wholly of an elementary character. Up to the present year the course of the more advanced of the two classes in Drumcondra has been the course in Irish as an extra for pupils in National Schools.* The students in Drumcondra and Carysfort have been following exactly the same Irish course as the twelve-year-old youngsters in the

---

* For the forthcoming and future examinations the programme for teachers is more extensive. Hitherto it has been identical with the three years' course for pupils.

John Street National Schools! Nay, some of them are being taught precisely the same books as some thousands of pupils in the Infants' First, Second, and Third classes throughout the country!

Neither the Board nor the College authorities must be allowed any rest until this scandal ceases. Taking the school status of Irish for granted, we have Irish as a recognised *primary* subject, capable of being taught to the very youngest children from the moment of their first entry to school. It must therefore be laid down as incontrovertible that the treatment of Irish in the Training Colleges as to entrance, exit, and the intervening stages, should be based on the treatment accorded to subjects which like it are primary, and not on the treatment accorded to subjects which unlike it are purely extra. It will, of course, be urged on the other side that Irish, though a primary, is not a compulsory or a universal subject, and cannot therefore claim equality of treatment with the subjects which are unanimously made essential and universal. We answer that we have not demanded that Irish be made compulsory in the Training Colleges. We merely demand that, as it occupies a special position in the schools, being a primary yet not a compulsory subject, it should occupy the same position in the training of teachers. In other words, all teachers who desire training in Irish should have provision made for them in the ordinary, and not in the extra, curriculum of the Training Colleges.

If this is obtained, the immediate result may be an apparent diminution of the number of candidates who 'take up' Irish. The real effect will be to get rid of a kind of training in Irish which can only lead to vicious results. Statistics favourable on the surface to Irish may suffer, but the general interests of the language will gain enormously.

A WELSH SYLLABUS
10.6.1905

Under the leadership of the Welsh Language Society — a Cymric imitator of the Gaelic League — our cousins in Wales are just now engaging in an effort to extend and systematise the teaching of Welsh in their primary schools. The status of Welsh in the educational programmes of the principality is not yet by any means satisfactory, especially with regard to its use as the medium of instruction in the Welsh-speaking districts. Bilingual education is, indeed, much more of an actuality in Wales than it is here; but, if it is so, it is because public sentiment is more favourable to Welsh than is our education code to Irish. In point of fact, the Gaelic League has during the past few years fought the National Board to such purpose that Irish now obtains quite as full official recognition from the central education authority as does Welsh in Wales. Nay, we have wrested a Bilingual Programme from the Commissioners, whereas in Wales the bilingual principle receives only a permissive sanction from the authorities. There is no official Bilingual Programme, nor is there any special legislation which puts Welsh in a more favourable position than any other non-essential subject.

Wales is not recognised as a separate entity for educational purposes, being subject like any English shire to the Code of Regulations for Public Elementary Schools issued by the Education Department at Whitehall. Under this Code it is possible for Welsh to be taken as an additional subject in any public elementary school provided that H.M. Inspector is satisfied that the conditions required by the Code to be fulfilled before any special subject may be included in the curriculum, are fulfilled. These conditions are:

(1) That the subject is suitable to the age, circumstances and capacities of those scholars who take it;

(2) That it can be taken without interfering with the general course of instruction;

(3) That it can be efficiently taught;

(4) That the instruction will be given in accordance with a suitably graduated Scheme.

Beyond these general instructions, which apply to all special subjects, the Board does not issue any particular instructions with regard to the teaching of Welsh. The language is, however, recognised as a medium of instruction in Welsh-speaking districts, and is widely utilised as such. The present campaign of the Welsh Language Society has for its object the extension and systematising of the use of Welsh in this way, and its more efficient teaching as a special subject. As the immediate problem in Wales — i.e., the inducing of the managers and teachers of the schools to take the fullest advantage of the facilities allowed by the education code — is precisely the immediate problem which confronts us in Ireland, a glance at the maxims and methods which command the adhesion of our confrères of the Welsh Language Society will prove helpful.

We have been favoured with a draft of certain 'Suggestions for a Welsh Syllabus', which are at present engaging the attention of the Society. They are the work of a prominent Welsh educationist, and will be read with the greatest profit by everyone interested in the drawing-up of working Bilingual Programmes for Irish schools. In Wales the duty of preparing Schemes of Instruction lies with the Local Education Authority for each autonomous area, and in these 'Suggestions' the Society indicates how Welsh may most usefully be worked into such Schemes, having regard to (1) Welsh districts, where Welsh is the home language of all or very nearly all the inhabitants; and (2) all other districts in Wales where it has been decided that Welsh should be taught. With regard to Welsh districts we read: —

> 'In the Infant Schools and classes the medium in which the instruction is generally imparted should, of course, be Welsh. It must be remembered, however, that even in the Welshest parts of Wales the children hear some English, and it may be thought advisable that one lesson each day should be given in Englsih. This should be by the now well-known 'direct method', in association with pictures or objects.
>
> It is important to observe that, with the exception of the specified English lessons, not only the whole of the teaching, but also the whole of the intercourse between children and their teachers from "Good morning" to "Good night" should be in Welsh.
>
> If the example of good English schools is followed, the principle of correlation will be adopted, and a thoroughly Welsh programme would set something like the following for the work of the week, the lessons all assisting the central idea "Spring". (There follows a very interesting Welsh programme for a week, the various lessons, hand-and-eye lessons, etc., — having this in common, that they all directly or indirectly illuminate the subject 'Spring", chosen as the theme for the week).

Besides these subjects there will, of course, be physical exercises, games, and songs, the words all in Welsh, and also arithmetic. . . .

STANDARD I. The children now go up to the upper school, being able to read and write simple Welsh and to speak a limited amount of English.

Their education in the ordinary Code subjects will be continued for the first year in Welsh mainly.

One lesson each day will, as before, be devoted to conversational English, which will gradually be made the vehicle of information on various topics, and to English recitation. . . .

STANDARD II and III. The time now given to English must be increased. English reading and writing will be commenced in addition to object lessons, geography, recitation, and perhaps arithmetic lessons in English. It will be advisable to give one-third of the available time to English. This will amount to about eight hours.

Welsh will take up the remaining six hours, i.e., during this time the children will be reading, writing, composing, or speaking in Welsh, just as, in the time above apportioned to English, the whole of their mental and oral processes will be carried on in the latter language.

Every lesson given in the Time Table should be labelled either "Welsh" or "English". It may be found useful to use different coloured inks according as a particular subject, as geography or arithmetic, is conducted in one language or the other, in order that the arrangement may be definite and intelligible.

STANDARDS IV, V, VI, and VII., It is suggested that the school time should, for the higher Standards, be divided equally between English and Welsh. The same division should also apply to each subject so that the scholars should do as much English as Welsh reading, as much English as Welsh composition, recitation, singing. It will be possible at this stage to give very useful instruction in the grammar of the two languages, with comparison as to their structure, idioms, etc.'

Obviously, a child of ordinary capacity, carefully and intelligently instructed on the lines here suggested, would at the end of his course of seven Standards, leave school a correct and fluent speaker, reader and writer of both Welsh and English. He would be an educated bilingualist, speaking Welsh, his mother tongue, by choice, but with a perfect and ready command over English, the acquired tongue. The adoption and intelligent working of the Bilingual Programme in Corca Dhuibhne or Erris or Irish-speaking Donegal would lead to a parallel result.

In a further article we shall deal with the Society's suggestions for a Syllabus for a district other than strongly Welsh-speaking.

MORE POINTS FROM WALES
17.6.1905

It is not to be understood that the Bilingual Programme contemplates merely the utilisation of Irish for the purpose of teaching English and other subjects to Irish-speaking children. Neither does it contemplate merely the teaching of Irish. Its object is the education of the Irish-speaking child; and as a necessary incident to the process of education on bilingual lines, the Irish-speaking child will be given a thorough grip both of Irish and of English as spoken and as literary tongues. A pupil of ordinary intelligence, instructed bilingually, ought at the end of his course to be able to speak, read and write the two languages with fluency and correctness, and to have in addition a good general acquaintance with their literatures. Let this be as clearly understood in Ireland as it is in Wales.

We have seen that the best Welsh educationists recommend that in the upper forms in Welsh-speaking districts half the school-work be done in each language. The teaching of Welsh should, of course, always be through the medium of Welsh, and the teaching of English always through the medium of English. The instruction in subjects other than Welsh and English should be commenced in the familiar language, the new language being gradually introduced, until when Standard IV or V is reached, the two speeches are used in the general school work in equal proportions. Applying these principles to a Welsh-speaking district, the Infants would be taught solely in Welsh, except during the short period each day which would be devoted to easy lessons in English on the direct method. There would be an increasing amount of English until Standard IV was reached, and from Standard IV to Standard VII Welsh and English would be used in equal proportions.

Let us see how the scheme would work out in a district in which English, and not Welsh, is the vernacular of at least a large proportion of the school-going children. A parallel district in Ireland would be the less Irish-speaking portion of Erris, the town of Galway, the greater part of the Déise, West Cork (with the exception of such spots as Gougane and Ballingeary, which might fairly be ranked as exclusively Irish). The following are the Welsh Language Society's recommendations for 'Districts other than strongly Welsh':—

'This is a very mixed class, as it includes not only the bilingual parts of the country, but also those where Welsh is all but extinct.

The Society's suggestions with respect to these widely varying districts are based on the principle that time spent in teaching Welsh will be almost wasted unless it leads to a solid result. The time must be adequate and the teachers must be thoroughly competent.

Infant Schools — The medium of instruction will be English, as a rule, but when the conditions as regards the sentiment of the locality and the composition of the staff make such a step possible and profitable, one lesson a day may be given to conversational Welsh, on the same lines as English was taught in the purely Welsh Infant Schools.

STANDARD I. — The Welsh daily oral lesson should be continued in Standard I, in combination with blackboard reading and word-building.

STANDARD II-VII. — A fourth of the available time should now be devoted to Welsh in the same way as was described in connection with English in Welsh schools, the subject being divided between the languages in a similar ratio. This fraction will represent about six hours, and will be enough to give a very satisfactory knowledge of Welsh to the children who pass through the whole of the course.

If to some it will appear to be too much, it should be recollected that with steady and expert teaching, the Welsh language will have become, say from the Third Standard, a vehicle of information, so that there will be no loss on that side.

It is doubtful, however, whether as much can be said when only two or three hours a week are devoted to the language, as is too often the case.'

For our part, we would go even further than do these very moderate recommendations of the Welsh Language Society. We do not see why fully one-half of the school work should not be done in Welsh or Irish, as the case may be, after the Fourth or Fifth Standard is attained. If Welsh speaking children are supposed to have acquired sufficient English to enable them to do half their work in that language after Standard IV is reached, surely English-speaking children at a similar stage ought to have acquired enough Welsh to enable them with profit to do half their work in Welsh. Nevertheless, we should be well satisfied were even one-fourth of the school time devoted to teaching through the medium of Irish in the 'bilingual' districts of Ireland. In the strongly 'Irish-speaking' districts — districts, that is, of the type of Aran, all Iar-Connacht, the greater part of Erris, Glenties, Corca Dhuibhne, part of West Cork, the Ballinagaul area in Waterford — we should rigidly insist on the minimum required by the Welsh Language Society for 'Welsh' districts.

REFORM OF THE NATIONAL BOARD
15.7.1905

That the Board of National Education stands badly in need of reform is now admitted on all sides. The Gaelic League has been saying so for years, and the Protestant teachers of the north have recently added their voice to the chorus of dissatisfaction. At a meeting lately held in Belfast they indicated very clearly that even they had become disgusted with the deplorable state to which primary education had been reduced by the gross incompetency and mismanagement of the National Board. And they suggested as a remedy that that Board should be abolished and a Department of Education established in its stead. Now, in our opinion, this would never do. In homely *parlance* it would be simply 'getting out of the frying-pan into the fire'. We are certain that such a settlement of the question would not be at all acceptable to the vast majority of the Irish people who are quite cognizant of the danger with which such an arrangement is fraught. And we know that any attempt at a solution of the problem on these lines could only result in even still greater disorganisation and dissatisfaction than exist at present.

We were told some time ago that this country should in future be 'run' according to Irish ideas. Now, there is absolutely no subject in connection with which it would be more necessary to put this intention into practice than the subject of education. And here is a splendid opportunity to translate this good pious intention into practical action.

Everybody agrees that the time has come when something must really be done with the National Board as at present constituted. We do not, of course suggest its abolition, but we think that in the interest of education a drastic change in the personnel of the Board is a matter of pressing necessity. This unrepresentative, irresponsible body appears to be absolutely indifferent to, and out of touch with, the interests of the classes who use the primary schools, as well as being apparently unacquainted with the educational needs and wishes of the country generally. And we think the time has arrived when a serious and strenuous demand should be made for the establishment of a Board on representative lines. No argument can be advanced in favour of the continuation of the Board as at present. It has been tried and found sadly, deplorably wanting. Sooner or later it must go and we are convinced that the only statesmanlike and acceptable solution of the problem will be to set up in its stead a Board which shall represent the managers, the teachers and the taxpayers of Ireland. The selection of this Board would involve no violent straining of electoral machinery. A certain number of seats might be allotted to, say, the Managers' Associations, the teachers' organisation, the County Councils (through their General Council), and the Gaelic League. There can be no doubt but that a Board so selected would be thoroughly representative of the country and would therefore command the utmost confidence. Besides the method of its selection, which is simplicity itself, would involve but a minimum of trouble or delay. Some people may say it would be rather ungrateful to treat the present Board in so abrupt and summary a fashion, but we think that if these gentlemen went tomorrow there would be very few indeed amongst the Irish people who would view their exeunt with regret.

A NATIONAL BOARD MINUTE
26.8.1905

Thanks to the indefatigable energy of the Ard-Rúnaidhe of the League, practically the whole story of the shameful conspiracy to oust the national language from the schools of Ireland has now been laid bare. Today we are in a position to publish a further material document. The Commissioners of National Education and the British Chief Secretary will no doubt be amazed to see it in our columns. It is the actual minute of the meeting of the National Board at which the unholy compact with the arch-enemy of Ireland was entered into. Here are the terms of the resolution adopted by the Commissioners:-

'(1) The Commissioners are of the opinion that in districts where Irish is the home language of the majority of the children attending primary schools, instruction in Irish, and the teaching of English through the Irish idiom, are of great educational importance. In districts where it is not the home language, Irish must be considered, to a great extent, an unknown tongue, and the Commissioners are aware that it is difficult to find a precedent for the teaching of a second language, which is not the home language, in elementary schools to children of tender years. But, on the other hand, there is at present a strong sentiment in favour of Irish in a large number of primary schools, and the Commissioners believe that the study of a language in which the teachers and pupils are keenly interested has an educational value, even though, strictly speaking, it may be considered outside the programme of an elementary school.

(2) As to the propriety of discontinuing the fees for all extra subjects, the Commissioners offer no opinion, but they will consent to such a policy only on the condition that the savings thereby effected

shall not be applied to reduce the vote, but shall be devoted to the purposes of Irish national education.'

In forwarding a copy of this minute to the press the Ard-Rúnaidhe of the League writes: —

'I beg to send you for publication copy of the resolutions adopted by the National Board in connection with the question of the withdrawal of fees for Irish. These resolutions are a summary of the communications forwarded by the Board to the Treasury and conclusively establish the accuracy of my précis of the famous Board-Treasury correspondence.

The utmost precautions were taken to prevent the publication of this correspondence.

I have succeeded in securing the Board's side of the story, and hope to be soon in a position to place before your readers a copy of the communications forwarded by the Treasury to the Board.'

It will be seen that everything took place exactly as, in the teeth of the British Chief Secretary, we said it took place. In one respect only we did the National Board more than justice. It caved in to the clerks at Whitehall more quickly and more ignominiously than we had imagined. Having stated the case for Irish with an energy and an effect which would have done credit to a League organiser, it promptly surrendered. The question arises: Why did not the Board, believing as it did that 'in districts where Irish is the home language of the majority of the children attending primary schools, instruction in Irish, and the teaching of English through the Irish idiom, are of great educational importance', and believing further in the 'educational value' of Irish as a subject of study in English-speaking districts, — why did not the Board, believing all this, join issue with the Treasury? Why did it not fight? Why did it make a formal protest, and then run away? Why did it not take the people of Ireland into its confidence, appeal for their support on this and other large questions in dispute between it and the Treasury, and atone in some measure for its disastrous past by putting itself at the head of a national movement for the freeing of Irish education from the domination of a foreign bureaucracy? This would have been manly, this would have been honourable, this would have been to keep faith with the Irish public and with its own conscience. But the course actually pursued is a course which covers the Board and its members with infamy; — its members, we say, for everyone who continues to sit on the Board is responsible before the public for its acts. The Resident Commissioner has eaten his own words; the members believed to be friendly to the language movement are — unless there be some strange explanation of their silence which we have not heard — either traitors or cowards.

In the fight which is about to be entered upon the National Board may be eliminated as a factor. It has ceased to think and to act for itself. It is functionless. We have to fight the British Treasury and the British Government. The Gaelic League called for reform in the personnel of the National Board: the British Lord Lieutenant has replied by nominating for membership — Mr. Richard Bagwell. Irish Ireland will not forget the insult.

WHAT WE WANT
9.9.1905

At its meeting on Friday evening last the Education Committee of the Coiste Gnótha considered the situation created by the recent official announcement as to the withdrawal of special fees for Irish as an extra subject in national schools. It goes without saying that the unanimous voice of the Committee was for war, — war to the knife. The only question was as to method of procedure. Should the Treasury and the Commissioners be attacked on the comparatively narrow issue of the continuance or discontinuance of special fees for Irish, or should the opportunity be availed of for the purpose of pushing forward the League's programme with regard to the reformation of the National Board? Remembering that the recent Ard-Fheis had adopted a resolution declaring that in its opinion the National Board should be replaced by a Board in the election of which the people of Ireland should have a voice, the Committee felt itself bound to recommend the Coiste Gnótha to press ahead with its long-cherished project of a national agitation directed against the present method of appointing Commissioners of Primary Education.

The National Board might, if it had so elected, have allied itself with the Irish people and bid the British Treasury defiance. It has not done so. It has chosen its part, — the ignoble part of a lackey to some clerk in the Treasury Office. We could have wished otherwise. We should have entered on this fight with greater willingness had it been a clear issue between English officialdom and the unanimous public opinion of Ireland. As matters stand, there are some on the other side who should be with us. The Board still includes within its ranks men whom most Irishmen respect. Such are the Bishop of Kildare and Leighlin, Lord Chief Baron Palles, Sir Henry Bellingham, Lord Killanin, Mr. W. R. J. Molloy, and Mr. Edward Gwynn. It is for these gentlemen to consider their own position. For our part, we have no hesitation. The National Board *as a whole* has proved itself unworthy of the confidence of the Irish nation. It has betrayed the interests confided to its care. It has, in the teeth of its own expressed conviction, acquiesced in the Treasury scheme for driving the Irish language out of the schools of Ireland. It has permitted an external body to usurp its functions. It has allowed the teachers of Ireland, whose rights it should have been its duty and privilege to vindicate, to be plundered and pauperised. It has gone further, and itself passed absurd and childish regulations for no other purpose than the degradation and humiliation of its own teachers. Such a Board has no claim on our generosity, — not even on our pity. As constituted at present, it must go.

Let us not be misunderstood. We do not call for the total abolition of the National Board, or for the erection of an education department under Dublin Castle, or under a minister responsible to the British Parliament. We have long ago made clear what it is we do want. We want to see a drastic change in the mode of appointing Commissioners of National Education, and in the class of person appointed. We want to see duly-accredited representatives of the school managers, of the teachers, and of the people of Ireland on the Board. We want to see the deadheads and the bigots, the castle lawyers and the fox-hunting squires, fired out. We want educationists on the Board, and we want *men* on the Board. We want a body of Commissioners who will grapple boldly and masterfully with the immense problems of Irish primary education; who will think largely and

89

generously; who will face the situation in the Irish-speaking districts; who will place Irish on a proper basis in the non-Irish-speaking districts, whether by restoring the special fees, or by adopting other and more educationally satisfactory measures; who will make it their business to protect the interests of the teachers and of Irish education generally; who, in short, will realise in theory and carry out in practice what is required of a *National Board of Education*.

This we want, and this, be the cost what it may, we must get.

HOW TO SOLVE THE EDUCATION PROBLEM
16.9.1905

In the agitation for the reform of the National Board and for the freeing of Irish primary education from the illegal domination of the British Treasury, the decision to withdraw the special fees for Irish must, of course, form one of the main counts in Irish Ireland's indictment of the two conspirators. But the final objective of the campaign must be, not the restoration of the fees, but the placing of the whole system of primary education in this country on a satisfactory basis. We believe that this can be done, simply and expeditiously, by a drastic reform in the personnel of the National Board. We are not in favour, under present circumstances, of the introduction of the principle of local control, and still less of an interference with the existing managerial arrangements. We simply ask that the Board itself be brought into line with public opinion in Ireland; that it be strengthened on the educational side; and that it be freed from the control of anti-Irish politicians in London.

The Gaelic League is by no means bound to the system of encouraging the teaching of Irish by the payment of special fees. The actual arrangement – a three years' course of intruction with fees at the rate of ten shillings per head for every unit in a class which passes – is far from ideal. We ourselves suggested many months ago an alternative scheme – viz., a four years' course with a graduated scale of fees – which, we believe, was on the point of being adopted by the National Board, when the Treasury stepped in with its ukase that fees of all kinds were to cease. But it would be possible to devise a scheme for the adequate teaching of Irish which would have as its *motif* a far sounder guiding principle than the essentially vicious one of payment by results. It had been our intention to develop such a scheme during the course of our articles on the bilingual system of Belgium. Let us here anticipate ourselves just so far as is necessary for the purpose of putting our readers in possession of the main essentials of the suggestion.

The Belgian Government lays down as the cardinal principle of its educational system that every Belgian child is entitled to be taught first to speak, read, and write his mother tongue ('langue maternelle'). If the child be a Fleming, he is entitled from the moment of his first entry into school to be taught Flemish; if he be a Walloon he is entitled from the first moment to be taught French. The Government further lays down that every Belgian ought to be taught a second language ('seconde langue'). In theory this second language may be anything; in practice it is always French in the case of Flemings, and Flemish in the case of Walloons. The Government actively encourages the acquiring of the 'two national languages' by every Belgian; it insists that the teaching of the second language be commenced at the earliest possible stage in the child's school career; and it insists that the teaching be on the direct method. The system so works out that, whereas the Flemish child goes to school speaking only Flemish, he leaves it an educated bilingualist, speaking, reading, and writing, both Flemish and French; whilst similarly the Walloon child, who on entering school speaks only his *patois*, emerges from his school career with a thorough written and spoken knowledge of both French and Flemish.

There is nothing to prevent the application of this system, *mutatis mutandis*, to Ireland, — nothing, that is, except the 'National' Board and the British Treasury. If we had in this country a really *National* Board of Primary Education, we should expect it to deal with the language problem somewhat in this way: —

Every Irish child is entitled to receive his earliest instruction in the language of his own home. Accordingly, in Irish-speaking districts the first steps of the child's education must be taken in Irish; in English-speaking districts, they must be taken in English. But, from the earliest possible moment, each child must be taught 'a second language', and that second language must be taught as a living tongue according to sound modern methods. In theory, this second language might be anything; in practice, it would be in Irish-speaking districts be English, and in English-speaking districts Irish. In some Ulster schools, and in a few Protestant schools elsewhere, French or German would possibly be adopted as the second language, until such time as the language movement should have captured — as it inevitably will capture — even the strongholds of Orangeism. But in 80 per cent of the schools of Ireland, the languages taught would be Irish and English; they would be taught well and rationally, as spoken and as literary tongues; and the children — in Dublin no less than in Connemara, in Wexford no less than in Donegal — would leave school educated bilingualists.

Such a system would of course pre-suppose two things, — first, the proper training of the teachers, and secondly their adequate remuneration.

IRISH IN SECONDARY SCHOOLS
18.11.1905

The system of Intermediate Education in Ireland, considered as a system, exemplifies pretty nearly every fault of which a national education scheme could possibly be guilty. It yet remains true that that system provides the secondary schools of Ireland with a school programme capable of a sound and enlightened scheme of teaching.

The Intermediate system sins against fundamentals in its retention of the obsolete principle of payment by results, in its neglect to apply live tests of efficiency, as, for instance, personal inspection by a competent staff, and — not least — in its failure to appeal boldly to the more generous and exalted sentiments of the children for whom it caters. This is a strong indictment of an educational system, and it may at first sight appear impossible that the programme of studies emanating from such a system should be capable of utilisation to any good purpose whatsoever. Our criticism, however, concerns the Intermediate system as conceived by those responsible for its administration at headquarters; whereas, it is the staff of teachers who are actually charged with the working-out of the system in the schools that give it its tone and colouring as far as the individual child is concerned. In other words, it is our contention that, unsound as the Intermediate system undoubtedly is, unsympathetic as the majority of the Commissioners apparently are, and unsatisfactory as the programme in many important respects may be held to be, the schools and colleges working in connection with the Board are yet free to make the course of education within their walls practically as national and as rational as they choose.

The Intermediate Programme directly penalises Irish at several points. It is not reasonable that Irish boys and girls who elect to take up Irish, or that Irish schools and colleges which are anxious to give a genuinely *Irish* education, should be subjected to pains and penalties, — and their time-tables should be overloaded, or that their chances of winning honourable distinctions should be reduced by one-half. For this reason steady pressure must be kept on the Intermediate Board until Irish is placed on a footing of absolute equality with any and every other subject in every course and in every Grade. But in the meantime — we write advisedly — there is nothing in the rules or programme of the Commissioners which makes it impossible for Irish to be taught, if the heads of schools so will, to every child in every secondary school in Ireland. We are familiar from the inside with the working-out of the Intermediate system in actual practice; and we hold that if in a given secondary school, Irish is not taught to every boy or girl on the school roll the fault rests, not with the Commissioners, but with the head of the school.

It is perfectly true that, by taking up Irish in preference to some easier subject, a pupil may expose himself to a certain amount of risk, — under the new rule with regard to the awarding of 'Literary Exhibitions' he may even run the risk of losing an exhibition. That is a scandal and a shame which must be terminated. But the existence of this possible contingency — which, at worst, can arise in the case of only a comparatively small number of pupils — does not at all justify the exclusion of Irish from the curriculum of even a single child on the rolls of an Intermediate school. 'Am I, then,', asks the teacher, 'to allow a pupil to run the risk of losing a distinction for himself and for the school?' Yes, we answer, if necessary; for the primary object of an education system is not the winning of distinctions, but, — well, education. In keeping your eyes fixed on the Results List of the Commissioners you are losing sight of the main end and purpose of your work, — of all its noble significance, its gigantic responsibility, its astonishing possibilities. To cut a fine figure in the Results List is not necessarily an unworthy ambition: but for the true teacher there is a worthier and a higher one — the training up of boys and girls to be good and useful men and women. For Irish-born people to be good and useful men and women it is necessary for them to be good citizens of the Irish Nation. Hence the paramount, imperative duty on Irish teachers to make the school life robustly Irish, to give their rightful position to the national language, literature, and history, and — ignoring as far as may be necessary, merely selfish interests — to direct all their thought, all their energies, all their enthusiasm towards the training up of a generation of patriotic and intelligent Irish boys and girls.

In a future article we shall endeavour to show how such an inspiring educational programme may be carried out in our secondary schools; how, in short, secondary education in Ireland may be made vital and valuable, saddled though it be with the incubus of the Intermediate Board and its rules.

THE SECONDARY SCHOOL
25.11.1905

The most important factor in moulding the character of the education given in a school, whether secondary or primary, is the teacher. Programmes have their influence, codes of rules have their influence, examiners and inspectors have their influence, but the thing which matters most is the living personality of the teacher. It is possible for a good teacher to impart a sound and stimulating education under the worst programme that could be conceived: whilst no programme and no rules will galvanise into life and vigour the school system of a teacher who either does not know or does not love his work. Similarly, it is possible — though, we admit, not easy — for a genuinely Irish and national education to be given at the present moment in any primary school in Ireland, the 'National' Board not withstanding: whilst it is a matter of no very great difficulty to inform the school work in an Intermediate School with as Irish and as healthy a spirit as may be desired.

All that is presupposed is a sympathetic governing authority, and a staff of teachers not only sympathetic but competent. These granted, the education given in the school is national as a matter of course. True, the programme may not be altogether such as an Irish educationist, if left to himself, would be likely to devise; but the programme, we insist, is entirely a secondary matter. Far more important are the character, ideals, sympathies, enthusiasms, of the school *personnel*.

Our Intermediate teacher must, in the first place, be a man (or woman) of fine character and lofty ideal. He must, in the next, be warmly Irish in sympathy. This does not mean that he must of necessity be a rampant politician. It means only that he must know Ireland and love her with an intimate and discerning love; that he must regard himself as a worker for Ireland; that he must realise the awfulness and the responsibility of his position as one into whose hands it is given to mould for good or ill the characters of future Irish citizens. His patriotism must not be of a dour and repellent kind, but rather a generous and wholesome enthusiasm which will communicate itself to his pupils without any undue display of propagandism on his part. The children must be brought to feel that they are Irish children; that this is Ireland; and they are destined to become citizens of an Irish Nation; and that their allegiance and their love are due to that Nation, above every other secular person, institution, or conception.

We submit that it is easy, even under existing circumstances, for such a sane and strenuous gospel to be preached by the teacher of an Irish Intermediate School. We are convinced of this for two reasons, — first because there is nothing that we can see to prevent it, and secondly because we are acquainted with Intermediate schools in which the thing is done.

The Irishising of the general tone of school life we regard as of even greater importance than the set teaching of Irish and Irish history. But, of course, the school life cannot be genuinely Irish unless the course of instruction centres round the ample and proper teaching of the language and history of the country. To show how, under the existing Programme of the Commissioners, their proper place may be given to Irish language and history in the scheme of school work, will be the purpose of a future article. Meanwhile we may suggest some subsidiary ways in which what we call an Irish 'tone' may be given to secondary school life in Ireland.

In the first place, every pupil should be addressed only by his Irish name, and the children should be actively encouraged to use the Irish forms of their names in addressing one another. We know an Intermediate school in which one of the teachers commenced quite recently to call the boys 'Tomás,' 'Pádraic,' etc., instead of, as hitherto, 'Tom,' 'Pat,' and so on. Within a week the boys themselves had unconsciously dropped into the habit, and some of the other teachers had also adopted it. Again, the pupils should be encouraged to use their Irish signatures. The roll should be kept in Irish; and lists showing the order of merit at school examinations and the like should invariably be written in Irish. The common orders throughout the day should be in Irish, — the various stereotyped phrases, 'To your desks,' 'Take out your copies,' 'Open the books,' etc., uniformly so, and this not merely in the Irish classes but in all the classes, — except, perhaps, in the case of foreign language classes, where the foreign language itself should be utilised as much as possible. In the Irish class as large a portion of the teaching as is feasible should be done through the medium of Irish: when the teacher knows the way to go about it, he will find it quite easy to make the average Intermediate boy or girl follow grammatical and other instructions *in Irish*. Of this more anon. It goes without saying that where prayers are publicly recited in school they should invariably be recited in the national language. Finally, in the playground, the pupils should be urged to play Irish games — in fact, foreign games which actively compete with Irish games should be *prohibited* — and to use Irish as much as possible in their intercourse with one another.

All these things are possible in any and every Intermediate school in Ireland. If they are not done, the fault assuredly does not rest with the Commissioners.

ABOUT THE INTERMEDIATE
9.12.1905

Those of our readers who have followed the recent discussions provoked by the issue of the Intermediate Results for 1905 have heard much of the various 'courses' — Classical, Modern Literary, Mathematical, and Experimental Science — in which the exhibitions and prizes of the Intermediate Board are awarded. They are aware that this segregating of the candidates into 'courses' is responsible for some of the most grotesque anomalies in this year's Honours' List. The case of the student of St. Colman's College, Fermoy, who though he qualified for a first-class exhibition in three courses, was awarded only a second-class exhibition in a fourth course, is perhaps the most glaring of all. This student happened to have been entered in the Classical Course: therefore, according to the rules of the Board, he had to stand or fall by his answering in classics, his brilliant scoring in the other subjects availing him naught. Thus it comes about that the most distinguished student in the Intermediate schools of Ireland this year appears in the official results list only as a second-class exhibitioner. The process of selecting the 'course' in which a given student is to stand has been happily compared to the declaration of trumps in Bridge; but the Bridge player has very definite principles to guide him, whereas the Intermediate student must declare trumps almost at hazard, and without even seeing his cards.

The precise purpose of the rule it would probably take a Commissioner of Intermediate Education to tell — nay, some of the Commissioners themselves seem to be wondering why on earth they ever adopted so elaborate a piece of fatuity. To the outsider the whole thing seems no more than an ingenious device for making the Intermediate system absurd. It must not be imagined that a student who takes the Classical Course is specialising in classics, or that a student who takes the Mathematical Course is specialising in Mathematics. Whatsoever course he may select, the student studies practically the same subjects as he would have studied had he selected any other course. Thus, you will enter a schoolroom and will be told that quarter of the pupils are in the Classical Course, quarter in the Modern Literary, quarter in the Mathematical, and quarter in the Experimantal Science. Yet every pupil in the school is being taught practically the same subjects, it matters not whether he be labelled Classical, Mathematical, Literary, or Scientific! The 'classical' student learns nothing that the 'mathematical' student may not learn, and *vice versa*; the 'modern literary' student learns as much experimental science as the 'experimental science' student, and the latter as much modern literature as the former! All, too, are taught in common — we are taking the case of the average school in a country town or of one of the smaller schools in Dublin; and the pupils very often do not know themselves what course they are supposed to be studying! Yet the complicated piece of absurdity so works out that only the classical marks of one student count towards an exhibition, and only the mathematical marks of another, according as the headmaster may have happened to determinine when entering their names as candidates. Thus, the division does not materially affect the course of studies in a school: it only affects, and that very paradoxically, the allocation of prizes at the end of the year.

However, our present business is simply to point out that, whatsoever course a student may take up, it is quite easy for him to include Irish as one of his subjects. True, in certain of the courses Irish can come in only as a third language; and teachers will assert that it will 'pay' a weak student better to take up some easier subject. This constitutes a legitimate ground of grievance against the Board; but it does not, we submit, absolve the teacher from his *duty* to teach Irish, be the risks run what they may. Those risks, however, have been exaggerated. We do not believe that there is in the Intermediate schools of Ireland an Irish-born boy or girl who, given reasonably good teaching, is incapable of securing in twelve months such a knowledge of Irish as will enable him or her to pass in the subject with credit. Nor do we think that the compulsory branches will be detrimentally affected by the time taken from them and given to Irish; for the study of Irish will have such a stimulating effect on the child's mentality generally that he will apply himself with more diligence and intelligence to his ordinary school work.

Irish emphatically 'pays' in the Intermediate, — not that it is an easy subject or that, as its enemies have still the hardihood to assert, it is leniently marked, but simply that the teacher generally teaches it *con amore*. There exists, in short, a combination of circumstances which makes the acquisition of Irish a comparatively easy matter to Irish children. Everything works with the teacher — the mysterious forces of heredity, the very physical and mental conformation of the child, all his sympathies, predilections and enthusiasms, his very surroundings; — whilst, in addition, the teacher himself is generally much better qualified than the teacher of French or German in this country, — that is, he not only knows his work better, but likes it better. The amazing thing is that the heads of the Intermediate schools have not long ago realised all this: that they fail to see that, even from the purely pedagogic standpoint, they could do nothing better than make generous provision for the teaching of Irish in their schools.

For years we have been pointing out to the Intermediate schools and colleges that it is their *duty* to teach Irish. Perhaps it will be more profitable to endeavour to convince them that it will *pay* them to do so.

THE BRITISH LIBERALS AND THE IRISH LANGUAGE
16.12.1905

The British Ministry which sought to crush the Irish language movement has gone the way of all ministries. The language movement remains to confront its successor. As a rule we are not interested in the coming or the going of British ministries. Our work lies here in Ireland. But we are obliged from the nature of the case to take some account of political happenings in Britain; because, unfortunately, political happenings in Britain affect, and sometimes very materially affect, the interests of the Irish language. The shadow of the Palace of Westminster falls on Connacht hillsides and darkens the sunlight in Munster valleys.

Messrs. Arthur Balfour, Austen Chamberlain, and the other British politicians who plotted with the 'National' Board for the ousting of Irish from Irish primary schools are gone; with them are gone Messrs. Walter Long and John Atkinson who inspired the virulent police campaign against the use of Irish on vehicles and in public documents. How is the situation affected by their passing?

That we do not yet know. The British party which comes into power is labelled 'Liberal' and proclaims itself the friend of Ireland. But our objection to Messrs. Balfour and Chamberlain was not that they were Conservative or that they belonged to the party which is the hereditary foe of this nation. Our objection to them as controllers of the educational systems of Ireland was simply this, that they were British. Being British, they had no right to interfere with our schools. Morally, they were no more entitled to dictate what should be taught to children in Connemara than they were to dictate what should be taught to children in Yokohama. Obviously this objection applies to British Liberals equally with British Tories. But there is a difference between the two parties, and we must differentiate in our attitude accordingly. The Tories frankly governed Ireland in the interests of 'the Empire'. The Liberals profess a desire to govern Ireland in the interests of Ireland, to commit the management of Ireland's internal affairs to Irish hands. How far they will be in a position to carry that desire into effect we do not know. But there is one thing which they can do. There is one piece of 'devolution' which can be carried out with unanimous consent of everyone in Ireland, Gaelic Leaguer and non-Leaguer, nationalist and unionist. We refer to the committing of the administration of Irish education to the hands of a Board representative of and possessing the confidence of the people of Ireland. If there be any truth in Liberal protestations, the 'National' Board as at present constituted ought not to last a twelvemonth.

Mr. Walter Long is replaced in the British Chief-Secretaryship of Ireland by Mr. James Bryce. Mr. Walter Long was a machine, owned body and soul by a British party, and caring about as much for the things of the mind

96

as does the average member of the Royal Irish Constabulary. Mr. Bryce is a gentleman and a scholar. He is moreover — or was when in Opposition — convinced of the sanity and value of the Irish language movement. On July 31st, 1900, Mr. Bryce delivered the following speech in the British House of Commons, the occasion being the moving of a reduction in the vote for National Education in Ireland for the purpose of calling attention to matters connected with the teaching — or rather non-teaching — of Irish:—

'The question which had been raised was one of very wide and general interest and had really nothing to do with politics, though it might have been a political subject sixty or seventy years ago. He did not think any newspapers were published in Ireland in Irish: there were literary magazines. (An Irish member — "There are three newspapers.") Were they daily newspapers? (Irish members — "Weekly. The daily Press in Ireland have columns in Irish"). He was glad to hear that. The political side of the question might be dismissed altogether. The other remark which he wished to make was that this was no question of promoting the Irish language at the expense of the English. It was not suggested that anywhere except in Irish-speaking districts should the teaching of Irish become a regular part of the school work. he would not argue this question as a matter of national sentiment. He would think it a great misfortune if the Celtic language were altogether to disappear. In France there was the same wish not to let the ancient languages die out. There was a desire to keep the Breton and the Basque, and there had been an important revival of Provençal, in which had appeared the finest poem that France had produced in the last fifty years. Therefore, there was a great deal to be said for keeping the old language. But with all respect to the distinguished Irish literary man who recently wrote an interesting letter to *The Times*, he did not think there was much prospect at this time of day of making the ancient Celtic language a vehicle for modern literature. He did not think it would be much use trying to change the ancient language into a modern one. The experiment had been tried in Greece, and modern Greek had not been nearly so good a language since an endeavour had been made to bring in the old classical forms. He would not, however, discuss the question on these sentimental considerations, because though they appealed to him very strongly, he believed there was a strong practical case for the teaching of the old Celtic languages. Thirty-four years ago he was assistant commissioner of a commission which was to examine into the endowed grammar schools of Wales, and the schoolmasters, clergymen, and ministers, whom he consulted, all agreed that the bilingual system not only taught the children English better, but was useful in other respects. When we began to teach a child another language than its own, the child was obliged to transfer thought from one set of words to another and to get a much more exact idea of the meaning of words, of the genius of a language, and of the nature of transference of thought more than he otherwise could. That was why writing Latin prose was a valuable stimulus to the mind. The hon. member for East Down had asked why we should teach a language which was of no use, and whether there were any countries in Europe where the people spoke two languages. It is hard to find a country in Europe in which there are not many people using two languages.

97

Mr. Rentoul. — "I said the mechanics and working classes".

Mr. Bryce said there were a great many parts of Europe where the working classes spoke two languages. In Belgium a large number of people spoke Flemish and French: in Denmark a large number spoke German as well as Danish. In Germany there were large districts where the national language of the population was Slav where they also speak German, and all through the Austrian Empire it was the same.

Mr. G. W. Balfour. — "And in the Italian Alps".

Mr. Bryce. — The hon. member asked why the two languages should be taught when English was the language to be used. The proposal was to teach English through the medium of Irish, and it was really a great piece of good fortune that there was already a language which could be used in that way; and children will not learn English more slowly or less thoroughly through Irish than if Irish is neglected. Irish should be taught as a literary language. There should be Irish reading to translate the Irish into English and *vice versa*. In Scotland and Wales the teachers who are going to districts where Welsh or Gaelic is the commonest tongue, get special instruction. This ought to be done in Ireland. He submitted, therefore, that the demand which the Irish members made was a very reasonable and sensible demand. He would also point out that the larger the number to whom instruction was given in Irish the more prospect was there that in after life some would avail themselves of it to make use of the abundant and rich material that existed for the study of ancient Irish history and literature, which had been very insufficiently and inadequately made use of heretofore. Without venturing to express an opinion on the precise rules that ought to be made, he would suggest to the Chief Secretary that he should go fully into the subject. They were fortunate in having a Chief Secretary who was himself a man of high literary attainments, and he hoped that the right hon. gentleman, if he felt any doubt on the subject, would institute an inquiry into it, referring it to those who had practical knowledge, and that he would endeavour to induce the Commissioners to frame a scheme which would go far to meet the complaints made that day.'

All this is, in the main, admirable. The gentleman who so spoke in 1900 is now himself Chief Secretary for Ireland.

Remarkably enough, the only Liberal who prominently supported Mr. Bryce on the occasion was Mr. Hemphill, the announcement of whose appointment as Attorney-General for Ireland is momentarily expected. Mr. Hemphill said that: —

'As an Irish Protestant, he agreed in general with the view of this question put forward by the Nationalist members. He argued that it was a fallacy on the part of the Chief Secretary to say that the Government had no control over the National Board of Education; but if this was the case the same observation, at all events, could not apply to the action of the House of Commons. He also thought the Vice-President of the Board of Agriculture was not very ingenious because he seemed to convey that the Board by their new rules had initiated something in the direction of what Irish Nationalist members were seeking. The hon. gentleman was under a mistake, because the note to which he referred was a mere replica of the same note which had appeared in the code of the National Board ever since 1883, and which had resulted not in the promotion, but the gradual extinction of Irish in the schools. Any one who did not try to arrest such an evil was, in his opinion, guilty of a great historical crime. The Board should be compelled to make this change whereby English should be taught in Irish-speaking districts throught the medium of Irish. The other part of the demand was equally reasonable. Give a young Irishman an opportunity of learning the language of his own country, of reading its legends full of heroism, of the spirit that breathed in the pages of Homer, and you will not only elevate his character, but make him a better citizen.'

The two chief executive British officers in Ireland are now Mr. Bryce and Mr. Hemphill. Do not their words in 1900 warrant us in expecting that the prosecutions for the use of Irish on carts and in public documents will cease; that the Treasury decree which aims at banishing Irish from the primary schools will be annulled; and that the reform of the 'National' Board will be undertaken at the earliest opportunity?

LIVE TEACHING IN THE SECONDARY SCHOOL
6.1.1906

Now that the Secondary Schools are on the point of re-assembling after the Christmas Holidays we may fittingly add one or two further articles to those we have already written on the position and possibilities of Irish in the Intermediate curriculum.

We have maintained that, unsatisfactory as is the Board's Programme in many respects, it is still possible to teach Irish effectively in Secondary Schools: that it is possible to teach it to practically every child on rolls: and that it is possible to teach it at a profit. Two things only are needful: goodwill on the part of the school authorities and competence on the part of the teacher.

The opportunities of the Intermediate teacher are rather greater than those of the primary teacher. He has in most cases better material to work upon; he has larger freedom of action; he has a more attractive programme. Unlike the primary teacher, he has not as a rule to keep two or three classes in swing at one and the same moment: nor is his attention liable to be constantly distracted from the class in hands for the purpose of supervising monitors or pupil-teachers. It is said that Caesar was able to dictate seven letters simultaneously and to write his Memoirs at the same time. Similar feats are often attempted — not always successfully — in Irish Primary and Secondary Schools.

We must assume that our teacher has undivided control of his class; that during the lesson-hour in Irish he is free to concentrate his attention on that class only; and that he is capable of such concentration.

We must further assume that he knows Irish, — that is, can speak it; if he does not, he has no business where he is.

Now, knowing Irish, the teacher's first and most obvious duty is tc *speak* it in class. Gaelic League teachers now accept this as an axiom: it is high time that our secondary teachers accepted it also. It goes without saying that the children should be consistently addressed by their Irish

99

names: that all expressions of commendation or reproof should be in Irish: that the ordinary class directions — *'Suidhidh,' 'Éirighidh inbhur seasamh,' 'Fosglaidh na leabhra,' 'Léigh leat, a Shéamis!', 'An chéad duine eile!' 'Cuir Gaedhilg ar an méid sin!'* and so on — should be in Irish also. The facility with which a class of youngsters familiarises itself with such expressions is quite astonishing. Bye-and-bye the young folk will commence. almost without being told, to use the language themselves not only in their intercourse with the teacher but in their intercourse with one another. The fact is that — apart from the appeal of Irish to the child's national sense — the experience of using familiarly a new and unwonted language is so strange and interesting that children will, when quietly encouraged by the teacher, do so out of very glee and childish wonder. The *air of pride* with which we have heard Dublin boys answer the question 'Cia mhéid earráid in do cheacht, a Sheagháin?' with 'Níl acht aon cheann amháin, a mháighistir!' was something very pleasant to witness. We have often imagined, too, that the short phrase, 'Maith an buachaill, a Thomáisin!' has brought a happier flush to the cheek than would the corresponding English formula; whilst a firm but kindly reproof in Irish sinks much more deeply into a child's impressionable mind than would a much severer one in English.

At a later stage the teacher will be delighted to find that as he comes into class the pupils will volunteer him pieces of information in Irish. 'Bhí an ceacht an chruaidh aréir, a mháighistir!' 'Níl Máire Ní Bhriain ar sgoil indiu, a mháigistreás: tá si breoidhte'. 'Sgiob duine éigin mo pheann uaim!' Such confidences should never be repulsed, but rather encouraged. In fact, the teacher should invariably make the information so volunteered the starting-point of a little conversation. 'Cia sgiob do pheann uait?' 'Tuige nach raibh sé in do phóca agat?' 'Cia sgiob peann Sheagháinín?'

We have been in schools in which the pupils would as soon think of making a casual remark to the teacher as a prisoner in the dock of asking the judge on the bench to give him a light. Such a shrinking on the part of the children indicates an unhealthy state of affairs. The teacher should not be a man of terror to his pupils. Whilst never relinquishing his authority, or suffering himself to be 'played upon', he should appear to the children rather in the guise of a wise and tolerant and genial friend: one whose advice may be asked not merely on matters concerning the school and its studies, but also on subjects wholly foreign to the ordinary school work, yet not foreign to the office of teacher. The teacher of the infant school should exhibit a keen interest in the welfare of the kittens and puppies and other animal pets of his young charges; the teacher of the primary school should care a good deal for marbles and leap-frog; the secondary teacher should be an enthusiast on football and hurley. In the case of teachers of girls there should be corresponding enthusiasms. Furthermore, the teacher should be able and willing to talk on all these subjects, and should be glad to hear his pupils talk about them; and finally — which is our immediate point — all such conversation ought to be in whatever language happens to be on the stocks at the particular moment at which the conversation crops up, — in French if French is being taught, in German if German is being taught, in Irish if Irish is being taught. The Irish teacher, for example, on entering the classroom, asks genially: 'Seadh, a bhuachaillí, an raibh sibh ag bualadh peile aréir?' 'Bhiomar, a mhaighistir.' 'Cia bhuaidh?' 'Cia mhéid cúl a bhuaidh sibh?' 'Agus cia mhéid cúilín?' Should the unfamiliar word turn up — peil, for instance — its meaning should be made clear by a little pantomimic display on the part of the teacher, or by a rough sketch on the blackboard. As a rule there will be no need for translation.

'All this is admirable, says some Intermediate teacher amongst our readers, 'but impracticable — utterly impracticable.' Our only answer is that we ourselves, as a teacher in an Intermediate school, practised everything that we here preach.

THE SECONDARY SCHOOL: THOUGHTS AND SUGGESTIONS
13.1.1906

We have insisted that the first and most obvious duty of the secondary teacher who is in charge of an Irish class is to *speak* the language to his pupils. English need be used only for the more difficult explanations. Under an ideal system of language teaching there would be no necessity to use the known language even to this limited extent. The best German and Belgian teachers give all their grammatical explanations in the language which is being taught. Under present circumstances this course is not feasible in a secondary school in this country. The Intermediate Commissioners require candidates to translate from English into Irish and from Irish into English, as well as to answer questions on grammar in English. So long as the Intermediate programme is accepted by our secondary schools, its requirements must, of course, be complied with. Hence we admit the necessity, if not the desirability, of a certain amount of Irish grammatical teaching in English. Outside this no English need or should be spoken during the progress of the Irish lesson.

We suggest four hours per week as the minimum time which ought to be allotted to Irish in an Intermediate school. No lesson should last either longer or shorter than an hour. Sixty minutes is about the span that the average teacher can maintain himself at his very best, and that the average class will keep up unimpaired interest even in the most attractive teaching. On the other hand, no practical schoolmaster requires to be reminded of the disadvantages attending very short and skimpy lessons.

The first quarter of an hour of the class time will naturally be devoted to the correction of home work. Even here method is important. Too often the correction of the pupils' exercises is a performance of a very perfunctory character. The teacher reads in a sing-song voice the correct translation of the sentences or passages set, and the pupils with feverish haste mark each sentence 'right' or 'wrong' as the case may be. Then the teacher makes a tour of the class and administers 'slaps' to every pupil who has, say, more than four wrong. We are describing the method of procedure in many Christian Brothers' Schools and Diocesan and other Colleges. This is surely crude. In the first place, the *pupils* should themselves do the reading aloud, — each one reading a sentence or two. If a mistake is made another pupil should be called upon to read his version; if he is wrong yet another is called upon, and so on until a correct version is forthcoming. Only in the event of the entire class failing to provide a satisfactory rendering, should the teacher give his version. The why and the wherefore of each pupil's mistake should be pointed out, the blackboard, if necessary, being called into requisition for illustration purposes. All this, of course, will make the correction of exercises a longer (not necessarily more tedious) process than it generally is: but the teacher's aim should be not to get through things with the greatest possible rapidity, but — well, to *teach;* a point which,

101

though fairly obvious, is sometimes strangely overlooked. After all the sentences have been carefully dealt with in this way, the teacher may make his tour of the class, — but he should leave his cane behind. We have frequently seen masters — many of them wearing religious habits — systematically punishing boys for faults in their home work on the delightfully simple principle, 'one slap for each mistake'. The boy with four mistakes, gets four slaps, the boy with five, five; and so on. This is nothing short of criminal. To inflict corporal punishment *for a mistake* is surely the very acme of stupid and purposeless folly. Punish a boy for inveterate laziness or for gross and long-continued carelessness whether in home work or in school work, but *do not* try to teach the irregular verbs or to explain the difference between 'is' and 'tá' with the aid of a cane.

The exercises corrected, it remains to consider the disposal of the three-quarters of an hour or so which remains. One of the four weekly lessons might well be given up altogether to conversation; another might usefully be devoted to composition; the other two to text-reading with grammar and composition lessons founded thereon. Of course, a good deal of Irish will be talked incidentally during the progress of the composition and grammar lessons, so that the single lesson per week by no means represents the total time accorded to conversation in our suggested scheme. The following seems to us a fairly satisfactory time-table in Irish for, say, a Junior Honours Class which can afford no more than four lessons per week to the subject: —

> Monday. — Revision of Home Work. Composition.
> Wednesday. — Revision of Home Work. Text ('Cathair Chonroí' and 'Stair-Cheachta'), with grammar, etc., arising therefrom.
> Thursday. — Revision of Home Work. Conversation.
> Saturday. — Revision of Home Work. Text.
> Exercises in Dictation should frequently be substituted for those in Composition and Grammar; and one or two unprescribed texts should also be read in class during the year.

The above is not an ideal time-table: it is conditioned by the Programme of the Commissioners.

THE SECONDARY SCHOOL: MORE THOUGHTS AND SUGGESTIONS
20.1.1906

Subject to the proviso that — in order to comply with the requirements of the Intermediate Commissioners — there must of necessity be a certain amount of grammatical teaching in English, as well as a certain amount of translation from English into Irish and *vice versa*, all Irish teaching — as, indeed, all modern language teaching — in the secondary school should be on the Direct Method. Seaghán Ó Catháin will be glad to hear that he misunderstood us in imagining us to advocate any 'conglomeration' of the Direct and any other method. The Direct Method is the only one which we recognise as sane; and we hold that grammar, composition, and texts — including the despised O'Growney — can and ought to be taught on the Direct Method. In the ideal secondary school there would never be the slightest necessity for recourse to any other method; and — we would

102

repeat and underline it — our sole reason for countenancing, or rather tolerating, grammar teaching in the known language and translation from the new to the known is that these things are, as things stand, compulsory on all schools which accept the Intermediate programme.

By the Direct Method we do not mean Berlitz, nor yet Gouin, nor, for that matter, the Módh Réidh, the Módh Díreach, or any other published 'method' or 'módh' whatsoever. That is to say, we would not tie down our teacher within the four corners of any one system; we would not impose upon him the fads of any one maker of method-books. The good teacher must create his own method; and his own sympathy, insight and ingenuity will serve him in better stead than all the maxims of all the theorists. He will, of course, find much that is valuable and suggestive even in the most imperfect — which we take to be the Gouin — of the systems we have enumerated; but he must not slavishly follow even the best of them.

The essentials of Direct Method teaching may be put very briefly. The object is to connect the words and phrases of the new language, not with the words and phrases of some language already familiar, but with the *ideas* for which in the new language those words and phrases stand. With this end, names of things are taught, not by giving the equivalents in the known language, but by *showing the things themselves* (or pictures of them); names of qualities by showing things (or pictures of things) which possess the qualities and contrasting them with things which do not possess the qualities; names of actions by performing the action (or showing a picture representing its performance); abstract ideas by association, suggestion, illustration, pantomimic display; grammar, first incidently during the course of the conversation lessons, afterwards by formal lessons (always on a conversational basis) *in the language itself;* composition by means of little action-plays, pictures, 'images animées', the magic lantern, chalk sketches on the blackboard; texts by reading aloud, followed by questions *in the new language* on the subject-matter, as well as on grammar and idiom, and by composition exercises arising out of the text; spelling, etc., by dictation; and so on.

The system which embodies these principles best is undoubtedly that of Berlitz, as far as it goes; but Berlitz does not go the whole way. Moreover, his methods in their later devolopments are less attractive to children than are some of those referred to in the latter portion of the preceding paragraph, as well as others which have been or are to be described in our articles on the schools of Belgium. Berlitz undoubtedly teaches his pupils to *chat* in the language learned; to *understand* it when spoken; and to *read it*; but — unless his methods be considerably supplemented by the teacher — he does not impart to the pupil a sufficient mastery over the *writing* of the language, nor does he give an adequate and connected view of its *grammar*. These things need, in the later stages, to be taught formally by the devices we suggest.

In the course of our studies on Belgian methods we shall develop our ideas as to how conversation, reading, writing, spelling, grammar, and the rest, can best be taught by the Direct Method. Meanwhile, to bring to a conclusion the present series of articles on the secondary school, we propose to give, during the next few weeks, some general hints under each of the heads specified.

Here we may fittingly take the opportunity of expressing our appreciation of the many kindly things — as also of the two or three cross things — which have been written to us during the past few weeks by secondary teachers. '*An Claidheamh*,' writes one friend from the South, 'is my sole manual of method; and, by practising your instructions and utilising your hints and suggestions, I am, to my own and their delight, *making Irish speakers of my boys.*'

THE FUNCTION OF A TEXT-BOOK
27.1.1906

The article by Seaghán Ó Catháin in our last impression considerably widens — perhaps we should say completely changes — the issue raised by the editorial notes in *An Claidheamh* to which it was a reply. On reading Seaghán's article we became aware that he does not attach the same connotation to the word 'text-book' which we do. The text-book in his view is a manual of teaching. It should afford a basis for a complete course of instruction in a language. Put into the hands of anyone, it should make a teacher of him. His methods should instantly become 'live', and expert speakers of the language should quickly spring up around him. We fear that no such text-book had ever been written, or ever will be written. If it were written, it would not be a text-book in our meaning of the work. It would be a book for the teacher. By a text-book we understand a book for the pupil — a book which may be put into his hands during the class for reading, and which he may take home with him for purposes of reference. The teacher does the teaching *viva voce* and on the blackboard; the text-book is a mere adjunct. If Seaghán Ó Catháin on reflection accepts this — it may turn our that there is very little in dispute between us.

Language teaching must be on the Direct Method from start to finish. We take it that the first few weeks of a course should be devoted exclusively to conversation lessons and to phonetic drill. 'An Modh Réidh' is the best basis we have for a series of conversation lessons in Irish. Diarmaid Ó Foghludha's 'Mac-Léighinn' will undoubtedly afford a better basis. But, given the best imaginable method books, the teacher must largely plan his own conversation lessons and indeed work out his own methods generally. Such a book as *An Modh Réidh* or *An Mac-Léighinn* is valuable chiefly as showing him *how* to do this.

After a week or two of purely oral drill, a stage is reached at which it becomes necessary to put a book into the hands of the pupil for reading, and as the basis of further conversation and grammar teaching (the purely oral lessons being meanwhile continued). What book shall it be? The *Ceachta Beaga* are admirable, but they take you only a short distance. Dr. Henry is too difficult for the average student, and the intelligent reading of his exercises would necessitate a deal of advanced grammatical explanation which at so early a stage the pupil could not possibly follow in Irish, and which, in our opinion, *ought not* to be given in English. We have, thus, no alternative to O'Growney. O'Growney supplies a course of simple, fairly attractive, fairly well graduated, and in the main idiomatic reading-lessons proceeding (in Parts IV and V) to the best continuous passages that have yet been constructed as exercises in Irish reading.

It will be seen that we no more than Seaghán Ó Catháin would dream of working stolidly through O'Growney with a class, reading aloud the grammatical explanations, translating the Irish exercises into English, and *vice versa*. All our grammar would be taught incidentally, or rather made to reveal itself, in the course of the conversation lessons (the blackboard being freely utilised); at a later stage there would be formal grammar lessons founded on the text and on conversation, but always *in Irish*. Of translation from Irish into English we would have none; of translation from English into Irish, a little, but only after the pupils should have learned to think in Irish with ease.

Is O'Growney an ideal book for the purpose we have suggested as the proper one of a text-book? It is not; but we do not know one equally good which carries the pupil so far.

To come to closer quarters with Seaghán's criticism as far as they apply. (1) The O'Growney vocabulary is not all it might be, and certainly does not fit in with any series of conversation lessons on the Direct Method which it is easy to imagine. But what reading-book that we have gives us a vocabulary which does? (2) The Phonetic Key should simply be ignored. It will be observed that our suggested scheme of teaching implies no reference to it whatever. The teacher should teach the sounds orally and by blackboard demonstrations. (3) This objection is mainly a criticism of O'Growney as a *basis* for a course of instruction: we have never suggested that it should be used as such. Most of the faults specified are capable of remedy. (4) Any re-casting of O'Growney must, of course, provide for the introduction of the verb 'is' in the first lesson.

We suggest that O'Growney is capable of satisfactory revision in all these particulars. The grammatical matter (compressed and systematised) may remain for reference, and for the benefit of students who have to do without teachers.

One thing only will displace O'Growney from general use: the production of a text-book, equally good in other respects, based as to vocabulary and order of progress on some such book as Diarmaid Ó Foghludha's forthcoming *Mac-Léighinn*. Perhaps Diarmaid or Seagháin himself will give us such a book: none will welcome it more heartily than we.

For the rest, the teacher will always remain infinitely more important than the text-book. Good teachers will succeed despite bad books, bad teachers will fail, good books notwithstanding. It is largely because our teachers have *abused*, instead of *using*, O'Growney that of 400,000 purchasers of Part I we have probably no more than 500 new speakers. The main problem for us is to train our teachers; a point on which Seaghán and we are doubtless in full agreement.

THE SECONDARY SCHOOL: CONVERSATION-TEACHING
3.2.1906

There is no reason why all the 'live' methods of language teaching which have been advocated in *An Claidheamh* by ourselves and others should not be employed in the Secondary School. It is, in point of fact, when applied to the teaching of children that such methods are capable of their most interesting developments and are culculated to lead to the best results. In a class of adults there is nearly always a certain amount of constraint and self-consciousness on the part of both the teacher and of the taught. Neither the teacher on the one hand nor the pupil on the other can always quite 'let himself go'. But there are even more tangible difficulties. You cannot very well set a class of grown-ups including persons of both sexes and all ages, playing leap-frog or pegging tops. Nor can you use the same amount of freedom in describing persons and their clothes as you would in the case of a class of small boys. You would not care to tell a young lady pupil even in Irish that her hair is untidy, or to request a young gentleman in the presence of a class of cailíní to put his coat inside out. All such familiarities are possible and desirable in the course of a language lesson in a primary or secondary schoolroom.

To map out once more the general lines on which a Direct Method course must proceed. Your earliest conversation lessons concern themselves with the names of *things* around you in the classroom. You point to the various objects and name them. You then question the pupils in the new language, requiring correct answers in that language. From names of things you pass to names of *qualities*. Ideas of *position* come in at a very early stage — perhaps in the second lesson. Names of *actions* are soon proceeded to. The handling of abstract notions in the new language is being taught incidentally all along. So much for *principle*. As regards the *methods* most applicable to the conditions of a secondary school.

To teach *names of things;* Call out a boy and hold forth on him as follows: — 'An Gasúr. An Ceann. An Beál. An tSúil. An tSrón. An Chluas' — pointing to each part. Questions follow : 'An é sin an gasúr? An é sin an béal? An í sin an chluas?' And so on. The names of the chief articles of clothing are thus taught: only common and really useful words being introduced.

To teach *names of qualities:* 'Tá a cheann dubh. Tá a bhóna bán. Tá a chóta gorm'; and so on. Then two or more boys are compared: 'Tá Séamus dubh, tá Seaghán ruadh, tá Tomás donn, tá Séamus mór, tá Seaghán beag.' This comparative method is capable of indefinite development. To convey ideas of *position:* 'Tá Séamus ar an úrlár; tá Seaghán ar an stól. Tá an stól ag an doras. Tá Seaghán ar an stól ag an doras.' Notions of time — tá Séamus ar an stól *anois* — are similarly insinuated.

To teach *names of actions;* Tógaim an leabhar! A Shéamus, tóg an leabhar! Suidhim ar an stól. A Sheagháin, suidh ar an urlár! Cá suidheann Seaghán? Suidheann sé ar an urlár. Distinguish suidhim and táim 'mo shuidhe.

From these very elementary beginnings the lessons can proceed to practically any point. In the final stages the pupils will play marbles, peg tops, play leap frog, skip, jump, run, etc., names of objects, qualities, and actions, with as much abstract language as may be desired, being taught during the course of each lesson. The advantages of making the pupils themselves perform the actions are obvious. Needless to say, much useful teaching could be done by means of pantomimic display on the part of the teacher himself, or by means of pictures, blackboard sketches, models, etc; but, where possible, it is always best to allow the class to take an active part in *the giving of the lesson*. The pupils should be not merely listeners and spectators of but actual participants in all that goes on. In fact, pictures representing things or actions should be fallen back upon only when it is not convenient to produce the thing or to perform the action in the schoolroom.

The best substitutes for actual living things, performing actual actions, are undoubtedly the "images animées" which the Editor of this paper has introduced into the classrooms of the Ard-Craobh and into two or three secondary and higher schools in Dublin. The use of these ingenious contrivances — the invention of a primary teacher in Brussels — will be fully dealt with in the course of our articles on Belgian schools.

THE DUBLIN TRAINING COLLEGE
10.2.1906

The project for the establishment of an Irish Training College in Dublin has now taken definite shape. For some weeks past a Committee nominated by the Dublin Coiste Ceanntair and consisting of Eoin Mac Néill, Úna Ní Fhaircheallaigh, Pádraic Mac Piarais, and Seoirse Ua Muanáin — with Maire Ní Chinnéide who, however, was unable to attend the meetings — has been discussing the scope, organisation, and financing of the proposed institution. Detailed recommendations under all three heads were included in the report which was presented by the Committee to the Coiste Ceanntair at its meeting on Saturday last, and adopted by the latter body. It now remains to proceed actively with the work or organisation.

The object of the College will be to afford means by which present and prospective teachers of Irish, whether in League branches or in secondary and primary schools, may obtain a thoroughly efficient training in the most approved methods of language teaching as applied to Irish. Accordingly, the main course in the College curriculum will be the course in the method. It goes without saying that this course will not be theoretical merely, — it will resolve itself into a course of instruction in Irish on the Direct Method. All students of the College, whether Irish speakers or non-Irish speakers, will be expected to attend this course. 'Criticism lessons' will, needless to say, form a feature.

If all the students of the College were beginners in Irish, this single course would be sufficient for all purposes. The student would be conducted by a regular ascension from the bottom-most to the top-most rung of the ladder, — preceeding from *speaking* to *reading*, from *reading* to *writing*, and then on to the higher ranges of Irish scholarship. It is likely, however, that the students of the College will be of two classes: those who, whether native or non-native speakers, have already a fair grip of spoken and literary Irish, and those who are beginners or practically so. In view of this probability, it is proposed to conduct two courses of general literary instuction in Irish, one elementary and the other advanced. In these classes the system developed in the lectures on method will be applied, in the one case to supplementary instruction in Irish conversation, reading, and writing, and in the other to the study of advanced grammar, composition, and texts.

The treatment of Phonetics is of course only a branch of Method, and any well-considered scheme of oral language-teaching would make fitting provision for a thorough drill in sounds. Having regard, however, to the great importance of Phonetics and to the fact that it has hitherto been so sadly neglected in Irish schemes of teaching, the Committee suggests that a prominent and distinctive place be assigned to it in the College curriculum. There will, therefore, probably be a special course in Phonetics, in charge of an expert.

This scheme of teaching will be supplemented by occasional lectures and demonstrations by specialists in various subjects — pedagogics, literature, history, antiquities, topography, music, art, industries, and so on.

Whilst the main object of the College — the training of Irish teachers — will be kept steadily in view, it is not the intention of the promoters that attendance should be confined to teachers and prospective teachers. Furthermore, although the College will cater especially for the needs of the metropolitan area, it will welcome to its classes as many students residing outside that area as it can find room for.

From the nature of the case, the details of organisation must differ widely from those of the existing schools at Ballingeary and Tourmakeady. The class meetings will be held in the evening, and there will not be more than two class evenings per week (a third evening or afternoon in the week will, however, be devoted to special lectures by extern professors). All this for obvious reasons. The majority of those who are likely to enrol themselves as students are engaged, whether as teachers or otherwise, during the day; and it would be unreasonable to expect students, however ardent, to give up more than three evenings per week to the work of the College. The session will last from October till Easter, with a short recess at Christmas. For the complete session the fee will be £2 2s., but a scheme is being arranged in virtue of which pupils may be nominated by subscribing branches, classes, schools, and individuals at a reduced fee of £1 1s.

The handling of the extensive programme which has been outlined will involve a permanent staff of at least three, – a principal, a staff professor, and a registrar. In addition there will probably be need for one or more assistant professors, whilst, as already indicated, there will also be extern lecturers.

For the government of the College it is proposed to call into being a College Council or Committee of Management, to be appointed annually in the month of July, and to be constituted as follows: – Five members nominated by the Dublin Coiste Ceanntair, and one member each nominated by the following: – His Grace the Most Rev. Dr. Walsh, Archbishop, of Dublin; the Coiste Gnótha of the League; Cumann Gaedhealach na Múinteoirí Náisiúnta; the Managers of all subscribing Primary Schools; the Principals of all subscribing Female Secondary Schools; the Principals of all subscribing Male Secondary Schools; all general subscribers of £1 1s. or over; all subscribing League branches outside the area of the Dublin Coiste Ceanntair. It will be observed that the governing body will thus number thirteen, and that of these seven will be Gaelic League representatives. No change in this system of control is possible without the consent of the Dublin Coiste Ceanntair.

The nucleus of the governing body will be formed almost immediately. As soon as its appeal for funds goes forth the League public in Dublin will, we feel sure, respond generously. It is computed that the total annual cost of the College, exclusive of initial outlay will be £420.

THE CASE FOR BILINGUALISM
7.4.1906

Our readers do not need to be reminded that it is the settled view of *An Claidheamh* that the language problem in the schools can be solved in one way only, – that is to say, by the application of the Bilingual Programme to the whole of Irieland. The reasons which make the Bilingual Programme desirable in Connemara are only a shade more compelling than those which make it desirable in Dublin. Personally we would have all education bilingual from its earliest stages, while we would have the higher stages trilingual or quadrilingual. If the English were wise they would devise a Bilingual Programme for England. Germany, although, unlike Ireland, Wales, and Belgium, she is not confronted with the problem of two languages within her own borders, is already rapidly making her school system bilingual, –

associating French or English as 'second language' with German. Now, if bilingualism in education be desirable in such countries as England and Germany, it is absolutely necessary in Ireland: for Ireland, say what we will, is actually a bilingual country, — That is to say, a country in which there are two vernaculars. There is not a barony in Ireland in which two languages are not spoken. There is not a town in Ireland in which two languages are not read. There is scarcely a human being in Ireland to which either language can be said to be altogether unfamiliar. Ireland, as things are, emphatically makes use of two languages in doing her daily business. To neglect either of these two languages, to leave either out of the educational scheme, would be to commit an educational blunder of the first magnitude.

Thus, we would have education bilingual in Íbh-Ráthach and in Belfast, in Gleann Coluim Cille and in Rathmines. On account of the practical difficulties created by North-East Ulster and by the presence of small un-Irish minorities elsewhere, we should not make Irish the compulsory 'second' language in non-Irish-speaking districts. We should leave the local management an option of selecting French, German, or indeed any other modern language that might be thought suitable. Conversely, we should not force English on an Irish-speaking countryside which might happen not to be desirous of acquiring it, or on any local manager or teacher who might happen to think — as we do — that the acquisition of French or German would constitute a more stimulating and a more really useful mental training for the child. But, speaking broadly, our education scheme would be thus ordered from the point of view of language: —

A. *Districts in which Irish is the Home Language: First Language, Irish; Second Language, English* (with the option of French, German, etc., instead);

B. *Districts in which English is the Home Language: First Language, English; Second Language, Irish* (with the option of French, German, etc., instead).

Certainly in town schools, and probably in a large number of rural schools, a third language could usefully be added when the child is about half-way through his school course.

We believe that the problem will ultimately be settled on these lines; and that it is incapable of settlement on any other lines.

So much for our ideal. But we are face to face with the situation that at present the Bilingual Programme can be sanctioned only in Irish-speaking and bilingual districts, and that as a matter of fact it has actually been sanctioned only in about a score of schools. Next week we propose once more to take up the subject of the position and prospects of the Programme, with special reference to the points raised by the writer of the very valuable article which appears eslewhere in this issue.

THE BOOK DIFFICULTY IN BILINGUAL SCHOOLS
21.4.1906

Our contributor 'B[3]' and a correspondent who writes in our columns this week — both of them teachers in Irish-speaking districts — agree in regarding the dearness of Irish books as one of the main obstacles in the way of the widespread adoption of the Bilingual Programme. Their views are entitled to consideration; and if, on examination, the difficulty suggested is found to be real and of wide application it is certainly one which, at whatever financial loss, the Coiste Gnótha will be bound to make an effort to remove.

Our own impression is that whilst there is something in our contributors' complaint the grievance is not so great as they would appear to imagine. It is not really a question of inducing all the pupils in a school to buy a double set of school books. The various readers — historical, geographical, etc., — are required only for the pupils of the higher standards: in the lower forms history, geography, grammar, science, and so on, should invariably be taught by purely *viva voce* methods, and the only books which the children in these forms need buy are their literary readers, with perhaps a table-book and a catechism. As for the prices of the readers — of which four have now been issued by the Gaelic League — they have been fixed by the Publication Committee with special regard to financial conditions in the Irish-speaking districts; and the practice of supplying all books at two-thirds of the publishing price to pupils of bilingual schools further lightens the burden. *Stair-Cheachta* at 8p., *Leabhar ar Áireamh,* and *An Cruinneolaidhe,* at 4d., each, and *Ceachta Graiméir* at 2d., are certainly not prohibitive. By ordering a quantity of these books together the teacher may secure a further substantial discount.

There remains the important matter of the literary readers. Pending the completion of the League's bilingual series there is of course a double burden on the parent or teacher, as each child requires two reading-books, an Irish one and an English one. With the completion of the League's series this very legitimate grievance will practically disappear. Each book will be an Irish and an English reader combined, yet the price will be substantially the same as that now charged for the corresponding English reader alone. The Second Bilingual Reader, now in the press, will, it is hoped, be issued at 3d. — which will mean only 2d. to a school in which the Bilingual Programme is in operation. The Third Bilingual Reader, also in the press, will probably be issued at 6d., — possibly at 4d.: prices which are as revolutionary as the books themselves will be found to be in style, tone, and appearance.

At the moment it is not apparent to us that the Publication Committee or the Coiste Gnótha can do anything beyond cutting down the prices of books intended specially for bilingual schools to the lowest figure consistent with common sense; and this has been done. We cannot approve of the suggestion that books should be supplied *gratis* by the League to bilingual schools. Every teacher knows that children never value books which they can get for nothing; and we object on principle to anything which would tend to perpetuate the notion, already far too prevalent amongst Irish-speaking parents that, whilst the acquisition of English is something which they (the parents) ought to pay for, permission to allow them to acquire Irish is something for which they (the parents) ought to be paid. We must educate the Irish-speaking parent to the point of seeing that Irish is quite as valuable a thing as English: that it is his *duty* to teach his children Irish and to see that they are properly educated in it; and that the Gaelic League with a philanthropic public at its back is not going (indefinitely at least), to pay him for doing his duty. Since the advent of the Feis many Irish-speaking parents have come to regard themselves as having strong claims on public charity because they have taught their children (more or less) Irish: which in most cases simply means that their efforts to *prevent* their children from picking up Irish have not been altogether successful. We suggest to the teachers and managers in bilingual schools the desirability of a little plain speaking to the parents.

THE SCHOOLS
23.6.1906

Certain friends of ours have been disappointed at the lack of what we may call 'blood and thunder' in *An Claidheamh*'s references to the new scheme for the teaching of Irish in the primary schools. We are ourselves disappointed in these friends. We had hoped that we had educated the Gaelic League public up to the point of seeing that one can be strong without being violent. No sooner had Mr. Bryce's summary of the scheme appeared in print than we pointed out in clear, precise, and unequivocal terms the defects which, in our opinion, rendered it unacceptable. We might have gone on to demand Mr. Bryce's head on a charger, but that would have been mere 'sound and fury, signifying nothing'. We preferred to show where the scheme failed and how it might be amended; for we held — and still hold — that it is capable of such amendment as will make it a fairly satisfactory *ad interim* solution. The final solution can, in our view, take one shape only, the application of the bilingual principle to Ireland as a whole. That will come in time, — but not before the 'National' Board is swept into the Limbo of effete tyrannies and there is erected in its stead an education authority representative of and answerable to the people of Ireland.

The Coiste Gnótha has met since we last went to press and in its criticism of Mr. Bryce's proposals it brings together the objections already urged in two or three issues of *An Claidheamh*. The following is the Coiste's manifesto: —

'The Coiste Gnótha of the Gaelic League has had under consideration the Chief Secretary's statement with reference to the proposed new scheme for teaching Irish. The Coiste Gnótha regards the scheme with the gravest dissatisfaction, for the reasons below stated, and expresses its conviction that the scheme will arouse determined and widespread opposition, until it is amended and improved: —

I. Infants and first class have been excluded.

II. The proposed fees are so small as to be quite nugatory.

III. The total expenditure in remuneration of the teaching of Irish has been reduced from about £12,000 to under £6,000, and perhaps to a much smaller amount.

IV. The services of a large number of extern teachers, teaching a much larger number of schools, have been put an end to and rejected by the new scheme, and nothing is done to supply their place.

V. The public, the school managers, and the teachers have had no opportunity of expressing their wishes and views with regard to the proposed regulations, until the regulations have been adopted as final and operative. We specially complain of this, inasmuch as the Chief Secretary has informed, us that "he considers it reasonable that the Gaelic League should have an opportunity of expressing their views on the proposals in question before they are finally promulgated'.

VI. With regard to the teaching of Irish on the bilingual system, we regret that the public is still in the dark as to what is proposed.

One or two further valuable points are made in the following statement unanimously adopted at a special meeting of Cumann na Múinteoirí: —

'That as practical teachers of Irish we strongly condemn the new scheme for (it is strangely alleged) "the more efficient teaching of Irish".

'The compulsory portion of the School Programme in ordinary subjects requires more time than the official school day affords. From July 1st., 1906 (on which date the new scheme comes into force), this compulsory programme instead of being shortened is still further overloaded. The result will necessarily be that, except in cases of schools taught by teachers who are prepared to sacrifice their professional prospects for the language's sake, Irish teaching will cease in the great bulk of our schools.

The fees offered can only be described as insulting alike to the teacher and the National Language. If the teaching of Irish at 10s. per head was "inefficient" we fail to see how the teaching can be made more efficient at a fee ranging from one shilling to two-and-sixpence. The fee now offered would not be sufficient to cover the cost of the books, in most cases supplied at the expense of the teachers.

'We would, therefore, recommend that this sham system of payment be immediately withdrawn; that Infants and First Standard should be taught Irish and paid for at a reasonable rate, that the fees offered in other Standards should at least be quadrupled, that provision should be made in the scheme for the retention of extern teachers, who have done such excellent work, as those of us who have examined pupils at Feiseanna can testify.

We appeal to our fellow-teachers not to relax their efforts in the face of this disheartening scheme, but rather to redouble their energies in performing a manifest national duty. We believe that the scheme carries its condemnation on its own face and must be withdrawn.'

We are not, as our reader will be prepared to hear, in entire agreement with every expression of opinion contained in the foregoing statement. For instance, we are not convinced that teachers who continue to give instruction in Irish under the new scheme — as we hope the great body of teachers will do — will necessarily jeopardise their 'professional prospects': Irish Ireland must see to it that such teachers suffer nothing at the hands of the Board and its inspectors. Neither are we inclined to call for the 'withdrawal' of the new scheme: rather we demand that it be amended in the directions pointed out by us, by the Coiste Gnótha, and by Cumann na Múinteoirí itself. We cordially associate ourselves with the Cumann's appeal to the teachers of Ireland to stand firm and loyal in this crisis. On them rather than on any other element in the community depends the success of the fight which must now be waged. It would be simply fatal if there were any general move towards abandoning the teaching of Irish on account of the inadequacy of the proposed scale of remuneration. Father Augustine in his great address at Kinsale struck the note that is required: — 'Let us put our faith not in the Government, but in God, in Ireland, and in ourselves, and the cause will go on slowly but surely, as we wish it to go on, till it begins its swift progress and triumphal march. It is now too late to expect any change in the new scheme before the 1st July, but while making the most of the new scheme, we ought all to press for its reform along the lines I have marked out'. This is sound generaliship and sound sense. Let Irish teaching go on and extend in the schools as if no Special Fees had been withdrawn, as if no miserably inadequate substitute had been offered to us. The question is: does the Nation want Irish to be taught to its children? If it does, we believe that no power on earth can say it nay. The wresting of a satisfactory scheme from the Government will be a mere question of time. But if, in a mad panic, managers, teachers, and parents agree to discontinue Irish because it is announced that its teaching will no longer be paid for as liberally as before, they will put it into the mouth of the enemy to say that there is not and never was a national demand for the teaching of the language, and the whole movement will stand self-convicted a fraud and a sham.

Our obvious duty, therefore, is to work ahead as best we can with the scheme that is imposed upon us, whilst leaving no stone unturned to have that scheme amended in accordance with our desires. Let the agitation for its amendment commence at once in every corner of the country. Let every Craobh of the League and every individual member of the league; every local public body and every individual member of a local public body; every teachers' or managerial association and every individual member of such an association, take concerted action. The Nation, as we believe *Wills* a certain thing: if it does not, we have no case. And the Government has yet to be invented which can indefinitely withstand a Nation's *Will*.

The fight upon which the organisation and the country now enter will have as its immediate object the adequate amendment of the new scheme. But its ultimate aim must be larger than this. Agitation must not cease in Ireland until the baleful influence of Death and the Nightmare Death-in-Life — the British Treasury and the 'National' Board — is once and for all removed from Irish schools. This week the Coiste Gnótha gives to the public one of the most remarkable correspondences ever published in this or perhaps any other country. That correspondence reveals a Chief Secretary bubbling over with sympathy but avowing himself powerless in the hands of the 'National' Board; a 'National' Board as bitterly hostile to the Gael and the things of the Gael as it was in the days of Whately, yet itself apparently the bound serf of the British Treasury; a Treasury as cynically indifferent to the views of a 'sympathetic' British Minister as it is to those of mere Ireland. The Gaelic League urged that it was entitled to be consulted before the new scheme was finally approved of. Mr. Bryce agreed, and referred the League to the Resident Commissioner. The Resident Commissioner informed the League that he would receive two representatives named by it, to whom he would deign to 'explain' the proposed new scheme. The League replied that it could send representatives only on the understanding that the scheme was still open to amendment if found unsatisfactory as the result of the interview. The Resident Commissioner intimated that it was impossible for him to receive a deputation on any such understanding, 'having in view the fact that the scheme has already received the sanction of the Treasury and that it cannot be altered by the Commissioners'. The whole thing was an elaborate performance of the game known amongst children as 'Send the Fool Farther'. Needless to say, no deputation from the League will go to hear Dr. Starkie's 'explanation' or to engage with him in an academic discussion on a scheme already sanctioned by the Teasury. In fact. the time for discussion is past. We must now *Act*. It is war to the knife between the Gael of Ireland and the Board of 'National' Education.

As we close up for press we see Mr. Bryce's reply to Seaghán Ó Beoláin's question in the British House of Commons on Tuesday evening. From Mr. Bryce's statement it appears that the new scheme is still open to amendment and that during the next few months the Chief Secretary will be happy to consider the whole question. Surprising, to say the least, is Mr. Bryce's suggestion that he does not know what the Gaelic League wants. The League's views have been put before him again and again.

AN EDUCATIONAL POLICY
24.11.1906

We were recently asked for a compendious statement of the League's educational demands. The most compendious statement we can give is 'Educational Home Rule'. Now, Educational Home Rule involves two things: —

(1) The freeing of Irish education from the illegal domination of the English Treasury and of all other bodies external to Ireland.

(2) The erection of a central Irish Education Authority, controlling Irish education in all its grades, and composed of men and women elected by and responsible to the people of Ireland.

To which may be added:—

(3) The repayment to Ireland of the educational monies wrongfully withheld from her.

We think these demands cover everything. Their granting would leave us free to deal in our own way with the language question and all the other questions that cry aloud for solution. Recent happenings ought to have convinced Gaels of the futility as things stand of agitating for the settlement of individual phases of the education difficulty: be it ever so willing, the English Government is unable to settle our grievances for us, for it is unable to understand either us or them. Let us first get control of the educational system: then let us set about solving our problems ourselves. We shall find their solution wonderfully easy.

Our first demand is understandable enough. The domination complained of is, we believe, illegal from the standpoint even of the British Constitution. Ireland is united in opposition. The Boards themselves chafe under it; the Catholic and Protestant Hierarchies join in protesting against it; Orangemen and Nationalists stand pledged to hostility to it.

With regard to the second demand, the view has been expressed that the Gaelic League should be more explicit, — that it should, in short, come forward with a concrete scheme around which it might rally the country. This the League as a corporate body has not seen fit to do. There is no reason why it should. The essentials of its demand are plain and explicit enough. As far as primary education is concerned, the League, while not proposing to disturb the existing arrangements with regard to local management, calls for a central Board composed of persons in sympathy

114

with Irish opinion, and representative, directly or indirectly, of the managers, the teachers and the ratepayers of Ireland. It is obviously unnecessary and would probably be unwise for the League to say how it thinks such a Board should be elected; how many representatives it would like to see assigned to the managers, how many to the teachers, and so on. Any detailed scheme, especially in view of the fact that next year's measure of Devolution, Extended Local Government, or whatever it may be called, is likely to bring into existence a set of totally new circumstances, the nature of which it is impossible to forecast. The League's part is obviously done when it clearly and unmistakeably indicates the general conditions which any settlement must satisfy in order to be acceptable.

While this is so, no harm can be done, and a great deal of good may be done, by an informal discussion in these columns of the lines which a settlement of the Irish education question might take: a discussion which we hope to initiate next week.

AN IRISH EDUCATION BOARD
1.12.1906

If Ireland were an independent Republic, or a self-governing member of the confederacy known as the British Empire, she would probably entrust the administration of her educational affairs to a single Minister responsible to her Parliament. This is what is done in most countries in which there is constitutional government. With such a Minister she might or might not associate a Council of Education; and such a Council, if established, might be either responsible or purely consultative. A 'Ministry of Education' for Ireland has recently been talked about by British statesmen, and quite possibly forms part of next year's Devolution scheme. We must be on our guard in coming to close quarters with any such proposal. Who will appoint the Minister? To whom will he be answerable? What will be his relation to the 'Council of Ireland' which the future holds in its womb, and how far will that Council itself be a representative and popular body? It is obvious that until answers are forthcoming to these questions, the Gaelic League cannot declare for a Ministry of Irish Education. We might pull down the 'National' and Intermediate Boards only to erect a new tyranny in their stead.

Any solution of the education question which is within the range of practical politics must provide for the formation of a Central Education Board of some sort. Such a Board must be elective, wholly or in great part. It must be responsible to Irish public opinion, either *de facto* as is, say, the Coiste Gnótha of the Gaelic League, or formally and legally, through some such body as a really representative 'Council of Ireland' or the present General Council of County Councils. It must consist of men and women who are in touch with Irish life generally, and with the work of Irish education in particular. The qualification for membership must be competency to direct the administration of education, and not the possession of particular political or religious beliefs. The new authority, therefore must know nothing of the 'half-and-half' principle on which the 'National' and Intermediate Boards are contrived. Again, the Board must, of course, have undisputed control of the expenditure on Irish education, subject to no authority outside the four seas of Ireland. Finally, it must be entrusted with the general superintendence of education in all its phases —

115

primary, secondary, higher, technical. In other words, it must take over the powers in regard to education at present exercised by about a dozen independent authorities, of which the chief are the 'National' Board, the Intermediate Board, the Board of Education (controlling the Endowed Schools), and the Department of Agriculture and Technical Instruction. In a normal State the work which these various autocracies are engaged in doing – or rather in preventing from being done – would be attended to by a single Minister, with perhaps three responsible subordinates, and a moderate staff of clerks. Our representative Irish Board might, and doubtless would, appoint sub-committees of its own body to deal with the various sub-divisions of its work, but it is essential that the general control of the educational machine should be in the hands of a single authority. The education of a country should be looked upon as a whole: the traditional division into 'primary', 'secondary', and 'higher' corresponds to no actuality and has no justification philosophically.

AN IRISH EDUCATION AUTHORITY
8.12.1906

An Irish Education Board, as we wrote last week, must be composed of men and women in touch with Irish life generally and with the work of Irish education in particular; it must be answerable either mediately or immediately to Irish public opinion: it must be free from the control of any person or body not responsible to that opinion; and it must be entrusted with the general superintendence of Irish education in all its grades.

The League has definitely put forward the claim that the whole or a substantial majority of the membership of the Board must be elective. It has gone so far as to indicate the classes in the community which have a right to direct representation. Roughly speaking, we have to consider in the first place *The People* – the parents and rate-payers – and in the second the persons and institutions actively engaged in the work of education or having a special *locus standi* in educational matters. The parents and ratepayers might be represented through the General Council of County Councils or (should next year's Bill happily materialise) through the 'Council of Ireland', provided that body be so constituted as to prove really representative. One or other of these authorities might elect a proportion – say one third – of the members of the Board. The rest might be nominated, in due proportion, by (1) the Universities; (2) the Heads of Secondary Schools; (3) the Secondary Teachers; (4) the Managers of Primary Schools; (5) the Primary Teachers; (6) the Conductors of Technical Schools; (7) the Council of Agriculture (we assume that the control of technical education would be taken away from Sir Horace Plunkett's Department and handed over to the new authority). A Board of twenty-one members would thus be constituted somewhat as follows: –

Representatives of:	No.
Ratepayers and Parents	7
Universities	4
Heads of Secondary Schools	2
Secondary Teachers	2
Managers of Primary Schools	2

It would be quite easy to organise the managers, teachers, etc., into elective constituencies. Care should be taken to ensure due representation of girls' colleges and schools and of women's interests generally. To provide for the 'representation of minorities' (religious and otherwise) power to co-opt, say, four additional members might be accorded to the Board, whose full strength would, thus, be twenty-five.

We make Mr. Bryce a present of these suggestions. We do not anticipate that he will adopt a single one of them. But they will, we trust, show him how thought is running in Ireland, and they will take out of his mouth the complaint that the Gaelic League is 'vague' and 'indefinite' in its suggestions. Neither he nor the public is, of course, to look on these speculations as the formal demands of our organisations. *An Claidheamh*'s status in this discussion was explained a few weeks ago. As for the League's official statement of its claim, we may as well repeat it: —

'We demand such measures of reform as will secure that a majority, and not as at present, a small minority, of the Commissioners of the Board dealing with Irish education shall be in sympathy with the principles of the people of this country, and understand their educational needs.'

THE ENGLISH-SPEAKING TRADITION
15.12.1906

Our leading articles for the past three months have been devoted to an examination of the actual situation in the Irish-speaking districts, and to the suggestion of remedies for the deplorable state of affairs revealed by that examination. We have seen that, speaking generally, vernacular Irish continues to die in spite of the fact (we again speak generally) that the public opinion of the Gaedhealtacht, so far as such a thing exists, has been converted to the view that it ought not to be allowed to die; that it continues to die, in other words, primarily and chiefly because *the habit* of speaking English has become ingrained in Irish speakers and that the eradication of that habit has so far proved a task beyond the strength of the language movement. We have seen the habit in full force in the home, in the school, in the church, on the political platform, in the public boardroom. We have seen that it imposes its tyranny on teachers who spend themselves in the effort to impart a reading and writing knowledge to their pupils; on priests who are thoroughly convinced that the maintenance of the language is essential to the spiritual, intellectual, and material welfare of their flocks; on politicians who subscribe to the full programme of the Gaelic League; on League workers known throughout the length and breadth of the land as eager and effective writers, students, teachers, or propagandists. In theory, we all admit that Irish should be spoken; in practice we all — or nearly all — go on speaking English. In the Galltacht this is only ridiculous: in the Gaedhealtacht it is not ridiculous but tragical.

The unchecked continuance of the English-speaking tradition for another ten years will mean the death of the Irish language.

Let the tradition, then, be attacked on every League platform, in every League classroom, in every newspaper and periodical which the Gaelic League can influence. Let it be attacked from the pulpit, from the political platform, in the boardroom, in the schoolroom. Let it be attacked directly and indirectly, in season and out of season, night, noon, and morning.

This is a programme in which every Gaelic Leaguer can take part — it is a programme in which every Gaelic Leaguer *must* take part. It was by adopting a strenuous and utterly uncompromising attitude in a similar crisis that the Czechs succeeded in saving the spoken tongue in Bohemia. At the present day a Czech will reply to a foreigner who addresses him in German, but he will not reply to a Czech who does so. In Poland a hundred thousand children strike from school because they are required to repeat the Catechism in German. In Wales the audience at a political meeting storms the platform because it is addressed in English by the member for the constituency. We want a little of the Czech's, or the Pole's, or the Welshman's thoroughness, stiffneckedness, and contempt for "respectability".

THE STARVATION POLICY
2.2.1907

Early in their report on the 'National' Board Training Colleges for the period 1904-5, Messrs. Purser and Hynes, Chief Inspectors of the Commissioners of 'National' Education, make the following pregnant remarks: —

'The failures on the part of the men were again very numerous, due largely to inferior candidates having to be admitted. The students were arranged in three classes, according to their marks. Of those in the final year there were:—

	Men	Women
Placed in 1st Class	11	20
Placed in 2nd Class	54	182
Placed in 3rd Class	124	108

Of those at the end of the first of the two years' course there were: —

	Men	Women
Placed in 1sr Class	6	16
Placed in 2nd Class	74	182
Placed in 3rd Class	109	123

Further down occurs the following sentence: —

'Many King's scholars, on leaving the Training Colleges, continue to find employment in Great Britain, so that the Irish colleges help to make good the deficiency of trained teachers across the channel.'

Here we have fresh official testimony to a truth which *An Claidheamh Soluis* commenced to preach some two years ago, and which is now beginning to dawn on the country at large. This truth constitutes by far the

118

gravest fact in the educational outlook of Ireland today. No tendency that it is easy to imagine could possibly be more unhealthy. Nothing that the 'National' Board, the British Treasury, or a British Government could conceivably plan would more momentously threaten the future of Irish education, and consequently the whole moral, intellectual, and industrial future of the Irish nation.

The fact is that as the inevitable and logical outcome of the Starvation Policy of the English Treasury — a policy silently acquiesced in not merely by the 'National' Board, but by Irish political and other leaders, by the Irish press, and by the Irish public generally, until the Gaelic League drew attention to it the year before last — the quality of the work done in Irish schools is steadily deteriorating, and that for the all-sufficient reason that the quality of the teachers is steadily deteriorating. The Training Colleges now find the greatest difficulty in filling up their vacancies; they are obliged to accept inferior candidates — candidates who would have been scouted from their doors ten years ago; and these, having scraped through the college course, are let loose on the country to 'educate' it. Of those who pass the college tests with anything like credit, a large and increasing proportion emigrate as soon as they are certificated — 'to make good,' as the Inspectors naively put it, 'the deficiency of trained teachers abroad'. According to a statement recently issued by the Executive of the Teachers' Organisation the number of such emigrants during the past five years has been 242; the net money loss to Ireland being £20,000. The facts thus are — an inferior class of candidate is now seeking admission to the profession of primary teaching; of those who do seek admission and successfully pass through the course, the best, having been trained at the expense of Ireland, emigrate. All this obviously, points to the fact that in, say, five or ten years' time, the boys' schools of Ireland will be staffed with a body of teachers seriously inferior in mental calibre as well as in acquired culture to the present teaching staff.

And the cause of it all? It is not far to seek. The prospects of remuneration and promotion, under the new Starvation regime, are not such as to attract able, educated, and generously ambitious men to the service of primary education in Ireland; and the degrading conditions of servitude which the 'National' Board would fain impose on its teachers are sufficient to turn away from the profession most of those who, despite even meagre emoluments and certain prospects, would take up the work for love.

TRINITY AND THE GAEL
9.2.1907

There is much that is interesting — though, in view of the fact that the Government's plans are already cut and dry before the public, the interest is mainly of an archaeological nature — in the bulky and belated volume of evidence published as an appendix to the Final Report of the late Trinity College Commission. The only portions of it which immediately concern us here are those dealing with the attitude of Trinity towards the historic Irish Nation for which, in all its aspects, the Gaelic League stands. This phase of the question appears to have been seriously dealt with only by the Gaelic League's own spokesmen, Eoin Mac Neilll and T. W. Rolleston. It does not seem to have entered the heads of the vast majority of the witnesses that there

119

exist profound objections to Trinity apart altogether from the objections on the religious ground, and that the setting up of a College or a University as Catholic as Trinity is Protestant might conceivably leave the provision for *Irish* higher education as unsatisfactory as it is today. In the circumstances it is fortunate that Irish Ireland was represented not merely on the Commission itself but at the witness table.

The fundamental objection to Trinity on the national ground was concisely stated by Eoin Mac Neill in one of his opening sentences: 'The College and the University are a provincial and British institution, not a national and Irish one;' a statement in support of which he gave conclusive arguments, citing the testimony of, among others, the Provost and Vice-Provost of the College: —

'The present Provost has repeatedly asserted his favourite doctrine that Ireland consists of two nations, a view which clearly harks back to the period of conquest. One of the two is the historical Irish nation, the other is the nation of Trinity College. The Vice-Provost in a letter to the press has described Trinity College as the "the only successful British institution in Ireland". (*Irish Times*, October 22, 1903). One of the Senior Fellows (Appendix to First Report, page 48) cannot imagine any meaning in that "pompous expression" a National University. . . .". He has never heard of the "National" Universities of England. It is clear, at all events, that no suspicion of nationality attaches to the University of his experience. If Dublin University were in any appreciable degree as distinctively Irish as Oxford and Cambridge are distinctively English, my evidence would be unnecessary.'

'What Might Have Been'.

To condemn Trinity it is enough to state that it is the only successful British institution in a country which is not British. Eoin Mac Neill went on to contend that the maintenance in Ireland of such a University as the only real University in the country, was harmful not merely to education but to the public peace and welfare. Having dealt with the shady history of the Irish Chair, he proceeded to dwell on Trinity's lost opportunities: —

'The attitude of the College towards Irish studies is in sharp contrast with its opportunities. Dublin is the very centre of what may be called modern Celtdom, the one spot from which the monuments of Celtic antiquity as well as the existing Celtic languages are most accessible. Trinity College has ignored these opportunities because it is inspired by a firm tradition of hostility to whatever stands for an Irish nation — a primitive spirit of racial antagonism kept alive in a modern seat of learning. . . . Sir Henry Maine, M. D'Arbois de Jubainville, and others have shown the importance of (Irish) studies in the history of law. They have just the same importance and for the same reasons in the history of literature, politics, and other branches of social science. In all these respects, the study of Irish brings us into touch with an unbroken and almost independent tradition leading back to the beginning of civilisation. A short time ago, the Italian archaeologist Boni discovered in an Irish poem the key which he had sought for in vain elsewhere to the problem of that hearth of civilisation, the Roman forum. I may add that the sole copy of the poem referred to has been preserved in the library of Trinity College.'

The irony of the story is that Trinity itself has severely suffered for its aloofness from Ireland, just as Ireland has suffered through the aloofness of Trinity. Said Eoin MacNeill towards the close of his evidence: —

'Its (Trinity's) contempt for everything Irish has recoiled on its own head. If the College had been animated by a national spirit, if it had even responded to the national spirit such as existed among the Protestant gentry and men of wealth up to a century ago, if it had done anything to make them feel that they were Irishmen, they and their children and their children's children would have chosen it before any other place. Trinity College would have maintained its prestige and would have benefited itself to no small extent. It would have benefited Ireland still more. In that case, we should not have seen the almost complete divorce between wealth, property and rank, on the one side, and the national interest and public duty on the other. The agrarian, economic, and social evils of the country would have been softened and mitigated. Dublin would have remained in some degree what it was before the Union, one of the brightest, most intellectual and cultured, and most progressive capitals in Europe.'

Next week we shall quote from the evidence of Mr. Rolleston, the other spokesman of the League, as well as from the very interesting views of the Professor of Irish in Trinity.

INSPECTORS ON THE LANGUAGE
9.2.1907

We have already given some excerpts from the recent volume of Reports by 'National' Board Inspectors. Below we collect practically all the references to Irish which the book contains, including these already quoted in *An Claidheamh*: —

'There are a few classes in mathematics in the circuit, but they are not so numerous as I should wish. There are many classes in Irish, but as I do not examine in the subject I am unable to pronounce any opinion upon the worth of the instruction. In one large school, however, I had to complain of the training and answering of a large staff of monitors. I was informed that the monitors were learning Irish, and had not time to study their own programme.'
— Mr. Stronge, Dublin (2) Circuit.

'Irish is taught in a large number of schools, and mathematics in a small number. French has been taught in two schools.'
— Mr. M'Elwaine, Ballinasloe Circuit.

'Extra branches are taken up sparingly. Irish is most common round Carlingford Lough and in South Armagh. French and mathematics are taken up in not more than a dozen schools in the whole circuit.'
— Mr. Hogan, Dundalk Circuit.

'Irish is taught in a large number of schools; mathematics, with fair

121

results, in somewhat less than 30; French in three, to a small number of pupils.'

'Mr. Heron writes:— "About half-a-dozen schools in the district have taken up mathematics as an extra subject with success. About the same number in the neighbourhood of the Glens of Antrim have taken up Irish, and have been inspected by Mr. Mangan. One teacher taught mathematics with fair success. Irish is taught in a few schools amongst the Londonderry uplands, under the inspection of Mr. Mangan.'

— Dr. Beatty, Ballymena Circuit.

'In section 14A mathematics and Irish are the only extras presented. About half-a-dozen schools presented mathematics, and about 30 per cent Irish. . . . Mr. Tibbs, says of section 14C: — "A few of the schools take mathematics with fair success; book-keeping in a few schools with like results; Irish is taught in about 20 schools." '

— Mr. Smith, Dublin (1) Circuit.

'The extra subjects taken up are Irish, mathematics, French and Latin. Only the first of these occupied much of the Inspectors' time.'

— Mr. Brown, Clonmel Circuit.

'The extra subjects usually taken up are mathematics, and Irish; the former in 24 schools and the latter in 25. The classes in Irish wore inspected and examined by Mr. Lehane, who has special charge of this branch of school work. . . . French was taught in two schools.'

— Mr. Craig, Longford Circuit.

'As to extra subjects, Mr. Welply says: "The optional and extra branches taught were Irish, mathematics, and in one school French. The examinations in Irish are conducted by Mr. Duffy. Mathematics are not taken up as often as they ought to be. . . Mr. Martin writes: "Irish is taught in a large number of schools, but I am unable to speak of the proficiency of the pupils in this branch. Mathematics and French were taken up in a small number of schools, and the proficiency in these subjects was, as a rule, good. In the rest of the circuit mathematics have been taught in one or two schools, and French in one school, but not in the latter instance with a view to obtaining a special fee. Latin is not taught. Irish is taught as an extra branch, but only in the higher standards and out of school hours. It is a curious fact that the bilingual programme of instruction to be followed within school hours by the lowest as well as the highest standards has been adopted by only one school in the circuit. Irish is in parts of the Co. Kerry a living language — sometimes the only language. In Dingle on a market day nine-tenths of the transactions are conducted in Irish. It is the language of the home, and children lisp in Irish at their mother's knee. It should, therefore, be the language of the school from the earliest moment. English should be taught through the medium of Irish, and as the child grows up he would naturally and easily become the possessor of two tongues instead of one." '

— Mr. Connolly, Killarney Circuit.

'Irish and mathematics are the only extras taught. Mr. Cromie states "that the former subject is taught in about thirty schools, and the latter in less than half that number. As a rule the work done in both branches is a satisfactory character." In section A Mr. Kyle says: "Irish is taught in about 40 per cent of the schools, but as the classes have been in all cases inspected by Mr. Duffy, I am not in a position to express any opinion as to the degree of success attained. I have myself inspected and examined a great many Irish classes, and in nearly every case I was able to recommend the payment of the full fee. As a rule the teachers did not confine themselves to the limits of the programme, but gave practice in conversation from the beginning. In the section of which I have charge there are many districts where the grown-up people speak Irish habitually yet there is none in which the majority of the children can speak it, and there is no school in which the Bilingual Programme could be advantageously taken up. One school in Mr. Kyle's section took that Programme and was examined by Mr. Duffy. Without touching on other aspects of the question, I may be permitted to express the opinion that the study of Irish has helped by the contrasts of grammar and idioms to a better comprehension of many points in English." '

— Mr. O'Connor, Cork (2) Circuit.

'Mathematics, French, and Latin are efficiently taught in section B. . . . In Section A. . . . three classes in French, one in Latin, and fifteen in mathematics (1), and eleven in mathematics (2), were conducted with more or less success. There are a few classes in Irish. In Section C algebra and geometry are taught in eight schools, and algebra alone in seven of these. Irish is taught in about four schools, and Latin in one.'

— Mr. Kelly, Belfast (1) Circuit.

'Mr. Brown reports: — "I have no statistics as to the teaching of Irish, but the other extra subjects have been so little taught that I am glad to see them discontinued as extras." Mr. Little remarks: — "There are nearly 70 schools in Section C attended by Irish-speaking children. In some the language is but little used by the pupils, in others it is the language for all except school purposes; between these extremes are found schools of varying degrees of proficiency in the vernacular. Irish as an 'extra' was attempted successfully in 18 schools and unsuccessfully in 12. The number seems small, considering the facility of earning a fee, but some of the schools are under teachers who do not know the language, and others under teachers who have a native or acquired knowledge, but have not certificates of competency; in an appreciable number of schools the attendance is so very bad that the few pupils above third standard do not make the minimum attendance to qualify for fees in the subject. . . ." In Section A . . . . I found French in, I think, two schools, and Latin in one. In a few cases a number of pupils have been prepared in Irish, but, as this subject has been inspected by Mr. Mangan, I am not aware of the result."

— Mr. O'Riordan, Londonderry Circuit.

THE IRISH FEES
23.3.1907

We have at length, from the lips of the Minister responsible for the government of Ireland, a statement as to the actual position of affairs with regard to what are compendiously known as the Irish Fees. In anticipation of Mr. Birrell's announcement we deferred last week our comments on the situation raised by the previous statement of the Financial Secretary to the Treasury. The question can now be dealt with at leisure and as a whole.

It will be useful, at the outset, to remind the public of the past history of the Irish Fees. It is a history extending over twenty-eight years. Irish was first placed on the programme of Irish National Schools in 1878. It was given the status of an 'Extra Subject', and remuneration for its teaching was fixed at the rate of 10s. per pass per pupil annually on a three years' course. These fees were paid uninterruptedly from 1878 to 1906. Once more we re-print the always instructive table showing the at first slow and afterwards astonishingly rapid rise in the popularity of the language in the schools. As to the period 1885-1899 — the reign of the 'individual pass' — the following are the numbers of the pupils who passed and in respect of whom fees were paid in each of the years mentioned:

1885	1886	1887	1888	1889	1890	1891	1892	1893
161	321	371	443	532	531	515	575	609

1894	1895	1896	1897	1898	1899
676	706	750	882	1012	1317

In 1900 individual passes were abolished, and the ten-shilling fees were thenceforward paid on the basis of the number of pupils *in average attendance* at a *class* which passed. In that year 2,256 pupils presented themselves. The number of pupils is not available for 1901, but the schools in which the language was taught for fees numbered at least 212. From 1902 on, the fees were paid as follows — mark the now phenomenal rise in the numbers both of the schools and of the pupils presented: —

In 1902 in   235 schools to   4,092 pupils.
In 1903 in   553 schools to 11,175 pupils.
In 1904 in 1,185 schools to 25,984 pupils.
In 1905 in 1,204 schools to 24,918 pupils.
In 1906 in 1,410 schools to 31,741 pupils.

Early in 1905 Mr. Walter Long became Chief Secretary for Ireland. He had scarcely entered on office when he decided that the teaching of Irish in the primary schools — or at any rate the remuneration of the teachers for its teaching — should cease. At the time the public was inclined to attribute this ukase to the British Treasury, but in an address to his present constituents, delivered in Dún Laoghaire Town Hall on January 2nd, 1906, Mr. Long arrogated the entire credit — or discredit — to himself.

At the instance, then, of Mr. Walter Long the Treasury, in March, 1905, made an Order declining to sanction the payment of fees for Extra

Subjects after June 30th, 1906. The National Board protested in the memorable resolutions in which the Commissioners reiterated their opinion as to the great educational importance of instruction in Irish and of the teaching of other subjects through Irish in Irish-speaking districts, and, in view of the strong sentiment in favour of the language and the interest taken in it by teachers and pupils, its educational value as a school subject even in non-Irish-speaking districts. This expression of opinion was ignored by the Treasury, and the Board, in the popular parlance, 'lay down' under the insult.

In December, 1905, Mr. Walter Long went out of office. The Minister sent to Ireland by the new Liberal Government was an Irishman, and was known to be interested in the Irish language, whose cause he had vigorously championed from the opposition benches. In answer to the protests against the withdrawal of the fees with which the country had been ringing during the previous six months, Mr. Bryce promised to go into the matter at an early opportunity.* He did so, and as the result of negotioations between Tyrone House, Dublin Castle, and the British Treasury, he soon announced that a new scale of fees had been decided upon in lieu of that which had been withdrawn at the instance of Mr. Long. It had also been decided to offer thirty prizes for proficiency in Irish in connection with the King's Scholarships Examinations, and to recognise the Gaelic League's Irish Training Schools by awarding prizes to their successful students. The scale of fees proposed to replace the withdrawn ten-shilling fees was, however, so ludicrous that a roar of indignation and repudiation went up from the country. In place of a three years' course, with a fee of 10s. per year, there was substituted a course extending from the 2nd to the highest Standard, the remuneration per head on the average attendance being fixed at 1s. in the 2nd and 3rd Standards, and at 2s. 6d. per head in the higher Standards. Under this scheme a teacher with an average attendance of 50 pupils could earn, at the most, £2 for a year's work in teaching Irish; and his remuneration for passing a pupil through the entire Irish course from beginning to end would be 9s. 6d., as against 30s. under the old system! True, Irish could now be taught within the technical 'school hours', and not merely as an extra; but, as against this, the compulsory part of the ordinary programme was so long and exacting as to make the proper teaching of Irish impossible in a large number of schools, especially as a considerable section of the Board's Inspectors were actively opposed to it. Moreover, the utter inadequacy of the fees offered was such as to endanger, or render impossible, the continuance of the admirable work which had been done under the old system by 'Extern' Teachers, employed under the aegis of the Gaelic League.

The League and the public interested in the schools plainly told Mr. Bryce that his scale of fees would not do. He replied that he would be glad to reconsider the whole matter, and requested the League to submit him an alternative scheme. The Coiste Gnotha accordingly drew up a programme of instruction, embracing the whole school course and providing for the remuneration of the teachers at a scale of fees ranging from 2s. in the Infants' and 1st Standards to 8s. in the 6th Standard. This scheme was

* The restoration of the fees was demanded by over 100 public bodies in Ireland, by the Archbishops and Bishops, and by the Teachers' and Managers' Associations. A Memorial from 616 Managers, representing 3,095 schools, was forwarded to Mr. Bryce on February 10th, 1906.

backed by an expression of opinion from the managers, teachers and elective boards of the country.

Here the public history of the controversy ends until it re-opens twelve months later. In the meantime, however, *An Claidheamh* was able to tell its readers that Mr. Bryce had been led to believe that the Treasury was willing to restore the withdrawn fees, or their equivalent, if approached on the subject by the National Board: that at a meeting held just before Christmas last the Board had decided so to approach it; and that a sliding scale of fees (not identical with, but based upon, the recommendations of the Gaelic League) had been approved of both by the Board and by the Irish Government. The Board's application for the expenditure, together with applications for other and much larger expenditure (on buildings and other things), came before the Treasury in due course; but — the previous half-promises notwithstanding — was rejected.

So much we gave the public to understand. And in the House of Commons on Tuesday last Mr. Bryce's successor confirmed the accuracy of all our information. The restoration of the full grant and the adoption of a satisfactory scale of remuneration had been agreed upon between the Board and Mr. Bryce when, at the eleventh hour, and after Mr. Bryce had laid down office, the Treasury stepped in with its '*non possumus*'. Mr. Birrell's statement is remarkable. It is as follows: —

'I wish to make the position of the Irish Government quite clear on the subject of fees for teaching Irish. Since July, 1906, fees for Irish as an extra subject in in National Schools have been abolished. Irish is now an optional subject, which can, with the consent of the managers, be taught in every National School either outside or during school hours. Other teachers may be employed if the teachers of the school are not competent to teach the subject. According to the new scale of fees, which came into force on 1st July, 1906, one shilling per scholar is paid for Irish in the lower standard, and two shillings and sixpence in the higher standards. The Commissioners of National Education are of the opinion that Irish can be best taught by the ordinary teachers of a school, and in order to provide a sufficient number of competent teachers they award thirty prizes yearly in the Training Colleges for the encouragement of Irish. In these Colleges Irish is an optional subject, so far as the National Board is concerned, but it is open to the managers of the Colleges to make it compulsory if they so desire. The supply of National School teachers competent to teach Irish is at present very defective, so much so that the Commissioners are unable in many instances to enforce the new rule requiring teachers appointed to schools in Irish-speaking districts to have a knowledge of Irish. This seems to point to the necessity of the managers of Training Colleges making the learning of Irish compulsory in these institutions. The Commissioners of National Education being of the opinion that the scale of fees which I have just mentioned was insufficient for the remuneration of extern teachers, made a proposal for an increase in the scale in connection with the estimates for 1906-7, and these proposals were supported by the Irish Government. The Treasury, however, felt unable to sanction these proposals, as my hon. friend the Secretary to that Department has already informed the hon. member."

In reply to a further question addressed to him by Tomás Ua Domhnaill, Mr. Birrell admitted that the school curriculum would require 'some adjustment' before Irish could be satisfactorily taught as an ordinary subject. We should think so, indeed.

It will be observed that the blame for the refusal to restore the fees is thrown by the Chief Secretary on the Treasury. This is technically accurate. But has the Treasury no master? Does the British Constitution recognise within the state a power which is supreme alike over the Ministry, Parliament, and people of Great Britain and Ireland? We do not believe so. It is absolutely certain that if Mr. Birrell were thoroughly determined that the Irish fees should be restored, he could bring about their restoration by a whisper in the ear of the Treasury. Of whom, in point of fact, does 'the Treasury' consist? It consists of Sir Henry Campbell-Bannerman, First Lord; Mr. H. H. Asquith, Chancellor of the Exchequer; and Messrs. J. A. Pease, J. H. Lewis, J. M. F. Fuller, and Capt. C. W. North, M.P.s, Junior Lords. But these are Mr. Birrell's colleagues in the Ministry; these, like him, are committed to the policy of 'governing Ireland in accordance with Irish ideas'; these are, assuredly, men open to be convinced by the sweet persuasiveness and, as we are still willing to believe, honesty and earnestness of purpose of the Chief Secretary for Ireland.

We pitch our remarks in a key which is intentionally moderate. We write with calmness and dispassion. We call no hard names. But we assure Mr. Birrell and all others on both sides of the controversy that we, and the organisation for which we stand, are in deadly earnest. The National Board and Mr. Bryce have been flouted; the Gaelic League shall not be flouted. By every legitimate means in our power we will bring continuous and un-yielding pressure on the Government until our demands are conceded. The full grant must be restored. A satisfactory scale of fees must be sanctioned. A live and progressive programme of instruction must be adopted. These three things we want and these three things we mean to have. We look to the country to rally round us. The Coiste Gnótha have given the lead. Its resolution of a fortnight ago has now been followed up by a memorandum reciting the facts of the controversy and accompanied by a call to the branches of the League, to the representative public bodies of the country, to the press and to the managers and teachers, to range themselves behind the Irish Ireland demand. In Baile Átha Cliath on Saturday last the President of the League made a rousing appeal for the support of the nation on this great national issue. If that support be forthcoming in due measure, no Government — much less one professedly anxious to govern Ireland 'in accordance with Irish ideas' — can long remain inactive.

Mr. Birrell and his colleagues have now been put in possession of 'Irish ideas' on this particular question. Will they yield to them? They will have an opportunity of doing so gracefully on this (Thursday) afternoon, when, as we understand, the Irish Educational Estimates come up for discussion in the House of Commons. We presume that the matter of the Irish fees will be raised by the Irish members: and if the Government refuses to pledge itself to see them restored, we shall know the value of its 'sympathy'.

THE TEACHERS
13.4.1907

Last week we expressed the hope that the national language would be frequently heard — and not merely *heard of* — during the deliberations of the National Teachers' Congress' in Baile Átha Cliath. We cannot say that the hope has been fulfilled. So far as we can make out the only speeches delivered in Irish from beginning to end of the proceedings were that of one of the representatives of the City Council — who happens also to be the manager of this paper — on the opening day, and those of Tomás Ó hAodha and Domhnall Ó Duibhne, both of them prominent members of the Gaelic League, on the Wednesday. We realise that the time has not yet come when one can reasonably expect an All-Ireland body with the limitations of the Teachers' Organisation to conduct its business wholly or even mainly in Irish; on the other hand, one is entitled to look for something better than a mere formal recognition of the existence of the national language from the teachers of the nation assembled in their annual Congress. There is really no reason why the agenda and annual report should not be bilingual; why Irish should not be accorded a prominent place in the opening ceremonial; and, especially, why every Gaedhilgeoir among the delegates should not freely make use of the national language in addressing the Congress.

The teachers of Ireland have not yet, we fear, nailed the colours of the Irish Nation to their masthead. They are wont to regard themselves as the civil servants of a foreign power, rather than as 'captains in Israel'. They plead for the redress of their grievances from much the same point of view and in much the same tone as might, say, the Irish Post Office Clerks, 'English and Scotch teachers receive so-and-so and so-and-so; therefore we are entitled to so-and-so and so-and-so'. This, we suggest, is not the true point of view, nor is this the tone which becomes the situation. Rather let the teachers say — not so much to the British government as to the Irish people: 'We are entrusted with the most important secular care that could be entrusted to any body of men within the nation: it is your bounden duty, *as it is within your power,* to insist that we be suffered to discharge that duty untrammelled by outside interference, whether taking the form of British Treasury stinginess or of "National" Board tyranny. We call on you to rally to our support, not as an act of grace to us, but as an act of duty which you owe to your children and, therefore, to the nation. We, on our part, are pre-pred to take our stand definitely with Ireland and against foreignism."

We conceive that such language as this, addressed by the teachers of Ireland to the fathers and mothers of Ireland, would awaken a very definite response; and we are not at all sure that its immediate effect on the British Government and the 'National' Board would not be at least as decisive as that of the lengthy resolutions and the *pour-parlers* with Chief Secretaries which have hitherto been the order.

THE WORK OF THE SCHOOLS
20.4.1907

In his address at the public competitions in connection with Feis Bhaile Átha Cliath on Saturday evening last An Craoibhín delivered a powerful indictment of the educational ideals and methods which still prevail in our secondary and primary schools. His severest criticism was directed against the Intermediate system of examination 'by pen and ink'. Under that system examinations in modern languages, as in all other subjects, are carried out entirely by way of written question and answer. 'I call that', said An

Craoibhín, 'a hideous and appalling mockery of learning. The whole Intermediate idea of testing by examination alone without inspection is a blot on Irish education and on the name of education everywhere: but their system of examination in modern languages is the *ne plus ultra* of stupidity.

It is significant that this sytem is forced on the Intermediate Board by — the British Treasury. The Treasury it was that, by stopping supplies, compelled the Board to dismiss its staff of temporary Inspectors a few years ago; the Treasury it is that, by refusing a grant for the purpose, prevents the Board from appointing a permanent staff, as it has repeatedly proposed to do. As surely as one of our Education Boards exhibits an all too rare gleam of intelligence, as surely as one of them proposes to do something useful and progressive, so surely does the British Treasury step in with its 'I forbid'. At every point and in every department of Irish administration that impassive and relentless tyranny bars the path to reform.

True as is An Craoibhín's indictment, we are not sure that, when all is said, the most valuable work that has so far been done for Irish in the schools has not been done in the domain of secondary education. Certain it is that the percentage of pupils who are taught Irish in the Intermediate schools and colleges is far in excess of the percentage under instruction in the language in the primary schools, and less than five out of every hundred are presented for examination in it. As for the quality of the teaching, it is difficult to dogmatise: but we believe that, proportionately to the numbers attending them, the Intermediate schools have turned out far more speakers of Irish during the past five years than the National schools. We could name off-hand a dozen secondary schools from which every pupil who passes through an Intermediate course emerges an Irish speaker of some sort: are there yet a dozen primary schools in the non-Irish-speaking parts of the country of which a similar remark could truthfully be made?   The fact is that, speaking generally, the National schools are not yet making Irish speakers of the children, even where the language is taught as part of the ordinary programme, and where the teacher is an Irish speaker, and enthusiastic to boot. And the causes seem to be three: insufficient time devoted to the study; failure on the part of the teachers to utilise the language during the course of the general school-work; and in spite of the Coláistí Múinteoireachta and *An Claidheamh's* propaganda for the past four years — antiquated teaching methods.

Once more — for the preaching of all gospels consists in the re-inculcation of known truths — we propose to take up each of these points in detail, and to hammer away at them during the next few months.

EDUCATIONAL HOME RULE?
11.5.1907

At last there is a Bill before the British Parliament which proposes to give effect to the Gaelic League demand for educational Home Rule. On Tuesday afternoon the Chief Secretary for Ireland moved the first reading of the Irish Government Bill. That Bill, if placed on the Statute Book, will call into being an Irish Council, three-fourths elective, which will have virtual control of Irish Education. The National and the Intermediate Boards will be swept away, and will be replaced by an Education Department answerable to the Irish Council. An Education Committee will immediately superintend the work of the Department. The bulk of the members of this Committee, will, we gather, — but the point is rather obscure in the Chief Secretary's statement, — be elected by and from the Council, though the Lord Lieutenant will have power to nominate persons with educational experience as additional members, — such nominated members, however, not to exceed one-fourth of the whole. Finally, an Irish Treasury is to be created and the sum of £4,000,000 per annum will be placed at its disposal, subject to the control of the Council.

He would be a bold man who would venture to prophesy that these proposals are actually about to be carried into effect. One thing is certain: if they, or anything like them, reach the Statute Book, we shall be on the eve of the greatest and most beneficient revolution in the modern history of Ireland. *The schools will be ours*. The shadows of Death and the Nightmare Death-in-Life will have passed away from the Irish landscape.

Would it not appear that there is work — mighty work, glorious work — awaiting our hands during the next few weeks?

THE BILL
18.5.1907

To the superficial observer Mr. Birrell might appear to have accomplished the hitherto impossible, — to have united Ireland. Men and newspapers that have never previously been known to agree on any single topic are at one in anathematising his Bill. The long chorus of denunciation goes on from morning till night, the deep bass of the true-blue Tory being for once in harmony with the light treble of the moderate Nationalist, and both with the sharp, clear, defiant notes of the aggressive Sinn Féiner. The very Ishmaelites of Irish politics have come in from the wilderness and are howling in concert with the pack.

We are loth to break in on this pleasant harmony by striking a discordant note. Yet we fear we must do so. It would no doubt be an infinitely easier and an infinitely more popular thing for us to join our voice to the chorus, and to point out that from the Gaelic League point of view Mr. Birrell's Bill is mischievous and machiavellian. It would, however, be dishonest — it would be to write what we do not believe. When we took charge of this paper we resolved that, though it might cost us our position and — a thing we value far more highly — the friendship of our fellow-Gaels, we would never shrink from taking up an unpopular attitude and never stoop to write a lie. Now, we believe in our heart and soul that the passing of the Irish Council Bill, even in its present form, would be for the advantage of Ireland as a whole, and for the particular advantage of the Irish movement which *An Claidheamh* exists to advocate. Believing this, it is as impossible for us to remain a dumb dog as it would be for us to proclaim that we believe the contrary.

When, last week, we wrote that the effect of Mr. Birrell's Bill, if placed on the Statute Book, would be to give the people of Ireland virtual control of their own education, we did a very bold thing, for we had no guarantee that a single man, woman, or child in the country would agree with us, or, agreeing, would have the courage to say so. This week our position is less precarious. With the exception of the Bishop of Limerick no one on the Irish side has taken serious exception to the educational clauses of the Bill. The most eminent educationist in Ireland has cordially welcomed them. As

130

for the Gaelic League, they propose to give it precisely what it has been demanding for the past five years: an education authority representative of the people of Ireland, answerable to Irish public opinion, and free from the domination of the British Treasury. Whosoever has reason to be disappointed with the Bill, the Gaelic League has none.

Here, in brief, are the educational proposals. As soon as may be after the passing of the Act, there will be constituted an Education Department for Ireland, to which will be transferred the powers at present vested in the Boards of National and Intermediate Education, — which two Boards will be dissolved. The new Education Department will pass under the jurisdiction of the Irish Council, when the Council comes into existence. The Council will delegate the immediate superintendence of the work of the Department to an Education Committee. The bulk of the membership of this Committee will be chosen by and from the members of the Council, but the Lord Lieutenant will have the power to nominate as additional members persons (including clergymen and women) of social educational experience, — such nominated members not to exceed six or one-fourth of the whole, whichever is greater.

It is our deliberate opinion that an Education Department working under a Committee so constituted, and controlled in final resort by the Irish Council, will be adequately representative of Irish views and adequately responsible to Irish public opinion. When we say 'controlled in final resort by the Irish Council', we assume, of course, that the clause which proposes to give the ultimate control of everything to the Viceroy will be withdrawn or, as suggested in an English contemporary, so 'modified' as to to be modified out of existence.

It seems to us that under no conceivable circumstances could anti-Irish Irishmen secure a majority either on the Education Committee or on the Irish Council. The Gael would dominate the situation from the outset, and his power would be a steadily increasing quantity. Such matters as the general introduction of the Bilingual Programme in the Gaedhealtacht; the Gaelicising of the Training Colleges; the proper training of the teachers to teach the language; the revision of the school programme and the making of ample provision for the (remunerated) teaching of Irish as an Ordinary Subject; the Gaelicising of the Inspectoral Staff, etc., etc., would be speedily attended to; and the extension of the Bilingual Programme to the country as a whole would be only a matter of a few years.

As for the secondary schools, the ruinous results system is specifically abolished by the Bill, and we may take it that examination 'by pen and ink' will become a thing of the past as soon as an Irish Education authority independent of Dublin Castle arrives on the scene.

Finally, the teachers will cease to be British Civil Servants and will become the servants of the Irish people: one of whose first cares will be to accord them that status in the commonwealth which they are entitled to and which the dearest interests of the nation demand that they should receive. And, in this and other connections, it will be necessary from the new vantage ground of the Irish Council to commence a struggle for financial justice to Irleand.

All this will be possible if the Bill becomes law. If it does not, we shall be — where we are.

THE DEAD BILL AND OURSELVES
25.5.1907

The Nation Convention has rejected the Irish Council Bill. We regret the decision, and we believe that the time will come when everyone who recorded his vote in favour of it will equally regret it. The rejection seems to us to mean the postponement, perhaps for twenty years, of any possibility of the Irish people's gaining control over the administration of their own affairs. In this we may be mistaken. Miracles, we suppose, are always possible. The British Liberals may withdraw their Bill and introduce a Home Rule Bill. They may go to the country and the country may give them that 'mandate' for Home Rule which it refused at the last General Election. The House of Lords may be converted, reformed, bullied, or abolished. The Sinn Féin party in Ireland may rouse the nation against the Parliamentarians; the latter may withdraw from Westminster; the General Council of County Councils may develop into an Irish Parliament. All things, we say, are possible. But we are dealing now with probabalities, and the probability is that Ireland will not again find herself within measurable distance of even a partial control of her own educational and other affairs 'for' — in the words of Mr. John Redmond — 'a generation'. The prospect is truly enlivening.

A few brave words, spoken by some responsible and trusted Irish leader before the public chagrin at the non-fulfilment of foolishly-formed hopes had had time to explode, would have saved the Bill. But no one who was at once sufficiently strong and sufficiently popular opened his lips except to condemn. So the Bill goes, and we are where we were twenty-five years ago. And we shall probably be in the same position — with, of course, a diminished population and fuller work-houses and lunatic asylums — twenty-five years hence.

For our part, we spoke out the faith that was in us and, whatever the consequences, we shall have the satisfaction of knowing that we did our duty as it presented itself to us. We saw and see that the passing of the Bill would have meant (amongst other things) the control of Irish education by the Irish. We did not see, and do not see, that its passing would have retarded the attainment of the Irish political ideal by a single hour. On the contrary, it would have hastened it.

We are aware that our attitude has been a scandal and a stumbling-block to many valued friends. Several of those have written to us this week, but unfortunately their letters are so long that in the interval between receipt of them and our going to press it is a physical impossibility to put them in type. However, as the Bill is dead, there is all the less necessity to enter into a controversy as to whether it would or would not have been for the benefit of Ireland if it had been allowed to pass.

Alderman Mac Cumhaill asks us to state that our editorials in our last two issues were published without our having first consulted with the Coiste Gnótha or its Advisory Committee 'as to whether anything should appear, and, if so, what, in regard to the Irish Council Bill in the official organ of the League'. We gladly make the statement; adding the explanation that, as we are the Editor of this paper, we are not in the habit of consulting with anyone as to what should appear and what should not appear in it, nor is any such requirement attached to the appointment. We try as best we can to interpret the spirit of the League, and to define what is, in our opinion, its true policy; but we should be the veriest serf did we bind ourselves to record here from week to week, not our own views and convictions, but the views and convictions of someone else. In final resort, everyone must recognise that an official organ, unless it be edited by a mere machine, can guarantee to do no more than speak for the individual who is its Editor. The measure of its authoritativeness is simply the measure of that individual's grasp of the principles of the organisation.

We have received from the Right Rev. Mgr. Hallinan, P.P., a letter which is, we regret to say, too late for publication or reply in this issue. A similar remark applies to a letter which has reached us from Seosamh Ó Riain, and which, for the rest, is rendered out-of-date by the decision of the National Convention. Coiste Ceanntair Co. Mhuigheo has adopted the following resolution: — 'That we express our disappointment at the views expressed by the Editor of *An Claidheamh Soluis* in connection with the educational portion of the Irish Council Bill. That we totally disassociate ourselves from the views put forward, and that we regard such an expression of policy from the official organ as detrimental to the interests of the Gaelic League throughout the country.' We are sorry to have to differ from friends whom we respect as much as we do the members of Coiste Ceanntair Mhuigheo. We must differ from them again in holding that the Gaelic League throughout the country is not so puny a growth as to suffer any serious detriment from the spleen of such half-friends and whole enemies as may attempt to make our legitimate, though possibly unpopular, attitude on a question which vitally affects the welfare of our movement, an excuse for their own inveterate distrust or hate.

A FORWARD MOVE
29.6.1907

We hear with satisfaction that in many quarters of the Gaedhealtacht the schools are preparing to raise the standard of Bilingualism. The Programme is to be introduced throughout several important stretches of Tír Chonaill, notably in the schools of the Right Rev. Monsignor Walker, P.P., of Ailt an Chorráin (Burtonport). It is also to be introduced in one or two of the parishes of Corca Dhuibhne — a far cry from Tír Chonaill — and at isolated points elsewhere in the South, including Béal Átha an Ghaorthaidh and at least one school in the Déise. We hope that the number of bilingual schools in Ireland will at least double itself during the educational year if, as we understand, one of the main duties of the new Organisers of Irish Training is to be to pioneer the Programme in the more Irish-speaking districts.

Considerable misapprehension still appears to prevail with regard to the function and scope of the same Programme. Now, its aim is certainly *not* to teach English to Irish speakers. Neither is it precisely to teach Irish or to forward the interests of Irish at the expense of any really useful school subject. Its aim is simply to *educate* the child through the medium of both Irish and English, applying to him a double intellectual stimulus, bringing him into contact with a two-fold culture, placing before him a view-point at once healthily national and broadly human. Incidentally the child educated on bilingual lines in an Irish National School will acquire a thorough vernacular and literary acquaintance with both Irish and English; he will be taught, not merely to speak, read, and write both languages, but to discuss in both history, geography, grammar, mathematics, elementary natural science, Christian Doctrine, and every other subject that comes within the purview of a primary education. It is to be distinctly understood that in every school in which the Bilingual Programme is taken up, the teacher must forthwith commence to give portion of his or her instruction in Catechism, in History, in Geography, in Science, in Hygiene, in Physical Drill, in Needlework, and so on, *through the medium of Irish.* The order in which Irish is to be applied to the various subjects, and the extent to which it is to be introduced during the first year, are matters which must be decided upon in view of the local circumstances — the linguistic conditions of the school, the extent to which Irish has been previously taught, the confidence of the teacher in his own ability. At first, a certain grouping of standards must be allowed, as it would not be easy to set a full seven-years' course in motion all at once. The Infants can work at the first eight lessons in An Chéad Leabhar, Part I; the First Class should be able to cover An Chéad Leabhar, Parts I and II. The Second and Third Standards might be grouped, with 'An Dara Leabhar' as literary class-book; and (for the first year) 'An Treas Leabhar' would probably make a sufficiently advanced Irish reader for the Fourth, Fifth, and Sixth Standards grouped. The widest discretion is allowed in the matter of the selection of further reading-texts for the higher standards.

Whatever is wanting, books are certainly not wanting. In addition to the series of Bilingual Literary Readers, we have now two Irish History Readers; an Irish Geography Reader; a first Irish Arithmetic; a first Irish Grammar; a book of Bilingual Object Lessons; and a set of Irish Reading Charts. Before the end of the year we shall have in addition a Bilingual Science Primer, a first Irish Euclid, an Irish Map of Ireland, Irish Natural History Charts, and (probably) a second Irish Geography and a second Irish Arithmetic. The equipment in the matter of publications of the bilingual primary school will then, for all practical purposes, be complete.

We look for a forward move in the non-Irish-speaking districts also. There no longer remains anything to prevent the teaching of Irish to every child on the rolls of every school in Ireland in which there is a teacher willing and qualified. If the teacher in a given place is not willing, it is for the local Gaels to ask why; if the teacher is not qualified, it is for him to qualify himself, which he may do by attending a month's course at one of the Irish Colleges. The four Summer Colleges open in the first week of July, and it should be possible for every teacher who is really anxious to take up Irish teaching this year to arrange to spend July or August at one or other of them.

We want genuine teaching this time. We want the Irish instruction begun in the very earliest classes even though no fees be available until Standard III is reached — it is necessary to begin early if the children are to be given a real grip of the language; it is politic to begin early in order to make sure of the fees later on. We want profitable and progressive programmes; we want adequate provision for the Irish lesson in the school time-tables — the minimum should be half-an-hour daily, preferably between 10 a.m. and 11 a.m.; we want attractive and up-to-date methods; we want the language *spoken* by the teacher to the pupils and by the pupils to the teacher; we want Irish songs, Irish hymns, Irish prayers, Irish words of command at drill, the school-roll called in Irish, Irish rallying cries in the recreation-ground. All these things are allowed by the rules of the Board; none of these can be stopped by a Board Inspector, — the Inspector who as much as frowns at them will do so at his peril. In a word, we want a forward policy in the schools; we look to the managers and the teachers to co-operate with us, and we do not intend to allow the Board or anyone else to thwart or check us.

THE DUTY OF THE SCHOOLS
7.9.1907

Last week we drew attention to the large facilities for Irish teaching which are allowed by the new Rules and Regulations of the Commissioners of National Education. It goes without saying that Irish Ireland will expect those facilities to be fully availed of by the managers and teachers. The Code is not a perfect one, but at least it allows the school managements full liberty in the matter of the introduction of Irish. Theoretically, there has been such liberty for a number of years past; but practically this liberty has been discounted by the existence of penal statutes, by the known or suspected hostility of the Board's Inspectors, by the length of the compulsory programme, and by the absence of a financial inducement sufficient to make it worth the teacher's while, from a business point of view, to take up the language. All this has been changed. Irish is in fashion at Tyrone House. The hostile Inspectors are under caution. There are eight or ten Gaels on the existing inspectoral staff, and six more are about to be appointed. It has been made known that, where necessary, the compulsory programme can be lightened in order to make room for Irish. The financial inducement to teach the language is not all that it might be, but still it is considerable. Teachers will be facilitated in attending courses at the Irish Colleges, where they will be trained in the most up-to-date methods of language instruction. The road, as we said last week, is clear for the universal introduction of Irish. It is for the managers and the teachers to do their duty.

That duty, however, does not end with the placing of Irish on the school programme. Rather it only begins there. It does not end even with the conscientious teaching of Irish as a set subject whether from books or by the most up-to-date and 'direct' of Direct Methods. More important than any programme, more important than any course of formal instruction, more important than any mere 'subject', even though that 'subject' be the national language, is the creation in the schools of an Irish atmosphere, the Irishising of the hearts and minds of the children, the kindling in their souls of the quenchless fire of patriotism, the setting before them of a great and glowing ideal of *Duty*. Here it is that the schools have most disastrously failed in the past, and here it is that their help is most urgently needed now and in the future. Their task under the new and favourable condition of affairs must be less the training up of a generation of linguists and grammarians than the breeding, for the weal of Ireland, of a race of patriots.

THE NEW RULES
5.10.1907

The long-delayed *Rules and Regulations* of the Commissioners of National Education for 1907-8 have just reached us. They contain nothing startling from our particular point of view, the rules affecting Irish being

135

precisely as printed in our issue for August 31st last. The following summary will make the future position clear. Irish may henceforth be taught: —

(A). As an Ordinary Subject, within the technical 'school hours', to every child in every National School in Ireland;

(B). As an Extra Subject, outside the technical 'school hours', to pupils in Standards III, IV, V and VI; in which case its successful teaching is remunerated by substantial fees, irrespective of the fact whether the language is also taught to the same pupils as an Ordinary Subject or not.

(C). Under the Bilingual Programme, in Irish-speaking districts and districts where Irish and English are both commonly spoken; in which case fees for Irish as an Extra are not earnable, but valuable special fees are payable in respect of each pupil receiving bilingual instruction.

(D). To every pupil in every Evening Continuation School in Ireland; in which case book-prizes are awardable to the pupils for proficiency in the language.

In connection with (A.), 'Irish as an Ordinary', the Commissioners publish two specimen programmes, which we reprint on another page. The first is a complete course covering Standards I — VII, and is graduated on the assumption that the pupils in each standard have mastered the courses prescribed for the preceding standards. The second is a very useful 'Modified Programme', intended to meet the case of schools where Irish has not hitherto been taught to pupils of all standards. Two different groupings are suggested according as the pupils in the senior standards have, or have not, gone through the 1st, 2nd, and 3rd Extra Courses in Irish.

The specimen programme for (B.), 'Irish as an Extra' is as printed in *An Claidheamh* of August 31st. We may remark that the drafters of the various programmes included in the Commissioners' 'Rules and Regulations' have obviously studied their *Claidheamh* to good effect. In several instances the graduation is precisely as suggested by us, and the notes and hints to teachers are taken almost *verbatim* from our columns.

The specimen Bilingual Programme (C) remains unchanged. The teacher who regards it as a little 'stiff' is referred to the numerous alternative programmes, allowing for grouping of standards and so on, which have from time to time appeared in *An Claidheamh*. (D), 'Irish in Evening Schools', speaks for itself.

Last week we confidently wrote that under the new scheme fees for Irish as an Extra would certainly be payable in respect of children to whom the language is also taught as an Ordinary Subject. To make assurance doubly sure, the Ard-Runaidhe had previously addressed a query on the point to the National Board. The answer, which had not come to hand when we went to press last week, entirely bears out our reading of the rules. The Secretary to the Commissioners writes: —

'In reply to your communication dated 12th inst., regarding the regulations for the teaching of Irish as an Extra Subject in National Schools, I am directed to inform you that no objection will be raised to the payment of fees for Irish taught as an Extra Subject outside school hours in respect of pupils who are taught Irish as an Ordinary Subject within school hours'.

The point is thus settled. Teachers will also read with relief the following answer to another query of the Ard-Runaidhe's: —

'With reference to your inquiry as to whether fees will be paid in full for the current school-year in cases where, owing to the new programme not having been issued earlier, Irish was not taught as an Extra Subject until September, I am to state that the circumstances of each case will be duly considered and that a reduction of the fees will not necessarily take place owing to instruction in Irish not having been given during the months of July and August in the manner proscribed by the new regulations for Extra Subjects'.

One further point and we trust we shall have laid to rest the fears and forebodings of the morbidly-imaginative correspondent who has seen in the recent rules the 'banishment' of Irish from primary schools. The Commissioners state (Schedule I, p. 58), that the fees for Irish as an Extra will be paid at the rate of 3s., 6s., 9s., and 12s., respectively, 'per unit of the average attendance at the Irish class'. Further down they stipulate that 'at least forty hours' instruction must be given, and the teaching of the Extra Branch must continue throughout the entire school year'. Connecting these two provisions, many teachers have assumed that each pupil must put in forty hours' attendance at the Irish class. This is not the true reading. The class must be in progress at least forty hours, spread over the entire school-year, — say two half-hours per week; but the fees will be paid for every unit of the average attendance at the class, many children counting towards running up the average attendance who have not put in anything like forty hours. The rule is this respect much more favourable to the teacher than the old rule, under which each child had to make a hundred attendances.

Two half-hours of 'Extra' instruction per week will, we have seen, meet the requirements of the National Board. Will the Gaelic League be so easily satisfied? Certainly not. We shall expect Irish to be taught for a full hour per day in every school in Ireland. A minimum of two half-hours outside the 'school day' can be set apart as the time for the official instruction in Irish as an Extra (to qualify for fees): the remaining four hours may be within or without (preferably, of course, within) the ordinary 'school day', as suits the local situation.

IRISH IN THE SCHOOLS
12.10.1907

The time is now ripe for a forward move all round towards getting Irish firmly established and properly taught in the schools and colleges of this country. We trust that where the necessity exists every supporter of the language movement will henceforward exert himself unceasingly until the desired end is brought about. Reasonable facilities and encouragement are on the whole now afforded for the introduction of Irish teaching into our schools. Apart from patriotic reasons, which should, of course, be the main incentive to teach Irish, and from the educational value of knowing a second language, there is now a distinct commercial value attaching to Irish owing to its position on the programmes of examination for a large and rapidly increasing number of appointments, including clerkships in the four principal railway companies of Ireland, the Munster and Leinster and Hibernian Banks, the teaching profession in all its branches, solicitors' apprentices, the Dublin Corporation, and many other public boards, in various scholarship schemes, etc., etc. Its commercial value, too, is being steadily established in business circles, though it would, we might remark *en passant*, be infinitely more so than it is, if the majority of those who are or profess to be supporters of the language did not overlook one of the most powerful levers which could be moved in its favour, viz., the use of Irish consistently in purchasing or ordering goods, thereby compelling firms to use Irish in some degree and creating a necessity for the employment of persons knowing it. There are difficulties no doubt in the matter of getting Irish effectively taught in the schools in many districts, but in no case are they insurmountable, and if the 'will' is there it only requires a certain amount of intelligence to find the 'way'. In very many places there are no difficulties, the 'way' is quite clear but the 'will' is wanting. What is being done in so many districts of varying circumstances all over Ireland, North, South, East, and West, in town and country, where Irish is being effectively taught can be done in the remaining districts by adopting similar measures. The great requirement everywhere is someone who will move, even *one* man or woman who will take up the cudgels determinedly for Irish and never relax brain or energies until the work is done, until every boy and girl in the district is being taught Irish, one who will at the same time act wisely and discreetly in endeavouring to bring this about.

The Means

The practical steps to be taken are outlined in a circular letter being issued by the ever watchful Education Committee of the League which points out that 'with the increased scale of fees for teaching Irish in National Schools 3s., 6s., 9s., and 12s. per head on the average attendance as an ordinary subject and 4s., 6., and 8s. for Bilingual Programme now in operation there is no longer any reason why Irish should not be taught in every school, and that the present being an opportune time for moving to extend the teaching of Irish in the schools every Craobh is requested to take steps without delay to ensure that the language is placed on the programme and time-table of all schools in its district where it has not hitherto been taught.

'Craobhacha are also asked to secure (1) that Irish History is regularly taught in the schools; (2) that text books of an Irish character are used; (3) that patriotic books and *An Claidheamh Soluis* and the other Irish Ireland papers are placed in the hands of the senior children; (4) that the pupils are encouraged to support Irish industries and manufactures.'

The circular further advises that "at least half an hour per day should be demanded for the teaching of Irish in all standards and that half hour preferably in the early part of the day while the children are fresh. It may be taught partly within and partly outside school hours in the case of the upper standards to qualify for results fees. The importance of teaching Irish orally on the Direct Method beginning with the most practically useful words and phrases should be laid stress upon. Memorising simple pieces of prose and poetry is also useful, provided the pupils are got to understand the meaning of each word and to pronounce it accurately.

'Branches are requested to hold a special meeting at the earliest possible date to urge on the schools the national and educational importance of teaching the language and history of Ireland amongst the rising generation. If necessary a deputation of parents should be appointed to wait on the managers and teachers in the matter. Managers requiring teachers qualified to teach Irish for their schools may as a rule obtain suitable persons through the Gaelic League by writing to the General Secretary, who will be glad to receive timely information whenever a vacancy occurs in any of the National Schools in the district.

'Where the National Teachers are not qualified to teach Irish on the Direct Method teachers' Irish Classes should be organised. The teachers should also be urged to arrange to attend a month's course of training at one of the Irish Colleges (Ring, Ballingeary, Partry, Cloghaneely), the certificates of which are now accepted by the National Board as satisfactory qualification in Irish to earn fees.

'If there is not already a Múinteoir Taistil in the district the fees for Irish make it comparatively easy for any three or four active branches combining together to employ such a teacher and so greatly advance the effectiveness of the organisation and of the Irish teaching in the district. Suitable young fellows or cailíní to teach may be obtained through this office at very moderate salaries.'

Patience

Whilst we feel that for some time to come there must be patience taken with many places where Irish is not taught until circumstances alter and make its introduction comparatively easy, still we shall not hesitate to give special prominence in future as in the past to instances where the language remains untaught through sheer hostility or negligence. Even in many of these latter cases it will be well to realise that hostility and negligence more often than not proceed from ignorance, and hence the first essential in certain places is to spread the light by means of propagandist literature or lectures. Possibly the most prudent step for sympathisers willing to work in these untilled fields would be to obtain supplies of Gaelic League pamphlets for circulation amongst persons likely to derive benefit therefrom or else to arrange for a few explanatory lectures on the Irish language movement in the local hall or schoolroom where none exists.

The measures to be taken will vary according to the district, but we hope someone will be found everywhere to move promptly and practically in this all-important matter of the education of the rising generation on Irish lines. We look forward to beholding this year a record advance both in the learning and using of the Irish language which are, when all is said and done, the two main issues to be kept constantly in view by every true Gaelic Leaguer.

THE BILINGUAL PROGRAMME AT WORK
19.10.1907

This article is being written from a home in a Western parish into which the custom of speaking English to the children has not yet penetrated. There are about four thousand souls under the care of the sagart pobail. Within a radius of five miles the only genuinely bilingual children are those of the schoolmaster, and even these speak Irish better than English. Every other gasúr or gearr-chaile in the parish is, for all practical purposes, monolingual, — *i.e.*, exclusively Irish-speaking. There are grave and revered seniors in the movement who will doubt these statements. Let them come and see. We have spent the morning in a vain search for an English-speaking child who has not been to school — not that we should have been glad to find one, but that we wanted to discover for ourselves whether such a being existed in the parish. Our search has been crowned by a glorious failure. Irish is the language in which every mother who comes to Mass at Ros Muc or Camus, or Leitir Mhór, sings her children to sleep, praises them, scolds them, rules her little domain. The result is that the children come to school purely Irish-speaking. But the Bilingual Programme is in swing in the parish, so that each child is taught both Irish and English at school. Taking into consideration the fact that the children here rarely remain in school beyond the Fourth Standard, and very rarely indeed beyond the Fifth, they are given during their short school course a very fair literary knowledge both of Irish and of English. On leaving school, Irish remains their language, but they are able and willing to speak English to strangers. In other words, things are developing in this Western parish precisely as we foretold they would develop five years ago when we first began to organise the movement in favour of bilingual education. Irish *is not* being killed. It *is not* being displaced by English. English is being learned as a 'second language' and is being kept strictly in the place of a 'second language'. Irish, on the other hand, is being learnt as a literary as well as a spoken tongue, and the young lads and (to a lesser extent) the girls are eager readers of such Irish books and papers as reach them — indeed, they, in several instances, are commencing to produce Irish prose and poetry themselves. Ros Muc is thus demonstrating not merely the feasibility but the absolute success, from the Irish no less than from the general point of view, of bilingual education.

THE BILINGUAL PROGRAMME: A NEED
2.11.1907

We have little doubt that the Bilingual Programme, carefully and intelligently worked, and backed by a reasonable amount of public opinion favourable to the language, will spell the salvation of living Irish in the Irish-speaking districts. We have simply to educate a generation of Irish speakers on really Irish lines, and the language and indeed the whole tradition of Irish nationality will be safe as regards that generation and the generations springing from it. The education — in Irish — of the young Irish speaker: we might almost sum up the entire task of the movement in these words.

It is very possible that there is not yet a school in Ireland — if we except the League's own secondary school at Rinn — in which an Irish education in a really adequate sense is being given to the pupils. But we have personal experience of a number of schools in which, under circumstances of peculiar difficulty, a courageous attempt is being made by the teaching staff to give an education predominantly Irish in tone rather than English; in which Irish is the ordinary medium of intercourse between teacher and pupils; in which the Irish lessons are the most important events of the day; in which Irish is used rather more than English in giving instruction in such subjects as geography, mathematics, elementary natural science, and so on; in which English is taught as a 'second language' more or less on the direct method, as French is taught in the Flemish-speaking districts of Belgium.

There are two things which prevent the work in these schools from being as efficient as the work in even the more backward schools in Flanders. The first is the National Board, with its machinery of Senior Inspectors, Junior Inspectors, and so on, still in the main hostile; the second and more serious is the lack of special training on the part of the teachers themselves. This is a lack for which the Board and not the teachers must be blamed. The bilingual teachers, considering their disabilities, have done wonders. But bilingual education will not march until the teachers in the Gaedhealtacht are given an opportunity of qualifying themselves to conduct it on strictly scientific lines. We trust we are right in assuming that the training of the bilingual teachers in the specialist knowledge required for the proper handling of the Bilingual Programme will be the first task taken up by the new organisers of the National Board.

WITH OR AGAINST?
9.11.1907

Last week we commented with some reserve on the report that the Bishops had adopted a resolution which, in effect, removes Irish from the list of obligatory subjects at Maynooth. We were loth to believe that such a proposal had been made to their Lordships by the administrative authorities of the College; still more loth to think that the Bishops, or any committee or sub-committee of the Bishops, had as much as considered such a proposal, if made. Even still we find it difficult to give credence to the story, repeated though it has been with circumstance. We are informed that the President of the College formally applied to the governing body for authority to dispense from the obligation of taking Irish any student who finds (which really means who alleges that he finds) the study of the language hampering him in his general course; that this authority was granted; that about fifty students have already applied for and received permission to discontinue Irish; and that even more students are about to apply for and will doubtless obtain the same dispensation. If all this is true, it means that the national language has now been degraded to a lowlier position than it has ever occupied in the official curriculum of Maynooth. It will stand henceforward just where it stands in Trinity — an extra, an exotic, a stranger just tolerated within the gates ('so long as it does not interfere', etc.); its study will be a matter for the enterprise and enthusiasm of the individual student; the seoinín and the staigín will be afforded every facility, will be granted every consideration, in their retreat from the Irish class-room.

Once more, is it true? If it is true, it becomes necessary for us to ask in all seriousness whether Maynooth is with us or against us. We had thought it was with us. The most brilliant of its Professors are certainly with us. The great bulk of the clean, brainy young Irish manhood which fills its class-rooms is with us no less certainly. But is the College as an institution with us? Is its immense influence on the spiritual, intellectual, social, and political life of Ireland to be thrown into the scale for us or against us? Is Maynooth going to stand in Ireland for the Gael or for the Gall? If it has made up its mind to stand for the Gael, why its *volte face?* Why this re-tracing of steps taken laboriously Irishwards during the past few years? Why this eating of fine professions, this cooling down of ardent enthusiasm? Why this turning of the back on the grave of O'Growney?

The situation is serious. The Irish language is dying. The most effective — we do not say the most deliberate or the most culpable — agent in its destruction is the non-Irish-speaking priest in the Irish-speaking district. Every sermon preached in English to an Irish-speaking congregation, every chance word, every kindly salutation, every piece of fatherly advice addressed in English by a priest to an Irish-speaking parishioner, is a nail in the coffin of vernacular Irish. The priest who does these things is not always to be blamed. He may not know Irish. It was not spoken to him at home, it was not taught to him at school, or at the Diocesan College, or at Maynooth. He is too old or too busy — or imagines himself to old or too busy — to learn it. Perhaps he knows it, but has fallen out of the habit of speaking it. In this respect he is no worse than many of his neighbours — landowners, doctors, solicitors, well-to-do farmers, shopkeepers, schoolmasters and schoolmistresses. But whilst no more culpable than these — perhaps less culpable, all things considered, than most of them — he is, in point of fact, a greater menace to the life of the language than any of them; and this just because of the respect and reverence which are due and so freely rendered to him by his flock. 'The priest speaks English: why not we?' This, in substance, is the retort of nine Gaedhilgeoirí out of ten whom a layman reproaches for addressing his children in Englsish.

There are those who hold — we believe that the Cardinal Primate is amongst the number — that were the Irish language to die in Ireland, with it would disappear the surest earthly safeguard of the faith of Ireland. Now the Irish language will die unless a generation of Irish-speaking priests be sent abroad into the Gaedhealtacht. We had thought that Maynooth had taken upon herself the proud and holy task of breeding up such a generation. Were we mistaken? Are priests, in the future as in the past, to go forth from the College of O'Growney to preach in the language of Queen Elizabeth from altars around which only Gaedhilgeoiri kneel?

The Gaelic League and the Irish public will require to know Maynooth's attitude. The matter is too vitally important to the interests of the race, and (if the Cardinal is right) to the interests of faith also, to be decided behind the backs of the public in a closed room. All Ireland is interested, and has a right to be interested, in the training given to her future priests in the National Seminary. In the name of Ireland the Gaelic League claims that instruction in the national language shall form an integral portion of the education of every Irish priest. It will not be so easy to 'kick the Gaelic League down stairs' as some people in high place imagine.

MAYNOOTH AND IRISH
16.11.1907

We have received ample confirmation of the amazing tidings from Maynooth on which we commented in our last two issues. It is all too true. The Bishops of Ireland, at the instance of the President of the College, have virtually degraded the national language to the status of a purely voluntary and extra subject in the National Seminary. The only attempt at an explanation of or an apologia for their Lordships' action which has reached us is the following from a correspondent who desires to be known as 'X': —

'Dear Sir — I should feel obliged to you if you would give me space for a few observations on the article in your last issue in which you dealt with Maynooth and its attitude to Irish. You say: "We are informed that the President of the College formally applied to the governing body for authority to dispense from the obligation of taking Irish any student who finds (which really means who alleges that the finds) the study of the language hampering him in his general course; that this authority was granted . . . . ." The words which appear in brackets suggest that any imaginary excuse will suffice, but as I understand the matter, a dispensation will be granted only when the President feels satisfied that the reasons alleged by the student are such as entitle him to relief. You may take it for granted that the President is no enemy of Irish and will exercise his power with all regard for the true interests of the language. At all events I think you should judge him by the manner in which the rule has worked under his direction, in the present year.

'Irish hitherto has been obligatory only in the Junior House, that is, during the first two years of the College Course, but the real work and the genuine enthusiasm have always been found in the two higher divisions. I do not wish to minimise the work done in the Junior classes. It is highly valuable as a preparation for more serious study and if there were the least likelihood that such work would cease through the operation of dispensing power or in any other way, many voices would be justly raised in protest.

'You say that about fifty students have already been dispensed. That, I believe, is true. I do not believe, however, a further statement which you make that many more will apply for or receive dispensations. You seem to be unaware that some, how many I cannot say, have applied and have been refused. Of the fifty students dispensed one-third are students who have already failed or are in grave danger of failing at their examinations. You must bear in mind that, in a large College like Maynooth, a rather considerable fraction of the students belong to the class who cannot succeed at their examinations without devoting all their time and energy to the effort. Of the remainder I cannot speak, but I should hope that they were relieved for valid reasons.

'The regulation made by the Bishops at their last meeting may not be permanent. I have no doubt that if a better regulation be suggested by the Professors or by the President it will be at once accepted.'

'X'

It is desirable that we should recall the history of Irish at Maynooth somewhat more fully than is done by our correspondent. Since the foundation of the College there has been in existence a rule by which all the students coming from dioceses in which Irish is spoken — that is to say, more than half the dioceses of Ireland — have been bound to attend Irish classes during portion of their College career. For some fourteen years past — since, we believe, the appointment of An tAthair Eoghan Ó Gramhna to the Irish chair — *all* the students of the College have been bound to attend Irish classes, at first for three years and more recently for two years of their course. A few years ago, as most of our readers will remember, the Bishops proposed to make Irish a purely voluntary subject and actually adopted regulations to that effect; but so strong a protest was made by the Gaelic League and the Irish Ireland public that these regulations were rescinded, and the language remained a compulsory subject of study for all students in the Junior House. The effect of the decision just arrived at is to gain possession by a flank movement of the position which it was then sought to carry by a frontal attack. Under the former legislation the student could drop Irish without formality: now he must go through the form of applying to his Bishop, through the President, assigning reasons.

True, our correspondent points out that a dispensation will be granted only when the reasons alleged by the student are such as, in the President's opinion, entitle him to relief. He assures us that the President is no enemy to Irish and asks us to judge him by the manner in which the rule has worked out, under his direction, in the present year. Now, this is a test which we are perfectly willing to apply. As far as we can ascertain, no dispensation which has been applied for up to the present has been refused, putting aside the cases of students from the dioceses of Waterford, Kerry, and Galway. The Bishops of these three dioceses have declined to permit any of their students to drop Irish. These exceptions apart, the dispensations asked for appear to have been granted wholesale. They have been granted, we gather, to students from the dioceses of Armagh, Dublin, Clogher, Cork, Tuam, Cashel, Ferns, Derry, Dromore, Achonry, Ardagh, Killaloe, Kilmore, and Ossory — and, as we believe, granted in every instance in which application was made, — granted in all to some fifty students, or about one-third of the total number to which the compulsory regulations applied. This does not point to a careful and perfectly impartial consideration of the reasons alleged by the students in favour of dispensation. It points rather to a promiscuous rush for dispensations from several dioceses and to an indiscriminate grant of such dispensations by the College authorities.

Our correspondent further points out that about one-third of the exempted students were students who had already failed or were in grave danger of failing at their examinations. But what of the remaining two-thirds? And with regard to this one-third who had failed or were in grave danger of failing at their examinations, was it not possible to lighten their load by exempting them from some subject of less comparative importance than the Irish language? There are other compulsory subjects at Maynooth which, when it comes to a question of choosing between them and the national language, might well be thrown overboard. Why was Irish selected for sacrifice in preference to, say, Logic? Logic is important: but can it compare in importance with the national language? Can it, for an Irish priest, compare in importance with the language which is the trusty vehicle of the faith of Ireland? Can it, for a priest who is to work in the Gaedhealtacht, compare in importance with the language which is the *only* tongue of a portion of his flock and the more intimate and familiar tongue of his whole flock?

Incredible as the statement may appear, Irish has now, for the first time in the history of Maynooth, ceased to be a compulsory subject of study even for future priests whose missions will lie in Irish-speaking districts. As already mentioned, students from the dioceses in which Irish is vernacular have, ever since the foundation of the College, been obliged to study the language during a portion of their College course. Henceforward, even such students may be dispensed: nay, numbers of such students (notably from the dioceses of Tuam and Killaloe) *have* been dispensed within the past few weeks. This means that priests ignorant of the veriest rudiments of Irish will during the next few years be sent out from Maynooth to minister in Irish-speaking districts. Matters in this respect have, in all conscience, been bad enough in the past: in the future they will be worse. Heretofore the student has had at least to sit out his Irish lectures: henceforth he is free even from this obligation. Irish sinks lower than it has ever been in Maynooth, lower than it is in Trinity College. In Maynooth Irish becomes a voluntary subject: it is no worse off in Trinity. In Trinity there are valuable

144

sizarships and scholarships for the encouragement of Irish studies: in Maynooth, as far as we know, there is nothing of the kind. One cannot become a clerk under the Dublin Corporation without knowing Irish: one can become a priest and minister in Aran or Garumna without knowing a syllable of it.

And those who seek to inflict this huge wrong on Irish education, on the Irish language, and on the faithful simple people who speak Irish as their vernacular are not the 'National' Board, nor the Intermediate Board, nor Trinity College, nor Dublin Castle, nor the British Treasury. They are the Bishops of Ireland. The decision was come to at a plenary meeting. It was, we presume, sent forward for the Agenda of that meeting by the Board of Visitors, consisting of the four Archbishops, with the Bishops of Ferns, Raphoe, Clonfert, and Cloyne, — all, or practically all, of whom have prominently identified themselves with the language movement. Are we to understand that these prelates were present when the recent legislation was passed and they acquiesced in it? It seems incredible. But how in their absence, or in the teeth of their opposition, could it have become law?

The part which has been played by the President of the College in bringing about this most calamitous decision is one of the most disquieting and regrettable phases of the whole question. Dr. Mannix is a young man. Instinctively one feels that he should be with the Gael. We, in common with most Irishmen who hailed with satisfaction the announcement of his appointment to the Presidency of Maynooth, hoped for much from his energy, progressiveness, clear-sightedness, and broad national sympathies. Can it be that where Irish Ireland hoped to find a friend she has found an enemy, and an enemy who is in a position to do her untold harm? We are unwilling to believe it. Rather, we imagine that Dr. Mannix has been led away by his anxiety for the success of his College on the academic battle-ground of the Royal University. He conceived that the necessity of having to take Irish was a handicap to a number of his students, and, doubtless without adverting to the disastrous consequences inevitably entailed, proposed to the Bishops his scheme for lightening their programme. We would all wish to see Maynooth hold her own against the Queen's Colleges and her other competitors in the Royal University and elsewhere; but there are things more important than academic success. A national language is more important, a nation's life is more important, the spiritual welfare of 600,000 Irish speakers is more important. What shall it profit Maynooth to cut a fine figure in the Royal University Results List if the Irish language dies in the Gaedhealtacht and with it the old, pure, unquestioning, strenuous faith of Ireland?

THE SITUATION AT MAYNOOTH
23.11.1907

Can things at Maynooth be altogether as bad as our recent leading articles have made out? This is the question which, in one shape or another, some thousands of Gaels have been putting to one another during the past few weeks. We wish we were in a position to reassure them. Unfortunately, we are not. The following letter from a correspondent *who knows his facts thoroughly* goes to show that in our anxiety not to overstate our case we have, far from magnifying the gravity of the situation, rather understated it:

145

'I have been following with intense interest the series of articles in *An Claidheamh* for the last few weeks, concerning the recent decrees of the hierarchy of Ireland regarding the study of Irish in Maynooth. I would like to add yet another article. Let me discuss the letter of 'X' in your issue of November 16th, and see how far his is right and how far he is wrong. It may turn a new side to the gaze of some people.

Irish is now put on the same level with German, Italian, etc., in Maynooth! What reason for this step? Well, one of the members of the council of studies in the National Seminary has come to our rescue. "Irish should not be compulsory while the students are graduating in the R.U.I."

The idea the authorities have in their heads is this, that Irish is hampering the efforts of those who, otherwise, would shine in the Result Book of the R.U.I., and therefore to give the greatest possible freedom to those students, they may, by application, on sufficient grounds (whether alleged or otherwise), be dispensed from the obligation of learning Irish. Let us see what has happened. 'X' says fifty dispensations were granted. I can say with certainty not more than five, if at all five, were refused dispensations! — He says one-third were those who were in danger at their examinations. I say not half one-third of these were in danger. If they were in danger, or if they had already failed, it was not because they were learning Irish, but because they were not learning Irish or anything else. They were attending lectures, but nothing more. If they worked moderately at their subjects, I say even moderately, they would not fail.

What about 'X's' remaining two-thirds? I have a greater number to account for, but I will do so. Some got dispensation for the sake of making (in Maynooth parlance) a "howl" at the examinations. These were the guns (?) who came in with either French or Greek honours in the Intermediate and who would not let this Irish movement interfere with their smashes.

Those of this class who did happen to do Irish in the small seminary, and who perhaps, had been fairly successful — I shall go farther and say they had been very successful — gave up Irish because the total marks assigned to Greek is higher in the R.U.I. examinations (at least in I and II Arts). This is patriotism, isn't it? To give up all chance of learning our own tongue for the low mean reason of self-interest! But someone will say: later on these young priests with their classical degrees, etc., etc., etc., will be an ornament to their Church and country. I hope they will be an ornament to their Church and country but will they be anything else? Will they remain ornaments? Will they teach the people? Will they confess the people? Will they fulfil thir duties as priests to the people as mediators between the Creator and his creatures? How can they, if they do not know the language of the people?

So much for the guns, who in the opinion of the President and their bishop had perfectly valid reason for leaving the house Irish classes and devoting all their energy to making examinations for the "howl" (I cannot help using the word; it expresses my meaning perfectly). What about another class? Well, to be brief, they are those who are too lazy to attend the class, for we have such in Maynooth as anywhere else. But there is a third division. They stated as their reason that they were hampered by the study of Irish. What did they do when they were free? Oh! hush — went and joined the Italian class, some even joined both Italian and German!!!! There is reason for you! If they got dispensed from Irish, why in the name of all that's wonderful and sacred and otherwise, should they be allowed into an Italian class? This is the manner in which the rule has worked up to this.

'X says: 'The real work etc. was done in the senior divisions! Certainly there is far more opportunity for doing work in those divisions, and I admit all Mr. X says about the real work etc. being done there. But what is that due to? It is due to the fact that Irish was learnt in the junior division.

'What does Mr. X mean by valid reasons? Could any reason be valid enough to defend a man who does not wish to study his own language?

'Mr. X also says the work in the junior division was (I presume he means when Irish was compulsory) highly valuable as a preparation for the more serious study. I believe him; what is going to happen now? Are we going to begin the preparation when we should be in the middle of the more serious work? If we are, I pity Maynooth. I pity the priests who leave it and go to the Irish-speaking people to lead them to salvation while ignorant of their tongue!...'

Our correspondent, we think, disposes of all the valid reasons for dispensation except one. It is stated that several of the exempted students, notably several of those from Tuam, have been exempted on the ground that they already know enough Irish! Now, we know the archdiocese of Tuam fairly well and we have yet to meet the priest or layman — not to mention that raw student from a seminary — who knows so much Irish that he is incapable of profiting by a two years' course of organised and carefully-directed Irish study. Who are these wonderful Tuam men who, at so very callow an age, are already whole and complete Irish scholars? Some of them are doubtless good Irish speakers. But is it not notorious that the most efficient agency in killing the irish language in the archdiocese of Tuam has been the preaching and teaching in English of Irish-speaking priests? And if you ask one of these priests why he preaches and teaches in English, he will answer: "The English comes easier to me. I have not the technical terms in Irish. I can talk about the weather and about the crops in Irish right enough, but when it comes to discussing sanctifying grace and the matter and form of the sacraments — well, I'm stuck". To put it bluntly, these priests, whilst fine Irish speakers, are illiterate in the language. They cannot read it or write it with any ease, — perhaps not at all. They have no acquaintance with its literature. They have not read the Gospels, or any devotional or theological works, in Irish. They know nothing of Dunleavy, or O'Gallagher, or the Irish *Imitation*. They know nothing of Keating, with his vast store of just such 'technical terms' as are required in preaching. In other words, they lack precisely that training, literary and 'technical', in the language of their flock which it should be the duty and the privilege of Maynooth to give them. And this is the state of affairs which it is now sought to perpetuate!

As we stated last week, dispensations have been granted to students from the dioceses of Armagh, Dublin, Tuam, Cashel, Clogher, Cork, Ferns, Derry, Dromore, Achonry, Ardagh, Killaloe, Kilmore, and Ossory. The Bishops of Waterford, Kerry, and Galway — all honour to them for it — have refused to dispense any of their students. It does not appear that

147

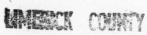

any applications for dispensation came from the dioceses of Meath, Limerick, Ross, Cloyne, Elphin, Clonfert, Kildare, Killala, or Raphoe – a fact which is infinitely to the credit of the students of these dioceses. We gather that the applications from Clogher, Dromore, Achonry, and Ossory, were inconsiderable in number, but those that were made were granted without difficulty. Applications have also been freely granted in the cases of Cork, Ferns, Derry, and Armagh. The applications and dispensations would seem to have been on a large – we might almost say a wholesale – scale in the cases of Dublin, Tuam, Kilmore, Ardagh, Cashel, and Killaloe. Kilmore and Ardagh appear in the same unenviable light in this matter as that in which a recent press paragraph places them with regard to the entrance examination. The action of Meath, on the other hand, seems to offset the figure which that diocese cut on the same occasion. The Dublin record is simply inexplicable. Sadder still is the rush of Tuam students to get dispensed, and saddest of all the *exercise* of such dispensing powers in the archdiocese of Mac Hale. It is all very disquieting. Missionaries to foreign countries must needs learn the language of their flocks. Missionaries to the Irish-speaking districts of Ireland are now definitely 'dispensed' from the same obligation.

IN THE SECONDARY SCHOOLS
23.11.1907

Úna Ní Fhaircheallaigh has rendered an important service to Irish education in general and to the study of the national language in particular by her vigorous and unflinching criticism of crude methods of language teaching and her continued protests against 'examination by pen and ink' in the striking series of reports which she has issued during her tenure of the Advising Examinership in Irish under the Intermediate Education Board. This year's report has been widely commented upon, though it only repeats and enforces the views energetically put forward in three or four previous reports. Even in the Intermediate schools there has been a wave of interest in rational teaching methods, and of this the Examiner finds ample evidence in the answer-papers of the candidates. But much has to be done ere Irish can be said to be taught as a really living language in even a majority of the secondary schools. The first and most obvious thing to do is to provide for efficient inspection and *viva voce* examination; the second, and finally more important, is to adopt means for the training of the teachers. It is one of the many anomalies of the Irish education system that whereas the primary teacher has to pass through a long course of training, the secondary teacher is called upon to conduct very much more advanced educational work with absolutely no training at all. Cheapness is the chief recommendation for a secondary teacher in Ireland. The National teachers have grievances enough in all conscience; but secondary teachers and secondary education groan, all unnoticed, under grievances immeasurably greater. There are reputable Intermediate schools which pay each of their 'professors' for a full week of six days, five or six hours a day, the stately sum of ten shillings – on which he has to feed and lodge himself and to look 'respectable'!

To return to Úna Ní Fhaircheallaigh's report. She gives a detailed criticism of the work done in the various grades, but the following sums up the general status of the language in the Intermediate schools: –

'Once again the increase in the number of entries marks the ever-spreading enthusiasm for the national language. There is much excellent work to report and some work that is very far from being excellent. The teaching in some of the schools, it is easy to see, is oral and on the Modh Díreach, but in a large number of schools the teacher still adheres to antiquated methods of teaching, the ear of the pupil is left untrained and the mind works at the language in the same way it might work at a proposition in Euclid or a sum in mental arithmetic. The examiners are powerless to cope with this evil as a whole. They can do little more under the present system of examination than check the tendency and point out the result.

There are two defects at the root of sight-teaching in language: (1) the want of training in method on the part of the teacher and (2) want of practice in the spoken language on the part of the pupil. If the success of a system in modern language teaching is to be guaged by the number of competent speakers of the language which it turns out, then the evident result of the Irish programmes in the Intermediate, though brilliant as compared with the results in other languages, still falls sadly short of what might be expected from the expenditure of energy involved. If Irish is to be taught as a living language in the secondary schools, it is absolutely necessary that the teachers be trained, and that the examination be oral as well as written.

At present the teachers who go to the trouble of studying method and of teaching on rational lines do so because of their personal conviction, not because there is anything in the system which forces them to work on those lines. As a matter of fact, rational methods are sure to be recognised indirectly in the quality and live force of the students' answering, but it is quite possible at present for the more easy-going teacher to fag the student's brains by memory work and to burden him with the weight of a dead language and yet be rewarded at the end of the year for the success of his school. No guarantee as to the teacher's competency is required and the examination is a written one, and that in spite of the repeated efforts of the Intermediate Board, which has tried, time and again, to reform matters in this direction. Until all this is changed there can be no real progress in language-teaching in the secondary schools.

More attention is being paid to the Irish forms of place names, but a great deal still remains to be done in this direction. As for personal names, the craze for translation into some English form vaguely resembling the original still remains amongst us. Tadhg, for instance, is variously rendered as Tim, Timothy, Thady, Teig, Tague, Thade, Tige, Tom and Thomas. It is for the teachers to cultivate a proper mental attitude on the part of the children towards native names and to warn them against random translations. Translations of names except in peculiar instances are quite unnecessary. We speak of a Frenchman as Jules or Jean, not as John or Jack, even in speaking English. Why should we try to render Séamus by James or Seaghán by John?'

MAYNOOTH
30.11.1907

What is Maynooth going to do? This is the question which is on the lips

149

of Irish Irelanders everywhere. The incredulity with which the first startling rumours were received has given place to anxiety and to vague, but very real, misgivings as to the future. Where do we stand? A fight between the Gaelic League and a British Government Department — the 'National' Board, the Intermediate Board, Dublin Castle, the Lords of the Treasury, — seems natural and commonplace. A battle royal with Trinity College is only an exhilarating diversion. We enter into these contests with a certain buoyancy and lightheartedness, the issue lying clear before us, the contestants each under his own colours, each raising his traditional war-cry. But here it is different. It is our own who have struck this blow at us. It is the beloved College of O'Growney that has declared itself with the Gall and against the Gael. Men whom we had thought trusty had failed us. Revered and honoured leaders have seemed to countenance their betrayal.

Let it not be thought that we are writing hysterically. Matters at Maynooth are as bad as they can be. We have the word of students, Professors, and at least one Bishop for it. We do not, of course, imagine that Irish study in the College is to come to a sudden standstill. In spite of, perhaps because of, the recent hostile legislation it will go on more ardently than ever amongst that not inconsiderable body of the students who have vowed their young intellects to the service of fatherland as they have vowed their young hearts to the service of faith. But Maynooth as an institution, the official Maynooth, has laid it down that success at the Royal University is of greater moment than the life of the Irish language, involving though it does the life of the Irish nation, and according to Cardinal Logue, the spiritual welfare of Irish-speaking men and women.

And of this attitude — taken up, as we believe, hastily and without forethought by the governing body of the College — the students of the Junior House, to the extent of one-third of their number, have availed to effect their retreat from the Irish classroom and, as we gather, are spending the time 'gained' in twiddling their thumbs and drumming their heels or (in the case of those studiously inclined) in learning a smattering of Italian and German — languages which they will never have occasion to speak even supposing (which is unlikely) that they ever acquire anything like a speaking knowledge of them.

And all the while Irish-speaking congregations are crying mutely for pastors willing and able to preach to them and to teach them in their own language. Irish-speaking penitents are struggling to utter the inmost thoughts of their souls in a speech which is unfamiliar to them. Dying sinners are longing in vain for a few words of kindly consolation in the language nearest and dearest to their hearts. The priest is by their bedside, but, as far as they are concerned, he is a dumb priest.

These are things we do not care to write, but they are things which must be written. We are not theorising or generalising from insufficient evidence, or building up a case on hearsay. We know our facts. We can give chapter and verse for our statements. The personal experience of scores of readers will bear us out.

Within our own knowledge a young priest, wholly ignorant of Irish, yet working in an Irish-speaking district, was called to attend the deathbed of a parishioner who knew no English. The dying man appeared to be troubled by some dark memory which he longed to confide to the minister of God. To his horror the priest was unable to understand him. The latter, much perturbed, gave absolution , but the dying man was not consoled: he felt, poor soul, the necessity of whispering his secret into the confessor's ear, not

150

understanding that in the circumstances of the case the Absolution was as efficacious as if the latter had understood all. His agony of mind was frightful to witness. Finally, the priest was obliged to call in a third person and to hear the confession through an interpreter.

We submit with the greatest respect that such should not be possible in holy Ireland. They are not only possible, but are inevitable as long as non-Irish-speaking priests are sent to minister in the Gaedhealtacht. At the present moment there are possibly not enough Irish-speaking priests to staff all the missions in the Irish-speaking territory. We had hoped, however, that Maynooth was marching full speed to the rescue. Was that hope a vain one? Is the Gaedhealtacht to be left for another generation at the mercy of the Béarlóir? And where will the Gaehealtacht be then?

It is our profound conviction that through her influence, direct and indirect, on Irish life Maynooth is in a position, if she chooses, to save the Irish language. To those who feel thus and have hoped accordingly it is like receiving a sudden blow in the face to be told that the hand of Maynooth is to be stretched forth, not to save the language, but to strangle it.

DR. MANNIX AND THE COISTE GNÓTHA
28.12.1907

At the meeting of the coiste Gnótha the Ard-Rúaidhe was instructed to write to the President of Maynooth College for information as to the truth or otherwise of the rumours with regard to the altered status of the National language in the College curriculum to which publicity has just been given by *An Claidheamh Soluis* and other newspapers. In pursuance of these instructions the Ard-Rúnaidhe, on December 7th, wrote to the President of the College as follows: —

The Gaelic League,
24 Upper O'Connell Street,
Dublin.
December 7th, 1907.

The Right Rev. Monsignor Mannix, D.D.,
 President, Maynooth College,
  Maynooth.

Right Reverend Sir,
 I have been desired by the Executive Committee of the Gaelic League to bring under your notice a statement made at their last meeting to the effect that a regulation had recently been made by the Maynooth College authorities, providing that students studying in Maynooth for the Examinations of the Royal University of Ireland may be dispensed from studying the Irish Language in the College, and also that many students had already been so dispensed. My Committee were much surprised at this statement, and sincerely hope that the R.U.I. Examinations will not be allowed to hamper, or in any way interfere with, the study in Maynooth College of a subject so extremely important as the national language. The Committee are deeply impressed with the gravity of the matter, being of the opinion that, apart from the question of the study of the language in Maynooth itself (which they, of course, do regard as of paramount

importance), the example of the premier ecclesiastical college in Ireland would undoubtedly have a seriously damaging effect on the study and status of the language in many schools and colleges throughout the country.

It was also stated that though there is, it is understood, a rule providing that students must have a reasonable knowledge of Irish when entering Maynooth, last year students were admitted whose knowldege of that language was practically nil.

I shall be obliged if you will kindly let me know at your earliest convenience how the matter stands.

Hoping there is no foundation for these rumours,

I am,
Your obedient servant,
Pádraig Ó Dálaigh,
General Secretary.

The following was Dr. Mannix's reply: —

St. Patrick's College,
Maynooth,
8th December, 1907.

Dear Mr. O'Daly,

I have received your letter of yesterday's date, in which on behalf of the Executive Committee of the Gaelic League, you made certain inquiries about the course of studies prescribed in this College. In reply, I desire to say that any information that I am in a position to give is to be found in a convenient form in the College Calendar, of which I shall gladly send you a copy.

I need scarcely assure your Committee that the interests of the Irish language are safe in the keeping of the Trustees and of the students of Maynooth College. And as I shall not be suspected of taking any credit to myself, I may be allowed to add, that it will be a day of joy and of hope for the friends of the national language when the Gaelic League, in its great work throughout the country, begins to follow the example and to rival the success of Maynooth. The Irish language will then be safe.

I am,
Dear Mr. O'Daly,
Very faithfully yours,
D. Mannix.

Mr. Patrick O'Daly,
General Secretary of the Gaelic League,
Dublin.

The copy of the college Calendar did not reach the Ard-Rúnaidhe until a few days after the December meeting of the Coiste Gnótha. When it did reach him it was found to contain no information whatever on the points covered by his queries. The Calendar, as a matter of fact, consists mainly of names and of programmes. It gives the Irish programme drawn up, for study within the College, and mentions Irish as one of the subjects in which candidates are supposed to pass an examination previous to entrance. It does not, however, state for what students Irish is a compulsory subject, or whether it is compulsory for any. For all the information the Calendar vouchsafes, Irish may be studied by every student in the College or it may be studied by none.

In acknowledging receipt of the Calendar, the Ard-Runaidhe wrote: —

The Gaelic League,
24 Upper O'Connell Street,
Dublin.
December 19th, 1907.

The Right Rev. Monsignor Mannix,
  St. Patrick's College,
  Maynooth.

Right Reverend Sir,

I beg to acknowledge the receipt of a copy of the Maynooth College Calendar for 1907-8, for which I am much obliged.

Having looked carefully through the Calendar, I regret to say I have failed to find therein the information required by my Committee. In my letter to you of the 7th inst. I stated that my Committee had been informed (1) 'that a regulation had been made by the Maynooth College authorities, providing that students studying in Maynooth for the Examinations of the Royal University of Ireland might be dispensed from studying the Irish language in the College, and also that many students had already been so dispensed'; and (2) 'that though there is, it is understood, a rule providing that students must have a reasonable knowledge of Irish when entering Maynooth, last year students were admitted whose knowledge of that language was practically nil'. Would you kindly refer me to the page of the Calendar where the information with respect to these points is to be found?

I am,
Right Reverend Sir,
Your obedient servant,
Pádraig Ó Dálaigh,
General Secretary.

To this Dr. Mannix, who is at least a punctual correspondent, replied as follows on the same topic: —

St. Patrick's College,
Maynooth,
19th December, 1907.

Dear Mr. O'Daly,

I have received your letter of this day.

I regret to learn that your Committee seems to require information regarding our course of studies which the College Calendar does not supply, for the purpose of the Calendar is to furnish all the information that can be reasonably required by those who are interested in the curriculum.

Apparently my previous letter was not quite clear. But I endeavoured to convey that I was not in a position to add anything to

153

the information given to your Committee and to the public generally in the College Calendar.

I am,
Dear Mr. O'Daly,
Very faithfully yours,
D. Mannix.

Mr. P. O'Daly,
General Secretary, Gaelic League.

It will be observed that the President of Maynooth takes up the attitude that the public is not entitled to any information as to what goes on in the College beyond that which is contained in the College Calendar. 'The purpose of the Calendar is to furnish all the information that can be reasonably required by those who are interested in the curriculum'. Does the President seriously mean to stand by this? Does he think that he *can* stand by it? The Calendar, as we have stated, contains no information that is really pertinent. It gives the programmes drawn up for study, but we know, as a matter of fact, that the programme in Irish is *not* studied by as many as one-third of those for whom it is drawn up. It specifies Irish as a subject in which an examination must be passed at entrance, but we know, as a matter of fact, that students were admitted last autumn whose knowledge of Irish was literally *nil* — who failed to secure a single mark at the Irish examination, and who have been heard boasting of the fact in the College quadrangle. May not those interested in Maynooth 'reasonably require' more information than is supplied by so very unsatisfactory a Calendar?

But, apart from the imperfections of the Calendar, we submit that the Irish public is entitled to know just as much as it wants to know about the studies — at any rate about the secular studies — of the students of Maynooth. Maynooth belongs to the Irish public. It is endowed by the money of the Irish public. The Church for whose ministry it is educating its students is voluntarily supported by the Irish public. Everyone in Ireland — non-Catholic as well as Catholic — has an interest in Maynooth, for Maynooth touches Irish life at every point, and affects, directly or indirectly, the destiny of every man and woman born in Ireland. The Irish public is no impertinent outsider in this matter, as the President would seem to suggest. It wants to know how its money is being spent, how its sons are being educated, how its vital interests are bing consulted or otherwise. The young men at Maynooth are our own, — our brothers, our cousins, our sons. It is we who send them to Maynooth; it is we who pay Maynooth for educating them; it is amongst us they will work when they emerge from Maynooth. Their spiritual education we are content, and shall always be content, to entrust to the hands of those whose special function it is to direct such things; but their secular education is a matter in which we claim to have a voice, — a claim which we intend to make good against all who impeach it. Dr. Mannix not only impeaches that claim, but impeaches our right to information as to the College curriculum. Every student in Maynooth might be expelled from the Irish class-room tomorrow morning and sent to learn Chinese or Choctaw, but, according to Dr. Mannix, the mere Irish public would not only have no right to intervene, but would have no right to any information as to what was going on! This is autocracy with a vengence.

It remains to be seen whether the Bishops will adopt a similarly haughty

154

than has hitherto been manifested in the primary schools, the Committee, on November 27th last, addressed a memorandum to the Resident Commissioner on the subject of the Direct Method, pointing out the desirability of its general introduction, and dwelling on the obstacles which, under existing circumstances, stand in its way. Foremost amongst these obstacles is the fact that the testing of Irish teaching in the schools is still carried out on the old-fashioned 'Text Book' or 'Translation' method, with the result, of course, that teachers who have already adopted Direct Method principles are discouraged from persevering and other teachers are deterred from commencing.

The Committee grouped under the following heads what it considered to be the main obstacles, under existing conditions, to the teaching and inspecting of classes on the Direct Method: —

1. The programme for Irish in National Schools does not make sufficient provision for teaching on the 'Direct Method'.
2. The inspection of classes is not conducted on such lines as would test the quality or results of teaching that has been based upon the 'Direct Method'. Classes taught on the 'Direct Method' have been inspected on the unsuitable lines of the 'translation' method.
3. The Inspectors, as a body, are not familiar with the principles of 'direct Method'.

By way of ameliorating this state of affairs, the Committee proceeded to urge the following recommendations:—

(a) That the 'Direct Method' be explicitly recognised in the School Programme for Irish, and that suitable provision be made for it therein.
(b) That the Inspectors should receive special courses in the principles of the 'Direct Method' of teaching languages analogous to the course in Science and Manual Training which they received upon the introduction of these new subjects in 1900. The Committee will be prepared to arrange for such a course, or courses in the Leinster College if it be considered desirable.
(c) That the inspectors be instructed to base their inspections upon the 'Direct Method' in classes in which it has been employed in teaching, and to encourage the use of this method.
(d) That in order to secure efficient teaching, and to prevent a continuance of the present anomalous discrepancies in the value of the certificates, the standard for the National Board's certificate of qualification to teach Irish should be raised to the standard set by the Gaelic Training Colleges for their certificates, and that the programme for those certificates should be based upon the 'Direct Method'.
(e) That in order to provide for the higher standard recommended in the preceding paragraph, a second modern language, in addition to English, be made compulsory at Entrance Examinations to the Training Colleges, and for all seeking teacher's certificates.
(f) That the regulation against the teaching of Irish for fees within ordinary school hours be withdrawn, as, amongst other grave objections, this official restriction militates against the employment of

extern teachers, many of whom have been trained in the 'Direct Method', and on the high standard of the Gaelic Training Colleges.

To these points Dr. Starkie replied as follows on December 12th: —

(a) The Commissioners are in favour of the use of the 'Direct Method', and the question of giving more prominence to this system of instruction will be considered in connection with the preparation of the next issue of the Rules and Regulations.

(b) The majority of the Irish Inspectors and organisers in the service of the Board are familiar with the 'Direct Method', but some Inspectors, from want of practice in the language, might find it difficult to employ it. Should the Committee arrange for special courses in the principles of the 'direct method' in the Leinster College, facilities will be afforded to any Inspector who may wish to attend.

(c) Inspectors, etc., will be instructed where necessary to base their inspection upon the 'direct method' in classes in which it has been employed, and to encourage the use of this method.

(d) The question of keeping the Board's Programme of Examination for Certificates in Irish, as well as the standard of marking, up to the level of the best of the Gaelic Training Colleges, will not be lost sight of. It appears that the standards of the certificates granted by the Gaelic Training Colleges vary from College to College.

(e) The inclusion of the second modern language in addition to English in the examination for entrance to Training Colleges and for all candidates seeking teacher's certificate, though, no doubt, very desirable, is not considered expedient at the present time; but the question will not be lost sight of.

(f) It is considered most inadvisable that the teaching of Irish as an extra subject within the ordinary school hours should be allowed, as the work to be accomplished within these hours is already sufficiently heavy. Complaints are frequently made in teachers' journals, etc., as to alleged overcrowding of the ordinary school programme in its present form.

Having expressed its satisfaction with the assurances (a) and (c) that more prominence would be given to the Direct Method in the new issue of the Board's 'Rules and Regulations', and that Inspectors, etc., would be instructed to employ it in inspections and to encourage its use, the Committee, in a letter dated January 10th, proceeded to make the following observations on the other points: —

(d) My Committee are pleased with your promise that the standard for the Board's Certificates in Irish will be kept up to the level of that of the Gaelic Colleges. Wtih reference to the alleged variation in the standards of the different Colleges, they wish to point out that the courses and standards for the Certificates of the Gaelic Colleges are kept fairly equal by the fact that many members of the staffs and governing bodies are closely associated with different Colleges. In addition, at a conference of representatives of Colleges held here on the 8th June, 1907, a minimum standard for the Certificates of all the Colleges was agreed to on the basis of such a knowledge of Irish,

Method of Teaching, and Phonetics as would be necessary for the proper teaching of the full programme for Irish submitted to the Board by the Gaelic Association of National Teachers.

(e) My Committee's interest in the suggestion as to a second modern language at the Entrance Examination for the Training College is, of course, confined to the Irish language, but they recognised the necessity of an alternative. They are convinced that if the standard for the Teachers' Certificate is to be on the same level as that of the Irish Colleges a fair knowledge of Irish on entering will be essential.

(f) My Committee's views on the question of teaching Irish for fees within ordinary school hours are expressed in the following resolution, which has already been forwarded to the Secretaries of the Board: —

'That it is the opinion of the Committee of the Leinster College of Irish that the regulations of the Commissioners of National Education preventing the teaching of Irish for fees within school hours is contrary to the spirit of the arrangement made in Parliament last year for payment of the teaching of Irish; and that it seriously interferes with the teaching of Irish in the schools, and that this restriction ought to be withdrawn immediately, and teachers and managers who prefer to teach Irish for fees within school hours be allowed to do so'.

The announcement of the Board's new policy with regard to the use of the Direct Method is, of course, very satisfactory. We have reason to know that the new 'Hints to Teachers' will embody much of the sound teaching as to the necessity of attractive *viva voce* methods, and their use in practice, which has appeared in *An Claidheamh Soluis* during the past few years. It is to be trusted that the Inspectors of the Board will avail to the full of the special course which is to be provided for them at Coláiste Laighean.

In his reply to point (f) Dr. Starkie is cryptic. The reasons he gives in support of the contention that it is most inadvisable that Irish should be taught as an Extra Subject (*i.e.*, we presume, for fees) within school hours, would, if valid, show that it is equally inadvisable to teach Irish as an Ordinary Subject within school hours. But the Board specifically provides for the teaching of Irish as an Ordinary Subject, supplies teachers with a specimen programme for Irish as an Ordinary, and instructs its Inspectors to promote the teaching of Irish as an Ordinary as a necessary supplement to its efficient teaching as an Extra. We trust that the Committee of the College will press Dr. Starkie to be more explicit and candid on this point. Is the Board for or against Irish teaching within school hours? If it is against it, then we must see to it that it revises its attitude; if it is for it, then the reasons which Dr. Starkie gives for declining to remunerate it cannot be the true reasons, — or rather they cease to exist.

WAITING
1.2.1908

Once more — such is the perverseness of her destiny — the eyes of Ireland are, not, as the old proverb has it, 'ar Bhaile Átha Cliath', but on —

Westminster. Once more a King's Speech is expected to make a momentous announcement with regard to the plans and intentions of British ministers for our future. Once more the fates and fortunes of unborn generations of Irish people are being discussed and settled by permanent secretaries and their clerks in Whitehall. Non-political as we are in these columns, we are not railing at or bewailing these facts: we are merely stating them. And lest the statement, growing prolix, lead us into forbidden ground, we may summarise it and get rid of it in one sentence by saying that once more an Irish University Bill is on the *tapis*.

We are not over-sanguine of the propects of this Bill, — we have seen and heard of so many of them. Yet we think it would be unwise, and we hope that Gaels in general will adopt a similar view, to throw unnecessary obstacles in its way or to dash an anticipatory douche of cold water in its direction before it even appears. For this reason we deprecate would-be-heroic resolutions proclaiming that the Gael will have nothing to do with this British-made University: the circumstances are all against it, yet there remains the chance that the Bill may pass into law and that it may embody the nucleus of a University settlement which Ireland, by judicious kneading and shaping, may ultimately mould into such a settlement as, if she were mistress of her own house, she might have herself evolved. At all events it behoves us to reserve our judgement until the measure is actually before us. When it appears we may find ourselves in a position to support it or we may find ourselves under a moral obligation to fight it. For the present we stand and wait.

But we need not stand idly. There is the off chance of an Irish University *in posse* if not *in esse*, — of a University, that is, capable of development into an Irish University, — and it seems to us to be the duty of Irish Irelanders, as individuals and as an organised body, to strengthen the chance as far as may be. True, it is an English minister who will give the Bill the shape in which it will be presented to the British Parliament; but we may assume that that minister, for the sake of the chances of his Bill if not for the sake of Ireland (though, for our part, we believe that Mr. Birrell has the interests of Ireland as much at heart as any foreigner can whose proper allegiance is first to his own country and next to his own party), — we may assume, we say, that Mr. Birrell will make an honest attempt to produce a Bill which will embody Irish ideals and opinions so far as he has been able to collect them? That he has been active in endeavouring to collect them we know: but has he succeeded? Have his advisors been the right advisors? Has he adverted to all the conditions of the problem? Has he, in particular, adverted to this very important one that Ireland is Ireland, and not merely a part of England which happens in the main to be Catholic in religious persuasion? Has he, in fact, realised that what Ireland wants, and what he has staked his reputation on supplying, is *not* a new West-British University which may satisfy seoinín Catholics, as Trinity satisfies seoinín Protestants, but a *National* University which Catholic and other Nationalists shall be able to enter without doing violence to any one of their religious or national convictions? The part which we suggest Irish Irelanders ought to play in the present conjuncture is to keep this fact before Mr. Birrell right up to the moment at which he introduces his Bill.

Of course, we do not expect that Mr. Birrell or any one else will be able to evoke an Irish University out of chaos and old night by the mere creative force of a British Act of Parliament. But we do demand as a condition governing the acceptance of any University he may offer us, that it shall be so constructed organically as to allow us liberty when we have once taken possession of it to create within it an Irish atmosphere for ourselves. We will not enter into it as the bound slaves of a Westminster-made or Dublin-Castle-made constitution, subject to the autocratic behests of a nominated oligarchy: we — the men and women of Ireland — must be its masters, and must have the moulding of its future. Put concretely, what is required is that the element known vaguely as the 'democratic element' should have its due share in shaping the courses, the *personnel*, and the general policy of the institution. The 'democratic element' must express itself mainly through the spokesmen of the rank-and-file graduates and professors, whose representation on the governing bodies of the University and of its constituent Colleges must be ample. A further channel (favoured, so it is rumoured, by the framers of the Bill; and to which we have no radical objection) would be through nominees of the local public authority, acting on the governing body of each College. The degree of autonomy with which each College is to be endowed, the relations of the College Council to the University Senate, the prestige and resources of the new Dublin College in the matters of buildings and finance, — are all points upon which, despite the existence of floating rumours, we are still almost entirely in the dark, and satisfactory assurances on which must largely govern the attitude of Irish Ireland towards the Bill.

It will be observed that we have not called on Mr. Birrell to make Irish the language of the new University or even to insert a clause in his Bill providing that after the lapse of a certain number of years the courses shall be conducted bilingually. These are matters which do not concern Mr. Birrell at all. They are matters which we Irish people must settle for ourselves, and what we are demanding from Mr. Birrell is *Liberty* so to settle them. Give us a University over which the men and women of Ireland shall be the masters and leave it to the men and women of Ireland to fashion its future. Give us anything else and you give us something which, far from benefiting us, will be a hindrance on the path which we have marked out for ourselves, and with which Irish Ireland at any rate will have nothing to do.

IRISH IRELAND AND THE UNIVERSITY QUESTION
8.2.1908

The King's Speech at the opening of the English Parliament (a Scotch Gaelic friend objects to our calling it the British Parliament) has announced the intention of His Majesty's Ministers to introduce legislation 'to improve and extend University Education in Ireland'. The official formula is elaborately vague and carefully colourless, — a trick which King's Speech announcement's have. It may cover anything or nothing. We cannot pretend to be palpitating with subdued excitement. We live in hope, — 'all men, we hope, live so'. Our duty at present is to do what in us lies to strengthen the somewhat slender chance of a settlement of the Irish University question which is promised by the announcement that has just been made. It is with a view to help Mr. Birrell rather than to throw obstacles in his way that we state Irish Ireland's demands as frankly as we do.

What Ireland wants is an Irish University. 'Explain yourself,' says Mr. Birrell. 'What do you mean by an Irish University? I ask for information. I am an Englishman, and I don't understand these things. You couldn't in reason expect me'. We don't, – hence our anxiety. But we shall try to give him light. Mr. Birrell is a Cambridge man. As Cambridge is English, so must our University be Irish. It must catch up an Irish tradition, it must be the seat of an Irish culture, it must be the nerve-centre of an Irish education system. It must be such that from the outset it shall fire and enthuse with a generous love of work for Ireland the young men and women who shall flock to its halls; that it shall give them a stimulus Ireland-wards whose force shall persist through all their lives to come; that it shall in the fullness of time become the breeding-place of generations of cultured Irish-speaking gentlemen and gentlewomen. 'God bless me!' we imagine Mr. Birrell exclaiming, 'do you expect me to do all this?' No, we don't – but we demand from him, and from those for whom he stands for the moment, *Liberty* to accomplish all this for ourselves.

And here we are back again at the point at which we stopped last week. Unless this University be handed over to the people of Ireland to fashion according to their will, then the people of Irleand would be well advised to have none of it. We have already indicated the ways and means by which, in our opinion, the people could be given such a control over its destinies as we demand. When we say the people we do not mean the benevolent fogies – medical men with expansive waistcoats and aggressive watchchains, elderly lawyers whose brains have become obfuscated in the dust of the Four Courts, clerics who for thirty years have not come into vital contact with the practical problems of Irish life at any one point – who pose, and whom we too often implicitly recognise, as the 'leaders of educated opinion' in Ireland. This must be a University of Young Men (and Women) if it is to do any good for Ireland. Lay and clerical, Catholic and Protestant, men and women, let those who are to guide the destinies of our National University belong to the new generation which has felt throughout its nervous system, however faintly as yet, the galvanic shock of a re-awakened national consciousness. Our faith in the younger men and women even of this anglicised generation in Ireland is unbounded. Give the young men and women that share in the government of the University, in the shaping of its courses, in the appointment of its *personnel*, which they are entitled to, and all will go well: commit its fortunes to the charge even of the best intentioned of the old-fashioned school and you predestine it to failure.

Some of the names we have heard mentioned as those of persons likely to be nominated to the Senate of the new University are not such as to inspire us with hope. Prominent are the names of one or two determined foes of Irish nationality. The men – there are no women – of Irish sympathies amongst them would, with one or two exceptions, appear to have been selected for personal amiability rather than for vigour. Some of them would be deadheads on the Senate; others the unconscious catspaws of the representatives of the garrison. It seems to us that now is the time to point out all this rather than when the names are officially announced.

There must be a Senate boldly Irish in sympathy to start with. There must be College Councils fully representative of the rank-and-file graduates and professors, and possessing a large amount of autonomy. The mode of appointment to professorships must be satisfactory – a suggestion that a vacant chair should be filled by election by the members of its own faculty, subject to the approval of the Senate, seems worth consideration. The independence and Irish 'atmosphere' of the University thus secured, we should have little fear of its future. The young men and women of Ireland might be trusted to mould it into a genuinely Irish — that is, a genuinely Gaelic — University. We take it for granted that from the outset Irish would be a compulsory subject at the Matriculation Examination; that there would be ample provision, in the way of scholarships, studentships, and so on, for the encouragement of Irish studies throughout the pre- and post-graduate courses; that in the later stages there would be special provision for the encouragement of Irish research; and that there would be Chairs of Celtic Philology (with special reference to Old and Middle Irish), Modern Irish Language and Literature, Ancient Irish History and Archaeology and Modern Irish History. This, we think, would be Irish Ireland's minimum demand. It is just as well that it should be stated.

THE SCHOOLS
15.2.1908

A short notice published by the Commissioners of National Education in the daily papers of Wednesday last is of momentous importance. It runs: —

'The Commissioners of National Education desire to give notice that it is their present intention that in the year 1911, and subsequently, candidates for admission to Training Colleges shall be required to undergo examination in one language, in addition. to English'.

This announcement marks the beginning of the end of the fight for the Training Colleges. It represents the happy fruition of an agitation which has been carried on by the Gaelic League publicly and privately for the last five years. The Irish language is not mentioned in the Board's carefully-drawn-up paragraph, but with the Gaelic League abroad in the land, the regulation will automatically work out in such a way as to make Irish the practically universally-studied 'second language' of candidates for admission to training. Before the rule comes into force the movement will be strong enough to see that *all* the Training Colleges make due provision for the continuance of their Irish studies by the students after they have entered training. The era of Bilingual Education for all Ireland has been brought appreciably nearer.

Indeed, there are now only one or two minor reforms to be pressed for preparatory to the great forward move for Bilingualism all round. One of these is already within sight. We mean the alteration of the existing rule with regard to the remuneration of Irish teaching in the case of schools where Irish is dealt with by an Extern Teacher. The Extern Teachers must be remunerated for Irish teaching even when done within school hours. The reasons for this demand are obvious. Except in favourable cases, the Extern Teacher cannot make a living wage unless remunerated for work done inside the school day. The half hour from 10 to 10.30 each morning — which he can and ought to supplement by another half-hour within the 'ordinary' hours — gives ample opportunity to the regular teacher of a school both to teach the language properly and to earn his fees. Not so with the Múinteoir Taistil who has six or seven schools to cover in a week, and cannot possibly give two half-hours (the minimum required) outside the school day to each of them. The League should therefore press with all its energy for the adoption of a rule whereby Extern Teachers shall be remunerated for Irish teaching, whether done inside or outside the 'ordinary' school hours. The demand is an eminently reasonable one and cannot long be refused.

Craobh an Chéitinnigh has just issued a 'Memorandum on the Teaching of Irish in the National Schools', which is interesting from the historical point of view, as containing a well-written *resumé* of the ups and downs of the Irish Fees, but proceeds to urge the movement to embark on a line of agitation which, in our opinion, would be most ill-advised, undignified, and possibly disastrous. It wants us to demand the payment of special fees for Irish when taught as an ordinary subject, even by the regular teacher of a school. It is a demand which we do not think the movement ought to make. *An Claidheamh Soluis* led the successful agitation for the granting of a Bilingual Programme. It led the successful agitation for the restoration of the Irish Fees. It led the successful agitation for the appointment of a staff of Organisers of Irish Teaching. It led the successful agitation for the making of a second language compulsory at entrance to training. It is prepared to lead the agitation for securing of the positions of the Extern Teachers. But — there is nothing like being frank — we are not prepared either to lead or to take part in an agitation for the remuneration of Irish teaching by the regular teacher of a school within the ordinary school day.

Our reasons are numerous. Strategically, it would be most ill-advised for the movement to embark on an agitation which has not the slightest chance of success. From the language point of view, success, even if possible, is undesirable. At present Irish can be taught both as an Ordinary and as an Extra subject. It is for the movement to insist that it be taught as an Ordinary Subject in every school in Ireland. There is no reason why the teacher should be specially remunerated for teaching it as part of his ordinary day's work. It is his duty to do so. To admit that the teaching of Irish within school hours by the regular teacher of a school is an extra and special service for which the teachers deserves extra and special pay is to give away our case that Irish is the National language. Irish can be taught and must be taught, just as English is taught, as part of the ordinary school work, for which the teacher is remunerated by his regular salary. If the salary is inadequate agitate for an increased salary all round, but *do not* for all time label the National language as a genuine 'extra' by demanding special fees for its teaching by the ordinary teacher within the ordinary school day.

Finally, we do not think it would be consonant with the dignity and public honour of the language movement to base a huge agitation on what most of us have all along suspected, and what we all now know, to have been a verbal slip on the part of the official who drew up the reply given by the Attorney-General for Ireland on May 16th last. The League did not ask for fees for Irish as an Ordinary Subject. It asked for the restoration of the fees for Irish as an Extra Subject, withdrawn by Mr. Walter Long — with the substitution, however, of a graduated scale. This is what we have got. There are one or two minor but important points in which this scheme can ·be amended, and for the amendment of which we mean to press. Our main business at present, however, is with the managers and teachers rather than with the Board. Quiet and steady work in the school for the next five years and then — the Bilingual Programme for the country at large. This is our policy.

THE MARCH OF BILINGUALISM
29.2.1908

The fact that the Bilingual Programme has already been established in a hundred and ten schools and that at least an equal number are preparing for its introduction at the opening of the new school year on July 1st, shows that the education question is slowly righting itself in the Gaedhealtacht. Indeed, when we remember how far off most people still thought bilingual education as recently as four years ago, 'slowly' seems scarcely the word to use. The fact is that we are advancing quite as rapidly as anyone can in reason have hoped we should. Five years ago, when *An Claidheamh* commenced to write up the subject, 'bilingual education' was a vague term denoting some very wonderful and revolutionary system of education in vogue in such impossibly 'advanced' and 'up-to-date' countries as Germany and Belgium. We recall the solemn head-shakings with which old-fashioned people inside and outside the League greeted our early articles, and the whispered question of the wiseacres. 'What new fad is this that *An Claidheamh Soluis* has taken up? Bilingual Education! Let us try to get Irish taught as a subject, as a school subject, first. In twenty years' time we may be talking of bilingual education'. Yet today bilingualism is a commonplace in Ireland, and the only important question that remains outstanding is when is it going to be applied to the Galltacht as well as to the Gaedhealtacht?

Last year we took part in an organising tour in Tír Chonaill. We visited parish after parish in which the Bilingual Programme was still merely a name — in some cases not even a name, for it had never been heard of. Everywhere we went we held little meetings of teachers and managers, explaining, advising, encouraging. Nearly all the teachers knew Irish, but not more than half were teaching it. Today if we were to go over the same ground our difficulty would be to find a school in which the Bilingual Programme has not been established, or in which, at any rate, the language is not being taught both as an Ordinary and as an Extra in preparation for the introduction of the Programme next year or the year after. The parish which was then the gloomiest in outlook has turned out the most progressive and hopeful of all. One school of which we all but despaired has just set the Programme going with — already — the happiest results. In appealing to the public spirit of the teachers we used to make the point: 'the Bilingual Programme is established in twenty-one schools in Co. Galway. In all Tír Chonaill it has been established so far only in one. What a contrast!' The contrast is now the other way about. The Programme is today in operation in as many schools in Tír Chonaill as it is in Galway and Mayo combined.

Iorrus has been stirring since last year, but much still remains to be done. A similar remark applies to Tír Amhalghaidh and to Umhall Uí Mháille. Moving into the most Irish part of Ireland, Conamara proper, Duthaigh Sheoighe, and Iar-Chonnachta badly need attention — especially the two former: in the last-named the Programme is in the ascendancy, though the teachers confessedly stand in need of expert advice and assistance in pioneering it. We wish it were possible to make Conamara the venue this year of a great educational organisation campaign similar to last year's most successful campaign in Tír Chonaill. Unlike Tír Chonaill, a large proportion of the teachers in Conamara are non-Irish-speaking and progress here will necessarily be slower. This is one of the main difficulties in the remote West. Tír Chonaill and the greater part of the Munster Gaedhealtacht raise their own teachers. The more Irish West has to import largely from the Galldacht, for rarely does a boy or girl from an Irish-speaking village in Aran or Iar-Chonnachta become a school-teacher. They have not the necessary funds, or they leave school too soon and go to America. Managers and teachers in the West should assist the League in endeavouring to remedy this state of affairs. One means of doing so is by co-operating with the Scholarship Scheme.

In Clare the Programme was at work in one school only last year. We have not detailed information as to its progress since, but we should hope that July next will see its establishment in at least those schools — unfortunately there are not many of them in Clare — in which the children are Irish-speaking. Kerry partly makes up by the excellence of the work done in some of its bilingual schools for the still comparatively small number which have adopted the Programme. It should be in operation throughout Corca Dhuibhne, Íbh Ráthach, and the greater part of Ciarraghe Luachra. Crossing the border into Cork, Béara, Corca Laighe, Musgraighe, Íbh Laoghaire, and the South-East corner bordering on the Déise are all districts in which the Programme should be universally established. True, the children are not Irish-speaking everywhere, but they come from semi-Irish-speaking homes, and Irish cannot be ignored as a factor in their mentality and intellectual environment.

Last the Déise. Waterford was the only Irish-speaking county unrepresented in last year's list of forty-two bilingual schools, but this year the standard of bilingualism has been raised in two or three improtant posts in Dúthaigh Dhéise. Even in Ring we expect developments.

THE SCHOOLS
7.3.1908

Coiste an Oideachais — a body whose silent work has been a more potent factor than most people are aware of in securing recent improvements in the status of Irish in primary education — has just sent out a very valuable and suggestive circular letter in which the branches of the League are urged to interest themselves more actively than ever in the work of securing its rightful position for the national language in the primary schools of the country. We have now large facilities for Irish teaching in the primary schools, and until these facilities are availed of by, at all events, the great majority of the teachers and managers, it would be premature to call a forward march against the Board. The points which the Branches are asked to attend to in their efforts to establish the teaching of Irish on a satisfactory basis in their respective districts are: —

1. Attractive and efficient methods of teaching.
2. Sufficient and suitable time for holding the lessons.
3. Cultivation of the right spirit amongst the pupils.
4. Home and other encouragement.

The circular goes on: —

'With regard to 1, every possible effort should be made to induce the teachers to attend a course at one of the Irish Colleges, so that they may study the 'Direct Method' and other essentials of successful language teaching. As is pointed out on page 123 of the Regulations of the Commissioners of National Education, 1907-8, *"Irish should be used as exclusively as possible during the Irish lesson. All directions should be given to pupils in Irish and all responses received from them in Irish. Explanation of Irish words and phrases through the medium of Irish should be attempted as early and as much as possible.* When writing Irish exercises, pupils should be taught to write their names and the dates in Irish." Not alone should Irish be used during the Irish lessons, but *it is absolutely essential that it be used frequently by all teachers and monitors throughout the day in school directions, etc.,* in order to produce fluency in the language on the part of the pupils. Memorising songs and short stories is also most desirable, provided due attention is given to securing that the pupils have the correct pronunciation and understand what they get off by rote.

'With regard to 2, at least half an hour per day should be provided for Irish in each class, and that preferably in the earlier part of the day whilst to the junior classes (Infants, 1st and 2nd Standards), *within what* constitutes the 'attendance', and in the case of the upper standards either from 10 to 10.30 every morning or partly within and partly outside the 'attendance'.

The Teaching of Patriotism

'Point 3. This is extremely important. In fact, without the spirit of patriotism animating both teachers and pupils, it is hopeless to expect much progress in Irish knowledge. Hence, side by side with the language teaching, the history and knowledge of everything relating to Ireland's past and present should be taught and expounded. The teacher who cannot, if he wishes, arouse a patriotic spirit in the breasts of Irish boys and girls is not worth his salt. This duty of fostering patriotism, it should be known, is officially insisted on in all the States of Europe and in the United States of America, and it is high time to insist, in the interests alike of education and of our national welfare, on its being attended to henceforward in Ireland. In the German Government Regulations for schools, it is laid down that 'the first duty of a German school is to foster an ardent spirit of true patriotism in the young'. The same Regulations acknowledge that 'the most priceless possession of a nation — its own individuality in the noblest and highest sense — is best represented in its language and its literature'. The children's minds should be fired by frequent narration of the stirring deeds of Brian, Art Mac Murrough, Red Hugh, Sarsfield, Michael Dwyer, and the many other heroes figuring in Irish history, and they should be taught to recite the stirring ballads and heroic poetry and legends of Ireland, such as are to be found in the "Spirit of the Nation" and other collections. They should be constantly reminded of and made to realise the fact that they are a separate race from England and that it is a disgrace and a badge of slavery for a race to use the language of any other in preference to its own. Needless to say, they cannot be convinced on this point unless they have a clear and vivid grasp of whom they come from, of what their country was like in the past, and of what nationality or distinctiveness of race consists in the natural order. Intelligent talks and lectures on these matters by teachers or others to the children are imperative. Nothing but a keen sense of nationality and national duty in the individual will ever bring a successful language revival,and the same thing applies to the movement for the revival of national industries. The wrong systems of education, etc., in vogue in this country in the past, by neglecting to foster a spirit of idealism and self-sacrifice in the schools in due proportion to the amount of positive knowledge imparted, have failed lamentably to evolve that sense of individual responsibility so essential to the well-being and progress of a nation. The pernicious systems of education are directly responsible for the advent of that mean, selfish, materialistic "what's the good of it anyhow" point of view which exists amongst large masses of our people. We do not, however, blame the Managers or the Teachers for this. The want of a National University which would voice our native ideals and national aspirations in the highest sense, from which secular education, primary and secondary, should spring and take its tone, and the failure of the Central Boards governing education in this country to make any attempt to supply its absence by providing to some extent in the Training Colleges for Teachers facilities for the cultivation of those branches of national culture such as the Language, History, and Literature, that have in all ages and in all countries been accepted next to Religion as the prime factors in liberal education, are responsible for this unnatural trend of affairs.

'No so-called "setlement" of Irish Educational questions, whether University, Primary or Secondary, can be accepted by the Gaelic League or will, we feel assured, ever finally satisfy the bulk of the people of this nation which does not freely recognise the individuality and ideals which have been handed down to us from the dim distant past of our race as inherent factors in the education of the nation. Any other "settlement" will be against both nature and experience, and, no matter how plausible it may appear in theory, will be sure to fail in practice.

"Éire Óg"
'With regard ot the fourth point, it is of extreme importance in the present stage of transition from Anglicisation (which is the only style of so-called "education" of which the living generations of Irish people have had any experience or knowledge) to the natural basis of Irishism, that there should be positive encouragement given to the youth of the country to step out on Irish lines. Hence the necessity for an active organisation to gain and hold the approval of the parents and of the public for the educational revolution rendered necessary by the wholesale blunders of the past.
'Branches of the Gaelic League should deal directly with the moulding of the character of the rising generation on Irish lines, in addition to working through parents, managers, and teachers. The last Ard-Fheis recommended that an "Éire Óg" Club should be organised in connection with every Craobh, in order to give the children a living interest in the national language, history, songs, dances and games. In this connection the Education Committee desire to suggest that your Committee arrange with the manager and

168

teacher of every school in your district in which Irish is taught for the holding of an examination or miniature Feis on Lá'le Pádraig, or on some other convenient day — provided prizes can be procured from local sympathisers. If possible, a Céilidhe or treat of some sort should be also given to the regular attendants at the Irish classes. The day should be made an annual fixture, and if held on other than 17th March, it is suggested that it be described as Caitlín Ní Uallacháin's Day. The children should be examined in comhrádh, léigh-theoireacht, sgríbhneoireacht, recitation of poetry, story-telling, seanráidhte, prayers and catechism, Irish history, singing and dancing.

"A simple discourse should be given them on love of Ireland and everything Irish. It should be carefully explained to them that the use of English in prefernce to Irish is the badge of conquest and slavery on the race, and why it is we are reviving Irish. The various duties expected of them in the matter of the language, such as salutations, Irish forms of names and addresses, use of Irish badges, mottoes and hatbands, etc., and also towards the industries and products of Ireland, towards Irish games, such as hurling and camóguidheacht, the national music, songs, dances, etc., should be briefly explained to them. The speaking and reading of Irish, and singing of Irish songs *at home*, should be laid stress upon. The other phases of the movement, such as temperance, cleanliness, use of healthy food, uprightness and good conduct, should be touched upon, and they should be warned against Anglicisation in all shapes and forms, emigration and other evils.

'The headings of the discourse might be written on a blackboard for them to copy and write letters or essays upon, subsequently, in describing the events of the day.

'In conclusion, the Education Committee desire your Branch to use its influence to secure that in all new appointments to the position of teacher, whether principal, assistant, or J. A. M., the deciding factor shall be capacity to teach Irish properly combined with proved sincerity, earnestness, and altruism, in the work of building up an Irish Ireland.'

SHOULD WE DEMAND FEES FOR IRISH AS AN ORDINARY
28.3.1908

It has become desirable that we should give the public in somewhat fuller outline than in our previous articles the reasons which have influenced the Coiste Gnótha in deciding not to embark on an agitation for the payment of special fees to the regular teachers of National Schools for the teaching of Irish as an Ordinary Subject. We believe that the views we are about to express will appeal to the common sense of the vast majority of our readers, as they appealed to the common sense of the overwhelming majority of the Coiste Gnótha when urged before it at its February meeting.

In the first place, the language movement should be sane and practical in its demands. We are playing for a tremendous stake, and we should be careful not to compromise ourselves or our cause in the eyes of sober and level-headed people by putting forward fantastic and impossible claims. We must be on our guard against taking up, in the excess of our zeal, any position which we cannot maintain against the world. The position into which it is now sought to force the organisation is untenable from the view-point of the sound educationist. It is untenable from the view-point of the sound administrator. It is, above all, untenable from the view-point of the language movement itself. We claim that Irish is the national language of Ireland. We claim that it should form an integral portion of the education of every Irish child. We claim that the first duty of the Irish teacher, after his duty in the matter of the child's moral training, is to teach the child Irish. The moment we admit that the teacher who does this — who performs this elementary and essential portion of his mimimum duty — is entitled to extra and special payment therefor, we surrender our fundamental claim, — we acknowledge that Irish, after all, is an 'extra' in the true sense and that its teaching is a special and remarkable and meritorious service for which special and meritorious pay is due.

So far as the rules of the National Board are concerned, Irish can at the present moment be taught as an Ordinary Subject to every child in every National School in Ireland. We want to see it so taught. We mean to see it so taught. It is the duty of the teachers so to teach it, just as it is their duty to teach the other subjects which form the essential portions of the education of an Irish child. They have no right to demand, and we have no right to demand for them, special remuneration for teaching this subject any more than for any other teaching which is done within the minimum 'school day' of four hours.

But Irish also enjoys the privilege of being recognised as an 'Extra Subject'. That is to say, in addition to teaching it within the ordinary school hours, the teacher can also teach it outside those hours; and when he does so successfully to children in the Third and higher standards he earns valuable fees in accordance with a scale ascending with the standards. 'Ordinary school hours' is a technical term denoting the minimum four hours that must be devoted to secular instruction in every National School. In the average school they commence at 10.30 a.m., — in many cases not until 11 a.m. Thus, under the existing rules, the teacher has available for the teaching of Irish the half-hour from 10 to 10.30 a.m. — the best half-hour in the whole day. At 10 a.m. the children are all assembled and they are all fresh. No arrangement could be more favourable to Irish than the arrangement which seems to mark out for it this hour above all others. The teacher can give his 'Extra' lesson from 10 to 10.30; having called the roll (in Irish), he can continue his lesson (as an 'Ordinary') until 11 a.m., or, if this is not convenient, he can give a second lesson in Irish later on in the day. We submit that in the average school Irish would not gain, but would lose, if it ceased to be an Extra and became an Ordinary merely. Only the *Ordinary* lesson would be given, and the amount of time devoted to the language would, speaking generally, be reduced by one-half. Conscientious teachers would gain nothing by the change, but lazy and half-hearted teachers would, for they would secure 'extra' remuneration without any 'extra' work.

In another column a contributor endeavours to make out a case for the payment of special fees for Irish as an Ordinary. His is the first attempt to argue his side of the question on its merits that we have seen, and it is not a very successful attempt. His whole argument rest on the *non-sequitur* in his fifth paragraph. He writes: 'All this means that the teaching of Irish during school hours involves far more extra study and labour on the part of the

170

teacher than if taught as an "Extra". Now 'all this' means nothing of the sort. Nothing that has been said in the preceding paragraphs leads up to the conclusion that the teaching of Irish within school hours involves "more extra study and labour on the part of the teacher." In point of fact, it is not the case that it is more difficult to teach Irish as an Ordinary than it is to teach it as an Extra, nor does the teacher who teaches it as an Ordinary require any more elaborate training than the teacher who teaches it as an Extra. *The same programme can be used for Irish as an Ordinary and for Irish as an Extra.* There is no difference in kind or quality between the two things, the sole distinction being as to the hour of the day at which the subject is taught. The teacher who is not competent to teach Irish at 10.30 a.m. is most assuredly not competent to teach it at 10 a.m. The teacher who is competent to teach it at 10 a.m. (and earn his fees) is competent to continue the lesson until 11 a.m., or to give a further lesson at 1 p.m. The contention, therefore, that extra time is required in preparing to teach Irish as an Ordinary, involving the sacrifice of remunerative private work, falls to the ground and with it the case for special payment built up upon it.

It is said, however,: 'We must take the teachers as they are: the majority will not teach Irish unless they are paid for doing it within ordinary school hours'. Now, we refuse to believe that the teachers of Ireland are as mercenary a lot as this contention would make them out. But, granting that they are, we can deal with them by bringing public opinion to bear upon them. We can give them clearly to understand that one of the chief reasons why Irish children are sent to school is that they may be taught Irish, and that Irish they must be taught. 'But this is coercion. Is the Gaelic League going to coerce the teachers to teach Irish?' We do not know that to take the line proposed could be called 'coercing' any more than it can be said that the managers 'coerce' the teachers to teach the Catechism or that the Board 'coerces' them to teach arithmetic. But, at the worst, we prefer to gain our end by 'coercion' of the sort we suggest than to gain it by bribery.

A further point which we should not lose sight of is, that the application of the existing scale of fees to Irish as an Ordinary would constitute a grave danger to the progress of the Bilingual Programme. Teachers in Irish-speaking and semi-Irish-speaking districts would find it at once easier and more profitable to teach Irish as an Ordinary than to adopt the Programme, involving as the latter does the teaching of everything else through the medium of Irish. Now, the most urgent task ahead of the League in the schools is to spread the Bilingual Programme throughout the Gaedhealtacht, and as soon as may be to tackle the problem of its extension to the rest of Ireland. Surely we are not going to tempt the teachers to abandon the Programme by making it easier and more profitable for them to take up something else infinitely less valuable to the movement?

We need hardly refer again to the consideration which we put clearly in a former article and which was urged with force at the meeting of the Coiste Gnótha. It would not become this great movement, standing as it does for a noble cause and speaking in the name of an honourable nation, to build up an agitation on a quibble, — to rouse all Ireland to support of demands having as their basis, not elementary right and justice, not anything that the good of the movement requires, but an alleged promise whose genesis has been traced to the blunder of an unfortunate clerk in a Government office.

Mr. Long withdrew certain fees: we entered on an agitation for their restoration: they have been restored. In common honesty, let us drop the agitation. In common sense, in common justice to our own organisation and our own work, let us settle down to *Do* things now that we have got the chance. 'Agitation' has been the bane of our movement. It has constantly distracted our attention from our own essential work of saving the language in the Irish-speaking districts and operating on the schools with a view to securing the full utilisation of the facilities for Irish teaching which exist. Out task during the next few years lies in the homes and in the schools of the Gaedhealtacht: there we can do more effective, if less showy, work than we possibly can by embarking on another long, and this time wholly unnecessary and absolutely mischievous 'agitation'. Some of us are in danger of yielding to the vulgar notion prevalent in pre-Gaelic League days that the whole duty of an Irishman is to be 'agin the Governmint.'

IRISH IN THE TRAINING COLLEGES
28.3.1908

The announcement upon which we recently commented that in and after 1911 entrants to the Training Colleges for National Teachers will be required to pass in a second language gives one to hope that we are at length nearing the period when the schools of Ireland will be staffed by trained bilingual teachers, – a condition of affairs which must, of course, precede our next great forward march – a march for which the appointed goal is Bilingualism all round. For the next few years the most profitable directions in which we can operate in the department of education are the *training of the teachers for the advent of Bilingualism and the inducing of the school authorities to avail to the full of the large facilities for Irish teaching afforded for by present regulations of the Board.*

The Training Colleges are still very far from what they should be. The most important of the Colleges for Men turned out last year only twelve teachers qualified to teach Irish. The most important of the Colleges for Women turned out only ten. In contrast with these records is that of the young and comparatively small College for Women in Belfast, which turned out fourteen. The De La Salle College, which has honourable traditions of long standing in the matter of Irish teaching, heads the list with twenty-seven. There is no reason in the world why Drumcondra and Carysfort should not do at least as well as this. In both places there is capable teaching power, and the only conclusion one can come to is that the working heads of the institutions are as determinedly hostile to Irish as they ever were – which is saying a good deal. The new College for Women in Limerick turned out last year five teachers certified in Irish. Marlborough-street turned out two. De La Salle, Waterford, and St. Mary's Belfast, are the only two of the six Colleges we can conscientiously congratulate.

THE FEES CONTROVERSY
4.4.1908

While we are thoroughly convinced of the wisdom of the Coiste Gnótha's decision not to embark on an agitation for the payment of special fees to the regular teachers of national schools for the teaching of Irish within

172

ordinary school hours, we have no desire to bar discussion of the whole question by readers of *An Claidheamh Soluis*. The view of Gaels who disagree with us are just as sure of a place in our columns as the views of Gaels who agree with us, always provided that the ordinary journalistic decencies are observed. 'Hear all sides' has been the motto of *An Claidheamh* since its foundation.

Cathal Brugha writes: —

A Chara,

I quite agree with Mr. Walsh's remarks with regard to the insolent tone adopted by you in a recent article on the above question. To call Gaelic Leaguers 'cranks' because they advocate the payment of fees for Irish, within school hours, is insolent coming from anyone, but it is ludicrous coming from the man who, on May 25th last, referred in the following terms to the scheme upon the carrying out of which the cranks are now insisting. "We think the League and the country may accept it as a fairly satisfactory solution of the question. To the average teacher it is better financially than the withdrawn scale of 10s. fees on a three years' course. It is much sounder educationally, and it has in particular these two enormous advantages: — first, in order to qualify for fees, the language need no longer (as under the 10s. regime) be taught as an extra, but may be taught as an ordinary subject; and, secondly, it extends to the Third Standard'.

Your remarks are all the more uncalled for owing to the fact that to the category of cranks they relegate numbers of influential public bodies, committees of Training Colleges, Craobhacha, Coisti Ceanntair, and the Coiste Gnótha itself of the Gaelic League, all of whom have passed resolutions demanding the carrying out of the same scheme. It is, to put it mildly, a rather unique mode of returning thanks to the outside bodies who backed up the Gaelic League's demand to tell them they are cranks for doing it.

In your article of last week's issue you say — 'We claim that the first duty of the Irish teacher, after his duty in the matter of the child's moral training, is to teach the child Irish". Quite right, but then there may be teachers who will neglect their duty to the Irish Language, just the same as the Editor of *An Claidheamh neglects it by not carrying out the definite instructions given to him by the Coiste Gnótha* — his employers. And whereas we should compel the editor of our paper to do his duty, we, unfortunately cannot compel recalcitrant teachers to do so, as we have no control over them. Consequently we can only induce them, and as we have been offered the means of inducing them by Mr. Birrell, we should be indeed very foolish were we to tamely submit to the National Board's interference now. The National Board do not want Irish taught as an ordinary subject (nor indeed as an extra if they could prevent it); but Mr. Bryce compelled them to have it taught and paid for as an ordinary last year, and Mr. Birrell promised to continue the same system with better payment this year. Is there anything cranky in demanding the fulfilment of this promise? Personally, I consider it humiliating to have to ask for, or accept any favour from, an English Government's representative, but we must submit to circumstances, and as any scheme for the payment of Irish must, unfortunately, have the sanction of the British Treasury, we should not, in my opinion, be acting wisely if we accepted a scheme that would cost them less than the one which, according to Mr. Birrell, they have already sanctioned. Goodness knows it is little enough we get out of our own money from England, without the editor of *An Claidheamh Soluis* starting to put excuses into the mouths of one of her Ministers, to enable him to back out of his promise. You say that the promise 'has been traced to the blunder of an unfortunate clerk in a Government office'. Will you tell us that it was an unfortunate clerk who was responsible for Mr. Birrell's speech on March 23rd, 1907, and for Mr. Cherry's statement on May 16th, just two months later?

You inform us that the moment we admit that a teacher who does his duty to the language by teaching it, is entitled to extra and special payment, we surrender our fundamental claim — we acknowledge that Irish after all is an 'extra' in the true sense, and that its teaching is a special and remarkable and meritorious service for which special and meritorious pay is due. We do nothing of the kind, but we have to admit that we cannot compel the teachers to teach Irish if they don't want to do so; and furthermore, we realise that most of the teachers who are at present competent to teach Irish have been rendered so at their own expense, and that teachers who are not competent to teach Irish already may not be induced to make themselves so at their own expense unless they receive remuneration. And we hold that the remuneration given should be given to them for teaching Irish during school hours, as it is *then* that the National language should be taught, and not as an extra outside school hours.

You think that in the average school Irish would not gain, but would lose if it became an Ordinary and ceased to be an Extra. Well, last year Irish became an Ordinary and ceased to be an Extra, and although the payment was only 2s. 6d. and 1s. per head, as against 10s. the previous year as an Extra, yet, according to the General Secretary of the Gaelic League, it was taught to over 50,000 more children last year than in any previous year.

You say 'the teacher can give his Extra lesson from 10 to 10.30; having called the roll (in Irish), he can continue his lesson (as an 'Ordinary' until 11 a.m., or, if this is not convenient, he can give a second lesson in Irish later on in the day'. I would like to know in how many schools it is being done at present; and in how many schools it would be likely to be done if the new idea be adopted of paying travelling teachers, but not school teachers, for teaching Irish as an Ordinary? The argument I have heard put forward by some school teachers, who did not want to teach Irish within school hours, was that the programme was already overcrowded. I can imagine what those teachers would say if you asked them now to do for nothing what the travelling teacher would be paid for. And even if we were satisfied with this fallacy of paying travelling teachers for work that you would expect a school teacher to do for nothing, you tell us that you have it on the highest authority that we must wait until the Lords of the Treasury sanction it. Perhaps you would give us an idea of how long that would be. The British Treasury are seldom over-anxious to sanction any scheme granting money to Ireland, and I suppose you do not mean to assert that the National Board are the people to hurry them up.

You have such a high opinion of the teachers of Ireland that you refuse to believe that 'the majority will not teach Irish unless they are paid for doing it within school hours', and yet you have such a poor opionion of teachers in Irish-speaking districts and semi-Irish-speaking districts that you think 'that the application of the existing scale of fees to Irish as an Ordinary would constitute a grave danger to the progress of the Bilingual Programme', because those teachers 'would find it at once easier and more profitable to teach Irish as an Ordinary than to adopt the Programme'. Well, I don't think you need have any grounds for fear in the latter direction. I have as high an opinion of the teachers of Ireland as anyone, and I thingk too highly of the teachers in the districts referred to to consider they would be so mercenary as to be influenced by such a matter, and even if they were, they would at once see that it would pay them better to adopt the Bilingual Programme, because the fees for it extend to the whole school, whereas as an Ordinary they only begin in the Third Standard.

You say 'Mr. Long withdrew certain fees; we entered on an agitation for their restoration; they have been restored. In common honesty let us drop the agitation'. The fees Mr. Long withdrew have not been restored, and even if they had, do you imagine that because the editor of our official organ has so little driving force in him that he would be satisfied, as his statement implies, that the condition of Irish in the schools this year should be the same as years ago, that Leaguers in general are of the same way of thinking?

You add that 'agitation has been the bane of our movement'. Had you said 'negotiation' you would have been nearer the mark. It was 'agitation' that caused the League's demand for the abolition of the National Board; it was 'negotiation' that lessened that demand, and sent a cap-in-the-hand deputation to the English House of Commons to wait on Mr. Bryce, which deputation so little impressed him as to the strength of the Gaelic League that he had the hardihood to bring in his miserable 2s. 6d. and 1s. scale — a scheme whose only merit was that the fees could now be earned inside schools' hours. Later on it was 'agitation' that forced Mr. Birrell to promise to continue the same scheme, with an increased scale of fees; and it the abandoning of 'agitation' and the restoring to 'negotiation' that resulted in the National Board's refusal to fulfil Mr. Birrell's promise. It would be well for the Gaelic League if its governing body included more 'agitators' and fewer 'negotiators'.

I may add in conclusion, that hitherto I have more than once found it necessary to express the opinion, that whatever the failings of the Editor of our official organ might be, he at any rate always acted from honest conviction. In spite of what has happened. I still adhere to that opinion, but let me tell you that I consider that had he been in the pay of this Shoneen Board, he could scarcely have done their work more effectively, and have still retained his present position.

If the expression 'crank' offends Cathal Brugha or any other honest Gael we unreservedly withdraw it. For ourselves, during our career as an active Gaelic Leaguer, we have been called pretty everything from a Castle Spy to a Modernist and it may well be that we under-estimated the sensitiveness of Leaguers who have not occupied so bad an eminence as the editorship of the 'official organ'. There are persons on Cathal's side of

175

the controversy who weekly impute the vilest motives to us and to those who agree with us, and the existence in our midst of such perennial pests of Irish movements makes it at times a little difficult for good friends like Cathal and ourselves to thresh out our differences of opinion with due kindness and mutual forbearance. In these notes we will studiously refrain from saying anything that might wound the feelings of even the most susceptible and unsophisticated of Gaels.

Unkind and unwary, in view of their extreme sensitiveness, it may have been to describe our opponents as 'cranks', but that it was either 'insolent' or 'ludicrous' Cathal has failed to show. The contention that our attitude now is inconsistent with our attitude in May last does not bear scrutiny. The scheme foreshadowed in Mr. Cherry's answer was in our opinion sounder educationally than the old scheme because it substituted a graduated for a uniform scale of fees: and the prospect of payment for Irish as an Ordinary was welcomed because it would secure the position of the Extern Teachers. It has since been made manifest that the position of the Extern Teachers can be secured in another way and, on this understanding and in view of the undesirability from several standpoints of the special remuneration of the regular teacher of a school for teaching given as part of his ordinary day's work, we — and the Coiste Gnotha — have come to the conclusion that it is not necessary and indeed would not be wise to press the agitation for the general payment of fees for Irish as an Ordinary. The point to bear in mind is that the demand which was backed up by the various public bodies referred to by our correspondent was essentially a demand made in the interests of the League's Travelling Teacher scheme. This is manifest if only from the terms of the resolution of January last in which the necessity of the payment of the Múinteoirí Taistil for work done within school hours was put forward as the basis of the plea for redress.

We regret that so honest a Gael as Cathal Brugha has been taken in by the unprincipled attempt that is being made to represent *An Claidheamh* as acting in opposition to the Coiste Gnótha on this question. We may be wrong, hopelessly wrong, criminally wrong, in our attitude, but if we are, the Coiste Gnótha is hopelessly wrong with us. As Cathal Brugha is, unfortunately, not a memeber of the Coiste, he cannot know its views except through its published utterances; and its latest public utterance on this question is an expression of the opinion that it is undesirable that the agitation for fees for Irish as an Ordinary should be proceeded with. Now, we are an officer of the Coiste Gnótha and one of our duties is to be present at its meetings in order that we may be able to interpret its views in *An Claidheamh*. We beg to inform Cathal that at the February meeting of the Coiste there was an all but unanimous expression of opinion that this agitation should not be proceeded with. It was *after* that meeting, and not until after it, that we publicly expressed the same opinion. At its March meeting the Coiste re-affirmed this opinion in a formal resolution. In view of these facts it is simply childish to pretend that *An Claidheamh* is guilty of 'disobedience', 'insubordination', 'misrepresenting the Coiste Gnotha', and so on. If we are guilty of these things the Coiste has the remedy in its own hands. It can pass at its next meeting a resolution repudiating us.

We not not propose to go over again the ground covered in our leading article of last week. That article answers most of Cathal's arguments. His only rejoinder to our main contention is a counsel of despair. He says, in effect: 'We can't get the teachers to teach Irish as an Ordinary unless we bribe them to do so. Let us bribe them'. We believe that we *can* get the

176

teachers to teach Irish as an Ordinary without bribing them; and even if we believed the contrary we would be no party to the bribing. Better that Irish remain untaught in the non-Irish-speaking districts until there arises a generation of teachers who will teach it because it is their duty to teach it.

Cathal wants us to tell him how many teachers have been teaching Irish both as an Ordinary and as an Extra to the same children, and how many are likely to do so in future. We cannot give him figures, but we are in a position to know that many hundred teachers have been and are doing so, and that the number is daily increasing. Cathal cannot be very closely in touch with the schools or he would know that it is a common and growing practice to teach Irish both as an Ordinary and as an Extra to the same children. Sometimes the same programme is taught under both headings and sometimes the Ordinary lesson consists mainly of oral and the Extra mainly of literary instruction. The knowledge that, if he failed to teach Irish as an Ordinary, the Extern Teacher might be introduced over his head, would be an incentive rather than a deterrent to a recalcitrant teacher. It is obvious that in all schools in which Irish is taught both as an Ordinary and as an Extra the transference of fees to Irish as an Ordinary would work in the direction of wiping out the Extra teaching, with the result that the time devoted to the language would be reduced by one-half. There are not many schools which could spare a full hour out of the Ordinary day for Irish, but every school can spare half-an-hour in conjunction with half-an-hour's Extra teaching. Our aim is to secure half-an-hour's Ordinary and half-an-hour's Extra teaching per day in every school, — with as much incidental teaching in the way of phrases, terms of command, and so on, as the teacher can work in.

The increase in the number of pupils taught Irish in 1906-7 was not due to, but was in spite of, the change in the official status of the language. Cathal seems to be unaware that there has been a continuous rise in the number taught Irish for many years past, and that the rise last year was less remarkable than the rise in several previous years. There will be a further rise this year. Arguing on Cathal's lines, we shall be able to claim next summer that the rise this year has been due to the withdrawal of fees for Irish as an Ordinary, and the restoration of fees for Irish as an Extra! That payment for Irish as an Ordinary during 1906-7 had nothing whatever to do with the increase in the number studying the language is proved by the fact that out of 161,740 children studying it, fees were claimed in the cases only of 24,712! The truth is that as the language movement advances Irish will be introduced into more and more schools, no matter what regulations the Board may or may not make with regard to remuneration for its teaching.

A simple arithmetical calculation will show Cathal that Irish as an Ordinary remunerated under the present scale of fees for Irish as an Extra would 'pay' the average teacher in an Irish-speaking district better than the Bilingual Programme. To suggest that the average teacher in an Irish-speaking district might possibly be influenced by this consideration is assuredly less insulting to the profession than it is to lay down that the general body of Irish teachers will not teach Irish as an Ordinary until they are bribed to do so.

'The fees withdrawn by Mr. Long have not been restored', says Cathal. They have been restored, Cathal, and more than restored, for fees are now available in the Third Standard, and the payment is in accordance with a graduated scale — a point long contended for — which works out more remuneratively for the teacher than the old scale. We are *not* satisfied, a Chathail, that the condition of Irish this year should be the same as years ago, nor does any statement we have ever made imply that we are. The condition of Irish in the schools has, in point of fact, improved enormously within the past year, and it is improving almost daily.

With the 'negotiations' which Cathal denounces we have had nothing to do, but if to them we may trace the present excellent prospects of Irish in the schools as compared with its prospects, say, three years ago, then the Gaelic League has no reason to regret having entered into them.

As to our doing the work of the Board, — well, Cathal will, we imagine, one day join us in a friendly laugh over that taunt.

Piaras Béaslaí writes:—

A Chara,

There are a number of serious mistatements in your article of March 21st, dealing with the Fees Question, which call for contradiction. Distinguishing between the payment of extern teachers and National Teachers, you say: — 'No one on the Coiste Gnótha or outside of it, a few cranks apart, is seriously in favour of giving extra payment to the teacher of a school for teaching the National Language as part of his day's work'. Let us see how this statement is borne out by the facts of the case.

In October of last year the following resolution appeared on the agenda of the Coiste Gnótha from a member, an experienced National Teacher: —

'That as the Commissioners of National Education recognise the teaching of Irish as an optional subject during ordinary schools hours, and as the programme of instruction therein is more difficult than that for the teaching of Irish as an Extra Subject for fees outside school hours, we consider that fees should also be paid in the third and higher standards when taught as an optional subject, should managers and teachers prefer to have it so taught.'

There is no mention of extern teachers in this resolution. Its wording makes it clear that it was the ordinary teacher that was meant, it being taken for granted, of course, that the extern teachers would be accorded the same treatment. Owing to the large agenda, this resolution did not come on at the October meeting, until an advanced hour of the night, and was then referred to Coiste an Oideachais for further consideration. Coiste an Oideachais unanimously recommended its adoption by the Coiste Gnótha; and at a later meeting held on November 11th, they decided to hold a public meeting in Dublin to plead, among other things for 'Díoluigheacht as Gaedhilg mar Ghnáth-adhbhar scoile' (payment for Irish as an ordinary school subject). At the meeting 'of the Coiste Gnótha on November 12th the resolution above quoted was *passed unanimously*.

A month passed, and at the Coiste Gnótha meeting in December it was officially stated that no reply had been received from the National Board to the request embodied in this resolution. General dissatisfaction was expressed at this, and a resolution was handed in demanding the fulfilment of the promise of the Government to pay for the teaching of Irish as an ordinary subject. At the January meeting this resolution, which was slightly amended in the course of

178

discussion, was passed by fourteen votes to seven, in the following form:—

'That, inasmuch as we have received no reply from the Commissioners of National Education to our unanimous resolution demanding the payment of fees for Irish as an ordinary subject in the National Schools, and inasmuch as the Government's Ministers promised in May last to pay such fees for Irish as an ordinary subject: and inasmuch as the regulations since made by the National Board deprive the Múinteoirí Taistil of any chance of performing their work properly; we bind ourselves to a vigorous agitation, and not to desist from it until the Government redeem its pledge to us; and we direct the Editor of *An Claidheamh Soluis* to explain the situation correctly to the public, and to assist in urging the people towards such an agitation.'

The wording of this resolution was clear and explicit, but the officials did nothing! Coiste an Oideachais did nothing! The *Claidheamh* did nothing! None the less the resolution had its effect, for at the next meeting of the Coiste Gnótha, three months after the adoption of the original resolution, a letter was received from Dr. Starkie, in which he promised preferential treatment of the extern teachers, should the National Board agree, and the Treasury sanction the expenditure.

Now, when at last the National Board was showing signs of feeling the pressure brought to bear upon it, would have been the time to force on more vigorously than ever the demand of the Gaelic League. Instead of this the *Claidheamh Soluis* on February 15th published an article in which the Coiste Gnótha were openly defied, and their directions, given in a clearly-worded resolution, were scouted. The Editor of the *Claidheamh* declined to support the agitation.

The *Claidheamh Soluis* now makes the plea that 'the January resolution was supported by a number of members solely on the ground that the granting of fees for the teaching of Irish as an Ordinary would secure the position of the Múinteoirí Taistil', and goes on 'It had not then occurred to these members that it would be possible to secure special treatment for extern teachers. Between the January and February meetings, however, the possibility, and indeed the probability, of being able to secure such treatment was made manifest, and when the Coiste met in February the *raison d'être* of the January resolution had ceased'.

This statement is entirely untrue. The Editor of the *Claidheamh* was present at the January meeting, and knows quite well that the Chairman of Coiste an Oideachais told us that she had it from Dr. Starkie himself that special treatment would be accorded to the extern teachers. This was made the ground of objection to the resolution by those who opposed it; and this question, which the *Claidheamh* now says had 'never occurred to these members at the time', was fully debated. The vote, showing the sense of a large representative meeting of the Coiste Gnótha, was a deliberate condemnation of accepting such a proposal. I go further and say that, as a matter of fact rumours of Dr. Starkie's intentions were being circulated for two months before his letter reached us, and were ineffectively used to prevent the Coiste Gnótha, and the Gaelic League, generally, from embarking on the agitation.

179

Now, as to the resolution of the March meeting which the *Claidheamh* says 'formally associated itself with *An Claidheamh*'s attitude on the question, I will give its history. On February 26th, subsequently to the *Claidheamh*'s disobedience of the Coiste Gnótha, a meeting of Coiste an Oideachais, consisting of three members was held at which the following resolution was ordered to be put on the agenda of the March meeting of the Coiste Gnótha –

'Mar gheall ar gurb' é baramhail an chruinnighthe dheireannaigh go mb'fearr leigint do cheist na Gaedhilge mar gháth-adhbhar scoile nó go socróchfaidhe ceist na múinteóirí taistil, an rún a bhaineann leis an nGaedhilg mar obair lae scoile a scriosadh amach agus ceist na múinteóirí taistil a chur ar aghaidh chomh tréan agus is féidir linn.'

(That as it was the opinion of the last meeting that it was better to drop the question of Irish an an ordinary school subject until the extern teachers question be settled, the resolution dealing with Irish as ordinary work of the day be rescinded, and the question of the extern teachers be advanced as strongly as we can).

It is a remarkable thing that although the three members who constituted this meeting were present at the February meeting of the Coiste Gnótha, they moved no resolution to test the opinion of the Coiste Gnótha on the subject; but that on February 26th, after the *Claidheamh's* act of disobedience of February 15th, they passed this resolution declaring what the opinion of the February meeting of the Coiste Gnótha was. This resolution of Coiste an Oideachais was practically the first important item on the agenda of the March meeting of the Coiste Gnótha, but it was not reached until the small hours of the morning. In the early part of the night there were twenty-seven members present, and the chair was occupied by Eoin MacNeill, our Vice-President. When the resolution came on there were only thirteen members present, in no mood to consider the question. Practically the only matter discussed was whether the resolution was in order or not. Several members objected on the ground that a motion to rescind a résolution already on the books, according to the standing orders, could not be rescinded for six months. These objections were overruled by the new chairman, who, I may add, had not attended a meeting of the Coiste Gnótha since August last, and consequently was technically not a member at all. When the chairman called for a show of hands on the resolution, the proposer of it, who had previously argued that it was perfectly regular and legal, rose and said that, as the legality of the resolution was doubted, she would substitute 'Leigint thairis' for 'scriosadh amach'. The chairman immediately accepted the resolution in its new form – another irregular proceeding – and put it to the meeting. It was passed by eight votes to five. Is it to be maintained seriously now that the passing by a snap division at a meeting of thirteen exhausted members over an hour after midnight, of a retrospective resolution which, even if regularly passed, only urges a temporary abeýance of the agitation, justifies the assertion that the *Claidheamh Soluis* was not 'misrepresenting the views of the Coiste Gnótha'.

Our correspondent goes on to set forth *in extenso* certain lengthy resolutions, including one which he moved and failed to carry, and others which he had on the agenda but declined to move at the last meeting but which, it seems, he contemplates moving at the next meeting. When these resolutions are adopted by the Coiste Gnótha we will give them due prominence in *An Claidheamh*. Our correspondent also intimates to all and sundry that, 'in view of the irregularities of the March meeting' of the Coiste Gnótha he is writing to the President and Vice-Presidents of the League 'asking them for such an expression of opinion as will prevent the repetition of conduct of this kind in future'. Ní beag sin,' he concludes. Ní beag, go deimhín.

Much of what we have written in answer to Cathal Brugha will stand equally well as an answer to Piaras Béaslaí. We cannot be expected to follow his letter paragraph by paragraph. We need only refer him to the wording of his own resolution of January to show him that the plea of the Coiste Gnótha at that meeting was essentially a plea for the Múinteoirí Taistil. Members of the Coiste distinctly stated at that meeting that they voted for the resolution solely with a view to urging forward the case for the Múinteoirí Taistil. In referring to the February meeting Piaras is guilty of very unworthy *suppressio veri*. He fails to state that the outcome of the discussion which arose on Dr. Starkie's letter was a consensus of opinion that the agitation for the fees for Irish as an Ordinary should not be proceeded with. It was, we repeat, in view of that consensus of opinion that in the following issue of *An Claidheamh* we stated that we could not support the agitation. So far from 'openly defying' and 'scouting' the Coiste Gnótha, we were simply carrying out its views. '*An Claidheamh*'s act of disobedience,' in fact, exists only in the heated imaginations of Piaras and one or two other Gaels.

We must attribute to the manifest excitement under which Piaras laboured during the course of the discussion his very inaccurate recollection of what took place at the March meeting. He states that when the resolution came on there were only thirteen members of the Coiste Gnótha present, and that the voting was eight to five. Now, there were at least fifteen members present, and the voting was ten to five. Piaras suggests that had the question come on earlier in the evening the result would have been very different. We are in a position to know that had the question come on earlier in the evening the majority in favour of the resolution would have been much more overwhelming than it actually was. The matured judgement of the Coiste Gnótha is, in fact, strongly against the continuance of this ill-advised agitation. On this point let there be no more doubt or misrepresentation.

As An Dochtúir Conchubhar Mag Uidhir is well able to defend himself, it is unnecessary for us to rebut the charges of irregularity in the conduct of the business of the meeting which Piaras has the ill-taste to bring so publicly against him.

We have received the two following further letters in continuance of the discussion: —

A Chara,

Your article in last week's *Claidheamh Soluis* proves conclusively why the teaching of Irish as an Ordinary Subject should not be paid for. The Gaelic League, after a long and persistent agitation, has succeeded in making Irish an important subject in a large number of schools. Still, a great deal more remains to be done, before we are in a position to stop agitation, and settle down to solid work, as you suggest. As long as Irish is left an optional subject, so long will

181

several teachers refrain from teaching it within school hours.

Teachers justly complain of an overcrowded programme. Yet they are compelled to teach Drawing, Drill, Singing, Science, and Object Lessons. There has been no demand for special fees for the teaching of these subjects. It is only when the National Language is concerned, that special fees are required. When Irish is made an obligatory subject — one, on which the awarding of increments will largely depend, — then, and not until then, shall it be taught successfully. The Gaelic League should then continue to agitate, until Irish is placed on a par with Reading, Writing, and Arithmetic. There are several unnecessary subjects on the school programme at present. Let those be weeded out so as to make room for the more important ones. The time and the hour for teaching Irish is engaging too much attention now-a-days. If the teacher is inclined to teach Irish, they generally present themselves.

In Irish speaking districts there is one great drawback to the teaching of Irish, as well as to education in general — one which it is high time to grapple with. I mean the irregularity of attendance at schools. Statistics show us that Irish is taught only to the senior classes in the majority of schools. Here in Mayo, and I suppose it is the same in other counties, only fifty per cent of the pupils ever reach third standard. The irregularity of attendance reduces this number again by at least fifty per cent, so in a school having one hundred on rolls, there are only twenty-five learning Irish daily. Of this number twenty or thereabouts remain at home when sixth standard is reached, so we have left five pupils out of one hundred who can lay a fair claim to a knowledge of Irish. We know schools in the semi-Irish-speaking districts of Mayo, in which twenty per cent of the pupils in the lower standards are Irish speakers, but one might search, and in vain, for an Irish speaker in senior standards. The indifference and carelessness and ignorance of the parents are of course, to blame for all this. They send their children to school not as a matter of duty, but merely to oblige the managers and teachers.

Now, where are we to seek a remedy for this lamentable state of affairs? While it is allowed to continue, the teaching of Irish, even by enthusiasts, cannot be productive of the best results.

The Gaelic League is the one educational organisation which can rouse and direct public opinion. It is not, I think, outside its sphere to take up the question of compulsory attendance. A number of public meetings held in various centres should prove effective, and would receive the whole-hearted support of all interested in Irish education, and the welfare of the country.

In schools where the teacher is enthusiastic things are not quite so bad, as all pupils are taught Irish, and what is still more important, they are enthused with a love for it, but unfortunately the number of enthusiasts is small, and will never of themselves succeed in restoring Irish to its rightful position. Where the teaching is half-hearted, the pupils are careless, and do not want Irish. The study of it is insipid, and lifeless, and involves extra trouble. They leave school with a smattering of Irish — just enough to teach them to despise it afterwards. This statement may appear strong and unfounded. But let us look to facts. How many pupils who have left school for the past eight years with a knowledge of two or three books of O'Growney, have since identified themselves with the language movement? How many have made any effort whatsoever to supplement that knowledge? They shun the Gaelic League classes,and after some time pluck up courage to question the utility of Irish.

It will take some time to remedy all this, but the sooner a vigorous agitation is begun the better. The Bilingual Programme should certainly be our goal, but as there is poor prospect of reaching it in the immediate future, we should make the most of present opportunities. Some people think that it is ridiculous to put the Bilingual Programme into operation in the English-speaking districts, yet they think it quite reasonable and justifiable to teach English only in Irish-speaking districts'.

Mise le mór-mheas
P. Ó Catháin, Máistir Sgoile.

Dear Sir,

I was amused at the note you wrote in reply to my letter in your issue of last week. The answer to the conundrum which you put to me is very simple. I am *not infallible.* You and I 'think that to demand "special" remuneration for the teaching of Irish as an ordinary subject would be to give away our whole case'; but since we are both liable to error, the mere fact of our agreeing as to a conclusion does not settle the question beyond yea or nay. A case may be quite arguable even though its merits are disputed by two such 'clever fellows' as the Editor of *An Claidheamh Soluis* and his old pupil, sincere friend, and warm admirer,

LOUIS J. WALSH.

(The answer to our conundrum is, indeed, very simple, but An Breathnach has not given it. He has answered instead another and entirely different conundrum of his own propounding. — F. an Ch.).

THE UNIVERSITY BILL
11.4.1908

Most Gaels will find it impossible to enthuse over Mr. Birrell's University Bill. It makes no appeal to the imagination. It will not stir a single pulse into passionate quickness. Trinity College, 'high and dry' above Ireland and the people, providing higher education for such Protestant Episcopalians as cannot afford to go to Oxford or Cambridge; a new Belfast University providing higher education for Ulster Nonconformists; a new University of the 'sprawling' type, with its extremities at Dublin , Cork, and Galway, supplying higher education for Catholics and perhaps for non-Catholics of Irish sympathies — these are scarcely the lines on which an Ireland working out her own destiny would have solved the University problem. And the irony of it is that Ireland could have settled the University question for herself at any time within the past twenty-five years. Had she even so recently as three years ago taken the advice given by the bolder spirits amongst her educationists she would now, instead of having to accept with the best face she can what is offered her by an English statesman, be in a position to compel the British Government to endow out of Irish moneys an Irish University embodying

183

Irish ideals and aspirations. This must now remain one of the great 'might-have-beens' of Irish history. We are where we are and we must make the best of it.

But whilst we cannot see much reason to enthuse, we see no ground for dismay or even for despondency. We are not getting a settlement which an Irish patriot might wish or an Irish stateman propose: but neither are we face to face, as some would have us believe, with a new and deep-laid plot of English politicians to pertetuate what one of them calls 'hell in Ireland'. This really seems to be an honest Englishman's honest attempt to settle the Irish University question in the best interests of Ireland as he sees them; and if we are not enamoured of it, if we have qualms and misgivings, as most of us have, — well, we are simply paying the penalty of having an Englishman to settle an Irish question. We may be wiser next time.

It is pretty certain that Mr. Birrell's main proposals will have been embodied in a statute before the end of the present year. The obvious duty of Irishmen is to set to work with a view to moulding the new Universities, especially the new Dublin University, while still plastic, into something in the semblance of National institutions and capable in the fulness of time of developing into institutions as Irish and as national as institutions can be. Trinity, so far as the present Bill is concerned, is to remain not merely as 'proudly Protestant' but as proudly English as ever; it is to be feared that the new Belfast University, if not quite so English as Trinity, will be at least as anti-Irish: Ireland's hope, then, must centre mainly in the Dublin-Cork-Galway institution. Of this institution, what are to be the standpoint, ideals, 'atmosphere'? Are they to be frankly Irish, frankly English, or frankly neutral? This is the question.

It is all very well to say that a University must be left to formulate its own ideals and that the 'atmosphere' is a thing which must be created mainly by the students. We agree, but our point is that liberty must be secured to the new institution to formulate Irish ideals and to develop an Irish 'atmosphere'. We do not want Mr. Birrell, or the British Parliament, to do these things for us: they could not do them, were they ever so willing. What we want is liberty to do them for ourselves. Does the proposed constitution allow us that liberty? If it does not, then in Heaven's name, let us have nothing to do with it.

Now, we are inclined to think it does leave us just that bare liberty and no more. It is by no means as democratic a constitution as we would wish. By democratic, in speaking of Universities, we do not mean representative of the butcher, the baker, and the candlestick-maker, — we mean representative to the full of University life and thought, from the lowest to the highest stage, — academically democratic. In this sense the Belfast constitution is more democratic than the Dublin one. Why? The direct representation of the rank-and-file graduates on the Senate of the Dublin University is only five members out of thirty-five. This does not seem sufficient. And students other than graduates are, apparently, allowed no representation, while they are in Belfast. Fourteen members of the Senate will be chosen by the Governing Bodies of the Colleges, — six by Dublin and four each by Cork and Galway. But what is the composition of these Governing Bodies themselves to be? This is a point on which the Bill affords no information. It is a most important point. Under what auspices are the 'ideals' of the Dublin College to be formed and the 'atmosphere' to develop?

The first duty of thoughtful Irishmen is to consider all these questions with a view to arriving at a matured opinion as to whether the constitution really commits the working of the new University, for good or evil, to the hands of Young Ireland. If it does, we need have no fears for the future.

There next comes the important matter of the *personnel* of the University, and of its constituent Colleges during the first critical five years. The Senate to which is to be entrusted the great task of pioneering the scheme is, judging from the lists which have been handed about in Dublin during the past few weeks, a singularly heterogeneous body. Some of the names on it are like the proverbial fly in amber, — one wonders how the dickens they got there. On the whole, however, it is a body of Irish sympathies. The inclusion of such Gaels as An Craobhín, Eoin MacNeill, Dr. Sigerson, Máire Ní Aodáin, Dr. M. F. Cox, Dr. Coffey, Stephen Gwynn, and William O'Brien, in conjunction with the announcement — which may be taken as definite — that Donnchadh Ó Cobhthaigh is to be the first President of the Dublin College, gives one to hope that the spirit animating the institution in its early years will be generously Irish and genuinely progressive.

Unfortunately, however, the Senate is not to have the appointment of the first body of Professors nor is it to have the drawing up of the statutes of the University. These two important tasks are to be entrusted to a Statutory Commission, four of whose seven members are to be named by the Senate and three by the Crown. This is one of the least satisfactory features of Mr. Birrell's Scheme. Some sort of Commission or Committee is no doubt necessary: but to hand over to a body consisting of three direct Crown nominees and of four others nominated by a body itself nominated by the Crown, the framing of the whole code of University statutes including, apparently, the statutes determining the position of the National Language and of Irish studies generally in the new University — this is a proposal which, we suggest, should be strenuously fought. What guarantee have we of Irish Ireland that these seven Crown nominees will as much as consider the National Language from the proper point of view?

GAELS AND THE UNIVERSITY BILL
25.4.1908

What should be the demands of the Gaelic League touching the position of Irish in the new University? As to our ultimate ideals we are, of course, all agreed: Irish must one day occupy the place of honour in an education system fully bilingual — in the University no less than in the primary school, in the technical school as well as in the secondary college. This ideal is, obviously, impossible of realisation just at present. But we must keep it steadily in view, nevertheless; and we must test every body of proposals that may be put before us with regard to any of the great branches of Irish education by the question — to adapt a formula familiar two years ago in another connection — 'Are they proposals consistent with and leading up to the realisation of that ideal?' This is why we think the attention of Gaelic Leaguers should in the first instance be directed to the constitution of the new University rather than to any details with regard to the possible position of Irish in its curriculum. Given a constitution sufficiently democratic in the academic sense, it will be possible for Young Ireland in due time to carry into effect its views, not merely in the matter of the

185

position of Irish, but in all other matters as well. In other words, the thing for which a stand must be made is genuine academic autonomy, – but academic autonomy in the form not of an oligarchy but of a democracy. Trinity, for instance, has academic autonomy of a type we do not ambition.

We know what the constitution of the University governing body or Senate is to be, and whilst by no means ideal, it is certainly tolerable. We are still in the dark with regard to a matter of almost equal importance, – the constitution of the governing bodies of the individual Colleges. Rumours have, indeed, reached us, but we prefer not to dogmatise on the strength of rumours. These bodies will exercise functions of the utmost responsibility in the University, not merely as directing the affairs of their respective Colleges, but as returning between them fourteen members to the Senate, – we might say, indeed, seventeen members including their Presidents, which means slightly more than one-half of the total membership. It is quite clear that no criticism of the constitution of the University as a whole can be final until the constitution of these three bodies is known. Neither can we be safe in congratulating ourselves on the personnel of the University for the first five years until we know what the personnel of these bodies is to be for the same period. Apparently there is to be admixture of the academic and of the external elements. In the West the names of the Archbishop of Tuam, the Very Rev. Canon Séamus Ó Dálaigh, D.D., Lord Killanin, Captain Shawe Taylor, and Colonel Nolan, ex-M.P., are being talked of in connection with the governing body of the Galway College. What authority for these names – not more than two of which could be regarded as entirely satisfactory by Gaels – may be we cannot say. It is to be feared that *An Craobhín's* ideal of a great Gaelic College on the Western seaboard is still far off.

Reverting once more to the list of Senators proposed for the Dublin University – to which we are confining our attention in this article – our readers will have noticed that some of the omissions are as extraordinary as some of the inclusions. The name of Father Thomas Finlay, for instance, does not appear. There is but one woman in the final list whereas there were originally two. Is one woman – would even two women or for that matter six women – be a sufficient representation of the interests of what is, after all, the more important half of Ireland's population, a half, too, which is bound to be largely represented amongst the students of the University? We think that some of the male deadheads might well give place to female brains and educational experience. And we should like to see it made clear that women will be eligible for the professorial chairs.

In connection with the Statutory Commission the Government is being credited with an intention which can only be described as extraordinary. It is to preclude from election as a Commissioner anyone who has expectations of a professorship or any other appointment in the University. This course has, no doubt, one superficial consideration in its favour, but there are a score of considerations, far more weighty, if not equally obvious, against it. The Commission, be it remembered, is to be charged not merely with the appointment of the staffs of the University and the Colleges, but with the drawing up of the statutes. Who more suitable to draw up the statutes than the men who are to administer them? Who more competent to shape the lines on which a new Irish University is to develop than the men who, under every difficulty and discouragement, have devoted their lives to the cause of higher education in Ireland in the past? Last week we mentioned eight or ten names of proposed Senators, and went on to say that it would be quite possible to select from a body comprising such distinguished Irishmen and educationists as these, four Commissioners in whom everyone who cares for the future of Ireland and of Irish education would have absolute confidence. But amongst these distinguished educationists are several whom the country will expect to see appointed to professorial chairs; and it now appears that, on that account, they will not be allowed to sit on the Commission! If this is really so, then there is far more cause for anxiety with regard to the powers and personnel of the Commission than even we, who have been criticising the Commission proposal from the start, had imagined.

All this closely concerns us in the language movement. There are, we know, many Gaelic Leaguers who think that the University question is solely a question for learned people with letters after their names living in Dublin, and that the ordinary workaday Gael in the field or in the schoolroom or behind the shop counter has nothing to say to it. This is a tremendous mistake, and if anything is destined to wreck the present prospects of a University settlement which shall in time be a real settlement on Irish lines, it is just this attitude on the part of Gaelic Leaguers. We submit that it is the clear duty of every individual amongst us to interest himself or herself actively and intelligently in the questions we have been discussing — the constitution of the University, its statutes, its personnel and the constitution, statutes and personnel of the individual Colleges. These are the things on which depends the final emergence of an Irish culture in Ireland. An undertaking is about to be carried out which must have a momentous bearing for good or evil on our work and on the whole future of our country. Are we to stand by without making an effort to secure that that bearing shall be for good and not for evil; without looking around to see how and where Irish Ireland may gain a foothold within the three institutions which will henceforward have charge of the higher education of the great bulk of our countrymen and countrywomen; without taking counsel as to what our immediate plan of campaign is to be with regard to the subject which comes specifically under our care, — the welfare of the Irish language? One thing is certain: if the Gaelic League does not interest itself in these things no one else will do so, and the chances are that we shall find Irish Ireland and the Irish language all but ignored by the commission-made statutes of the new University. *Then* we shall be powerless to do anything but pass resolutions of protest. *Now*, therefore, is the time for us to be up and doing. They call Ireland a land of lost opportunities. Let us not lose this opportunity of achieving, it may be, something, as noble as we have ever stood for on the tented field or in the deadly breach, — a measure of educational freedom which we can use, if we are wise, for the attainment of any other kind of freedom that at any time hereafter we may really desire.

THE FEES QUESTION
25.4.1908

It is as we suspected. A great many of those who have been favouring the launching of an agitation for the payment of special fees for Irish as an Ordinary Subject have been doing so under a misconception, — perhaps we should say under a series of misconceptions. They have been befogged by the unfortunate terminology of the Board, with its utterly misleading terms,

'Ordinary School Hours', 'Ordinary Subject', 'Extra Subject', and so on. A hazy view prevails that an Extra Subject is a subject which must be taught either at an unearthly hour in the morning or at an unholy hour in the evening, — that the children must be dragged out of thir innocent beds at cockcrow and made hurry to school to catch the Extra lesson, or else that they must be kept in for Irish in the evening when tired and hungry after the day and longing for home and dinner with all the yearning with which school-children long for these things once three o'clock strikes. Now all this is myth, pure and simple. There is no necessity to bring children to school at an exceptionally early hour in the morning or in the alternative to keep them in after three o'clock for an 'Extra' Irish lesson. The expression 'Ordinary School Hours' simply means the minimum four hours which *must* be devoted to secular teaching in every National School; but, as a matter of fact, every National School is open for at least six hours a day, of which one hour may be said to be divided between Religious Instruction and Recreation. The remaining hour is available for the (so-called) 'Extra' subjects.

'Ordinary School Hours' commonly begin at 10.30 a.m. But the school work always starts at 9 or at any rate 9.30 a.m., and in every school, town or country, in which the teacher is worth his salt, the children are all assembled long before 10 a.m. *Irish can be taught for fees in every non-Bilingual school in Ireland from 10 a.m. to 10.30 a.am., every day.* If the teacher, for any reason, prefers to devote this half hour to some other subject, he can *teach Irish for fees from 2.30 p.m. to 3 p.m.* In neither case are the children required either to come in before the normal hour or to remain in school beyond the normal hour. It will be seen that these facts dispose of the argument that under the present scheme Irish can be taught for fees only at an hour at which the children are not all assembled, or else at an hour in the late afternoon, after the end of the normal school day, when the children are tired and hungry, and their companions who are not old enough to earn fees have been dismissed.

We are informed that a number of Dublin teachers, when interviewed by a League Timthire, stated that they could not get the children in in time for the 'Extra' Irish lesson. We should like to know what are the Dublin schools in which the children are not assembled at 10 a.m. These teachers, if there be any truth in their complaint, are doubtless teaching Irish at 9 or at 9.30 a.m. *There is no necessity whatever for them to choose so unreasonably early an hour.* The can teach Irish if they like at 10 a.m., or — should their Roll Call be fixed for 9.30 or 10 — then they can teach it at 2 or 2.30 in the afternoon. There is not a single school in Dublin or anywhere else where either one or other of these arrangements is not feasible. The teacher who fixes Irish at an unreasonable hour does so of his own accord, and without any justification whatsoever in the rules of the Board.

This explicit statement may help members of the Dublin Coiste Ceanntair and others to find their bearings. Some of those who voted for Cathal Brugha's resolutions the other day were actually unaware of the fact that Irish can at the present moment be taught for fees from 10 to 10.30 a.m., or, in the alternative, from 2.30 to 3 p.m. They thought it had to be taught either at or before 9 a.m., or else at 3.30 p.m.!!!! Had they known the real facts they would have voted the other way. It is as we suspected.

The North Dublin Guardians have allowed themselves to be rushed into adopting a resolution demanding all round payment of fees for Irish as an

Ordinary, doubtless under the impression that they were supporting a demand officially made by the Gaelic League. The arguments used by the members of the Board who proposed and supported the resolution were again based on a complete misunderstanding of the actual facts of the case. One spoke about the 'exacting from the teachers to defer the teaching of the Natioanl language to a part of the day when they and their pupils were after the day's work', and another grew pathetic on the inhumanity of keeping 'poor little mites' in after school hours in order to teach them Irish. Now, no one 'exacts' any such thing from the teachers, and the necessity of keeping 'poor little mites' in at unreasonable hours exists solely in the imagination of ill-informed persons. It is a pity people do not read the rules of the National Board, or seek information from honest people who have read them, before making speeches and proposing resolutions condemning them.

An tAthair Peadar Ua Laoghaire has written a letter to a member of the Coiste Gnótha, in which he ridicules the argument that 'teachers should not be paid for teaching Irish to children within school hours, because that would be treating Irish as a foreign language'. He appears to attribute this argument to us! We need hardly say that we have never put forward any such argument. An tAthair Peadar owed it to himslef, no less than to us, to take the trouble to find out what we really did and do say. Our position is that a teacher should not be paid *twice over* for teaching Irish as an Ordinary Subject. He is already paid once for teaching it. The teacher's salary covers all work done within ordinary school hours. He cannot teach Irish as an Ordinary unless he drops some of his other subjects, or else curtails the time given to some one or more of them. This is self-evident. Room cannot be made for a new thing in a space already crowded without displacing something else. For the subject displaced the teacher received no extra pay; why should he receive extra pay for the subject replacing it? This argument would stand even if Irish did not enjoy in addition to recognition as an Ordinary remunerated subject, the special privilege (for privilege it is) of further recognition as a remunerated Extra.

An tAthair Peadair finds it impossible to argue 'without a feeling of humiliation' with the 'idea' which he attributes to us. As we have never entertained such an 'idea' in our life, his letter is a foolish piece of irrelevancy which coming from the Vice-President of the Organisation it is really humiliating to have to expose in these columns.

Since writing the foregoing we have seen in the *Freeman's Journal* a translation of a letter addressed to the Ard Rúnaidhe, in which An tAthair Peadar resigns the Vice-Presidency of the Gaelic League. Reluctant as we are to embitter matters, we must, in view of the terms and tone of An tAthair Peadar's unfortunate letter to the members of the Coiste Gnótha, allow the preceding paragraph to stand.

THE NEW DUBLIN UNIVERSITY: WHAT WE WANT
16.5.1908

Mr. Birrell's Universities Bill has been read a second time in the British House of Commons and committed, with the blessing of a majority of 314, to Grand Committee. In other words, the crucial stage has now been reached. It is while the Bill is in Committee that Irish opinion has its only opportunity of coming into play with a view to securing that, when it finally

189

emerges as a statute, the Bill shall provide us with the outer framework of a University which Ireland can enter into and make her own. Now is the moment for the country to speak out against the various objectionable features in the Bill and in the charters. Now, to come to our own immediate concern, is the moment for Irish Ireland to put forward unitedly, unequivocally, and determinedly its demands touching the position of the National Language and kindred interests in the new institutions.

We want in the first place Irish as an essential part of the curriculum of every student who passes through the Dublin University. Irish must be made a compulsory subject up to the point at which the student commences to specialise, — that is, up to the point at which English is likely to be made a compulsory subject. It will not do to call for Irish as compulsory merely at matriculation, for there is, we learn, the possibility that the University will hold no matriculation examination of its own, but will simply recognise one of the Intermediate examinations. Secondly, due provision must be made for the encouragement of Irish studies throughout the course by the institution on an adequate scale of scholarships, studentships, and fellowships in Irish. We throw out the further suggestion that there should be a special degree in Celtic subjects. Most Universities provide for a degree in Classics, a degree in Modern Literature, a degree in Mental and Moral Science, a degree in Physical and Physico-Mathematical Science, and so on. Why should not an Irish University have also a degree in Celtic study? A course embracing Celtic Philology, with Irish and one other Celtic language, would be at least as broad, as humanising, and in the best sense as useful as a degree, say, in Ancient Classics. Making this our third demand, our fourth is that there must be an ample Irish Faculty at each of the Colleges, including professors (with such assistant-professors and lecturers as may be necessary) in Celtic Philology and Old Irish; in Modern Irish Language and Literature; in Ancient Irish History and Archaeology; and in Modern Irish History, political, social, and economic. Fifthly, there must be due provision for the education in and through Irish of Irish speakers. Sixthly, with a view to the conversion of the University into one frankly bilingual as soon as the country is ripe for it, a date should be fixed after which none should be eligible for professorships or other offices unless able to conduct the teaching or other business of their offices in Irish. Finally, recognition of the courses given in the League's Training Colleges should be demanded on the same lines as recognition will doubtless be accorded to the courses in special subjects given in various outside institutions.

This, then, is the programme behind which we think Irish Ireland should rally. We may not be able to carry it in its every detail all at once, but carry its essential features we must, if the new University is to be a help and not a hindrance in our work of nation-building.

Since we went to press last week the draft charters of the three Colleges have been published. It will be recollected that, in commenting on the constitution of the Senate, we said that no criticism of the scheme as a whole could be final in the absence of information as to the composition of the governing bodies of the individual Colleges. This information is afforded by the draft charters. It may be said at once that the proposed constitution of these is such as to threaten the academic autonomy not merely of the Colleges but of the whole University. In the Dublin College, for instance, the professors and graduates are to have but ten representatives on a Governing Body of thirty-three, — the remainder being

190

nominated by the Crown or elected by extern authorities. The matter would be still more serious if there were not provision for an Academic Council, consisting of the President, Professors, and Lecturers, which 'subject to review by the Governing Body', shall have powers to manage the curriculum and generally to carry out the educational work of the College. This Council, we anticipate, will be the real centre of light and energy in the life of the place.

Some of the clauses in the Bill and charters are, on close examination, fraught with the gravest danger. It seems to us astonishing that there has not been an outcry against the failure on the part both of the Bill and of the charter; to make provision for the fixity of tenure of the professors, after the first probationary period; and a still louder outcry against the utterly preposterous proposal that all examinations should be conducted, not by the Professors of the University, but by extern examiners, – strangers, from Trinity, Edinburgh, London, Kamschatka, or the Lord knows where. This really means that the University is not to be trusted to confer its own degrees.

Coming to the nominations for the first Governing Bodies of the Colleges, we find that, from the Irish Ireland point of view, two at least of the proposed bodies are well-nigh impossible. In Cork, Irish ideas are scarcely represented at all; in Galway Irish ideas would probably command a bare majority; in Dublin, unless the Governing Body is materially strengthened on its Irish side, Irish ideas will be in a decided minority. This is a serious state of affairs. If those responsible for the nomination of the Governing Body of the Dublin College value the co-operation of the Gaelic League in carrying out their University scheme, they will be well advised to give the view-point for which the Gaelic League stands a more adequate representation. We mean, of course, a more adequate representation numerically, for the names of Gaelic Leaguers which actually figure in the list – including as they do the names of Eoin Mac Neill, Máire Ní Aodáin, and Una Ní Fhaircheallaigh – are, perhaps, the very names to which the League itself, if it were making the nominations, would give pride of place. But if the College is to flourish on Irish lines the representatives of the Gael on its Governing Body must receive a strong numerical reinforcement.

THE FEES QUESTION
30.5.1908

Craobh after Craobh and Coiste after Coiste are endorsing the policy of the Coiste Gnótha on the two main questions – apart from the larger question which, though not formally raised on the resolutions, will really be the central one at the special meeting of the Ard-Fheis (the question, that is, as to whether the elected leaders of the movement are to be allowed to lead or to give place to a faction of malcontents) – Craobh after Craobh and Coiste after Coiste are, we say, endorsing the attitude of the Coiste Gnótha on the two main questions, the Fees Question and the University Question, which have precipitated the summoning of the Ard-Fheis. Among bodies that have recently adopted resolutions supporting the Coiste on the Fees Question are Coiste Comhairle Cualann, Craobh na Carraige Duibhe, and Craobh na gCúigí, – all of them, like the Ard-Craobh, within the area of Coiste Ceanntair Bhaile Atha Cliath, which is represented as being solid against us. Our correspondence on the subject has, we are glad to say, dwindled considerably, now that really important issues have arisen. We need deal only with the letters adopting a view contrary to the Coiste Gnótha and our own.

Three weeks ago we asked: 'Will someone show where precisely the alleged impossibility of teaching the language at 10 a.m. comes in?' Two readers have attempted to show it, but have failed. They show only that certain teachers in their neighbourhood *will not* teach the language at 10 a.m., not at all that they *cannot*. Now, the best and shortest way of answering their arguments, and of showing that we have adverted to and made allowance for all the difficulties they suggest, is to print a skeleton time-table which fulfils all the conditions of the National Board and secures the desired half-hour for Irish. The following arrangement is actually in force in scores of National Schools: the particular school whose Time-Table we summarise teachers Irish with much success as an Extra and on its general merit secures the Board's highest mark: —

School opens at 9.15 a.m.
Ordinary Instruction commences at 10.30 a.m.
School closes at 3 p.m.
SUMMARY OF TIME TABLE
9.25 to 9.55. Optional for Junior Standards; Mathematics (Extra for Fees) for Senior Standards.
9.55 to 10.25. Irish for whole school.
10.25. Roll marked.
10.30 to 12. Ordinary Instruction ($1\frac{1}{2}$ hours.).
12 to 12.30. Religious Instruction.
12.30 to 3. Ordinary Instruction, including Recreation 1 to 1.30. (This gives $2\frac{1}{2}$ hours of Ordinary Instruction, making a total of 4 hours — all that is required by the Board).

The object in commencing the Irish lesson at five munutes to ten is to secure a full half-hour before the school roll is marked: the marking of the roll must be completed before the hour (10.30 a.m.) scheduled for the commencement of the Ordinary Instruction. One of our correspondents makes a great deal of fuss over the marking of the roll, for which he says ten minutes must be allowed! There is not a single school in Ireland in which the roll could not be marked within one and a half or two minutes. The marking of the special roll for Irish is a matter merely of seconds. We are not theorising, but are describing what we have seen both in rural and urban schools.

It may be objected that, though the half-hour's recreation may, according to the rules of the Board, count as portion of the minimum four hours' Ordinary Instruction, yet many teachers give, in lieu of it, an extra half hour of Ordinary teaching. In cases where this is done it simply becomes necessary to keep the children in school to 3.30 p.m. — the common time for dismissal in rural schools. The Irish half-hour is not interfered with. The necessity for keeping the children in to 3.30 does not in any way arise from the fact that Irish is taught as an Extra. Indeed, where the language is taught as an ordinary, this extra half-hour is even more necessary than in the other case, for the minimum four hours proper to the compulsory subjects have been infringed upon, and the teacher may have to make up his leeway by keeping the children in school half an hour longer. Thus, the effect of the teaching of Irish as an Ordinary, under present conditions, is often to lengthen the school-day, whereas its teaching as an Extra tends to shorten the school-day.

Our experience — and we have experience of schools in the very poorest, wildest, and most scattered districts in the country — is that, speaking generally, all the children who intend to come to school for the day are assembled by five minutes to ten. This is admitted by one of our correspondents, who, agreeing with us that the half hour from 9.55 to 10.25, is 'the best in the whole day', claims that, for that reason, it should be devoted to Religious Instruction. Where this is considered advisable, Irish (always as an Extra for Fees) can be taught during some later half hour, — say from 2.30 to 3. In neither case is there any hardship on the children nor any injustice to the language.

Are the arrangements we suggest possible? They are possible in every school in Ireland. They are in force in scores of schools, rural and urban, everywhere throughout the country, — in force, we daresay in a number of schools in every one of the thirty-two counties. For reasons best known to themselves, certain teachers *prefer* to teach Irish at 9 or 9.30 in the morning or after 3 in the evening; but under the present rules of the Board no set of circumstances is imaginable which would make it *necessary* for them to do so. *An hour is always available before 3 p.m. at which all the children are assembled and at which Irish may be taught and special fees earned for its teaching.*

SOME FOREIGN PARALLELS
30.5.1908

A few weeks ago we promised An tAthair Pádraig Ua Murchadha to give the details as to the positions of Gaelic, Welsh, and Flemish in the primary schools of Scotland, Wales, and Belguim respectively. The hullabaloo which has arisen on the Universities Bill and the excursions and alarums preparatory to the special meeting of the Ard-Fheis have since claimed so much of our space and attention that it is only this week we have been able to send our article on this interesting subject to the press. In dealing briefly with the matter in our issue of the 9th inst., we wrote: — 'In Scotland Gaelic is purely an optional and extra subject for which no special remuneration of any kind is given. Not a farthing is paid by the Scottish Education Department for the teaching of Gaelic in the schools either in Gaelic-speaking or in English-speaking districts. There is no genuine bilingual education at all. In Wales a bilingual system is optional in Welsh districts, and Welsh can also be taught as an optional subject throughout Wales generally. No special fees, or extra remuneration in any form, is given for the teaching of Welsh whether under a bilingual programme or as an optional specific subject in a non-bilingual school. In Belgium the 'vernacular' of the district (be it what it may) is compulsory, and a second language (to be introduced gradually as a vernacular) is optional. For the teaching of this second language no extra remuneration of any kind is given. When the second language is taught the school day is lengthened by from an hour to an hour and a half. These are the main facts of each case.'

To come to details. Gaelic does not officially figure amongst the list of subjects which may be taught in Scottish schools. The teacher may teach it if he chooses and if his local authority permits him, but he does so as a purely voluntary piece of exertion on his part, and receives no special or extra remuneration whatever, no matter at what hour of the day he may teach it or to what classes of pupils. This applies both to Gaelic-speaking and to non-Gaelic-speaking districts. Even in Gaelic-speaking districts the teaching of Gaelic is not compulsory, nor does anything exist which by any stretch of the imagination could be called bilingual education. Within the last few months the Scotch Education Department has refused to countenance the introduction of a bilingual sytem, and the utmost it could be induced to do was to agree to *recommend* that Gaelic-speaking children should be taught to read their language, — but for this teaching it will allow no special remuneration to the teacher. The Department gives a £10 grant to those schools in which the children know so little English that Gaelic has perforce to be used as a medium of instruction:* but not a farthing extra is paid to the teacher for teaching Gaelic whether in such a school or in any other.

That the official status of Irish in the Irish primary school system is out of all comparison more satisfactory than that of Gaelic in the Scottish system goes, therefore, without saying. Indeed, even the most sanguine amongst the Gaelic workers in the Highlands almost despair of reaching in the present generation the point which we in Ireland have already attained.

We come to Wales. The Welsh language is one of the ordinary subjects of instruction in Welsh schools. It is expressly laid down, however, that 'it is not necessary that all the subjects should be taught in every class, *nor in the case of the Welsh Language, in every school*'. In other words, while Welsh is an ordinary subject, it is not a compulsory subject. No special remuneration in any shape or form is given for its teaching. The teachers are, indeed, expected and encouraged to teach it, but they are neither compelled to do so nor specially remunerated for doing so. So far, therefore, as non-Welsh-speaking districts are concerned, Welsh stands in a much less favourable position on the curriculum than Irish does in the non-Irish-speaking parts of Ireland. For Irish, in addition to being a non-specially-remunerated (but non-compulsory) Ordinary — the exact position of Welsh in Wales— is also a specially remunerated Extra, which can be taught at a very favourable hour of the school day for fairly valuable special fees. Most of Wales is, however, Welsh-speaking; and in Welsh-speaking districts 'any of the subjects of the curriculum *may* . . . be taught in Welsh'. '*May* be taught': teaching through Welsh is not compulsory even in Welsh-speaking districts: and, needless to say, no special remuneration, in the shape of fees or otherwise, is given for Welsh or bilingual instruction in such districts. In Ireland the recent policy of the Board is to insist on the adoption of the Bilingual Programme in Irish-speaking and bilingual districts, provided the teaching staff be competent to work it, while valuable special fees are paid when this is done. Here again, the Irish Education Department, so far as its rules and regulations are concerned, is more advanced than the Welsh one. If teaching through Welsh is, in point of fact, more widespread in Wales than teaching through Irish in Ireland, the reason is to be sought in the fact that Wales is predominantly Welsh-speaking, and that the local authorities, teachers, and parents of Wales are resolved that she shall remain so.

* In certain counties, if the infant and children in the Junior Division are partly taught by a Gaelic-speaking teacher, whose services are not required in respect of the average attendance, the rate of the capitation grants (18s. and 20s. respectively per head on the average attendance) may be increased by 1s.

194

The attitude of the Belgian Education Department on the language question may be summed up in these propositions: (1) Every Belgian child has the right to be taught in his own mother-tongue, be that mother-tongue French or Flemish**; (2) every Belgian child ought to be taught as a 'second language' one of the other vernaculars spoken in Belgium; and (3) this 'second language' should be gradually introduced as a medium of instruction and intercourse in the general work of the school. The second language, be it noticed, is not compulsory, but in practice it is taught in all but the most backward of the rural schools. In theory the second language may be anything, but in fact it is nearly always French in the case of Walloons.*** The system, therefore, works out as follows: in Flemish-speaking districts Flemish is the 'first language' and French the 'second language'; in French-speaking districts French is the 'first' and Flemish the 'second language'; in border districts the vernacular of the majority of the pupils is selected as the 'first language', and the other vernacular becomes the 'second'. This is the true bilingual ideal, and an analogous state of affairs is what we must work for in Ireland. It is to be remarked, however, that in Belgium no extra remuneration is given for the teaching of the second language, even though its introduction requires the lengthening of the school day by from an hour to an hour and a half. So far as the encouragement afforded by special fees is concerned, Ireland, therefore, is in advance even of Belgium. Where, then, do we fall behind? First, in the *spirit* animating our Education Department (as apart from the letter of its rules and regulations) — though here we are gradually changing for the better; but chiefly in the facts that our teachers are not yet sufficiently trained for the work of Irish or bilingual teaching and that, speaking generally, both teachers and managers are partly unable and partly unwilling to avail of the facilities actually afforded by the rules and regulations of the Board, — facilities incomparably greater than those afforded in Wales, and — except as regards the use of the second language as a medium of instruction throughout the country as a whole — greater even than those afforded in Belgium.

What, then, are the lines for future work? To imbue the Board and its officials with the right spirit; still more, to imbue the managers and teachers with the right spirit; to teach the teachers Irish and to train them in the best methods of bilingual instruction; and finally to secure the extension of the Bilingual Programme to the whole country. Here are the objects for which we must strive. Here are the lines on which we shall ultimately secure a bilingual education system which, while making use of a 'second language' as an important part of its scheme of work, shall give the place of honour to the national language and be impregnated through and through with the national spirit.

BILINGUALISM
20.6.1908

The Gaelic League has emerged from the special Ard-Fheis of 1908 with the motto of 'Bilingualism' definitely inscribed on its banners. It remains for us to translate that motto from a mere pious aspiration into a vital and

** Or German in one small corner of the country.
*** French or Flemish in the case of German speakers.

practical policy. There are two main divisions of the question. Most urgent in point of time and importance is that which relates to the immediate establishment of the Bilingual Programme in the schools of the Gaedhealtacht: but behind this there is the need that all our efforts in the schools, whether in the Gaedhealtacht or in the Galltacht, should be directed towards hastening the advent of what we have called 'bilingualism all round'. Here is a proposition to which we ask the assent of every Gaelic Leaguer: Irish can never be restored as a living vernacular in the non-Irish-speaking districts as long as it remains a mere 'subject' in a unilingual, *i.e.*, purely English, teaching scheme. We must establish it as *a medium of instruction and intercourse* in every school in Ireland. Children who merely learn Irish for a half-hour or an hour in the day, even from the best possible teacher using the best possible methods, may, indeed, obtain a very fair grip of conversational and literary Irish, but if their contact with the living language ceases as soon as the Irish lesson is over and all the rest of their day's work and play is got through in English, they will remain to the end of their school course essentially English-speaking children and will grow up English-speaking men and women, the fathers and mothers of future English-speaking families. Our object, remember, is to make Ireland Irish-speaking, and if there be any possible way of making that portion of the country in which the language has ceased to be a vernacular, Irish-speaking again, save by re-introducing Irish as a vernacular through the schools, no one has yet mentioned it.

The alternative for the moment is not one between an Irish-speaking and an English-speaking Ireland. It is one between Bilingualism and Englishism. Is the next generation of Irish men and women to be a generation of educated bilingualists or a generation of English speakers with (or without) a smattering of Irish? That is the real question to which the movement must address itself.

In the *Leader* of last week we find a very thoughful and level-headed article on the subject from 'Marbhán'. He approaches the question from a somewhat new but very practical standpoint. We have been described as an 'educational theorist': now 'Marbhán' is the father of children who are growing up in an English-speaking city and he is confronted with the problem: 'How am I to get for my children an education which, whatever else it may secure them, will secure them Irish *as a living vernacular*?' He does not see where he can get such an education in the absence of a bilingual school system applying to Belfast equally with the Déise. We make no apology for quoting somewhat extensively from his article: --

'As far as I understand the matter, there are various sorts of bilingualism. Most of us from the South and West, for instance, were reared in a bilingual atmosphere, the atmosphere created by our parents speaking Irish to each other, and English to the dogs and to us. Many of us who went in for the Intermediate became acquainted with another sort of bilingualism — the bilingualism of learning, as we were supposed to do, modern European languages, without ever hearing a word of them spoken, and from teachers who had never heard a word of them spoken. There is, thirdly, the bilingualism that was in vogue during the past half century in many National schools in Irish-speaking districts, that, namely, by which children who knew no English were spoken to in, and taught everything through, English. Lastly, there is the bilingualism whose aim is to educate children bilingually — that is, to bring them up speaking, reading, writing, and finally mastering two languages. The question is — which of these bilingualisms is the Gaelic League going in for? And, that point being agreed upon, there is the further question — is the League wise, its great object being to get the people to again speak, and read, and write Irish as their native tongue — is it wise in troubling itself about any sort of bilingualism towards that end?

'For the benefit of such readers of the *Leader* as don't read *An Claidheamh Soluis*, I may say at once that the Bilingualism the Gaelic League is going in for (I am supposing the coming Ard-Fheis won't reverse the present policy of the League) is the fourth kind mentioned above. In other words, it is agitating for, and working towards, this end — that, in districts where the children know Irish, they shall be taught all subjects throught both Irish and English, just like the class first mentioned. Now, is that policy a wise one, the object of the Gaelic League being, let us always remember, to revive the Irish language?

'Well, for my part, I think it is a wise policy. I have read all that Father Dinneen has said in the *Leader* against it. I have also considered objections to it that I have not seen in print anywhere. Let me set down in my own way how the matter, as a whole, appears to me through the tangle of criticism that has been thrown round it. . . .

'As I say, I am myself in favour of the bilingual idea. Indeed, I don't see that we have any alternative in the matter. I confess that, if I had my own way, I would use only Irish in the schools in which the children understand that language. I don't, however, see any chance of getting any number of teachers, or managers, or parents, not to speak of the National Board, round to that way of thinking. I don't even find many Gaelic Leaguers desperate enough to speak *only Irish* to children. All that being so, and recognising that we have not Red Hugh O'Donnell now to sent round as a Timthire, I have reconciled myself to the conclusion that we must have English in the schools. And, as we must have it. I want to have it in the most useful way. The most useful way to have it is as a *working language*, not merely as an 'Extra', such as Irish is at present. Especially as — the children being now able to use it freely enough all over the country — it would require very little *teaching* in the strict sense, but would merely have to be used and developed — the children would merely have to be educated in it, in a word. I would, of course, insist that Irish should get pride of place in the school, should be the official language, so to say. As to that, however, I don't see that there need be much trouble. It ought, at any rate, be as easy to secure pride of place for it as it would be to secure the place altogether for it.

'I am reminded here that Father Dinneen urges that the use of two languages in a school would be mere waste of time. I don't see it. It isn't necessarily that the teacher would have to teach each lesson twice over. It would mean, rather, that he should teach half a lesson in one language and half in the other. With this advantage — that the children, not to speak of the sharpening effect of the speaking of two languages on their intelligences, would learn faster and at the cost of less mental weariness than they do at present. And, anyhow, as the object of education is to educate rather than to teach, the means, including the language or languages, by or through which children

197

are taught their lessons are, after all, of as much importance as the lessons taught. Few boys can see for what exactly they are put to learn Euclid. The learning of it has its own effect on them all the same.

'So much for the Irish-speaking districts; now as to the rest of the country. What the Gaelic League aims at for the rest of the country is that Irish shall be taught on the direct method in the schools, until gradually, as the children become at home in the language, the teaching shall become bilingual in the true sense. I don't think we could go in for anything more than that, things being as they are. One remark I will make, however. The idea of making those schools bilingual in the course of five years or so has been laughed at. I don't see anything in it to be laughed at. I have seen a school made bilingual in *one year*. And, as to the sense or nonsense of insisting on bilingualism as the end to be aimed at in connection with these schools, I am myself firmly convinced that, without such a fixed end in view, the teaching of Irish in the English-speaking schools will never be more than what it has been in the main up to the present – a failure. A million pounds a year spent on "special" fees for Irish would not save the language as a spoken tongue in one school in Ireland without a condition of the fee-earning being that the language be made, within a given period, a *working language* in the school. Indeed, I lean myself to the fear that the more "special" consideration Irish gets, in the absence of any more definite object than the vague teaching of the language, the more exotic and hothouse-natured the language will become in the country. And, as I said twice before, as we don't want to boycott English, but rather to educate the children as well as may be in it, the only programme we can sensibly lay out for the good of Irish in the schools all round is the Bilingual Programme. So, at least, it seems to me.'

Here is the case for 'bilingualism all round' irresistibly stated by a man who sees the necessity for it if his own children, whom he is endeavouring, in an unsympathetic atmosphere, to bring up Irish speakers, are not to be anglicised in their progress through a purely English school course.

We think it may be taken that working Gaelic Leaguers are practically unanimous in endorsing 'bilingualism all round' in the sense understood by 'Marbhán', by *An Claidheamh,* by the Coiste Gnótha, and by the Ard-Fheis. How to secure it is the question. Obviously, the first point of attack is the Gaedhealtacht, for which bilingualism is already the official policy of the National Board. We must establish the Bilingual Programme in as many schools as possible from the opening of the school year on July 1st. We must carry on an active propaganda throughout the coming twelve months with a view to impressing the parents, the managers, the teachers, the inspectors, the Board itself with the necessity of the universal adoption of the Programme throughout the Gaedhealtacht if anything like real education is to be imparted to the children in the schools. The parents must be appealed to both from the patriotic and from the 'practical' standpoints; the managers and teachers must be invited into friendly council with the League, the needs of the situation talked over with them, ways and means discussed: the Board and its inspectors, equally with the managers and teachers, must be induced to enter into the work of that divine enthusiasm which is necessary to the propagation of all great causes and which is especially essential in the pioneering of what is really the greatest and most far-reaching reform that has yet been attempted in Irish education.

The most urgent part of this campaign is, perhaps, the training of the teachers. This is a matter which, for the present, may best be attended to by the Irish Colleges. Coláiste Uladh proposes to deal with the problem in a very thorough and a very practical way. The school at Gort a' Choirce, within half-a-mile of the College building, has adopted the Bilingual Programme. It is intended, with the consent of everyone concerned, to utilise it as a demonstration school in bilingual methods for the benefit of the national teachers and others attending the College courses. Úna Ní Fhaircheallaigh, the Principal of the College, who has just returned from a series of visits to bilingual schools in North Wales, will, with the co-operation of Pádraic Mac Giolla Cearr, the teacher, — himself a noted exponent of sound method — give demonstration lessons in the teaching of Irish and English side by side to school children, and the bilingual teaching of history, geography, arithmetic, object lessons, and the other subjects which go to make up a primary school course. The students of the College will also be required to conduct bilingual lessons in the school subject to the criticism of the College staff. It is to be trusted that every member of Tír Chonaill's growing little army of bilingual teachers will make an effort to attend this most valuable course. It should be possible for the other Irish Colleges to attempt something similar. There are two bilingual schools in the immediate neighbourhood of Coláiste Chonnacht, and we understand that the Bilingual Programme is to be introduced in the Ballingeary Schools on July 1st. The scheme, therefore, should be feasible both at Túr Mhic Éadaigh and at Béal Átha an Ghaortaidh.

Reverting to a matter touched on last week, the Board, it is to be feared, is not yet at the right viewpoint on the subject of bilingualism in the Gaedhealtacht. Its *Rules and Regulations,* at any rate, lend colour to the theory that it regards the Bilingual Programme primarily as an instrument for facilitating the learning of English by Irish-speaking children. Irish Ireland strenuously dissents. A bilingual system contemplates the *education* of the child through two languages: but in the Gaedhealtacht Irish must be established and must remain the 'first language' throughout the whole of the course. The Education Committee of the Coiste Gnótha has been pressing the Board to withdraw the absurd rules referred to in our last issue which lay down that where the Bilingual Programme is adopted 'Irish should be mainly the medium of instruction for the junior standards (I to III) *and English mainly for the higher*;' and that 'the merit of the teaching is judged by the proficiency both in Irish and English, the former being, 'the main factor in the case of the junior classes *and the latter in the case of the higher*'. Let English be taught by all means, and the better it is taught the better pleased shall we, for one, be — for we agree that what is worth doing at all is worth doing well: but English must not replace Irish as the first and most intimate vernacular, or as the instrument of the higher culture, of Irish-speaking children, which seems to be what is .contemplated by these rules. Seán Ó Cuiv endeavoured to move a resolution on this subject at the Ard-Fheis, but did not succeed, as he had not placed it on the Agenda: we hope, however, that the whole organisation will rally behind the demand that these obnoxious provisions be removed from the *Rules and Regulations* for 1908-9, now going through the press. By its attitude towards this demand we shall be able to test the *bona fides* of the Board and the sanity of its conception of a bilingual system as applied to the Irish-speaking districts.

BILINGUALISM: ITS GREAT ADVANTAGES
11.7.1908

We recently published extracts from a striking report by one of the senior inspectors of the National Board, which was really an eloquent plea for a bilingual system of education in Irish-speaking districts. In the course of his remarks the inspector declared the unilingual (or English alone) method of teaching in Irish-speaking districts to be 'the clumsiest, the most irrational, and hopelessly ineffective'.

Welsh educationists have for many years advocated a system of bilingual education in that country; yet the British Education Department has not met them in any way to the same extent to that which the National Board has already met the Gaelic League in this country.

A writer in the *Cymmrodorian* as far back as January, 1882, says: — 'If proper advantage were taken of the peculiar bilingual conditions of the country the *elementary schools* of Wales might be placed at least on an equality with the *secondary schools* of England, as far as real mental culture is concerned. These latter differ from the elementary schools mentally by the fact that a little Latin and French are taught. But what advantage is this French and Latin? Only to this: that the average boy who leaves school for business, say at 16, is perhaps able to translate easy French into English; but as for translating a piece of English into French it is generally beyond his powers. In Latin his acquirements are much more moderate.

'Welsh which is easily and naturally acquired, enables the pupil to gain a better knowledge of English, and very soon it will be possible to exercise him in translation from one language to another, written and oral; an exercise acknowledged from the days of Cicero to be of the highest value as a mental training.

'If such a course were adopted, the boy who now leaves school comparatively ignorant of English, would go forth into the world with a power of using *two languages* with equal ease, and possess a far more grammatical knowledge of both.

'Need it be asked: which is the *more* valuable mental acquisition, such a practical and intelligent knowledge, or a mere smattering of French and Latin, which is soon forgotten? . . .

'If this right method were pursued, Welsh and English would become to the children of the Principality almost as two vernacular languages. In both they would be able to think, and express their thoughts with equal ease. This would be an attainment of the highest value from an educational point of view; as it would constitute a stimulus of mental activity that could not otherwise be supplied. For it is very rarely that such a knowledge of French or German is acquired at our grammar schools as enables a pupil to use either of these languages with any degree of facility, if at all. And until a language can be used freely as an exponent of thought, it has not served its higher purpose as an instrument of culture.'

Put the word 'Irish' for 'Welsh', and Ireland for Wales, and the foregoing pronouncement on this important question will apply with singular force to the conditions prevailing in many parts of our own country.

We trust that these words of the Welsh educationalist will be carefully pondered upon by everyone anxious to promote education in Ireland; and especially by managers in Irish-speaking districts who are now in a position to put this beneficial system of bilingual education in force in such a large number of elementary schools.

If further proof were needed of the immense advantages of bilingual teaching it would be found in a 'Report on Modern Language Teaching' issued by the English Education Board some five years ago.

The 'Report' deals with the system of teaching in vogue in Belgium, Holland, and Germany. In the former country owing to the 'Mouvement Flamand' or Flemish Language Movement, the system of education has been bilingual for some years. In Flemish-speaking districts, Flemish is the first teaching language, and French is introduced by degrees into the school curriculum until both are practically on a level: and the pupil on leaving school possesses a practical knowledge of the two languages. In French-speaking districts, French is naturally the first teaching language, and Flemish gradually introduced, when the same result is produced as in the former case: pupils with a practical knowledge of two languages.

In the official *Programme of Teaching* it is laid down that:

'The teaching of the second language (French or Flemish according to locality) should be by the "Direct" or Natural Method. This method consists in teaching a foreign language without having recourse to translation, except in special cases; and even then, a direct and intimate connection should always be maintained between words and ideas. The lessons should deal with things familiar to all the children (the family, clothes, furniture, etc.), or with things which have already been made the subject of lessons in the children's own language. Thus the whole attention can be concentrated on correct pronunciation and the construction of sentences. Care should be taken to keep before the children the objects which are mentioned, either by models or pictures, or blackboard illustrations. To make verbs intelligible, the action spoken of should be performed as far as possible, — by the teacher or the pupils themselves. Let us now glance briefly at the result of this system of teaching.'

The writer of the Report goes on to say: —

'On entering another primary school I heard a French lesson given to Flemish children, *mostly under eight*, who had only learnt about eight months.

'An outline picture was traced lightly on paper, with a piece of charcoal the teacher then filled in the various parts of the picture, speaking and asking the children questions (in French) all the time.'

In the Secondary Schools, the results of this bilingual system of teaching are still more striking. The Report referred to says: — 'In the well-known State School of Mlle. Gatti de Gamond in Brussells I heard an English lesson given to children (boys and girls), in the "Classe Maternelle", little children *under seven and eight*'.

During this and similar lessons a running conversation is kept up between teacher and pupils in the shape of questions and answers, 'questions being asked about the names and qualities of everything in the room'.

Such in brief are the methods, and such are the results of Bilingualism in a country where it is carried out as a *National Educational Policy*.

THE NEW UNIVERSITY: IRISH ESSENTIAL FOR MATRICULATION
22.8.1908

The new Coiste Gnótha lost no time in making arrangements to follow up the work of its predecessor in reference to the new University. At the very first meeting of the new Executive, a special committee was appointed to place the views of the League before the members of the Statutory Commission by means of a deputation, and to take active steps to secure the co-operation of the country in pressing forward their demands.

Fears have been expressed that possibly one or two members of the Commission, would not be agreeable to have Irish made a compulsory subject for Matriculation in the new University. Some people have a very curious idea of the word 'compulsory'; they call it 'coercion', and even stronger names; forgetting that nearly every action of our daily lives is more or less compulsory. In our student days, every text studied and every examination prepared for, a certain degree of compulsion had to be exercised. The vast majority of us daily fulfill duties with the greatest alacrity, which in the last analysis, are really compulsory. Whatever is necessary, is not compulsion, and should not be described as such.

The whole question reduces itself to this: Is the new University to be frankly and avowedly English only, or is it to be partly Irish and partly English — absolutely Irish it cannot be, for years to come. But we want the door open for this. English, and we presume Latin, will be compulsory for Matriculation; but no exception is taken to compulsion in reference to these; we want Irish to be in the same position — we cannot accept less. We acknowledge that English is necessary, but we consider Irish absolutely essential, and unless the new University is determined to follow the traditions of Trinity College, it will make Irish a subject for Matriculation, and that too, without any pressure from the outside public. The function of the new University should not be to turn out so many persons per annum entitled to write certain letters to their names; if it is to be any service to Ireland, its function will be to train the intellects of its students, lead them to aim at a high standard of culture, and inculcate lofty national ideals.

For generations our education has been shaped and moulded to a British pattern, and after a long trial, its very advocates admit that it is barren of results; the intellect of our people was directed into the wrong channel, and as a nation we stand today absolutely devoid of science, art or industry. If the new University is not to tread the same barren path, it will gladly respond to the wishes and ideals of the people for whom, presumably, it has been established, for if it is not openly with the Gael, the new University must necessarily be against him. There is no middle course, and any attempt to steer a middle course, even if there were such, would render the new institution useless — it would be 'neither flesh, fowl, nor good red herring'.

Intellectual freedom must precede political or national freedom: the first care of every race struggling to maintain their national existence, is to educate their people on national lines, and through the medium of their own tongue. It is inconceivable that our new University shall take an opposite course by closing the door upon our native language at the very outset? It can hardly place the English language on the pinnacle of honour, while the language of the people for whom the University has been founded is relegated to a corner, just to be picked up by whoever cares to do so? Yet if this course is adopted, and we protest against such treatment, we will be told that we want to coerce the Statutory Commissioners and the Senate. No, we want no coercion, but we want to see that justice shall be done. We want to see that our native tongue shall have its rightful place in the curriculum of the new University, and be made equal to English as a subject for the entrance examination. Let us not be misunderstood, this is only part of our demands but we want to be sure of the beginning. We look to the new University to make such provision as will raise up successors to Keating, Mac Firbis, and the O'Clery's, O'Curry, Petrie and O'Donovan; but as we have said, we must look to the beginning.

'Tús maith leath na hoibre.'

We freely and thankfully acknowledge that both the Statutory Commission and the Senate contain several who are anxious to make the new institution a genuine National University, but we feel that a clear and definite demand from the people of Ireland, that their native tongue must have its rightful place in the University curriculum, and especially in the matriculation examination, would materially strengthen the hands of our friends against any opposition that might be offered.

Surely, to ask that the Irish language should form an essential subject for matriculation in an Irish University, is not an unreasonable request.

The making of Irish compulsory for Matriculation may be regarded as a barrier to the admission of numbers of students. But in view of the numerous opportunities now afforded for acquiring the necessary knowledge, this excuse cannot hold for a moment. If the Statutory Commissioners at an early stage of their proceedings declare that Irish shall form an essential subject for Matriculation, colleges and students shall have practically two years to prepare for it. Surely the Matriculation examination of the new University will be equal to those of the Intermediate Education Board, that has now made a knowledge of a second language, together with English, compulsory for a pass in the Junior, Middle, and Senior Grades. Besides, the new institution should aim rather at quality than quantity — it is not the number of students that matriculate or graduate, that will reflect credit on the new University, but the standard of its examinations and the degree of culture attained.

Professor Kuno Meyer, speaking recently in Dublin, referring in the course of his lecture to the University of Liverpool, said: 'Our first act, when we had our Charter, was to *insist on a rigorous entrance examination,* which *excluded one-third* of those students on whom we had hitherto drawn. But within two or three years, a better class of students began to be attracted to us; the numbers rose rapidly, and have now far surpassed any previous record. Contrast this, for instance, with Durham University that opens its portals to any new comer without examination or test of any kind, and has never succeeded in attracting more than one hundred students.'

We think this is a conclusive reply to those who would lower the entrance examination to the new Irish University by excluding the Irish language from Matriculation. Furthermore, Irish as an entrance subject would materially help to forward bilingualism throughout the country. The fact that Irish was necessary for Matriculation as well as for other University examinations, would encourage secondary schools to take up the bilingual system, which as yet, they have not touched. On the immense advantages of bilingual education, we need not now dwell, except to point out that it is to this system of education that Belgium owes her eminence in commerce and industry.

Industrial and commercial prosperity can only come from the intellectual development of a people on national lines; intellectual patriotism is the foundation on which the industry and commerce of every nation has been raised. The man who is not a patriot, as well as a scholar, will never become a pioneer in any scheme for the elevation and betterment of his fellow countrymen; but when men are trained to love their country, and all that belongs to it, they will then be ready to devote their lives to her service, whether in the marts of commerce, the factory, workshop, or in the chemical laboratory.

If Ireland's new University commences its career, by brushing aside Ireland's language from its entrance examination, it will court defeat at the very outset; if, instead of drawing forth those intellectual gifts which the Gael possesses in abundance, the new University begins by teaching its students to content themselves with borrowing the language and ideals of another people, intellectual stagnation must be the consequence. But, as Professor Meyer said: 'If she will only be true to her genius, and *eschew like poison*, the baneful example of the older English University system, which Trinity College has so slavishly imitated, she (Ireland) may once more become what she was in her golden age, the home of learning of the Western World.'

Whatever attitude the Statutory Commissioners may ultimately adopt, we have confidence in the patriotism of the people that they will whole-heartedly support us in this most reasonable demand, that Irish shall be necessary for the entrance examination in the new University. English and Latin will be compulsory, is Irish to be 'boycotted'? It all depends on the people of Ireland. If they are *Irish*, their language will not be boycotted: as Dr. Hyde said at the Oireachtas: 'if the people are Irish, the University will be Irish; but if they are "Gallda", then the University will be Gallda', – and so, will be useless to Ireland.

IRISH IN THE NEW UNIVERSITY
5.9.1908

In a recent article we set forth the demands of the Gaelic League in reference to the place which Irish should occupy in the matriculation examination in the new University. A gentleman, who is not a member of the Gaelic League, though a sincere friend of the movement, expressed to us the opinion that while Irish should be essential for Matriculation, it was impossible at present to make it equal to English in this examination. Another gentleman, who is a Gaelic Leaguer, and an earnest and prominent worker in the movement, has raised the very same objection, and pointed out that at the present juncture, it was unwise to claim that Irish should be placed on the same footing as English, since the latter language must for some years, be the medium of examination for the various subjects.

It would appear from the foregoing that at least one passage in our first article has been misunderstood; and as we want no misunderstanding on the matter, it might be as well to refer briefly to the subject again.

In the first place, we quite recognise that English must, for some years, be the medium of examination in all subjects, at Matriculation, and other examinations, except for Irish itself. In these circumstances we quite understand that Irish cannot be placed at present, on exactly the same footing as English at any examination, until such time as the lectures in the various colleges and seminaries are given bilingually, or in Irish altogether; and for this ideal state of things, we must wait for some years. These were the facts we intended to convey when we said in reference to the University: 'absolutely Irish it cannot be for years to come'.

But, in bracketing Irish with English for Matriculation, we did so as 'a subject'. The words we used were: 'We want to see that our native tongue shall have its rightful place in the curriculum of the new University, and be made equal to English as *a subject for* the entrance examination'.

When we wrote these words, we had in mind, that, in addition to its being the medium of the various examinations, English would probably form a special 'subject' for Matriculation in the New University, as it does at present in the 'Royal', and in London and other English Universities, where students for Matriculation must pass a fairly searching examination in 'English Language' (its grammar, structure, and history) which examination is, of course, conducted through the medium of English itself. In the University of Sydney, Australia, and in Yale University, U.S.A., 'English' forms a special subject for the entrance examination. These were the facts which led us to ask Irish being placed in the same position as a 'subject' for entrance to the new University.

It is, however, quite possible, if not probable that since English must for the time being, be the medium of all examinations (except for Irish) the Statutory Commissioners may not make English a *special subject* for Matriculation at all. It is not so in Oxford, Cambridge, and other English Universities; while in others such as those of Leeds and Sheffield, 'English Literature' may be taken in lieu of 'English Language'.

However, from our point of view, it is immaterial whether or not, English is made obligatory as a special subject for Matriculation, but we must press as earnestly and as vigorously as we can, for the making of the National language of this country, an essential subject for Matriculation, in the new University. We want to be perfectly clear on this. What we ask is, that it be made obligatory on all students for Matriculation to pass an examination in oral and written Irish, which examination should be conducted through the medium of Irish itself. Examinations in Irish of a very elementary character have been conducted through the medium of the same language by the London Gaelic League; in the first, second, and third grades of the Gaelic League Scholarship examination, the same thing is done. In all the Gaelic Training Colleges, the instruction is not only through the medium of Irish, but the examinations are absolutely so. We would expect, therefore, that a fair amount of oral and written knowledge would be insisted on for Matriculation in the new University, so that students pursuing their Irish studies could follow lectures delivered in the language.

An early declaration on the matter from the Statutory Commissioners would not only set all doubts and misgivings at rest, but set practically every school and college in the land at once making preparations to meet the requirements of the University; and by the time the Matriculation examination had to be held, there would be no lack of students fully prepared in Irish, owing to the numerous facilities now offered for gaining a thorough knowledge of the language. In fact, once it was made definitely known that Irish would be required for Matriculation, there is every probability that most, if not all the Gaelic Colleges, would lengthen their sessions by some months, in order to prepare students in Irish.

205

The Rev. Dr. O'Daly speaking recently at Ballingeary, said in reference to the Gaelic College there:

> 'Some of those connected with it had ideas for its future development in connection with University Education. Under the recent University Act the Senate of the Dublin University would have power to recognise that College if it established a complete course of Arts studies and maintained a standard of teaching which would satisfy the Senate. They had already been doing University work at the College. Dr. Bergin's lectures last year on historical Irish grammar were up to University standard. Father O'Nolan taught elementary science and grammar, and he himself had taught the science of speech sounds. All this was University work. It was hoped to continue and extend this work from year to year until finally the whole course of Arts studies would be covered. They would then have a unique institution, a College in which University education would be imparted in the Irish language.'

The 'Leinster' and other Gaelic Colleges would probably follow suit, and vie with each other in the extent and variety of their Gaelic studies, so that the Statutory Commissioners need not fear but that ample opportunities would be available for preparing students for the Irish portion of the Matriculation examination.

Let every friend of the language bear well in mind all that depends on having Irish made an obligatory subject for entrance to the new University. The aim of every secondary school, of every college and seminary throughout the country, would be to meet the requirements of the Matriculation examination; what is obligatory in the University will naturally find the first and securest place in the college curriculum. Therefore, by making Irish essential for Matriculation, it would at once be placed in a position of honour and security in the colleges and seminaries of Ireland, such as it never before occupied within their walls.

Our readers will now, perhaps, realise that the refusal of the Commissioners to make Irish an essential subject for Matriculation, would have the most disastrous consequences for the Language: such a refusal would throw us back as it were, for some years, and seriously hamper the progress of the movement. As we have said, what is made obligatory in the new University, will be so in the curricula of the various colleges preparing students for its examinations, while so-called 'optional' subjects will have to take a back-seat.

If then, Irish should be brushed aside at the entrance to the new University, we may be certain that as far as the secondary schools and colleges are concerned, the position of the language will be precarious to say the least of it. No matter how desirous such schools and colleges may be to promote the language — and most of them are at present doing excellent work for it — they must shape their courses according to essential requirements.

Let every friend of the language bear well in mind all that depends on having Irish made an obligatory subject for entrance to the new University. The aim of every secondary school, of every college and seminary throughout the country, would be to meet the requirements of the Matriculation examination; what is obligatory in the University will naturally find the first and securest place in the college curriculum.

Therefore, by making Irish essential for Matriculation, it would at once be placed in a position of honour and security in the colleges and seminaries of Ireland, such as it never before occupied within their walls.

Our readers will now, perhaps, realise that the refusal of the Commissioners to make Irish an essential subject for Matriculation, would have the most disastrous consequences for the Language; such a refusal would throw us back as it were, for some years, and seriously hamper the progress of the movement. As we have said, what is made obligatory in the new University, will be so in the curricula of the various colleges preparing students for its examinations, while so-called 'optional' subjects will have to take a back-seat.

We have, however, every hope that the Statutory Commissioners will manfully stand by the Irish nation, and meet its demand that whatever else is required, Irish at least shall be essential at entrance, and up to the end of the first or second year in the University. We sincerely trust there will be no attempt made to put back the hands of the clock in Ireland. We have only asked a very reasonable position for the language; and any attempt to set it aside, or minimise it to any extent, would only create bitterness and disappointment, which would be a bad augury for the success of the new seat of learning.

FRIENDS AND FOES
5.12.1908

A crisis is upon us. The eventful period of the last fifteen years has come, if not to a climax, at least to a point at which we must distinguish our trustworthy friends from those who no longer deserve to be leaders or advisers. We have come to the parting of the ways, and all true men must feel that common sense, honesty, and devotion to our cause demand that we accompany no farther on the path of compromise those of our erstwhile friends who have joined forces with the enemy to prevent the new Dublin University being either Irish or National. In a nation like ours, made up of many political, racial, and religious elements, compromise, or the policy of 'give and take', is ever in the air. We all have passions, strivings, ideals, but we must be ever prepared to fine down our demands for the sake of unity, co-operation, and progress. Times come, however, when compromise becomes treason, when the fining down of demands becomes actual submission or betrayal, and we feel that those who believe in Irish nationality have now reached a point from which they cannot recede if even the minimum rights of the cause they love and serve are to be maintained.

A number of late events following hot upon one another's heels have indicated that very many have been living in a fool's paradise, regarding not only the probable attitude of the Senate of the Dublin University towards the national language, but regarding even the purpose which in the intention of the majority of the Senate the University should serve. Mr. P. J. O'Neill's little outburst was but as the kite before the storm. The intentions and attitude of many of those on the Senate were indicated in the startling speech of the Very Rev. Dr. Delany, S.J., at the University College Gaelic Society last Friday evening. Dr. Delany is opposed to the making of Irish a necessary subject on the University curriculum. His ideal for the future of the University can be neither pleasing nor encouraging to the majority of the community. His hope is to make it a University for the

English-speaking world, or, frankly, for the British Empire.

We cannot forget that Dr. Delany belongs to a religious order whose interests and activities are not confined to Ireland, and his position represents that of many others whose minds seem obsessed by the time-worn fallacy that the mission of our race is to keep English-speaking peoples straight in their morals. No other conclusion can be drawn from his speech and his statement that if Irish were compulsory foreign students would be deterred from coming to Dublin. He supplied no argument why a country so poor as ours should found and support a University for other lands. And his statement that because only six per cent of the Royal University students take up Irish, the making of Irish compulsory would exclude great numbers of native students from the new University was very misleading. He omitted to tell his audience that all medical students taking their degree at the Royal University are prevented from taking Irish by a rule which compels them to take, besides Latin, either French or German. Any student having three languages to prepare cannot be blamed if he omits to tack on a fourth which is only an optional subject, and not encouraged by his examiners. But Dr. Delany cannot have taken his own argument seriously, any more than we can take his assertion that we have no proper teachers of Irish, or any reliable or useful textbooks of the language. These statements are so opposed to facts as to suggest that their author took no pains to acquaint himself with the justice of the Gaelic League demands.

Dr. Delany is an old man and we have no hopes of converting him to our ideas. He was old when the Gaelic League was born and ere the re-awakened spirit of nationhood which it brought back had come. He and those of his way of thinking are the victims of seven centuries of Irish history, which, to some minds, go to prove that we are not a nation and never will be. Their opposition to Ireland's language is their denial of Ireland a nation. They cannot be convinced; they must be fought.

Having made due allowance for the conservatism of men to whom Gaelic League ideas and claims are new and revolutionary, we hoped that the Senate would meet us half way, and that the worst we had to fear was the delay of a few years until Irish would be a necessary subject for every student of the University, and an indispensable part of Irish higher education. The discovery that certain members of the Senate from whom we had hoped for support are opposed to our claims was startling and disappointing, and now comes the rumour that the decision to name the new University the 'National University' has been set aside, and that the name is to be the 'King's University". Should this be true it would seem to indicate that the purpose of those who sanctioned the founding of the new Universities was not to benefit Irleand, but rather to capture and control the hitherto independent portion of the system of higher education in this country, to oppose and nullify the effects on Irish education of the revival of the Irish language, and to strike a final and effective blow at the richest heritage of our fallen nationhood, the independence and freedom of Irish thought. Left the right to think for ourselves and the freedom to guide and mould the mind of young Ireland, we should never fear for the future; but deny us these and what remains? Territory without those rights is but an unhallowed thing and the people that acquiesces in their betrayal stoops its brow for the brand of the slave.

The thinking part of our people, those of them embraced by the Gaelic League, will not accept a new system of higher education in which the national language does not get a standing such as is due and becoming to a national language. They know that the future spirit and aims of our primary and secondary systems will eventually be determined by the University systems, and they must oppose any system of education the fundamental basis of which is not founded on the recognition of Gaelic civilisation, and the end and aims of which are other than the welfare of the people of Ireland, in Ireland.

The voice of the Gael on this matter has not yet been heard effectively, but it soon will. The Ard-Rúnaire has announced a public meeting which is to be held in the Rotunda on next Monday evening. The speakers will include An Craobhín and Eoin Mac Neill, and many others of the boldest and most trusted champions of our cause. Several prominent workers are coming from the country to join in the protest against the proposed degradation of Irish below the level of a dead language. Of Dublin Gaels we hope to see a great hosting, a gathering animated by a determined spirit, and of such proportions as will show that the Gaelic League is the strongest force working for the regeneration of the nation, and that no one and no party choosing to ignore its demands can hope for success. From Belfast and Cork comes the news that two great meetings are being organised in those centres, and when our three premier cities have spoken the voice of the nation will be no longer inarticulate.

On the Senate, and outside of those members who are also members of the Coiste Gnótha of the League, there is one man to whom Ireland looks with hope in this crisis. His Grace the Archbishop of Dublin has on more than one occasion successfully opposed the designs of powers greater than those we have now to fight. He has dared for the sake of truth and right to court the enmity of the greatest in the land, and we hope and feel that when the hour of trial comes he will be found on the side of his race.

THE NATION AND THE UNIVERSITIES
12.12.1908

During the next few weeks the Gaelic League must justify its existence as a force in Irish life. Judging from the way in which it has now addressed itself to its task, the justification will be a complete one. The Gaelic League is here to vindicate and to voice traditional Irish civilisation. It stands for the historic Irish Nation. It is in protest not against the Union but against the Conquest. Rather, it does not admit the Conquest. It claims that this broken and battered frame is still a Nation, bearing high on its brow all the august marks of Nationality, treasuring still in its heart the unconquerable desire to live its own life, to work out its own destiny. It is the business of the Gaelic League to assert this truth when and wheresoever it finds it contradicted. It is its business as far as it can to secure for this truth the allegiance of all the men of Ireland. How far that allegiance has really been secured is one of the questions that has haunted the sleep of the leaders of the language movement. It need haunt their sleep no longer. The events of the last few weeks are proving that Ireland — democratic Ireland, the Ireland that toils, the Ireland that thinks, the Ireland that *matters* — is with us. Our people are not yet all enthusiasts in this matter of conserving the historic Irish language as the seal and sacrament of historic Irish nationality. It may be years before they are all enthusiasts. But it is becoming daily clearer and clearer that the public sentiment of Ireland, so

209

far as that sentiment is at all articulate, is overwhelmingly with the Language Movement, — that, in fact, the people are willing to go as far and as fast as we are willing to lead them, and that the measure of their allegiance is simply the measure of our courage in claiming it.

Six months ago the League formulated its demands touching the position of Irish in the new Universities. To many men high in Church and State and academic dignity those demands appeared extravagant and preposterous. Not so to the people. The people straightway endorsed them. For months past the people have only been waiting for the League to put itself at their head and to march forward and claim their fulfilment. The League, exhausted for the time being as the result of a foolish internecine quarrel early in the year, lay quiescent during several months. At last, just at the psychological moment, it has roused itself to action. It finds the people ready to follow it. We believe that the people will follow it to the very end — to a victorious assault on the citadels of the Promised Land or, if need be, back into the desert again.

Monday's great meeting in the Rotunda shows how popular feeling is running. Only once before — when it was a question of defending our language in the primary schools against the attack of the British Treasury — did a mightier rally answer the summons of the Ard-Rúnaidhe. But the meeting of Monday evening perhaps surpassed and certainly equalled that other historic gathering in the representativeness of its character and in the stark vehemence of its determination. What other cause in Ireland could so pack that huge hall? What cause essentially intellectual could so pack such a hall in any other country? Noble things must needs be in store for that nation the democracy of whose capital takes so passionate an interest in a subject ordinarily considered as merely academic.

The Commissioners and Senators of the new Universities had best take note of all this. Let them realise once and for all that this question, which they had thought to settle quietly amongst themselves in a back room, has already been settled by public opinion. The men and women of Ireland want their national language an essential subject of study in their National Universities. It is not for any parcel of educational pundits to say them nay. The people in this matter are more advanced than the educationists. Some of the educationists, on their own admission, stand at the same point at which they stood twenty-five years ago. They are men of a past generation. But the people have been marching on while they have been standing still. Is it for men with ideas quarter of a century old to mould the character of the Universities into which the young men of this generation, with their newer, saner, broader ideas, their sounder, because more national point of view, all their fresh young hopes and enthusiasms, are about to press?

It is rumoured that certain high and mighty personages threaten to resign their seats as Commissioners or Senators if the demands of Irish Ireland are acceded to. If there be on the Commissions or Senates men who esteem their own prejudices as more sacred than the hopes and aspirations of the Irish Nation, then they had better go at once: they have no place in the economy of a University which is designed above all things to méet the legitimate aspirations and reflect the national sentiment of the Irish people. For the sake of their good names, it is to be hoped that Lord Chief Baron Palles and Professor S. H. Butcher are not amongst those who have been using the unworthy threats referred to.

It may be that these people, hugging themselves in the delusion that they are essential to the success of the Universities, have been endeavouring to

210

intimidate such of the Irish Ireland Senators as they regarded as least extreme by holding out threats of resignation with the possible consequence of shipwreck to the whole scheme. They know now that these weak Irish Ireland Senators are non-existent. In this question every Gaelic Leaguer stands where his President and Vice-President stand. An Craobhín has defined his position in a splendid phrase which will live. 'If we are to have the Confederation of Kilkenny over again, I stand by Eoghan Ruadh'. In the Dublin University the Gaelic League representatives to a man will demand that Irish be made an essential subject of study. In maintenance of that demand they will fight to the last ditch. Eoin Mac Neill almost scouts the possibility of failure; but, contemplating that possibility for an instant, he declares that, when the moment for such a decision comes, it will be for men and women of the language movement to determine whether their representatives in the Universities are to walk out or to continue the fight from within. The strength of the League's position consists largely in the fact that it has left itself absolutely free. Unlike its opponents it does not tie its own hands by preliminary threats.

The same note of uncompromising determination was struck by all the subsequent speakers. An tAthair Mathghamhain Ó Riain (the League's new Vice-President received a rousing reception from his first Dublin audience), Art Ó Grióbhtha, Ulliam Mac Giolla Bríde, and An tAthair Lorcán Ó Ciaráin, each standing at a different view-point, all enforced the utter unanimity of the Irish Ireland demand; and this unanimity was still further emphasised by the batch of letters and telegrams read by the Ard-Rúnaidhe. There were expressions of opinion from prominent leaders in every political party, almost in every political group, in Ireland; from prelates; from educationists; from distinguished scholars; from League Branches and Coistí Ceanntair at home and abroad; from political and other organisations of various types and complexions; from representatives of almost every phase and factor in Irish life. Maynooth voiced its sympathy through Connradh Chuilm Naomtha; Irish America spoke in terse and telling cablegrams from Father Yorke and the President of the Ancient Order of Hibernians; the leader of the young Scottish Gaelic Party assured us of the moral support of our brother Gaels of Alba; Mr. Lindsay Crawford gave welcome expression to the new Irish faith that is stirring in the heart of Young Ulster. Prominent amongst the communications read was a letter addressed by An tAthair Michael Ó hIceadha to Pádraic Ó Brolcháin. It reminded one of ancient rights fought and won to hear again once that stern resolute voice. It is significant of the graveness of the crisis that it should have tempted An tAthair Michael to break at last his self-imposed silence of six years. Once again the unity, the solidarity, the spirit of comradeship, the loyal co-operation in the face of danger which are characteristic of the Gaelic League are made splendidly manifest.

Dr. O'Hickey's letter was largely a vigorous elaboration of a thesis laid down by Eoin Mac Neill, and accepted, be it noted by such of our opponents as are represented by the Rev. Dr. Delany. Irish Ireland's case may be put thus. A knowledge of the language, literature, and history of Irish is admittedly essential to the liberal education of an Irishman. The function of the new Universities is admittedly to provide a liberal education for Irishmen. On what pretext then can we exclude the language, literature, and history of Ireland as essential subjects in the curriculum of the Universities?

Last week we warned those responsible of the terrible disillusionment they were preparing for themselves if they persisted in calling the new Dublin University by the title of 'The King's University'. The warning has been heeded, and at the last moment it has been decided to revert to the name of 'The National University of Ireland'. It is well. Nothing is more certain than that the new University would have been the most ghastly failure in Irish history had a name objectionable to the majority of the people of Ireland been persisted in. But it would be even more serious if the University were to commence its career in a spirit antagonistic to Irish national sentiment. For ourselves, we do not fear for the language. Sooner or later it will force its way into its proper place in the University and in University life. But the struggle may be a terrible one, and if there is a struggle the University is bound to suffer. Let those at the head of affairs take heed in time. And Eoin Mac Neill utters a warning which is still more grave. 'If a University is now established which, as has been commonly and with good authority stated, will be acceptable to the Catholics of this country as Catholics, and which will not be acceptable to the Irishmen of this country as Irishmen — if any such institution at this time of the day is set up here in our midst — it will be the most portentous danger to Irish life that has ever been seen in Ireland.'

IRISH AS AN ESSENTIAL: THE WHY AND THE WHEREFORE
19.12.1908

It appears to us that during the past few weeks the League has made considerable progress in convincing the public opinion of Ireland that it is a highly sane and reasonable thing to postulate that a knowledge of Ireland's language is essential to the liberal education of an Irishman. Not indeed that public opinion needed a violent conversion. In Ireland of recent years public opinion has largely regained that precision of intuition which characterises it in all healthy nations not labouring under abnormal excitement. The League's demand has, indeed, only to be stated in the form we have just given it to command the assent of all men in possession of ordinarily-developed thinking faculties. In this form, be it remembered, it commands the assent of the Rev. Dr. Delany. The Doctor's expression of approval when Eoin Mac Neill so stated it was emphatic. The League is simply asking Dr. Delany and those of his fellow-Senators who agree with him to carry their theory into practice. They hold, as we hold, that a knowledge of Irish is essential to the liberal education of an Irishman. But they are placed at the head of an institution whose raison d'etre is precisely to supply a liberal education for Irishmen. Is it not their clear bounden duty, on their own admission, to make Irish an essential part of the curriculum of that institution? If that is not done, how can the institution be said to be providing a liberal education for Irishmen?

There is really no getting away from this argument. The only attempt to meet it is a feeble appeal to expediency. 'Is it wise', we are asked, 'to force Irish down the throats of people who don't want it?' We answer in the first place that it is always wise to do the right thing, — the thing that principle dictates; our opponents, recollect, agree with us *in principle*. We answer in the second place that to assume that the young men and women who will come into the new University do not want Irish is to make an assumption wholly unwarranted. The Intermediate results lists, the class-rolls of the League Branches, of the Irish Summer Schools, of the

Irish Training Colleges, all prove that the young men and women of Ireland *do* want Irish. It is the one thing in their educational programme they are really keen about. We answer in the third place that it is no more tyrannical to force Irish down the throats of a (largely imaginary) minority who don't want it than it is to force Latin, English, Logic, Algebra, and a number of other things down the throat of everyone.

It may be retorted that if the young men and women of Ireland really want Irish there is no need to make it a compulsory subject. Let Irish be given fair play as between itself and the other modern languages. Let the student, as the Rev. Dr. Delany suggests, be allowed to select any two languages from a group of four or five of which Irish shall be one. Or let the student, — to discuss another scheme that has been hinted at as a possible solution — be required to stand an examination in six quasi-obligatory subjects, e.g., Latin or Greek, Irish, English, French or German, Mathematics, and Physics, with the proviso, however, that failure to pass in one of these subjects shall not involve failure to pass the whole examination, provided the answering in the other five subjects has been good.

Now, we must meet all such proposals with the query: 'Do they promise real equality of treatment for Irish or only an ostensible equality?' On examination, it will be found that they do not guarantee equality at all. Nominally, they leave the student who is so minded perfectly free to take Irish: in reality they weight the scales against Irish. Where a student has an option at Matriculation and First Arts he will almost certainly select the subjects which will be essential later on when he comes to specialise. This is how Irish has been squeezed out in the Royal University. A student who has in view a degree in Ancient Classics will at Matriculation select Latin and Greek as against Latin and Irish; a student who has in view a scholarship or studentship in Modern Literature will select French and German as against French and Irish or German and Irish; a student who is going on for law or for medicine will select English, Latin, and Greek, or English, Latin, and French, as against Irish and any two of these. This shows that the 'equality' held out by all such schemes is illusory. When the later courses are framed (as they must to a certain extent be framed) on lines of specialisation, a permissive grouping of subjects in the first or second year simply means that the student will in his own interests commence to specialise a year or two earlier: he will from the start pick out from the list of subjects amongst which he is allowed an 'option' those which he requires for his later purpose. It is obvious that there is no real option here. The ostensible 'equality of treatment' works out in such a way that the classical man, the scientific man, the legal man, the medical man, are one and all compelled — compelled in sheer self-defence — to omit Irish, however willing and anxious they may be to take it up.

There can be no acceptance of any such illusory scheme of 'equality', no matter by whom proposed. To offer us even real equality of treatment — *mere* equality of treatment for our *national* language — is an insult to our nationality; to offer us a sham equality is an insult to our intelligence. Let it be understood once and for all that mere equality of treatment between Irish and the minor subjects of the University course falls far short of what we require. It is simply preposterous to think that the demand of a nation for adequate recognition for its national language in the courses of its National University can be met by saying to it: 'Oh! we are placing Irish on a level of absolute equality with — physics'. *A knowledge of Irish is essential to the liberal education of an Irishman*: accepting this as

213

axiomatic, the new University must devise machinery for giving it effect in practice. It has no ground for a refusal to grant this demand unless it admit that its end and purpose are something other than the liberal education of Irishmen. And if its end and purpose be not the liberal education of Irishmen, what title has it to our respect or our support?

ENGLISHMEN FOR IRISH POSTS
19.12.1908

Last week we complained that the Intermediate Commissioners are not making Irish an essential qualification for the new inspectorships they are about to create. They do not even say that a preference will be given in a specified number of the appointments to candidates knowing Irish. The Commissioners could not have stopped the teaching of Irish in the colleges, but now they refuse to provide for inspection in this subject or to give colleges any credit for efficient teaching. This matter affects not only the interests of our language, but also the material interests of the colleges. Will the college authorities of Ireland put up with such treatment? For the sake of their own good repute and independence we hope they will not. The proposed appointment of inspectors who will be unable to examine in a subject in which 6,000 candidates are annually presented is an outrage that could happen nowhere on earth, perhaps, outside of English-governed Ireland. We see many complaints in the English papers of Russian methods in Poland and elsewhere, but where on the face of the globe could a parallel be found for the latest proposal of the butchers and bakers of the Intermediate Board?

The ignoring of Irish by the Board was disappointing, but not out of keeping with its history and prejudices. That, however, is not the worst. We learn that the Commissioners had intended to give all the appointments to Englishmen, and that they offered the new posts to the men they had here, temporarily, some years ago, but that some of these have refused to accept the price offered. Only three of them are willing to come, and so we have Irish appointments going begging in England while our own men and women — University graduates, too — are every day leaving the country. Neither the Castle nor the Government has a hand in this shameful betrayal of Ireland's interests. The guilty party is a body of Irishmen, who whatever their educational abilities be, should be cognisant of the difference between Irish and English interests. They should know that in the present state of our country every foreigner imported involves the exiling of an Irishman. And what is the purpose of our Universities, bad as they have been, if they cannot provide a half-dozen inspectors?

Whatever may be thought of the wits of the genuine Saxon, it must be acknowledged that the imitation Saxon, of the type found on the Intermediate Board, is entirely stupid. When men in responsible public positions despise their country it is an evil day for that country, unless those men are removed and replaced by others who, above all things else, have confidence in their nation and have its interests at heart. The Intermediate Commissioners appear to look upon England as their motherland. Would it not be relieving them of the pains of exile if, when the three Saxons come over, three of themselves were sent to Coventry? We recommend the suggestion to Lord Aberdeen. The proposal, if carried out,

214

would compensate in a small way the Sister Isle for the loss of three of her 'younger sons'. It would show that we are not an entirely ungrateful people, and that for some favours, at least, we are thankful.

THE UNIVERSITY AND THE SCHOOLS
23.1.1909

Perhaps the most important function which the new National University must discharge is the function of supplying a nerve-centre for the whole educational system of Ireland. If this be remembered, then the necessity for placing the National Language on a proper basis within the University becomes more evident than ever. If the purpose of a University were simply to manufacture M.D.'s and B.A.O.'s and promising candidates for the Indian Civil Service, then indeed something might be said for the view that Irish should not be included amongst the essential subjects of study in our new University. But the purpose of a University is something vastly higher and greater, and the purpose of an Irish University is nothing more nor less than the restoring of Ireland to her intellectual balance. How an institution in which genuine Irish culture shall not be predominant and all-pervading can do this it is not easy to imagine.

Prime amongst the functions of the new University must be, as we have suggested, the permeating of our primary, secondary, and technical school systems with a proper and adequate conception of their duty to the individual Irish boy or girl and to the Irish commonwealth as a whole; the setting before them of a lofty and true ideal; the bringing them into touch with all the currents of thought and activity which flow here and there throughout the educational world.

What is the matter with education in this country is that it is — except in so far as it has been affected by the language movement in recent years — completely divorced from the country and its life. It seems as *The Irish Homestead* put it last week, 'as if the system had been thought out amid the aether and interstellar spaces by someone who was doubtful as to what planet or country it might be worked in'. Irish schools are, on the whole, more efficient as mere teaching machines than English schools: they teach the Three R's better, they teach modern languages, classics, and higher mathematics better. Yet in spite of this, they do far less real educational work, — in many cases, if not the majority, the work they accomplish is the negation of education in the fine sense. And the reason is that there is no great national concept of education admitted by all concerned in the work of the schools from the highest to the lowest, and permeating through and through the entire school system. Such a concept can best grow up at and best be disseminated throughout the body at large from a National University, — the intellectual nerve-centre, as it has been called, of a nation.

The Homestead seems to suggest that by making a fuss about Irish in the Universities we are commencing at the wrong end. This would be true, perhaps, if a University were an isolated item in the national education system affecting only those who come into its halls. But a University affects both directly and indirectly the whole teaching community, and hence the whole population of the schools, secondary and primary, — in other words the whole future population of the country. We hope to see our secondary schools manned in the near future by the alumni of the new University: we hope in time to see even the primary schools, at any rate the larger ones,

215

staffed also with men and women who have imbibed the culture and assimilated the ideals of the University Colleges of Dublin, Galway, and Cork. If that culture and those ideals are to be foreign and not Irish, then the last state of Irish education will be worse than the first. An anti-national 'National' University, touching the machinery of Irish education at all points, will in a few years accomplish what Trinity College, aloof as it was from the people and their teachers, has not yet entirely accomplished in three centuries — the death of Irish thought, the crushing of Irish spirit, the overthrow of Irish hope. Should this thing come to pass then indeed the future is gloomy. But the Irish public has no intention of allowing it to come to pass. Already its coming to pass has been made well-nigh impossible. We have but to help on the fight to win an inevitable victory.

THE BISHOPS AND THE LANGUAGE
30.1.1909

The news that the Standing Committee of the Catholic Bishops is opposed to the national demand for essential Irish in the National University has been heard by Gaelic Leaguers with regret but without dismay. It simply means that their Lordships have not yet appreciated the vastness of the change that has come over Ireland since they were young men; that they have not yet realised the passionateness of the desire of so many men and women of our race that Ireland should again be her normal self; that they do not yet share in the new clearness of vision which makes the average citizen who thinks over these things, be he lettered or unlettered, see that as regards an Irishman or an Irishwoman higher culture divorced from the Irish language is a contradiction in terms. The most encouraging thing in the present controversy — the most encouraging thing in the recent history of Ireland — has been the readiness and the precision with which the Irish democracy has grasped this great question of principle, the promptness and the resolution with which the people have made up their minds: the most discouraging, though in a sense not the least understandable, is that the Bishops have not grasped the issue with equal readiness and precision, that they have not made up their minds with equal promptness and determination.

For we do not look upon the Standing Committee's pronouncement as final, even as regards the Committee itself. Closely examined, it will be seen that it does not touch the great question of principle at all. It is addressed altogether to the matter of the present expediency of making Irish — in their Lordships' phrase — 'compulsory'. Their Lordships are against this 'compulsion', as well, they suggest, in the interests of the language as in the interests of the University. But they ignore the fact that there is a larger thing at stake than even the immediate interests of the language. There is a question of principle which stands apart and which is the real question on which we have to make up our minds. That question is as to Ireland's duty in the matter of moulding the type of the higher education which for the first time in modern history she is now about to enjoy. Is that education to be Irish in complexion or is it to be foreign, or at best nondescript, in complexion? And can we have an Irish education in which the Irish language does not form an essential ingredient? If we agree — as all who call themselves Irish must agree — that of an Irish education the Irish language must be the very basis and fundament, — then we can answer only in one

216

way the question as to Ireland's duty with regard to making Irish an essential subject in the new University. The purpose of the University is avowedly to supply a proper University culture for Irishmen; in such a culture the Irish language forms and must form an essential ingredient. There would be no getting away from this, even if it could be shown that the immediate interests of the language seem to demand rather compromises and half-measures.

As we have suggested, the statement of the Standing Committee of the Bishops is unsatisfying and indeterminate because it shirks the question of principle and approaches the subject purely from the point of view of expediency. To reach the stage 'when the Irish language will again be spoken throughout the country, and will in consequence become largely the medium of instruction in the Constituent Colleges', the members of the Standing Committee 'consider that by far the best means is to set up in the Colleges bright centres of Irish study, that will, by their light and by their rewards, attract young Irishmen within the sphere of their Irish influence'. The only argument advanced in support of this contention is that 'the progress of Irish in our seminaries and in numbers of the Intermediate schools of the country, far from being an argument for compulsion, shows what the voluntary system, under our constant encouragement, has hitherto done, and what no doubt it will do still more successfully in the Colleges of the new University'. Father Forde has promptly and effectively disposed of this argument. In the seminaries and Intermediate schools in which Irish has flourished, there has been no 'voluntary system', properly so called; that is to say, the individual student has not been left an option. The head of the college has in each case decided the matter for all his pupils, and in point of fact Irish is virtually an essential subject, having been made so by the ruling authorities, in all the seminaries in which any considerable work for the language has been done. What we want to secure is that the authorities of the new University institutions should in a similar way make Irish an essential part of the curriculum for all *their* students.

The Standing Committee suggests that the case will be met by the erection in the University Colleges of 'bright centres' of Irish study. But there is a 'bright centre' of Irish study at Liverpool; there will shortly be a 'bright centre' of Irish study at London; there are 'bright centres' of Irish study in a dozen German, Scandandinavian, and French University cities. Do we require nothing more in Ireland? Do we not require that our whole system be Irish through and through, and can we have a system Irish through and through, without the Irish language as an essential? The Standing Committee's suggestion that nothing is needed beyond a few 'bright centres' shows how utterly and how unfortunately it has failed to grasp the issue which — and this is the strange and gratifying thing — the people have grasped so fully and so firmly.

We do not know how far the views of the Standing Committee are shared by the Bishops as a body. It is quite certain that the Bishops are not unanimous in the matter, for two at least have publicly endorsed the Gaelic League demands. But one thing is perfectly clear. Whether the Bishops are for or against us, the people are with us. This has been evident for weeks past. It has been made still more evident within the last few days. On the very morrow of the Standing Committee's pronouncement came the vigorous discussion culminating in the unmistakeable resolution of the Dublin Corporation. Since then the Waterford County Council, not to mention several Urban and Rural District Councils and other public bodies

217

in various parts of the country, have spoken with equal determination. If the people of Ireland were ever solid behind a demand they are solid behind this demand. That the Standing Committee of the Bishops does not realise this only shows how entirely it is out of touch with popular trends of thought in present-day Ireland. It is lamentable that a body occupying so exalted a position, wielding so large an influence, and so entitled to reverence as the leaders of the great Church which commands the allegiance of the majority of Irishmen, should nevertheless be governed in so important a matter by ideas which are as obsolete in the country as are the Penal Laws that gave them birth. But the fact remains.

As for the agitation, the Rev. Dr. O'Hickey has given us our watchword: 'on the cause must go!' The Gaelic League stands as firm as a rock. We believe, too, that, whatsoever pronouncements may be made, the elective boards and other representative bodies that have declared for Irish Ireland, will have the manhood to stick by their publicily-affirmed opinions. The Gaelic League gives the Standing Committee credit for the best intentions; it accords its opinion the respectful hearing which any opinion from such a quarter is entitled to; but, holding as firmly as ever to an opinion which is diametrically opposed to that of the Committee, the League will go on with its campaign just as if the Committee had not spoken. Keenly as we regret to find that we are not to have the countenance and support of prelates whom we revere so much as spiritual leaders and honour so much for their records of unselfish devotion to their people, we have nothing for it but to advance without them. We know that we have turned our faces towards a good fight, and we go on with that fight, fearing nothing.

WARNINGS
30.1.1909

We trust that there will be no disposition amongst Gaels to regard the pronouncement of the Standing Committee of the Bishops as the pronouncement of a body of men who are hostile to the language movement. The Committee expresses itself as most friendly to the general aims and aspirations of the Gaelic League, and states that it looks forward to the day when Irish will be commonly spoken throughout the country. We take it that their Lordships are thouroughly sincere in these professions, and are content to believe that they differ from us merely as to the best ways and means of realising our − and their − hopes. It is further to be borne in mind that their Lordships do not − and in fact cannot − claim for their pronouncement any sacrosanct authority, they expressly state that the question on which they proceed to give their opinion 'is a question for fair argument'. We hope and believe that their Lordships will carry out the letter and the spirit of this declaration, and in particular that priests in the various dioceses will be as free as heretofore to take part in the 'fair argument' and to express their convictions on one side or the other. Amongst some of the Bishops there would appear to be a disposition to discountenance the active participation of their priests in the Gaelic League campaign for essential Irish. The detailed statements we have received as to priests in one archdiocese who have been forbidden to attend meetings in support of the Gaelic League demands, and as to strong episcopal pressure exercised in another diocese to induce priests to withdraw from the agitation, may be true or false; but certain it is that priests in several dioceses no longer feel themselves at liberty to take an active part in the prosecution of the Gaelic League campaign. The Bishops owe it to these zealous priests and zealous Gaelic Leaguers to make it clear to them that on this question, admittedly one for 'fair argument', they have entire liberty of conscience and action.

Every day that passes serves to show more clearly than ever the unanimity and spontaneity of the desire of priests and people that the new University should be stamped once and for all as an Irish institutions by having Irish included in the basis of its education. The few opposing resolutions serve only to throw that unanimity and that spontaneity into higher relief. Take the resolution of the Donegal County Council, which turns out to have had a very extraordinary genesis. Out of a membership of thirty-two only eight were present, three of whom were Unionists. The proposer of the resolution had apparently been supplied with a copy of the Bishops' statement before the document had been made public, and from this he copied the 'bright centre' idea. The seconder of the resolution was Mr. Hanna, a Unionist, and one of the bitterest partisans in the north-west of Ulster. West Britain is welcome to the resolution but the public should know how it was obtained and that it in no way represents the opinion of Donegal. In the same county the Coiste Gnótha resolution has been adopted by the Letterkenny, Inishowen, and Milford District Councils, and by the Boards of Guardians in Letterkenny and Carndonagh, while the Donegal County Committee of the Gaelic League has asked that no rates shall be raised in aid of the National University until it makes Irish an essential subject.

The members of the Gaelic League will need tact and patience in the present crisis. The position of Gaelic League priests in particular is a delicate one. It is fortunate that the most notable of them have already declared themselves to be uncompromisingly on our side. The cause that has such backers as Canon O'Leary, Mgr. Hallinan, Canon Arthur Ryan, and the Rev. Dr. O'Hickey need not fear. The Bishops have, of course, a distinct right to express their own opinions on the University question, but it must not be thought that their opinions are binding on anyone but themselves. Priests may find it difficult to stand by the people, but the people themselves must continue the fight. Coolness and firmness are the needs of the time. Let there be no excuses given for charges of anti-clericalism, and let the strength and usefulness of the League be maintained at all costs. The last blow has not yet been struck, nor has the last Irish lesson been taught. Young Ireland — lay and clerical — is with us.

'FAIR ARGUMENT'
6.3.1909

In the statement issued by the Coiste Gnótha of the Gaelic League in reply to the pronouncement of the Standing Committee of the Catholic Bishops, their Lordships were asked for an assurance that the clergy, no less than the laity, are still in the fullest sense free to take part, according to their own convictions, in the public discussion of the question as to the position of Irish in the new Universities. No such assurance has been forthcoming. On the contrary, several Bishops, while leaving their priests free to oppose the national demand for essential Irish, have effectually constrained priests who are in sympathy with that demand from giving expression to that sympathy in public. Priests have been forbidden to attend meetings; priests have been censured for writing to papers; priests have been forced to withdraw resolutions of which they had given notice at public conventions. During the past week or ten days this campaign of coercion has entered on a new phase. Certain Bishops are now endeavouring not merely to silence their priests but to prevent the expression of all public opinion whatsoever on the question. The recent meeting of Dáil Uladh, presided over by the Rt. Rev. Mgr. O'Doherty, P.P., Omagh, decided to inaugurate a series of public meetings in Ulster in support of the national demand. In pursuance of this decision, the organisation of meetings in Derry and in Omagh was undertaken by the local Gaels, aided by the machinery of Dáil Uladh and the central body of the League. Both meetings have been 'proclaimed'. The local priests cannot take part in them, and cannot countenance their being held. The position of the Rt. Rev. Mgr. O'Doherty is a peculiar one, as he presided over the meeting which ordered the organisation of these public demonstrations: singular also is the attitude of Father McFeely, Adm., of Derry. A somewhat sinister light surrounds the activity of Father O'Doherty, P.P., of Strabane, who, we gather, has taken a prominent part in inducing brother priests to lend themselves to the suppression of public opinion. These are extraordinary developments to follow so fast on the episcopal declarations that the question is one for 'fair argument', and the Cardinal Primate's more recent dictum that people are 'free as the winds' to take which side they please in the controversy.

But the 'fair argument' treaty has now been openly repudiated by no less a member of the Hierarchy than his Grace the Archbishop of Tuam. It is our painful duty to direct public attention to the amazing proceedings which took place at the meeting of the Committee of the Connacht College, at Tuam on Thursday, the 25th ult., and of which we publish a report in another column. With Archbishop Healy's claim that Coláiste Chonnacht — an institution founded by the Gaels of Connacht at a public meeting in Galway, and controlled by a Committee appointed by and answerable to them — is his personal property, we must leave Connacht Gaels to deal as they think best and wisest. At present we are concerned only with the extraordinary attitude adopted by His Grace towards the resolution on the University question tendered by Colonel Moore. 'Is it a resolution from this Board — from this Committee?' said Dr. Healy, according to the report. 'I'll refuse to take any resolution on the question. I could not be a loyal bishop and do so; and I don't see how any priest who supports such a resolution can consider himself a loyal priest'. But, as Colonel Moore immediately pointed out, the Standing Committee of the Bishops had said that the question was one for fair discussion (he might have added that Cardinal Logue had written that people were 'free as the winds' to hold what opinion they chose); to which Dr. Healy replied: *It was a matter for fair discussion before they (the Bishops) spoke, but not now*.

So that when the Standing Committee said the question was one for fair argument, they really meant that it was no longer anything of the kind, since by a sort of ex-cathedra pronouncement hitherto unknown to theology they were settling it once and for all as finally and as irrevocably as if it were a question of faith being pronounced on with all formality and solemnity by the supreme voice of the Church! We doubt if there is a single member of the Standing Committee who will agree with Archbishop

Healy's interpretation of their words, or with his extravagant claim of a sacrosanct authority for a pronouncement on a subject on which, as Bishops, the Bishops have no more claim to pronounce with authority than the most ordinary member of that Irish public of which his Grace of Tuam speaks with so lordly a disdain. Cardinal Logue, at any rate, does not endorse a contention which to him as to other members of the Hierarchy must appear a veritable *reductio ad absurdum* of the Hierarchy's lawful claim to the allegiance, in the sphere of faith and morals, of the members of their Church.

Colonel Moore's mildly-put argument that the people of Ireland had spoken with no uncertain voice in favour of Irish, and that their opinion should be respected, was received by Dr. Healy with this outburst: 'The people of Ireland indeed! What do they know about it? Do you mean to tell me that the fellows who kicked football a few days ago, and held a meeting here, knew or understood what they were talking about? I would not give a pinch of snuff for their opinion; what do they know about it?'

Strange language for a prelate, in whose pronouncements, however bizarre, one would expect to find at least a little apostolic charity and humility. 'The people of Ireland indeed! What do they know about it?' We can assure His Grace that the people of Ireland, and especially of his own Archdiocese of Tuam, know a vast deal about this question, and have a paramount right to express themselves on it. They know, for instance, of priests sent to minister to them at the altar, in the confessional, and at the bedsides of their dying, who do not know a word of their language; they know of doctors who do patients to death because they cannot follow their descriptions of their symptoms; they know of school teachers who do not understand a single syllable uttered by their pupils during the day, while the pupils do not understand a single syllable uttered by them. And when this long-outraged, long-silent people see at last an opportunity of remedying these terrible wrongs, and determine to avail of it, their Archbishop, instead of proclaiming himself their leader, plants himself across their path, declares that he will thwart them if he can, and meets their just demands for redress with flouts and scoffs and jeers.

The people will remember.

THE TYRANNY OF PROGRAMMES
27.3.1909

The Report of the Advising Examiner in Irish to the Intermediate Board dwells strongly on the evidence afforded by the last examination of the continued prevalence of unenlightened teaching methods in the secondary schools. It may be that the criticism is unduly pessimistic, for we all know the high ideals in Irish scholarship for which the name of Dr. Bergin stands, and we can imagine his impatience with anything like slipshod work in any department. It is probable that Dr. Bergin and his staff of assistants were by far the most exacting of the various groups of examiners engaged in scrutinising the Intermediate papers this year, at any rate in the languages; for people used to the efficiency of Gaelic League teaching methods in the best centres naturally look for more in the way of colloquial knowledge and literary facility than do examiners whose standard of excellence is only the very mediocre one of the ordinary Intermediate school. This fact must be taken into account in comparing the report of the Advising Examiner in Irish with those of the Advising Examiners in other subjects. One thing is certain. The teaching of Irish in the secondary schools is far and away a more live and genuine thing than the teaching of French, or German, or any other modern language. The Irish boys and girls who are taught to talk French which a Parisian would understand are few indeed. Some hundreds of children leave the Intermediate schools each year with a conversational knowledge of Irish which would stand them in very fair stead in Baile na nGall or Inismeadhon.

But we are still far off the era of bilingual education in the secondary schools; and bilingual education alone can bring back the language to the Galltacht as a real vernacular. As things stand, bilingualism is impossible. A compulsory unilingual programme bars it out. This is one of several considerations which have made it necessary for Sgoil Éanna at the outset of its career to renounce the Intermediate Board with all its works and pomps. A school in which all the school subjects — Christian Doctrine, History, Natural Science, Mathematics, and the rest — are taught through Irish as well as through English, and in which all languages are taught on the Direct Method, would necessarily be handicapped in a race for Intermediate honours. The time given to the Irish side of the programme would, from an Intermediate point of view, be so much time wasted. The Intermediate system is vicious in its essence. Not only does it make proper Irish or bilingual teaching impossible, but it penalises sound teaching in modern languages generally, and relegates to the limbo of the impracticable and fantastic all that more important part of education which aims not at the mere imparting of knowledge but at the formation of the character and the kindling of the imagination. That affairs will materially improve under the new system of inspection we can hardly hope. Six Inspectors (only one of whom, by the way, is competent to inspect Irish) flying hither and thither through the country will hardly counteract the evil trend of a system which must continue to shape itself around the central idea of a written examination based on a rigidly-fixed programme.

The programme is the primal curse. That persons sitting round a table in Hume Street, Dublin, should prescribe in the minutest detail the subjects to be studied, the authors to be read, the books of each author, the chapters of each book, by every pupil in every Intermediate School in every corner of every province in Ireland, is an arrangement to which no true educationist can ever reconcile himself.

At Sgoil Éanna we take the view that we alone, in consultation with our pupils and their parents, have the right to decide what subjects we shall study, what books we shall read; and we have been willing to sacrifice to this precious liberty the certainty of valuable fees and possible fame as a successful Intermediate school. That a central education authority should have power to see that a suitable standard be maintained as the condition of state help is just and proper; that it should prescribe a programme for every school in the country is grotesque and anomalous. We do not allow Government Departments to dictate what we should put on our children's backs; why should we allow them to dictate what we should put into their heads?

WHITLEY STOKES
24.4.1909

The Dublin in which Whitley Stokes grew from boyhood to manhood was an intensely interesting city, with a very distinctive intellectual and artistic life of its own. Of this life the house of William Stokes (son of Whitley the friend of Tone) was the natural centre and focus. Stokes was himself one of the most famous physicians in Europe, and a literary man of wide and gracious culture. His circle of intimate friends included all that was best and rarest in contemporary Ireland. To Burton and Petrie and Ferguson his house in Merrion Square was a home: Davis often came there, and Gavan Duffy, and O'Donovan, and O'Curry, and Reeves; sometimes, too, like a ghost the worn figure of Mangan would pass in, bringing a breath of the misery of the Dublin slums into the midst of that quiet and ease. It is not wonderful that the thoughts of the children who grew up in such a home should turn very warmly towards Ireland; indeed the children of William Stokes were under such tutelage as no other children ever had. The mantle of O'Donovan and O'Curry fell on the eldest boy, Whitely; fostered by Petrie, Margaret became the most loving and conscientious of Irish antiquarians.

From school Whitley Stokes passed to Trinity College, from Trinity to the English Bar, from the English Bar to India, where finally he reached the Council of the Governor-General as Law Member in succession to Sir James Fitz-James Stephen. In the history of British India he will be remembered as one of the most brilliant of the brilliant band responsible for its monumental Law Code. But, unlike most Irishmen who elect to serve the Empire, the whole of his heart and the greater part of his genuis were reserved by Whitley Stokes for the dearer service of his own land and people. While yet a student at home, he had been attracted into the then almost untrodden wilds of early Irish literature; in India the glamour came upon him again, more powerful even than the glamour of the East; and if through those wilds there now leads many a beaten path today trodden by thousands of students, to the young adventurer of 1860 let the greater praise belong. O'Donovan and O'Curry had simply lifted the veil which separated the enchanted country from the ordinary haunts of men: Whitley Stokes boldly led his own generation into it.

We hope to publish in an early issue of *An Claidheamh* a complete bibliography of his work. The list is almost a staggering one. Remembering that we owe to him practically all the Old-Irish Glosses, and most of the Middle-Irish Lives and Homilies that have been published, The Féilire of Oengus, the Saltair na Rann, the Tripartite Life of St. Patrick, the Annals of Tighearnach, the Bruighen Da Derga, the Tógáil Troí, the Irish Marco Polo, Maundeville, and Fierabras, etc., etc., one understands that there was little exaggeration in the remark of the Irish scholar who said recently that there now remains no Old or Middle Irish of high literary value to be published — it has all been published by Stokes, if not in one of his great volumes, then in some article in the *Zeitschrift* or the *Revue*, in some obscure index or catalogue, or in some breezy critque on a colleague's work. But this is only part of Stoke's achievement. He practically recast the whole science of Irish Grammar. What Strachan did in our own day for the Irish verb, Stokes did twenty years ago for the Irish noun. Taken together, the work of Stokes and Strachan marks as great an epoch in the history of Celtic Philogy as did the work of Zeuss in the time of our grandfathers. All future Irish grammarians must follow what the Rev. Dr. Hogan has called the 'lines of light' traced out by them.

Among Celtic scholars Stokes stood in a class apart. He possessed in a degree rarely if ever equalled the two great and seemingly contradictory qualities which go to the making of a master-worker in the field he chose for himself, — relentless accuracy of scholarship and deep artistic insight. To the philological keenness of a Strachan he added the imagination of a Kuno Meyer or of a Standish Hayes O'Grady. He was the scholar and the poet in one. We do not know that he ever wrote anything in Irish, but as an interpreter in English of the beauty and strength of Irish prose and poetry he was unapproached. He wrote an English singularly nervous and beautiful, — an English in which, far more than in any recent warblings to the 'Celtic note', the authentic tone of Irish literature is caught and conveyed, as far as it ever can be caught or conveyed in a foreign idiom.

THE NATIONAL TEACHERS
24.4.1909

While it would be wrong of us to pretend that we are satisfied either with National Teachers or the National Board, we can give expression to sincere admiration, for the growing strength of the Teachers' Associations and for the success of their congress, which has just been held in Galway One of the first things necessary for success in fighting against the Government — and the fight of National teachers is almost invariably against Government forces in one form or another — is strength and courage. Until of late the claims which teachers put forward were very often, if not always, of professional interest, but now they have to a certain extent joined in the struggle for national resuscitation, and with this advance they have gained new strength within their organisation and sympathy and support from without. They are now fighting for fuller freedom to teach Irish in their schools, for the provision of a teaching faculty or a somewhat similar arrangement in the University, for better schools, for better attendance of pupils, and for their own civil rights, and they have joined us in the fight for the recognition of Irish as an essential subject in the University.

The claim for civil rights might be more effectively asserted by action than by words. The law — even the British law — gives no powers to any public department such as the Board of Education to interfere with the individual freedom of any citizen, and whatever regulations the National Board has made to debar teachers from exercising their ordinary political rights should be disregarded by the teachers, and broken on as many occasions as they find it possible to break them. The Board might thunder and threat, but it would not dare to penalise men and women for refusing to observe regulations that the clerks in the Education Office, who are directly under the Commissioners, would not tolerate even for a day. The Resident Commissioner is reported to have said that the managers were to blame for the Russian regulations, but the Rev. Father Curry, on behalf of the Clerical Managers, has denied this. It would be an evil day for Ireland if the managers were to join forces with any Government Board against a body of Irish citizens, and we are glad that the blame has now been placed on the guilty parties. But whatever the Board may say or do, the teachers of Ireland will be themselves to blame if by observing regulations for the existence of which there is no legal justification they allow new political fetters to be placed on Irishmen.

We hope that the claim made at the Congress for special provisions for teachers in the University will not end in the Galway resolution. If education is to be made a real live and useful instrument of progress we must have some better arrangement for the training of teachers than a two years' course in a cramming college, where little or no attention is paid to the teaching science itself, and where students are trained without any regard for the country in which they are to work and live. The new Universities should be for the use of all classes, and more particularly for the big majority, made up of many classes, that gets educated in National Schools. To serve these the Universities must open their doors to the teachers who, if they receive a sound University training, will make its benefits felt in the poorest homes in the land. At present an Irish teacher receives such a training as would hardly suffice to fit him for a junior post in a city office. This is the teachers' great grievance, greater even than starvation wages or the denial of political rights. It is for the righting of this wrong that all Ireland will come to their assistance, and this is the matter that needs their own most urgent attention.

We are not entirely convinced of the wisdom of compulsory attendance, particularly as it involves the patronising of the law courts. The low average attendance in rural Ireland might be supposed to discredit our supposed love of learning, but the real causes are to be found in the schools rather than in the people. The 'National' system has ever been foreign to the Irish child, and, the training of the teacher has been such as to emasculate his own Irish nature and render him incapable of interpreting the juvenile mind of his own race. An Irish primary teacher need know nothing of Ireland beyond its name, fifty per cent of National Teachers know little more. It is not then a great wonder that Irish children prefer the freedom of the hills and fields to the stern atmosphere of the Saxonised school. Then, the attitude of the teachers towards the people and their affairs is generally one of cold aloofness. The young teachers, especially of late years, show a decided disdain for the working population, the company of the policeman is too often preferred to that of the young farmer. The boys are given no practical instruction to serve them on the farm, and in two-thirds of the schools neither boys nor girls are taught to love home or given any interest to Irish affairs.

The very poor attendance in Irish schools is admittedly a shame, but the means of improving it lie very largely in the hands of the teachers themselves. School programmes can be made more attractive by the introduction of the national language and by the sympathetic teaching of Irish history. Irish songs are more pleasing to Irish children than the artificial music and language of English nursery rhymes. Irish and local geography can be made more interesting than a fairy tale, by the revival of Irish place names and by the teaching of history in connection with this subject. The pictorial advertisements of foreign goods which disfigure many Irish schools should be replaced by pictures of Irish scenery or of historical Irish men and women, and the battle of the two civilisations should be explained in every school until the pupils all become conscious workers in Ireland's cause. When the teachers become what many of them, we are glad to say, are at present, kindly and sympathetic guides to young Ireland, they will obviate the pain and shame of teaching before half-empty benches. On the other hand, not all the powers of British law will ever send young Ireland into anti-Irish schools.

COUNTY SCHOLARSHIPS
24.4.1909

We make no excuse for returning this week to the subject of County Scholarships, for the odds against our movement are so great that no available weapon can safely be neglected in the fight. To stay emigration and steady the social unrest that lies behind it, the life of rural Ireland must be reformed. The land must be given to workers, and, what is of equal importance, the workers must get the best instruction that is to be had. They must be told of the possibilities of Irish farming, taught the best methods in production and marketing, and have instilled into them the manliness and dignity of intelligent labour and honest business. The County Scholarships, if properly utilised, should enable us to send home annually from our Agricultural Colleges to each Irish county, a few well-instructed farmers who would soon become exemplars for their neighbours, and whose example in up-to-date methods would be followed by all with an eye to progress. Irish farming, like that of England, has been declining for a long time, and, what is perhaps more fatal to national life, the people who live on the land have begun to slide down the social scale.

The fiscal laws and the system of primary education, both of which have been imposed upon us by England, are the chief causes of this social and industrial fall of the farmer. In Germany, where different fiscal and educational systems prevail, the farming industry has been going steadily upwards for the past generation, and the lands of that progressive country are now among the most highly cultivated in Europe. In the whole of Germany there are over 5,500,000 holdings of not more than fifteen acres of fertile land each, and over 3,200,000 holdings each of three acres, and under, while seventy-per cent of the land is held by farmers owning not less than twenty-five acres each. It thus appears that small holdings are not necessarily a bar to success in farming, but the German farmer has the benefit of a highly organised system of agricultural education which the Irish farmer has not. In 'Modern Germany' by J. Ellis Barker, a book published in 1907, there is a stimulating account of rural industries in Germany, and of the schools that made her farmers the most successful in the world.

In Prussia alone, says Mr. Barker, there are nine Agricultural High Schools, where about 2,500 pupils are trained by 202 teachers. According to the latest returns, these High Schools were attended by 1,852 German students and by no less than 569 foreigners. Evidently these courses are very popular, not only with German agriculturists, who by-the-bye are very foolish not to keep their knowledge to themselves, but with foreigners also. The State aids these High Schools with grants of £40,860 per annum. Besides these there are 202 ambulant lecturers provided by the State, who teach scientific agriculture. Furthermore, there are in Germany 269 other agricultural schools, 1,803 teachers, and 15,811 pupils, and facilities are provided in every direction for spreading the scientific knowledge of agriculture far and wide. Many teachers in rural elementary schools voluntarily study agriculture in the High Schools in order to be able to teach some useful and valuable things to the country children and their parents. The Prussian Ministry of Agriculture spends yearly about £200,000 on agricultural education in all its branches, and the sum total spent by all the German Governments and local authorities in this direction should, at present, amount to about £500,000.

Last week, we recommended that half at least of our county scholarships should be set aside for young farmers, and that a number of them should also be earmarked for future teachers of primary schools. The great fault of the present primary system is that it has but little relation to the actualities of life and that the teachers of rural schools receive no special training to enable them to give any useful instruction to the school-going farming population. They do things better in Germany where,

226

according to Mr. Barker, many of the teachers voluntarily take up courses in agriculture in the High Schools. The National Board, which is of English origin, is followed by results very similar to those that the system of primary education in England itself has produced. In speaking of England, our author says: 'The general education in the rural districts of Great Britain is unfortunately too townified, and the little boys and girls are taught subjects at school which not only are useless, but which unfit the children for rural life. The boy who leaves the elementary schools has only too often been estranged from the country, and has been taught to turn up his nose at agriculture, the girl aspires to a situation in Kensington and the possession of a piano, and if she marries a countryman she reads penny novelettes, and thinks it beneath her dignity to milk a cow or look after chickens, for that would not be ladylike'.

The County Scholarships are at present tenable in Intermediate schools where the system of education is one of cram, and the curriculum suitable only for those preparing for the professions or for the University. The most necessary branch of education, apart from moral training, for young farmers is practical instruction in agriculture. But this they cannot receive in the Intermediate Colleges, and to make scholarships financed out of public funds tenable to these schools, is mere waste of money, and can result only in unfitting some of the most intelligent of our young people for their natural calling in life, and in giving a new impetus to the flow of emigration. It is only within the past few years, when they were fitted with laboratories, that many of these colleges became qualified to give what is called 'technical science'. Technical instruction of a practical kind they do not provide, neither can they be of any practical assistance to young farmers, and if our farmers are wise they will insist on the scholarships, or a large number of them, being made tenable in the Agricultural Colleges. There are branches of the Gaelic League in each of the thirty-two counties, and it is a matter of urgent importance that in every county where these scholarships are in being members of the League should use every legitimate influence to have the Irish language and Irish history made essential subjects of education, not only for examination, but for all scholarship courses, and, if possible, to have the other recommendations we have made adopted.

THE UNIVERSITY CRISIS
1.5.1909

The coming months will be eventful ones for Ireland. A great many things lie in the balance, but most of them, for the present at least, depend on one event, the settling of the position of Irish in the University. To the consideration of that question everyone who reads, thinks, and cares for Ireland should turn. It is a matter on which too much information cannot be had, and its settling will demand such persistency of purpose as we are seldom called upon to exercise. Some who have been thinking and working for the cause of the Irish language for years have been of one mind since before the University come into being. The have never been led astray by the paltry arguments that are prompted by either expediency or weakness. They have fought for a great principle, and have kept the issues so clear that, despite the almost countless attempts that have been made to emphasise little difficulties, only one matter concerning the University has now any interest for the public, and that is whether it is to be Irish or West British. The rank and file of our own organisation, and the people generally, have shown such singular unanimity of opinion as makes victory almost a certainty. To ensure that the issue shall be favourable it remains only to inform the public mind more perfectly on the causes which led to the decay of our language, on the history of the struggle against foreign systems of education, on the endeavours of the League to gain recognition for Irish in the schools, on the forces that are working against us, and on the fate that awaits race and country if once the English language gets a charter of superiority over Irish in the new University. The distribution of pamphlets dealing with all aspects of the question, and the holding of public meetings during the summer months, should help to inform and organise public opinion, and to this work we beg that all League Branches will now turn. Classes will soon disband, but before breaking up hundreds of pamphlets can be distributed, and public aeridheachta, taking the shape of propagandist and special meetings, can be arranged for. Patriotism and the needs of the time demand that all local disputes should be allowed to rest for the present. Honest and wise workers will nowhere enter into petty quarrels over minor matters during the coming year, knowing full well that the battle in which we are engaged is one affecting things above personality and party, and for which great sacrifice must be made. We must not waste against any wrong-doer or petty tyrant within our ranks the forces that should be used against the arch-enemy, and we say to all — I n-ainm Dé agus ar son na hÉireann — let all members of the Gaelic League work as brothers should for the coming year. We neither advise nor desire that matters wrong in principle should be permanently endured, or allowed to go on unchecked for ever; but we counsel patience. Time will right small things, and it would be madness to waste energy or split our forces on any minor affairs now.

It is not a mere figure of speech to say that Ireland is again at the crossroads. Often before in her sad history have her leaders stood at the parting of the ways, but now when leaders with courage to champion the cause of the old civilisation are few, the people themselves have come to the contest as they would come in defence of their religion, or the privacy or possession of their homes. The old race, beaten to the dust in the eighteenth and nineteenth centuries, is again coming to its own, determined that in the new Ireland that is coming no stranger language shall hold sway. The issue between the two civilisations does not indeed depend on the result of the present struggle so much as on the spread of that individual determination to give an active allegiance to Ireland which has made and which is the strength of our movement. The present struggle too, as well as the final one, can be won if we determine to sink minor grievances, and to do all that lies within reach to convince the Senate of the wisdom of our demands, and of our determination to hamper the success of the University unless those demands be granted. On the Senate there are three classes of members: those who have faith in Ireland and who think only of her interests; those who wish to serve Ireland but who are satisfied to see her become what Cardinal Newman wished her to be, a cultured English province; and those who, like Sir William Butler and Mr. Butcher, could not even entertain the idea of the resurrection and rehabilitation of Irish civilisation. The first class are few but determined. Those of the second stand to be convinced, but the third have in their hearts the dogged opposition of Britishers believing in the weakness of their opponents, and must be fought without compromise to the end. With the inner workings of higher politics and kindred matters the Irish public are unacquainted. They are and have ever been too willing to place an unquestioning trust in their leaders and often also in others in high office. We have many reasons for believing that great influences are being worked against the interests of the language in the University. The intriguers are determined to win over the support of those Senators who are honest, but weak and undecided. Against all the forces engaged against us our only weapons are an informed public opinion and a firmness of purpose, but we promise that against both weak friends and open foes a determined and united Ireland shall win.

The middle party of the Senate has no doubt been strengthened by the opinion to which a number of the Bishops gave expression early in the controversy. But many things have occurred since the publication of that opinion that should remove their Lordships' fears that our demands were premature, or that young Ireland was unprepared for the effort which the making of Irish essential would demand. The unanimity and determination of the people to have an Irish University, combined with the informed opinion of the priests and public men, who are almost entirely with us, cannot be disregarded. Irish-America demands that the language of the motherland shall be made an essential subject of University education, and in Australia we have the support not alone of the Irish people there, but of the head of the Catholic Church in that land, Cardinal Moran. In the gospel of the Revival several of the Bishops have little faith, and have but poor hopes of our chances of success. Many of them are men of an old school, disciples of Cardinal Newman in the matter of Ireland's future, and it should not have been expected that they would be enthusiastically on our side from the outset. Now, however, we have a right to hope for the withdrawal of their opposition, for they cannot, if they respect Irish opinion both at home and abroad, continue to advocate a University which no party in Ireland, save the upholders of British supremacy in all things desires. The Gaelic League itself with its fifteen years of work for temperance, industry, and education behind it has a right to be heard. When the hopes of Ireland were low it gave to the people new reasons for renewing the old struggle, and it taught them a self-reliance that has won for the name of Ireland respect throughout the world. At all times and in the face of unreasoning opposition it has been moderate in its methods. Always it has shown respect for the opinions and even the prejudices of the Catholic Bishops. Some of their Lordships we know to be with us, and we hope that in the present grave crisis they will act up to their own convictions, and to the high ideals that are the secret of new Ireland's strength and hopes.

But some priests and prelates hastily mistook the patriotic fervour aroused by the University question for anit-clericalism, and suddenly became active opponents of the Gaelic League policy, and in some cases of the Gaelic League itself. Charges of anti-clericalism have been made by clergymen against men and women in our movement whose religious sentiments are above reproach, and young priests who were our teachers and leaders, and to follow whom Young Ireland had deserted the squalor of party politics, were forbidden, and are still forbidden, to counsel or direct the people on a matter in which neither religion nor morals are involved, but which involves another matter second only to that of religion in importance, viz., duty to Ireland. Against these things we have, in the name of the Gaelic League, to protest. Our only aim is the restoration of self-respect and self-reliance to the Irish people. To teach them to turn away

229

from the slavish imitation of England is one of our first duties towards the accomplishment of our end, and we believe that an Irish Ireland freed from the worst influences of English civilisation with its open irreligion and veneered heathenism, would be a truer friend of religion than a West British Ireland in which the English language and English ideals would be supreme. The declaration of Cardinal Moran on the University question, will, we hope, hasten the return of the Irish Bishops to the side of the people. The Catholic clergy and people of Ireland are old allies, and they have seldom been found in opposition to each other. There is no reason for opposition now, and it would be a pity if the continued opposition of the Standing Committee of the Bishops should delay a victory over the old enemies of the race, and of its historic religion.

IRISH HISTORY IN INTERMEDIATE SCHOOLS
1.5.1909

What is being done for Irish history in the Intermediate schools may be judged from the following extracts from the report of the advising examiner, Máire Ní Aodáin, in Geography and History: — 'Irish history seems to have been greatly neglected in many of the schools. Students in the Preparatory Grade generally knew more about Peter the Hermit or Boadicea than they did about Cormac Mac Art; while to those in the Middle John Wilkes was usually a more familiar personage than was Henry Flood. Almost all the examiners comment in their reports on the painful ignorance displayed by a large number of the students when the questions related to the history of their own country. Some attempted, I may say without success, to make bursts of fiery patriotism supply the place of correct information.' Of the Junior Grade (Pass) she says: — 'The answers in Irish history were especially wretched'. In the Junior Grade (Honours) 'Irish history, though weak, was better than in many of the other papers'. In Question 4, Middle Grade (Honours) 'A list of persons, of whom three were Englishmen and two Irishmen, was given, and particulars regarding any three were asked for. Few selected the Irishmen, and those who did generally knew very little about them. The blot on the paper was the answering to Question 5, which ran as follows: — 'Give a short account of Grattan's Parliament, explaining clearly what extension of legislative independence was given to Ireland'. Many omitted this altogether, and scarcely any of those who answered it seemed to have any clear idea of what constituted the difference between this Parliament and those which came before it . . . . That Irish boys and girls should show so little understanding of so important an event in their country's history, especially considering that the period set for them to study is only 100 years (1689 to 1789), is most lamentable and extraordinary.'

Who is to blame? and with whom lies the remedy? are questions which naturally occur to anyone interested in Irish education on reading Máire Ní Aodáin's critical and valuable report. The Intermediate Commissioners seem to be under the spell of cast iron English models. They frame their programmes not with any intention of relating Intermediate education to the necessities of Irish life, but in rigid conformity with English precedent, as if they were the high priests of a cult, from the ritual of which it would be heresy to vary. The Board, doubtless, has high educational ideals, but it is bitterly opposed to the ideals of the Irish people. The Intermediate system was framed ostensibly to assist and regulate secondary education; but its founders had a distinct intention, of which their successors have never lost sight, of making the system a machine for the forcing of the English language and ideals on the Irish people. The subsidy based on the the results was the bait on the trap into which the secondary schools of Ireland, almost without exception, have fallen. For the sake of this bribe the directors of our secondary schools have thrown Irish interests to the winds, and some of them appear to outstep even the Board in their disregard for such subjects as Irish history and the Irish language. The Intermediate colleges in a large measure are responsible for the most contemptible generation of Irishmen that this country has known. They have given us the men and women who despise their own country, who ape the manners and pleasures of a race that is in many ways inferior to our own, who worship the success that money brings, and mistake the tinsel of artificiality for the realities of life.

It would be demanding too much courage of those who control the Intermediate schools to cut themselves free of the Board and its iniquitous programmes. Even the Christian Brothers, who have maintained their primary schools independent of the National Board, have bound themselves body and soul to the Intermediate Commissioners. The schools, in truth, have gone so far in accommodating themselves to the requirements of the Intermediate system that they have all but ceased to be susceptible to patriotic sacrifice. Why the interests of Irish secondary education should be crucified on a cross of monetary interests and Anglicisation is a question which those who now demand an Irish University have often considered and their desire to kill the Anglicisation of the Intermediate schools is one of their strongest reasons for demanding that Irish shall be an essential subject of the National University, for its curriculum will inevitably influence the programme of Intermediate education no matter how unsympathetic the Commissioners may remain. The alien system of education which pervades many of the Colleges explains the opposition of their directors to an Irish University. The force of circumstances however, usually breaks down the opposition of even the materially minded, and nothing except the Irishing of the Intermediate Board itself could have such a beneficial effect on the Intermediate colleges as the making of Irish and Irish history essential for entry to the new University.

THE ISSUE UNCHANGED
5.6.1909

The Statutes of the New University have not we trust deceived a single member of the Gaelic League into the belief that the Senate will do what we want it to do without any further pressure on our part, or lead anyone to conclude that all is well because the Statutory Commissioners have endowed a few chairs of Irish studies. All is not well, and now, when the curriculum is about to be settled, we need more than ever to be on our guard against compromise and the acceptance of any plausible but unsatisfactory settlement. It is well to remember that the public have been utterly deceived by the manner in which many on the Senate professing popular sympathies have forgotten their allegiance to the nation and have joined the avowed opponents of a distinctive nationality for this country. The people have expressed and reiterated the demands put forth by the Gaelic League but these demands have been ignored, and sneered at even by men who profess to act only on the mandate of the people, and there remain on the Senate only the few faithful ones in whom we may place implicit trust. These few are in a minority and their only hope for success lies in the strength of the support they get from the workers outside. The time for argument has gone by; we have to fight the battle straight and hard now, and the earlier we get through with it the better, for Ireland. We have argued long and patiently; we have employed only square methods; and now when the time for the final settlement is approaching, if the Senate has not improved its intentions, as expressed by many of its members, we shall have to counsel the use of methods that are bound eventually to be successful. Men who call themselves Irish but who oppose the most essential things of nationality and would have us adopt at our own expense, a foreign system of higher education are enemies of Ireland, and we must henceforth act towards them as enemies. Should the Senate decide against essential Irish, it as a body will have joined our opponents and we must treat it as an enemy — a dangerous enemy, also, for it will control one of the greatest educational machines in the country and will use it against us and the advancement of our ideas. We must be prepared to prove our earnestness by making it felt. We must treat the new University if it start out on its course in antagonism to our wishes, as a foreign institution. We must give it no financial aid or moral patronage, and must on every possible occasion treat it as we would a dangerous opponent of our national aims. A University with national sentiment opposed to it may do a little harm, but it will never become a dangerous foe to nationality. The country is no longer either ignorant or indifferent to its requirements, and it has come to recognise that one of its most urgent needs is a system of national education and it will have none of the un-Irish-second hand schemes that some would foist upon us. The people, in spite,of the nefarious work of the seoinín schools, have ceased to be ashamed of their country and they will now insist on having national schools and national universities also. They have become proud of the name Irishman, or Irishwoman, and they will no longer willingly acquiesce in a campaign of mind murder, character murder, nation murder, which is the end and aim of West British education.

We are told that men of sound nationality and patriotism are opposed to us on this question. We deny the statement. Our opponents on and off the Senate are our old enemies the seoiníni, the West Britons, and the craven souls who pay their homage to the stranger and have never known the independence of mind that a manly patriotism gives. They are the men who have given us the West British school, and who have turned two generations of Irish people out on the world without a thought for their motherland, and devoid of the protection which allegiance to it brings.

What the Senate will do we do not know, but we have said what Ireland should do, and must do, or suffer the strengthening of a dangerous enemy at our own expense. To a patriotic Senate we could promise the loyalty and support of Irish Ireland, but for a craven body, we shall have only unchanging enmity. Wexford, as it often in the past gave the lead, has again pointed to the course we must follow. At the Loch gCarmain Feis on Sunday last a resolution, proposed by the Rev. Father Fitzhenry and seconded by the Hon. William Gibson, pledging the Gaels of that county to give no moral or material support to the University until it became a *national* institution was adopted. The Gaelic League is the strongest organisation in Wexford and the only one having the support of all classes in the county. Whatever its leaders undertake to do they usually carry through, and it is certain that Wexford will stand by the pledge they have given. We trust that a big majority of our thirty-two counties will follow Wexford's example.

THE DISMISSAL OF DR. O'HICKEY
26.6.1909

At their meeting on Tuesday last the Trustees of Maynooth College — which means the Catholic Bishops of Ireland — dismissed the Rev. Dr. O'Hickey from the Irish Chair in the College on account of certain letters on the question of Irish in the National University written by him to the promoters of various public meetings and afterwards published in the pamphlet *An Irish University or Else* —. This is not all the news from Maynooth. A number of students have been refused orders, ostensibly because of some breach of College discipline but in reality because of their advocacy of essential Irish in the new University. Last week we were aware of recommendations to this effect which the Right Rev. Mgr. Mannix, President of the College, was making to the Trustees, but we could not believe that the Bishops of Ireland would dare to lend themselves to the vile work of the suppression, in the interests of West Britain, of Irish intellect and Irish freedom of thought. There is, however, no longer room for doubt. The Bishops have done their worst against Irish Ireland. It is not Irish Ireland that will suffer. Neither is it the noble priest whom the Bishops have turned out of their College — the bravest man of all the men of Maynooth who, from O'Growney to the young students so shamefully penalised today, have been building up the Gaelic League and the Irish language movement. It is the good name of the Bishops of Ireland that will suffer; it is, we fear, the good name of the Catholic Church, that will pay the penalty of the folly and shortsightedness of those who represented it in Maynooth on Tuesday last. Dr. O'Hickey has long been respected, even by those who differed most materially from him as to points of policy within and without the League, as the most brilliant and fearless champion of the movement among the priesthood of Ireland. Today he has earned a new fame and a new title to love and veneration. There is not a hamlet in the Gaedhealtacht, there is not a city in Ireland or Britain or America or Australia in which brave and patriotic and religious Irishmen will not bless the Irish priest who dared to meet tyranny face to face, answering it back with words as proud as its own, and refusing to budge one inch from the position which fortified by his own conscience and by the approbation of his countrymen, he had deliberately taken up. O'Growney's successor leaves Maynooth with a glory greater than O'Growney's and a place next to O'Growney's in the heart of Ireland.

Dr. O'Hickey, we take it, will without delay place before his countrymen a full statement of his shameful persecution and of his eviction from Maynooth. Until we have his story before us we prefer not to go into details. Of the central pitiable fact we are only too sure. The Trustees building their charge against him on certain paragraphs in the letters collected in *An Irish University, or Else* —, adopted a resolution dismissing the Rev. Dr. O'Hickey from the Irish Chair, Dr. O'Hickey having presumably refused either to withdraw what he had written or to resign.

233

The thing that amazes one most is the horrible fatuity of the men responsible for this piece of tyrannical blundering. In the counsels that swayed the decision of Tuesday last there was no scintilla, we shall not say of statesmanship, but of elementary commonsense or of recognition of things as they are. Do the Bishops think that the Irish people are babes in swaddling-clothes? Has the splendid history of their own Church not taught them that a cause can in no way be so surely and swiftly advanced as by giving it a martyr? Tomorrow morning the name of Dr. O'Hickey will be a rallying-call throughout Ireland. What a calamitous thing it is that so noble a name should be used as a rallying-cry against the Bishops of the Church in defence of whose faith and discipline three out of every four Irishmen would joyfully lay down their lives!

After what we have written, it is hardly necessary for us to state the attitude of the Gaelic League. Speaking here as the spokesman of that great organisation, we have to say to the Bishops of Ireland that the men and women of the League will not stand tyranny. We will fight it as resolutely as Dr. O'Hickey has fought it. We will answer it back as he has answered it back. We cannot, of course, restore Dr. O'Hickey to Maynooth, but we can carry to a triumphant success the cause for which he suffers. This struggle of ours is a struggle against the unholy things that are destroying our race and nation. It shall not be strangled by secret persecutions of Irish-Ireland priests whom God has inspired for the saving of a people. The power of the Bishops may be used against priests. It may be used against laymen. But the movement need not fear; for, as a priest beloved by Ireland has told us, the hand of God is with us, — yea, even though, for the moment, the hands of the Bishops may be raised against us.

THE MAYNOOTH DEBACLE
3.7.1909

The dismissal of Dr. O'Hickey has not smashed the Gaelic League or even weakened the fight for Irish in the University. Instead, it has had results entirely opposite to those which its authors expected it to produce. Men who until now scarcely knew they had a country are beginning to inquire into Irish affairs and are finding that there are only two parties and two interests in this country — English and Irish. They fail to see why Maynooth should join the enemy, and the natural result is that Maynooth and those who control it have fallen in the respect of all who value fair play and admire patriotism. Less than six months ago the Standing Committee of the Bishops went out of their way to state that the question of essential Irish was a matter for fair argument, but before and since that statement was made they have been employing all the powers which Church discipline gives them to crush fair argument, and, as we have seen, they have not stopped even at suppression. The late president of the Columban League, the Rev. Fr. Walsh, was refused ordination and excluded from Dunboyne (to which his brilliant college career had won him the right to enter) by the Maynooth authorities because he had publicly expressed the opinion that in the National University the national language should be treated fairly. Several other students were refused minor orders, and now the young priests of the Dunboyne Establishment who are suspected of patriotism are to be sent out of Ireland, not in accordance with the ordinary regulations of their dioceses, but because they are hateful to West Britain.

234

One of these young priests, An tAthair Aindrias Ó Ceileachair, is a man of whom his Church and the country of his birth may well be proud, for he has trained and developed, to a high degree, the gifts God gave him to use in the service of both. He has a rare knowledge of the Irish language, and if left in Ireland would have done much-needed work for Irish scholarship and literature. With some other students in Dunboyne he joined in sending a message of sympathy to the promoters of the students' meeting held in Dublin last Spring. For that little incident he is suspected of patriotism — the latest crime — and is being sent on a foreign mission, so that the foreigner's mind, no less than the foreigner's rule, may hold sway in his native land. The clever and patriotic priest is to be ostracised and exiled, and men who are not suspected of patriotic ideals will be kept at home, and considered good enough for the Irish mission. There was a period in Irish history when Dublin Castle allowed no patriotic priests to remain in Ireland. Are the penal laws it administered to be revived by the Irish Bishops?

The persecution of Irish-Ireland priests will serve one good purpose. It will draw a sharp line of distinction between West Britain and Ireland. The Bishops may remain on the wrong side for some time, but we are confident that the determination of Irish Ireland to have no trucking with the Garrison will, sooner or later, convince Irish churchmen that Catholics mean to have as much freedom to fight for national ideals as those who deny Ireland's right to nationhood employ to suppress them. We hope that Irish Catholics will always remain good Catholics, but we must say that the man who would make his religion an excuse for disloyalty to his country deserves all the odium which is ever the lot of the traitor or the apostate.

The feeling excited by the petty persecutions of the Bishops is one of sorrow and anger, and we believe that their foolish and unpatriotic action will have no other result than that of strengthening the case for an Irish University. Even those Senators who have been strongest in their opposition to Irish denounce the tyranny that has been employed against the League, and many who are in no way interested denounce the methods that have been employed against it. What makes the affair so painful to patriotic Irishmen is the consideration that it is not Dublin Castle, nor the Grand Orange Lodge that has employed such methods, but a body of Irishmen who claim to be patriotic, and that they have used them not against an anti-Irish or irreligious organisation, but against the Gaelic League.

It was said of the Bourbons that they would never learn from experience. We trust that the Irish Bishops will be wiser. They have betrayed a great dread of Irish Ireland and have failed woefully in the attempt to transfer the feeling to the object that inspired it. The resolution of the Dublin Coiste Ceanntair shows how Dublin Leaguers feel. The testimonial to Dr. O'Hickey to which the resolution refers will be supported as a duty by every Gael worthy of the name. His fearless courage in defence of the Irish language, and his action in resisting a tyranny, that would deprive every Catholic of freedom of speech have placed all Ireland under a debt to him that this generation cannot repay.

FAIR ARGUMENT
3.7.1909

Whether it be good for the Irish Language Movement, and good for the

New University, to make Irish compulsory, is a question for fair argument.
The Standing Committee of the Bishops, (20th January, 1909).

These are questions on which each one is free as the winds to hold his own opinion.
Cardinal Logue, (In the *Freeman's Journal,* February 24th, 1909. Letter
on *Irish in the University)*

I am in sympathy with the National Convention held in Dublin, and with the various Irish Corporations who have expressed the opinion that the Irish Language should be made a compulsory subject in the New National University.

Cardinal Moran.

COOL HEADS AND STRONG HEARTS
3.7.1909

We hope that the unfortunate events of the past two weeks will not turn one worker aside from the path of duty to the Gaelic League, or cause even a single one to lose faith in its cause. The thoughtless and heartless injustice that has been done to Dr. O'Hickey, and to the Irish-Ireland students of Maynooth and Dunboyne, for the purpose of terrorising the Gaelic League into meek submission to West Briton, we cannot repair; but we can do more needful and greater work. We can multiply our activities in the work of our organisation, and make it stronger and greater than it yet has been. We can increase our own subscriptions, and assist in collecting for the Language Fund. We can start new classes for the teaching of the language and of Irish history, and revive old ones. Many of us can spend our holidays at the Gaelic Colleges and prepare for assisting in Branch work during the coming winter. There is no one who cannot do something to forward the work of nationhood. The old can encourage, and the young can study and teach, and all should remember that it is only through sacrifice that any oppressed nation ever came to its own. Miss Hayden tells in our columns this week the story of how the Dutch let the sea overrun their country to scourge the Spanish conqueror over its borders. The sacrifice was great, but the Dutchmen did not flinch. They preferred no land to an enslaved land, and today neither foreign nor domestic tyrants oppress them. The sacrifice which we ask Irishmen of every creed and class to make, and which we feel they must make or else lose their race and country, is not one of land or life. It is no more than the sacrifice of a little time and effort. It is nothing more than to join in promoting the study of the national language and national history, and in becoming so informed on Irish affairs that they may be able to lead lives by which they will be known from the slaves who know no country, and never call their soul's their God's, or feel that when He gave them a land, a language, and a nationality, that He gave them a stewardship to guard and care.

No worker, young or old, need have any doubt regarding the justice of our cause, and although we cannot now help concluding that the machinery of the Catholic Church may be used against patriotic priests and laymen directly under control of the Bishops, we promise that no Bishop will dare to condemn Irish nationality. No churchman will have the courage to publicly champion British civilisation in Ireland. Secret influences will be used to crush out the national spirit so as to assure our British Governors of Ireland's loyalty, but we must keep our heads cool and never forget our purpose, which is not the reform of the Church, but the resurrection of our national civilisation. Against that purpose no honest man will raise his hand. If priests and others are forbidden to join us, as many have been, we, ourselves, must go on with the work. We shall answer every outrage that is committed on our rights, not by reprisals, but by renewed efforts in the cause for which MacHale refused to touch the West British Catholic University, for which O'Growney died, and for which today Dr. O'Hickey has been sacrificed to West Britain. Already the cry of anti-cleric has been raised. A western Bishop has told his clergy in conference that the Gaelic League is no longer worthy of support, because of its anti-clericalism. We need not heed such baseless charges, and our only care in the matter should be to give no provocation for such charges, no matter how great our own provocation may be. We are working in the cause of nationhood, and our opponents can find no justification for their disloyalty to Ireland in the Catholic religion, or, indeed, in any other.

A MATTER OF EDUCATION
24.7.1909

The aims of the Gaelic League resolve themselves in practice into an educational campaign. However sincere men may object to the compelling of Irish children to study their native tongue none can oppose our objection to systems of education which cater for our country in much the same manner as if it were a British colony in Asia or Africa, or as if our identity were one with that of Cumberland or Kent. To tolerate such a system any longer would be to acquiesce in the placing of our children in the grip of a mental vice that would teach them to regard their race, their country, its language and history, with less pride than they might those of the children of any European nation. Such a system has been that of the primary school. Such a system is that of the Intermediate Board, and such a system has been that of the Universities. Intelligent men of every creed and class are agreed in condemning such mind murder as those systems involved. Ireland has a history: why should it be suppressed? Ireland has a language: why should it be destroyed? Ireland has a nationality, written even on her physical outlines by the hand of Providence: why close our eyes to the fact? Whatever be the political fate of our country, there can be only stagnation in national affairs until there be a more general recognition of the essentials of nationality. To set our people back on the way of sanity will need a revolution. The revolution has been begun already, but it must be carried into the schools and conducted mainly in them. The conference on Bilingual Education which has been arranged by the Coiste Gnótha for Oireachtas week is a hopeful sign for the future of the schools, or for a large number of them at least. Bilingualism is a matter of ways and means, but ways and means so important, that the neglect of them would mean the neglect of the most valuable educational weapon within our grasp. The progress of Bilingualism in the schools marks, very largely, the real progress of the language movement. The great bar to the progress of both is the lack of skill in methods of language teaching, and of a good knowledge of the Irish language itself. The pioneers in Bilingual teaching are largely the most efficient workers in the revival, and we may expect that from the

Oireachtas they will send out a call to teachers generally for an immediate stride forward in a knowledge of Irish as well as for the adoption of Bilingual school methods.

Bilingualism, however, is not the only end to be aimed at. A resolution will come before the Ard-Fheis to recommend that more attention be given to the teaching of Irish history in the schools. The subject of the resolution deserves calm and earnest consideration. Bilingualism will give us Irish methods of education, but the teaching of our national history should exercise almost as great an influence in Gaelicising the Anglicised juvenile mind as that which is exercised by the teaching of the language itself. The old style of history — lists of battles and broken treaties with the English — must be set aside. The broad scientific history which shows us as a branch of the Aryan race that played a big part in early European history and later as a nation isolated politically from the rest of Europe, but having every interchange with outside nations which progress demanded, receiving and giving, must take the place of the date book and agony column style of history which has taught Irishmen to hate their foes but not to love each other.

The Gael is slowly coming to his own. In education two new subjects, viz., our language and history, have been added to school programmes. Education itself is being radically altered both in purpose and methods. Socially new dress costumes and native song and dance are replacing those of the *allmhurach*; and intellectually, the dignity of using our own minds is so widely recognised, that one may now hope for anything from Young Ireland. The few thousand active workers who have had the courage to come into the market place and challenge the right of a world-wide civilization to dominion in our little country have done something that appeals to the spirit of resistance in all brave men. They took upon themselves a battle in which giants might engage and find stressful work to do. That is why the Gaelic League is gathering to itself the best workers that exist in the country. Its work is so noble, unselfish, and demands such sacrifice that every strong-brained man and woman who comes to know of it becomes impatient for participation in the struggle, and envious for a share of the honour that falls to all who serve their country. If the League and the movement which it has set going be wisely piloted we may hope to see within a few years the best minds of all creeds and political parties under the spell of the revival. The Ireland of old drew its people from many lands. The new Ireland, our Ireland, is welding a composite race from men of many parties and creeds, but they are all 'Ireland men'. We all must suffer the pains of the purifying Gaelic fire, and out of the seething pot will come a new Irish mind, a new Irish character, a new race whose home and the centre of whose activities will be Ireland.

THE BISHOP OF GALWAY
24.7.1909

The Most Rev. Dr. O'Dea, the new Bishop of Galway, received a public welcome from the people of his new see last week. Many of the addresses of welcome were in Irish and in replying to that from the Gaelic League, his Lordship spoke entirely in Irish. He spoke enthusiastically of the aims and efforts of the League, and promised that as far as his judgement and capabilities would admit, he would do 'a man's part in the work'. Dr.

O'Dea is not, we believe, a friend of compulsory Irish either in the University or in secondary schools, but he is reported to have made the following statements regarding the Land Question: —

> 'I have been an advocate of *legal compulsion*. I regard *compulsion and compulsory purchase* as the logical extension of the principle of the compulsory fixing of fair rents. The Act of 1881 *compulsorily altered the landlord's income*, and I do not see anything *sacrosanct about capital* which would exempt it from compulsion rather than income. That is the principle of the thing. And then, as to the need of it, anyone who knows the state of things, in the West of Ireland especially, will admit that *the public good requires that there should be compulsion* in order that landlords *who may be unreasonable* may not be allowed to stand in the way of a complete and final settlement of the Land question.
>
> '*Why could not you take the whole land away on principle if the public good requires it?* It is a *principle of ethics* and *theology* that if *the public good requires it*, the State can take away property. I believe that here in the West of Ireland especially, the public good requires it, and no one landlord should be allowed to stand in the way of a complete and final settlement of the Land question.'

If it be good and necessary to apply compulsion in a matter affecting the nation's material interests, why should it not be also wise and needful. to apply the same principle when the interests of the nation's soul are at stake? Dr. O'Dea is not a man who would connive at any barter of principle for material gains, and if he would only consider how great is the need of the Irish language for succour, he should inevitably favour compulsion in the schools and University, just as he now favours compulsory sale of land. Leaving Irish optional is handing over to students the power to determine what place Irish shall occupy in education. Are students competent to decide such an important question? No one will assert that they are; yet all who oppose the principle of essential Irish, fail apparently, to see that the result of their policy whould be to make students the arbiters. In St. Joseph's College, at Ballinasloe, over which Dr. O'Dea, until very lately exercised control, students were not compelled to study Irish. The language was not neglected by all the students, but, is his Lordship satisfied, from the results, that freedom of choice for students is good for the life of the language?

THE FACTS ABOUT DR. O'HICKEY
24.7.1909

The facts of Dr. O'Hickey's case are simple, and will be stated over and over again as often as necessary. It is clear that some influence is at work endeavouring to mystify and confuse the public about this case. To avoid all misunderstanding, let us say that so far as we are aware, this influence is not being employed by any of Dr. O'Hickey's superiors. But it is being employed by certain people, and, at least, one weekly paper, in order to curry favour with the Maynooth authorities whether they be right or wrong, and to avoid the unpleasant duty of taking a clear stand on the side of Irish Ireland. The public is familiar with this sort of patriotism that wants

239

to be on the side of the hare and the hounds at the same time.

The facts are these: —

Dr. O'Hickey published a pamphlet entitled *An Irish University or Else*.

When the Board of Visitors (consisting of Bishops) met last month at Maynooth College, Dr. O'Hickey was called before them to answer for his pamphlet and for certain statements contained in it. He has stated publicly in a letter to the *Independent,* in correction of a statement in that paper, that no other charge was brought against him or mentioned, or suggested, except on the sole evidence of this pamphlet.

Two days later, Dr. O'Hickey was again cited before the Board of Trustees of the College, i.e., before the body of the Irish Hierarchy acting as Governors of the College. On this occasion again, the pamphlet, and the pamphlet alone was the evidence relied on against him, and the statements contained in the pamphlet were the whole and only basis of indictment. Particular weight was attached to certain passages on pages 9, 10, 20, 30, and 31 of the pamphlet.

On this occasion, Dr. O'Hickey was presented by the Trustees with a resolution which they had adopted before hearing him. The resolution called on him to resign his professorship, on pain of dismissal.

It was stated two days later in the *Irish Times* that Dr. O'Hickey had resigned. He did not resign and he has not been dismissed. In a brief letter to the *Irish Times* he contradicted the report of the resignation. The *Irish Times* explained that they had published the statement 'on the highest official authority', and no repudiation on the part of any official authority has since been forthcoming. No living person doubts the absolute truth of Dr. O'Hickey's published words.

Nothing could be more unfair than the suggestion now going the rounds that Dr. O'Hickey has been brought to judgement for some obscure internal collegiate matter about which the public are in ignorance. The public are in possession of the entire facts of the case brought against him. That case is entirely in the pages of his pamphlet which is on public sale.

Dr. O'Hickey, like the other professors of Maynooth, holds a life appointment. He does not hold his appointment at the pleasure of the Trustees, and is not liable to dismissal merely because something he says or writes causes them displeasure. He can only be dismissed for incapacity or misconduct of a kind that renders him unfit to hold the Chair. The public can judge whether Dr. O'Hickey's pamphlet, the sole evidence against him, contains proof of such misconduct as to render him worthy of being ignominiously kicked out of his livelihood and out of an honourable position which he has held for many years.

If his misconduct was of this kind, why was Dr. O'Hickey allowed to remain unmolested, without any accusation brought against him, and without any notice of any accusation, for the greater part of the past academical year?

The whole proceedings against Dr. O'Hickey show every appearance of haste and irregularity. It is almost certain that these proceedings would be instantly quashed by any court, ecclesiastical or civil, properly constituted. It is certain that no other authority could venture to dismiss the holder of a life appointment on such terms. Dr. O'Hickey has been threatened with dismissal — that is all — on the grounds of his pamphlet. His case is not sub judice in any judicial sense, and there is no reason why it should not be publicly discussed.

It would be absolute cowardice to pretend that the question at stake is purely a private one between Dr. O'Hickey and the College authorities. If Dr. O'Hickey's action, which is well known to the public, is approved of then it will be a public scandal if he is deserted and left to fight out his battle — which is really the nation's battle — in the obscurity of a private dispute. The public knows well that a grave blunder was committed by the Bishops' Standing Committee when they took one side, and that one the anti-national side, in the University question, and when the clergy over a great part of the country were at the same time prevented from advocating the opposite side, which their conscience and their patriotism had impelled them to join. The second blunder — for a blunder it is — arises directly out of the first, and that is the whole story. As the nation refused to be misled or confused by the first blunder, it will also refuse to be misled or confused by the second. Let every one who now knows the facts insist on stamping out every attempt to muddle or misrepresent them. We shall soon know 'who is afraid'.

THE BISHOPS' STATEMENT
7.8.1909

At a meeting of the Catholic Archbishops and Bishops of Ireland held at Maynooth College on the 29th ult., the following statement was unanimously adopted:

'The Bishops, finding that there is a serious misconception in the country, based upon misrepresentation of the nature of certain steps which they have recently found it necessary to take for the maintenance of discipline in the National Ecclesiastical College of Maynooth, where their young ecclesiastical students are trained for the priesthood, wish to remove that false impression.

'The steps in question were taken solely in discharge of the episcopal duty of maintaining ecclesiastical discipline in the College, and had no connection whatsoever with the views of anyone as to whether the Irish language should or should not be an obligatory subject at certain examinations, or in certain courses, of the National University of Ireland.

'Considering the course which, especially of late, is being pursued in this and similar matters by certain newspapers — including one which is generally reputed to be the official organ of the Gaelic League — the Bishops feel it to be a sacred duty to warn the people committed to their charge against allowing themselves to be misled by writings the clear tendency of which is antagonistic to the exercise of episcopal authority and which, in some instances, are calculated to bring into contempt all ecclesiastical authority, not even excepting that of the Holy See itself.'

(Signed),
+ MICHAEL, CARDINAL LOGUE,
Chairman,

+ RICHARD ALPHONSUS,
Bishop of Waterford and Lismore.
+ ROBERT,
Bishop of Cloyne,
Secretaries to the Meeting.

On the same day the Bishops in their capacity as Trustees of the College finally dismissed the Rev. Dr. O'Hickey from the Irish Professorship.

Why has Dr. O'Hickey been dismissed? We are asked to believe that he has been dismissed solely for the purpose of maintaining ecclesiastical discipline in the College. His dismissal, and the other steps that have been taken, have 'had no connection whatsoever with the views of anyone as to whether the Irish language should or should not be an obligatory subject at certain examinations, or in certain courses of the National University of Ireland'. The point would seem to be that Dr. O'Hickey has been dismissed not for *holding* his view on the question of Essential Irish but for having *expressed* those views in the way in which he did — the mode of his expression having in some way interfered with the maintenance of ecclesiastical discipline in the College. This, no doubt, is the light in which the matter presents itself to the minds of the Bishops. The Irish public cannot and will not draw such fine distinctions. For them the broad fact remains that Dr. O'Hickey has suffered because of his fearless and brilliant championship of the Irish language. No one can pretend that if he had not taken the stand he took on the question of Essential Irish he would have been driven from Maynooth. The only charges brought against him were charges based on certain paragraphs in his published letters and lectures. If those passages had not been written he would still be the occupant of the Irish chair. It is trifling with words and paltering with the commonsense of men to maintain that his expulsion is anything but the direct consequence of his advocacy of an Irish University.

The Bishops find it their duty to warn their flocks against writings in certain papers, 'including one which is generally reputed to be the official organ of the Gaelic League', 'the clear tendency of which is antagonistic to the exercise of episcopal authority'. *An Claidheamh Soluis* is the official organ of the Gaelic League. No word antagonistic to the exercise of episcopal authority has ever appeared in its columns. We are the mouthpiece of a non-sectarian organisation, and as such we have no standing in any matter concerning the exercise of episcopal authority within its own sphere. But we claim and will always exercise the right to criticise any action of the Bishops, as of any other body of Irishmen, which affects the welfare of the Irish language. The Irish language is our charge and to that charge we will be faithful. We spoke out strongly against the recent action of the Bishops, an action which seems to us to have been at once a terrible wrong and a terrible blunder. Our words had in them, as the occasion demanded, a certain passion, but they had in them nothing of disrespect for episcopal authority, nothing of disrespect for the Bishops either in their episcopal or in their personal capacity. The strongest thing we said was that we will fight what seems to us to be tyranny even as Dr. O'Hickey has fought it. If there was any doubt in anyone's mind as to whether we authentically voiced the feeling of our organisation, that doubt has been dispelled by the great meeting of Tuesday last, presided over by the founder of the Gaelic League. The meeting unanimously agreed to the following resolution: 'That we adopt the proposal of a testimonial to the Rev. Dr. O'Hickey in recognition of his services to Irish education, and in particular with reference to the National University'. The men and women of the League will, as Eoin Mac Neill said, stand by the man who has stood by them. 'If we do not we need never face another fight nor look for respect or sympathy from any man in Ireland.'

AGRICULTURE IN SCHOOLS AND THE TRAINING OF TEACHERS
16.10.1909

An announcement in an English newspapers shows how in England reform in education works from above, not from below, as happens almost invariably in Ireland. The announcement says: — 'The Boards of Agriculture and Education have arranged to improve and extend specialised instruction of all grades bearing on agriculture. A Rural Education Conference is to be constituted, as "Much remains to be done to bring the facilities for agricultural education at the disposal of British agriculturalists to the level of those enjoyed by many of their competitors elsewhere".'

A few weeks ago the Catholic clerical school managers of Connacht adopted a resolution recommending the teaching of agriculture in the primary schools. The first matter to which we wish to draw public attention in regard to this resolution is that it focuses attention on a subject the teaching of which is of vital importance in an agricultural country, and that it, inevitably, implies that the National Board has been and is doing next to nothing to fit the country boys, either technically or mentally, for an occupation which fifty per cent of them at least should follow. The Board, as it is at present constituted and financed, will, we are sure, show very little tendency to improve, and it is hardly fair to expect teachers to take on additional work for the teaching of which they have not been trained, and for which no training facilities that we know of exist at present. It would lead to further crowding of programmes and further muddle.

We hold, however, that the study of agricultural conditions and requirements should form a special feature of the educational equipment of Irish primary teachers, because in Irish land agriculture is our greatest and most general industry. The spirit of primary education should aim at fitting our rural children mentally, if not technically, for life on the land. The spirit, as we know it, of the education now given in the primary schools aims at nothing, if not Anglicisation. Reform can come only through the teachers, and to 90 per cent of them it must come through training. The resolution of the Connacht clerical managers cannot, therefore, in our opinion, effect any immediate good, but it will serve the purpose of helping to expose one of the many grave faults of primary education. What we have to consider is how reform might be effected. If there were any immediate chance of gaining administrative control over our educational system we might wait for years, because a body composed of persons of intelligence and patriotism would set matters right in a few months; but there is no sign of such a desirable change and we may, by continuous and vigorous agitation, get the present Board, the Department, and the Universities to direct their powers and finances to the raising of the efficiency of the men and women who are responsible for the working of the primary schools. We want to reconstruct rural life, which many forces, some of them at work for centuries, have been destroying. Education is our chief instrument, and we could scarcely devote too much money or attention to its welfare. At present we spend 6s. 7d. per head of population for police, and 1d. per head less for education. In Scotland the cost of police per head of population is 2s. 6d., and education costs 8s. 8d.

When we assert that the methods and spirit of primary education must be changed we should remember that the change cannot come without a

243

change in the system of training our teachers, and our first and principal aim should be to improve the teachers' opportunities for fitting themselves for the important, though underpaid, posts they hold. It is considered necessary for a grocer's assistant to spend three years learning how to serve customers with common commodities, such as tea, sugar, and whiskey; a veterinary surgeon spends at least four years in training; a doctor often spends many more, while a clergyman may be ten or twelve years preparing for his calling. To our teachers, the men amd women who have the training of our children, we give two years of hard 'grinding', and then expect them to teach everything from languages to cookery. The present state of things is intolerable to all thoughful people, and it is perhaps due as much to the indifference of the public as to the cheeseparing policy of the British Treasury. The two years' course at present given in the Training Colleges is not in reality a training at all. It is an educational course, absolutely essential, but not a training. When Drumcondra, Blackrock, and other similar colleges have done with the young teachers it should be made possible for them to spend two additional years in higher and better-equipped schools in which they could make a special study of the science of teaching, of the national language, of history, and of the elements of national economics, including, of course, the principles of agriculture.

The Treasury would not readily consent to finance any such scheme as we have suggested, even if the Board were ready and anxious to set it going. But our hopes are not all centred in the Board. The Department of Agriculture has power to incur expenditure for agricultural education, and we are sure that the Universities, especially the new Universities, might, if they chose, establish a teaching faculty both in Dublin and Belfast for the purpose of giving us properly trained and generously educated teachers. The National Board, the Department, and the Universities might combine to bear the financial burden of such a faculty. If the Universities and the County Councils contribute a rate-in-aid there could be no safer expenditure and no surer means of ensuring to the rural taxpayer a return for his money than by assisting primary teachers to undergo a University course. Both the Queen's and the 'National' University are closed to teachers, except as ordinary students. The teachers themselves seem to have taken the matter with indifference; but it is not a matter of indifference either to them or to the country. The most necessary qualities in a teacher, apart from his knowledge of subjects and of teaching methods, are finish and strength of character, and a tolerant and cultivated mind. For the gaining of these the present Training Colleges afford no opportunity, but in the University they would come almost naturally. We look forward hopefully to the time when our teachers will have opportunities for culture and the development of character, when every parish and little town will have a continuation school, a step above, but not far removed from the primary school, and when the education of the country will be in the hands of men and women of wide knowledge and of generous and lofty aims. The education they will give will be Irish through and through. It will be conversant with all things concerning our race and our country, and the most influential and most respected citizens in the new Ireland will be the trainers and instructors of the new nation's children.

COLÁISTE LAIGHEAN
23.10.1909

The opening of Coláiste Laighean took place on the evening of October 14th. The event, notwithstanding the fact that Irish colleges have now become quite numerous, was one of more than ordinary importance, for it was the occasion of several speeches of a kind that are too infrequent even on Gaelic League platforms — speeches free from platitudes and charged with commonsense and courageous sincerity.

The Irish colleges were referred to by Eoin Mac Neill, who was one of the speakers, as the flower of Gaelic League endeavour. They are certainly the best instruments we have forged for the working out of our purpose. Their staffs consist of teachers who are expert in knowledge and method, and they are engaged in the training of other teachers who will carry on in school and college the work of revival. The result of the struggle in which we are engaged will depend very largely on the efficiency and the extent of the means we employ to attain the desired end. On the application of means depends victory, and by employing only the surest means we ensure against failure. The Irish colleges are to the League what military colleges are to an army. They train the officers of our movement in knowledge and in methods and give them courage and resourceful individuality for their work. Before the advent of the colleges, in spite of the enthusiasm and sincerity of many workers, much energy was wasted in unfruitful endeavour to teach Irish without the skill of the language teacher. Now no teacher who has not studied the latest methods in the teaching both of sounds and of language is held to be competent or expert, and public opinion is so strongly in favour of expert training that it has become essential for every teacher of Irish to become possessed of the certificate of one of the Irish training colleges.

So far as the six colleges have been able to reach they have found useful work to perform. Their slender resources have scarcely served for the purpose of providing salaries for the teachers, and were it not for the voluntary labours of men like Seoirse Ó Muanáin, and An tAthair Ó Ronáin, who give much of their time to the drudgery of committee work the chances of success would be reduced to a minimum. Coláiste Laighean is not or could not be self-supporting, as the summer colleges in the Gaedhealtacht are rapidly becoming. Its session is a winter one, and for this and other reasons its roll of students does not exceed 100 by any large figure. The fees from such a number of students amount to only a slender sum which has had to be supplemented every year since the foundation of the college. As our progress depends almost entirely on the number of efficient teachers we are able to turn out, two duties become particularly urgent on Dublin and Leinster Gaedheals: these are to subscribe to the college funds as freely as our purses allow, and to use whatever influence we possess to get teachers to attend its classes.

The colleges have subsisted on the fees of students and on the small subscriptions — with a few exceptions — of poor but generous subscribers. They have made a science of producing great results at a minimum of expense, and in this they have followed the example of the teachers, Irish and foreign, of other ages when the aim of the school was to give the greatest possible amount of teaching at a nominal cost. The wealthier educational establishments are, the greater will be their usefulness in spreading education amongst the comparatively poor. No school should be locked with a golden key against the poor scholar. The generosity of Irish chieftains in the old days made education practically free, within the tribe at least, but modern circumstances, and the lack of patriotism and generosity amongst our wealthy classes, who never dream of endowing a school, make free education, except in the primary schools, almost impossible. But we are overcoming the difficutly in Irish Ireland. The outlay which out teachers make is not necessarily large; their fees are moderate, and they are true to the ideal of Irish education through the medium of the Irish language. That is the chief aim of the Gaelic League, not indeed, its ultimate purpose, for it looks on education as but a means of 'perfecting Ireland'.

The task of Gaelicising Irish education is a large one, but if we be prudent and energetic as we have been in the past, we need not fear for the final result. We have already worked wonders. Our cause is a just one, and our work is absolutely necessary to the life of the nation. But a negative prudence will not be sufficient. We must be courageous enough to speculate, and energetic enough to execute new plans for the futherance of our aims. The Irish colleges are the best weapon we can command today; tomorrow, or next year, we may need other weapons with the use of which we are as yet unacquainted. Let us not be unprepared.

Ar aghaidh libh, a Ghaedheala!

IRISH IN THE INTERMEDIATE
13.11.1909

His Grace the Archbishop of Tuam, if he spoke with a knowledge of why the majority of the Intermediate Board refused a re-examination of the Irish papers, gave their case completely away when last week he said that the 'was not surprised that the Commissioners had declined to review these examinations, because it would be a very dangerous precedent to set up, and on the whole, perhaps, it is better to tolerate the injustice of this year than throw discredit on their whole system of examinations'. His Grace is, apparently, in favour of policy before justice to Irish students and teachers. It might be very bad policy for the Board to attempt to satisfy everyone who complains of its administration, but it will be fatal to its standing as a public department if a wrong admitted on all sides be not corrected. Mr. Cherry has announced that the rule behind which German is being elbowed into the Intermediate system and Irish crushed out is to stand for the coming year. The Lord Lieutenant has given it his approval, and it must, therefore, stand, for the law is almighty. Its abolition might bring the Lord Lieutenant's office into disrepute, as a re-examination of the Irish would destroy the respect of the public for the Intermediate Board. The truth is that if Mr. Cherry or the Lord Lieutenant or the majority of the Intermediate Commissioners set any value on the good-will of the Irish public, they would willingly attempt to govern Ireland in accordance with Irish ideas.

Canon O'Ryan has suggested that the Gaelic League and the Headmasters should raise a fund to compensate those pupils whose marks entitled them to exhibitions, but who were penalised through the working of this iniquitous rule. The suggestion is excellent, for worthy pupils should not be allowed to suffer through the Board's contrariness; but, the Coiste Gnotha could scarcely undertake to subscribe for such a purpose money

246

that has been subscribed for other and more pressing ones. The income of the Gaelic League is very slender, and the central body could not, in any case subscribe extensively to such a fund as Canon O'Ryan suggests. It has not, up to the time of writing, even considered the suggestion, but, should it do so, and approve of the raising of the fund, the difficulty could be overcome if the Branches would subscribe as much as a pound each. It has been calculated that the Intermediate students of Irish were deprived of £700 in exhibitions at the last examinations, but it should not be necessary to compensate more than those students who have been deprived of the means of education by the unfair awards. The whole struggle for the revival of the national language has been one of sacrifice, and the Intermediate schools and pupils must be prepared to take their blows in turn. They should stand by Irish no matter what the Board does, just as Ring College and St. Enda's are standing by it. If, however, the suggested fund finds favour the Branches and Headquarters could easily raise the required amount.

The rule was originally created, it is said, to prevent the Catholic schools that taught Irish running away with all the exhibitions in the Modern Literary course. It was found that students of Irish, even when the set texts were difficult and archaic, were able to beat students of the Continental languages, and as a consequence the Protestant schools which, unfortunately, do not teach the national language, came out of the annual examinations only a poor second. We do not thing that it would be wise to force them into teaching Irish because their history and political creeds prevents them, just yet, appreciating its value in education and nationality. They should, however, see that their refusal to admit Irish into their schools implies a belief of their own superiority over the Gaelic population of this country. It is unnecessary to assert that they possess no such superiority except in the circumstance that they are occasionally more favoured by our British governors because of their anti-Irish feelings. It would be wise for our Protestant fellow-countrymen to abandon this pretence of superiority and to join us in the effort to snatch our educational systems from the hands of English Rationalists, whose aims in educational matters, when not political, are anti-religious. The tendency in England is to drive religion out of education. The same tendency will become manifest among the heads of our own systems if the power of nomination remains continually in the hands of the British. The duty of Protestant and Catholic is to unite against the British Rationalist or both may be ultimately destroyed by him. The Irish language, instead of being a bone of contention, should be a link of unity between the followers of the two creeds. That the Board has taken objection to the Protestant indifference to the national language to emphasise the racial and religious split is not to be wondered at. It is in keeping with British policy in Ireland from the very start. National progress we cannot make while we remain divided within ourselves, and while the Catholic and Nationalist should be willing to allow the Protestant and Unionist full freedom for political and religious opinions, the Protestant should recognise that outside of his religion and politics there are duties to Ireland, the observance of which is as binding on the Unionist as on the Nationalist. Loyalty to the Irish language is one of these. Neglect of it implies that Protestants mean to isolate themselves from their fellow-countrymen and to remain a British garrison. While they maintain this attitude we shall remain a straw for every British breeze to blow about, and the Protestant and Catholic will be trampled under foot by every British Minister.

THE MEANING OF BISHOP DAY'S ATTACK
27.11.1909

At the annual meeting of the Protestant Training College for Teachers, held in Dublin last week, under the presidency of the Most Rev. Dr. Peacocke, a resolution recommending a modification of the National Board's rule which will require candidates for Training to know a second language after next year was adopted. The resolution itself was a mild affair, but the speech by Dr. Day, Bishop of Clogher, was neither mild nor discreet, and it is because of this, and because we believe that the resolution in question is nothing more than an indication of an effort that is being made to make the Board withdraw the rule altogether that we write.

Last year the Board gave notice that after three years all candidates for Training would be required to present a second language at the entrance examination. There were many reasons for making such a rule. The chief one, perhaps, was that teachers without Irish found it difficult to get employment in most parts of the country, for there is a growing demand for the teaching of Irish among the parents of at least two-thirds of school-going children. Another and very obvious reason was that no one knowing only English can be either cultured or well educated. No English or American educationalist would admit that it is possible to devolop, train and inform the mind without a second language. A third reason would be that in the large towns and cities there is always a slight demand for the teacher of French and German. The rule was not adopted without good and sufficient reason, and three years' notice of its enforcement has been given. This is sufficient for all classes from whom the candidates for training are drawn, and we need not regard seriously the recommendation for the 'gradual' enforcement of the rule. The speech of Bishop Day indicates a purpose and determination which the resolution does not express. Those who are opposed to Irish ideals, and who are content to be mere imitation Englishmen, while they draw their sustenance from this country, have generally been able to have their aims carried out in all Government departments. British ministers nominate them on Castle Boards, or present them with sinecures at the public expense, because of their political prejudices, and without reference to their qualifications. They ruled the old Royal University, and they have a majority on the Intermediate and National Boards. They can if they choose secure the abolition of the new language rule to which Bishop Day objects, and we regard the attack on the Irish language at the Protestant Training College as an indication of secret influences at work to secure this end.

We ask our readers to remember that the new rule will impose no hardship on any candidate, that it will not compel any candidate who might be opposed to Irish to learn that language, that it is a much-needed step forward in the raising of the qualifications of candidates for teacherships, and that there is a growing demand in all parts of Ireland for bilingual teachers. Remembering these facts, it is perfectly plain that the attack of Bishop Day, who was frequently applauded by his listeners, was inspired not by any sense of fear or injustice which might be caused by the rule, but by that bigotry which has always, unfortunately, characterised a large section of his class. His bigotry cannot be attributed to ignorance in the ordinary sense of the word, for bishops are, as a rule, men of culture and understanding. It is due primarily, perhaps, to political hatred. The Irish language is associated with Irish nationality. It must, therefore, be opposed, even though it be the national language of the country in which Bishop Day lives, but which he despises. That was the belief and the sentiment voiced by this Protestant divine, and applauded by his hearers. It does not matter to him that a knowledge of Irish makes Catholic boys mentally superior to Protestant boys, and he appeals to Irish Protestant teachers not to learn or teach it. He prefers that ignorance, intellectual incapacity, and inefficient training of teachers should prevail rather than see Irish Protestants join their Catholic fellow-countrymen in an endeavour to raise Irish ideals and Irish intellect out of the unhonoured track of a second-hand civilisation. But he does not speak for intellectual Protestantism. Some of the best workers in our movement are Protestants, and the makers of the industrial revival are very largely of that creed. Even as we write the Protestant students of Trinity College are assembling for the inaugural meeting of the College Gaelic Society. That the Protestants will yet come to realise the need and value of a national language we have not the least doubt. Their conversion will, necessarily, be gradual. The vigour of our fight will hasten rather than retard it. We need not, then, be diffident in protesting against Bishop Day's attack, and against the secret attempts that, we are confident, are being made to have the new language rule of the National Board abolished. Bishop Day and his friends will not rest at the passing of a resolution, but, just as they secured the creation of the iniquitous rule which destroys the equality of Irish among modern languages in the Intermediate, they will now do their utmost to destroy the new rule of the National Board.

TEACHING AND ITS RESULTS
4.12.1909

We judge any method of teaching or system of education by its ultimate results. We have already been long enough teaching in the Gaelic League to review the work of years just left behind and to inquire into its effectiveness. Less than ten years ago the few who cried out for common sense in language teaching were looked upon by many as uneasy spirits sent among us to worry honest, earnest workers and prevent progress. Today their will has prevailed, and the teacher in the country who has not acquainted himself with the Modh Díreach in language teaching either feels keenly the want of it or is indifferent to all method. Miss Hayden, lecturing before the Dublin Educational Society last week, spoke with natural pride of the great things that we have achieved on the most slender resources. She told of the hundreds of teachers who have studied in the Gaelic League Colleges and of the tens of thousands of children who are now being taught a second language on the most scientific methods, and that language their mother tongue. One result of our work, and the methods in which it is done is plain: it is that the revival of Irish as a spoken tongue is being achieved everywhere the approved methods of teaching have been adopted. This fact is satisfactory in the sense that it relieves us of all doubt as to the possibility of realising our aims. The fate of the revival depends on our common sense and industry. To be worthy of success we have only to adopt the best methods and to employ them continually, and, in our case, deserving success will be commanding it. Another pleasing result, although an incidental one, of the movement for science and sanity in language teaching is the beneficial effects which it is producing on teaching generally. It is helping to dissipate the idea of Tom Tulliver's master that teaching came naturally, like the habits of the beaver. The idea is still very widespread, but it is rapidly giving way to the true idea that teaching is an art which can be perfected only by careful study and practice. Of this change the teaching of Irish is largely the cause. The sight of a teacher employing all his powers of suggestion and demonstration to make himself unterstood is a standing surprise to both the teacher and the taught. Under the old system the rod was often employed to drive fine points home. Under the new the teacher depends on his skill to make his pupils appreciate the finest points imaginable. The old-time teacher — the man without method — was an unskilled worker; the new up-to-date teacher is an artist. The pupils under the old system dreaded the teacher and hated their tasks. Under the new system they admired the teacher's skill which, by obviating their difficulties, makes them love the pursuit of knowledge. Now, this change which, if it has not been brought about, has been precipitated by the introduction of the new methods of language teaching and is influencing education generally. The teacher who learns method to teach Irish soon sees the advantage of method for instruction in other subjects, if he has not already got it, as well, and we may hope to have in the near future a body of teachers who will be not less skilled or successful than those of any other country. A third effect of the revival work is the kindling among large masses of people of a love of the higher kinds of knowledge. It is a noble achievement to have won hosts of men and women in the busy pursuits of life for the study of their country's language and history. The result of the study is the great quickening of thought which is making the present period the most remarkable one of our modern history. This awakening seems to be dreaded by some. But they need not fear, if they be friends of truth and justice. These are the things we seek, and it is not our purpose to destroy those who befriend them.

While the results of our efforts have been so satisfactory in several ways there is one desirable effect which they are not always producing: They are not producing in all the shrewdness, the willingness to sacrifice, the fortitude, and the courage which are so essential and so frequently absent from the national character. What we mean to convey is that a superficial knowledge of Irish does not always carry with it a keen sense of the obligations imposed on us by our duties to patriotism and a willingness and spirit in the fulfilment of them, such as should result from a good system of national education. Were the revival of Irish our only aim, then we might be satisfied at the fruits of our labours; but it is the revival of the nation that we ambition, and we should on that account endeavour to make the teaching of Irish more and more telling in its influence on education generally, and education itself we should employ, in the first place, for the training of good men and women, and after that, and before all else, for the training of patriotic citizens. Our teachers must not rest satisfied with the ability to turn out Irish speakers in one or two years; nor must students be content with a colloquial knowledge of the language.With the teaching of Irish must go a knowledge of our literature, and with both a knowledge of our history. In a letter, which we publish elsewhere, to the Secretary of the Ring Secondary School, Mrs. J. R. Green expresses the hope that the teaching of Irish history will figure in the education of the future. We are confident that it will, but we must not wait for its introduction until it pleases the National and Intermediate Boards to show it more than bare consideration in their programmes. As we founded the Training Colleges to revolutionise teaching methods so we must make Irish literature and history subjects of instruction and examination for the students who pass through them and desire their certificates. It is time for the College Committees to aim higher than the mere training of Modh Díreach teachers. It is essential to give teachers reasons for the faith that is in them.

In one of his recent lectures in Trinity College Professor Culverwell stated that a language might be taught as an art or as an exact science. To acquire a spoken language of any tongue was to learn an art. To study a language as Latin and Greek were studied was to study a science. The effect of any art on its possessor was to improve not only his knowledge but his culture, and usefulness in society. The chief, or one of the chief, effects of the scientific study of a language was to improve mental activity, and to train the mind in the ways of logical thought. The art of speaking a living language affects for the most part the ear and tongue; but a deep knowledge of a language gives mental training and enlargement. There is a great danger that in our eagerness, praiseworthy though it be, to give teachers a hurriedly acquired knowledge of Irish the deeper side of Irish study may be neglected. The gift of perfect language comes largely from the study of masterpieces. In Greece it came from the public recitations of the Iliad. In England it came largely from the English Bible. Amongst our own race it was the possession of the stories of the seanchaidhe and the poems of the bard that preserved the language in a comparatively perfect state, even on the lips of the people. The power to teach a language does not often mean that a teacher either appreciates or has the power to interpret its literature. Unless our teachers know Irish literature neither themsleves nor their pupils will help to create a new literature; nor will the knowledge of the spoken language be either vivid or extreme. It is evident then that the deeper study of Irish is absolutely necessary. Our colleges have done great things, but greater things lie waiting to be done. They must not be satisfied with the teaching of a colloquial knowledge of Irish, however perfect. They must not neglect the advanced study of the language, and they can only neglect the teaching of literature and history at the risk of missing half the fruits of thier labours. The spoken language is the key to the deeper knowledge, and the experience of past ages that will give strength and beauty and restore its Gaelic charm to the character of the rising generation.

THE SCHOOL AND THE NATION
1.1.1910

Everything the British Government originates and arranges for the people of Ireland may not be calculated by the English themselves to injure our welfare or retard our progress, but there cannot be the shadow of a doubt concerning the evils that have followed, and are still resulting from the wholesale acceptance of systems of English education by all classes and creeds of our people. While public education was forbidden the majority of the nation, and while the Irish language was widely spoken, the people retained a keen and vivid sense of their wrongs and of the artificial limitations placed upon them in every walk of life. They were able to distinguish Ireland's friends from her foes, and her interests from those of her rival, England. Catholic Emancipation was followed by a system of primary education which was cunningly designed to destroy our nationality. Its originators did not formally teach that Ireland, her language, literature, history, and industry, were unworthy of the attention even of Irish children, and consequently of the Irish people; but, by ignoring them, and by concerning Irish education with the affairs of England, and of her Empire, they attained the desired result quite as effectually, and without the arousal of suspicion among the masses, or among the teachers or school managers, indeed the general fear was that there would be any difficulty or delay in doing as our British masters wished us to do, viz., to get rid of every trace of our nationality, from our speech and accent to our Irish clothing and food. The Intermediate system, planned and worked to make the children of the middle classes really 'respectable', we accepted also without demur. It had nothing to show that it was a system of secondary education suited to the needs and pecularities of this country. It would not have suited any country on the face of the globe. It was designed to complete the destruction of national ideals, but it was arranged with such little regard for correct educational principles in the abstract that it inevitably led also to the destruction of mental powers and capacity for the acquirement of knowledge. Ireland, after the long night of the Penal Laws, needed special educational treatment. The tradition of school life and of teaching had been broken and the high ideals of the early Gaels who fostered each other's children had been lost sight of. Religion itself had fallen on evil days, and our people, through poverty and the evils and shame of subjection, had lost not knowledge only, but many of the noblest traits of the race also. To raise a fallen nation, to give its people knowledge, ideals, dignity, and national pride, was the work that should have been begun after the cessation of religious persecution. But there was no educationalist in power with either the wisdom or patriotism to teach young Ireland how to respect herself, or to defend. Instead, there were in office nation destroyers and mind murderers who planned for the further degradation of an already degraded and impoverished people. The Penal Laws were the sword that struck down the strong man; but the educational systems originated and directed for us by foreigners during the past century under English control were the slow poison administered to the enfeebled and unsuspecting wounded warrior.

These evil systems are still with us, and although teachers and managers are no longer the willing tools of the anglicisers, evil results continue to follow from systems that were never planned for Ireland's good. They are still in the main unconcerned with Ireland. Those who direct them are content to follow the slow meandering march of English educationalists. The state of education in the United States is by no means ideal, but Dr. McNamara, a prominent English educationalist, declared a few years ago that American schools and teachers were fifty years ahead of those of England. In educational matters, at least, we must have independence, and freedom to work out our own ideas, and strive for our own ideals. The Intermediate system turns the schools that adopt it into educational mills which earn money for their owners, but at the cost of national ideals and of Irish originality and genius. The programme of the Intermediate Board, no less than the Board itself, needs instant and radical reform. Of this need there is a growing consciousness amongst those who are deeply interested and concerned in Ireland's educational welfare. Last week the Most Rev. Dr. O'Dwyer, Bishop of Limerick, dealt severely but sensibly with the methods that prevail in the Intermediate. He said: —

'If a bureau in Dublin was to have control at all of all the schools of the country, inspection was about the best way they could exercise it. The system of an annual examination in writing simultaneously in every school in the country, and exactly identical, was a retrograde and an antediluvian system for managing the education of a country. He could not conceive anything better calculated to bring about the results that the Intermediate system brought about in Ireland, of cramming and deadening the intelligence of the boys and girls. The only other country in which examinations were conducted entirely by writing was the Empire of China, but China was now progressing and was throwing over the old literary examinations. The inspection examined the education of a school as consisting of living processes for the development of the child all round — to give it "mens sana in corpore sano". The written examination system simply meant testing the amount of information that might be got into a child's mind in a certain time, and could be expressed on paper. Those two systems exclude one another. One of them would have to go. He hoped it would be the written examination system, which was a gross absurdity. As regards competitive examination, they were good enough for the civil service or things of that kind, but as a test for the ordinary education of children the system was a preposterous humbug, and under it the children would be racing against each other instead of being educated properly. What his lordship would like to do was to let every school teach what it liked, and teach it in his own way — let every school work out its own salvation, strike out its own course of studies, and if they had that they would have a real emancipation over Irish schools, and would have in a generation a greater development of Irish ability than they had for the last thirty years under the Intermediate system. When the children's education was completed they might have a leaving examination to see finally what amount of scholarship and developed ability the schools had produced in the children while they were there, and that final examination might well be conducted under the auspices of our new National University.'

This is a courageous lead from an able and responsible man, one who is no unwise revolutionary, but a respecter and guardian of tradition and of authority. When will those who control our secondary schools follow?

Belgium and its Schools

AN CLAIDHEAMH SOLUIS
5.8.1905

The Germ of Things

The history of most European nations — Ireland is one of the three or four exceptions — begins with Julius Caesar. It is in the Commentaries that we first catch a clear glimpse of the facts and processes which were to eventuate in modern Europe. It is in the Commentaries that we first make the acquaintance of many an obscure tribe, Celtic or Teutonic, which was afterwards to give its name to some famous nation or to some illustrious province in the European commonwealth. When, marching victorious from his encounters with the Helvetii on the Rhone and with the Suevii on the Rhine, Caesar came face to face with a new confederation of tribes, known to him as the Belgae, the history of Belgium began. These Belgae, hailed by their conqueror as the most valiant of the Gauls, held sway in those days over a wide territory which swept from the right bank of the Seine to the bank of the Rhine. The north-east corner of this domain forms today the Dutch province of Brabant; its south-west part belongs to France, and a broad strip on the east to Germany. The rest is Belgium.

The Belgae, when Caesar knew them, were by no means a political unity, nor were they either racially or linguistically a homogeneous people. They were in part Celtic and in part Teutonic, as they remain today. The Celts had ruled in the low countries for many centuries when Germanic tribes commenced to push across the Rhine, partly expelling the Celtic clans from their homes, partly fusing with them. This went on during many generations. There resulted a loose congeries of tribes, loosely known as the Belgae. To the north of a line cutting modern Belgium horizontally, and passing through Courtrai and Louvain, Gallia Belgica* was predominantly Teutonic; south of that line it was predominatingly Celtic. This division, fundamental and far-reaching, has persisted to the present hour; it explains all Belgian history; it explains why Belgium is today a nation with two national languages, why its education scheme is ordered on bilingual lines, and why these articles are being written. Thrown together in a contact first

---

* The Gallia Belgica of Caesar's time must be distinguished from the later imperial province of the same name, which was much larger, extending southward to the Rhone.

254

hostile and afterwards friendly, the two races, though differing so profoundly from each other in blood and language, were destined never to part company: all their future history was to be lived in common. Together they were to pass under the dominion successively of the Roman, the Frank, the Burgundian, the Spaniard, the Austrian, the Frenchman, and the Dutchman; and finally, achieving independence, they were to form together the free, gallant, and prosperous Kingdom of Belgium.

The Teuton, living northward of the line through Courtrai and Louvain, spoke a Germanic dialect akin to the Old Frisian, but forming an independent development of an older Low-German speech. The Celt, living southward of that line spoke the language of Gaul. The Roman came and conquered. From the legionaries quartered amongst them the Celtic tribe soon learned to speak Latin, and in the course of time the native idiom disappeared, as the Celtic vernacular disappeared everywhere on the Continent except in steadfast Brittany. In Gallia Belgica, under the same influences, it eventuated in a dialect which came to be known as Walloon. Walloon bears about the same relation to French as Lowland Scotch does to English. Lowland Scotch is a separate Anglo-Saxon development, influenced by Gaelic and Norse; Walloon is a separate Romance development, influenced by Flemish and Spanish. The word 'Walloon' means 'foreign': it is cognate with 'Walachian', 'Welsh', etc., and, like those words, is one of the designations bestowed by the Germans on peoples alien to them in race. Formerly all the Celts were 'Walloons' (Walah) to the Germans, but the word has long been restricted to the Celts of Belgium.

Whether gifted with a greater staying power, or because Roman civilisation pressed on them with less severity, the Teutonic speakers of the northern half of Gallia Belgica, unlike the Celts of the south, retained their ancestral speech. They retain it to the present day. It is a strange and eloquent fact in history that, except on the frontiers of their empire – in North-West Armorica and in Western Britain – the language and civilisation of the Celts were everywhere submerged and obliterated by the language and civilisation of Rome; whilst on the other hand the tide of Roman conquest, sweeping over the Teutonic lands, rolled back again, and left them as Teutonic as ever. The explanation is probably this, that when the terrible legions of Rome appeared in their midst, the Celts were already a decadent race: they had passed their prime, had aged and grown ineffective; only the daring clans who had found distant homes in the Isles of the West retained the ancient vigour of the stock. The Teutons, on the other hand, were a newer people than the Italics themselves: theirs was the buoyancy of young manhood, the self-confidence of a coming race; they had still their history before them, whilst the history of the continental Celts was all behind them. The Celt of Caesar's time was no longer the magnificient barbarian who had sacked Rome and given Alexander pause. His day was over.

All this is ancient history, but it is ancient history which we must bear firmly in mind if we would understand the Belgium of today. The germ of the actual situation in Belgium is to be found in the Gallia Belgica of Caesar. The Teutonic speaker on the sea-board who, the Roman conquest notwithstanding, retained his Low-German dialect is the ancestor of the Fleming; the Gallic speaker of the forests and uplands who abandoned his Celtic mother-tongue for the vernacular of the Roman legionaries, is the ancestor of the Walloon. And Fleming and Walloon are the opposing forces in the Belgian language war of today.

BELGIUM AND ITS SCHOOLS
12.8.1905

The Making of Belgium

When the Roman Empire crumbled to pieces, the Low Countries became swordland to a race of fair-haired and blue-eyed warriors from the North. These were the Franks. In the heart of Belgium was the home — won by the strong hand — of the most famous of all the Franks, — the Salians. It was the destiny of this tribe — which did not at the time muster more than 5,000 fighting men — to throw up one of the great empire-builders of the world. Clovis, King of the Salian Franks, evoked order and unity out of the chaos which followed on the break-up of the Roman dominion in the West. He pushed his conquests northward to the Rhine and southward to the Mediterranean, bringing under his sceptre almost every acre of Gallic territory that had once owned the supremacy of Rome. Dying in 511, he left his dominions to be divided amongst his sons. This was a reversion to chaos, and during the three centuries which followed Belgium changed hands as often as a prince arose who felt himself strong enough to wrest it from whatsoever descendant of Clovis happened to hold it at the moment. Thus, chance and change held sway until there sprang from Belgian soil a second and greater empire-maker, — Charlemagne. Under Charlemagne, Aix — then regarded as a Belgian town — became the capital of a dominion stretching from the Baltic to the Mediterranean and from the Atlantic to the mountains of Bohemia.

But Charlemagne died, and his death was followed by another partition of territories, and by another reversion to chaos, Belgium fell to Lothaire, grandson of the conqueror. Later on it was contended for by the Emperors of Germany and the Kings of France. In 953 the Emperor Otto conferred it on Bruno, Archbishop of Cologne, who divided it into two duchies, Upper and Lower Lorraine. In the list of the rulers of Lower Lorraine occurs the famous name of Godfrey de Bouillon, King of Jerusalem.

In the eleventh century we find Belgium split up into a multiplicity of countries, marquisates, and duchies, governed by feudal chiefs owning a nominal allegiance to the empire, but in reality independent and absolute. Strife reigns on all sides. France and Germany still contend for the overlordship, the Walloons of Luxemburg, Namur, Hainaut, and Liège generally siding with the former, the Flemings of Brabant and Flanders usually with the latter. When the dividing line through Courtrai and Louvain is kept well in mind, much that is dark and involved in the story becomes clear and intelligible.

During the twelfth and thirteenth centuries a new and significant movement began to manifest itself. This was the rise of the great industrial municipalities. Bold merchant princes brought wealth and fame to the towns of Flanders and Brabant: Antwerp and Ghent and Bruges became the marts or manufactories of Western Europe. With prosperity came a sense of importance, an impatience of tyranny, a contempt for the wastrel nobles. Each city developed into a miniature republic governed by its Guilds. Princes sought alliances with these civic communities, and foreign nations — England amongst the number — entered into treaties with them. Sometimes the cities went to war with one another, and sometimes they combined and chastised the nobles. These are the picturesque days which relive in the pages of Conscience. At Courtrai in 1302 the municipalities triumphed over the aristocracy; but at Roseberque in 1382 the men of

Ghent, fighting under gallant Philip van Artevelde, suffered a disastrous defeat, and feudalism received a new lease of life.

Two years later, Flanders and Artois came into the possession of the Dukes of Burgundy. Within half a century Holland, Zealand, Hainaut, Brabant, Limburg, Antwerp and Namur had been added to the domain of the same house. Luxemburg, Guelders and Friesland followed. To this splendid inheritance succeeded in 1467 Charles the Bold, the great protagonist of Louis XI of France. Charles dreamed of adding Alsace, Lorraine, and Liège to his dominions, and of exchanging a ducal for a royal crown. He and his projects perished at the battle of Nancy in 1477.

With the accession of Mary, the daughter of Charles, Belgian history enters on a new phase. By Mary's marriage with the Archduke (afterwards Emperor) Maximilian, the Low Countries were brought under the shadow of the mighty house which then ruled Austria and was soon to succeed to the gigantic empire of Spain. Under Philip the Fair, Maximilian's son and representative, Belgium flourished apace; but the ambitions of Charles V (a Netherlander born) — added to the religious discords of the sixteenth century — were soon to plunge it into a new turmoil. In 1540 the Netherlands were inseparably united to the crown of Spain. Fifteen years later Charles was succeeded by his son, Philip II, and into Belgian history comes the sinister figure of the Duke of Alva. Alva is the Cromwell of the Low Countries: he had the thoroughness, the ruthlessness, the dour and sombre genius of the man of Drogheda and Wexford. The Spanish occupation was Belgium's trial by fire. She passed through it, scathed indeed, but unbroken in spirit. Alva, after all, was less thorough than Cromwell.

A further period of vicissitudes followed. The Northern Netherlands, under William the Silent, achieved independence. By marriages, deaths, and treaties, the Belgian Netherlands passed from Spain to Austria, from Austria to Spain, and from Spain back to Austria again. They were twice conquered by the armies of Louis XIV; they were many times overrun by the English; they shook beneath the tread of Turenne and Condé, of William III and Marlborough, of Prince Eugene and Marshal Saxe; they were coveted and fought for by Holland, Spain, Austria, Germany, France, and England. As the outcome of all this warring, portions of northern or Flemish Belgium fell to Holland; a good deal of southern or Walloon Belgium to France; the rest remained to Austria. A desperate attempt to loosen the Austrian grip was crushed in 1790.

But meantime Europe had been shaken by the cataclysm at Paris. One of the first acts of revolutionary France was to pour her armies into the Netherlands. Belgium quickly exchanged an Austrian for a French yoke and was straightway parcelled out into French departments. The Abbé Siè obligingly provided a constitution. And now the destinies of Belgium become interwoven with those of a more tremendous conqueror than either Clovis or Charlemagne. When Napoleon ruled France, he sent his brother Louis to reign in the Low Countires. As part of Napoleon's colossal empire Belgium flourished again: the Emperor, who visited it repeatedly, laboured strenuously for its advancement, and dreamed of making Antwerp in wealth and commerce the rival of London. Finally, it was on Belgian soil that Napoleon fell, fighting alone against Europe. Belgians do not love his memory. They forget that he made them prosperous, recollecting only that he made them slaves. He ranks with Alva in the Flemish imagination as an impersonation of foreign conquest. In the Wiertz Gallery at Brussels there

257

is a terrific picture which shows the soul of Napoleon in hell. He is surrounded by the bleeding victims of his wars, who point accusing fingers at him; on his drawn brow is the imprint of an immortal sorrow. It is Belgium's unjust, but not unnatural, verdict on the last and greatest of her conquerors.

The Treaty of Paris (in which she had no say) united Belgium to Holland as the Kingdom of the Netherlands. One would have thought that the union had in it the seeds of permanance, for the Fleming and the Dutchman were akin, and spoke the same language. But the Walloon had to be reckoned with. The Walloon could have borne the supremacy of France, but to bend the knee to a Dutchman was not in his nature. The Dutch, with blind stupidity, proscribed the speech of the Walloon, prohibited its use in courts of justice and in official life, packed the public service with Dutchmen, and in every way acted to perfection the part of 'predominant partner'. Walloon sentiment flamed into madness; encouraged by the success of the French Revolution of 1830, the populace of the Walloon towns of the South broke into revolt; the Dutch troops, at first successful near Brussels, were compelled to retire before the advancing bands of insurgents. Then – an unexpected, though not an inexplicable development – the Flemings of the North, akin though they were to the Dutch in race and language, made common cause with the Walloons, and before a united Belgium the Dutch power went down. A National Convention met in Brussels drew up a Consitituion, and offered the crown of free Belgium to Prince Leopold of Saxe-Coburg. He accepted. The Belgian Revolution was accomplished, and a new State entered into the European Commonwealth.

BELGIUM AND ITS SCHOOLS
19.8.1905

A Revolution and its Aftermath

The Belgian Revolution of 1830 is one other instance of a political upheaval of the first magnitude which has owed its origin to a language question. The *causa causans* of the Revolution was the attempt of the Dutch Government to outlaw the speech of the Walloon. This attempt the Walloon passionately resented; so passionately, indeed, that when his own day of power came he was in no humour to deal considerately with the vernacular of the Fleming, practically identical as the latter was with the hated *Nederduitsch*. And thereby hangs a tale which shall be recurred to anon.

A preliminary question presents itself. How came it that the Flemings, who were own brothers to the Dutch, so spiritedly threw in their lot with the Walloons in 1830, and thus made the Revolution a possibility? The chief reason that weighed with them was doubtless the sentimental one (sentiment, when all is said, has been the great shaping force in history), that they and the Walloons had been companions in weal and woe ever since they had faced together the legions of Rome. Their union had been hallowed by twenty centuries of common history. There was between them this further tie that both peoples were Catholic, whereas the Dutch oppressor was vigorously Protestant. The Reformation had been preached in Flanders early in the sixteenth century, and for a moment it had seemed as if the Belgic as well as the Dutch Netherlands, were to be lost to the Universal Church. But the movement passed away, leaving the bulk of the

Flemings as Catholic as ever. They remain Catholic to this hour. And their Catholicism is not a thing of forms and ceremonies, but an abiding faith which illumines their daily lives. Only the Irish-speaking peasant of Connacht and Munster is more essentially Catholic in spirit than the Flemish-speaking peasant of Flanders and Brabant. So untrue is the dictum that Catholicism is 'the Celtic form of Christianity' that it is amongst non-Celtic peoples, — Slavs in Poland and Bohemia, and Teutons in Germany, Austria, and Flanders — that one finds the most intensely Catholic populations of the Continent. But this is by the way.

The memories of a common past and the enthusiasms of a common creed bound, then, the Fleming to the Walloon. This double tie of sentiment was strengthened by the fact that the Fleming, almost equally with the Walloon, had suffered from the Dutch plan of thrusting Dutchmen into places of emolument in Belgium. There were further minor points in which Flemish and Walloon interests agreed in running counter to Dutch interests, but a discussion of these is not necessary to the understanding of the story. Suffice it to say that the three-fold fact that they had passed together into the furnace of persecution; that they were both Catholic with the thoroughness with which men were Catholic in the Middle Ages; and they they both chafed under a galling ascendancy, formed a sufficiently firm basis for a union of hearts between Fleming and Walloon. Their union, as the union of the elements in any subject nation must inevitably be, was followed by the downfall of the foreign tyranny. No intelligent people which is at one with itself can be indefinitely governed against its will.

The Revolution of 1830 settled a language question, but settled it in such a wise that a new language question promptly arose. It is this second language question which chiefly concerns us in these articles. As we have seen, the Revolutionary movement was in its inspiration, and conduct essentially a Walloon movement. It was the revolt of the Romance-speaking Celt against the intellectual and political domination of the (in this instance) Dutch-speaking Teuton. Nothing more natural, therefore, than that the whole movement should be militarily Walloon in tone. French was the language of the Revolutionary leaders; French was the language of the National Congress, and of free Belgium. Flemish, tainted by its close relationship with Dutch, was not recognised. Here, then, were the seeds of a new language war, which was not long in breaking out. The Fleming, disregarding ties of blood and speech, had united with the Walloon and helped him to oust the Dutchman; the Walloon showed his gratitude by endeavouring to impose his intellectual yoke on the Fleming. The Fleming, who was a fighter from of old, resisted. His struggle to assert himself is the theme of the inspiring story which remains to be told.

BELGIUM AND ITS SCHOOLS
16.9.1905

The Call to Arms

We have seen that the opposing forces in the Belgian language war are on the one hand the Fleming and on the other the Walloon. The opposing languages, however, are not Flemish and Walloon, but Flemish and French. For Walloon was from the outset, and is still, a mere *patois*. I have said of it that it bears to French somewhat the same relation which Lowland Scotch bears to English. But unlike Lowland Scotch it has never developed a literature. The Walloon peasants, indeed, chant rude songs in their own idiom as they work in the fields or in the forests, or foregather around the firesides in the winter evenings. But no great poet or dramatist has clothed his thoughts in Walloon; no great master-mind, leaving its impress upon it, has made it immortal. French is the language of the educated Walloon; in the large towns, it is the language of the Walloon, whether educated or not. As a *patois* Walloon will continue to live in the country places of Romance Belgium, just as *patois* live, and will continue to live, in France and Germany and England. But it has never occurred to anyone, and probably never will occur to anyone, to demand official recognition for it. The Walloon accepts French as his language, and is content to retain Walloon as his *patois*. It was French — not Walloon — which the Revolutionists of 1830 exalted at the expense of Flemish. It is against the domination not of Walloon, but of French, that the Fleming struggles.

Flemish, as we already know, is a language of ancient lineage and honourable fame. It sprang from some old Teutonic speech, which was the parent also of Old Frisian. At first and for many centuries Dutch and Flemish were one, and even today they are practically identical. A Dutchman can understand a Fleming somewhat more easily than a Donegal Irish speaker can understand a Gaelic-speaking Highlander. The Taal of the Boer is perhaps still nearer to Flemish than is classical Dutch. I have heard Boers and Flemings converse together with practically no difficulty in making themselves mutually understood.

Down to the Spanish occupation Dutch and Flemish have a common literary history. The term 'Nederduitsch' or 'Vlaamsch' covers both. The oldest literary monuments of Netherlandish speech come in fact from Belgian soil. These are an ordinance of the town of Brussels dated 1229, and the poem of 'Reinaert de Vos'. Towards the close of the thirteenth century Jacob van Maerlant brought the language to a high point of literary cultivation; but the Burgundian domination, which set in in the fourteenth century, spelt eclipse for the Taal. It was only when the fierce struggle for national existence against Spain had again fanned Netherlandish patriotism to fever heat, that the native language commenced once more to flourish. This revival was permanent in Holland, which now began a literary life of its own. In the Belgian Netherlands the Taal still drooped, and for two centuries produced little literature of note. Amongst those who helped to keep the lamp of learning and literature alight during these, the Dark Ages of Flemish-speaking Belgium, was one Abbé Ahearn who evidently hailed from Munster. I questioned leading Flemings about him, but they could tell me little that was definite. He had written poetry in Flemish, and someone had read a paper about him at a meeting of the Flemish Academy. That, in substance, was all that I gleaned. Some day I may succeed in disinterring his works.

The Revolution of 1830 came, and the Fleming found himself numerically the predominating, but intellectually and politically the less important factor in the new and free State. He at once entered on a struggle to assert himself. And like the hard-headed and far-seeing Teuton that he was, his first care was to revive and cultivate his native speech. At the call of Willems, Bloomaert, Van Ryswych, and Conscience, Flanders awoke anew to intellectual life. As in every country in which there has been a national revival, poets and dreamers had to prepare the way for the men of action.

BELGIUM AND ITS SCHOOLS
23.9.1905

Conscience

In the year 1811 there was serving in Napoleon's navy as *chef de timonerie* one Pierre Conscience, a native of Besançon. By one of those 'chances' which alter the destinies of nations he was in that year appointed harbour-master of Antwerp, then a city of the French Empire. He he married a Flemish wife — one Cornelia Bahen — and here in the next year was born to him a son whom he called Henri. When the French withdrew from the Netherlands in 1815, Pierre remained on in Antwerp. His occupation as harbour-master was, of course, gone, and by way of earning a livelihood he commenced to buy and break up old vessels with a view to selling their fittings. As a side-line to this business he opened a small shop which he stocked with marine stores and unsaleable books. In these surroundings grew up Henri — or Hendrik as he afterwards learned to call himself. One figures the boy with his pale and delicate features, French rather than Flemish in type, his dark, comtemplative eyes, and his 'long smooth hair', — one figures him day-dreaming in that dim old shop of which the exact counterpart may be seen half-a-dozen times repeated in any one of the quaint and narrow streets which today as then crowd the space lying along the river between the Cathedral and the Church of the Dominicans; or one imagines him stealing up to the attic to devour in secret the dusty old romances which Pierre had stored there because the shop was too small to hold them; or, again, escaping from home to surreptitiously pick up Flemish from the street *gamins*, for his father remained a Frenchman to the end of his days and, though he had married a Flemish wife, professed an intellectual contempt for Flemings and Flemish.

Later on Pierre Conscience sold up his shop and retired to the Kempen or Campine, that drab and dreary plain which stretches between Antwerp and Venloo. Young Hendrik is next heard of as a tutor in Antwerp, where the Revolution of 1830 found him. Then an extraordinary thing happened. So had the mind and character of the Flemish folk amongst whom he lived won on him, that the son of the Frenchman took up arms as a soldier of Belgian independence. His camp and barrack life made him better than ever acquainted with the thoughts and view-points of Flemish-speaking people, and in 1830 we find him writing: — 'I do not know how it is, but I confess I find in the real Flemish something indescribably romantic, mysterious, profound, energetic, even savage. If I ever gain power to write, I shall throw myself head over ears into Flemish composition'.

The recent history of Ireland affords more than one parallel to that strange resolve on the part of a youth whose paternal language was French. As a matter of fact, Conscience's first literary efforts were made in his own and his father's native tongue; but, his soldiering done, he returned home filled with the quixotic resolution to perform the feat of writing a book in Flemish, — a thing it had never occurred to anyone to do for perhaps a generation. As the fruit of this resolve he produced *In't Wondejaar,* a book which is a holy book in Flanders today. So enraged was the stern old ex-officer of Napoleon to find his son had written a book in Flemish that he incontinently turned him out of doors. With two francs in his pocket and a bundle of clothes under his arm Hendrik started for Antwerp. The Flemish Revival had begun.

Probably the hand of God was in the Flemish movement, as it has been said to be in ours. Certain it is that young Conscience almost immediately gained powerful friends in Antwerp; and though during the next few years he was often perilously near starving, he produced book after book, — *The Lion of Flanders* in 1838, *How to become a Painter* and *What a Mother can Suffer* in 1844, *Siska van Roosmael* in 1844, *Lambrecht Hensmans* in 1847, *Jacob von Artevelde* in 1849, *The Conscript* in 1850. At first his books brought him in little or no money. In order to keep the pot boiling he had to turn his hand to many things besides the creation of a literature. For thirteen months he worked as a common gardener, and his avocations ranged from this rather humbler one up to the Secretaryship of the Academy of Fine Arts in Antwerp, — his appointment to which post ensured him at long last a competence. Meanwhile fame was coming, first slowly, afterwards more rapidly. In 1841 a Flemish Congress at Antwerp hailed his writings as containing the seeds which gave the surest promise of a crop of Flemish literature. Followers commenced to gather round his standard, — amongst others Ledejanck, whose *Three Sister Cities* is one of the classics of Flemish literature, and Jan Frans Willems, who, though an older man, declared himself a disciple of Conscience.

Works continued to flow from his pen. In 1850 came his *Blind Rose,* and his *Rikketikketak;* in 1851 *The Poor Gentleman;* in 1853 *The Miser.* About this time translations of his books commenced to appear in various European tongues. His later activities need not be chronicled in detail. Before he laid down his pen he had given to Flemish literature eighty independent works. His seventieth birthday was solemnised by all Belgium as a national festival; and when in the next year — 1883 — he died, his people followed him to the grave in tears.

Conscience is not, from the purely aesthetic point of view, one of the greatest figures in literary history. His pictures of Flemish home life are, indeed, exquisite, and his historical romances live and glow with something of the movement and colour of Scott. But his fame rests less on the intrinsic merits of his own work than on his influence on the intellectual and political future of his adopted people. He raised a decayed and despised speech to the dignity of a literary language; though not a Flemish speaker born, he laid deep and strong the foundations of a modern Flemish literature; he inspired a movement of national revival, literary, artistic, social, and finally political, which, continuing to our own day, is one of the most striking and humanising influences in contemporary Europe.

BELGIUM AND ITS SCHOOLS
30.9.1905

The Revival

The writings of Conscience awakened many unseen fires in Flanders. Desolate country places became vocal with song, and peasants began to produce literature. Jan Frans Willems, declaring himself a follower of Conscience, exercised an influence second only to that of the master himself. Ledejanck celebrated the Three Sister Cities of Antwerp, Ghent, and Bruges in strains which will live as long as the Flemish language. Tony Anton Bergmann attracted European attention by his *Ernest Staas, Advocaat.* The sisters Rosalie and Virginie Loveling wrote tales full of a sweet and fresh simplicity as of country ways and gardens. Jan van Beers, a poet, showed that Flemish could be tender and pathetic as well as virile and rugged. Bloomaert, Van Ryswyck, Delecourt, Van Duyse, Snellaert,

Snieders, De Laet, Dedecker, Vervier, David, Bormans, combined much eager propagandist work with the production of not a little pure literature. Dramatists arose, none commandingly great, it is true — perhaps the age of great dramas, like the age of great epics, is past — but many respectable, and some few excellent, Flemish theatres were builded in all the cities; Flemish clubs, 'cercles', reading-rooms sprang up in the towns and villages; Flemish newspapers began to issue from the press; the Flemish Academy came into existence.

In a remote country place, a priest and a man of the people, Guitto Gezelle, commenced to produce a new and distinctive poetry. He was at first ignored, and later on laughed at, for he wrote in literary Flemish and not in the dialect of his countryside. Today he is acknowledged not merely in Flanders but in Holland, as the greatest poet that the Low Countries have produced. His nephew, a working baker who lives near Courtrai, is the most considerable literary figure in contemporary Flanders. He writes poetry, and a rich and striking prose which has been compared to Carlyle's.

Such a movement as this could not and did not long continue a literary movement pure and simple. Flemings, now that they had poets, and dramatists, and journalists amongst them, began to demand official recognition for their speech. Forming a majority of the population, and intellectually as vigourous as their Walloon fellow-citizens, their demands could not long be resisted. By successive steps Flemish established itself in the law courts, in the civil service, in the Houses of Parliament. Fifty years ago the whole administration of public affairs in Belgium was as French in tone as the administration of public affairs in this country is English. Today a knowledge of Flemish is compulsory for every civil servant, for every municipal official (at least in the Flemish country), for every post-office clerk. No judge who does not know Flemish may sit on the bench in Belgium, and no advocate ignorant of Flemish need hope for a lucrative practice. In the Walloon country French is the language of the courts, in the Flemish country Flemish. In the High Courts in Brussels cases are conducted in French or Flemish according as the one or the other is the vernacular of the litigants. In the Chambers, French is still heard oftener than Flemish, but many of the Flemish deputies and senators uniformly speak in their native language. All public documents are bilingual. In the churches, Flemish is used as the vernacular in Flemish districts, French in Walloon. In the large cities both French and Flemish-speaking priests are attached to every parish. Briefly, Flemish has gained substantive equality with French — in five or ten years more it will have gained absolute equality. It has taken the Flemings exactly three-quarters of a century to accomplish this. How long will it take Ireland to reach a corresponding stage? We do not know; but this we do know, that in twelve years we have travelled well-nigh as far as the Flemings — notwithstanding the immense initial advantage of a Flemish-speaking population which actually outnumbered the non-Flemish-speaking population — had travelled in twenty-five.

BELGIUM AND ITS SCHOOLS
7.10.1905

'In Flanders Flemish'
In many respects the Flemish language movement has developed on

lines parallel with those pursued by our own. But it must always be remembered that the two movements differ widely in scope. In Belgium there is not, and there never has been, a question of preserving a language from almost imminent extinction. When the Flemish movement began the speakers of Flemish were actually a majority of the population of Belgium. They still remain a majority, having neither gained nor lost in relative numerical strength during the seventy-five years that have elapsed. The aims of the movement have simply been, first, the creation of a modern Flemish literature, and secondly, the securing for Flemish of official recognition as full and ample as that accorded to French. Let it be frankly realised that Ireland's problem is vastly more difficult. We have to rescue a language from the very brink of the grave. We have to instil a spirit of national pride and self-reliance into a people broken by political conquest and demoralised by a system of education designed and administered in the interest of a foreign civilisation. We have to fight against the apathy of public opinion at home, and against the avowed and secret opposition of an alien government and its agents. The Flemings were citizens of a free state and their whole task was merely to convince their non-Flemish-speaking fellow — citizens of the reasonableness of admitting their language to equal rights with French in school and state. There was no question of *restoration;* no question of prevailing on non-Flemish speakers to learn Flemish; no French-speaking territory to be evangelised; it was simply a matter of securing fair play for that one of the two national vernaculars which an historical accident had placed in a subordinate position in the commonwealth.

The fact that the Flemish movement differs thus widely in scope from our own explains why its organisation is so different. In Belgium there is no body corresponding to the Gaelic League. That is to say, there is no vast popular organisation, with its headquarters in the capital and branches ramifying throughout the country, taking charge of a national movement for the rehabilitation of a national language. There is no need for such a body. No campaign having for its end the inducing of Flemish speakers to speak Flemish has to be carried on in the Flemish-speaking districts. No teaching work has to be done in the non-Flemish districts. The literary interests of the language are looked after by the Flemish Academy. The teaching is done in the schools. Flemish clubs and 'cercles' exist everywhere, but their objects are social and religious as much as linguistic. The actual fighting is carried on in Parliament by the Flemish deputies and senators, and outside Parliament through the medium of the Flemish press. There are at least six Flemish dailies, and a host of Flemish weeklies, whilst there are also Flemish reviews, literary, social, and religious. The Flemish press is in reality the first fighting line of the movement. I met at Louvain Emile Vlieberghe, the editor of the leading Flemish review — *De Dietsche Warande en Belfort* — and a pillar of the movement. Of him, and of his views on the Flemish and Irish questions — for he has studied the Irish movement — I may write hereafter.

I have said that the Flemish movement simply sought to secure for Flemish absolute equality of treatment with French in every department of national life, and that this object has now been substantively attained. Let us see how matters work out linguistically in the Belgium of today. Belgium is often referred to as a bilingual country. If by 'bilingual country' we mean a country in which two languages are spoken side by side, then the description is accurate enough; but if we mean a country whose inhabitants are bilingualists the description is far from accurate. The Belgians, as a people, are not yet bilingualists: in a generation or two, however, their system of bilingual education will have made them so.

North of a line stretching from near Warneton on the Lys eastward to Visé and the Meuse Belgium is Flemish-speaking; south of that line it is French-speaking; in the single arrondissment of Arlon it is German-speaking.* For practical purposes, therefore, the country is divided into two well-defined parts — Flemish and Walloon.

This fact is taken cognisance of by the State, the municipalities, and the Church, all of which now adopt as their motto, 'In Flanders, Flemish; in the Walloon country, French'. But they further recognise that even in the Walloon country Flemish must get official recognition, and that even in the Flemish country French must get official recognition, — for Belgium, in the words of the government decrees, has 'deux langues nationales'. Accordingly, everywhere all official notices and documents are bilingual; but in the Flemish country, Flemish gets the place of honour, and in the Walloon country French gets the place of honour. Thus, in Brussels French figures first on the street nameplates and Flemish afterwards; whilst in Antwerp the Flemish name is put first and the French name beneath. In the case of public announcements, the two languages are placed side by side in parallel columns, — in Brussels the French being on the right, and the Flemish on the left, whilst in Antwerp the positions are reversed. This arrangement extends to every public or semi-public document from a Royal proclamation down to a tram-ticket. It is adopted by all the government departments, including the post office and the state railways system; by all the municipal authorities; by the banks; by public companies and private traders; by the Church. In the city the destination of every tramcar is announced in French and Flemish, or in Flemish and French, as the case may be: in the museum, the inscriptions under the pictures and statues are usually bilingual, as in the Churches are those under the Stations of the Cross and on the Confessionals. Everywhere it is Flemish and French in Flanders, and French and Flemish in the land of the Walloons.

BELGIUM AND ITS SCHOOLS
21.10.1905

The Fight for the Schools

It goes without saying that at an early stage the *Flamingands* — for so the Walloons nickname the Flemings, who retort by calling them *Fransquillons* — raised the war-cry 'In Flanders Flemish' outside the school doors. A long struggle, of which the end is not yet, ensued. For years the whole tone of education in Flanders had been militantly French. Flemish was a proscribed idiom. Not, indeed, that pains and penalties were incurred by its use; not that little children were flogged in school if they let fall a word of Flemish; not that the tally, the ferule, and the cane were requisitioned for the purpose of establishing the supremacy of French. These enlightened methods were reserved for the use of the Russian in Poland, of the German in Alsace-Lorraine, and of the Anglo-Saxon in

---

* There were in 1890, 2,744, 271 Belgians, who spoke Flemish only; 2,485,672 who spoke French (Walloon) only; 32, 206 who spoke German only; and but 700,997 bilingualists (French and Flemish).

Ireland. In Belgium the schools never passed under the power of a virulent enemy of Flemish nationality. They never lent themselves to a conspiracy for the crushing of the native speech. They simply did not recognise it. It was not taught as a school subject. It was not officially sanctioned (though of necessity frequently used) as a medium of instruction. In other words, the Flemish-speaking child was treated by the school authorities as if he were a French speaker. A hardship; — but only part of the hardship under which, up to quite recently, the Irish-speaking child has suffered uncomplainingly.

However, the battle-cry of the Flamingand — 'In Flanders Flemish' resounded through the land. First, the primary schools gave way; next, the state secondary schools; finally the *private* secondary schools — those, that is, which are controlled by the religious orders. These latter, indeed, are not yet quite conquered. Some of them, the convents especially, still cherish the delusion that Flemish is not so respectable a language as French. Accordingly, Flemish is not yet compulsory even in those of the higher private schools which are situated in purely Flemish territory. When I was in Belgium public opinion was in a ferment on this very question. M. Cooremans, deputy for Antwerp, had introduced in the Chamber of Representatives a Bill to make the teaching of Flemish compulsory in all denominational or private secondary schools in Flanders. He was being bitterly opposed by the Walloons on the ground that many Walloon children attend these schools and that it is not fair to compel these to learn Flemish whether they like to or no. He was also opposed by the school authorities themselves, who represented that if the Bill were passed the Walloon children, and also the children of foreigners who were sent to Belgium to learn French, would be withdrawn and that the schools would suffer financially. The issue of the struggle is still doubtful. Those with whom I conversed on the matter — and they included leading thinkers on both sides — inclined to the opinion that a compromise of some sort will eventually be accepted.

Apart, however, from the denominational or private schools, which are not under direct State or municipal control — though they are subject to government inspection — Flemish has now, throughout the entire primary and secondary school system of Belgium, attained substantive equality with French. One may sum up the attitude of the State, of the municipal bodies (which, under government supervision, control elementary education), and of educated Belgian opinion somewhat as follows: —

(1) Every Belgian has the right to be taught first to speak, read, and write in his own mother-tongue, be that mother-tongue French or Flemish.

(2) Every Belgian ought to be taught to speak, read, and write a second language.

(3) Belgium having, as the outcome of its remarkable history, two national languages — French and Flemish — every Belgian ought to be taught, as a second language, that one of these which he is not taught as his mother-tongue.

(4) All language-teaching ought to be on the 'direct method'.

I do not assert that there are any acts of the Belgian Parliament which decree all this in so many words. In theory the 'second language' may be anything, — German or English, for instance. In practice, however, it is nearly always Flemish in the case of Walloons, and French in the case of

Flemings.* The one point insisted on is that the child's *Mother-tongue*, shall, in any event, be the basis of his earliest instruction.

These concessions were not wrung from the Government without a fight. The fight, in point of fact, was protracted and bitter. But the Government, and the Walloon party generally have long been converted to the view of the Flamingands that Flemish is entitled to full equality with French. The Government appears to be carrying out the principle of equality all round in the spirit as well as in the letter. I have before me a ministerial circular to the Inspectors of primary schools, dated July 31st, 1899. Its purpose was to promote the more extensive and (especially) the more effective teaching of the second language, and to this end it enjoined on the Inspectors the necessity of seeing that all language teaching should be on the direct method. From the issue of this document, indeed, dates the great wave of enthusiasm in Belgium in favour of bilingual teaching on sound lines. My thanks are due to M. Charles Rémy, Directeur in the Department of the Interior and of Public Instruction, who placed this and other documents, together with a mass of invaluable information, in my hands. He is himself an enthusiast in education, – just such a man as *ought* to occupy a high place in a national education bureau, and just such a man as we should expect *not* to see in such a position in Ireland.

I translate the opening paragraphs of the Circular (which is of course bilingual): –

'M. l'Inspecteur,

The Central Section of the Chamber of Representatives charged with the examination of the budget of the Department of the Interior and of Public Instruction makes inquiries each year as to the number of schools in which a second language is taught. *It, as well as the Legislative Assembly from which it derives its authority, attaches a high importance to the diffusion of our national languages* (in Flemish, 'in de verspreiding onzer landstalen'; in French, 'à la diffusion de nos langues nationales').

Each year also my administration is happy to be able to count a greater number of schools on the programme of which a second language has a place, whether as an obligatory or as an optional branch. Nevertheless, the movement in favour of the teaching of a second language in the various institutions of public instruction is neither so widespread nor so active as the Government would wish; it must be admitted that the progress made and the results attained do not correspond with the extension which has been given to this teaching in the primary and normal schools (Training Colleges), nor to the efforts of the staff appointed to superintend its introduction.'

The Circular goes on to point out that the main cause of this failure is to be found in the defective and old-fashioned teaching methods which so late as 1889 still prevailed in the majority of Belgian schools; and it then makes a series of valuable suggestions from which I shall quote more than once during the course of these papers. The Circular concludes:

'The diffusion of the languages spoken in Belgium is a powerful

* In the case of the handful of Belgians whose mother-tongue is German, French or Flemish is usually the 'second language'.

means of national education, an important factor in public prosperity; that is why it is to the interest of the country that a second language should be taught in a practical and really useful manner in our primary and normal schools. To this end, I appeal to the zeal of the teachers and professors, for they alone are in a position to carry out this truly patriotic work. Possibly the abandonment of the classical method will cause them some regrets, and the adoption of the natural method will call for greater efforts on their part: they will find a valuable reward in the conforting reflection that, thanks to their devotion, an increased number of their fellow-countrymen will understand and be able to speak two of our national languages, and that closer bonds will thus unite one to the other the members of the Belgian family.'

The Circular is signed by the Minister of the Interior and of Public Instruction.

Fancy the 'National' Board addressing such a Circular to its Inspectors! The 'Circulars' of which we have had recent experience in this country have been documents of quite another complexion.

BELGIUM AND ITS SCHOOLS
28.10.1905

The School System

The administration of the educational system of Belgium is intrusted to the Minister for Home Affairs, whose official title is 'Ministre de l'Intérieur et de l'Instructio publique'. The Ministère occupies the greater part of one wing of the Palais de la Nation in Brussels, where are housed the Senate, the Chamber of Representatives, and the various Ministries. Each of the three grades of education – higher, secondary, and primary – is in charge of a Directeur responsible to the Minister, who, in turn, is responsible to Parliament. The cabinets of these three Directeurs, who may be called the working heads of the Belgian educational system, are within a few yards of one another, so that consultations are easy. This fact, together with the fact that the three grades of education are under the supreme control of one responsible Minister, secures almost as a matter of course that necessary 'co-ordination' and unity of purpose throughout the educational scheme of which in this country we hear so much and know so little.

Apart from the University system, which does not concern us here, the State schools of Belgium may be divided into two classes – primary and secondary. The primary schools are in the hands of the Communes or municipal bodies; the secondary schools are under the direct control of the State. The central Government, however, exercises a certain amount of supervision even over the primary schools. It publishes 'specimen programmes' (*programmes types*), and takes other steps necessary to secure uniformity of standard throughout the kingdom; it *inspects* all schools, including even the *écoles privées* conducted by religious bodies; and it issues from time to time official returns, reports, suggestions, etc., for the information and guidance of teachers. In other words, the Directeur-Général of Primary Schools controls (under the Minister responsible to Parliament) the *general policy* of elementary education: the details of administration are intrusted to the local civic bodies. The system of intermediate education, on the other hand, is administered direct from Brussels by the Directeur-Général of Secondary Schools.

The elementary schools are of three types: we have the École Froebel or Kindergarten, the École primaire, and the École primaire supérieure. The names of the Kindergarten and the ordinary Ecole primaire explain themselves. The École primaire supérieure, example of which exist in many of the large towns, is an institution designed to give an education somewhat higher and more literary in type than they would otherwise receive to the more distinguished and deserving pupils of the ordinary primary schools whose circumstances do no permit of their taking a secondary school course.

Primary education in Belgium, whilst free, is not compulsory. This rather surprising fact goes part way to explain the circumstance that the percentage of illiterates in Belgium is still large.* But the non-recognition up to a comparatively recent date of the Flemish language as a medium of education is probably the real cause of much of Belgium's illiteracy, so far at least as Flanders is concerned. We in Ireland know that there are such things as illiterates who have spent six years at school.

The secondary schools of Belgium are of two types: the École moyenne or Middle School, and the Athénée. The École moyenne aims at giving a thorough commercial education; the Athénée, which corresponds to the German Gymnasium, gives an education of the type known as 'liberal'. Attached to the École moyenne there is generally a preparatory school. Both the École moyenne and the Athénée are 'écoles payantes', – that is, they charge fees. The amount of these varies in different districts, the average for an École moyenne being as low as £3 per annum.

It will thus be seen that the École primaire and the École primaire supérieure supply between them a *free* course of education for the children of the less wealthy section of the community; whilst the children of the more well-to-do can choose between the École moyenne offering a 'commercial' and the Athénée offering a 'liberal' education. Of course, there are many well-to-do and even wealthy parents who prefer to send their children to the École primaire; and, on the other hand, poor parents occasionally send their children to the 'écoles payantes'. The main consideration with the practical parent is naturally 'What type of education will best prepare my child for a career which he is likely to adopt?' If he is to be a farmer or an artisan, the École primaire will suit him; if he is destined for commercial life, the École moyenne is the thing; if for the learned profession, he ought to go to the Athénée.

Naturally, the Athénée is the usual stepping-stone to the University.

BELGIUM AND ITS SCHOOLS
18.11.1905

The Primary School
We have seen that the scheme of primary education in Belgium embraces schools of three types — the École Froebel or Kindergarten, the École primaire, and the École primaire supérieure. It does not follow that every commune is provided with schools of all three types. In many cases

* In the Belgian army there were recently 130 illiterates per 1,000 soldiers, as against 8 per 1,000 in the Swiss, and 2 per 1,000 in the Danish army.

the Infant School is attached to the ordinary École primaire, forming a sort of preparatory school to it; whilst the École primaire supérieure exists only in the wealthier and more populous centres, its object being, as we have said, to provide a special advanced course, free of charge, for the more distinguished pupils of the École primaire.

The details of school organisation in a given commune are entrusted to the communal authority. All schools, however, must be organised and conducted in accordance with a 'règlement type', issued by the Central Education Department in Brussels. The complete course in the primary school proper extends over six years and the pupils are grouped as follows, according to their standing: —

Degré élémentaire { Two Divisions { 1st year. 2nd year.

Degré moyen { A Single Course (3rd and 4th years joined), or Two Divisions { 3rd year. 4th year

Degré Supérieur { A Single Course (5th and 6th years joined), or Two Divisions { 5th year. 6th year.

To this six years' course of three degrees the commune may, at its discretion, add a fourth degree (Degré complémentaire) open to pupils who have successfully passed through the Degré supérieur.

This very elastic scheme permits of a simple or of an elaborate organisation as local circumstances — the number of pupils, the numerical strength of the staff, etc. — may suggest.

A child will enter the Infant School at the age of, say, four. At six he will pass to the École primaire, where he will spend, normally, from six to eight years. From the École primaire he may proceed to the École primaire supérieure, and thence possibly to the University.

The primary school system aims at giving an education which will prepare the child for a useful career in one of the humbler walks of life, whether as an agriculturalist, an artisan, a shopkeeper, a clerk, or the wife of one of these. Its scope will be understood after a glance at a specimen programme. The details of the actual programme in a given locality are, needless to say, determined upon by the local authority; but all primary school programmes must follow the general lines of the subjoined 'programme type' issued by the Central Department, and must make provision for the teaching of the subjects specified therein as 'obligatory': —

Obligatory Branches
1. Religious Instruction.
2. Reading and Writing.
3. *The Mother Tongue* (French, Flemish, or German, according to the circumstances of the locality).
4. Arithmetic, and the legal systems of Weights and Measures.

5. Geography (*With special reference to Belgium*).
6. The History of Belgium.
7. Elementary Drawing.
8. Elementary Hygiene.
9. Singing.
10. Gymnastics.
11. Needlework (girls only).
    Elementary (practical) Agriculture (in rural schools, and for boys only).

Optional Branches
1. Elementary Science (in urban schools as an alternative to agriculture).
2. *Second Language* (French, Flemish or German).
3. (Practical) Domestic Economy (girls only).

Truly, a practical and a well-balanced school programme. It is to be noted that amongst the compulsory subjects are *The mother tongue* (be it what it may), *Belgian Geography*, and *Belgian History*; whilst the second language, though nominally only optional, is in practice taught almost everywhere (indeed in many primary schools a *third language* — German or English — is taught in addition).

Practical teachers will be interested to see a specimen school Time Table. Here is one, provision being made only for the obligatory branches: —

Subjects	Degré Intérieur		Degré Moyen		Degré Supérieur	
	Boys	Girls	Boys	Girls	Boys	Girls
Religious Instruction	3	3	3	3	3	3
Reading and Writing	6	6	5	5	5	5
Mother Tongue	5	5	4	4	4	4
Arithmetic	4	3	4	3	3	3
Geography	1	1	1	1	1	1
Belgian History	—	—	1	1	2	1
Drawing	2	1	2	1	2	1
Hygiene	1	1	1	1	1	1
Singing	1	1	1	1	1	1
Gymnastics	1	1	1	1	1	1
Agriculture	1	—	2	—	2	—
Needlework	—	3	—	4	—	4
Hours	25	25	25	25	25	25

It is to be understood that the 'Reading and Writing' are in the mother tongue (Belgian educationists, unlike Irish 'educationists', *do not* interpret 'reading and writing' to mean the reading and writing of a foreign language); and further that the general instruction is, especially in the earlier stages, mainly in the mother tongue. This lest the number of hours — from four to five — assigned to the 'langue maternelle' in the foregoing time-table should appear too scant.

In a school in which 'optional branches' are taught the number of working hours per week will naturally exceed the minimum of 25. It may

271

range from 28 or 29 to 33 or 34. Two typical programmes — one from Brussels, and the other from Antwerp — will show how the time is divided between the two languages in a genuine bilingual school. Here is the Brussels table:

	1st year	2nd year	3rd year	4th year	5th year	6th year
Mother Tongue	$10\frac{1}{2}$	9	$7\frac{1}{2}$	7	6	7
Second Language	3	5	$4\frac{1}{2}$	$4\frac{1}{2}$	$3\frac{1}{2}$	$4\frac{1}{2}$
Total hours in school per week	$29\frac{1}{4}$	$29\frac{1}{4}$	$29\frac{1}{4}$	$30\frac{3}{4}$	$31\frac{1}{2}$	$33\frac{1}{2}$

And here is the Antwerp one (it will be observed that in this case the second language — French — is not commenced until the *second* school year):

	1st year	2nd year	3rd year	4th year	5th year	6th year
Mother Tongue (Flemish)	10	10	6	6	6	6
Second Language (French)	—	$2\frac{1}{2}$	5	5	6	6
Total hours in school per week	28	28	31	31	34	34

These tables show that the 'second language' holds an important place on the school programme, and that its teaching is no mere make-believe. We find from $3\frac{1}{2}$ to 6 hours per week accorded to it in the upper stages. The Belgian minimum — $3\frac{1}{2}$ hours — may be said to be the Irish maximum: for here, even amongst those schools in which Irish holds a fairly satisfactory position, it is the exception rather than the rule to find as many as $3\frac{1}{2}$ hours per week assigned to it.

BELGIUM AND ITS SCHOOLS
25.11.1905

A Circular from the Belgian Education Department
The function of the Director-General of Primary Schools and his staff in guiding, less by actual legislation than by suggestion, criticism, and the diffusion of information, the general policy of primary education in Belgium, will be understood from the following circular issued by the Minister to his Inspectors in 1899. From its issue dates the all but universal movement in Belgium in favour of live methods of language teaching. The first part we have already quoted in another connection: —

'M. l'Inspecteur,
The central section of the Chamber of Representatives charged with the examination of the Budget of the Department of the Interior

and of Public Instruction makes inquiries each year as to the number of schools in which a second language is taught. It, as well as the Legislative Assembly from which it derives its authority, thus attaches a high importance to the spread of our national languages.

Every year, therefore, my Department is happy to be able to count a larger number of schools in the programme of which a second language has a place, whether as an obligatory or as an optional branch. Nevertheless, the movement in favour of the teaching of a second language in the various institutions of public instruction is neither so widespread nor so earnest as the Government would wish; it must be admitted that the progress made and the results attained do not bear any proportion either to the important place given to this subject in the curriculum of the Primary and of the Normal Schools, or to the efforts of the staff charged with its promotion. In many of these schools the study of the second language is either without fruition in result, or else the little learned by the pupils is destined to be soon forgotten.

This almost negative result is due to various causes, amongst which there is one in the pedagogic order which it may be well to point out to the teaching staff, because it depends on it to make it disappear. This cause is the abstract and too exclusively grammatical character of the lessons and exercises.

The system generally followed is that which begins and proceeds by way of rules, themes, and translations. Such instruction, from its theoretic and cold nature, is bound to prove sterile: in place of causing a desire to learn a second language to spring up and grow in the pupil's breast, it makes its lessons a bugbear to him. It fails in vitality and force, because, confined within the domain of grammatical abstractions, it does not awaken those concrete ideas which are directly and immediately associated with the words and forms of the language.

The true intuitive method to employ in language teaching is that suggested by the maternal instict. The mother excites the attention and curiosity of her child, not only by the sounds and inflexions of her voice, but also by gesture and look. She first addresses herself to those senses which at an earlier stage and to a greater extent than the others are made use of in the acquisition of ideas, — hearing and sight. Thus she makes clear impressions on the child, and these she frequently awakens and strenghtens by the ingenious mimicry which always accompanies her words. And her language is not that of grammar, it does not clothe the dry and rigid form of a theme or a translation; it is first a word, often even a syllable, which the child smilingly makes an effort to pronounce, in order to show his mother how happy he is to be able to enter into intimate converse with her. Little by little, the child thus acquires a knowledge of the more usual words of the mother tongue, and to each of these terms there corresponds *an idea*, or at least *an impression* which will soon become an idea. He feels more and more the need and the pleasure of understanding and of being understood: he makes efforts to speak, and by dint of these repeated attempts — which his mother elicits and encourages — he succeeds at length in making his thoughts intelligible.

The pupils of our Primary Schools, and also those of our National

Schools, are generally, as regards the acquisition of a second language, in a less favourable position than the child to whom his mother teaches his mother tongue. True, they have already acquired their first ideas; but they are at a total loss for words and turns to express these ideas; their ears are not attuned to the sounds and inflections of the new language, and their vocal organs still lack the skill to enunciate them correctly. By the very fact that they are in a position where they can always understand and make themselves understood (by using the known language), they do not feel keenly the necessity of learning the second language; moreover, they hesitate to express themselves in a language which is still unfamiliar to them, their mistakes in which would, as too often happens, excite the merriment of their fellow-pupils and sometimes of their masters. There is here a combination of causes calculated to render language lessons both dull and useless, unless enlivened by the powerful attraction of an intuitive, natural, and living method. Therefore, it is the maternal method which the primary teacher and the professor in the Normal School must imitate if they wish that the first efforts of their pupils in the learning of a new language be encouraged by an appreciable degree of success.'

All this reads like a breezy homily on teaching method from Seaghán Ó Catháin. To us, with the lucubrations of the 'National' and the Intermediate Boards in mind, the document sounds the unlikeliest thing in the world to a circular from a central education authority. In Ireland it is reserved for lone enthusiasts like Seaghán and others to think out teaching and kindred problems, and they are laughed at for their pains by the 'educationists': in self-governing Belgium the central educational department really leads educational thought and is a source of light and inspiration to the whole country.

BELGIUM AND ITS SCHOOLS
2.12.1905

The Direct Method

The ministerial circular goes on to give a series of valuable hints on the teaching of the second language by the direct method: —

'A little at a time: a few concrete ideas — ideas of *persons or of things*, ideas of *qualities*, ideas of *actions* — springing from an attentive observation of the surroundings or circumstances in which the pupils are placed, the most everyday forms and words which the language provides for the expression of these ideas, — these, it seems to us, are the essential elements of the method. . . . No grammar rules, but extremely simple chats about the class, what is to be seen there, what is being done,; about the home, about the scenes of domestic or rural life, in a word about subjects *coming within the pupils' range of observation*, so that, in the exercises, the mind, the eye, the ear, and the vocal organs always take part, energetically and simultaneously, in the conception and in the expression of the ideas. The aim should not be to teach much in a few lessons: it should be rather to convince the young pupils that it is possible for them, if they only persevere, to enter into communication with others through the

274

medium of a second language. Their perseverance is assured if their first successes are the obvious outcome of the use of attractive methods: as soon as they reach the stage in which they find pleasure in being able to express themselves otherwise than in their vernacular, there will spring from this pleasure the irrestible need of extending their vocabulary. Then, if they know that they can count on the good-natured assistance of their teacher, as the little child can on that of his mother, they will grow bold, they will "let themselves go", and the greatest difficulty will be overcome.

Experience has already clearly shown the superiority of the natural over the classical method. I desire that it be generally adopted in the Normal Schools (Training Colleges) in order that the number of teachers capable of giving instruction in a second language with advantage may be increased. This secured, it will be possible to include French and Flemish, or French and German, as obligatory branches on the programme of many Primary Schools, or at any rate to organise special courses to prepare the young to study this language with success from the moment of their entry into the Normal School, the Middle School, the College or the Athénée.

It need scarcely be said that this teaching of a second language on the direct or natural method by no means implies the abandonment of all set grammatical instruction. The latter is employed concurrently with the former as soon as the pupils are fit for it. A time comes when it is necessary that grammatical notions should be brought in to confirm or correct the linguistic forms acquired through the medium of conversation; the utility of these grammatical notions is then better understood and they have not that dryness which always characterises the first teaching of a living language solely by way of grammar.

'The spread of the languages spoken in Belgium is a powerful medium of national education and an important factor in public prosperity; that is why it is in the interests of the country that a second language should be taught in a practical and really useful manner in our Primary and Normal Schools. To this end, I appeal to the zeal of the teachers and professors, for they alone have the power to carry out this eminently patriotic work. Possibly, the abandonment of the classical method will cause them some regrets, whilst the adoption of the natural method will demand greater efforts on their part; they will find a rich reward in the stimulating thought that, thanks to their devotion, a greater number of their fellow-countrymen will understand and be able to speak two of our national languages, and that thus closer bonds will unite one to the other, the members of the Belgian family.'

This document — which is, of course, bilingual — is signed by the then Minister of the Interior and of Public Instruction.

BELGIUM AND ITS SCHOOLS
23.12.1905

A Summing Up and Some Acknowledgments
From the preceding chapters the reader will have collected a fair general notion of the education scheme in modern Belgium. He will have learned

that there exist side by side two school systems, – one a voluntary and the other a state system; that even over the voluntary schools, which are conducted mainly by religious corporations, the Government exercises a certain amount of supervision; and that the state school system comprises (a) Infant and Primary Schools administered immediately by the local authorities, but guided as to their general policy by the central department at Brussels, and (b) Intermediate and Higher Schools administered direct from Brussels. He will further have learned that a rational bilingual system is the ideal of every Belgian educationist: the principles laid down being (1) that every Belgian child is entitled first and foremost to be taught his mother-tongue; (2) that every Belgian child is entitled to be taught in addition one of the other languages spoken in Belgium; and (3) that all language teaching ought to be on the 'direct method'.

Bearing all this in mind, the reader will be in a position to follow intelligently the account I propose to give of visits which I paid to Belgian schools during the summer of 1905. I visited in all upwards of a score of state schools, secondary and primary; some infants' schools; two or three voluntary schools, including the Jesuit College de Saint Michele in Brussels; one industrial school; and two of Belgium's five Universities.

A few further words by way of preface to the actual accounts of the visits. Letters with which I had been furnished by friends in Dublin procured my introduction to the bureau of the Minister of the Interior and of Public Instruction. To the Minister – M. de Trooz – I am in the first place indebted for permission to visit the schools and otherwise pursue my inquiries. M. van der Dussen de Kestergat, Directeur Général of Secondary Education, of whose geniality I retain kindly memories, furnished me with a number of valuable reports and other official documents, and gave me a letter authorising me to visit the Écoles moyennes and Athénées in the Brussels, Antwerp, Ghent, and Bruges districts. M. Coremans, Directeur Général of Primary Education, committed me to the care of his head Inspectors. My visits to primary schools in the Brussels district were made in company with M. Mestdagh, Chief Inspector for the Province of Brussels; and my visits to primary schools in Antwerp and its neighbourhood were made in company with M. Heinz, Chief Inspector for that Province. No Inspector accompanied me to the Intermediate and Higher Schools. To MM. Mestdagh and Heinz I owe grateful thanks; and I should also acknowledge my obligations to M. Charles Remy, Directeur in the Ministry of the Interior, who keenly interested himself in my mission and gave me, in particular, much valuable information on the subject of the direct method and its introduction into Belgian schools. Other obligations will be acknowledged during the course of the chapters, which follow. Suffice it here to say that I met with nothing but courtesy and kindliness from everyone with whom I had dealings during·the course of my inquiry, from the Minister down to the humblest teacher – nay, down to the tiniest garçonnet – in the smallest of rural schools. One and all contrived to convey the impression that in seeking permission to visit their schools and to inquire into their methods of work I was, in their opinion, conferring rather than asking a favour.

BELGIUM AND ITS SCHOOLS
30.12.1905

A Belgian Kindergarten

To begin at the beginning, I start this record of my experiences in Belgian primary and secondary schools with an account of a visit to an Infant School. As has been already mentioned, whilst in rural places the Infants' Schools, as commonly in Ireland, are attached to the ordinary Primary Schools, there exist in the large and populous centres Kindergartens or Infants' Schools totally apart from these latter, and catering only for infants. In Antwerp, for instance, there are seventeen schools for infants under the direct control of the communal authorities, and sixteen in the hands of the Catholic body; whilst there are forty communal Primary Schools and thirty Catholic. It is not, of course, to be assumed that the communal schools are of the type known as 'godless': in all of them provision is made for religious instruction, the local authority determining the character of the religious instruction to be given. In practice, this instruction is nearly always Catholic. Thus, the 'communal' schools stand to the 'Catholic' or voluntary schools pretty much in the same relation as our 'National' schools to the primary schools of the Christian Brothers.*

As a fair average type of a Belgian Infants' School I select the École Froebel or Kindergarten in the Rue de l'Empereur, Antwerp. Antwerp is a Flemish-speaking city, Flemish being the vernacular of nine-tenths of the children attending its Primary Schools. Accordingly, the Infants' Schools of Antwerp are purely Flemish. As soon as the École primaire is reached French is taught to Infants. This is in accordance with the general principle so often referred to, that the *first steps* in the child's education are made *in his vernacular*, be that vernacular French or Flemish; the second language is commenced only in the second or third school year. Applying this principle to Ireland, we should have children in Connemara and Corca Dhuibhne taught *Irish only* as long as they remain in the Infants' Class, whilst shortly after their promotion to Standard I they would commence English as 'second language'. Conversely, in Dublin and Belfast, children would be taught Irish as a 'second language' from Standard I up.

This particular school is not a pretentious building, unlike many Belgian primary schools of more recent erection. Entering the street door we pass by the concierge's lodge, and walking along a paved passage arrive at the bureau of the head-mistress. In plan, the school consists of a number of moderately-sized class-rooms enclosing a neat court. The court, into which the class-rooms open, is used as a playground. A separate mistress is, of course, in charge of each class-room, having under her care not more than thirty or forty children. Needless to say, no sane Belgian would dream of herding from 130 to 150 children into the same schoolroom, as is often done in the large city schools in this country.

Brightness, neatness, and scrupulous cleanliness are the dominant notes in the *tout ensemble* of the class-room. There are some plants and flowers; a few attractive pictures; a bust or painting or photograph of the King of the Belgians. The time-tables, the inscriptions on the wall-charts, and all the other notices displayed are *in Flemish only*; for this is Flanders, and 'in

---

* The parallel is not quite exact, for the 'Catholic' schools in Belgium, unlike the Christian Brothers' Schools here, are subject to Government inspection.

Flanders Flemish'. The head-mistress speaks to the children and to the class-mistresses in Flemish only. The class-mistresses use only Flemish in their intercourse with the children.

BELGIUM AND ITS SCHOOLS
6.1.1906

A Belgian Kindergarten (Continued)

The successful teaching of infants presupposes gifts and acquirments of a very special kind in the teacher. It demands infinite sympathy, infinite tact, infinite patience; an intimate understanding of the child mind and the capacity to come down to its level; an attractive and winning manner; and finally considerable talents as a draftsman, a mimic, and a *raconteur*. All this means that, from a true standpoint, the really good Kindergarten teacher belongs to a higher order than the ordinary primary teacher, and is proportionately rarer. British and West-British educationists imagine that anyone can teach infants. It is one of the many British and West-British heresies. The monitor and the pupil-teacher are peculiar to these enlightened islands. No continental in his right senses would dream of setting youngsters to teach youngsters only a little younger than themselves; least of all would he dream of setting them to teach infants. Accordingly, we find that some of the most gifted members of the teaching profession in continental countries are in charge of Infants' Schools. The same will apply very largely to America. Neither in the Écoles moyennes nor in the Athénées of Belgium did I meet with more interesting personalities or with more suggestive methods of work than I did amongst the teachers of the Infants' Schools and of the lower forms in the Primary Schools. For obvious reasons the teachers of the Kindergartens are almost invariably women.

In my Kindergarten in the Rue de l'Empereur I found the principles I have just enunciated held in due honour. The staff — consisting of eight or ten ladies working under a Head-Mistress — realised that their lessons, to be rally valuable, must have a two-fold aim: they must both amuse and educate — the former in order that the latter might be possible. Accordingly, all the lessons were in the first place *attractive* — appealing to the child's love of colour, of movement, of music; in the second place all had a *purpose*, and were not given merely to fill up time, — the purpose being the enkindling of the child's imagination, the awakening of his faculties, the training of his hand, his eye, his ear, his intelligence. All the instruction given with this end was *useful* in the best sense; some of it, as will immediately appear, was highly practical even in a more restricted application.

To come to the concrete. The first lesson at which I assisted belonged to a type which it is difficult to classify. It was a lesson which aimed at awakening the children's powers of observation: it was a lesson in language; it was a lesson in very elementary domestic economy. I can best convey an idea of its scope by reproducing as nearly as I can the actual questions asked and answers given — a method to which I shall frequently have recourse in future papers.

Teacher (in a pleasant conversational tone). — I suppose you all had breakfast this morning, children?

Omnes — Yes, teacher!

T. — So had I! I never forget my breakfast. Do you Hendrik?

H. (promptly) — No, teacher! (a laugh ripples through the desks).

T. — Well, what did you have this morning, Hendrik?

H. — Soup!

T. — Very good! Emile and Marie will get us the soup-plate and the other things required.

Emile and Marie leave their places, approach a cupboard, and bring forth a simple breakfast-service, consisting of a soup-plate, cup and saucer, knife, fork, spoon, table-cloth, etc. A less experienced teacher would have done this herself, but this teacher knew, as all good teachers do, that it is an excellent plan to allow the children to help as much as possible in the giving of the lesson. This amuses them, gives them a pleasant sense of self-importance, keeps their attention wide awake, and fixes things in their memory. The lesson goes on: —

T. — Jules, show me the plate! Quite right! Louise, the spoon! Hendrik, the cup! Emil, the *top* of the cup! Marie, the *bottom* of the cup! Josef, the *inside* of the cup! Jan, put the cup *upside-down*! (And so on and so on: each child coming forward when his or her name is called and indicating the required object or performing the required action).

T. — Now, Hendrik, where was your soup put this morning?

H. — In the plate!

T. — Where was the plate put?

H. — On the table!

T. — Was not something else put on the table *before* the plate? (Hendrik looks puzzled).

Louise — Teacher, I know!

T. — What, my child?

L. — The table-cloth!

T. — Quite right! Now come, my dear, and spread the table-cloth on the table. (Louise with an air of considerable self-importance trips forward and performs the action).

T. — You will make an excellent housekeeper, Louise. Now, where is the cup put?

Jules. — On the table! (Several hands go up).

T. — I see, Jules, that some of your friends don't agree with you. Where would you put it, Marie?

Marie — I should put the saucer on the table and the cup on the saucer.

T. — and where the spoon? In the cup?

M. — Oh no! In the saucer!

T. — Do so, my dear.

Marie trips forward and performs the action; and thus the lesson goes on. By the time it is concluded a neat little breakfast-table has been set in the school-room by the united efforts of the children, every one of whom, if possible, takes part in the operation. It will be seen that the little ones are — albeit it is all play to them — being trained up as careful little housekeepers.

The particular lesson I have described was given in the children's vernacular (Flemish); but the teaching of a new language could quite obviously have been linked with it. In point of fact, precisely similar lessons will at a later stage be given to these very children in French; whilst in French-speaking districts similar less are given in Flemish. But of all this more anon. I am here dealing with the Infants' School, in which only the vernacular of the district is heard.

Imagine the revolution were lessons like this *in Irish only* the order in Infants classes in Iar-Chonnachta and the Déise.

A Belgian Kindergarten (Continued)

Another lesson at which I assisted in the Kindergarten in the Rue de l'Empereur was an interesting variant of a common enough type of lesson in continental schools. The application of the method to a language lesson is obvious.

The teacher, taking a piece of chalk, sketched on the blackboard an admirable little marine view. A few bold lines served to suggest a rolling sea, with sails in the offing; in the foreground were the end of a pier, a lighthouse, some marine objects. A moon was riding in the sky; across her face clouds were hurrying. This delightful little study was the work of a few moments and the eager pleasure of the children as they saw the picture grow under the teacher's hand may be more easily imagined than described.

The next step, of course, was to question the children as to the picture and what it represented. 'What do you see on the blackboard?' , 'A sea.' 'Anything else?' 'Yes, a lighthouse.' 'What is the lighthouse for?' And then the class launches into a fascinating discussion on lighthouses, storms at sea, wrecks, and so on, the teacher so framing her questions as rather to *evoke* the ideas of the children than to give them ideas. This subject being exhausted, a further reference to the picture opens up a new train of thought. 'What are these?' 'Sails.' 'To what do these sails belong?' 'To boats.' 'What sort of boats do you think they are?' 'Fishingboats.' The possibilities for conversation in this subject are obvious. The excitement and perils of a fisherman's life; the sorts of fish caught; their uses; the distinction between salt water and fresh water fish; the fishing fleet and fish-market of Antwerp, and so on almost *ad infinitum*. Again, the moon and' the clouds in the sky are the starting point of yet a new discussion; the sea itself; its terrors, its hidden wonders, of another; what lies beyond the sea — strange lands and strange peoples — of still another. Possibly a week's conversation lessons will be founded on this little blackboard sketch: and all the time the little ones are using their eyes, their ears, their tongues, their reasoning faculties; they are being trained in the right use of language; their powers of observation are being developed; their descriptive powers are being brought out; their imaginative sense is being appealed to, — and they are enjoying themselves hugely.

It is to be noted that all the objects represented in the picture were objects which might be expected to come within the ordinary ken of the children. Antwerp is a seaport town, and every Antwerp *gamin* is familiar with ships and boats. The great North German Lloyd steamers come into the harbour; the fishing fleet on its way up or down the river is a common sight; the favourite evening airing of Antwerp folk of all ages and classes is across the Schelt in the ferry to take coffee or light beer in one of the cafés in Tête de Flandre. It is, of course, a maxim of good teaching that the lessons should as far as possible concern themselves with things that come within the children's daily experience. Only in Ireland is it considered intelligent to give object lessons on the habits of the cassowary and on the method of roofing houses in Cochin-China to children who are never likely to see a cassowary either dead or alive, and are still less likely in the ordinary course of events to engage in building operations in Cochin-China.

In some of the more up-to-date Belgian schools I found the *croquis* coming into vogue as an attractive and valuable exercise for children of Kindergarten standing. A *croquis* is a rough bold sketch. There are special *croquis* classes in many of the Paris studios, the students being required to make rapid sketches of a model who throws him or herself into various attitudes. In its simplest form the *croquis* in the primary school is something very similar. The children are asked to make a sketch of a cat, a dog, a horse, a bird, a man, a table, a house, — sometimes with and sometimes without the model before them. Another form of *croquis* lesson is this: the teacher tells a little story in very simple language, and each child is asked to illustrate it by a sketch on a slate or on paper. Yet another: the teacher draws an imaginary *croquis* in the air, using both hands; the pupils facing her, reproduce her motions, each drawing before him or her, in the air, a similar figure; then, turning round, they transfer the idea so obtained to slate or paper.

'Somewhat fantastic', the old-fashioned teacher will observe. Yet teachers in the United States and in France find it very valuable for training the eye, for developing the sense of form, and for inducing a feeling for the beauty of lines. The Belgian school in which I saw the system most intelligently used was the Infants' School attached to the École moyenne for girls at Schaerbeek, near Brussels. A fascinating book has been written on the subject by a French teacher.

BELGIUM AND ITS SCHOOLS
20.1.1906

A Belgian Kindergarten (Continued)

The exercises in Manual Training which I saw in this and other infants' schools were devised on an equally ingenious plan and carried out with equal address and resource. The educational value of a well-considered scheme of Hand and Eye Training few will deny. We must not allow the unhappy experiments in this direction which have been made in Ireland to prejudice us against a means of education which is held in high honour by all sound teachers on the continent. This is exactly what was lacking in Ireland.

A Hand and Eye lesson, to be of any value, must in the first place be of such a nature that it *does* actually 'train' the hand and eye — and also the intelligence — of the child. It must in the second place — especially if addressed to very young children — be sufficiently attractive to capture the attention and interest of the class; else, like all other lessons, it becomes a weariness of the flesh. Many Hand and Eye lessons which I have seen in this country failed in the former of these two requirements; still more in the latter; and not a few in both.

The Belgian teachers whose Hand and Eye classes I attended exhibited a good deal more originality, versatility and adroitness than I had been accustomed to see in Ireland. Each teacher thought out schemes for him or herself; skilfully availed of local circumstances; adapted his lessons to the geographical or social *locale* of his pupils; and, generally, depended more on his own native fund of ingenuity and sympathy than on the formulas of text-books. One principle which all seemed to bear in mind was that the objects made by the children in school, whilst of such forms as to be capable of utilisation as the basis of simple lessons in geometry, mensuration, drawing, and so on, should also be in themselves objects capable of being put to some practical use, whether as toys, as articles of household ornament, or as portions of the school equipment. Thus, the children feel that they are *doing something*; and at the end of each lesson there remain to them, to be carried proudly home or to be placed still more proudly in the school musuem, interesting little monuments of their skill and diligence. I found this idea carried to its highest development in a Brussels primary school in which nearly all the school furniture — desks, maps, geometrical figures, book-cases, book-covers, etc., — had been made during school hours by the boys themselves; of which more anon. Here I speak of something a good deal more elementary.

Most of us have, as schoolboys or schoolgirls, fashioned birds from paper and — during temporary absences of the teacher from the schoolroom — amused ourselves by making them 'fly'. To be discovered generally meant punishment in some form or other. Having lively recollections of such stolen schoolboy pleasures — and of their consequences — I was interested on my visit to the Kindergarten in the Rue de l'Empereur, to find the lowest class busily engaged in manufacturing paper birds under the superintendence of a lady teacher who seemed an enthusiast on the industry. The symmetry of shape and marvellous flying powers of the birds turned out would have moved my envy had I seen them fifteen years ago. The manner of the lesson was as follows: — Each child was provided with a sheet of white paper. The teacher, similarly provided stood at the top of the classroom. Without mentioning what she was about to make the teacher commenced to fold her paper into mysterious shapes. Thirty pairs of bright eyes eagerly followed her every motion; thirty pairs of nimble hands deftly imitated her every turn and twist. As the work neared completion, the teacher asked whether they knew what they were making. There were a few bad guesses, at which all laughed. At length one, having critically regarded his embryo for some time, suddenly cried out: 'Teacher! it will be a bird!' 'A bird!' was echoed in delight from desk to desk; and the work went on with renewed zest. Finally, thirty neatly-fashioned white birds lay in rows along the desks, each little maker regarding the result of his or her handicraft with considerable complacence.

The questions and criticisms from the teacher 'What is this?' 'His bill.' 'And this?' 'His tail.' 'Jan, your bird has no eye.' 'Louise, you have given yours too big a head.' Finally, the teacher asks: 'Have our birds wings?' 'Yes.' 'What are wings for?' 'To fly with.' 'Then our birds must be able to fly! Let us try!' And with a skilful cast the teacher sends her bird sweeping gracefully through the air. 'See whether yours can fly as well as mine!' Each child casts his or hers, the younger being instructed in the art by their elders or by the teacher. There is a cloud of white paper birds in the air; cries of pleasure from the children. 'Mine flies the best ' 'Hendrik, yours wobbles!' 'Now, each one bring me his or her bird! See whether you will know your own!' cries the teacher. There is a rush: a scramble on the floor; perhaps a few disputes as to ownership. The teacher, whilst taking care that there is no undue roughness, by no means attempts to check the noise. For two or three minutes seeming confusion reigns; but, when the proper moment comes, a word from the teacher suffices to hush the din, and a second to recall each little one to its place, — each bearing in triumph his or her own particular bird.

On similar lines lessons are given in the manufacture of paper dogs, cats, horses, carts trams, chairs, tables, houses, windmills, boats, hats, dolls — in short, any and everything that ingenious brains and deft fingers can fashion

282

out of paper. The best specimens of the children's handiwork are kept to be added to the school museum, or to be sent as models to other schools; the rest are taken home by the young makers, to be proudly shown to admiring parents, and — in the case of the more elaborate articles — to find a permanent place amongst the household adornments.

BELGIUM AND ITS SCHOOLS
27.1.1906

A Belgian Kindergarten (Continued)

It remains to deal with the other side of Kindergarten work — that which aims more directly at the *amusement* of the child, although not without an important educational purpose also. Here there is less need for detailed description, as the forms of exercise to which I have to draw attention do not materially differ from those in vogue in the best Kindergarten in this country. The chief difference in favour of Belgium is to be found in the superior education, skill and resource of the Belgian teacher. And this is explained mainly by the fact that there is in Belgium a National Education Department in full sympathy with popular ideals, thoroughly abreast of modern educational progress, and looking after the training of its teachers with solicitous care. In fact, if I were asked to sum up in a sentence the message which I carry home from the primary and secondary schools of Belgium I should say: 'Train the teacher'. But in order that we may be able to train our teachers exactly as they ought to be trained, it is necessary for us to get control of the supreme educational authorities in the country — our two precious 'Boards'. So that, whilst I hope that these articles may incidentally prove helpful to my fellow-teachers, I intend them primarily as a plea for a national education authority of, and responsible to, the Irish people.

To return. There are educationists in this country whose idea of a Kindergarten is a place in which very young children may conveniently be herded in order that they may be 'kept our of mischief' during the day, — a sort of glorified crêche. The continental ideal is widely different. The kindergarten, rightly conceived, continues and supplements the process of education commenced on the mother's knee. It seeks to draw forth the varied and mysterious faculties of the child's mind; to awaken in him an interest in the brave and beautiful world round about him; to fill his imagination with fair and gracious pictures; to make both his body and his mind things of beauty and grace and health. It is in order that it may do all these things that the Kindergarten, in even a greater degree than the ordinary primary school, must be a place of brightness and of flowers; of sunshine, of warmth, and of colours; of smiling faces and of happy hearts. For these reasons also the exercises must be so ordered that, whilst educative, they are attractive, and, whilst entertaining, never entertaining merely. The formal instruction should have the allurement and zest of a game; on the other hand, the games should have some object other than the mere filling up of time, the mere 'keeping the little ones out of mischief'.

Imagine yourself again with me in the École Froebel in the Rue de l'Empereur. We are in a bright and pleasant room opening on to a sunny courtyard. Without, the children are trooping ready for their 'march in'. A teacher seats herself at a piano and plays a few bars of an old Flemish patriotic song. Then she glides into a merry quickstep, and in file the children — forty or fifty two by two. Each little boy is paired with a dimunitive maiden. The first little girl carries in her arms a huge doll. She and her partner are the leaders of the revel. The rest are divided into parties, — some with balls, some with skipping ropes, some with hoops, some with nets, and so on. A ring is formed. The child with the doll steps forward and deposits her charge in the centre of the circle. Then she commences a pretty little song in Flemish celebrating the amiability and charms of her doll. A lullaby follows. The whole circle joins in the refrains of both. The Doll Song finished, one of the children with the india rubber balls commences a Ball Song, running round the ring and hopping his ball, — the rest, standing in their places, also hopping theirs in time. A Skipping Song, similarly illustrated, follows. Then there is a Hoop Song, a Net Song, and so on until the list of games is exhausted. At the conclusion of each song there is a chorus and a general dance round. Finally, the quickstep recommences, and all trip happily out.

The exercise has been palpably entertaining, — we submit that it has also been educational. Further, it has been in the vernacular, whilst twenty years ago it would almost certainly have been in French.

Another game which I saw performed by the same children was the common enough one of 'Guard the Handkerchief'. It was at times a little boisterous, but the mistress was always present to prevent anything like downright roughness.

Due attention is, of course, given to Physical Drill. In the Écoles primaires and moyennes and in the Athénées all the most approved forms of gymnastic training are seen in practice. In the École Froebel the exercise with which I was most struck was a very pretty drill in which white and blue hoops were made use of. These hoops were also employed in various dances and marches.

On the whole, I don't think I ever saw a merrier band of school children than these in the Rue de l'Empereur. As I stood amongst them and heard them chatter in their mother-speech without fear of the teacher's cane or the inspector's frown, I thought of Connemara and — swore! Fortunately, neither the teacher nor the children understood Irish.

BELGIUM AND ITS SCHOOLS
3.2.1906

The Primary School: The 'Series'

In our Antwerp Kindergarten we have seen the Belgian education machine at work on the very youngest generation of future Belgian citizens. We have noted that in this bilingual system the first phase is purely unilingual. Only the vernacular of the district is heard within the walls of the Belgian Infant School. It is in the lowest class of the Primary School proper that the bilingual principle is first introduced.

My type of a Belgian Primary School shall be the École Communale at Etterbeek, a suburb of Brussels. I select it for several reasons. First, the district is genuinely bilingual, the Walloons being in only a slight majority over the Flemings: the district is thus analogous to a border countryside in Connacht or Munster in which English has already secured a slight advantage — perhaps the average type of what we are accustomed with some looseness to call an 'Irish-speaking district'. Secondly, the school is, I think, fairly representative of its class in Belgium. And thirdly, the staff at

Etterbeek includes a teacher who makes a speciality of certain educational methods which I long to see introduced into the primary schools of this country.

This teacher — M. Basile De Cleene — I found in charge of the lowest classroom in the Boys' School at Etterbeek. His little flock consisted of some thirty happy-faced youngsters aged between six and seven. They were in their first school year, having passed from the Kindergarten at six. The reader must not be surprised to find a man of University standing , with a growing reputation as an educationist, filling no loftier post than that of teacher of thirty little boys all under seven. In Belgium, as I have already suggested, some of the most cultured and interesting personalities in the whole educational service are to be found amongst the teachers of the infant and primary schools. And this is as it should be: for assuredly it is in its earliest years that the child requires the kindliest and most sympathetic handling, the most skilful and attractive teaching. If I had my way, I would choose the very finest minds — the noblest and most cultured men and women — of the race to place in charge of the primary schools of my country. The best that we have is not too good for the service of our children.

M. de Cleene's school-work was ordered in accordance with a scheme which is a sort of expansion of the common enough 'series' method. A central idea is selected as a point of reference for all the lessons of the week. The instruction in drawing, in geometry, in arithmetic, in manual training, in geography, in language, even in singing, must all for the space of a week centre round and be illustrative of some subject proposed at the beginning. On the occasion of my visit to Etterbeek the theme for the week happened to be 'The Wind'. Every lesson which I saw given had, therefore, direct or indirect reference to the Wind. The object-lessons of the week were given on a paper windmill. The manual exercises of the week were concerned with the manufacture of paper windmills. Drawing, geometry, and simple calculation were taught incidentally to this process of manufacture. Some elementary notions of geography and of physiography were worked in during the course of simple chats on the wind, — what it is, where it comes from, what it does. The singing-lessons for the week centred round the acquirement of a 'Song of the Wind'. Finally, all these lesson were lessons in language, for all were conducted bilingually. I proceed to details.

Taking a well-made paper windmill from the school museum (the work probably of a former pupil) the teacher proceeds to give an object-lesson upon it *in French*. This finished, and the pupils exhaustively examined on the subject-matter, he proceeds to give another *and different* object-lesson upon it *in Flemish*. This second lesson, be it observed, is not a translation of the first. It has, in fact, no connection with the first beyond that of a common theme. Totally different points with regard to the windmill are dealt with in the Flemish demonstration, which thus resolves itself, so far as the non-Flemish-speakers are concerned, into a lesson in Flemish on the Direct Method. (For the non-French-speakers the French demonstration just concluded has been in effect a similar lesson). A good deal of useful conversation is, of course, built up around the windmill: names of objects, qualities, actions, and even of abstract ideas being freely introduced in both languages. Thus, in addition to an object-lesson on the form and uses of a windmill, we have a sort of double language-lesson on the Direct Method, — the Flemings being taught to talk about the windmill in French, and the Walloons in Flemish. There is, be it again remarked, no translation, the words 'wind' and 'windmill' themselves being practically the only ones which occur in both lessons. It is to be added that *both* lessons are addressed to the *whole* school; and that both the Walloons and the Flemings are questioned *in French on the French lesson*, and *in Flemish on the Flemish lesson*.

BELGIUM AND ITS SCHOOLS
17.2.1906

The Primary School: The 'Series' (Continued)

The windmill, having served as the subject of an Object Lesson, is now made use of as the basis of an elementary lesson in Drawing. Each child is required to draw a square in pencil on paper, and to put in the diagonals. The teacher maintains a fire of questions all the time, making use now of French, now of Flemish. 'Que faites-vous?' 'Nous faisons les diagonales'. 'Que venez-vous de faire?' 'Nous venons de faire les diagonales', etc. Next , a simple lesson in Geometry is given on the square. What is this? A square. What is a square? What is a right angle? How many right angles in a square? How many degrees in a right angle? Is this angle larger or smaller than a right angle? — all this bilingually. The operation of finding the centre of the square is gone through first in French and afterwards in Flemish. In the same way a little simple Arithmetic is introduced. The sides and diagonals are measured, the figures added, subtracted, multiplied, divided, — again all bilingually. Thus, every lesson is to a certain extent a lesson in language.

By way of exercise in Manual Training, the children are required to cut out their squares neatly, to slit up the diagonals, to pierce the necessary holes, and finally to fold over the flaps, and attach each improvised windmill to a little stick by means of a pin. This done, they are allowed a few minutes to amuse themselves by making the windmills revolve. Both languages are freely used by the teacher in giving the necessary directions for the carrying out of all these operations.

The toy windmill completed, a Flemish landscape introducing two or three windmills is shown. This is the starting-point of further conversation. Are real windmills, like those in the picture, made of paper? If not, of what? Is it the wind which causes them also to revolve? What are they for? Are they common in Belgium? In what neighbouring country are they also common? Why are they so much used in the Low Countries? By chats such as this the pupils' intelligence is quickened and their powers of observation and reasoning developed. The teacher does not fail to seize every opportunity which the lesson affords for a reference to the history, scenery, or industrial activities of Belgium.

Finally, as has already been noted, the song for the week is a *Song of the Wind*, with a fine swinging chorus lending itself to use as a marching tune. The song may be in Flemish or in French as circumstances suggest. Most of the singing I heard was in Flemish. Young as they were, all M. de Cleene's pupils could read the tonic sol-fa notation admirably at sight.

Apart from the general course, which, as we have seen, is bilingual all through, M. de Cleene gives formal instruction in language. It need hardly be said that he uses the Direct Method. During my visit he gave some very attractive lessons on colours. For the purposes of the lessons he used chalks of various colours, and also the revolving disc. The pupils were able to tell in both languages what colours are got by combining yellow and red, blue and red, blue and yellow, and so on.

M. de Cleene is an enthusiast on Hand and Eye Training. His school contains a most interesting little museum of objects made by the children — geometrical forms, toys, knick-knacks, etc., etc., in clay, paper, and wood. Many of the objects have actually been designed by the children themsleves, and very quaint and pretty some of them are.

Still more valuable, and, to me, more interesting are M. de Cleene's experiments in another direction. Nature-study holds a prominent place in his school programme. Under his guidance, his pupils make frequent expeditions into the fields and woods, some excursions being for general observation, others having for their aim the collection of objects of a particular kind. Thus, on one afternoon each pupil may be instructed to bring home the root of a particular plant; on another, the fruit of a particular tree; on a third, the grub of a particular insect. On the occasion of my visit the life-story of a butterfly was being studied at close quarters. The caterpillar was shut up in his cocoon, and the children were eagerly awaiting the day when he would burst forth from his lowly dwelling and flit out of the school window a glorious butterfly.

I have an uneasy notion that if M. de Cleene were an Irish teacher he would fail to secure the award 'Fair' from a National Board Inspector, because he teaches his pupils to *observe* and *think* before he teaches them to read and write; or else he would be dismissed by his manager as a faddist. The Belgian Education Department, less enlightened, is following M. de Cleene's experiments with much interest, and I more than once heard the Chief Inspector for the Province of Brussels warmly recommend his ideals and methods to other teachers.

BELGIUM AND ITS SCHOOLS
3.3.1906

The Bilingual Principle in Practice

In our École Froebel at Antwerp we have seen the Belgian child entering on his school life. We have duly noted that his very first steps are taken in his mother tongue, — that, in fact, as long as he remains in the Infant School he hears no other. We have seen, however, that the teaching of the second language is commenced almost as soon as the Primary School is reached, — that is to say, at the age of six or seven. We have further seen that the teaching of the second language is conducted on the Direct Method from the outset; and that in such up-to-date schools as that of M. de Cleene at Etterbeek special devices of a very attractive and interesting kind are made use of by the teacher.

From this point on the second language enters ever larger and more largely into the scheme of school work. Let us say that three hours per week are devoted to it during the first school year. In the second school year this time will have been increased to four or four-and-a-half hours; in the fourth or fifth school year, to five or six. Furthermore, the second language is after the first year and (as will have appeared from my account of my experiences at Etterbeek), in many cases from the very first moment, freely employed in giving instruction in other branches, — mathematics, geography, manual training, etc. Either of two plans may be adopted, according as circumstances or the inclination of the teacher may suggest:

either *all* the lessons may be given bilingually, as is done by M. de Cleene, or in the alternative certain lessons may be set apart to be given in the vernacular, and certain others to be given in the second language. Thus, it is common to find geography, history, and manual training dealt with in Flemish, whilst mathematics and science are taught in French. The plan of bilingualism all through seems preferable, provided always that the teacher is skilful and conscientious enough to avoid the temptation to have his French lesson a mere translation of his Flemish lesson and *vice versa*. Yet another device would be to use the languages on alternative days, but I do not remember to have seen this employed. I need hardly add that there is no such thing, at least in the more progressive schools, as bilingual *language* lessons. French, as a set subject, is taught *through French,* Flemish through Flemish. This applies also to foreign languages like German and English when they come to be taken up in the higher standards.

It will be seen that a child commencing at the age of six such a course as I have described will, at the end, have acquired a thorough mastery over the two languages, both as written and as spoken tongues. It has been doubted whether a language can really be learned at school: I have satisfied myself by observations both in Ireland and in Belgium that it can. A child who spends half his school time for six years thinking in and speaking a language must of necessity know that language at the end of the six years. It is all a matter of getting him really *to think in* the language: and this again is all a matter of good teaching.

Let me briefly describe my experience amongst a class of Belgian children who had been subjected to such a process as I suggest for six years. I take the highest class in the École de Filles at Etterbeek. These girls were in their sixth school year. Their ages ranged from twelve to fourteen. Some of them were Flemings, some Walloons. The latter being in excess, French had been selected as the 'vernacular' for school purposes. I was present at lessons in Flemish, in French and in other subjects. During the Flemish reading-lesson the mistress used only Flemish in addressing the class, whether in giving directions, in correcting mistakes, or in commenting on the passages read. The reading finished, 'explanation' followed: Flemish only being used in discussing the lesson whether in reference to meaning, to grammar, or to subject-matter. M. de Vliebergh, the Chief Inspector for the Province. who was present, afterwards questioned the class — also in Flemish.

During the French lesson which followed French only was used: there was first reading, next 'explanation', finally questions from the Inspector, — all in French. The children appeared equally at home in both languages: and even the Inspector, himself a Fleming, had often difficulty in detecting which of the two languages was the actual vernacular of a given child.

I afterwards assisted at a geography lesson in Flemish and at a mathematical lesson in French. Of the methods employed in teaching these subjects more anon.

BELGIUM AND ITS SCHOOLS
29.9.1906

In the series of articles on this subject which I contributed to *An Claidheamh Soluis* last year I described the organisation of the Belgian school system, primary and secondary, and explained in detail the bilingual principle summarised in the four propositions:

1. Every child ought to be taught his mother-tongue;
2. Every child ought to be taught at least one other language as soon as he is capable of learning it;
3. Such second language should be gradually introduced as a medium of instruction in other subjects;
4. All language teaching should be as far as possible, on the Direct Method.

In this second series of articles I propose to describe the *methods of teaching* which I observed in use in the primary and secondary schools of Belgium. At the outset there will necessarily be a certain amount of repetition of matter contained in the original series. I should add that the methods about to be spoken of have been used by me in elementary and advanced classes in University and Alexandra Colleges and, during the last session, in an advanced class in the Ard-Chraobh.

A Direct Method Lesson

The primary schools which gave me the greatest pleasure of the score or more that I visited during my stay in Belgium were those at Molenbeek St. Jean in Brussels. The district is a thoroughly Flemish one, and the great majority of the children know only Flemish on first coming to school. At the end of their course of six years they can speak, read and write Flemish, French and at least one other language — German or English. The Principal of the Boys' School is M. Jacques Mehauden, the soundest educationist and one of the most interesting personalities that I remember to have met in Belgium. I shall have to speak of him later on in connection with his invention of *L'Image Animée*. His wife, Mme. Mehauden, is Principal of the Girls' School. My account of my experiences in Molenbeek will occupy several of these chapters.

The simplest type of language lesson on the Direct Method, as given in this or any other up-to-date school in Belgium, may be described as follows:—

The teacher, standing at the head of the class-room, calls out a boy and stations him on a chair or stool in full view of the whole class. Pointing to him (the children are Flemish speakers and are being given their first lesson in French), she* pronounces distinctly the words 'Le garçon'. She then points to another boy and says 'garçon'; to yet another and another repeating the word each time. She displays some pictures of boys, pronouncing 'garçon' as she points to each. Long before she is done the dullest child in the room has learned to associate the word 'garçon' — not with the vernacular word 'knaapje' which has not been mentioned at all — but with the concrete, living thing which the teacher points to each time she pronounces the word. This first step attained — the child's *reason* as well as his memory having been called into play in the very first moments of the lesson — progress becomes easy, and the teacher passes on with surprising rapidity to enumerate in the new language various parts of the garçon's body, pointing to each. In the first lesson she will probably confine herself to the head. The words selected might be these: —

Le garçon

La tête.	Le nez	L'oeil.
La bouche.	Le cou.	L'oreille.

* Women teachers are generally — and properly — employed to teach the very juvenile classes even in boys' schools.

289

Note that two words taking 'la,', two taking 'le', and two taking 'l' are selected; also that, in the early stages, the definite article is invariably used before each noun. These words are repeated by the teacher several times and always in the same order.

Now comes the second great difficulty. Pointing to the boy, the teacher asks, making her voice as interrogative as possible and suggesting by the expression of her face that she is really in doubt: 'Qu'est-ce que c'est que cela?' and answers immediately, speaking in a didactic tone as if she were imparting information: C'est le garçon'. Again she asks, pointing to the boy's head, 'Et qu'est-ce que c'est que cela?' and answers: C'est la tête' So on with other parts. This may be repeated several times. Hitherto the children have been silent. Suddenly, addressing the class the teacher asks in her most interrogative tone, as she points to the boy: 'Qu'est-ce que c'est que cela?' Prompted a little by the teacher, if necessary, the class answers in unison: 'C'est le garçon'. 'Bon!' exclaims the teacher approvingly, and every child present infers instantly that this new word 'bon!' is an expression of commendation. The lesson proceeds. The teacher (pointing to the garçon's head): 'Qu'est-ce que c'est que cela?' The class in chorus: 'C'est la tête'. And so on with the other parts. After a while the order of the words is varied, the teacher taking care that the correct form of the article is used with each noun.

The next step is to question individual children, first using the words in their original order, afterwards, varying them. If a child makes a mistake another is asked to correct him.

Next, to further impress the connection between the *word* and the *thing* it stands for, the teacher calls out another boy, and he becomes the subject of the object-lesson, the same words and phrases being repeated. The teacher will then pass through the class rapidly pointing to the head, neck, ear, etc., of different pupils and asking 'Qu'est-ce que c'est que cela?' getting now the class in a body and now an individual child to answer. She will also ask the questions pointing to her own head, neck, ear, etc. Finally she will produce pictures of boys and go through the same performance with these as points of reference.

The lesson will conclude with a short drill on the sounds introduced. Not a syllable of the known language has been spoken throughout.

The words selected for a subsequent lesson might be:

La poitrine.	Le Dos.
La main.	Le corps.
La jambe.	Le genou.
	Le pied.
	Le doight.
	Le menton.

The teacher will be cautious to introduce only useful words of everyday occurrence and such as will fit in with the scheme of future lessons. It would, of course, be absurd and almost fatal to commence to teach a new language by giving an exhaustive catalogue of the parts of the human body. In the next article the purpose served by the introduction of the words 'main', 'jambe', 'pied', and 'doight' will be made clear.

I have found the piquancy of taking one of themselves as the subject of the first object-lesson to appeal to children. In the case of a class of adults I should prefer to commence, as is done by most Direct Method teachers, with such simple objects as books, pens, paper, chairs, tables, etc. The more personal note struck in the lesson described above appeals to the child's imagination and sense of humour. I have often been amused by the glee with which an Irish child has heard that his chin is called 'smig' in Irish and his nose 'srón': with similar glee did the Flemish children in Molenbeek St. Jean realise that the strange words 'menton' and 'nez' denoted in French those interesting parts of their chubby physiognomies.

BELGIUM AND ITS SCHOOLS
13.10.1906

Comparison — L'Image Animée

Apt and piquant comparisons play a large part in good language teaching. The teacher who has taken 'Le garçon' as the theme of his first two object lessons will take as the theme of his third some common quadruped between which and the garçon he will draw a number of broad and striking contrasts. In Belgian schools the horse is the animal most commonly selected.

Should the school be in the country the teacher, keen to seize the opportunity of an effective and realistic object-lesson, will march the whole class into the playground, into which he will introduce an actual horse. In Ireland, 'asailín an mháighistir' would probably be more easily available than a horse, and would form quite as interesting a theme of discourse. Should the master not be fortunate in the possession of an asailín, the parents of one of the children would very gladly lend the services of the family beast of burden. The class groups itself around the somewhat astonished quadruped, and one of the youngsters is called out to stand beside it as the joint theme of the lesson. The point-by-point comparision of their school-fellow's outer anatomy with that of the asailín is bound to appeal to the children's senses of curiosity and humour.

Should it be inconvenient to provide a real horse or donkey a model or even a toy could be used. Excellent models of all the commoner domestic and wild animals can be had from at least one school-furnishing house in Dublin. In the absence of a model a picture would do, or even a rough blackboard sketch. But the best of all substitutes for the living animal is undoubtedly the *Image Animée*.

The *Image Animée* is the joint invention of M. J. Mehauden, the Principal of the École Communale of Molenbeek St. Jean, and M. G. Wynincx, Professor at the School of Industrial Design, Ixelles. It is a cardboard figure, realistically coloured, and furnished with movable joints. In the hands of a skilful teacher its possibilities are endless. It can be utilised in every imaginable form of Direct Method teaching (including, of course, the teaching of grammar); in that useful type of lesson which has as its object the cultivation of the observing and reasoning faculties and imparting of 'general information'; and finally — this being its most characteristic and interesting use — in the teaching of composition, whether in the vernacular or in a new language.

The complete collection of Images Animées published for Mm. Mehauden and Wynincx by J. Lebègue et Cie., 46 Rue de la Madeleine, Bruxelles, includes animals, men, women, children, simple household articles (chairs, baskets, boxes, bags, cans, sweeping brushes, etc.), carts, wheelbarrows, saddles, guns, swords, toys of various kinds, caps, hats, etc., etc. Each cardboard figure can be fastened to the blackboard by means of a drawing pin. The hats and caps can be placed on the heads of the men and boys; the guns can be put in their hands; the horses can be saddled and yoked; the wheelbarrows can be pushed along. The objects form, in fact, a set of cardboard marionettes which can be manipulated pretty much as the operator likes. With the complete collection (which costs, I think, twenty francs), is issued a book in Flemish and French, which explains the system and includes a number of interesting specimen lessons.

To proceed. The teacher, in the absence of a real horse, attaches the Image Animée of a horse to the blackboard. Beside it she (we again for reasons already explained drop into the use of the feminine pronoun) pins one of the cardboard boys from her collection. She then, having first tested the pupils' knowledge of the previous day's lesson, submits them to a further test by asking them to name on the cheval parts already named in the case of the garçon, — la tête, le cou, l'oeil, etc. She will not fail to draw attention to the fact that the cheval possesses an appendage which the modern garçon does not, — la quene. Next she concentrates attention on the legs, — les jambes. She counts the legs of the horse, — un, deux, trois, quatre. The brighter children have realised at once what she is doing, aided by the similarity of the names of the numerals with those in their mother-tongue. For the benefit of the slower pupils the teacher counts up to four on her fingers and on the ball frame. She calls out four pupils and counts them. She counts four chairs, four windows, four marbles, four pennies. She makes four strokes on the blackboard. She writes down the figures 1, 2, 3, 4. She raps the desk four times. The more readiness and resource she displays, the more she varies her processes and hits on new and startling devices the better.

Having impressed her meaning clearly, the teacher announces:
'Le cheval a quatre jambes.'
She now refers to the garçon's nether limbs: un, deux, and announces:
'Le garçon a deux jambes.'
Endless play for conversational drill is afforded by these two sentences. Again: Paul a deux jambes: Henri a deux jambes: Etienne a deux jambes. Paul a aussi (a new word dropped incidentally; its meaning is soon apparent to the class) deux *mains*. Etienne a deux mains. Moi aussi (pointing to herself), *j'ai* deux mains. Nous (making a wide sweep of the whole class) *avons* deux mains. Le cheval a quatre jambes. *Nous avons* deux jambes.

The sentences are next made interrogative and negative; conversational practice follows; and the whole concludes with a short phonetic drill.

Note the early stage at which the verb *to have*, with three of its forms in the present tense, is introduced. In one instance I heard the forms of 'have' introduced in the very first lesson: the language being taught, however, was English, and there was little grammar to be remembered, owing to the absence of inflection in the article, etc., In teaching Irish I should reserve 'have' for a later stage, harping in the earlier lesson on the verb 'to be', which is, of course, a much greater crux in Irish than in English or French.

BELGIUM AND ITS SCHOOLS
27.10.1906

Qualities: Colour
The first few lessons of a well-conceived Direct Method course will

292

concern themselves with *objects*. From objects the teacher will pass to the *qualities* possessed by objects. And the quality most easily dealt with, and lending itself to the most striking and interesting treatment, is colour.

Some attempts at Direct Method lessons on colour which we have seen given at various times and places have been far from successful. Here is a common type. The teacher holds up a book and says: 'Tá an leabhar glas. *Bhfuil* an leabar glas?' 'Tá an leabhar glas!' choruses the class, and the teacher complacently passes on to another word, thinking that he has taught the meaning of 'glas'. The pupils know indeed that the book is 'glas', but as to whether 'glas' has reference to its size, shape, weight, material, price, or what not, they have not been afforded an inkling. The fact that *colour* is now on the *tapis* has not been brought home to them.

It may be brought home to them in various ways. The Berlitz teacher from whom we took our first German lessons produced a book and turned to a page on which were printed a succession of coloured bands. Passing his hand rapidly across these, he said 'Farben', and at once proceeded to enumerate the 'Farben'; grün, rot, gelb, schwartz, blau, braun, weiss, etc. In a moment he had taught us more than the laborious exertions of many Direct Method teachers would have taught us in half-an-hour. In Belgian schools we have seen the revolving disc so familiar in the science classroom utilised with admirable success for a similar purpose. Another device is the employment of ribands of various colours which are hung on the blackboard. Yet another — and in Belgium the favourite one — is the use of coloured chalks: a stroke being made with red chalk as the word 'rouge' is repeated, with green chalk as 'vert' is said, and so on. The most elaborate device of all is the employment of the Magic Lantern to cast various colours on a white screen; these are combined in endless ways — blue and yellow to form green, red and blue to form purple, etc., — and thus a little simple science teaching worked into the language lesson. Often all these devices with half-a-dozen others will be called into requisition in the course of the same lesson, — the skilful *varying of methods* being, as so often noted, one of the secrets of successful teaching, more especially in the elementary schools.

Opportunities for practice in the use of the newly-acquired names of the colours are endless. A pupil is called out and the colour of the various parts of his attire pointed out — new and useful nouns being thus introduced. Then each child is required to name the colours of his own clothes or of those of a fellow-pupil. Such dialogues as the following will take place: —

'What colour is your tie, Jean?'
'Mademoiselle, it is red.'
'Etienne, who else has a red tie?'
'Mademoiselle, Henri has also a red tie.'
'Is Pierre's tie red?'
'No, Mademoiselle, it is blue.'
'What girls in the class have blue frocks?'
'Marie, Therese, and Louise have blue frocks.'
'And what colour is Lucie's frock?'
'Mademoiselle, it is black.'
'Is her ribbon also black?'
'No, it is white.'

Note that from the outset of the French lessons the children are addressed by the French forms of their names; during the Flemish part of the programme they are addressed by their Flemish names; and when, at a later stage, they are being taught German or English, 'Jan' or 'Jean' is replaced by 'Johann' or 'John' as the case may be.

Note also that in the early stages the pupils are required to speak in *complete sentences*. This is useful for impressing genders, etc., and also gives practice in the syntax of the verb. Later on the abbreviated, ejaculatory, and allusive scraps of which ordinary conversation so largely consists will, of course, be tolerated.

BELGIUM AND ITS SCHOOLS
17.11.1906

Qualities (continued): Comparison

In dealing with the qualities possessed by objects it is especially necessary to proceed methodically and gradually, appealing at every step to the observative and reasoning faculties of the pupils, and availing of the natural association of ideas in their minds. It is simply fatuous to hold up a book and say: 'Tá an leabhar glas. Tá and leabhar mór. Tá an leabhar trom. Tá an leabhar daor', — expecting the pupil to grasp the meaning of 'glas', 'mór', 'trom', and 'daor', as soon as they are informed that another book held up for their inspection is *not* 'glas', 'mór', 'trom', nor yet 'daor'. Each idea must be approached gradually, and must be treated of in association with kindred ideas. We have discussed devices for teaching the names of colours. Other qualities are dealt with similarly. As illustrating the principle that there should be a gradual and methodical approach to a new idea, let us take the case of *size*. It is desired to familiarise the pupils with the words in the new language which render the ideas conveyed by the English words 'large', 'small', 'long', 'short', 'broad', 'narrow', 'thick', 'thin', etc. I will describe a lesson on size which I witnessed in a Belgian school. The language being taught was German. Some of the children were Walloons, Some Flemings, but neither French nor Flemish was spoken during the lesson. It was, in substance, a language lesson on the Direct Method of the type familiar in the Berlitz schools.

The teacher was armed with a long and rather wide ruler (Lineal) and a short slender lead pencil (Bleistift). Carefully comparing them is size he announced: —

Das Lineal ist *lang*. Der Bleistift ist *kurs*.

The quicker pupils grasped the idea at once. For the benefit of the slower, the teacher gave further illustrations, — drawing long and short lines on the blackboard, comparing his middle finger with his little finger, comparing one boy's hair with another's, and so on. In the same way, drawing attention by expressive gestures to the respective widths of the two objects, he brought the pupils to realise the facts expressed in the sentences:—

Das Lineal ist *breit*. Der Bleistift ist *enge*.

Further practice in the use of the new words was given before the next stage was approached. Pupils were required to point out objects in the room which were 'lang', 'kurz', 'breit', or 'enge'; negative and interrogative sentences introducing the terms were formed; a proverb in which the word 'lang' occurs was written on the blackboard.

Next, enforcing his meaning with the aid of vigorous and eloquent gestures, the teacher went on: —

Das Lineal is *lang und breit*: es ist *gross*.

Whereas: —

Der Bleistift is *kurz und enge*: es ist *klein*.

A host of further illustrations of the meaning of the words 'gross' and 'klein' were given. A big boy was compared with a little one; an elephant was compared with a mouse (a picture of the two being produced); two houses — a large and a small — were sketched on the blackboard, as also were a variety of odd little pairs of figures, one being always smaller than the other, — two pigs, two ducklings, two men dancing, two boats in full sail. Needless to say, there were thus afforded endless opportunities for useful and entertaining conversation.

By precisely similar methods the pupils were brought to understand the meaning of: —

Das Buch ist *dick*. Das Papier ist *dünn*.

Similarly with:—

Das Buch ist *schwer*. Das Papier ist *leicht*.

The next step was the teaching of *comparison*. With a less intelligent class, or one new to Direct Method instruction, this might be reserved for a separate lesson. In the instance I refer to the pupils had no difficulty in following, almost as soon as they were pronounced, such sentences as: —

(1). Der Bleistift ist *lang*. Die Feder ist *länger*. Das Lineal ist *am längsten*. (So with kurz, kürzer, am kürzsten).

(2). Die Feder ist *länger als* der Bleistift. Der Bleistift ist *kürzer als* als die Feder.

(3). Der rote Bleistift ist *eben* so lang *wie* der gelbe.

(4). Der Bleistift ist nicht so gross *wie* das Lineal.

To translate the type-sentences into Irish for the benefit of those unacquainted with German: —

Stage A.	Tá an riaghail *fada*. Tá an peann luaidhe *gearr*.
	Tá an riaghail *leathan*. Tá an peann luaidhe *caol*.
Stage B.	Tá an riaghail *fada agus leathan*: tá sí *mór*.
	Tá an peann luaidhe *gearr agus caol*: tá sé *beag*.
Comparison.	(1) Tá an peann luaidhe *fada*, tá an peann *níos fuide*, *'sí an riaghail is fuide* (so with gearr, níos giorra, is giorra).
	(2) Tá an peann *níos fuide* (*is fuide* an peann) 'ná an peann luaidhe. Tá an peann luaidhe *níos giorra* (is *giorra* an peann luaidhe) 'ná an peann.
	(3) Tá an peann luaidhe dearg *chomh* fada *leis* an bpeann luaidhe buidhe.
	(4) *(a)* Níl an peann luaidhe *chomh* mór *leis* an riaghail.
	(b) Níl an peann luaidhe *chomh mór agus bhí* sé.

All this is treated admirably in 'Feargus Finn-bheil's' *Mac-Léighinn,* which is, as far as it goes, by far the best adaption of Direct Method principles to a course of instruction in Irish.

BELGIUM AND ITS SCHOOLS
24.11.1906

Position

Objects, Qualities, Actions, — these three key-words suggest the order of progress in any well-considered scheme of language teaching on the Direct Method. As we have seen, however, the skilled teacher will as he proceeds incidentally introduce a vast amount of matter which comes under none of these three main heads. Expressions of commendation or blame, salutations, short references to the state of the weather, health, etc., exclamations of various sorts, proper names of persons and places, numerals, simple proverbs, — all these will be worked in as occasion offers, advantage always being taken of any chance observation made in class or any trend given to the conversation by a pupil; for though the conscientious teacher will always prepare his lesson beforehand, yet he will ever be on the alert to seize opportunities presented to him by some unexpected incident occurring during class time or by some passing event of school interest. Thus, if a feast-day happens to come round, its name in the new language will be given to the children; as the various games come into season their names and some of the more important technical terms employed in them will be mentioned and written on the blackboard; if a stranger happens to visit the school — especially a foreigner — a few references to his nationality, his occupation, or the business of his visit will always interest the class. My visists to Belgian schools were generally made the occasions of little lectures about Ireland — an island in the Atlantic, the most westernly of European countries, with a beautiful capital called Dublin; and the teacher rarely failed to remind the children that the Irish, like the Flemings, were making a great stand for their language. 'What would you do', a class was asked in my hearing, 'if the Government sent you to prison for writing your names on your carts in Flemish?' 'We wouldn't stand a Government which would do any such thing,' replied one of the boys; whereat the master turned smilingly to me and said, 'A home thrust, my friend: you know that *our* Revolution was mainly precipitated by a language question'.

Most of the good teachers I have seen took up the important subject of *position* before passing on to deal with actions. References to the situation of things and their external circumstances generally, spring naturally enough out of conversation concerning itself with their qualities; and from talking of their positions one proceeds instinctively to talk of their *changes* in position, — in other words, one passes on to *action*. So that lessons dealing with the preposition form an intermediate stage and supply a useful connection between those dealing with the adjective and those dealing with the verb. I will again take a German lesson witnessed in an Antwerp school as a specimen.

The children had on the previous day learned in the new language a number of facts about the book, — Das Buch. After a brief examination of the class in general, the teacher asked one of the pupils to sum up all he was able to say in German about Das Buch: 'Hier ist das Buch. Das Buch ist lang und weit: es ist gross. Es is grösser als die Karte, aber nicht so gross wie der Tisch. Das Buch ist dick: das Papier ist dünn. Das Buch ist schwer: der Papier ist leicht. Das Buch ist schwartz: das Papier ist weiss'. Here was quite a little dissertation made by a child who four weeks previously had never heard a word of German!

The book was now laid on the table by the teacher and the pupils informed: —

Das Buch ist *auf dem Tisch*

It was placed on the paper and the pupils told: —

Das Buch ist *auf dem Papier.*

It was transferred to the floor and the sentence given: —

Das Buch ist *auf der Boden.*

(Note that one noun of each gender was selected: more were afterwards added for the sake of practice).

In a similar way the meaning of the other prepositions were taught: —

Das Buch ist			*in der Schachtel.*
,,	,,	,,	*An* der Wand.
,,	,,	,,	*Unter* dem Tisch.
,,	,,	,,	*vor* der Tafel.
,,	,,	,,	*Hinter* dem Stuhl.
,,	,,	,,	*neben* der Thür.
,,	,,	,,	*zwischen* dem Bleistift *und* der Feder.

Etc., etc.

Next conversational drill: —

Wo ist das Buch? Das Buch ist auf dem Tisch. Ist das Lineal auf dem Tisch? Nein, das Lineal ist auf dem Stuhl. Wo ist der Stuhl? Auf der Boden. And so on.

The resourceful teacher would vary these sentences in countless ways, calling all his ingenuity and sense of humour to his aid in devising fresh and interesting illustrations of his meaning. Thus a coin which the teacher had left 'auf dem Tisch' would be discovered 'in der Tasche' of one of the pupils, — having been slipped in by the teacher; and in punishment for the supposed delinquency the Knabe might first be sent to stand 'hinter de Thür' and afterwards incarcerated 'in dem Schrank'. Such dialogues as this might take place:-

Wo ist Wilhelm? Er ist in dem Schrank. Varum ist Wilhelm in dem Schrank? etc., etc.

Again a pyramid of chairs and stools might be erected on the table and an athletic Knabe made to balance himself on the top of the pile: —

Wo ist Karl? Er ist auf dem Stuhl. Wo ist der Stuhl? er ist auf dem Lehnstuhl. Wo ist der Lehnstuhl. Er ist auf dem Tisch. Wo ist der Tisch. Er ist auf der Boden *or* in dem Zimmer. Again. Was ist unter Karl? Der Stuhl. Was ist unter dem Stuhl? Der Lehnstuhl. And so on.

The teaching of the prepositions in German is complicated by the fact that some govern the accusative, some the dative, some the accusative or dative according as *motion to* or *rest at* is implied and some the genitive. In Irish these difficulties are practically non-existent, but there is to make up for them the difficulty of eclipsis. This had better be faced boldly at the outset. The student will at first be puzzled when he hears 'mbord' where he had expected 'bord', and 'urlár' when he had expected 't-urlár', but he will very soon learn to expect and to observe these changes just as the German student learns to expect and to observe the still more bewildering changes in the form of the article.

297

Action Teaching

The methods by which *the verb* is handled were among the most interesting that came under my notice in Belgian schools. The simplest and most straight-forward was a mere adaptation of the method of Berlitz. The teacher performed some common action, describing it in the new language. Thus —

I *lift* the book.

I *open* the book.

I *shut* the book.

I *lay down* the book.

Or again —

I *stand*.

I *walk*.

I *run*.

I *sit down*.

I *rise*.

Next a pupil is asked to perform the actions and to describe them. Then the teacher, addressing him, says —

You lift the book.

You open the book.

Etc., etc.

Addressing the class, and pointing to the pupil who is performing the action, the teacher continues:—

He lifts the book.

He opens the book.

Etc., etc.

The plural persons are taught similarly. Questions follow —

Do I lift the book?

Yes, monsieur, *you lift* the book.

Does Jean lift the book?

No, monsieur, *Jean does not lift* the book.

Jean, *lift* the book!

Does Jean lift the book now?

Yes, monsieur, *Jean lifts* the book now.

This is an action-lesson in its simplest form. Usually the teacher imports a little more originality, in order to awaken and retain the pupils' interest and attention. Thus —

Henri, come here!

Henri leaves his place and stands befor the class.

Take off your coat!

The verb 'take off" not having been previously taught, Henri is at a loss what to do. The teacher shows him in pantomime what he means. Henri very quickly understands, and with some shyness removes his coat.

Questions and answers then proceed —

What does Henri do?

He takes off his coat.

Do I take off my coat?

No. monsieur, you do not take off your coat.

Do you take off your coat, Etienne?

No, monsieur, I do not take off my coat.

Who takes off his coat?

Henri takes off his coat.

Etienne, come here!

Etienne stands beside Henri.

Etienne, take off your coat!

Further conversational drill; then —

Henri, put on Etienne's coat.

Amid much laughter, Henri dons his companion's coat, which probably fits him very badly.

What does Henri do?

He puts on a coat.

Whose coat does he put on?

He puts on Etienne's coat.

Etienne, put on Henri's coat.

Etienne dons Henri's coat, amid renewed laughter, and the conversational drill proceeds.

The following is a more advanced lesson on the same plan. It was witnessed in the Boys' School in the Rue Six Jetons, Brussels: —

Who has a top?

Monsieur, I have! (from several pupils).

Emile, come here and spin your top. Describe what you do.

Emile (as he performs the actions): I stand up, I leave my seat, I come before the class.

Teacher: What does Emile do?

Class: He stands up, he leaves his seat, he comes before the class.

Teacher: Proceed, Emile.

Emile (as he performs the actions): I put my hand in my pocket. I take out my top.

Teacher: What does Emile do?

Class: He puts his hand in his pocket, etc.

Emile (performing the actions): I put my hand in my pocket again. I take out a piece of twine. I wind the twine round the top. I raise my hand. I throw the top. I spin the top thus. The top spins.

Teacher: What does Emile do?

Class: He winds the twine round the top, etc.

Emile returns to his place with a word of commendation, and another boy is called upon to describe what his schoolfellow has just done, — an exercise on the *past tense* being thus introduced —

Emile stood up, he left his place, he came before the class. He put his hand in his pcoket, he took out a piece of twine. He wound the twine round the top. He raised the top. The top spun.

A theme for a similar lesson was the striking of a match and the lighting of a candle. The pupil, performing each action as he speaks, proceeds as follows, being interrupted now and then in order that the class may be questioned —

I take up a box of matches. I open the box. I take out a match. I draw the match across the box. The match kindles. I put the match to the candle. The candle lights. I blow out the match. I throw the match in the fire.

All this was gone over in the *past* and in the *future*: and as a home exercise the pupils were required to write out the lesson (in the three tenses) from memory.

Next week I will describe some of the later and more elaborate developments of the method.

L'Image Animée in Action Teaching

The schools which have adopted the Image Animée make free use of it in Action Teaching. Indeed, it is here that its many advantages over the ordinary wall-chart are most apparent. With the Image Animée it becomes possible to enact on the blackboard scores of dramatic little scenes which it would be invonvenient — not to say impossible — to perform in the school-room with living actors, and very difficult to represent, as is sometimes attempted, by a series of pictures. I shall describe three or four of those I saw enacted, proceeding from the more simple to the more elaborate. It was in the school at Molenbeek St. Jean — presided over by M. Mehauden, joint inventor of the method — that most of these were observed.

The following is an elementary Action Lesson given with the aid of the Image Animée. Its object, of course, is to teach the various tenses of the verb: —

Henri and his Horse

The teacher sketches on the blackboard a house, with a garden gate, opening on a country road. A cardboard horse from the collection of Images is pinned on the board, seeming to stand outside the gate. The teacher announces in the new language: —

Then —

What does the horse do?

He stands at the gate.

What stands at the gate?

The horse stands at the gate.

Where does the horse stand?

At the gate.

A similar little catechism is gone through after the introduction of each new verb.

Next a cardboard figure of a boy is made to issue from the garden gate. The teacher announces: —

Henri *comes out.*

Then questions: —

What does Henri do?

He comes out.

Who comes out?

Henri.

The cardboard figure is pinned on the board and made to perform the various movements described in the following sentences: —

Henri *stops.*

He *raises* his head.

He *sees* the horse.

He *turns* round.

He *goes in.*

The figure comes out again wearing a hunting-cap and carrying a whip (all these objects are included in the collection): —

He *comes out* once more.

He *wears* a riding-cap.

He *carries* a whip.

He *mounts* the horse.

The horse *commences* to *walk.*

300

The horse *walks*.

Henri *strikes* him with the whip.

He *commences* to *trot*.

He *trots*.

Henri *strikes* him again.

He *commences* to *gallop*.

He *gallops*.

He *takes fright*.

He *runs* away.

Henri *becomes nervous*.

He *catches hold* of the horse's neck.

The horse *rears*.

He *plunges*.

He *throws* Henri.

Henri *falls* to the ground.

He *loses* his cap and whip.

He *lies* on the ground.

The horse *escapes*.

Figures of men are brought on and made to lift the supposed inanimate form of Henri and carry him away: —

Men *arrive*.

They *see* Henri on the ground.

They *lift* him up.

They *carry* him home.

Pupils are now asked to relate what they have seen taking place. This brings in the *past tense*: —

A horse *stood* beside the gate, Henri *came out*. He *raised* his head and *saw* the horse. He *went in* and *came out* again. This second time he *carried* a saddle, etc., etc.,

The story is then repeated in various other tenses — the lesson, if necessary, being extended over two or three days; and finally, the pupils are required to write it out (say in the past and in the future) as a home exercise.

It need hardly be said that abundant incidental conversation is introduced during the course of the series.

In the next two chapters I will describe the two most interesting and characteristic uses of the Image Animée, — its use as the basis of general conversation lessons of a very attractive nature, and its use in the teaching of composition. Both of these I saw exemplified in the admirable schools at Molenbeek St. Jean. They form the most elaborate development of the Action Lesson with the Image Animée.

NOTE

A number of National School teachers, Múinteoirí Taistil, and others, have written to us for information as to where the Images Animées referred to in these articles can be procured. The publishers are J. Lebègue et Cie., 46 Rue de la Madeleine, Bruxelles. The price of the complete collection is, if we remember aright, twenty francs.

BELGIUM AND ITS SCHOOLS
26.1.1907

How to Teach Children

The most interesting teaching to be seen in Belgian schools is probably that of M. de Cleene at Etterbeek; that in the Boys' School in the Rue Six Jetons, Brussels; and that in the Boys' and Girls' Schools at Molenbeek St. Jean. I am about to describe two experiences of mine in the last-named place, — one in the Boys' and the other in the Girls' School.

I find myself in a bright and pleasant room in which are assembled some thirty little Flemings aged from seven to nine. They are nearing the end of their first school-year and have been just ten months at French. Their teacher (a lady, of course) is Mdlle. de Paduwa, who, I think, is the best language-teacher I have ever known — with one exception; the exception being a certain Gael with a soft Connacht voice who will probably read these lines on a Swiss mountainside overlooking the Simplon Pass. (Bhfuil aithne agaibh air?). I recall Mdlle. de Paduwa as a dark girl with obvious traces of Southern blood both in her face and in her manner, and distinguished by just that mingling of animation and self-possession which marks the bearing of the ideal teacher. I believe she is literally worshipped by each and every one of the thirty garçonnets who form her little flock.

I translate into somewhat feeble and colourless English the lively French of one of her lessons to these little students of ten months' standing. Remember that *all* this takes place in the new language, of which the pupils have never heard a word until they came under her care in the preceding October: —

Teacher: Do you know where I was yesterday evening, children?

Class: No, mademoiselle!

Teacher: I was in the country. Were you ever in the country, Jean?

Jean: Yes, mademoiselle!

Teacher: Where were you?

Jean: At Aasche.

Teacher: Ah! And what did you see there?

Jean: I saw fields, and trees, and farmhouses, and cows, and cocks and hens.

Teacher: Good! Now, I was in a farmhouse yesterday evening, and what do you think I saw?

Emile: The farmer!

Teacher: What else?

Henri: His wife!

Teacher: What else — in the farmyard, I mean?

Etienne: A cow!

Teacher: What else?

Emile: A pig!

Teacher: What else?

Jean: A hen!

Teacher: Ah! Exactly! I saw a hen, and here's the hen. (Pins Image Animée of Hen to blackboard; sketches with chalk a little farmyard scene — outhouses, etc., in background, litter on ground. Gets children to name various parts of hen — this being repetition of a previous lesson — and to mention the colours of the parts. Then: Now what do you think I saw along with then hen?

Henri: The cock!

Teacher: No, the cock wasn't there. I think the cock was out walking. Or perhaps he was fighting with some other cock. What did I see? Come, now! What does one see along with the hen?

Pierre: Her chickens!

Teacher: Ah! Quite so. I saw the chickens. And here they are! (Pins Image Animée of Chickens to blackboard in various positions). Count them, children!

Class: One, two, three, four!

Teacher: Four little chickens! How many, Etienne?

Etienne: Four, mademoiselle.

Teacher: Four what?

Etienne: Four little chickens.

Teacher: See, one is on the hen's back! What colour is he?

Class: He is black, mademoiselle.

Teacher: And what colour is this one?

Class: He is white.

Teacher: How many white are there, Henri?

Henri: There are two white, mademoiselle.

Teacher: Is he right, Paul?

Paul: No, mademoiselle, there are three white.

Teacher: Ah! And how many black, Emile?

Emile: There is only one black, mademoiselle.

Teacher: Which one is that, François?

François: The one on the hen's back, mademoiselle.

Teacher: Good! Now, watch. (Makes Hen bend on the ground). What is the hen doing? Robert? — Jean? — Jules?

Jules: She is scratching.

Teacher: Precisely. She is scratching. What is she doing, Robert?

Robert: She is scratching.

Teacher: Jean?

Jean: She is scratching.

Teacher: All repeat!

Class: She is scratching.

Teacher: But why is she scratching? Come, now!

Pierre: Mademoiselle, she is looking for food!

Teacher: Good! Hens scratch for food, do they not?

Class Yes, mademoiselle.

Teacher: Watch again (makes Hen raise her head and draws a little wriggle in chalk to represent a worm in her beak). She has found something! What has she found?

Jean: Mademoiselle I know!

Teacher: Well?

Jean: A worm!

Teacher: Quite so. She has found a worm. All repeat!

Class: She has found a worm. (The class in general is frequently made to repeat a good answer, or an answer, introducing a new word or form).

Teacher: And what does she do with the worm?

Auguste: She eats it!

Teacher: Oh! for shame!
Surely she would not be so greedy? (A long pause, then):

Robert: Oh! mademoiselle! She give it to one of the chickens!

Teacher: Of course she does! Look here. (Makes Hen and Chicken go through the performance on the blackboard). Isn't she a kind hen?

303

Class: Yes, mademoiselle!

Teacher: Would you care for a worm for breakfast, Jacques? (Laughter).

Jacques (emphatically): No, mademoiselle!

Teacher: No, but the little chick does. See how he gobbles it up! Poor worm! Aren't you glad you're not a worm, Antoine?

Antoine: Yes, mademoiselle. I'd rather be the chicken!

Teacher: And eat worms? Fie! (More laughter).

This — with, of course, a good deal of repetition and explanation — forms Part I of the Lesson; Part II is reserved for next day. I will describe it in a further article.

BELGIUM AND ITS SCHOOLS
2.2.1907

How to Teach Children (Continued)

I give an English rendering of Mdlle. de Paduwa's second lesson on 'The Hen and her Chickens'. The preceding lesson having been gone over by way of 'repetition', the thread of the story is taken up as follows: —

Teacher: Well, children, as you see, the good mother hen is scratching in the ground for food, and also teaching her little ones to scratch. Some of the chicks are very lively and playful. Watch this one (makes one of the chickens mount on the Hen's back). What is he doing, Jules?

Jules: He mounts on the hen's back.

Teacher: Who mounts, Henri?

Henri: The chicken, mademoiselle.

Teacher: Good! Now, look here (makes Chicken fall, much to the merriment of the class). What happens, Paul?

Paul: The poor little chicken falls from the hen's back.

Teacher: Is he hurt?

Paul: No, mademoiselle, not that I know (the idiomatic little bit of French 'Pas que je sache' was unexpectedly introduced by Paul — a French student of ten months' standing — deservedly gaining him a special word of commendation from the teacher).

Teacher: Now, children, watch carefully. Something terrible is going to happen (a sudden eagerness and tenseness of expectation among the class; the Image Animée of a ferocious dog appears on the scene, and is made to face the Hen in a threatening manner; a murmur of interest and apprehension runs through the desks). What happens, Jean?

Jean: A big dog arrives.

Teacher: Good! What happens — all together?

Class: A big dog arrives.

Teacher: Exactly! A big dog dog arrives. What sort is this dog, Pierre?

Pierre: Mademoiselle, he is white, with black spots, and a black ear.

Teacher: Precisely. What about the poor hen?

Joseph: She is frightened, mademoiselle.

Teacher: And the chickens?

Joseph: They are frightened also.

Teacher: And what does the hen do?

Charles: She runs away.

Teacher (pretending to be shocked): What! and leaves her poor little chickens to the dog. Surely not? What does the good hen do? (A silence; then):

François: Mademoiselle, she calls the chickens to her!

Teacher: What does she say? (François makes an excellent if ludicrous attempt to imitate the Hen's frightened cry, — much to the delight of his playmates). Splendid, François. Try you, Thomas. And you, Jacques. Listen to me now. (The sound is imitated with varying degrees of success by several pupils and by the teacher). Now, all together! (A veritable babel of discordant cackling, developing into a roar of laughter, in which the teacher joins merrily. Silence restored): Yes, that is what the hen says. And the chickens?

Robert: They run to her.

Teacher: And where do they go, — Jules? — Charles?

Charles: Under her wing, mademoiselle.

Teacher: Ah! Precisely! All the little chickens run under the wing of the hen. Come and help put them in, Charles (Charles delightedly runs forward to aid the teacher in stowing the cardboard forms of the chicks under the Hen's wing; the latter is made to crouch down on the ground in imitation of the reality). Excellent, Charles! I see you know how to manage chickens. Watch this now! (The Dog is made to snap fiercely at the Hen, who pecks back at him in self-defence). What happens, Auguste?

Auguste: The dog snaps at the hen.

Teacher: And the hen ⁻Henri?

Henri: She pecks at the dog.

Teacher: Is she afraid, Pierre?

Pierre: Yes, mademoiselle.

Teacher: Why then does she peck?

Pierre: To defend her little ones.

Teacher: Ah! Gallant hen! Is she not brave?

Class: Yes, mademoiselle.

Teacher: What does the dog say, Alphonse?

Alphonse: He says 'Bow, wow, wow!'

Teacher: All repeat. (Chorus of barking from the class, ending in peals of laughter. Re-establishing silence, the teacher proceeds): So the brave hen fights to defend her little ones from the wicked dog. It is a hard battle. But look what happens! (The Image Animée of the Cock is brought on the scene: delighted cries from the class). Who arrives?

Class: The big cock!

Teacher: The big cock! And what does he do? (Puts figure through actions described) — Jules?

Jules: He flaps his wings.

Teacher: Yes. And? —

Jules: He runs at the dog.

Teacher: Yes. And what does the dog do, Etienne?

Etienne: He turns and runs.

Teacher: Who made him run, Jacques?

Jacques: The big cock.

Teacher: And so you see the good hen and all her little chickens are saved. What does the cock do? (puts figure through the action) — Robert?

Robert: He opens his wings, he stretches out his head, and and he says,

Teacher: What does he say? (Amid renewed laughter Robert imitates the crow of the cock). Good! Listen to me now! All together, to wind up!

Amid a din of crows the lesson comes to a merry end.

This is how languages are taught on the Direct Method at Molenbeek St. Jean.

The Teaching of Composition

In the Girls' School at Molenbeek St. Jean, of which the Principal is Madame Mehauden, I saw singularly interesting language teaching. Here there are separate classes for the Walloons and the Flemings for the first three years of the school course, but from the fourth year on all are taught in common — the Walloons having by that time learnt enough Flemish, and the Flemings enough French, to enable them to follow a lesson in either language. The lesson which I select for description is one which will illustrate the use of the Image Animée for the purpose of teaching Composition.

The classroom in which I now find myself holds almost as pleasant a place in my memory as that of M. de Cleene at Etterbeek or that of Mdlle. de Paduwa in the Boys' School at Molenbeek. It is presided over by Madame Beudin, who has in her charge some thirty little girls aged from twelve to fourteen. They have,of course, passed their third school year, and consequently Walloons and Flemings are united: and they are being given a lesson in French composition. Here is what happens: —

Madame Beudin, without speaking a word, sketches on the blackboard the interior of a room, showing a stove, a mantel-shelf, a table, some pictures, and a closed door. At one side she pins the cardboard Image of a chair. Next she takes the Image of a little girl, in whose hand she places a sweeping brush; this figure she moves backward and forward across the board, conveying the idea that she is sweeping the floor. The children are now asked to write on their slates an account of what they see taking place before them. Each thus commences to write a little story. There is no imitation, copying, or memorising, for every child is using her own powers of observation, reasoning, and description. Thirty different and independent accounts of the little drama which is being enacted on the blackboard are, in fact, being compiled. The teacher does not speak. Each child is left to give her own interpretation of the actions performed, and her own colouring to the story. After the first few actions have been gone through, members of the class are called upon to read what they have written. One little girl reads: — 'Louise was a very industrious child. Whenever her mother went out, she would seize the sweeping brush and commence to sweep the floor'. Another has written: — 'One day Mathilde's mother went out to shop. Before leaving home she told her little daughter to have the room tidied and the floor swept by her return'. And so on. If any inelegancy of style or a mistake, whether in grammar or as to the facts of the story, occurs in any child's version, a companion is asked to correct it: any difficult word occurring, or any particularly good sentence or idiom, being written on the blackboard for the benefit of the class. Thus the lesson proceeds — the teacher silently putting the figures through their performance on the blackboard, the pupils busily recording what takes place, the whole being stopped now and then in order that what has been written may be read, criticised, and corrected. The following are the bald events which each child thus works up into a pleasant little story: —

Louise is seen sweeping the floor. The door opens and her mother enters. The mother walks across the floor and places a bag on the mantel-shelf; she leaves the room again. She walks on tip-toe to the door and looks through the key hole. She goes over to the chair, lifts it, carries it to the mantel-shelf, and mounts it. She opens the bag (which contains flour), upsets it, and is covered with white. Her mother enters. Scolding. Louise weeps.

All this is enacted by the Images Animées, like so many marionettes, on the blackboard, and recorded with more or less ornamental details, additions, and comment by the children. When the thirty little essays are finished, some of the young writers are asked to read out their pieces *in extenso*, and the class in invited to criticise them both from the point of view of their language and of their faithfulness to the general facts of the little drama as enacted on the blackboard. Next each child is asked to select a title for her story. Some of thoses selected on the occasion I am describing were very clever and amusing. 'La Curieuse' was the commonest. Others said: 'La Curieuse Attrapée'. Others: 'La Curiosité Punie'. One put it: 'La Curieuse Bien Eprise'; and yet another hit on the difficult piece of French: 'La Curieuseprise en flagrant délit'. This so pleased the teacher that she wrote it on the board, and got the child who selected it to explain its meaning to the class.

Next each child was asked to write *the moral* of the tale, — and these again were in many cases very interesting and amusing. Finally, the story was set as a home exercise, to be written out fairly on paper, the various criticisms embodied, and the grammatical and other mistakes corrected.

It is obvious that the method cultivates at once the powers of observation, deduction, expression, and criticism, and that, above all, it encourages originality. The children, in a word, are trained *to think for themselves* instead of being asked to memorise the thoughts of others.

BELGIUM AND ITS SCHOOLS
2.3.1907

Reading; Grammar

With regard to the teaching of reading, grammar, etc., I saw little in Belgium that will be startlingly new to up-to-date Irish teachers. The Direct Method is generally used — that is to say, all the explanation, literary and grammatical, in connection with the reading lesson is in the language which is being taught; further, as soon as the students reach an age to appreciate them, formal grammar lectures are given — always *in* the language which is under study, be it the mother tongue, the second language, or a third (or foreign) language. There are still, of course, a number of Belgian teachers — chiefly older men and in country schools — who have not yet fully mastered Direct Method principles, and in some cases I heard a good deal of the vernacular used in the course of lessons in the 'seconde langue' or in German or English. This, however, is steadily discouraged by the Education Department through its staff of Inspectors, and in a few years the Direct Method will probably have been firmly established in every school in Belgium.

In the early classes the grammatical instruction is, needless to say, incidentally introduced in the course of the conversation and reading lessons. I have already fully described the devices by which the genders and plurals of nouns and pronouns and the moods and tenses of verbs are taught on the Direct Method. This teaching is carefully followed up when the pupils commence to read. A passage is read aloud by a member of the class. If a mistake is made another pupil is called upon to correct it. Next, questions are put to the members of the class (individually) for the purpose of testing their knowledge of the subject matter, — these questions, of course, being in the language of the lesson. Next come grammatical questions, — point out the objects and predicates, the nouns and verbs; give the plural of this noun, the comparative of that adjective, the subjunctive of this verb, the derivation of that proper name; pluralise the whole sentence; throw it into the past or into the future, and so on. Expand that clause; give the sense of this sentence in your own words. This process, covering the whole ground of the passage both from a literary and from a linguistic standpoint, is called *Rédaction*. In addition to testing the pupils' knowledge, it has the important object of *making them talk*.

Often, too, during the course of a conversation or a reading lesson a pupil is called out to the blackboard and asked to decline some pronoun or conjugate some verb which occurs. The grammar teaching thus springs directly and naturally from something that is being said or read in the schoolroom, and is not introduced, so to speak, *a propos* of nothing in particular. For instance, a teacher in my presence asked a boy: 'As-tu mangé ce matin, Henri?' The boy replied: 'Oui, monsieur, j'ai mangé ce matin'. 'Moi aussi', said the teacher, '*j'ai* mangé ce matin. *Tu as* mangé ce matin, Henri. Paul, *il a* mangé ce matin. *Nous avons* mangé ce matin', and so on through all the persons of both numbers. Again, in a reading lesson in German at which I was present, the sentence: 'Ich leiste ihm éinem Dienst' occurred. The teacher seized the opportunity of putting a number of pupils through several tenses of the verb, *the context being retained throughout*. This is a rule observed by all good teachers, the retention of the object, extensions, etc., giving life and interest to the otherwise dull process of conjugation.

In blackboard work chalks of different colours are used in order to make the grammatical teaching more explicit and graphic. Thus the nouns may be written in red, the verbs in blue, and so on. Again in teaching Walloons to syllabise Flemish (French speakers invariably find a difficulty in separating and properly accenting the syllables of other languages) it is common to write each syllable in a different chalk. Sometimes one syllable will be eliminated and the pupils asked to supply it. Of course the common devices of Direct Method grammar teachers — the dropping of a word, or the writing of a verb in the infinitive, — are frequently resorted to, the pupils being required to supply the missing word or to give the verb its proper mood and tense.

In teaching spelling, the best teachers use the phonetic method. That is to say, a word is not 'spelled' by the repetition of the conventional names of the letters by which it is represented in writing, but by the repetition of the *sounds* composing it. I saw a most interesting lesson in phonetics given on the sentence, 'Les moineaux sont des oiseaux tapageurs' — culled, of course, from the reading lesson of the day.

Almost everything else that struck me as far as grammar-teaching is concerned has already been referred to in the course of these papers.

BELGIUM AND ITS SCHOOLS
9.3.1907

The Teaching of Geography

It goes without saying that in the teaching of Geography the best Belgian teachers proceed 'from the schoolroom outwards'. The schoolhouse with its court and garden constitutes an ample map on which the points of the compass, the distinction of latitude and longitude, the divisions of land and water can be graphically pointed out. (In many of the schoolrooms which I visited the walls were marked — bilingually — 'north', 'south', 'east', and 'west'). From the school one proceeds to the parish, then to the district, next to the province, finally to the country, to the continent, to the world. In the earlier stages the geographical teaching consists largely in the conveying of elementary notions of physiography. Of the mere dry-as-dust enumeration of placenames there is very little.

In describing my experiences in the École Froebel in the Rue de l'Empereur, Antwerp, I dealt in some detail with the methods by which very young children are interested in geography. A marine sketch is drawn in chalk on the blackboard, or a picture of a port or a railway station is hung up, and class and teacher proceed to chat familiarly on the various objects composing the view, wandering off into endless trains of entertaining and instructive conversation. The development of this method is seen at a later stage in the use of the Magic Lantern. Let me describe a geography lesson given to a class of boys aged from twelve to fourteen. It was in Flemish, but might equally have been in French on some subsequent day. (In some schools certain subjects are uniformly taught in Flemish and others — science and the like — uniformly in French: other teachers prefer to use both languages in every lesson, or to give lessons in each on alternate days).

The schoolroom is darkened, and the magic lantern (which forms portion of the equipment of every up-to-date school) throws on the screen a picture representing a busy, bustling port. The class is informed that this is a view of Antwerp. Then questions and answers commence. What do they see in the picture? Water. What is it — a river, a lake, or a sea? Obviously a river? The Scheldt. Antwerp, then, stands on the River Scheldt. What do they observe on the river? Ships and boats. Are there many of them? Oh, yes; an immense number. Are they large ships? Very large. Antwerp, then, is an important seaport. Do they see the huge ship in the middle of the river? Yes. That is one of the famous North German Lloyd liners. So Antwerp is a port of trans-Atlantic call. What are all these small craft with dark sails? Fishing boats. Yes; in fact they are portion of the great Antwerp fishing fleet. So Antwerp is an important fishing centre. You see the buildings on the far side of the river? Yes. That is Tête de Flandre, where Antwerp people go very evening to take supper and listen to music in the cafés. You observe a steamer crossing the river? Yes. That is the Antwerp ferry. It carries people, horses, carriages, motor cars, everything, from Antwerp to Tête de Flandre. You see the spire? Yes. That is the famous Cathedral of Antwerp. Let us look at it more closely.

A second view shows the Cathedral, which gives rise to a little digression on the history of Antwerp. A view of the interior of the Cathedral follows. The pictures on the walls are by Rubens. Then a visit is paid to the Art Gallery, where some of Rubens' and Van Dyck's masterpieces are shown. Rubens' statue, too, the Stein Museum, and the Hotel de Ville are inspected in turn. Some busy streets are shown, the fact that Antwerp is populous and wealthy commented upon, and an idea of the population given by comparing it with that of the town or village in which the school is situated. Finally, a visit is paid to two or three factories in Antwerp, and its cottons and silks shown in process of manufacture.

It is quite obvious that from this lesson the most heedless pupil carries away the information that Antwerp is a large and improtant seaport; that it manufactures cotton and silk; that it is very old and has had a most interesting history; that it was the home of the great painter Rubens, and that it preserves in its Cathedral and in its Art Gallery many of his and of Van Dyck's most famous pictures. Nor is it likely that this information imparted in so striking and attractive a manner, will be easily forgotten.

Physiography, political geography, commercial geography, and history are all taught more or less in connection. I noticed in a rural school (a convent school at Aasche) an interesting device for teaching the productions and manufactures of Belgium. A specimen of the characteristic product or manufacture of each district or town was attached to the map of Belgium in the required locus. Thus at Brussels a scrap of lace was tacked on: at Antwerp a scrap of cotton; at Ghent a piece of linen; at Tournai a tiny patch of carpet; to the spot marking Liege pieces of coal, iron, and wool were attached; at Bruges there was a miniature brick; at Dinant a fragment of black marble. The maps in question are supplied by the school publishers, but any ingenious Irish teacher could easily make a similar one for himself. A patch of linen and a little model of a boat at Béal Feirste; a plough at Loch gCarmain; a bullock in Meath: and — a miniature porter-barrel at Baile Átha Cliath!

Maps and globes in relief — some of them very large and handsome — are seen in the bigger Belgian schools.

310

Education in the Gaeltacht

IRISH IN THE SCHOOLS*

Dear Sir,

Now that the air is rife with talk of reform in our primary school system, the trumpet call of Rev. Dr. O'Hickey comes with singular appropriateness. I am convinced that if we succeed in bringing home clearly to the Irish public (i) the present state of education in the Irish-speaking parts of Ireland; (ii) the two-fold demand put forward by the Gaelic League, the country will not be slow in making up its mind to support strenuously and whole-heartedly that demand. The second point has, I think, been made sufficiently clear by Dr. O'Hickey, and the object of this letter is to set forth as lucidly as may be a few concrete facts which will show the condition of affairs actually existing in the Irish-speaking area at the present moment. This is not a matter which demands fine writing or indignant declamation. Let us regard the facts of the case calmly, sanely. Naked facts speak with an eloquence more moving than the rhetoric of orators.

For the present I confine myself to those districts where Irish is the language of the children's homes. Let us take the case of the child who, on entering for the first time the door of a national school, knows only Irish. Irish is the language which he has imbibed with his mother's milk; Irish is the language of his home, of his companions, of his prayers, of his pastimes, the language in which he thinks and lives. From the very hour in which he enters the National School he is set to learn a foreign and unfamiliar speech; and worse still, he is set to learn this foreign and unfamiliar speech through the medium of itself — the unknown through the medium of the unknown.

To realise what this means let us take a parallel case. Suppose that I wish to learn French and that I have not, at present, the most elementary knowledge of that language. Suppose that I get a Frenchman, who knows no English and that we seat ourselves at a table. How long should I take to learn French? Should I ever succeed in mastering it? Pick up a few words,

---

* This letter to the press by Pearse was part of the campaign initiated by the Gaelic League in February 1900.

a few phrases, I might — a parrot could do that much — but as to mastering the language, as to assimilating its idioms, as to making it part and parcel of my intellectual being, as to learning to think in it, to read in it with intelligence, to write it — the feat would be impossible. Why? Because between me and the Frenchman there is no bond, no means by which we can communicate one with the other, no common medium through which he can impart his knowledge to me. This is exactly the condition of affairs in scores of schools in the north-west, west and south of Ireland at this moment. I have been in schools where the children did not understand one word the master uttered and the master did not understand one word the children uttered.

'But', it will be said, 'can any Board calling itself a Board of Education tolerate, much less sanction, such a system? So the Commissioners make no provision for purely Irish-speaking children?' Yes, the Commissioners do make a provision; they actually concede that, where a child fails to grasp the meaning of a lesson, the master — if he happens to be able — may explain the subject-matter in Irish. This permission, as officially interpreted, means nothing more than that the teacher is at liberty — always provided that he is able — to explain an English word or phrase by the corresponding Irish expression. Even this limited power is to a large extent a dead letter, as most of the teachers do not know Irish.

And, of this system, ignoring as it does the only language with which the child is familiar, or at least, the language with which he is most failiar, and which in the normal course of events should form the basis of his education, what as a matter of practical working are the results? It is found that either one or other of two things happens, according as the system is applied in an exlusively or almost exclusively, Irish-speaking district, or in a district already partially Anglicised. In the former case, whatever smattering of English and other subjects the child, parrot-like and by mere imitation, happens to acquire at school, is within a year or two after leaving school completely forgotten; it has been mere memory work, the reasoning faculties have not come into play at all, and hearing nothing but Irish in the home, the child soon forgets whatever little he has learned in school. In other words the net result is that he lapses into absolute illiteracy. I have seen in the West of Ireland young men and women, who after six years spent at a National School could neither read nor write, and did not know the meaning of the English word 'man'. I have met boys who could tell me that c-o-w spelt 'cow' that 'cow' was a common noun, third singular, feminine gender; but who were profoundly ignorant of what the word 'cow' meant, and, of course, had not the faintest conception of the signification of the terms 'noun', 'common', 'singular', 'feminine' or 'gender'. I remember on one occasion meeting in a remote district in Connacht a little fellow of twelve, who was absolutely the most intelligent child I have ever met. I happened to be collecting the names of wild flowers in Irish, and the boy went out of his way to show me all sorts of wild plants, telling me their names and properties with an ease and accuracy which to me was amazing. I asked him, out of curiosity, if he knew English. No, not a word. Had he ever been to school? Yes, for four years. How was it, then, that he had no English? 'He could never make out what the mistress used to be saying'. This is 'education' in the West of Ireland.

In the partially Anglicised districts the results of the National School system are even more appalling. There the product of the National Schools is that worst of human monstrosities — the being who has a smattering of

312

two languages, but knows neither sufficiently well to be able adequately to express himself in it. Surely it is not an exaggeration to say that the system which allows all of this is an abnormity — that the whole thing from top to bottom, is at once a colossal blunder and a colossal crime? The impression which an examination of it at close quarters leaves on the observer is that no other civilised country in the world would stand it for a single hour. Ireland has stood it for over half a century.

One other incident, and I have done. Some three or four years ago two Intermediate students, alumni of a certain well-known college in the West of Ireland, were passengers on the steamer which plies between Galway and Aran. They were discussing the difficulty of the Senior Grade Trigonometry paper which had been set at the late exam. Beside them sat a peasant lad who had no English and did not, of course, understand a word of the conversation. Suddenly he caught the word 'Trigonometry' and his face lit up. He asked one of the students, who happened to be Irish-speaking, what they were saying about Trigonometry. The case was explained to him, and having asked for the paper, he worked out all the problems with absolute accuracy. He had, it transpired learned the science during the winter evenings from an old Irish-speaking schoolmaster.

What does this incident show? It is not, perhaps, a very brilliant achievement to tackle successfully a Senior Grade Trigonometry paper. No, but the moral of the story is this: six years at a National School had failed to teach that boy English, whilst a few evenings by the fireside had given him a respectable knowledge of a difficult branch of mathematics, because he had been taught through the medium of the language he understood.

Educate on rational lines the mountaineers and glensmen and islemen of Irish-speaking Ireland and in these, even the children of the Pale will admit, that we have the bone and sinew — aye, and the brain —of Ireland; teach any other useful subject you choose through the medium of that language and watch the results. Perpetuate the present system, and you perpetuate illiteracy — and worse.

Let the people, the parents, the school managers of Ireland speak; let them fearlessly voice their demands through their representatives in Parliament, through their elective bodies, through the Press; let them take action, action determined, strenuous, persevering; above all let them move now — it is the psychological moment.

I am, dear sir, faithfully yours,
P. H. Pearse.

Sandymount,
Co. Dublin.
February 1900.

'EDUCATION' IN THE WEST OF IRELAND

I find myself on a long stretch of mountain road in remotest Iar-Chonnacht. I am in the heart of the lonely silent land in which the Gael maintains his last firm foothold. Anglicisation, as a living energetic fact, is at least a score of miles behind me. I should have to travel the distance, either to Galway or to Oughterard, to find a community whose daily speech is English. In the cabins which dot these brown hillsides, or which lie along the shores of these sheltered bays, Irish is the only language

313

known. The thought makes my journey pleasant. In the kindly Irish west I feel that I am in Ireland. To feel so in Dublin, where my work lies, sometimes requires a more rigorous effort of imagination than I am capable of.

But even in Iar-Chonnacht Anglicisation has its busy agents. A car approaches, driving rapidly to catch the Galway train at the roadside station ten miles off. As it passes me the driver, a country lad in báiníns, salutes me cheerily in Irish. The passenger, an important-looking person enveloped in a huge overcoat, salutes me neither in Irish nor in English. He favours me instead with a supercilious stare. In the west it is not customary for two strangers to pass on the road without exchanging greetings. But allowance must be made for the difference in status between the important-looking gentleman and myself. I am a mere member of the general public. He is an Official Personage. He is the representative of the English State. He stands for Civilisation. He incarnates Education. To be precise, he is an Inspector of 'National' Schools.

He is evidently returning from 'inspecting' the 'National' which lies half a mile ahead on the roadside. I marked it when I passed this way twelve months ago. I knew it to be a 'National' School by its ugliness. Moreover, as I cycled past, I heard the loud voice of a man talking in English. It is only inside 'National' Schools that one hears English in Iar-Chonnacht.

Scarcely has the car rattled by when in front of me on the road there arises a cheerful clamour. Plainly, the children let loose from school. The din grows nearer. I catch lively interchanges in Irish. 'Togha fir, a Sheaghain!' 'Do shlán fút, a Mháirtín!' 'Ara, a Chuilm, a dhiabhail, céard tá tú a dheanamh?' It sounds wondrously pleasant, this sudden and jocund uproar amongst the silent hills. There is still life and joy in Ireland. Even a spell of five hours a day in a 'National' School does not avail to still the song of youth in the heart of the child. 'Is breagh an rud an óige, agus is breaghtha 'na sin an tsaoirse!' says a recent Irish writer, recalling school days spent in this very region which I am traversing. So these boys feel now, though the thought may not shape itself into so many words. But there is a special reason for this sudden and vociferous outburst of Irish on the part of these liberated scholars. They have spent five hours in a 'National' School. This means, my Scottish Gaelic reader, that for five mortal hours they have been precluded from exchanging as much as a syllable with one another or with any one else in the only language they know. And why? Understand that they are being 'educated'. We have unique and wonderful 'educational' methods in the west of Ireland. One of them is to ignore the only language spoken by the pupils. Another is to pretend that there is no such place in the world as Ireland. A third is to inculcate that the English Government is Almighty Providence, and that America is an El Dorada in which gold is to be picked up in the streets. So our children, who enter school with an abundant store of pure and vivacious Irish, leave it 'educated' into ignoramuses who speak no language, who own no country, who have but one ambition in life — to shake the dust of Ireland off their feet as soon as they can; mere atrophied intelligences; countryless waifs; industrial inefficients carefully and labouriously manufactured under the aegis of the State and at the expense of Irish ratepayers.

But I digress. The merry group of school boys approachers. These are but in process of 'education'. Intelligence has not yet been 'educated' from their countenances, nor laughter from their hearts. That will come all too soon. In school, indeed, they are blocks, stones, clods. But here, with the mountain road beneath their bare feet and the mountain breeze blowing in their faces, they have hearts, they have intelligences, they have — as my ears tell me — voices. Facts which my genial friend the Inspector, who has spent some hours in vain endeavours to induce them to speak English, is doubtless far from suspecting.

The clamour is hushed into comparative decorum as the group draws near me. As each passes he salutes me shyly but pleasantly in Irish. Most of them know by sight the 'duine uasal' from Baile Átha Cliath who stayed in the village last year, who went boating with some of their fathers and elder brothers, and who so often made one of the fireside group at Conn...'s evening céilidh. So they have a merry nod and a smile for me, and give me voluble answers to my questions, which range from the state of the parish priest's health to the recent improvements in the handball court behind Pat ....'s shop.

The group passes on with renewed outburst of joyous clamour. A race is started, and they soon disappear over the brow of the hill in the road. As I approach the schoolhouse, I descry coming towards me a solitary straggler from the merry band — a small gasúr, in bare feet and báiníns like the rest. He comes along slowly, and as he draws near I perceive that he is crying bitterly. Now I recognise him as the little son of Máire ..... at the crossroads. He it was whom I took with me as my companion when I climbed Cnoc ..... last year. Naturally, I stop him to renew acquaintance, and to inquire the cause of his tears.

'Céard tá ort, a Sheagháinín?'

'Bhu-bhu-bhuail an máistir mé'

'O-o. Agus céard rinne tú as an mbealach?'

'L-labh-labhair mé Gaelhilge leis an "Inspecthor" '.

The child had been caned — cruelly caned, as I learned afterwards — because, in a moment of confusion, he had spoken Irish to the Inspector!

If these things happened in Poland or in Finland or in Alsace-Lorraine these islands would ring with denunciations. The British and the West British and — for aught I know — the North British press would report the facts under scare headings. We should hear of the 'Language War in Finland', or of the 'Reign of Terror in Polish Schools', or of 'German Aggression in Alsace-Lorraine'. But when Connacht is the theatre of tyranny the outside world hears nothing, for England controls the press agencies.

I want my Scottish Gaelic friends to realise the sterness of the fight which is being waged in Ireland. We have nearly 700,000 Irish speakers. Over one-third of the area of the country Irish is the language of the majority of the homes. We have wide districts west, and north-west, and south-west, in which for practical purposes Irish is the only language known. Yet the school system in these districts still, broadly speaking, ignores Irish as an instrument of education. In only thirteen schools in all Ireland has the Bilingual Programme, recently wrested from the Commissioners of 'National' Education, been officially sanctioned. Not one-sixth of the schools in the Irish-speaking area make a genuine effort to utilise the vernacular as a medium of instruction. There are still schools in purely Irish-speaking localities in which Irish has absolutely no place whatever on the school programme. There are still schools in which, whilst the pupils speak no English, the teachers speak no Irish — schools, that is to say, in which the instructor and the instructed have no means of communicating

315

one woth the other. There are still schools in which children are punished for speaking Irish — furtively, of course, for if the facts were made known it would, in the present state of public opinion, be rather awkward for the teacher and the manager. Finally, the general progress of Irish-speaking children is everywhere tested by inspectors who know no Irish, and permission to teach Irish as an 'extra' subject is conditional on a favourable report as to general progress from these incompetent and often hostile Inspectors!

Such is 'Education' in the West of Ireland!

Pádraic MacPiarais

P. H. Pearse

Editor of *An Claidheamh Soluis*.

St. Enda's 1908-1913

FROM THE PROSPECTUS OF SCOIL ÉANNA
1909

1908.

Purpose and Scope of School

St. Enda's School was founded last year with the object of providing an elementary and secondary education distinctively Irish in complexion, bilingual in method, and of a high modern type generally, for Irish Catholic boys. The programme of the School at once arrested attention, and, whether judged by the number of pupils who have come to it or by the satisfaction expressed by their parents with results of its system, St. Enda's has already achieved a remarkable success. In order to provide for the growth and expanding needs of the School, an important building scheme has been carried out during the summer vacation, including the erection of a spacious Study Hall, a new Refectory (to permit of the conversion of the existing Refectory into a Library), a Physico-Chemical and a Biological Laboratory, and a small Chapel. The School now stands fully equipped for the great educational work which lies before it.

Formation of Character

St. Enda's, apart from its distinctively Irish standpoint, has brought the experience of its founders to bear on an effort to extend the scope and improve the methods of secondary education in this country. The central purpose of the School is not so much the mere imparting of knowledge (and not at all the 'cramming' of boys with a view to success at examinations) as the formation of its pupils' characters, eliciting and development of the individual bents and traits of each, the kindling of their imaginations, the placing before them of a high standard of conduct and duty, in a word, the training up of those entrusted to its care to be strong and noble and useful men. While a wide and generous culture is aimed at, and classical studies are assigned a prominent place in the curriculum, the education provided by the School is on the whole 'modern' in type. The course enters at every point into relations with actual life and is framed with particular reference to the needs and conditions which prevail in our own country at the present day.

Religious Training

Since the function of education is to prepare for life, and since the most

317

important part of life is that which centres around the profession and practice of Religion, the first care of St. Enda's is to provide a proper religious and moral training for its pupils. The religious instruction is under the superintendence of a Chaplain approved by His Grace the Archbishop of Dublin. The Boarders attend daily Mass. The School opens and closes with prayer, and the Rosary is recited in the School Chapel every evening. A Guild of the Apostleship of Prayer and of the Arch-Confraternity of the Sacred Heart has been formed in the School in connection with the local Church of the Holy Name, Cullenswood. Pupils are prepared at the proper age for First Confession, First Holy Communion, and Confirmation.

Half-an-hour each day is devoted to the teaching of the Christian Doctrine, and a weekly Catechetical Instruction is given by the Chaplain. In addition to this formal doctrinal teaching, the School Staff constantly exerts itself to promote amongst the boys an active love and reverence for the Christian virtues, especially for the virtues of purity, temperance, fortitude, truth, and loving-kindness. A spirit of chivalry and self-sacrifice, gentleness towards the weak and courtesy and charity towards all, kindness towards animals and respect for their lives and well-being, as also a love of inanimate nature and of everything in the world that is fine and beautiful — these are amongst the virtues and sentiments which the teachers of St. Enda's most sedulously endeavour to implant in the hearts of their pupils. A manly self-reliance and a healthy ambition to plan and achieve are not only inculcated in theory but fostered in practice by the system of organisation and discipline which is adopted in the schoolroom and on the playground. The School Staff directs earnest efforts towards the awakening of a spirit of patriotism and the formation of a sense of civic and social duty.

Irish the Language of the School

In the general curriculum the first place is accorded to the Irish Language, which is taught as a spoken and literary tongue to every pupil. The teaching is by attractive modern methods. Object Lessons, Action Games, Pictures, Working Models, 'Images Animées', the Magic Lantern, and other devices of up-to-date Continental teachers being freely adopted. Irish is established as the official language of the School, and is, as far as possible, the ordinary medium of communication between teachers and pupils.

Direct Method Teaching of Modern Language

All Modern Language teaching is on the Direct Method. To boys who are Irish-speaking to start with, English is taught on the Direct Method; and to boys who are English-speaking to start with, Irish is taught on the Direct Method. Foreign languages other than English (French, German, Italian, and Spanish) are taught on the same attractive lines. Under this system it is hoped that every pupil who passes through St. Enda's will, at the end of his course, have obtained a good oral and literary knowledge of at least three modern languages. Latin is taught to all boys in the upper forms, and Greek and Old Irish to such as exhibit an aptitude for classical studies.

Bilingual Teaching of Other Subjects

All teaching other than language teaching is bilingual, — that is to say each subject is taught both in Irish and English. This applies to Christian Doctrine, History, Geography, Nature-study, Experimental Science,

318

(Chemistry and Physics), Mathematics (Arithmetic, Algebra, Euclid, and Trigonometry), Handwriting, Drawing, Manual Instruction, Hygiene and First Aid, Book-keeping, Shorthand, Typewriting, Elocution, Vocal and Instrumental Music, Dancing and Physical Drill.

Selection of Course

From the foregoing subjects a suitable course is selected for each pupil. In making this selection, not only the wishes of the parents or guardians, but also, to a certain extent, the wishes and inclinations of the pupil himself are carefully consulted. No pupil of St. Enda's is forced into a groove of study for which he evinces no special talent or native inclination. Where parents so desire pupils will this year be sent forward for the examination of the Intermediate Board, but in no instance will course or programme of the Board be allowed to interfere with the pursuit of the distinctive ideals of the school. The curriculum in the higher forms is co-ordinated with that of the Universities, and classes will be prepared this year for the Matriculation Examination of the National or of the Royal University (whichever hold a Matriculation Examination in 1910). Pupils are also prepared for the various professional preliminary examinations.

Younger Pupils

In the case of younger boys, the course is framed with a view to capturing their imaginations, quickening their powers of observation and reasoning, and giving them a pleasant interest in the world of life round about them. Their earliest instruction is purely oral, and is directed towards helping them to marshal their thoughts and to express themselves with intelligibility and accuracy. The formal study of literature as such is led up to by an attractive course of hero and fairy tales and of simple poetry. Similarly, the beginnings of a knowledge of physical science are made, not in the classroom or with the aid of books, but in the presence of nature itself by means of object lessons conducted in the School Garden or in the course of country walks.

History and Geography

The study of History, especially Irish History, forms an important part of the curriculum. European and general History is also dealt with, but from the first the pupils' attention is concentrated on their own land. The legends, literature, and history of Ireland are treated of in close association with the geography and physical features of the country. By 'Half-Holiday Lectures', illustrated by the Magic Lantern, alternating with excursions to spots of scenic, historic, or antiquarian interest, as well as by constant incidental teaching, it is sought to instil into the minds of the pupils an intimate and lively love of their fatherland. The History teaching thus merges into Geography teaching, and Geography again into Nature-Study. The School Garden, Orchard, and Playing Field, form an ample map on which geographical demonstrations of a very interesting kind are given. Globes, charts and maps in relief, and realistic models are used in the class work, and the Magic Lantern is called into requisition to help the pupils visualise the scenery and life of foreign countries. The geography of Ireland is thoroughly taught, and in this connection the industrial conditions and possibilities of the country are carefully dealt with.

319

Nature-Study and Physical Science

Nature-Study forms an essential part of the work at St. Enda's. The instruction, however, does not take the form of a mere dry-as-dust teaching of the rudiments of zoology, botany, and geology, but consists rather in an attempt to inspire a real interest in and love for beautiful living things. The study is commenced in the School Garden and is continued during frequently-organised outings to suitable spots within an easy radius of the School. Practical Gardening and Elementary Agriculture are taught as part of this scheme. Each pupil who so desires is allotted a plot of ground, which he is at liberty to plan out and cultivate according to his own taste, but under skilled direction. The new Biological Laboratory will give facilities for the prosecution of more advanced Nature-Study, and the new Physico-Chemical Laboratory completes the equipment of the School for the proper teaching of Experimental Science. Arrangements are being made by which pupils desirous of pursuing higher scientific studies can enjoy the advantages of a course in the Royal College of Science.

School Museum

In connection with this side of the programme there has been established a School Museum, containing zoological, botanical, and geological specimens, together with some illustrations of industrial processes and a few objects of historical and antiquarian interest. The pupils are encouraged to collect specimens for this Museum during their country rambles.

'Half-Holiday Lectures'

A feature of the school work is the series of weekly 'Half-Holiday Lectures' on Irish and general History. Literature, Art, Science, and so on, illustrated, where possible, by the Magic Lantern. These Lectures are sometimes given by members of the School Staff, and sometimes by distinguished outside specialists, of whom a number have promised their services for the coming year. Lectures in school are frequently replaced by visits to the city Museums, Art Galleries, and Zoological and Botanical Gardens, where demonstrations are given.

A Magazine under the title of *An Macaomh* has been established as a medium for the publication of work done in the School.

Physical Culture

Careful attention is devoted to Physical Culture. All the boys are taught Drill and the various exercises of the Gymnasium. The chief outdoor games are Hurling, Gaelic Football, and Handball. Irish Dancing forms a part of the ordinary curriculum. The boys are taught to prize bodily vigour, grace, and cleanliness, and the advantages of an active outdoor life are constantly insisted on. In the summer months as much as possible of the school work is done in the open air.

Chess is encouraged as an indoor game.

Music

Choral singing in Irish and English is taught to all pupils. Instrumental Music (Harp, Violin, Piano, or Pipes) and a special course in Solo Singing are taught on special terms.

Manual Training

Drawing is taught as part of the ordinary curriculum. Instruction in Modelling and in Practical Carpentry is given on special terms.

Commercial Course

A course in Shorthand, Typewriting, Book-keeping, and Commercial Arithmetic has been arranged to suit boys intended for a commercial career.

Association of Pupils with Administration

The organisation of the School embodies some new and improtant principles. With a view to encouraging a sense of responsibility amongst the boys, and establishing between them and the masters a bond of fellowship and *esprit de corps*, the pupils are as far as possible actively associated with the administration (though not with the teaching work) of the School. They are consulted with regard to any proposed departures in the curriculum or system of organisation, as to schemes of work or play. At the beginning of each school term they are asked to elect from their own ranks a School Captain, a Vice-Captain, a Secretary, a Librarian, a Keeper of the Museum, Captains of Hurling and Football, and a House Committee, their choice being limited merely by the condition that only boys of good conduct are eligible for office. An 'Éire Óg' Club, or juvenile Branch of the Gaelic League, was established in the School during the first term.

Prizes and Distinctions

Prizes and distinctions are awarded at the end of each school year on the basis, not of the results of an examination, but of the good conduct and progress in studies of the pupils during the year, of which a record is kept from day to day.

The Grounds

Cullenswood House is situated in the healthiest part of the southern suburbs of Dublin, in a neighbourhood which combines rural amenities with the advantages of close proximity to the city. The Clonskea, Palmerston Park, Dartry Road, Terenure, and Landsdowne Road to Kenilworth Road tram lines all pass within three minutes' walk of the gate. The Rathmines and Ranelagh Railway Station on the Dublin and South-Eastern line is within one minute's walk. The grounds, which command a delightful prospect of the Dublin Mountains, include a lawn, a flower garden with vinery and conservatories, a vegetable garden, an orchard, a playing-field, a handball court, and an open-air gymnasium.

The Schoolhouse

The house itself is large and the rooms spacious and airy. The boy's quarters comprise a study hall, five classrooms, physico-chemical and biological laboratories, a library, a chapel, a playroom, a gymnasium, a refectory, three dormitories, and an infirmary, together with bathrooms, lavatories, etc. A handsome new lavatory has been erected during the sumer recess. The sanitation is in perfect order and is fully certified.

The internal decoration and furnishing of the School have been carried out in accordance with a carefully-considered scheme of colouring and design. The object held in view has been the encouraging in the boys of a love of comely surroundings and the formation of their taste in art. In the classrooms beautiful pictures, statuary, and plants replace the charts and other paraphernalia of the ordinary schoolroom.

The equipment is up-to-date in every respect.

Domestic Arrangements

It is not proposed to allow the School at any time to grow as large as to make it impossible for individual care and attention to be devoted to each pupil. For the present and for some time to come the number of Boarders will not be permitted to exceed thirty, or the number of Day Boys eighty. The School will always maintain a private and homelike character. The resident pupils live rather under the conditions which prevail in a large family than under the somewhat harsh discipline of ordinary boarding-schools. An important point is that their domestic welfare is in charge of ladies, a fact which, in conjunction with its private character, renders the School specially suited for the education of sensitive or delicate boys.

Summer School in an Irish-Speaking District

In connection with St. Enda's there has been established a Summer Holiday School in an Irish-speaking district. It is housed in a cottage romantically situated on the shores of Lough Alooragh in South Connemara. Here a limited number of St. Enda's boys can be given an annual holiday in a purely Irish-speaking atmosphere and amid the finest scenery of the West. The terms may be had on application to the Head Master. Boys other than pupils of St. Enda's will be allowed to join the party under certain conditions. Application should be made befor June in each year.

BY WAY OF COMMENT
Cullenswood House, June 1909

An Macaomh, of which we hope to publish a number every Midsummer and another every Christmas, will record the fortunes of our adventure at Sgoil Éanna and supply us with the means of preserving in an accessible form the work, artistic and scholarly, done at the school. Its purpose will thus be wider than, and to some extent essentially different from, that of the ordinary school magazine. I mean not merely that it will be a genuine Review, educational and literary, rather than a glorified Prospectus, but that it will be a personal mouthpiece in a sense that is quite uncommon among kindred publications. It will form a vehicle for the expression of opinions which in their every detail are proper to myself, but in their general scope are fully shared in by all the friends associated with me in the work of Sgoil Éanna. We are not a religious community, but I do not think that any religious community can ever have been knit together by a truer oneness of purpose or by a finer comradeship than ours. It was the memory of this companionship in a year's pioneer work, very pleasant as I look back over it, that, I think, prompted the use of the word 'adventure', a moment ago, rather than any feeling that our work has partaken of the nature of an experiment or that we are entitled to figure as heroes as having set our hands to something very difficult or very dangerous.

Some of my friends have been looking forward to *An Macaomh* for my story of how Sgoil Éanna came to be. There is very little to tell. Various high and patriotic motives have been assigned to me in the press and

322

elsewhere. I am conscious of one motive only, namely a love of boys, of their ways, of their society; and a desire to help as many boys as possible to become good men. To me a boy is the most interesting of all living things, and I have for years found myself coveting the privilege of being in a position to mould, or help to mould, the lives of boys to noble ends. In my sphere as journalist and University teacher, no opportunity for the exercise of such a privilege existed; finally I decided to create my opportunity. I interested a few friends in the project of a school which should aim at the making of good men rather than of learned men, but of men truly learned rather than of persons qualified to pass examinations; and as my definition of a good man, as applied to an Irishman, includes the being a good Irishman (for you cannot make an Irish boy a good Englishman, or a good Frenchman), and as my definition of learning as applied to an Irishman, includes Irish learning as its basis and fundament, it followed that my school should be an Irish school in a sense not known or dreamt of in Ireland since the Flight of the Earls. This project, I say, appealed to two or three friends whose hearts were pat with mine; and Sgoil Éanna is the result.

I feel very grateful when I remember how fortunate I have been in all the things that are most important to the success of such an undertaking as mine. I have been fortunate in the site which accident threw in my way; I have been fortunate in the fellow-workers whom I have gathered about me; I have been fortunate in my first band of pupils, seventy boys the memory of whose friendship will remain fresh and fragrant in my mind, however many generations of their successors may tread the class-rooms of Sgoil Éanna.

And first, it is a pleasant thing to be housed in one of the noble old Georgian mansions of Dublin, with an old garden full of fruit trees under our windows, and a hedgerow of old elms, sycamores, and a playing field. Cullenswood House has memories of its own. A hundred years ago it was the landmark in the district where two centuries previously the Wood of Cullen still sheltered Irish rebels. That Wood is famous in Dublin annals, for it is under its trees that the Irish, come down from the mountains, annihilated the Bristol colonists of Dublin on Easter Monday, 1209; whence Easter Monday was known in Dublin as Black Monday, and fields on which our school-house looks down got their name of the Bloody Fields. A fresh colony came to Dublin from Bristol, and in 1316 the citizens took revenge for Black Monday by defeating a new ambuscade of the O'Tooles in Cullenswood. But all that is an old story. In 1833 Cullenswood House was bought from Charles Joly, the then proprietor, by John Lecky, grandfather of the historian. John Lecky was succeeded by his eldest son, John Hartpoole Lecky; and John Hartpoole Lecky's son, William Edward Hartpoole Lecky, was born at Cullenswood House on March 26th 1838. So our school-house has already a very worthy tradition of scholarship and devotion to Ireland; scholarship which even the most brilliant of our pupils will hardly emulate, devotion to Ireland, not indeed founded on so secure and right a basis as ours, but sincere, unwavering, lifelong.

It has been a pleasure, then, to work in Cullenswood House. It has been a greater pleasure to work with colleagues who are in the truest sense friends and comrades. And it is a still greater pleasure to be able to give the noble words 'colleague' and 'friend' and 'comrade', an extension which will include pupils as well as masters in its scope. I who, throughout the year, have often enough been critical and exacting may here once and for all, let myself go in praise. It is very likely that by driving a little harder, by packing a little closer, we could have compressed more information into our boys' heads than we have actually done; but I do not think that we could by any possible means, or with any possible school staff, have gained a more willing and intelligent co-operation or laid a sounder and more enduring basis for future work. I admit that our opportunities were unique. In no other school in Ireland can there be, in proportion to its size, so much of the stuff out of which men and nations are made. There is hardly a boy of all our seventy who does not come from a home which has traditions of work and sacrifice for Ireland, traditions of literary, scholarly or political service. If every boy in the Boy Corps of Eamhain Macha was the son of a hero, nearly every boy in the Boy Corps of Sgoil Éanna is the son or brother or nephew or cousin of some man or woman who is graving a mark in the history of contemporary Ireland. That in itself is a very splendid inspiration. It is much for a boy to start life with the conscious knowledge, 'I am the son of a good father'.

Again, we have here the advantage of a unique appeal. We must be worthy of our fame as the most Irish of Irish schools. We must be worthy of Ireland. We must be worthy of the men and women whose names we bear. We must be worthy of the tradition we seek to recreate and perpetuate in Éire, the knightly tradition of the macradh of Eamhain Macha, dead at the Ford, 'in the beauty of their boyhood', the high tradition of Cúchulainn, 'better is short life with honour than long life with dishonour', 'I care not though I were to live but one day and one night, if only my fame and my deeds live after me;' the noble tradition of the Fianna, 'we, the Fianna, never told a lie, falsehood was never imputed to us', 'strength in our hands, truth on our lips, and cleanness in our hearts'; the Christ-like tradition of Colm Cille, 'if I die, it shall be from the excess of the love I bear the Gael'. It seems to me that with this appeal it will be an easy thing to teach Irish boys to be brave and unselfish, truthful, and pure; I am certain that no other appeal will so stir their hearts or kindle their imaginations to heroic things.

The value of the national factor in education would appear to rest chiefly in this, that it addresses itself to the most generous side of the child's nature, urging him to live up to his finest self. I think that the true work of the teacher may be said to be to induce the child to realize himself at his best and worthiest, and if this be so the factor of nationality is of prime importance apart from any ulterior propagandist view the teacher may cherish. Even if I were not a Gaelic Leaguer, committed to the service of a cause, it would still be my duty, from the purely pedagogic point of view, to make my school as Irish as a school can possibly be made.

What I mean by an Irish school is a school that takes Ireland for granted. You need not praise the Irish language — simply speak it; you need not denounce English games — play Irish ones; you need not ignore foreign history, foreign literatures — deal with them from the Irish point of view. An Irish school need no more be a purely Irish-speaking school than an Irish nation need be a purely Irish-speaking nation; but an Irish school, like an Irish nation, must be permeated through and through by Irish culture, the repository of which is the Irish language. I do not think that a purely Irish-speaking school is a thing to be desired; at all events, a purely Irish-speaking secondary or higher school is a thing that is no longer possible. Secondary education in these days surely implies the adding of some new culture, that is, of some new language with its literature, to the culture enshrined in the mother tongue; and the proper teaching of a new language always involves a certain amount of bilingualism — unless, indeed, we are to be content with the construing from the new language into our own, a very poor accomplishment. The new language ought to become in some sense a second vernacular; so that it is not sufficient to speak it during the limited portion of the school-day that can be devoted to its teaching as a specific subject; it must be introduced during the ordinary work of the school as a teaching medium, side by side with the original vernacular. This argument justifies bilingualism as an educational resource, always and everywhere; but in Ireland, where there are already two living vernaculars, bilingualism is an educational necessity. Obviously, too, it is the one irresistible engine at the disposal of those who would restore Irish as a living medium of speech to the non-Irish-speaking three-fourths of the country.

Bilingualism in practice implies the teaching of the vernacular of the pupils; the teaching, in addition, of a second language and the gradual introduction of that second language as a medium of instruction in the ordinary curriculum, with the proviso, however, that any further languages taught be taught always on the direct method. This is the bilingualism I have been advocating in *An Claidheamh Soluis* for the past six years; this, is the bilingualism of Sgoil Éanna.

It must be remembered that bilingualism, as thus explained, requires, as indeed any sane teaching scheme must require, that the very earliest steps of a child's education be taken in the language of the child's home. In Connemara, and parts of Tirconnell and Mayo and Kerry and Waterford, that language is Irish; in Dublin it is English. When I was in Belgium I observed that most of the teachers delayed the introduction of the second language until the second school year was reached; at Sgoil Éanna we introduce it right on the first day, but in homeopathic doses, and so pleasantly presented as to appear always as a pastime to be enjoyed and never as a task to be learned. In the infant stage, little use can be made of the new language as a teaching medium; but as soon as the names of ordinary objects and qualities and the manner of predicating one thing to another have been learned, the bilingual principle comes into play.

To be concrete, at Sgoil Éanna, every child is taught Irish. Of thirty in the Infant's and Junior Division only one child uses Irish as a vernacular, so that English is necessarily the basis of the elementary instruction; but Irish has been taught even to the youngest mites since the first day the School opened, is used freely in the schoolroom, and is cautiously employed in giving Nature-Study, and Physical Drill. In the Senior School, the instruction throughout (with the exception of that in Higher Mathematics, and Mathematical Science, where English must necessarily predominate until we have Irish text-books and a recognized body of technical terms) is fully bilingual. That is to say, Irish, English and other modern languages are taught, each through the medium of itself; subjects other than modern languages are taught through the medium both of Irish and English. As regards procedure, occasionally a lesson is given in Irish only or in English only; but the rule is, whether the subject be Christian Doctrine or Algebra, Nature-Study or Latin, to teach the lesson first in Irish and then repeat it in English, or vice-versa. In such subjects as Dancing and Physical Drill English can practically be dispensed with. As a general medium of communication between masters and pupils in the schoolroom Irish is the more commonly used of the two vernaculars.

This system has been at work since September last. We have yet to

325

perfect it in many of its details, but it is not likely that we shall ever find it necessary to modify many of its principles. Already it has justified itself by its results. Boys who came to us on September 8th wholly ignorant that such a language existed, have now a good working command of Irish conversation, and can easily follow a lesson in Algebra or in Euclid conducted in Irish. At the same time I believe we have taught English and French (especially on the conversational side), Latin and Greek, Physical Science and Mathematics, at least as well as they are taught in any of the unilingual schools, while we have added a whole phase of work in History, Geography and Nature-Study, to which there is no parallel in the curriculum of any school in Ireland.

I mentioned at the commencement that our boys now number seventy. It has been very pleasant to watch the steady accessions to the little band of forty that mustered on the first morning. We started with four classrooms but had to add a fifth, a larger one than any except the main one, before the year was half-way through. Even the space thus secured is too small for our growing numbers. We have in hands a building scheme which includes the erection of an Aula Maxima for purposes of general assembly, of a Physical and Chemical Laboratory and of a new Refectory (for we propose to convert our present Refectory the fine old dining-room of Cullenswood House, into a library). We are also anxious to build a School Chapel, in order that we may have the great privilege of the presence of the Blessed Sacrament in our midst, and of daily Mass within our walls. How much of this scheme we shall be able to carry out before our boys return in September is a matter which is at present exercising my mind. Sometimes I wish that a millionaire would endow us with a princely foundation, and sometimes I feel that it is better to build up things slowly and toilsomely ourselves.

Our first attempt at the presentation of plays was at our St. Enda's Day celebration on March 20th, 21st, and 22nd last, when in the School Gymnasium, converted for the occasion into a beautiful little theatre, our boys performed *An Craoibhín's An Naomh ar Iarraidh* and Mr. Standish O'Grady's *The Coming of Fionn*. We had an audience of over a hundred each evening, our guests on the third evening including Sir John Rhys, Mr. Eoin MacNeill, Mr. W. B. Yeats, Mr. Stephen Gwynn, and Mr. Pádraig Colum. All these, especially Mr. Yeats, were very generous in their praise of our lads, who, I hope, will not be spoiled by the tributes they received from such distinguished men. The Press notices, too, were very kindly. *The Irish Independent* and the *London Sphere* published photographs. *The Freeman's Journal* dwelt on the beautiful speaking of the actors, which, it said, had none of the stiffness and crudeness usually characteristic of schoolboy elocution. Mr. D. P. Moran wrote in *The Leader:* 'There was a prologue to each piece, and both were excellently spoken. Dr. Hyde's little play, *An Naomh ar Iarraidh,* was well done, and particularly well staged. *The Coming of Fionn* was likewise a striking performance. We are not enamoured much of the cult of words on the stage, that has to fight for existence in the world, but words and their delivery are all important in school-plays. The players in *The Coming of Fionn* spoke their words excellently, and half the pleasure of a pleasant performance was the distinct and measured declamation. Indeed, we can write with enthusiasm — though some cynical people don't think we have any — of the plays at Sgoil Éanna. The stage and costumes emanated from the school, and the costumes were striking. . . . '. In the *Nation* Mr. W. P. Ryan wrote: 'The whole environment and atmosphere were delightful, but the human interest aroused by the boys is what remains kindliest in the memory. Boys as players are often awkward, ill at ease, and unnatural, as if they could not take kindly to the make-believe. The boys in the Sgoil Éanna plays for the most part were serenely and royally at home. An Craoibhin's delicate and tender little drama was delicately and tenderly interpreted; it had a religious sense and atmosphere about it, and the miracle seemed fitting and natural. In the *Coming of Fionn* one could easily lose sight of the fact that it was dramatic representation; the boys for a time were a part of the heroic antiquity; dressed in the way they were, and intense and interested as they were, one could picture them in Tara or Eamhain without much straining of the imagination. The heroic spirit had entered into their hearts and their minds, and one realized very early indeed that the evening's life and spirit were not something isolated, a phase and charm to be dropped when they reappeared in ordinary garb. The evening's sense was a natural continuation of that and many other evenings and days when the spirit of Fionn and his heroic comrades had been instilled into their minds by those for whom the noble old-time love had a vivid and ever-active and effective meaning. Fionn and Cúchulainn and their high-heroic kin had become part of the mental life of the teachers and the taught. With much modern culture they had imbibed things of dateless age, things that time had tested and found perennially human and alive.' And Mr. Pádraic Colum wrote in *Sinn Féin:* 'The performance of *An Naomh ar Iarraidh* gave one the impression that the play could never be better produced. It is out of the heart of childhood, and it has the child's tears, the child's faith, the child's revelation. In this performance there was a delight that must always be wanting in the great art of the theatre; the child actors brought in no conscious, no distracting personality. It was like the enacting of one of the religious songs of Connacht. It was Gaelic from the beautiful traditional hymn sung at the opening to the prayer that closes the play. Standish O'Grady's masque is really for the open air. The scene is nominally a hut, but the speeches and sentiments demand spaciousness; the plain with forest for a background. After childhood with its inner life, here was youth with its pride in conquest and deliverance. The language of *The Coming of Fionn* is noble, but it is not quite dramatic speech. In the production there was no professionalism, no elaborate illusion. It was one with all noble art, because it came out of a comradeship of interest and inspiration; the art was here not rootless, it came out of belief, work and aspiration.'

In the notes which I prefix to the programme of the plays I said that our plans included the enacting of a Pageant in the early summer and of a Miracle Play at Christmas. The early summer has come, and with it our Pageant. It deals with the Boy-Deeds of Cúchulainn, I have extracted the story and a great part of the dialogue from the Táin, merely modernising (but altering as little as possible) the magnificent phrases of the epic. I have kept close to the Táin even at the risk of missing what some people might call dramatic effect, but in this matter I have greater trust in the instinct of the unknown shapers of our epic than in the instinct of any modern. I claim for my version one merit which I claim also for my episode of the Boy-Deeds in the Táin, namely, that it does not contain a single unnecessary speech, a single unnecessary word. If Conall Cearnach and Laoghaire Buadhach are silent figures in our Pageant, it is because they stand silent in the tale of events as told by the Ulster exiles over the camp-fire of Meadhbh and Aileall. For Feargus I invent two or three short speeches, but the only

327

important departure (and these have a sufficiently obvious purpose) from the narrative of the Táin are in making Cúchulainn's demand for arms take place on the playgreen of Eamhain Macha rather than in Conchobar's sleeping-house, and in assigning to the Watchman the part played by Leabharcham in the epic. For everything else I have authority. Even the names of the boy-corps are not all fanciful, for around Follamhan, son of Conchobar (he who was to perish at the head of the macradh in the Ford of Slaughter) I group on the playground of Eamhain the sons of Uisneach, of Feargus, and of Conall Cearnach, boys who must have been Cúchulainn's contemporaries in the Boy-corps, though older than he. On how many of those radiant figures were dark fates to close in as the tragedy of Ulster unrolled!

The Chorus and the Song of the Sword have been set to music by Mr. MacDonnell, the latter to an arrangement of the well-known Smith song in the Petrie Collection, the former to an original air. I feel this music gives dignity to very common-place words. My friend Tadhg ÓDonnchadha has kindly checked over the verses in bad Rannaigheacht Bheag which I put into the mouths of the Chorus. Obligations of another sort I owe to my brother, who is responsible for the costumes grouping and general production of the Pageant, and to my nephew, Mr. Alfred McGloughlin, for help in the same and other directions. Mr. McGloughlin's name does not figure among the School Staff, but he might truly be called a member of the Staff without Portfolio. He is at our service whenever we want anything done which requires artistic insight and plastic dexterity of hand, be it the making of plans for an Aula Maxima or the construction of a chariot for Cúchulainn.

It may be wondered why we have undertaken the comparatively ambitious project of a Cúchulainn Pageant so early in our career so soon, too, after our St. Enda's Day Celebration. The reason is that we were anxious to crown our first year's work with something worthy and symbolic; anxious to send our boys home with the knightly image of Cúchulainn in their hearts, and his knightly words ringing in their ears. They will leave St. Enda's under the spell of the magic of their most beloved hero, the Macaomh who is, after all, the greatest figure in the epic of their country, indeed, as I think, the greatest in the epic of the world. Whether the Pageant will be an entire success I cannot venture to prophesy, but I feel sure, too, that Éamonn Bulfin will be duly beautiful and awful as Cathbhadh the Druid; that Denis Gwynn will be gallant and noble as Conchobar MacNeasa, Conchobar, young and gracious, as yet unstained by the blood of the children of Uisneach; and that Frank Dowling will realise, in face and figure and manner, my own high ideal of the child, Cúchulainn; that, 'small, dark, sad boy, comeliest of the boys of Éire', shy and modest in a boy's winning way, with a boy's aloofness and a boy's mystery, with a boy's grave earnestness broken ever and anon by a boy's irresponsible gaiety; a boy merely to all who looked upon him, and unsuspected for a hero save in his strange moments of exaltation, when the seven-fold splendours blazed in his eyes and the hero-light shone above his head.

BY WAY OF COMMENT
Cullenswood House, December 1909

During the past six or seven years I have grown so accustomed to having an organ at my disposal for the expression of my views and whims that I have come to look on an organ, as some men look on tobacco and others on motor cars and aeroplanes, as among the necessities of life. Use is a second nature, and the growing complexity of civilization adds daily to the list of indispensible things. I have a friend who wonders how I manage to exist without a Theatre of my own to 'potter about' (being a poet in his public capacity he relaxes by being slangy in conversation), and another who marvels that I find the running of a School more interesting than the running of a Palaestrina Choir. But Providence gives each of us his strength and his weakness, his wisdom and his folly, his likes and his wants as different, one's from the other's as the markings on the palms of our hands. I have never felt the need of tobacco or of an aeroplane (I am sure that both one and the other would make me dizzy), but I do find the possession of a School and of an organ necessary at once to my happiness and to my usefulness; a School for bringing me into contact with the wisdom of children, and an organ for the purpose of disseminating the glad and noble things I learn from that contact. Whether those to whom I preach will place the same value on my preaching as I do myself is another question: enough for me that my tidings are spoken, let the winds of the world blow them where they list.

It will thus be understood that it is a fortunate thing for me, if not for the public, that I founded *An Macaomh* before I descended from the bad eminence of the editorship of *An Claidheamh Soluis*. I have still my organ; and it is a luxury to feel that I can set down here any truth, however obvious, without being called a liar, any piece of wisdom, however sane, without being docketed a lunatic. *An Macaomh* is my own, to do as I please; and if through sheer obstinacy in saying in it what I think ought to be said, I run it against some obstruction and so wreck it, at least I shall enjoy something of the grim satisfaction which I suppose motorists experience in wrecking their thousand guinea Panhards through driving them as they think they ought to be driven.

A slight change in the sub-title of *An Macaomh* hints at a slight, a very slight, widening of its scope. The Review will remain identified with our adventure at Sgoil Éanna as long as the two endure, but I think it will become less and less of a school magazine (at least in the accepted sense) as time goes on. My hope is that it will come to be regarded as the rallying point for the thought and aspirations of all those who would bring back again in Ireland that Heroic Age which reserved its highest honour for the hero who had the most child-like heart, for the king who had the largest pity, and for the poet who visioned the truest image of beauty. I think I shall be able to give *An Macaomh* this significance without departing from my original intention of admitting to its pages the work only of those who are in some way associated with Sgoil Éanna. Nearly everyone whose name stands for high thought or achievement in any sphere of wholesome endeavour will in his turn address our boys in their Study Hall; and these addresses will find a place in *An Macaomh* along with the work of the masters and pupils. It may be that the most precious boon enjoyed by the boys of St. Enda's is the way they thus come in personal touch with the men and women who are thinking the highest thoughts and doing the highest deeds in Ireland today.

Philosophy is as old as the hills, and the science of today is only a new flowering of the science that made lovely the ancient cities and gardens of the East. With all our learning we are not yet as cultured as were the

Greeks who crowded to hear the plays of Sophocles; with all our art institutions we have not yet that love for the beautiful which burned in the heart of the middle ages. All the problems with which we strive were long ago solved by our ancestors, only their solutions have been forgotten. Take the problem of education, that is the problem of bringing up a child. We constantly speak and write as if a philosophy of education were first formulated in our own time. But all the wise peoples of old, faced and solved that problem for themselves, and most of their solutions were better than ours. Professor Culverwell thinks that the Jews gave it the best solution. For my part, I salute the old Irish. The philosophy of education is preached now, but it was practised by the founders of the Gaelic system two thousand years ago. Their very names for 'education' and 'teacher' and 'pupil' show that they had gripped the heart of the problem. The word for 'education' among the old Gaels was the same as the word for 'fostering'; the teacher was the 'fosterer' and the pupil was a 'foster-child'. Now to 'foster' is exactly the function of a teacher: not primarily to 'lead up', to 'guide', to 'conduct through a course of studies', and still less to 'indoctrinate' to 'inform', to 'prepare for exams', but primarily to 'foster' the elements of character already present. I put this in another way in the first number of *An Macaomh* when I wrote that the true work of the teacher may be said to be, to help the child to realize himself at his best and worthiest. One does not want to make each of one's pupils a replica of oneself (God forbid), holding the self-same opinions, prejudices, likes, illusions. Neither does one want to drill all one's pupils into so many regulation little soldiers or so many stodgy little citizens, though this is apparently the aim of some of the most cried-up of modern systems. In point of fact, man is not primarily a member of a State, but a human individuality — that is, a human soul imprisoned in a human body; a shivering human soul with its own awful problems, its own august destiny, lonelier in its house of clay than any prisoner in any Bastille in the world. The true teacher will recognise in each of his pupils an individual human soul, distinct and different from every other human soul that has ever been fashioned by God, miles and miles apart from the soul that is nearest and most akin to it, craving, indeed, comradship and sympathy and pity, needing also, it may be, discipline and guidance and a restraining hand, but imperiously demanding to be allowed to live its own life, to be allowed to bring itself to its own perfection; because for every soul there is a perfection meant for it alone, and which it alone is capable of attaining. So the primary office of the teacher is to 'foster' that of good which is native in the soul of his pupil, striving to bring its inborn excellence to ripeness rather than to implant in it excellences exotic to its nature. It comes to this, then, that the education of a child is greatly a matter, in the first place, of congenial environment and, next to this, of a wise and loving watchfulness whose chief appeal will be to the finest instincts of the child itself.

It is a long time since I was first attracted by the Gaelic plan of educating children. One of my oldest recollections is of a kindly grey-haired seanchaidhe, a woman of my mother's people, telling tales by the kitchen fireplace. She spoke more wisely and nobly of ancient heroic things than anyone else I have ever known. Her only object was to amuse me, yet she was the truest of all my teachers. One of her tales was of a king, the most famous king of his time in Ireland, who had gathered about him a number of boys, the children of his friends and kinsmen, whom he had organized into a little society, giving them a constitution and allowing them to make their own laws and elect their own leaders. The most renowned of the king's heroes were appointed to teach them chivalry, the most skilled of his men of art to teach them arts, the wisest of his druids to teach them philosophy. The king himself was one of their teachers, and so did he love their companionship that he devoted one-third of all the time he saved from affairs of state to teaching them or watching them at play; and if any stranger came to the dún during that time, even though he were a king's envoy demanding audience, there was but one answer to him: 'the king is with his foster-children'. This was my first glimpse of the Boy-Corps of Eamhain-Macha, and the picture has remained in my heart.

In truth, I think that the old Irish plan of education, as idealised for boys in the story of the Macradh of Eamhain and for girls in that of the Grianán of Lusga, was the wisest and most generous that the world has ever known. The bringing together of children in some pleasant place under the fosterage of some man famous among his people for his greatness of heart, for his wisdom, for his skill in some gracious craft — here we get the two things on which I lay most stress in education, the environment, and the stimulus of a personality which can address itself to the child's worthiest self. Then, the character of free government within certain limits, the right to make laws and maintain them, to elect and depose leaders — here was scope for the growth of individualities yet provision for maintaining the suzeranity of the common weal; the scrupulous co-relation of moral, intellectual, and physical training, the open-air life, the very type of the games which formed so large a part of their learning — all these things were designed with a largeness of view foreign to the little minds that devise our modern makeshifts for education. Lastly, the 'aite', fosterer, or teacher, had as colleagues in his work of fosterage no ordinary hirelings, but men whom their gifts of soul, or mind, or body, had lifted high above their contemporaries — the captains, the poets, the prophets of the people.

As the Boy-Corps of Eamhain stands out as the idealization of the system, Cúchulainn stands out as the idealization of the child fostered under the system. And thus Cúchulainn describes his fostering: 'Fionnchaomh nourished me at her breast; Feargus bore me on his knee; Conall was my companion-in-arms; Blai, the lord of the lands, was my hospitaller; fair-speeched Seancha trained me in just judgement; on the knee of Amhairgín the poet I learned poetry; Cathbhadh of the gentle face taught me druid lore; Conchobar kindled my boyish ambition. All the chariot-chiefs and kings and poets of Ulster have taken part in my bringing up'. Cúchulainn may never have lived, and there may never have been a Boy-Corps at Eamhain; but the picture endures as the Gael's idealization of the kind of environment and the kind of fostering which go to the making of a perfect hero. The result of it all, the simplicity and the strength of true heroism, is compressed into a single sentence put into the mouth of the hero by the old shaper of the tale of Cúchulainn's Phanton Chariot: 'I was a child with children; I was a man with men'.

Civilization has taken such a queer turn that it might not be easy to restore the old Irish plan of education in all its details. Our heroes and seers and scholars would not be so willing to add a Boy-Corps or a Grianán to their establishments as were their prototypes in Ireland from time immemorial till the fall of the Gaelic polity. I can imagine how blue Dr. Hyde, Mr. Yeats, and Mr. MacNeill would look if their friends informed them that they were about to send their children to be fostered. But, at least, we can bring the heroes and seers and scholars to the schools (as we

331

do at Sgoil Éanna) and get them to talk to the children; and we can rise up against the system which tolerates as teachers the rejected of all other professions, rather than demanding for so priest-like an office the highest souls and the noblest intellects of the race. I think, too, that the little child-republics I have described, with their own laws and their own leaders, their life face to face with nature, their care for the body as well as for the mind, their fostering of individualities yet never at the expense of the commonwealth, ought to be taken as models for all our modern schools. But I must not be misunderstood. In pleading for an attractive school-life, I do not plead for making school-life one long grand picnic: I have no sympathy with sentimentalists who hold that we should surround children with an artificial happiness, shutting out from their ken pain and sorrow and retribution and the world's law of unending strife; the key-note of the school-life I desiderate is effort on the part of the child itself, struggle, self-sacrifice, self-discipline, for by these only does the soul rise to perfection. I believe in gentleness, but not in softness. I would not place too heavy a burden on young shoulders, but I would see that no one, boy or man, shirk the burden he is strong enough to bear.

As for the progress of things at Sgoil Éanna, our Boy-Corps now numbers just a hundred, which is two thirds the muster of the Boy-Corps of Eamhain. When we reach Eamhain's thrice fifty I think we shall stop. I do not know that any man ought to make himself responsible for the education of multitudes of children; at any rate, to get to know a hundred and fifty boys as a master ought to know his pupils is a task that I feel sufficiently big for myself at present. The work is fascinating. One's life in a school is a perpetual adventure, an adventure among souls and minds; each child is a mystery, and if the plucking out of the heart of so many mysteries is frought with much in labour and anxiety, there are compensations richer than have ever rewarded any voyagers among treasure-islands in tropic seas.

In the Midsummer number of *An Macaomh* I threw out a modest hint to millionaires that Sgoil Éanna was in need of an endowment. I am afraid no millionaires read *An Macaomh*. Of the wealthy people who do read it none of them took my hint. I begin to fear that it is only poor men who are generous. Or perhaps, the explanation is that wealth and ideas do not consort. At any rate, except that one kind friend has undertaken to provide us with a School Chapel, we have been left the proud privilege of carrying out our new building scheme unaided. We have now our Study Hall, built to hold thrice fifty with room and verge to spare; our Art Room; our Physico-Chemical Laboratory; a new Refectory, the old Refectory having been converted into a Library (where we have already two thousand volumes); and a new Museum. I do not know that we need much else in the way of accommodation or equipment for teaching, except, perhaps, a special room for Manual Instruction. that will, doubtless, come in good time. We have a way of getting things done here, and are commencing to eliminate the word 'impossible' from our vocabulary.

The original Prospectus of Sgoil Éanna announced that where the parents so desired pupils of the School would be prepared for the examinations of the Board of Intermediate Education. Nevertheless, having no guarantee that we would receive any credit for our direct method teaching of languages or for our bilingual methods of instruction in other subjects, we decided last year with the concurrence of the parents of our boys, to hold aloof from the Intermediate. The establishment of a system of oral inspection by the Intermediate Board has brought about a new state of affairs which makes it possible for us to avail of the Board's grants, without sacrificing any of our principles. We have not converted the School into an Intermediate School pure and simple, but we are prepared to fulfil the announcement in our first Prospectus, that is to say, to send forward for the examinations of the Intermediate Board such boys as we think its programme suits, always pre-supposing the willingness of the parents. The only change in our method of working which this entails is that towards the end of the year we shall have to devote a few weeks to translating the prescribed language texts into English: for the rest, all our language teaching will be done on the direct method. Our classes in Physics and Chemistry have been placed under the inspection of the Department of Agriculture and Technical Instruction: here unfortunately, English must reign until Irish evolves a body of technical terms in these subjects. This cannot be done in a day or a year. As a preliminary we want Irish-speaking students to study Physical Science and then to write text-books. I would advise the Gaelic League to interest itself in the training of Irish speakers as Science Teachers. To an advertisement last year for a Science Master 'with a knowledge of Irish', I received no reply; to an advertisement making no stipulation with regard to Irish I received forty. The explanation is not far to seek. The fact that Irish does not form part of the essential basis of education in Ireland, not being essential for entrance to the Universities and hence not essential in the secondary schools, means of course that students who intend to specialize in Science neglect Irish as unnecessary to their purpose.

Nothing has given me greater pleasure during the past session than to watch Sgoil Éanna developing as it has been doing on the Athletic side. Our boys must now be amongst the best hurlers and footballers in Ireland. Wellington is credited with the dictum that the battle of Waterloo was won on the playing fields of Eton. I am certain that when it comes to a question of Ireland winning battles, her main reliance must be on her hurlers. To your camáns, O boys of Banba!

The first number of *An Macaomh* appeared on the eve of our Cúchulainn Pageant and the Distribution of Prizes. The Pageant was a large undertaking but we seem to have satisfied everyone except ourselves. We had over five hundred guests in our playing-field, including most of the people in Dublin who are interested in art and literature. I think the boyish freshness of our miniature Macradh, and especially the shy and comely grace of Frank Dowling as Cúchulainn, really pleased them. Mr. Colum wrote very generously of us in *Sinn Féin,* Mr. Ryan in the *Irish Nation,* and Mr. Bulfin in *An Claidheamh Soluis. The Freeman's Journal,* in addition to giving a special report, honoured us with a leading article from the pen of Mr. Stephen MacKenna.

Mr. MacNeill distributed the prizes, and he, Mr. Bulfin, and Dr. Henry addressed the boys and our guests. I have a grievance against the reporters for leaving before the speeches. They were only speeches at a school fete, but they contained things that were better worth recording than all the news that was in the newspapers the next day. I did not go beyond what I felt when, in tendering the speakers the thanks of the master and the boys, I said that our year's work would have been sufficiently rewarded if it had received no other recompense than the high and noble things Mr. MacNeill had just spoken in praise of it.

Our plays this year will take place somewhere between St. Brigid's Day and the beginning of Lent. They will consist of a Heroic Play in English and a Miracle Play in Irish. Mr. Colum is writing the English Play for us: its subject is the doom of Conaire Mór at Bruidhean Da Dearga. The Miracle Play will probably be the dramatized version of *Íosgán* which I print in this number of *An Macaomh*.

In writing the Cúchulainn Pageant I religiously followed the phraseology of the Táin. *Íosagán* I have as religiously followed the phraseology of the children and old men in Iar-Connacht from whom I have learned the Irish I speak. I have put no word, no speech, into the mouths of my little boys which the real little boys of the parish I have in mind — boys whom I know as well as my pupils at Sgoil Éanna — would not use in the same circumstances. I have given their daily conversation, anglicisms, 'vulgarisms', and all: if I gave anything else my picture would be a false one.

The story which I now dramatize has been described by an able but eccentric critic as a 'standard of revolt'. It was meant as a standard of revolt, but my critic must pardon me if I say that the standard is not the standard of impressionism. It is the standard of definite art form as opposed to the folk form. I may or may not be a good standard bearer, but at any rate the standard is raised and the writers of Irish are flocking to it.

Íosagán is not a play for the ordinary theatres or for the ordinary players. It requires a certain atmosphere, and a certain attitude of mind on the part of the actors. It has in fact been written for performance in a particular place and by particular players. I know that in that place and by those players it will be treated with the reverence due to a prayer. In bringing the Child Jesus into the midst of a group of boys disputing about their games, or to the knee of an old man who sings nursery rhymes to children, I am imagining nothing improbable, nothing outside the bounds of the everyday experience of innocent little children and reverent-minded old men and women. I know a priest who believes that he was summoned to the death-bed of a parishioner by Our Lord in person; and there are many hundreds of people in the countryside I write of who know that on certain nights Mary and her Child walk through the villages and if the cottage doors be left open, enter and sit awhile in the firesides of the poor.

BY WAY OF COMMENT
The Hermitage, Rathfarnham, Christmas 1910.

When I sent the last number of *An Macaomh* from Cullenswood House I had no more idea that within twelve months I should be sending out this number from a slope of the Dublin mountains than that I should be sending it from the plains of Timbuctoo. Yet very soon afterwards I had convinced myself that the work I had planned to do for my pupils was impossible of accomplishment at Cullenswood. We were, so to speak, too much in the Suburban Groove. The city was too near; the hills too far. The house itself, beautiful and roomy though it was, was not large enough for our swelling numbers. The playfield, though our boys had trained themselves there to be the cleverest hurlers in Dublin, gave no scope for that outdoor life, that intercourse with the wild things of the woods and the wastes (the only things in Ireland that know what Freedom is), that daily adventure face to face with elemental Life and Force, with its moral discipline, with its physical hardening, which ought to play so large a part in the education of

334

a boy. Remember that our ideal was the playgreen of Eamhain, where the most gracious of all education systems had its finest expression. In a word, St. Enda's had the highest aim in education of any school in Ireland: it must have the worthiest home.

To these considerations was soon added another. The parents of some of my boys were pressing me to establish a similar school for girls. I had hoped that this burden would be taken up by someone else; but, though many were eager to join us, no one seemed quite sufficiently detached from the claims of other service to become the standard bearer of this new adventure. Then it came to me, with the clearness of a call to action, that by taking one very bold step I could at once achieve a more noble future for St. Enda's, and make it possible for a sister-school to come into being, with similar potentialities of growth. If I could transplant St. Enda's to some wide and beautiful place among or near the hills, Cullenswood House (which was fortunately my property) would naturally become the cradle of a girls' school, even as it had cradled St. Enda's. Here was a great possibility. All those interested in my work agreed as to its desirability. I have constantly found that to desire is to hope, to hope is to believe, and to believe is to accomplish. I wrote to some friends, poor but generous people who had helped me in other causes; I consulted those of the parents of my boys whom it was my privilege to know personally; a sufficient number of those thus appealed to shared my desire transmuted, through hope, to faith; and our faith has found its inevitable fruition in accomplishment. St. Enda's has now as noble a home as any other school in Ireland can have had either in old time or new; and Cullenswood House shelters its sister school of St. Ita's. Thus the adventure of three years ago is seen to have been a forerunner of a new order; and *An Macaomh*, hitherto the organ of a school, becomes in some sense the organ of a movement.

The permanence of that order is not yet guaranteed; the issue of that movement I do not see. Wise men have told me that I ought never to set my foot on a path unless I can see clearly whither it will lead me. But that philosophy would condemn most of us to stand still till we rot. Surely one can do no more than assure oneself that each step one takes is right: and as to the rightness of a step one is fortunately answerable only to one's conscience and not to the wise men of the counting-houses. The street will pass judgement on our enterprises according as they have 'succeeded' or 'failed'; but if one can feel that one has striven faithfully to do a right thing does not one stand ultimately justified, no matter what the issue of one's attempt, no matter what the sentence of the street?

In most of the enterprises of life a fund is a more valuable asset than a sum in Consols. Many years ago I knew a parish priest who wanted to build a church. He went to his bank for a loan. When asked by the bank manager what security he had to offer, he made the simple and natural reply: 'St. Joseph will see you paid'. 'St. Joseph is an estimable saint', said the bank manager, 'but unfortunately he is not a negotiable security'. The mot passed into a proverb among the commercial folk of Dublin, and the bank manager gained the reputation of a wit. Both bank manager and priest have since gone down to dusty death; but the priest's dying eyes saw his church walls rising slowly, and today the church stands, grave and beautiful, in the midst of the people. The laugh, to speak without irreverence, is on the side of St. Joseph. So does the spiritual always triumph over the actual (for the spiritual, being the true actual, is stronger than the forms and bulks we call actual), and a simple man's faith is found more potent than a negotiable instrument. If sometimes this does not seem to hold, it is because of some wavering on the part of those who profess the faith, some shrinking from an ultimate heroism, some coming home to them of an old and forgotten sin. That is why in the history of the world the tales of its lost causes move us most and teach us best. Each of our own souls has its own unwritten annals of causes lost and won. Some of us might fight our silent interior battles more stubbornly if we realized that the issue of each one of them has a bearing on the issue of every battle that shall ever again be fought for all eternity. The causes, earthly and divine, which we champion suffer from every defeat that Right has ever undergone in the fortresses of our hearts. Lonely as each soul is in its barred house, it is part of a universal conscription, and its every disgrace brings dishonour on the flag. It can best be true to its causes, and to the great cause, by being true to its finest self.

So much depends on what we only half know and on what we know not at all in ourselves and in those about us, that no man can be certain how his schemes will eventuate. But be sure that if we do manfully the thing that seems right to us we must in the long run rise to some achievement. It may not be the achievement we dreamt of; it may, to the world, and even to ourselves, wear the aspect of a failure. But the world is not our judge, and a weary and disappointed spirit is often unjust to itself. My friends and I hope and believe that we have founded in Sgoil Éanna and Sgoil Íde two noble schools which for many years to come will send out Irish boys and girls filled with that heroic spirit which in old days gave Macha strength to run her race and prompted Enda to leave a king's house for the desolation of Aran, and which in the days of our great-grandfathers sent Emmet with a smiling face to the gibbet in Thomas Street, and nerved Anne Devlin to bare her back to the scourges of Sirr's soldiery. A new heroic age in Ireland may be a visionary's dream, or it may come about in some other way than that which we have planned; our schools may pass away or degenerate: but at least this attempt has been made, this right thing has been striven after, and there will be something to the good somewhere if it be only a memory and a resolve in the heart of one of the least of our pupils.

I am not sure whether it is symptomatic of some development within me, or is merely a passing phase, or comes naturally from the associations that cling about these old stones and trees, that, whereas at Cullenswood House I spoke oftenest to our boys of Cúchulainn and his compeers of the Gaelic prime, I have been speaking to them oftenest here of Robert Emmet and the heroes of the last stand. Cúchulainn was our greatest inspiration at Cullenswood; Robert Emmet has been our greatest inspiration here. In truth, it was the spirit of Emmet that led me to these hillsides. I had been reading Mr. Gwynn's book, and I came out to Rathfarnham in the wake of Emmet, tracing him from Marshalsea Lane to Harold's Cross, from Harold's Cross to Butterfield House, from Butterfield House to the Priory and the Hermitage. In Butterfield Lane, the house where he lived and where Anne Devlin kept her vigil stands; the fields that were Brian Devlin's dairy farm are still green. At the Priory John Philpot Curran entertained and talked, and there Emmet came and raised grave pleading eyes to Sarah Curran. Across the way, at the Hermitage, Edward Hudson had made himself a beautiful home, adding a portico and new wing to the solemn old granite house that is now Sgoil Éanna, and dotting his woods and fields with the picturesque bridges and arches and grottoes on which eighteenth century proprietors spent the money that their descendants (if they had it) would spend on motorcars. The Hudsons and the Currans were friends; and, so the legend runs, Emmet and Sarah met oftener at the Hermitage than at the Priory, for they feared the terrible eye of Curran. Old people point out the places where they walked and sat: the path that runs through our wood to the left of the avenue is known as Emmet's Walk, and the pseudo-military building occupied as one of our lodges is called Emmet's Fort. A monument in the wood, beyond the little lake, is said to mark the spot where a horse of Sarah Curran's was killed and is buried. I have not troubled to verify these minute traditions; I doubt if they are capable of verification. The main story is true enough. We know that Emmet walked under these trees (some of them were already old when with bent head he passed beneath their branches up the walk, tapping the ground with his cane as was his wont); he must often have sat in this room where I now sit, and, lifting his eyes, have seen that mountain as I see it now (it is Kilmashogue, amid whose bracken he was to crouch the night the soldiers were in Butterfield House), bathed in a purple haze as a yellow wintry sun sets, while Tibraddon has grown dark behind it. I do not think that a house could have a richer memory to treasure, or a school a finer inspiration, than that of that quiet figure with its eyes on Kilmashogue.

Edward Hudson's son, William Elliot Hudson, was born in this house on August 11th 1796. He lived to be the friend of Davis and Duffy, and whenever any good cause they had at heart was endangered for want of funds, Hudson's purse was always open. The Celtic and Ossianic Societies found him an unwearying patron. He died in 1857, having a few months before his death endowed the Royal Irish Academy with the fund for the publication of its still unfinished Irish Dictionary. He also left the Academy his library. If ever we have money to spare we will place a bust of that good man in one of our halls (the Academy has, I think, a marble bust of him by Christopher Moore). It is a strange and symbolic thing that the house in which William Hudson was born should after a hundred and fourteen years become the locus of such an endeavour as ours, and that his father's grottoes and woodland cells, though they never (as Hudson seemed to have hoped posterity might believe) resounded to chant of monk or voice of Mass-bell, should re-echo the Irish war-cries of eighty militant young Gaels who find them admirably adapted for defence in the absence of cannon. Edward Hudson in the eighteenth century had his eyes on the sixth century, but he was building for us in the twentieth. His quarrying had ends he did not foresee, and his piled stones have at last their destined use.

One of the Hudsons married James Henthorne Todd, whose place is the next to ours on the Dublin side. On the other side of us stretches Marley, through which our stream comes from Glensouthwell and the Hills. 'Buck' Whaley's more modest mansion is beyond the Priory. They were noble homes, those eighteenth-century mansions of County Dublin. An aroma as of high courtesy and rich living, sometimes passing into the riotous, still adheres to them. The Bossi mantle-pieces, the great spaces of hall, the old gardens, with their fountains and sun-dials, carefully walled in from the wilderness, all this has a certain homely stateliness, a certain artificiality if you will, not very Irish, yet expressive of a very definite phase in Irish, or Anglo-Irish, history. In such mansions as these lived those who ruled Ireland; in such mansions as these lived those who sold Ireland.

A prayer for Edward Hudson who made this home for us. A prayer for him for the spaciousness of soul which, while he was sufficiently the creature of his day to wall his inner gardens with walls as straight and square as every eighteenth-century formalist loved, prompted him to fling his outer walls now near, now far, up hill and down dale, so as to include within their verge not only the long straggling wood, and the four wide fields, but a winding strip of mountain glen with rushing stream at its bottom. Perhaps I ought to say that I am not really sure that it was Hudson who built these walls: indeed walls were here half a century before his time; but there is a fashion at Sgoil Éanna of attributing everything ancient and modern to Edward Hudson who has become a sort of local equivalent to the Roman guide's Michaelangelo. ''Tis wonderful the life a bit of water gives to a place', said my predecessor's gardener when conducting me on my first tour over the Hermitage. The stream makes three leaps within our grounds, and over each cascade thus formed a bridge has been thrown. When the river is in spate, as now, I hear the roar of the nearest cascade, a quarter of a mile off at night from my bedroom. It reminds me of the life out there in the woods, in the grass, in the river. And in truth I don't think more of wild life can be crowded into fifty acres anywhere else so near Dublin. It is not merely that the familiar birds of Irish woods and gardens seem to swarm here in numbers that I do not remember to have seen paralleled elsewhere, but that the shyer creatures of the mountains, and hidden places abide with us or come down often to visit us, as if they felt at home here. With a smothered cry a partridge or a snipe will sometimes rise from your feet in the wood; when you come through the fields on some wild place of the stream you will not seldom surprise a heron rising on slow wings and drifting lazily away; often a coot will splash in the water. But the glory of our stream is its kingfishers. You catch athwart the current, between the steep wooded banks, a quiver of blue, a blue strange and exotic amid the sober greys and browns; then another and another, sometimes as many as five at a time, like so many quivering blue flames. We are all under geasa to cherish the rare, beautiful creature that has made our stream its home. There are fiercer and stronger fishers that haunt the stream too. Once or twice I have seen the little eager form of an otter gliding behind the sallies where the stream cuts deep. I think it is partly to that freebooter we owe it that the trout are not as numerous now as they were of yore. Yet we will not intervene between him and the fish; let them fight on their old war, instinct against instinct. Sometimes rabbits come out and gambol under the trees in the evening; and they are happy, in the foolish way of rabbits, till one of the river rats wants his supper. So day and night there is red murder in the greenwood and in every greenwood in the world. It is murder and death that make possible the terrible thing we call physical life. Life springs from death, life lives on death. Why do we loathe worms and vultures? We all batten on dead things, even as they do, only we, like most of our fellow creatures, kill on purpose to eat, whereas they eat what has been killed without reference to them. All of which would be very terrible were death really an evil thing . . . The otter and the river rats had made me forget the gentle squirrels. They share our trees with the birds, and try in vain to teach them (and us) their providence. A flying hurley ball has no terror for them, and sometimes they disport in the chestnut tree in the playfield even while a hurling match is in progress. They have a distant outpost beyond the walls. Often I see one running across the road from the Priory woods to ours. Long may their little colony flourish.

If our boys observe their fellow-citizens of the grass and woods and water as wisely and lovingly as they should, I think they will learn much. That was one of my hopes in bringing them here from the suburbs. Every education must be said to fail which does not bring to the child two things, an inspiration and a certain hardening. Inspiration will come from the hero-stories of the world and especially of his own people; from the associations of the school place; from the humanity and great-heartedness of the teacher; from religion, humbly and reverently taught, humbly and reverently accepted, if it be really a spiritual inspiration schools fulfil well the first part of their task. But they have more to do than this.

No dream is more foolish than the dream of some sentimentalists that the reign of force is past, or passing; that the world's ancient law of unending strife has been repealed; that henceforward the first duty of every man is to be dapper. If I say that it is still the first duty of every man to be good, I shall be accused of being trite; but I am not more sure of the rightness of this than I am that it is the second duty of every man to be strong. We want again the starkness of the antique world. There will be battles, silent and terrible, or loud and catastrophic, while the earth and heavens last; and woe to him who flinches when his enemy compasses him about, for to him alone damnation is due. If this is true, it is of the uttermost importance that we should train every child to be an efficient soldier, efficient to fight, when need is, his own, his people's, and the world's battles, spiritual and temporal. And the old Ossianic definition of efficiency holds good: 'Strength in our hands, truth on our lips, and cleanness in our hearts'.

'Strength in our hands'. Our boys at Sgoil Éanna (and our girls at Sgoil Íde) have been seeking and gaining strength in their hands and all that strength of hand connotes for the Ossianic story teller meant the phrase to cover much, in many places and by divers ways, chiefly on their playing-fields and by wielding their camáns. My salient recollection of last year will always be of a sunny hurling field and the rush of our players up it; of the admiration of the onlookers to see such light boyish figures, looking whiter and slighter in their white jerseys and knickers than they really were, pitted against young men, yet, going into the field so nonchalantly; of the deep cheer often repeated as their opponents piled up points; of Maurice Fraher, grand in defence, rallying a losing field; of the battlecry 'Sgoil Éanna' ringing out in clear boyish voices as Éamonn Bulfin received the ball from Vincent through Fred O'Doherty; of breathless suspense at a passage of miraculous passing between Éamonn Bulfin, Brendan O'Toole and Frank Burke, back and forward, forward and back, all the world wondering; of Jerome Cronin standing ready, a slight figure, collected and watchful; of Burke, daring as Cúchulainn (whom he resembles in his size and in his darkness) outwitting or prostrating some towering full-back; of a quick pass to Jerome Cronin, Jerome's lightning leap, his swift swinging stroke, and the ball singing into the goal as the heavens rang to the shout of 'Sgoil Éanna'! Some such rally as this (it was like Cúchulainn's battle-fury when Laegh reviled him) brought us absolute victory or changed rout into honourable defeat on many a hurling and football field last year. We fought our way through the season, winning the leadership and medals in the Juvenile Hurling League, and losing them in Minor Hurling and Football only in the finals.

This year we have called into existence (or rather Dr. Doody has called into existence on our behalf) a Leinster Inter-College Championship in Hurling and Football, which will further stimulate Sgoil Éanna to excel at its chosen games. And I am seeing to it that all our lads learn to shoot, to fence, to march, to box, to wrestle, and to swim. I hope that the other schools and colleges will follow us here, too. Every day I feel more certain that the hardening of her boys and young men is the work of the moment for Ireland.

The National University is at work, and Irish is part of its essential basis of work. The banner of Sgoil Éanna has been carried proudly into it by Denis Gwynn. At the examination in October for Entrance Scholarships at University College, Dublin, he won the first of the Classical Scholarships (£50), fighting, like our hurlers, a boy against men. His subjects were Greek, Latin, and Irish. This, of course, is the highest academic distinction open to any pupil of a secondary school in Ireland. We may do memorable things in the years that are to come, but nothing more memorable, nothing more gallant, than the achievement of Denis Gwynn's in the first year of the National University. Frank Connolly, Joseph Fegan, and William Bradley have also matriculated, so that something of our soldier spirit will soon be surging through Irish student-life outside these walls.

We sent forward some of our boys for the Intermediate last year, deviating from our maxims so far as to devote some weeks towards the end of the year to translating Irish and French texts into English. In the issue, John Dowling won an Exhibition in the Modern Literary Course of the Junior Grade, qualified for a prize in the Science Course, and won a Composition Prize in Irish. If we had concentrated on Intermediate work and adopted Intermediate methods I have no doubt we should have done even better. But we have not concentrated on Intermediate work, and have no intention of doing so; and as for methods, it is for the Intermediate Board to adopt ours, not for us to adopt theirs. In this coming year we shall use the Intermediate even more sparingly, convinced that our boys will be the gainers.

If we had been believers in luck we should never have left Cullenswood House, seeing that we achieved there last year the highest academic distinction and also the highest athletic distinction achievable by a secondary school in Ireland. Whatever tradition of success clings around the place our boys magnanimously bequeath to their sisters and little brothers who now sit in their old classrooms and play in their old field. Of these newcomers in Cullenswood House, little can be written here, for they have yet their history to make. When I go to see them I find them full of the eagerness to attempt something, to accomplish something, if need be to suffer something. I think that is the right spirit in which to begin the making of history.

It seems a far cry now back to our plays of February last, on the little stage at Cullenswood House, and their subsequent performance in the Abbey Theatre. Mr. Colum's dramatization of one of the high tragedies of the Gael, *The Destruction of Da Derga's Hostel,* was in the mood of great antique art, the mood of Egyptian sculpture and dán díreach verse, solemn, uplifting, serenely sad like the vigil of those high ones who watch with pitying but unrelenting eyes the awful dooms and dolours of men. The other play, my dramatization of my own *Íosagán* owed whatever beauty it had, a beauty altogether of interpretation, to the young actors who played it; and they did bring into it something of the beauty of their own fresh lives, the beauty of childhood, the beauty of boyhood. I fear that we shall find it difficult in the future to achieve anything finer in acting than was achieved by Sorley MacGarvey, Éamonn Bulfin, Desmond Ryan, and Denis Gwynn, in *The Destruction of the Hostel* and by Patrick Conroy and the whole group of children in *Íosagán.* And an almost higher achievement was the vast solemnity, the remote mysteriousness put into the chant of the Three Red Pipers by Fred O'Doherty, John Dowling and Milo MacGarry. We performed the plays three times in our theatre during February. In April we repeated them at the Abbey with Dr. Hyde's *An Naomh ar Iarraidh* and Mr. O'Grady's *The Coming of Fionn.*

We brought the year to a close by going down to Cúchulainn's country and performing the Cúchulainn Pageant at the Castlebellingham Feis. I think that was the most spacious day in all our two years since we had come together to Sgoil Éanna. I shall remember long the march of the boys round the field in their heroic gear, with their spears, their swords, their hounds, their horses; the sun shining on comely fair heads and straight sturdy bare limbs; the buoyant sense of youth and life and strength that were there, There was another march with our pipers and banners to the station; and then a march home through the lamplit streets of Dublin. It was our last march to the old Sgoil Éanna. We have a larger school now, in a worthier place; but the old place and faces in that march (for some who marched that night have never since answered a rally of Sgoil Éanna and never will again as schoolboys) are often in my mind; and sometimes I wonder whether, if ever I need them for any great service, they will rally, as many of them have promised to do, from wherever they may be, holding faith to the inspiration and the tradition I have tried to give them.

BY WAY OF COMMENT
The Hermitage, Rathfarnham, May 1913

I have roused this *Macaomh* of mine again, having allowed him to slumber for two years. Like those panoplied kings that are said to sleep in Aileach, he has only been awaiting a call. I send him out now to publish tidings of sundry pageantries, pomps, and junketings: festivities to which my friends and I are inviting the men of Ireland, not altogether out of the largeness of our hearts, but with ulterior motives appertaining to the weal of a certain College. I send him out too in order that with his hero's voice he may utter three shouts on a hill in celebration of the completion of the fifth year of a certain gallant adventure.

To be plain, St. Enda's College has now been at work for five years, and we propose to commemorate the achievement of the lustrum by making a very determined effort to reduce the wholly preposterous debt which we incurred in our early months for buildings. There are some adventures so perilous that no one would ever go into them except with the gay laughing irresponsibility of a boy; they are not to be 'scanned' beforehand; one does one's deed without thinking, as a boy on the playfield strikes for goal. and whether one wins or fails, one laughs. It is really the only thing to do. Such an adventure, I think, has been St. Enda's and such the spirit in which we have gone into it. Not that we have not had a very serious purpose and a very high conception of our duty, but that we have found these things compatible with hearts as merry as the hearts of the saints; or rather supportable only by a hilarity as of heaven. Such burdens as we undertook five years ago would assuredly have crushed us if we had been wordlings, persons oppressed with bank balances and anxious about the rise and fall of stocks or the starting prices of racehorses. Fortunately the cares of competency have never existed for us, hermits of a happy hermitage. Having no little things to be troubled about, we have been able to busy ourselves with great adventures. Yet, we are worldly enough to desire to lighten our burdens, and generous enough to admit others to a share in our perils. Whence these excursions and alarums of ours at the Abbey Theatre, at Jones's Road, and elsewhere: it is our way of helping others to achieve sanctity.

It has been sung of the Gael that his fighting is always merry and his feasting always sad. Several recent books by foreigners have recorded the impression of Ireland as a sad, an unutterably sad country, because their writers have seen the Gael chiefly at his festivals: at the Oireachtas, at a race meeting, at a political dinner addressed by Mr. John Dillon. And it is a true impression, for the exhilaration of fighting has gone out of Ireland, and for the past decade most of us have been as Fionn was after his battles — 'in heaviness of depression and horror of self-questioning'. Here at St. Enda's we have tried to keep before us the image of Fionn during his battles — careless and laughing, with that gesture of the head, that gallant smiling gesture, which has been an eternal gesture in Irish History; it was most memorably made by Emmet when he mounted the scaffold in Thomas Street, smiling, he who had left so much, and most recently by those Three who died in Manchester. When people say that Ireland will be happy when her mills throb and her harbours swarm with shipping, they are talking as foolishly as if one were to say of a lost saint or of an unhappy lover: 'That man will be happy again when he has a comfortable income'. I know that Ireland will not be happy again until she recollects that old proud gesture of hers, and that laughing gesture of a young man that is going into battle or climbing to a gibbet.

What I have just written has reminded me of a dream I had nearly four years ago. I dreamt that I saw a pupil of mine, one of our boys at St. Enda's, standing alone upon a platform above a mighty sea of people; and I understood that he was about to die there for some august cause, Ireland's or another. He looked extraordinarily proud and joyous, lifting his head with a smile almost of amusement; I remember noticing his bare white throat and the hair on his forehead stirred by the wind, just as I had often noticed them on the hurling field. I felt an inexplicable exhilaration as I looked on him, and this exhilaration was heightened rather than diminished by my consciousness that the great silent crowd regarded the boy with pity and wonder rather than with approval — as a fool who was throwing away his life rather than a martyr that was doing his duty. It would have been so easy to die before a hostile crowd: but to die before that silent, unsympathetic crowd! I dreamt then that another of my pupils stepped upon the scaffold and embraced his comrade, and that then he tied a white bandage over the boy's eyes as though he would resent the hangman doing him that kindly office. And this act seemed to me to symbolise an immense brotherly charity and loyalty, and to be the compensation to the boy that died for the indifference of the crowd.

This is the only really vivid dream I have ever had since I used to dream of hobgoblins when I was a child. I remember telling it to my boys at a school meeting a few days later, and their speculating as to which of them I had seen in my dream: a secret which I do not think I gave away. But what recurs to me now is that when I said that I could not wish for any of them a happier destiny than to die thus in the defence of some true thing, they did not seem in any way surprised, for it fitted in with all we had been teaching them at St. Enda's. I do not mean that we have ever carried on anything like a political or revolutionary propaganda among the boys, but simply that we have always allowed them to feel that no one can finely live who hoards life too jealously: that one must be generous in service, and withal joyous, accounting even supreme sacrifices slight. Mr. J. M. Barrie makes his Peter Pan say (and it is finely said) 'To die will be a very big adventure', but, I think, that in making my little boy in *An Rí* offer himself with the words 'Let me do this little thing', I am nearer to the spirit of the heroes.

I find that in endeavouring to show that we are joyous at St. Enda's I have become exceedingly funereal. One of my pupils has accused me of 'sternly organizing merrymakings'. The truth is that it is from the boys that live in this place that its joyousness comes and if we share in the joy it is by rising to their height from our own slough of despond. When we attempt to be joyful on our own account the joy sometimes hangs fire. Mr. MacDonagh has told me how, when we were preparing the first number of *An Macaomh,* I came to him one evening with a face of portentous gravity and begged him to be humorous. I explained that *An Macaomh* was too austere, too esoteric: it needed some touch of delicate Ariel-like fancy, some genial burst of Falstaffian laughter. Mr. MacDonagh is one of the most fanciful and humorous men, but even he could not become Ariel-like or Falstaffian to order. He and I sat in our respective rooms for a whole evening lugubriously trying to be humorous; but our thoughts were of graves and worms and epitaphs, of unpaid bills, of approaching examinations, of certain Anglo-Irish comedies: the memory of it is still dreary. The next day at luncheon the clear voice of a boy spoke and the imp humour was in our midst: he told us the history of the Peacock of Hyderabad; and *An Macaomh* was saved.

I believe that many teachers fail because instead of endeavouring to raise themselves to the level of their pupils (I mean the moral, emotional, and imaginative level), they endeavour to bring their pupils down to theirs. For a high, if eccentric moral code, a glad and altruistic philosophy, a vision of ultimate beauty and truth seen through the fantastic and often humorous figments of a child's dreams, the teacher substitutes the mean philosophy of the world, the mean code of morals of the counting houses. Our Christianity becomes respectability. We are not content with teaching the ten commandments that God spake in thunder and Christ told us to keep if we would enter into life, and the precepts of the Church which He commanded us to hear: we add thereto the precepts or commandments of Respectable Society. And these are chiefly six: Thou shalt not be extreme in anything — in wrongdoing lest thou be put in gaol, in rightdoing lest thou be deemed a saint; Thou shalt not give away thy substance lest thou become a pauper; Thou shalt not engage in trade or manufacture lest thy hands become grimy; Thou shalt not carry a brown paper parcel lest thou shock Rathgar; Thou shalt not have an enthusiasm lest solicitors and their clerks call thee a fool; Thou shalt not endanger thy Job. One has heard this shocking morality taught in Christian schools, expounded in Christian newspapers, even preached from Christian pulpits. Those things about the lilies of the fields and the birds of the air, and that rebuke to Martha who was troubled about many things are thought to have no relevancy to modern life. But if that is so Christianity has no relevancy to modern life, for these are of the essence of Christ's teaching.

The great enemy of practical Christianity has always been respectable society. Respectable society has now been reinforced by political economy. I feel sure that political economy was invented not by Adam Smith, but by the devil. Perhaps Adam Smith was the human instrument of whom that wily one made use, even as he made use of the elder Adam to pervert men to the ways of respectability. Be certain that in political economy there is no Way of Life either for a man or for a people. Life for both is a matter, not of conflicting tariffs, but of conflicting powers of good and evil; and what have Ricarde and Malthus and Stuart Mill to teach about this? Ye men and peoples, burn your books on rent theories and land values and go back to your sagas.

If you will not go back to your sagas, your sagas will come to you again in new guise: for they are terrible immortal things, not capable of being put down by respectable society or by political economy. The old truths will find new mouths, the old sorrows and ecstacies new interpretation. Beauty is the garment of truth, or perhaps we should put it that beauty is the substance in which truth bodies itself forth; and then we can say that beauty, like matter is indestructible, however it may change in form. When you think that you have excluded it by your brick walls it flows in upon you, multitudinous. I know not how the old beauty will come back for us in this country and century; through an Irish theatre perhaps, or through a new poetry welling up in Irish-speaking villages. But come back it will, and its coming will be as the coming of God's angel, when:

> '. . . . seems another morn
> Risen on mid-noon. ....'.

I have to perform here the noble duty of giving thanks. First, there is a friend of St. Enda's whom I do not name, for I do not know that he would like me to name him. He and two others friends of older date have made St. Enda's a fact: for, though not what the world calls very wealthy, they have enabled me, whom certainly the world would call very poor, to found and to carry on this College. And I have to thank many other friends ranging from little boys up to church dignitaries, and including the parents of nearly all my pupils, for an unshaken loyalty to an ideal and to a place which by many are still misunderstood and distrusted.

Then coming to quite contemporary events. I have to thank the good people who looked to the organization of the St. Enda's Fete and Drawing of Prizes. And I have to thank Mr. W. B. Yeats and his fellow-workers at the Abbey Theatre for a very great generosity − a special performance which they arranged to give for us on the evening of May 17th. Mr. Yeats, in a lecture on Rabindranath Tagore, had spoken of Mr. Tagore's school for Indian boys as 'the Indian St. Enda's'. A friend of mine, interested by this, suggested that we should go to Mr. Yeats and ask him whether his Theatre could not do something to help St. Enda's. We had hardly time to frame our project in words when Mr. Yeats assented to it; and then he did a more generous thing still, for he offered to produce for the benefit of St. Enda's the play of Mr. Tagore's to the production of which he had been looking forward as to an important epoch in the life of the Abbey − the first presentation to Europe of a poet who, he thinks, is possibly the greatest now living. And he invited me to produce a St. Enda's play along with Mr. Tagore's. I understood then more clearly than ever that no one is so generous as a great artist; for a great artist is always giving gifts.

The play we decided to produce along with *The Post Office* was my morality, *An Rí*. We had enacted it during the previous summer, with much pageantry of horses and marchings, at a place in our grounds where an old castellated bridge, not unlike the entrance to a monastery, is thrown across a stream. Since that performance I had added some speeches with

344

the object of slightly deepening the characterization; and our boys were already rehearsing it for indoor production. Of Mr. Tagore's play I knew nothing except what I had heard from Mr. Yeats, but, I saw that both of us had had in our minds the same image of a humble boy and of the pomp of death, and that my play would be as it were antiphonal to his. Since I have seen Mr. Tagore's manuscript I have realized that the two plays are more similar in theme than I had suspected, and that mine will be to his in the nature of an 'amen'; for in our respective languages, he speaking in terms of Indian village life, and I in terms of an Irish saga, we have both expressed the same truth, that the highest thing anyone can do is to serve.

ST. ENDA'S

I have been asked to write here something about St. Enda's College and its boys and masters. It is too early for me to make any 'confessions'. And I have had certain deep joys and certain keen disappointments at St. Enda's which I shall never 'confess', at least to the public. Also, there have been humorous passages in the history of the past five years which would make excellent reading, but which to recount here and now would detract from the grave and decorous character that parents and the public expect in a headmaster. In the spacious leisure of a future when the Intermediate shall cease from troubling and the Department be at rest, I will write a school story whose incidents shall have all the wild improbability that only truth can have. The existence of St. Enda's itself is one of the most improbable things imaginable, and yet it is a fact.

Belfast Gaels will hear with interest that the first definite encouragement to me to start St. Enda's came from one of themselves. I sufficiently indicate whom I mean when I describe him as the dominant personality in Gaelic Belfast, and perhaps the strongest and sanest personality in the whole language movement. I remember that when I wrote round to my friends saying that I proposed to open near Dublin a school which should be more Irish in spirit than any school that had been opened in Ireland since the Flight of the Earls; which should be bilingual in method; which should teach modern languages orally; which should aim at a wider and humaner culture than other Irish secondary schools; which should set its face like iron against "cramming" and against all the evils of the competitive examination system, which should work at fostering the growth of the personality of each of its pupils rather than at forcing all into a predetermined groove; when I say, I wrote all this to my friends, most of the answers that came back might be summed up in the word 'Don't'. From Belfast came the gallant message, 'Do; and I will send you my boys'. The next word of encouragement was from Buenos Aires — from the late William Bulfin, with a similar promise. And the third was from an illustrious member of the Catholic Hierarchy. All this is sufficiently improbable; and our subsequent history has been of a piece.

Three Ulstermen (giving Ulster its Irish, not its Anglo-Irish geographical boundaries) have shared with me the main brunt of the financial burden of St. Enda's; and one of these Ulstermen is a non-Catholic, while St. Enda's is a Catholic school. Improbable again. And three of my most valued colleagues in our actual teaching work have been Ulstermen by birth or adoption. Add to this that if I were asked to select the six most promising of our pupils at the present moment, I should have to name four Ulster lads among the six. Ulster again is supposed to be the 'dour' province; but my experience of Ulster boys and Ulster men is that they have more of the Celtic gaiety than the boys and men of any other part of Ireland, and also that their gaiety is more joyous and less mocking than the gaiety of the South. I speak of Celtic Ulster — Donegal and the non-planted parts of the other counties.

It was very improbable that when a person who (although he had been a teacher all his life) was known chiefly as a journalist and secondarily as a lawyer, announced that he was about to open a school which should challenge the whole existing education system of Ireland, any pupils should be sent to him. Yet forty pupils rallied to St. Enda's on its opening day, and the number has increased in a steady ratio up to the present year. The time was in fact ripe for such an experiment, and it only remained to see whether the right people had taken it in hands. Several improbable things that have happened since go to show me that we were the right people. We have accomplished the miracle of making boys so love school that they hate to leave it. I do not think that any boy has ever come to St. Enda's who has not in a short time grown fond of it. It is not that we make things unduly easy for our lads: they work as hard in the study hall and on the games' field as it is healthy for any lads to work. I think that part of our success is due to the real comradeship that exists between boy and master. I mean not merely that we masters fraternise with the boys when off duty, but that we have put ourselves definitely into such a relationship with them that every boy is always sure that his point of view will be seen by the master and his difficulties sympathetically considered. And I have rarely found boys trying to evade punishment for faults committed; on the contrary, boys have many times come to me spontaneously, confessed faults, and asked to be punished. The reason is that they would consider it mean towards me and mean towards their companions to take shelter behind the excuse, 'I wasn't asked who did it.' Boys are proverbially honourable in their dealing with one another; our achievement has been to bring the masters within the magic circle, and thus give a new extention to 'schoolboy honour.'

It is improbable enough that the school whose main subject is the Irish language, and which leans rather to the 'modern literary' than to the 'classical' type of programme, should have gained the first Classical Entrance Scholarship in University College, Dublin; and it seems grotesquely improbable that we should have established a sort of 'corner' in Kildare County Council Scholarships. But these things we have done. It was a comparatively easy matter for us to make our boys the best athletes of their age in Ireland, and to win and hold the Dublin championships in football and hurling; and this success prepared us for the innately improbable event that our captain was selected to captain the Leinster Colleges against Munster.

I think our performances of Irish and Anglo-Irish plays, and especially our Passion Play of last Easter twelvemonth — intended to be a triennial event and due again at the Easter of 1914 — have meant something, not only in the development of our boys, but in the development of dramatic art in Ireland. As Mr. Pádraic Colum has written of us, we have gone back to the beginning of drama instead of trying to transplant the full-grown art from an exotic soil.

Achievements such as these have made the first five years of St. Enda's College memorable, but after all our main success must be looked for in the characters and daily lives of our boys, for the teaching that does not affect conduct is only so much empty breath. So I hope that what Mr. Eoin MacNéill said of us three years ago will always remain true, that St. Enda's has been a success, not only in its classrooms and on its playing fields, but firstly and chiefly in the homes of its pupils.

Analysis, Criticism and an Ideal 1912-1914

EDUCATION UNDER HOME RULE

A man stopped me in the street the other day and said to me: — 'Will the Gaelic League really insist upon making Irish a compulsory subject in the schools when Home Rule comes?' I replied: 'Ask me that question again when the Home Rule Bill is law'. I hope no one has come here this evening expecting me to answer that particular question or any similar question. If so, my reply must be that I have not the faintest idea what the Gaelic League will insist upon doing in a certain event whose time is still in what grammarians call the future indefinite. Nor would the mooting of such questions at this stage be very profitable. Speculation of the sort has always, no doubt, a certain fascination. We have all known girls of ten and twelve to decide the professions to be followed by their future sons, and the dresses to be worn on thier wedding days by their future daughters; and one has seen heated discussions in the papers as to whether a free Ireland ought to be a republic or a monarchy. But such speculations have nothing to do with practical politics. Home Rule, it is true, now looms very near: one hears in imagination the cheering of the crowds in College Green. Yet we shall probably all agree that it were too soon to commence the drawing up of an education code for a Home Rule Ireland. To me especially would it seem a work of supererogation, for part of my argument tonight is to be that under Home Rule we ought to have no education code to speak of: that instead of that we ought to have — education.

It is because I believe that in Ireland at present we have in strict language hardly any such thing as education, scarcely even the beginnings of an education system, that I think certain truths as to what education really is may usefully be enunciated here and now: while the swords clash at Westminister let the men of Ireland sit down in their camp as one among them tells them, in part, what the battle is about; so in ancient Ireland the hosts were wont to sit and talk while their champions battled at the fords.

I have just said that in Ireland at present there is no education system. I mean this. I mean that the work awaiting the Minister of Education in an Irish Parliament is not a work of reform, not a work of reconstruction, but a work of creation. You cannot reform that which is not; you cannot by any process of reconstruction give organic life to a negation. In a genuine and literal sense the task of our Irish Minister of Education will be the task of a creator; for out of chaos he will have to evolve order, and into a dead mass he will have to breathe the breath of life.

The speculations one has seen as to the probable effect of Home Rule on education in Ireland only show one how inadequately the problem is grasped. To some the advent of Home Rule would seem to promise, as its main fruition in the field of education, the raising of their salaries; to others the supreme thing it brings in its train is the abolition of Dr. Starkie; to some again, it holds out the delightful prospect of Orangemen, or rather Orange boys and girls, being forced to learn Irish; to others it means the dawn of an era of commonsense, the ushering in of the reign of a sound modern education, suitable to the needs of a progressive modern people.

I confess that of all the views the last is the one that irritates me most. The first view is not so selfish as it might appear, for between the salary offered to teachers and the excellence of a country's education system there is, indeed, a vital connection. And the second and third forecasts at any rate open up picturesque vistas: the passing of Dr. Starkie would have something of the pageantry of the banishment of Napoleon to St. Helena, and the prospect of the children of Sandy Row being taught to curse the Pope in Irish, pronounced with a Belfast accent is rich and soul-satisfying. These things we may, or may not, see when Home Rule comes. But there is one thing I hope we never shall see: I hope we shall never see Home Rule Ireland committed to an ideal so low, so false, so unworthy, of a nation with Ireland's tradition in education, as that underlying the phrase 'a sound modern education'.

It is, indeed, a vile phrase, one of the vilest I know; and yet we find it in nearly every school prospectus, and it comes pat to the lips of nearly everyone that writes or talks about schools. Now, there can be no such thing as a 'sound modern education': as well talk about a 'lively modern faith', or a 'serviceable modern religion'. It should be obvious that the more 'modern' an education is the less 'sound', and that the more 'soundly' it is 'modern' the less it is education. For in education 'modernism' is as much a heresy as in religion. In both medievalism were a truer standard. We are really too fond of clapping ourselves on the back because we live in modern times, and we preen ourselves quite ridiculously and unnecessarily on our modern progress: but it has been won at how great a cost? How many precious things have we flung from us that we might lighten ourselves for that race?

And in some directions we have progressed not at all, or we have progressed in a circle; perhaps, indeed, all progress on this planet, and on every planet, is in a circle, just as every line you draw on a globe is a circle or part of one. Philosophy is as old as the hills, and the science of today is only a new flowering of the science that made lovely the ancient cities and gardens of the East. With all our learning we are not yet as cultured as the Greeks who crowded to hear the plays of Sophocles; with all our art institutions and art coteries we have not yet that love for the beautiful which burned in the heart of the Middle Ages. Where we think ourselves refined we are only squeamish; where we think ourselves profound we are only muddled. Modern speculation is often a mere groping where ancient men saw clearly. All the problems with which we strive, I mean all the really important problems, were long ago solved by our ancestors, only their solutions have been forgotten. There have been states in which the rich did not grind the poor, although there are few such democracies now; there have been free self-governing democracies, although there are few such democracies now; there have been rich and beautiful social organisations, with an art and a culture, and a religion in every man's house, though for such a thing today we have to search out some sequestered people living by a desolate seashore or in a high forgotten valley among lonely hills — a hamlet in Connacht or a village in the Austrian Alps. Mankind, I repeat, or some section of mankind, has solved all its main problems somewhere and at some time. I suppose no universal and permanent solution is possible as long as the old Adam remains in us, the Adam that makes each one of us, and each tribe of us, something of the rebel, of the freethinker, of the adventurer, of the egoist. But the solutions are there, and it is because we fail in clearness of vision or in boldness of heart, or in simpleness of purpose that we cannot find them.

II

As the Boy-Corps of Eamhain stands out as the idealisation of the Gaelic system, Cúchulainn stands out as the idealisation of the child fostered under the system. And thus Cúchulainn describes his fostering: 'Fionnchaomh nourished me at her breast; Feargus bore me on his knee; Conall was my companion-in-arms; Blai, the lord of lands, was my hospitaller; fair-speeched Seancha trained me in just judgement; on the knee of Amhairgin the poet I learned poetry; Cathbhadh of the gentle face taught me druid lore; Conchobhar kindled my boyish ambition. All the chariotchiefs and kings and poets of Ulster have taken part in my bringing up'. Such was the education of Cúchulainn, the most perfect hero of the Gael. Cúchulainn may never have lived and there may never have been a Boy-Corps at Eamhain; but the picture endures as the Gael's idealisation of the kind of environment and the kind of fostering that go to the making of a perfect hero. The result of it all, the simplicity and the strength of true heroism, is compressed into single sentences put into the hero's mouth by the old shaper of the tale of Cúchulainn's Phantom Chariot: 'I was a child with children; I was a man with men'.

How often a phrase or an aphorism in an Irish tale lights up as with a lantern a whole phase of old Irish thought, or throws sharply into relief some characteristic Irish attitude! Thus Cúchulainn found in Emer the six gifts of perfect womanhood: the gift of wisdom, the gift of chastity, the gift of beauty, the gift of sweet speech, the gift of music, the gift of household work. I do not know that the twentieth century has any ideal at once so sane and so lofty. I do not know that in any Irish school of today girls are being as truly educated as they were in the Grianán where Emer worked with her foster-sisters.

Civilisation has taken such a queer turn that it might not be easy to restore the old Irish plan of education in all its details. Our heroes and seers and scholars would not be so willing to add a Boy-Corps or a Grianán to their establishments as were their prototypes in Ireland from time immemorial until the fall of the Gaelic polity. I can imagine how blue Dr. Hyde, Mr. Yeats, and Mr. McNeill would look if their friends informed them that they proposed to send them their children to be fostered.

The mere fact that the idea strikes us as ludicrous shows how definitely we have adopted the modern conception of education. The modern conception is that the state provides schoolrooms to which it compels you

350

to send your children to be taught certain subjects, regarded as useful, by persons placed there by the State for the purpose and paid (or under-paid) by the State for thier work. The Irish conception (I may add the classical conception and the medieval conception, but most emphatically the Irish conception) was essentially different. Among the old Gael a school always gathered around a personality. A school was less a place than a little group of persons, a Master and his disciples. The school might not always be in the same place, it might even be peripatetic. This idea, as I have suggested, was the idea of the East, too, and to some extent of ancient Greece, and to a large extent of the Middle Ages throughout Europe. I always think of Christ and His friends as they wandered through Palestine as of a sort of a school; and was not their name for Him 'the Master', and were not they His disciples, His pupils? In the Middle Ages there were everywhere little groups of persons clustering round some beloved teacher; and thus it was that men learned not only the humanities but all gracious and useful crafts. There were no State art schools, no State technical schools; men became artists in the studio of some master artist, technical schools; men became artists in the studio of some master artist, men learned crafts in the workshop of some master craftsman. It was always the individual inspiring, guiding, *fostering* other individuals; never the State usurping the place of father or fosterer, dispensing education like some universal provider of readymades, aiming at turning out all men and women according to regulation patterns. In Ireland, the older and truer conception was never lost sight of. It persisted into Christian times when a Kieran or an Enda or a Colmcille gathered his little group of foster-children (the old word was still used) around him ; they were collectively his family, his household, his clann, many sweet and endearing words were used to mark the intimacy of that relationship. It seems to me that there has been nothing nobler in the history of education than this development of the old Irish plan of fosterage under a Christian rule; when to the old Pagan ideals of strength and truth there were added the Christian ideals of love and of humility. And this, remember, was not the education system of an aristocracy but the education system of a people. It was more democratic than any education system in the world to-day. Our very divisions into primary, secondary, and university crystallise a snobbishness partly intellectual and partly social. At Clonard, Kieran, the son of a carpenter, sat in the same class as Colmcille, the son of a king.

To Clonard or to Aran or to Clonmacnois went every man, rich or poor, prince or peasant, who wanted to sit at Finnian's or at Enda's or at Kieran's feet and to learn of their wisdom. Always it was the personality of the teacher that drew them there. And so it was all through Irish history. A great poet or a great scholar had his foster-children who lived at his house or fared with him through the country. Even long after Kinsale the Munster poets had their little groups of pupils; and the hedge-schoolmasters of the nineteenth century were the last repositories of a high tradition.

I dwell on the importance of the personal element in education. I would have every child not merely a unit in a school attendance, but in some intimate personal way the pupil of a teacher, or, to use more expressive words, the disciple of a master.

It will be seen that I claim that the ancient Irish system possessed pre-eminently two characteristics: first, freedom for the individual; and, secondly, an adequate inspiration. Without those two things you cannot have education, no matter how well you may elaborate educational machinery, no matter how you may multiply educational programmes. And because those two things are pre-eminently lacking in what passes for education in Ireland, we have in Ireland strictly no education system at all; nothing that by any extension of the meaning of the words can be called an education system. We have an elaborate machinery for teaching persons certain subjects, and the teaching is done more or less efficiently; more efficiently, I imagine, than such teaching is done in England or America. We have three Universities and four Education Boards. We have some thousands of buildings, large and small. We have an army of teachers , mostly under-paid. We have an army of inspectors, mostly over-paid. We have a compulsory Education Act. We have the grave and bulky code of the Commissioners of National Education, and the slim impertinent pamphlet which enshrines the wisdom of the Commissioners of Intermediate Education. We have a vast deal more in the shape of educational machinery and stage properties. But we have, I repeat, no education system; and only in isolated places have we any education. The essentials are lacking.

And first of freedom. The word freedom is no longer understood in Ireland. We have no experience of the thing, and we have almost lost our conception of the idea. So completely is this true that the very organisations which exist in Ireland to champion freedom show no disposition themselves to accord freedom; they challenge a great tyranny but they erect their own little tyrannies. 'Thou shalt not', is half the law of Ireland, and the other half is: 'Thou must!'

III

Nowhere has the law of 'Thou shalt not' and 'Thou must' been so vigorous as in the schoolroom. Surely the first essential of healthy life there was freedom. But there has been and there is no freedom in Irish education — no freedom for the child, no freedom for the teacher, no freedom for the school. Where young souls, young minds, young bodies demanded the largest measure of individual freedom the largest measure of individual freedom consistent with the common good, freedom to move and grow on their natural lines, freedom to live their own lives — for what is natural life but natural growth? — freedom to bring themselves, as I have put it, to their own perfection, there was a sheer denial of the right of the individual to grow in his own natural way, that is, in God's way. He had to develop, not in God's way, but in the Board's way. The Board, National or Intermediate as the case might be, bound him hand and foot, chained his mind and soul, constricted him morally, mentally, and physically with the involuted folds of its rules and regulations, its programmes, its minutes, its reports and special reports, its pains and penalties. I have often thought that the type of Irish education was the Laocoon; that agonising father and sons seem to me like the teacher and the pupils of an Irish school, the strong limbs of the man and the slender limbs of the boys caught together and crushed together in the grip of an awful fate. And Irish education has seemed to some like the bed of Procustes; the bed on which all men that passed the way must lie, be it never so big for them, be it never so small for them; the traveller for whom it was too large had his limbs stretched until he filled it, the traveller for whom it was too small had his limbs chopped off until he fitted into it — comfortably. It was a grim jest to play on travellers; a grimmer jest to play on the children of a nation.

Our Irish sytems took, and take, absolutely no cognizance of the differences between individuals, of the differences between localities, of the differences between urban and rural communities, of the differences springing from a different ancestry, Gaelic or Anglo-Saxon. The programme denies freedom to the school; the school denies freedom to the individual pupil. Every school must conform to a type — and what a type! Every individual must conform to a type — and what a type! The teacher has not been at liberty, and in practice is not yet at liberty, to seek to discover the individual bents of his pupils, the hidden talent that is in every normal soul, to discover which and to cherish which, that it may in the fulness of time be put to some precious use, is the primary duty of the teacher.

Once a colleague of mine summed up the whole philosophy of education in a maxim which startled a sober group of visitors: 'If a boy shows an aptitude of doing *anything* better than most people, he should be encouraged to do *that*, and to do it as well as possible; I don't care what it is — scotch hop if you like'.

The idea of a compulsory programme imposed by an external authority on every child in every school in a country is the direct contrary of the root idea involved in education. Yet this is what we have in Ireland. In theory the primary schools have a certain amount of freedom; in practice they have none. Neither in theory nor in practice in such a thing as freedom dreamt of in the gloomy Limbo whose presiding demon is the Board of Intermediate Education for Ireland. Education indeed, reaches its nadir in the Irish Intermediate system.

IV

At the present moment there are fifteen thousand boys and girls pounding at a programme drawn up for them by certain persons sitting round a table in Hume Street. Precisely the same text-books are being read tonight in every secondary school and college in Ireland. Two of Hawthorn's *Tanglewood Tales,* with a few poems in English, will constitute the whole literary pabulum of three-quarters of the pupils of the Irish secondary schools during this twelvemonth. The teacher who seeks to give his pupils a wider horizon in literature does so at his peril. He will, no doubt, benefit his pupils, but he will infallibly reduce his results fees. As an Intermediate teacher said to me: 'Culture is all very well in its way, but if you don't stick to your programme your boys won't pass'. 'Stick to your programme' is the 'strange device' on the banner of the Irish Intermediate system; and the programme bulks so large that there is no room for education.

The first thing I plead for, therefore, is freedom; freedom for each school to shape its own programme in conformity with the circumstances of the school as to place, size, personnel, and so on; freedom, again, for the individual teacher to impart something of his own personality to his work, to bring his own peculiar gift to the service of his pupils, to be, in short, a teacher, a master, one having an intimate and permanent relationship with his pupils, and not a mere part of the educational machine; a mere cog in the wheel; freedom finally for the individual pupil, and scope for his development within the system and within the school. And I would promote this idea of freedom by the very organisation of the school itself, giving a certain autonomy not only to the school, but to the particular parts of the school: to the staff, of course, but also to the pupils, and, in a large school, to the various sub-divisions of the pupils. I do not plead for anarchy. I plead for freedom within the law, for liberty, not licence, for that true freedom which can exist only where there is discipline, which exists, in fact, because each, valuing his own freedom, respects also the freedom of others.

And that this freedom may be availed of to the noble ends of education there must be, within the school system and within the school, an adequate inspiration. The school must make such an appeal to the pupil as shall resound throughout his after life, urging him always to be his best self, never his second-best self. Such an inspiration will come most adequately of all from religion. I do not think that there can be any education of which spiritual religion does not form an integral part; as it is the most important part of life, so it should be the most important part of preparation for complete life. And inspiration will come also from the hero-stories of the world, and especially of our own people; from literature enjoyed as literature rather than studied as 'texts'; from science and art if taught by people who are really scientists and artists and not merely persons with certificates from Mr. T. W. Russell; from the associations of the school place; finally and chiefly from the humanity and great-heartedness of the teacher.

V

The value of the national factor in education would appear to rest chiefly in this, that it addresses itself to the most generous side of the child's nature, urging him to live up to his finest self. If the true work of the teacher be, as I have said, to help the child to realise himself at his best and worthiest, the factor of nationality is of prime importance, apart from any ulterior propagandist views the teacher may cherish. The school system which neglects it commits, even from the purely pedagogic point of view, a primary blunder. It neglects one of the most powerful of educational resources.

It is because Irish education has forgotten the importance of the national factor that it has so terrifically failed. Or rather it is because it has remembered the importance (from its own point of view) of forgetting it that it has so terrifically succeeded. For it has succeeded: succeeded in making slaves of us, if that was its object. Mr. John MacNeill has been more suggestive in discussing Irish education than anyone I know. He has compared the Irish education system to the systems of slave education which existed in the ancient pagan republics side by side with the systems intended for the education of freemen. To the children of the free were taught all noble and goodly things which would tend to make them strong, proud, and valiant; from the children of the slaves all such dangerous knowledge was hidden — they were taught, not to be strong, proud, and valiant, but to be sleek, to be obsequious, to be dexterous: the object was not to make them good men, but to make them good slaves. And so in Ireland. Our education system was designed by our masters in order to make us smooth and willing slaves. It has succeeded; succeeded so well that we no longer realise that we *are* slaves. Some of us even think our chains ornamental, and are a little doubtful as to whether we shall be quite as comfortable and quite as respectable when a few of the links are knocked off by the passing of the Home Rule Bill. It remains the crowning achievement of the National and of the Intermediate systems that they have wrought such a change in this people that once loved freedom so passionately. Three-quarters of a century ago there still remained in Ireland a stubborn Irish thing which Cromwell had not trampled out, which the Penal Laws had not crushed, which the horrors of '98 had not daunted, which Pitt had not purchased; a national consciousness enshrined mainly in a national language. After three-quarters of a century's education that thing is nearly lost; so nearly, indeed, in these recent years, that it sometimes seems that Home Rule, if come it does, will come to late to save it.

VI

The new education system in Ireland has to do more than restore a national cutlure. It has to restore manhood to a race that has lost it. Along with its inspiration it must, therefore, bring a certain *hardening*.

I would bring back some of the starkness of the antique world. No dream is more foolish than the dream of some sentimentalists that the reign of force is past, or passing; that the world's ancient battle laws have been repealed; that henceforth the first duty of every man is to be dapper.

And the old Ossianic definition of efficiency holds good: 'Strength in our hands, truth on our lips, and purity in our hearts'. 'Strength in our hands'. The Gaelic Athletic Association, with all its faults, is more truly an educational body than any of our Education Boards.

And, finally, I say, inspiration must come from the teacher. If we can no longer send the children to the heroes and seers and scholars to be fostered, we can at least bring some of the heroes and seers and scholars to the schools. We rise up against the system which tolerates as teachers the rejected of all other professions rather than demanding for so priestlike an office the highest souls and noblest intellects of the race. I remember once going into a schoolroom in Belgium and finding an old man talking quietly and beautifully about literature to a silent class of boys; I was told that he was one of the most distinguished of contemporary Flemish poets. Here was the sort of personality, the sort of influence one ought to see in a schoolroom; not, indeed, that every poet would make a good schoolmaster, or every good schoolmaster a poet. But how seldom here has the teacher any interest in literature at all; how seldom has he any horizon above his time-table, any soul above his results fees!

The fact is that, with rare exceptions, the men and women who are willing to work under the conditions as to personal dignity, freedom, tenure, and emolument which obtain in Irish schools are not the sort of men and women likely to make good educators. This part of the subject has recently been so much discussed in public that I need not dwell upon it.

355

You are all alive to the truth that a teacher ought to be paid better than a policeman, and to the scandal of the fact that many an able and cultured man is working in Irish secondary schools today at a salary less than that of the Lord Mayor's coachman.

And now, I have sufficiently indicated the general spirit in which I would have Irish education re-created. I say little of organisation, or mere machinery. That is the least important part of the subject. We can all foresee that the first task of an Irish Parliament must be destructive; that the lusty strokes of Gael and Gall, Ulster taking its manful part, will hew away and cast adrift the rotten and worm-eaten boards which support the grotesque fabric of the Irish education system. And then will come the work of reconstruction. We can all foresee that, when an Irish Cabinet is constituted, there will be an Irish Minister of Education responsible to the Irish Parliament; that under him Irish education will be drawn together into a homogeneous whole, — an organic unity will replace a composite freak in which the various members are not only not directed by a single intelligence, but are often mutually antagonistic, and sometimes engaged in open warfare one with the other; like the preposterous donkey in the partomime whose head is in perpetual strife with his heels because they belong to different individuals.

THE EDUCATION PROBLEM IN THE HOME RULE PARLIAMENT

Mr. John Dillon has declared that one of the first tasks awaiting a Home Rule Parliament is the recasting of the Irish education system. The declaration has alarmed the Bishop of Limerick, who has replied in effect that the Irish education system does not need recasting — that all is well there.

The positions seem irreconcilable. And yet it may be that there is somewhere common ground between these two distinguished Irishmen, and that the duty of the Home Rule Parliament with regard to education may be stated in such a way as to command the assent of both. I would put it that what Irish education needs is less a reconstruction of its machinery than a regeneration in spirit. The machinery has doubtless its defects, but what is chiefly wrong with it is that it is mere machinery, a lifeless thing without a soul. Dr. O'Dwyer is probably concerned for the maintenance of portion of the machinery, valued by him as a Catholic Bishop, and not without reason; and I for one would leave that particular portion untouched, or practically so. But the machine as a whole is no more capable of fulfilling the function for which it is needed than would an automaton be capable of fulfilling the function of a living teacher in a school. It is as inadequate to the salvation of the nation as was the Mosaic Law to the salvation of mankind; and it needs just what the Mosaic Law needed — not a repealing of its Ten Commandments, but the in-breathing of a new spirit, divinely human.

One of the most terrible things about the Irish education system is its ruthlessness. I know no image for that ruthlessness in the natural order. The ruthlessness of a wild beast has in it a certain mercy — it slays. It has in it a certain grandeur of animal force. But this ruthlessness is literally without pity and without passion. It is cold and mechanical, like the ruthlessness of an immensely powerful engine. A machine vast, complicated, with a multitude of far-reaching arms, with many ponderous presses, carrying out mysterious and long-drawn processes of shaping and moulding, is the true image of the Irish education system. It grinds night and day; it obeys immutable and predetermined laws; it is as devoid of understanding, of sympathy, of imagination as is any other piece of machinery that performs an appointed task. Into it is fed all the raw human material in Ireland; it seizes upon it inexorably and rends and compresses and remoulds; and what it cannot refashion after the regulation pattern it ejects with all likeness of its former self crushed from it, a bruised and shapeless thing, thereafter accounted waste.

Our common parlance has become impressed with the conception of education as some sort of manufacturing process. Our children are the 'raw material'; we desiderate for their education 'modern methods' which must be 'efficient' but 'cheap'; we send them to Clongowes to be 'finished'; when 'finished' they are 'turned out'; specialists 'grind' them for the Civil Service and the so-called liberal professions; in each of our great colleges there is a department known as the 'scrap-heap', though officially called the Fourth Preparatory — the limbo to which the debris ejected by the machine is relegated. The stuff there is either too hard or too soft to be moulded to the pattern required by the Civil Service Commissioners or the Incorporated Law Society.

In our adoption of the standpoint here indicated there is involved a primary blunder as to the nature and functions of education. For education has not to do with the manufacture of things, but with fostering the growth of things. And the conditions we should strive to bring about in our education system are not the conditions favourable to the rapid and cheap manufacture of readymades, but the conditions favourable to the growth of living organisms — the liberty and the light and the gladness of a ploughed field under the spring sunshine.

In particular I would urge that the Irish school system of the future should give freedom — freedom to the individual school, freedom to the individual teacher, freedom as far as may be to the individual pupil. Without freedom there can be no right growth; and education is properly the fostering of the right growth of a personality. Our school system must bring, too, some gallant inspiration. And with the inspiration it must bring a certain hardening. One scarcely knows whether modern sentimentalism or modern utilitarianism is the more sure sign of modern decadence. I would boldly preach the antique faith that fighting is the only noble thing, and that he only is at peace with God who is at war with the powers of evil.

In a true education system, religion, patriotism, literature, art and science would be brought in such a way into the daily lives of boys and girls as to affect their character and conduct. We may assume that religion is a vital thing in Irish schools, but I know that the other things, speaking broadly, do not exist. There are no ideas there, no love of beauty, no love of books, no love of knowledge, no heroic inspiration. And there is no room for such things either on the earth or in the heavens, for the earth is cumbered and the heavens are darkened by the monstrous bulk of the programme. Most of the educators detest the programme. They are like the adherents of a dead creed who continue to mumble formulas and to make obeisance before an idol which they have found out to be but a spurious divinity.

Mr. Dillon is right in looking to the advent of Home Rule for a chance to make education what it should be. But I hope that he and the others who will have power in a Home Rule Parliament realise that what is needed is not a revolution, but a vastly bigger thing — a creation. It is not a question of pulling machinery asunder and piecing it together again; it is a question of breathing into a dead thing the breath of life.

IRISH EDUCATION

It is because I believe that in Ireland at present we have, in strict language, hardly any such thing as education scarcely even the beginnings of an education system, that I think certain truths as to what education really is may usefully be enunciated here, and now; while the swords clash at Westminster let the men of Ireland sit down in their camp as one among them tells them, in part, what the battle is about; so, in ancient Ireland, the hosts were wont to sit and talk while the champions battled at the fords.

I have just said that in Ireland at present there is no education system. I mean this. I mean that the work awaiting the Minister of Education in an Irish Parliament is not a work of reform, not a work of reconstruction, but a work of creation. You cannot reform that which is not; you cannot by any process of reconstruction give organic life to a negation. In a genuine and literal sense the task of our Irish Minister of Education will be the task of a creator; for out of chaos he will have to evolve order and into a dead mass he will have to breathe the breath of life.

The speculations one has seen as to be the probable effect of Home Rule on education in Ireland only show one how inadequately the problem is grasped. To some the advent of Home Rule would seem to promise, as its main fruition in the field of education, the raising of their salaries; to others the supreme thing it brings in its train is the abolition of Dr. Starkie; to some again it holds out the delightful prospect of Orangemen, or rather Orange boys and girls, being forced to learn Irish; to others it means the dawn of an era of common sense, the ushering in of the reign of a sound modern education, suitable to the needs of a progressive modern people.

I confess that of all the views the last is the one that irritates me most. The first view is not so selfish as it might appear, for between the salary offered to teachers and the excellence of a country's education system there is, indeed, a vital connection. And the second and third forecasts, at any rate, open up picturesque vistas — the passing of Dr. Starkie would have something of the pageantry of the banishment of Napoleon to St. Helena, and the prospect of the children of Sandy Row being taught to curse the Pope in Irish is rich and soul-satisfying. These things we may, or may not, see when Home Rule cmes. But there is one thing I hope we shall never see — I hope we shall never see Home Rule Ireland committed to an ideal so low, so false, so unworthy, of a nation with Ireland's tradition in education, as that underlying the phrase, 'a sound modern education'.

It is, indeed, a vile phrase — one of the vilest I know. And yet we find it in nearly every school prospectus, and it comes naturally to the lips of nearly everyone that writes or talks about schools. Now, there can be no such thing as 'a sound modern education' — as well talk about a 'lively modern faith' or a 'serviceable modern religion.' It should be obvious that the more 'modern' an education is, the less 'sound' , and that the more soundly 'modern' it is the less is it education. For in education 'modernism' is as much a heresy as in religion. In both medievalism were a truer standard. We are really too fond of clapping ourselves upon the back be-

358

cause we live in modern times, and we preen ourselves quite ridiculously and unnecessarily on our modern progress. There is, of course, such a thing as modern progress — but it has been won at how great a cost? How many precious things have we flung from us that we might lighten ourselves for that race?

And in some directions we have progressed not at all, or we have progressed in a circle; perhaps, indeed, all progress on this planet, and on every planet, is in a circle, just as every line you draw on a globe is a circle or part of one. Philosophy is as old as the hills, and the science of to-day is only a new flowering of the science that made lovely the ancient cities and gardens of the East. With all our learning we are not yet as cultural as were the Greeks who crowded to hear the plays of Sophocles; with all our art institutions and art coteries we have not yet that love for the beautiful which moved in the heart of the Middle Ages. Where we think ourselves refined we are only squeamish; where we think ourselves profound we are only muddled. Modern speculation is often a mere groping where ancient men saw clearly. All the problems with which we strive — I mean all the really important problems — were long ago solved by our ancestors, only their solutions have been forgotten. There have been States in which the rich did not grind the poor, although there are no such States now; there have been free self-governing democracies, although there are few such democracies now; there have been rich and beautiful social organisations, with an art and a culture and a religion in every man's house, though for such a thing to-day we have to search out some sequestered people living by a desolate seashore or in a high forgotten valley among lonely hills — a hamlet in Connacht or a village in the Austrian Alps. Mankind, I repeat, or some section of mankind, has solved all its main problems somewhere and at some time. I suppose no universal and permanent solution is possible as long as the old Adam remains in us, the Adam that makes each one of us, and each tribe of us, something of the rebel, of the free-thinker, of the adventurer, of the egoist. But the solutions are there, and it is because we fail in clearness of vision or in boldness of heart or in singleness of purpose that we cannot find them.

I am interested here in the problem of education — the problem, that is, of bringing up a child. We constantly speak and write as if a philosophy of education had been first formulated in our own time. But all the wise peoples of old faced and solved that problem for themselves, and all their solutions were better than ours. Professor Culverwell thinks that the Jews gave it the best solution. For my part, I take off my hat to the old Irish. The philosophy of education is preached now, but it was practised by the founders of the Gaelic system two thousand years ago. Our grave treatises on the new science of child psychology seem to me as futile beside some of the tales of the Red Branch as a ponderous treatise on theology beside a gospel parable or the life of a saint. In the treatise a system is talked about; in the tale or parable the system lives.

A language expresses a people's outlook and inlook in many subtle ways; and the very words our forefathers used when speaking of education show that they had gripped the heart of this particular problem. Their word for 'education' was the same as their word for 'fostering' — the teacher was a 'fosterer' and the pupil was a 'foster-child'. Now, to 'foster' is exactly the function of the teacher, not primarily to 'lead up', to 'guide', to 'conduct through a course of studies,' and still less to 'indoctrinate', to 'inform', to 'coach', but primarily to 'foster' the elements of character already present.

This, some time ago, I put in another away, by saying that the true work of the teacher is to help the child to realise himself at his best and worthiest and not want to make each of one's pupils a replica of oneself (God forbid), holding the self-same opinions, prejudices, likes, illusions. Neither does one want to drill all one's pupils into so many regulation little soldiers or so many stodgy little citizens, though this is apparently the aim of some of the most cried-up of modern systems. In point of fact, man is not primarily a member of a State, but a human individuality — that is, a human soul imprisoned in a human body; a shivering human soul with its own awful problems, its own august destiny; lonelier in its house of clay than any prisoner in any Bastille in the world. Now, the true teacher will recognise in each of his pupils an individual human soul, distinct and different from every other human soul that has ever been fashioned by God, miles and miles apart from the soul that is nearest and most akin to it, craving, indeed comradeship and sympathy and pity, needing also, it may be, discipline and guidance and a restraining hand, but imperiously demanding to be allowed to live its own perfection; because for every human soul there is a perfection meant for it alone, and which it alone is capable of attaining. So the primary office of the teacher is to 'foster' that of good which is native in the soul of his pupil, striving to bring its inborn excellence to ripeness rather than to implant in it excellences exotic to its nature. It comes to this then, that the education of a child is greatly a matter, in the first place, of congenial environment and, next to this, of a wise and loving watchfulness whose chief appeal will be to the finest instincts of the child itself.

It is a long time since I was attracted to the Gaelic plan of educating children. One of my oldest recollections is of a kindly grey-haired seanchaidhe, a woman of my mother's people, telling tales by a kitchen fireplace. She spoke more wisely and nobly of ancient heroic things than anyone else I have ever known. Her only object was to amuse me, yet she was the truest of all my teachers. one of her tales was of a king, the most famous king of his time in Ireland, who had gathered about him a number of boys, the children of his friends and kinsmen, whom he had organised into a little society, giving them a constitution and allowing them to make their own laws and elect their own leaders. The most renowned of the king's heroes were appointed to teach them chivalry, the most skilled of his men of art to teach them arts, the wisest of his druids to teach them philosophy. The king himself was one of their teachers, and so did he love their companionship that he devoted one-third of all the time he saved from affairs of State to teaching them or watching them at their play; and if any stranger came to the dún during that time, even though he were a king's envoy demanding audience, there was but one answer for him: 'The king is with his foster children.'

In truth, I think that the old Irish plan of education, as idealised for boys in the story of the Macraidh of Eamhain, and for girls in that of the Grianán of Lusga, was the wisest and the most generous that the world has ever known. The bringing together of children in some pleasant place under some man famous among his people for his greatness of heart, for his wisdom, for his skill in some gracious craft — here we get the two things upon which I lay most stress in education, the environment, and the stimulus of a personality which can address itself to the child's worthiest self. Then, the charter of free government with certain limits, the right to make laws and maintain them, to elect and depose leaders — here was scope for the growth of individualities, yet provision for maintaining the suzerainty of the common weal; the scrupulous co-relation of moral, intellectual and physical training, the open-air life, the very type of the games which formed so large a part of their learning — all these things were devised with a largeness of view foreign to the little minds that devise our modern makeshifts for education. Lastly, the fosterer or teacher, had as colleagues in his work of fosterage no ordinary hirelings but men whom their gifts of soul, or mind, or body, had lifted high above their contemporaries — the captains, the poets, the prophets of their people.

II

As the boy corps of Eamhain stands out as the idealisation of the Gaelic system, Cúchulainn stands out as the idealisation of the child fostered under the system. And thus Cúchulainn describes his fostering:- 'Fionnchaomh nourished me at her breast; Feargus bore me on his knee; Conall was my companion-in-arms; Blai, the lord of lands, was my hospitaller; fair-speeched Seancha trained me in just judgment; on the knee of Amhairgin, the poet, I learned poetry; Cathbhadh of the gentle face taught me druid lore; Conchobhar kindled my boyish ambition. All the chariot-chiefs and kings and poets of Ulster have taken part in my bringing up.' Such was the education of Cúchulainn, the most perfect hero of the Gael. Cúchulainn may never have lived and there may never have been a boy corps at Eamhain; but the kind of environment and the kind of fostering that go to the making of a perfect hero. the result of it all, the simplicity and the strength of true heroism, is compressed into a single sentence put into the hero's mouth by the old shaper of the tale of Cúchulainn's Phantom Chariot:- 'I was a child with children; I was a man with men.'

How often a phrase or an aphorism in an Irish tale lights up as with a lantern a whole phase of old Irish thought, or throws sharply into relief some characteristic Irish attitude! Thus Cúchulainn found in Emer the six gifts of perfect womanhood: the gift of wisdom, the gift of chastity, the gift of beauty, the gift of sweet speech, the gift of music, the gift of household work. I do not know that the twentieth century has any ideal at once so sane and so lofty. I do not know that in any Irish school of to-day girls are being as truly educated as they were in the Grianán where Emer worked with her foster-sisters.

Civilisation has taken such a queer turn that it might not be easy to restore the old Irish plan of education in all its details. Our heroes and seers and scholars would not be so willing to add a boy corps or a Grianán to their establishments as were their prototypes in Ireland from time immemorial until the fall of the Gaelic polity. I can imagine how blue Dr. Hyde, Mr. Yeats, and Mr. Mac Néill would look if their friends informed them that they proposed to send them their children to be fostered.

The mere fact that the idea strikes us as ludicrous shows how definitely we have adopted the modern conception of education. The modern conception is that the State provides school rooms to which it compels you to send your children to be taught certain subjects, regarded as useful, by persons placed there by the State for the purpose, and paid (or under-paid) by the State for their work. The Irish conception (I may add the classical conception and the medieval conception, but most emphatically the Irish conception) was essentially different. Among the old Gael a school always gathered around a personality. A school was less a place than a little group of persons, a master and his disciples. The school might not always be in the

361

same place, it might even be peripatetic. This idea, as I have suggested, was the idea of the East, too, and to some extent of ancient Greece, and to a large extent of the Middle Ages throughout Europe. I always think of Christ and his friends as they wandered through Palestine as of a sort of school; and was not their name for Him 'the Master', and were not they His disciples, His pupils? In the Middle ages there were everywhere little groups of persons clustering round some beloved teacher, and thus it was that men learned not only the humanities but all gracious and useful crafts. There were no State art schools, no State technical schools; men became artists in the studio of some master artist, men learned crafts in the workshop of some master craftsman. It was always the individual inspiring, guiding, fostering other individuals; never the State usurping the place of father or fosterer, dispensing education like a universal provider of readymades, aiming at turning out all men and women according to regulation patterns. In Ireland the older and truer conception was never lost sight of. It persisted into Christian times when a Kieran, or Enda, or a Colmcille gathered his little group of foster-children (the old word was still used) around him; they were collectively his family, his household, his clann — many sweet and endearing words were used to mark the intimacy of that relationship. It seems to me that there has been nothing nobler in the history of education than this development of the old Irish plan of fosterage under a Christian rule when to the old Pagan ideals of strength and truth there were added the Christian ideals of love and humility. And this, remember, was not the education system of an aristocracy, but the education system of a people. It was more democratic than any education system in the world to-day. Our very divisions into primary, secondary, and university crystallise a snobbishness partly intellectual and partly social. At Clonard, Kieran, the son of a carpenter, sat in the same class as Colmcille, the son of a king. To Clonard, or to Aran, or to Clonmacnois went every man, rich or poor, prince or peasant, who wanted to sit at Finnian's, or at Enda's or at Kieran's feet and to learn of their wisdom.

Always it was the personality of the teacher that drew them there. And so it was all through Irish history. A great poet or a great scholar had his foster-children who lived at his house or fared with him through the country. Even long after Kinsale the Munster poets had their little groups of pupils; and the hedge schoolmasters of the nineteenth century were the last repositories of a high tradition.

Always it was the personality of the teacher that drew them there. And so it was all through Irish history. A great poet or a great scholar had his foster-children who lived at his house or fared with him through the country. Even long after Kinsale the Munster poets had their little groups of pupils; and the hedge schoolmasters of the nineteenth century were the last repositories of a high tradition.

I dwell on the importance of the personal element in education. I would have every child not merely a unit in a school attendance, but in some intimate personal way the pupil of a teacher, or, to use more expressive words, the disciple of a master. And here I nowise contradict my first position that the main object in education is to help the child to be his own true and best self. What the teacher should bring to his pupil is not a set of readymade opinions, or a stock of cut-and-dry information, but an inspiration and an example; and his main qualification should be, not such an over-mastering will as will impose itself at all hazards upon all weaker wills that come under its influence, but rather so infectious an enthusiasm as will kindle new enthusiasm. The Montessori system, so admirable in many ways, would seem at first sight to attach insufficient importance to the function of the teacher in the schoolroom. But this is not really so. True, it would make the spontaneous efforts of the children the main motive power, as against the dominating will of the teacher which is the main motive power in the ordinary schoolroom. But the teacher must be there always to inspire, to foster. If you would realise how true this is, how important the personality of the teacher, even in a Montessori school, try to imagine a Montessori school conducted by the average teacher of your acquaintance, or try to imagine a Montessori school conducted by yourself!

It will be seen that I claim that the ancient Irish system possessed pre-eminently two characteristics: first, freedom for the individual; and, secondly, an adequate inspiration. Without these two things you cannot have education, no matter how you may elaborate educational machinery, no matter how you may multiply educational programmes. And because those two things are pre-eminently lacking in what passes for education in Ireland, we have in Ireland strictly no education system at all; nothing that by any extension of the meaning of words can be called an education system. We have an elaborate machinery for teaching persons certain subjects, and the teaching is done more or less efficiently; more efficiently, I imagine, than such teaching is done in England or America. We have three universities and four boards of education. We have some thousands of buildings, large and small. We have an army of inspectors, mostly over-paid. We have a compulsory Education Act. We have the grave and bulky code of the Commissioners of National Education and the slim impertinent pamphlet which enshrines the wisdom of the Commissioners of Intermediate Education. We have a vast deal more in the shape of educational machinery and stage properties. But we have, I repeat, no education system; and only in isolated places have we any education. The essentials are lacking.

And first of freedom. The word freedom is no longer understood in Ireland. We have no experience of the thing, and we have almost lost our conception of the idea. So completely is this true that the very organisations which exist in Ireland to champion freedom show no disposition themselves to accord freedom; they challenge a great tyranny, but they exact their own little tyrannies. 'Thou shalt not' is half the law of ireland, and the other half of it: 'Thou must.'

Now, nowhere has the law of 'Thou shalt not' and 'Thou must' been so rigorous as in the schoolroom. Surely the first essentials of healthy life there was freedom. But there has been and there is no freedom in Irish education – no freedom for the child, no freedom for the teacher, no freedom for the school. Where young souls, young minds, young bodies demanded the largest measure of individual freedom consistent with the common good, freedom to move and grow on their natural lines, freedom to live their own lives, for what is natural life but natural growth? – freedom to bring themselves, as I have put it, tó their own perfection, there was a sheer denial of the right of the individual to grow in his own natural way, that is God's way. He had to develop not in God's way, but in the Board's way. The Board, National or Intermediate as the case might be, bound him hand and foot, chained his mind and soul, constricted him morally, mentally, and physically with the involuted folds of its rules and regulations, its programmes, its minutes, its reports and special reports, its pains and penalties. I have often thought that the type of Irish education was the Laocoon; that agonising father and his sons seem to me like the teacher and the pupils of an Irish school, the strong limbs of the man and the slender limbs of the boys caught together and crushed together in the grip of an awful fate. And Irish education has seemed to some like the bed of Procustes; the bed on which all men that passed that way must lie, be it never so big for them, be it never so small for them; the traveller for whom it was too large had his limbs stretched until he filled it; the traveller for whom it was too small had his limbs chopped off until he fitted into it — comfortably. It was a grim jest to play upon travellers; a grimmer jest to play on the children of a nation.

Our Irish systems took, and take, absolutely no cognisance of the differences between individuals, of the differences between localities and rural communities, of the differences springing from a different ancestry, Gaelic or Anglo-Saxon. the programme denies freedom to the individual teacher. Every school must conform to a type — and what a type! Every individual must conform to a type — and what a type! The teacher has not been at liberty, and in practice is not yet at liberty, to seek to discover the individual bents of his pupils, the hidden talent that is in every normal soul, to discover which and to cherish which, that it may in the fulness of time be put to some precious use, is the primary duty of the teacher. I knew one boy who passed through several schools a dunce and a laughing-stock; the National Board and the Intermediate Board had sat in judgment upon him and had damned him as a failure before men and angels. Yet a friend and fellow-worker of mine discovered that he was gifted with a wondrous sympathy for nature, that he loved and understood the ways of plants, that he had a strange minuteness and subtlety of observation — that, in short, he was the sort of boy likely to become an accomplished botanist. Once a colleague of mine summed up the whole philosophy of education in a maxim which startled a sober group of visitors: 'If a boy shows an aptitude for doing *anything* better than most people, he should be encouraged to do *that*, and to do it as well as possible; I don't care what it is — scotch-hop, if you like.'

III

The idea of a compulsory programme imposed by an external authority on every child in every school in a country is the direct contrary of the root idea involved in education. Yet, this is what we have in Ireland. In theory the primary schools have a certain amount of freedom; in practice they have none. Neither in theory nor in practice is such a thing dreamt of in the gloomy Limbo whose presiding demon is the Board of Intermediate Education for Ireland. Education, indeed, reaches its nadir in the Irish Inter-mediate system. At the present moment there are 15,000 boys and girls pounding at a programme drawn up for them by certain persons sitting round a table in Hume Street. Precisely the same text-books are being read to-night in every secondary school and college in Ireland. Two of Hawthorne's *Tanglewood Tales,* with a few poems in English, will constitute the whole literary pabulum of three-quarters of the pupils of the Irish secondary schools during this twelve-months. The teacher who seeks to give his pupils a wider horizon in literature does so at his peril. He will, no doubt, benefit his pupils, but he will infallibly reduce his results fees. As an Intermediate teacher said to me: 'Culture is all very well in its way, but if you don't stick to your programme you boys won't pass.' 'Stick to your pro-gramme' is the 'strange device' on the banner of the Irish Intermediate system; and the programme bulks so large that there is no room for education.

The first thing I plead for, therefore, is freedom; freedom for each school to shape its own programme in conformity with the circumstances of the school as to place, size, personnel, and so on; freedom again for the individual teacher to impart something of his own personality to his work, to bring his own peculiar gifts to the service of his pupils, to be, in short, a teacher, a master, one having an intimate and permanent relationship with his pupils, and not a mere part of the educational machine; a mere cog in the wheel; freedom finally for the individual pupil, and scope for his development within the system and within the school. And I would promote this idea of freedom by the very organisation of the school itself, giving a certain autonomy, not only to the school, but to the particular parts of the school; to the staff, of course, but also to the pupils and, in a large school, to the various sub-divisions of the pupils. I do not plead for anarchy. I plead for freedom within the law, for liberty, not licence, for that true freedom which can exist only where there is discipline, which exists in fact because each, valuing his own freedom, respects also the freedom of others.

And that this freedom may be availed of to the noble ends of education there must be, within the school system and within the school, an adequate inspiration. The school must make such an appeal to the pupil as shall resound throughout his after life, urging him always to be his best self, never his second-best self. Such an inspiration will come most adequately of all from religion. I do not think that there can be any education of which spiritual religion does not form an integral part; as it is the most important part of life, so it should be the most important part of education, which some have defined as a preparation for complete life. And inspiration will come also from the hero-stories of the world, and especially of our own people; from science and art if taught by people who are really scientists and artists, and not merely persons with certificates from Mr. T. W. Russell; from literature enjoyed as literature and not studied as 'texts', from the associations of the school place; finally and chiefly from the humanity and greatheartedness of the teacher.

A heroic tale is more essentially a factor in education than a proposition in Euclid. The story of Joan of Arc, or the story of Young Napoleon, means more for boys and girls than all the algebra in all the books. What the modern world wants more than anything else, what Ireland wants beyond all other modern countries, is a new birth of the heroic spirit. If our schools would set themselves *that* task, the task of fostering once again knightly courage and strength and truth — that type of efficiency rather than the peculiar type of efficiency demanded by the British Civil Service — we should have at last the beginning of an educational system. And what an appeal an Irish school system might have! What a rallying cry an Irish Minister of Education might give to Young Ireland! We must re-create and perpetuate in Ireland the knightly tradition of Cúchulainn; 'better is short life with honour than long life with dishonour," 'I care not though I were to live but one day and one night if only my fame and my deeds live after me; the noble tradition of the Fianna, 'we, the Fianna, never told a lie, false-hood was never imputed to us;' 'strength in our hands, truth on our lips, and purity in our hearts;' the Christ-like tradition of Colmcille, 'If I were to die it would be from excess of the love I bear the Gael.' And to that antique evangel should be added the evangels of later days; the stories of Red Hugh, Robert Emmet, and Eoghan O'Growney. I have seen Irish boys and girls moved inexpressibly by the story of Emmet or the story of Anne Devlin, and I have always felt it to be legitimate to make use for educational purposes of an exaltation so produced.

The value of the national factor in education would appear to rest chiefly in this, that it addresses itself to the most generous side of the child's nature, urging him to live up to his finest self. If the true work of the teacher be, as I have said, to help the child to realise himself at his best and worthiest, the factor of nationality is of prime importance, apart from any ulterior propagandist views the teacher may cherish. The school system which neglects it commits, even from the purely pedagogic point of view, a primary blunder. It neglects one of the most powerful of educational resources.

It is because Irish education has forgotten the importance of the national factor that it has so terrifically failed. Or rather it is because it has remembered the importance (from its own point of view) of forgetting it that it has so terrifically succeeded. For it has succeeded — succeeded in making slaves of us, if that was its object. Mr. John MacNeill has been more suggestive in discussing Irish education than anyone I know. He has compared the Irish education system to the systems of slave education which existed in the ancient Pagan republics side by side with the systems intended for the education of freemen. To the children of the free were taught all noble and goodly things which would tend to make them all strong, proud, and valiant; from the children of the slaves all such dangerous knowledge was hidden — they were taught, not to be strong, proud, and valiant, but to be sleek, to be obsequious, to be dexterous; the object was not to make them good men, but to make them good slaves. And so in Ireland. Our education system was designed by our masters in order to make us smooth and willing slaves. It has succeeded; succeeded so well that we no longer realise that we *are* slaves. Some of us even think our chains ornamental, and are are a little doubtful as to whether we shall be quite as comfortable and quite as respectable when a few of the links are knocked off by the passing of the Home Rule Bill.

It remains the crowning achievement of the National and Intermediate systems that they have brought such a change in this people that once loved freedom so passionately. Three-quarters of a century ago there still remained in Ireland a stubborn Irish thing which Cromwell had not trampled out, which the Penal Laws had not crushed, which the horrors of '98 had not daunted, which Pitt had not purchased; a national consciousness enshrined mainly in a national language. After three-quarters of a century's education that thing is nearly lost; so nearly, indeed, in these recent years that it sometimes seems that Home Rule, if come it does, will come too late to save it.

The new education system in Ireland has to do more than restore a national culture. It has to restore manhood to a race that has lost it. Along with its inspiration it must, therefore, bring a certain hardening. I would bring back some of the starkness of the antique world. No dream is more foolish than the dream of some sentimentalists that the reign of force is past, or passing; that the world's ancient battle laws have been repealed; that henceforward the first duty of every man is to be dapper.

And the old Ossianic definition of efficiency holds good: 'strength in our hands, truth on our lips, and purity in our hearts.' 'Strength in our hands!' The Gaelic Athletic Association, with all its faults, is more truly an educational body than any of your Education Boards.

And, finally, I say, inspiration must come from the teacher. If we can no longer send the children to the heroes and the seers and scholars to be fostered, we can at least bring some of the heroes and seers and scholars to the schools. We can rise up against the system which tolerates as teachers the rejected of all other professions rather than demanding for so priest-like an office the highest souls and noblest intellects of the race. I remember once going into a schoolroom in Belgium and finding an old man talking quietly and beautifully about literature to a silent class of boys; I was told that he was one of the most distinguished of contemporary Flemish poets. Here was the sort of personality, the sort of influence, one ought to see in a schoolroom. Not, indeed, that every poet would make a good schoolmaster or every good schoolmaster a poet. But how seldom here has the teacher any interest in literature at all; how seldom has he any horizon above his time table, any soul above his results fees!

The fact is that with rare exceptions, the men and women who are willing to work under the conditions as to personal dignity, freedom, tenure, or emolument which obtain in Irish schools are not the sort of men and women likely to make good educators. This part of the subject has recently been so much discussed in public that I need not dwell upon it. You are all alive to the truth that a teacher ought to be paid better than a policeman and to the scandal of the fact that many an able and cultured man is working in Irish secondary schools at a salary less than that of the Lord Mayor's coachman.

And now I have sufficiently indicated the general spirit in which I would have Irish education recreated. I say little of organisation, of mere machinery. That is the least important part of the subject. We can all foresee that the first task of an Irish Parliament must be destructive: that the lusty strokes of Gael and Gall, Ulster taking its manful part, will hew away and cast adrift the rotten and worm-eaten boards which support the grotesque fabric of the Irish education system. And then will come the work of re-construction. We can all foresee that, when an Irish Cabinet is constituted, there will be an Irish Minister of Education responsible to the Irish Parliament; that under him Irish education will be drawn into a homogeneous whole, — an organic unity will replace a composite freak in which the various members are not only not directed by a single intelligence but are often mutually antagonistic, and sometimes engaged in open warfare one with the other; like the preposterous donkey in the pantomime whose head is in perpetual strife with his heels because they belong to different individuals. The individual entities that compose the Irish educational donkey are four: the commissioners of National Education, the Commissioners of Intermediate Education, the Commissioners of Education for certain Endowed Schools, and last, but not least, the Department of Agriculture and Technical Instruction — the modern Ioldánach which in this realm protects science, art, fishery, needlework, poultry, foods and drugs, horse-breeding, etc., etc., etc., etc., and whose versatile chiefs can at a moment's notice switch off their attention from archaeology in the Nile Valley to the Foot and Mouth Disease in Mullingar. I must admit that the educational work of the Department as far as it affects secondary schools is done efficiently; but one will naturally expect this branch of its activity to be brought into the general education scheme under the Minister of Education. In addition to the four Boards I have enumerated I need hardly say that Dublin Castle has its finger in the pie, as it has in every unsavoury pie in Ireland. And behind Dublin Castle looms the master of Dublin Castle, and the master of all the Boards, and the master of everything in

Ireland — the British Treasury — arrogating claims over the veriest detail of education in Ireland for which there is no parallel in any other administration in the world and no sanction even in the British Constitution. You perceive the need of getting rid of British Treasury influence, and of taking measures to prevent any undue influence even of the future Irish Treasury. You perceive the need, too, of building up the whole system and giving it a common impulse. Under the Minister there might well be chiefs of the various sub-divisions, elementary, secondary, higher, and technical; but these should not be independent potentates, each entrenched in a different stronghold in a different part in the city. I do not see why they could not all occupy offices in the same corridor of the same building. The whole government of the kingdom of Belgium is carried on in one small building. A Council of some sort, with sub-committees, would doubtless be associated with the Minister, but I think its function should be advisory rather than executive: that all acts should be the acts of the Minister. As to the local organisation of elementary schools, there will always be need of a local manager, and personally I see no reason why the local management should be given to a district council rather than left as it is at present to some individual in the locality interested in education, but a thousand reasons why it should not. I would, however, make the teachers, both primary and secondary, a national service, guaranteeing an adequate salary, adequate security of tenure, adequate promotion, and adequate pension: and all this means adequate endowment, and freedom from the control of parsimonious officials.

The schools should have autonomy. The function of the central authority should be to co-ordinate, to maintain a standard, to advise, to inspire, to keep the teachers in touch with educational thought in other lands. I would transfer the centre of gravity of the system from the education office to the teachers; the teachers in fact would *be* the system. Teachers, and not clerks, would henceforth conduct the education of the country.

I need hardly say that the present Intermediate system must be abolished root and branch. Competitive examination in its present form must go. Well-paid teachers, well-equipped and beautiful schools, and a fund at the disposal of each school to enable it to award prizes on its own examinations based on its own programme — these would be among the characteristics of a new secondary system. Manual work, both indoor and outdoor, would, I hope, be part of the programme of every school. And the internal organisation might well follow the models of the little child-republics I described in the beginning, with their own laws and leaders, their fostering of individualities yet never at the expense of the commonwealth, their care for the body as well as for the mind, their nobly-ordered games, their spacious outdoor life, their intercourse with the wild things of the woods and wastes, their daily adventure face to face with elemental Life and Force, with its moral discipline, with its physical hardening.

And then, vivifying the whole, we need the divine breath that moves through free peoples, the breath that no man of Ireland has felt in his nostrils for so many centuries, the breath that once blew through the streets of Athens and that kindled, as wine kindles, the hearts of those who taught the learned in Clonmacnois.

The words and phrases of a language are always to some extent revelations of the mind of the race that has moulded the language. How often does an Irish vocable light up as with a lantern some immemorial Irish attitude, some whole phase of Irish thought! Thus, the words which the old Irish employed when they spoke of education show that they had gripped the very heart of that problem. To the old Irish the teacher was aite, 'fosterer', the pupil was dalta, 'foster-child', the system was aiteachas, 'fosterage'; words which we still retain as oide, dalta, oideachas.

And is it not the precise aim of education to 'foster'? Not to inform, to indoctrinate, to conduct through a course of studies (though these be the dictionary meanings of the word), but, first and last, to 'foster' the elements of character native to a soul, to help to bring these to their full perfection reather than to implant exotic excellences.

Fosterage implies a foster-father or foster-mother — a person — as its centre and inspiration rather than a code of rules. Modern education systems are elaborate pieces of machinery devised by highly-salaried officials for the purpose of turning out citizens according to certain approved patterns. The modern school is a state-controlled institution designed to produce workers for the state, and is in the same category with a dockyard or any other state-controlled institution which produces articles necessary to the progress, well-beling, and defence of the state. We speak of the 'efficiency', the 'cheapness', and the 'up-to-dateness' of an education system just as we speak of the 'efficiency', the 'cheapness', and the 'up-to-dateness' of a system of manufacturing coal-gas. We shall soon reach a stage when we shall speak of the 'efficiency', the 'cheapness' and the 'up-to-dateness' of our systems of soul-saving. We shall hear it said 'Salvation is very cheap in England', or 'The Germans are wonderfully efficient in prayer', or 'Gee, it takes a New York parson to hustle ginks into heaven'.

Now, education is as much concerned with souls as religion is. Religion is a Way of Life, and education is a preparation of the soul to live its life here and hereafter: to live it nobly and fully. And as we cannot think of a church without its Teacher, so we cannot think of a school without its Master. A school, in fact, according to the conception of our wise ancestors, was less a place than a person: a teacher with a little group of pupils clustering round him. Its place might be poor, nay, it might have no local habitation at all, it might be peripatetic: where the master went the disciples followed. One may think of Our Lord and His friends as a sort of school: was He not the Master, and were not they His disciples? That gracious conception was not only the conception of the old Gael, Pagan and Christian, but it was the conception of Europe all through the Middle Ages. Philosophy was not crammed out of text-books, but was learned at the knee of some great philosopher; art was learned in the studio of some master-artist, a craft in the workshop of some master-craftsman. Always it was the personality of the master that made the school, never the state that built it of brick and mortar, drew up a code of rules to govern it, and sent hirelings into it to carry out its decrees.

I do not know how far it is possible to revive the old ideal of fosterer and foster-child. I know it were very desirable. One sees too clearly that the modern system, under which the teacher tends more and more to become a mere civil servant, is making for the degradation of education, and will end in irreligion and anarchy. The modern child is coming to regard his teacher as an official paid by the state to render him certain services; services which it is in his interest to avail of, since by doing so he will increase his earning capacity later on; but services the rendering and acceptance of which no more imply a sacred relationship than do the rendering and acceptance of the services of a dentist or a chiropodist. There is thus coming about a complete reversal of the relative positions of master and disciple, a tendency which is increased by every statute that is placed on the statute book, by every rule that is added to the education code of modern countries.

Against this trend I would oppose the ideal of those who shaped the Gaelic polity nearly two thousand years ago. It is not merely that the old Irish had a good education system: they had the best and noblest that has ever been known among men. There has never been any human institution more adequate to its purpose than that which, in Pagan times, produced Cúchulainn and the Boy-Corps of Eamhain Macha and, in Christian times, produced Enda and the companions of his solitude in Aran. The old Irish system, Pagan and Christian, possessed in pre-eminent degree the thing most needful in education: an adequate inspiration. Colmcille suggested what that inspiration was when he said, 'If I die it shall be from the excess of the love that I bear the Gael'. A love and a service so excessive as to annihilate all thought of self, a recognition that one must give all, must be willing always to make the ultimate sacrifice — this is the inspiration alike of the story of Cúchulainn and of the story of Colmcille, the inspiration that made the one a hero and the other a saint.

The Murder Machine

.

I

THE BROAD ARROW

A French writer has paid the English a very well-deserved compliment. He says that they never commit a useless crime. When they hire a man to assassinate an Irish patriot, when they blow a Sepoy from the mouth of a cannon, when they produce a famine in one of their dependencies, they have always an ulterior motive. They do not do it for fun. Humorous as these crimes are, it is not the humour of them, but their utility, that appeals to the English. Unlike Gilbert's Mikado, they would see nothing humorous in boiling oil. If they retained boiling oil in their penal code, they would retain it, as they retain flogging before execution in Egypt, strictly because it has been found useful.

This observation will help one to an understanding of some portions of the English administration of Ireland. The English administration of Ireland has not been marked by any unnecessary cruelty. Every crime that the English have planned and carried out in Ireland has had a definite end. Every absurdity that they have set up has had a grave purpose. The Famine was not enacted merely from a love of horror. The Boards that rule Ireland were not contrived in order to add to the gaeity of nations. The Famine and the Boards are alike parts of a profound policy.

I have spent the greater part of my life in immediate comtemplation of the most grotesque and horrible of the English inventions for the debasement of Irleand. I mean their education system. The English once proposed in their Dublin Parliament a measure for the castration of all Irish priests who refused to quit Ireland. The proposal was so filthy that, although it duly passed the House and was transmitted to England with the warm recommendation of the Viceroy, it was not eventually adopted. But the English have actually carried out an even filthier thing. They have planned and established an education which more wickedly does violence to the elementary human rights of Irish children than would an edict for the general castration of Irish males. The system has aimed at the substitution for men and women of mere Things. It has not been an entire success. There are still a great many thousand men and women, in Ireland. But a great many thousand of what, by way of courtesy, we call men and women, are simply Things. Men and women, however depraved, have

371

kindly human allegiances. But these Things have no allegiance. Like other Things, they are for sale.

When one uses the term education system as the name of the system of schools, colleges, universities, and what not which the English have established in Ireland, one uses it as a convenient label, just as one uses the term government as a convenient label for the system of administration by police which obtains in Ireland instead of a government. There is no education system in Ireland. The English have established the simulacrum of an education system, but its object is the precise contrary of the object of an education system. Education should foster; this education is meant to repress. Education should inspire; this education is meant to tame. Education should harden; this education is meant to enervate. The English are too wise a people to attempt to educate the Irish, in any worthy sense. As well expect them to arm us.

Professor Eoin MacNeill has compared the English education system in Ireland to the systems of slave education which existed in the ancient pagan republics side by side with the systems intended for the education of freemen. To the children of the free were taught all noble and goodly things which would tend to made them strong and proud and valiant; from the children of the slaves all such dangerous knowledge was hidden. They were taught not to be strong and proud and valiant; but to be sleek, to be obsequious, to be dexterous: the object was not to make them good men, but to make them good slaves. And so in Ireland. The education system here was designed by our masters in order to make us willing or at least manageable slaves. It has made of some Irishmen not slaves merely, but very eunuchs, with the indifference and cruelty of eunuchs; kinless beings, who serve for pay a master that they neither love nor hate.

Ireland is not merely in servitude, but in a kind of penal servitude. Certain of the slaves among us are appointed jailors over the common herd of slaves. And they are trained from their youth for this degrading office. The ordinary slaves are trained for their lowly tasks in dingy places called schools; the buildings in which the higher slaves are trained are called colleges and universities. If one may regard Ireland as a nation in penal servitude, the schools and colleges and universities may be looked upon as the symbol of her penal servitude. They are, so to speak, the broad arrow upon the back of Ireland.

II

THE MURDER MACHINE

A few years ago, when people still believed in the imminence of Home Rule, there were numerous discussions as to the tasks awaiting a Home Rule Parliament and the order in which they should be taken up. Mr. John Dillon declared that one of the first of those tasks was the recasting of the Irish education system, by which he meant the English education system in Ireland. The declaration alarmed the Bishop of Limerick, always suspicious of Mr. Dillon, and he told that statesman in effect that the Irish education system did not need recasting — that all was well there.

The positions seemed irreconcilable. Yet in the Irish Review I quixotically attempted to find common ground between the disputants, and to state in such a way as to command the assent of both the duty of a hypothetical Irish Parliament with regard to education. I put it that what education in Ireland needed was less a reconstruction of its machinery than a regeneration in spirit. The machinery, I said, has doubtless its defects, but what is chiefly wrong with it is that it is mere machinery, a lifeless thing without a soul. Dr. O'Dwyer was probably concerned for the maintenance of portion of the machinery, valued by him as a Catholic Bishop, and not without reason; and I for one was (and am) willing to leave that particular portion untouched, or practically so. But the machine as a whole is no more capable of fulfilling the function for which it is needed than would an automaton be capable of fulfilling the function of a live teacher in a school. A soulless thing cannot teach; but it can destroy. A machine cannot make men; but it can break men.

One of the most terrible things about the English education system in Ireland is its ruthlessness. I know no image for that ruthlessness in the natural order. The ruthlessness of a wild beast has in it a certain grandeur of animal force. But this ruthlessness is literally without pity and without passion. It is cold and mechanical, like the ruthlessness of an immensely powerful engine. A machine vast, complicated, with a multitude of far-reaching arms, with many ponderous presses, carrying out mysterious and long-drawn processes of shaping and moulding, is the true image of the Irish education system. It grinds night and day; it obeys immutable and predetermined laws; it is as devoid of understanding, of sympathy, of imagination, as is any other piece of machinery that performs an appointed task. Into it is fed all the raw human material in Ireland; it seizes upon it inexorably and rends and compresses and re-moulds; and what it cannot refashion after the regulation pattern it ejects with all likeness of its former self crushed from it, a bruised and shapeless thing, thereafter accounted waste.

Our common parlance has become impressed with the conception of education as some sort of manufacturing process. Our children are the 'raw material'; we desiderate for their education 'modern methods' which must be 'efficient' but 'cheap'; we send them to Clongowes to be 'finished'; when 'finished' they are 'turned out'; specialists 'grind' them for the English Civil Service and the so-called liberal professions; in each of our great colleges there is a department known as the 'scrap-heap', though officially called the Fourth Preparatory — the limbo to which the debris ejected by the machine is relegated. The stuff there is either too hard or too soft to be moulded to the pattern required by the Civil Service Commissioners or the Incorporated Law Society.

In our adoption of the standpoint here indicated there is involved a primary blunder as to the nature and functions of education. For education has not to do with the manufacture of things, but with fostering the growth of things. And the conditions we should strive to bring about in our education system are not the conditions favourable to the rapid and cheap manufacture of readymades, but the conditions favourable to the growth of living organisims — the liberty and the light and the gladness of a ploughed field under the spring sunshine.

In particular I would urge that the Irish school system of the future should give freedom — freedom to the individual school, freedom to the individual teacher, freedom as far as may be to the individual pupil. Without freedom there can be no right growth; and education is properly the fostering of the right growth of a personality. Our school system must bring, too, some gallant inspiration. And with the inspiration it must bring a certain hardening. One scarcely knows whether modern sentimentalism or modern utilitarianism is the more sure sign of modern decadence. I would boldly preach the antique faith that fighting is the only noble thing, and that he only is at peace with God who is at war with the powers of evil.

In a true education system, religion, patriotism, literature, art and science, would be brought in such a way into the daily lives of boys and girls as to affect their character and conduct. We may assume that religion is a vital thing in Irish schools, but I know that the other things, speaking broadly, do no exist. There are no ideas there, no love of beauty, no love of books, no love of knowledge, no heroic inspiration. And there is no room for such things either on the Earth or in the heavens, for the Earth is cumbered and the heavens are darkened by the monstrous bulk of the programme. Most of the educators detest the programme. They are like the adherents of a dead creed who continue to mumble formulas and to make obeisance before an idol which they have found out to be a spurious divinity.

Mr. Dillon was to be sympathised with, even though pathetically premature, in looking to the then anticipated advent of Home Rule for a chance to make education what it should be. But I doubt if he and the others who would have had power in a Home Rule Parliament realised that what is needed here is not reform, not even a revolution, but a vastly bigger thing — a creation. It is not a question of pulling machinery asunder and piecing it together again; it is a question of breathing into a dead thing a living soul.

III

"I DENY"

I postulate that there is no education in Ireland apart from the voluntary efforts of a few people, mostly mad. Let us therefore not talk of reform, or of reconstruction. You cannot reform that which is not; you cannot by any process of reconstruction give organic life to a negation. In a literal sense the work of the first Minister of Education in a free Ireland will be a work of creation; for out of chaos he will have to evolve order and into a dead mass he will have to breathe the breath of life.

The English thing that is called education in Ireland is founded on a denial of the Irish nation. No education can start with a Nego, any more than a religion can. Everything that even pretends to be true begins with its Credo. It is obvious that the savage who says 'I believe in Mumbo Jumbo' is nearer to true religion than the philosopher who says 'I deny God and the spiritual in man'. Now, to teach a child to deny is the greatest crime a man or a State can commit. Certain schools in Ireland teach children to deny their religion; nearly all the schools in Ireland teach children to deny their nation. 'I deny the spirituality of my nation; I deny the lineage of my blood; I deny my rights and responsibilities'. This Nego is their Credo, this evil their good.

To invent such a system of teaching and to persuade us that it is an education system, an Irish education system to be defended by Irishmen against attack, is the most wonderful thing the English have accomplished in Ireland; and the most wicked.

AGAINST MODERNISM

All the speculations one saw a few years ago as to the probable effect of Home Rule on education in Ireland showed one how inadequately the problem was grasped. To some the expected advent of Home Rule seemed to promise as its main fruition in the field of education the raising of their salaries; to others the supreme thing it was to bring in its train was the abolition of Dr. Starkie; to some again it held out the delightful prospect of Orange boys and Orange girls being forced to learn Irish; to others it meant the dawn of an era of commonsense, the ushering in of the reign of 'a sound modern education', suitable to the needs of a progressive modern people.

I scandalised many people at the time by saying that the last was the view that irritated me most. The first view was not so selfish as it might appear, for between the salary offered to teachers and the excellence of a country's education system there is a vital connection. And the second and third forecasts at any rate opened up picturesque vistas. The passing of Dr. Starkie would have had something of the pageantry of the banishment of Napoleon to St. Helena (an effect which would have been heightened had he been accompanied into exile by Mr. Bonaparte Wyse), and the prospect of the children of Sandy Row being taught to curse the Pope in Irish was rich and soul-satisfying. These things we might or might not have seen had Home Rule come. But I expressed the hope that even Home Rule would not commit Ireland to an ideal so low as the ideal underlying the phrase 'a sound modern education'.

It is a vile phrase, one of the vilest I know. Yet we find it in nearly every school prospectus, and it comes pat to the lips of nearly everyone that writes or talks about schools.

Now, there can be no such thing as 'a sound modern education' — as well talk about a 'lively modern faith' or a 'serviceable modern religion'. It should be obvious that the more 'modern' an education is the less 'sound', for in education 'modernism' is as much a heresy as in religion. In both mediaevalism were a truer standard. We are too fond of clapping ourselves upon the back because we live in modern times, and we preen ourselves quite ridiculously (and unnecessarily) in our modern progress. There is, of course, such a thing as modern progress, but it has been won at how great a cost? How many precious things have we flung from us to lighten ourselves for that race?

And in some directions we have progressed not at all, or we have progressed in a circle; perhaps, indeed, all progress on this planet and on every planet, is in a circle, just as every line you draw on a globe is a circle or part of one. Modern speculation is often a mere groping where ancient men saw clearly. All the problems with which we strive (I mean all the really important problems) were long ago solved by our ancestors, only their solutions have been forgotten. There have been States in which the rich did not grind the poor, although there are no such States now; there have been free self-governing democracies, although there are few such democracies now; there have been rich and beautiful social organisations, with an art and a culture and a religion in every man's house, though for such a thing today we have to search out some sequestered people living by a desolate seashore or in a high forgotten valley among lonely hills — a hamlet of Iar-Connacht or a village in the Austrian Alps. Mankind, I repeat, or some section of mankind, has solved all its main problems somewhere and at some time. I suppose no universal and permanent solution is possible as long as the old Adam remains in us, the Adam that makes each one of us, and each tribe of us, something of the rebel, of the freethinker, of the adventurer, of the egoist. But the solutions are there, and it is because we fail in clearness of vision or in boldness of heart or in singleness of purpose that we cannot find them.

V

AN IDEAL IN EDUCATION

The words and phrases of a language are always to some extent revelations of the mind of the race that has moulded the language. How often does an Irish voacable light up as with a lantern some immemorial Irish attitude, some whole phase of Irish thought? Thus, the words which the old Irish employed when they spoke of education show that they had gripped the very heart of that problem. To the old Irish the teacher was aite, 'fosterer', the pupil was dalta, 'foster-child', the system was aiteachas, 'fosterage'; words which we still retain as oide, dalta, oideachas.

And is it not the precise aim of education to 'foster'? Not to inform, to indoctrinate, to conduct through a course of studies (though these be the dictionary meanings of the word), but, first and last, to 'foster' the elements of character native to a soul, to help to bring these to their full perfection rather than to implant exotic excellences.

Fosterage implies a foster-father or foster-mother — a person — as its centre and inspiration rather than a code of rules. Modern education systems are elaborate pieces of machinery devised by highly salaried officials for the purpose of turning out citizens according to certain approved patterns. The modern school is a State-controlled institution designed to produce workers for the State, and is in the same category with a dockyard or any other State-controlled institution which produces articles necessary to the progress, well-being, and defence of the State. We speak of the 'efficiency', the 'cheapness', and the 'up-to-dateness' of a system of manufacturing coal-gas. We shall soon reach a stage when we shall speak of the 'efficeincy', the 'cheapness', and the 'up-to-dateness' of our systems of soul saving. We shall hear it said 'salvation is very cheap in England', or 'The Germans are wonderfully efficient in prayer', or 'Gee it takes a New York parson to hustle ginks into heaven'.

Now, education is as much concerned with souls as religion is. Religion is a Way of Life, and education is a preparation of the soul to live its life here and hereafter; to live it nobly and fully. And as we cannot think of religion without a Person as its centre, as we cannot think of a church without its Teacher, so we cannot think of a school without its Master. A school, in fact, according to the conception of our wise ancestors, was less a place than a little group of persons, a teacher and his pupils. Its place might be poor, nay, it might have no local habitation at all, it might be peripatetic; where the master went the disciples followed. One may think of Our Lord and His friends as a sort of school; was He not the Master, and were not they His disciples? That gracious conception was not only the conception of the old Gael, pagan and Christian, but it was the conception of Europe all through the Middle Ages. Philosophy was not crammed out of text-

376

books, but was learned at the knee of some great philosopher; art was learned in the studio of some master-artist, a craft in the workshop of some master-craftsman. Always it was the personality of the master that made the school, never the State that built it of brick and mortar, drew up a code of rules to govern it, and sent hirelings into it to carry out its decrees.

I do not know how far it is possible to revive the old ideal of fosterer and foster-child. I know it were very desirable. One sees too clearly that the modern system, under which the teacher tends more and more to become a mere civil servant, is making for the degradation of education, and will end in irreligion and anarchy. The modern child is coming to regard his teacher as an official paid by the State to render him certain services; services which it is in his interest to avail of, since by doing so he will increase his earning capacity later on; but services the rendering and acceptance of which no more imply a sacred relationship than do the rendering and acceptance of the services of a dentist or a chiropodist. There is thus coming about a complete reversal of the relative positions of master and disciple, a tendency which is increased by every statute that is placed on the statute book, by every rule that is added to the education code of modern countries.

Against this trend I would oppose the ideal of those who shaped the Gaelic polity nearly two thousand years ago. It is not merely that the old Irish had a good education system; they had the best and noblest that has ever been known among men. There has never been any human institution more adequate to its purpose than that which, in pagan times, produced Cúchulainn and the Boy-Corps of Eamhain Macha and, in Christian times, produced Enda and the companions of his solitude in Aran. The old Irish system, pagan and Christian, possessed in pre-eminent degree the thing most needful in education; an adequate inspiration. Colmcille suggested what that inspiration was when he said, 'If I die it shall be from the excess of the love that I bear the Gael'. A love and a service so excessive as to annihilate all thought of self, a recognition that one must give all, must be willing always to make the ultimate sacrifice — this is the inspiration alike of the story of Cúchulainn and of the story of Colmcille, the inspiration that made the one a hero and the other a saint.

VI

MASTER AND DISCIPLES

In the Middle Ages there were everywhere little groups of persons clustering round some beloved teacher, and thus it was that men learned not only the humanities but all gracious and useful crafts. There were no State art schools, no State technical schools: as I have said, men became artists in the studio of some master-artist, men learned crafts in the workshop of some master-craftsman. It was always the individual inspiring, guiding, fostering other individuals; never the State usurping the place of father or fosterer, dispensing education like a universal provider of readymades, aiming at turning out all men and women according to regulation patterns.

In Ireland the older and truer conception was never lost sight of. It persisted into Christian times when a Kieran or an Enda or a Colmcille gathered his little group of foster-children (the old word was still used) around him; they were collectively his family, his household, his clann —

377

many sweet and endearing words were used to mark the intimacy of that relationship. It seems to me that there has been nothing nobler in the history of education than this development of the old Irish plan of fosterage under a Christian rule, when to the pagan ideals of strength and truth there were added the Christian ideals of love and humility. And this, remember, was not the education system of an aristocracy, but the education system of a people. It was more democratic than any education system in the world today. Our very divisions into primary, secondary, and university crystallize a snobbishness partly intellectual and partly social. At Clonard Kieran, the son of a carpenter, sat in the same class as Colmcille, the son of a king. To Clonard or to Aran or to Clonmacnois went every man, rich or poor, prince or peasant, who wanted to sit at Finnian's or at Enda's or at Kieran's feet and to learn of his wisdom.

Always it was the personality of the teacher that drew them there. And so it was all through Irish history. A great poet or a great scholar had his foster-children who lived at his house or fared with him through the country. Even long after Kinsale the Munster poets had their little groups of pupils; and the hedge schoolmasters of the nineteenth century were the last repositories of a high tradition.

I dwell on the importance of the personal element in education. I would have every child not merely a unit in a school attendance, but in some intimate personal way the pupil of a teacher, or, to use more expressive words, the disciple of a master. And here I nowise contradict another position of mine, that the main object in education is to help the child to be his own true and best self. What the teacher should bring to his pupil is not a set of readymade opinions, or a stock of cut-and-dry information, but an inspiration and an example; and his main qualification should be, not such an overmastering will as shall impose itself at all hazards upon all weaker wills that come under its influence, but rather so infectious an enthusiasm as shall kindle new enthusiasm. The Montessori system, so admirable in many ways, would seem at first sight to attach insufficient importance to the function of the teacher in the schoolroom. But this is not really so. True, it would make the spontaneous efforts of the children the main motive power, as against the dominating will of the teacher which is the main motive power in the ordinary schoolroom. But the teacher must be there always to inspire, to foster. If you would realise how true this is, how important the personality of the teacher, even in a Montessori school, try to imagine a Montessori school conducted by the average teacher of your acquantance, or try to imagine a Montessori school conducted by yourself!

VII

OF FREEDOM IN EDUCATION

I have claimed elsewhere that the native Irish education system possessed pre-eminently two characteristics: first, freedom for the individual, and, secondly, an adequate inspiration. Without these two things you cannot have education, no matter how you may elaborate educational machinery, no matter how you may multiply educational programmes. And because those two things are preeminently lacking in what passes for education in Ireland, we have in Ireland strictly no education system at all; nothing that by any extension of the meaning of words can be called an education system. We have an elaborate machinery for teaching persons certain subjects, and the teaching is done more or less efficiently; more efficiently, I imagine, than such teaching is done in England or in America. We have three universities and four boards of education. We have some thousands of buildings, large and small. We have an army of inspectors, mostly overpaid. We have a host of teachers, mostly underpaid. We have a Compulsory Education Act. We have the grave and bulky code of the Commissioners of National Education, and the slim impertinent pamphlet which enshrines the wisdom of the Commissioners of Intermediate Education. We have a vast deal more in the shape of educational machinery and stage properties. But we have, I repeat, no education system; and only in isolated places have we any education. The essentials are lacking.

And first of freedom. The word freedom is no longer understood in Ireland. We have no experience of the thing, and we have almost lost our conception of the idea. So completely is this true that the very organisations which exist in Ireland to champion freedom show no disposition themselves to accord freedom: they challenge a great tyranny, but they erect their little tyrannies 'Thou shalt not' is half the law of Ireland, and the other half is 'Thou must'.

Now, nowhere has the law of 'Thou shalt not' and 'Thou must' been so rigorous as in the schoolroom. Surely the first essential of healthy life there was freedom. But there has been and there is no freedom in Irish education; no freedom for the child, no freedom for the teacher, no freedom for the school. Where young souls, young minds, young bodies, demanded the largest measure of individual freedom consistent with the common good, freedom to move and grow on their natural lines, freedom to live their own lives — for what is natural life but natural growth? — freedom to bring themselves, as I have put it elsewhere, to their own perfection, there was a sheer denial of the right of the individual to grow in his own natural way, in God's way. He had to develop not in God's way, but in the Board's way. The Board, National or Intermediate as the case might be, bound him hand and foot, chained him mind and soul, constricted him morally, mentally, and physically with the involuted folds of its rules and regulations, its programmes, its minutes, its reports and special reports, its pains and penalties. I have often thought that the type of English education in Ireland was the Laocoon: that agonising father and his sons seem to me like the teacher and the pupils of an Irish school, the strong limbs of the man and the slender limbs of the boys caught together and crushed together in the grip of an awful fate. And English education in Ireland has seemed to some like the bed of Procustes, the bed on which all men that passed that way must lie, be it never so big for them, be it never so small for them: the traveller for whom it was too large had his limbs stretched until he filled it; the traveller for whom it,was too small had his limbs chopped off until he fitted into it — comfortably. It was a grim jest to play upon travellers. The English have done it to Irish children not by way of jest, but with a purpose. Our English-Irish systems took, and take, absolutely no cognizance of the differences between individuals, of the differences between localities, of the differences between urban and rural communities, of the differences springing from a different ancestry, Gaelic or Anglo-Saxon. Every school must conform to a type — and what a type! Every individual must conform to a type — and what a type! The teacher has not been at liberty, and in practice is not yet at liberty, to seek to discover the individual bents of his pupils, the hidden talent that is in every normal soul, to discover which and to cherish which, that it may in the fullness of time be put to some precious use, is the primary duty of the teacher. I knew one boy who passed through several schools a dunce and a laughing-stock; the National Board and the Intermediate Board had sat in judgement upon him and had damned him as a failure before men and angels. Yet a friend and fellow-worker of mine discovered that he was gifted with a wondrous sympathy for nature, that he loved and understood the ways of plants, that he had a strange minuteness and subtlety of observation — that, in short, he was the sort of boy likely to become an accomplished botanist. I knew another boy of whom his father said to me: 'He is not good at books, he is no good at work; he is good at nothing but playing the tin whistle. What am I to do with him?' I shocked the worthy man by replying (though really it was the obvious thing to reply): 'Buy a tin whistle for him'. Once a colleague of mine summed up the whole philosophy of education in a maxim which startled a sober group of visitors: 'If a boy shows an aptitude for doing any-thing better than most people, he should be encouraged to do that, and to do it as well as possible; I don't care what it is — scotch-hop, if you like'.

The idea of a compulsory programme imposed by an external authority upon every child in every school in a country is the direct contrary of the root idea involved in education. Yet this is what we have in Ireland. In theory the primary schools have a certain amount of freedom; in practice they have none. Neither in theory nor in practice is such a thing as freedom dreamt of in the gloomy limbo whose presiding demon is the Board of Intermediate Education for Ireland. Education, indeed, reaches its nadir in the Irish Intermediate system. At the present moment there are 15,000 boys and girls pounding at a programme drawn up for them by certain persons sitting round a table in Hume Street. Precisely the same textbooks are being read tonight in every secondary school and college in Ireland. Two of Hawthorne's Tanglewood Tales, with a few poems in English, will constitute the whole literary pabulum of three-quarters of the pupils of the Irish secondary schools during this twelvemonths. The teacher who seeks to give his pupils a wider horizon in literature does so at his peril. He will, no doubt, benefit his pupils, but he will infallibly reduce his results fees. As an intermediate teacher said to me, 'Culture is all very well in its way, but if you don't stick to your programme your boys won't pass'. 'Stick to your programme' is the strange device on the banner of the Irish Intermediate system; and the programme bulks so large that there is no room for

The first thing I plead for, therefore, is freedom: freedom for each school to shape its own programme in conformity with the circumstances of the school as to place, size, personnel, and so on; freedom again for the individual teacher to impart something of his own authority to his work, to bring his own peculiar gifts to the service of his pupils, to be, in short, a teacher, a master, one having an intimate and permanent relationship with his pupils, and not a mere part of the educational machine, a mere cog in the wheel; freedom finally for the individual pupil and scope for his development within the school and within the system. And I would promote this idea of freedom by the very organisation of the school itself, giving a certain autonomy not only to the school, but to the particular parts of the school: to the various sub-divisions of the pupils. I do not plead for anarchy. I plead for freedom within the law, for liberty, not licence, for that true freedom which can exist only where there is discipline, which exists in fact because each, valuing his own freedom, respects also the freedom of others.

380

VIII

BACK TO THE SAGAS

That freedom may be availed of to the noble ends of education there must be, within the school system and within the school, an adequate inspiration. The school must make such an appeal to the pupil as shall resound throughout his after life, urging him always to be his best self, never his second-best self. Such an inspiration will come most adequately of all from religion. I do not think that there can be any education of which spiritual religion does not form an integral part; as it is the most important part of life, so it should be the most important part of education, which some have defined as a preparation for complete life. And inspiration will come also from the hero-stories of the world, and especially of our own people; from science and art if taught by people who are really scientists and artists, and not merely persons with certificates from Mr. T. W. Russell; from literature enjoyed as literature and not sudied as 'texts'; from the associations of the school place; finally and chiefly from the humanity and great-heartedness of the teacher.

A heroic tale is more essentially a factor in education than a proposition in Euclid. The story of Joan of Arc or the story of the young Napoleon means more for boys and girls than all the algebra in all the books. What the modern world wants more than anything else, what Ireland wants beyond all other modern countries, is a new birth of the heroic spirit. If our schools would set themselves tha' task, the task, of fostering once again knightly courage and strength and truth — that type of efficiency rather than the peculiar type of efficiency demanded by the English Civil Service — we should have at least the beginning of an educational system. And what an appeal an Irish school system might have! What a Rally cry an Irish Minister of Education might give to young Ireland! When we were starting St. Enda's I said to my boys: 'We must re-create and perpetuate in Ireland the knightly tradition of Cúchulainn, "better is short life with honour than long life with dishonour"; "I care not though I were to live but one day and one night, if only my fame and my deeds live after me"; the noble tradition of the Fianna, "we, the Fianna, never told a lie, falsehood was never imputed to us"; "strength in our hands, truth on our lips, and cleanness in our hearts"; the Christ-like tradition of Colmcille, "if I die it shall be from the excess of the love I bear the Gael".' And to that antique evangel should be added the stories of Red Hugh and Wolfe Tone and Robert Emmet and John Mitchel and O'Donovan Rossa and Eoghan O'Growney. I have seen Irish boys and girls moved inexpressibly by the story of Emmet or the story of Anne Devlin, and I have always felt it to be legitimate to make use for educational purposes of an exaltation so produced.

The value of the national factor in education would appear to rest chiefly in this, that it addresses itself to the most generous side of the child's nature, urging him to live up to his finest self. If the true work of the teacher be, as I have said, to help the child to realise himself at his best and worthiest, the factor of nationality is of prime importance, apart from any ulterior propagandist view the teacher may cherish. The school system which neglects it commits, even from the purely pedagogic point of view, a primary blunder. It neglects one of the most powerful of educational resources.

It is because the English education system in Ireland has deliberately eliminated the national factor that it has so terrifically succeeded. For it has succeeded — succeeded in making slaves of us. And it has succeeded so well that we no longer realise that we are slaves. Some of us even think our chains ornamental, and are a little doubtful as to whether we shall be quite as comfortable and quite as respectable when they are hacked off.

It remains the crowning achievement of the 'National' and Intermediate system that they have wrought such a change in this people that once loved freedom so passionately. Three-quarters of a century ago there still remained in Ireland a stubborn Irish thing which Cromwell had not trampled out, which the Penal Laws had not crushed, which the horrors of '98 had not daunted, which Pitt had not purchased: a national consciousness enshrined mainly in a national language. After three-quarters of a century's education that thing is nearly lost.

A new education system in Ireland has to do more than restore a national culture. It has to restore manhood to a race that has been deprived of it. Along with its inspiration it must, therefore, bring a certain hardening. It must lead Ireland back to her sagas.

Finally, I say, inspiration must come from the teacher. If we can no longer send the children to the heroes and seers and scholars to be fostered, we can at least bring some of the heroes and seers and scholars to the schools. We can rise up against the system which tolerates as teachers the rejected of all other professions rather than demanding for so priest-like an office the highest souls and noblest intellects of the race. I remember once going into a schoolroom in Belgium and finding an old man talking quietly and beautifully about literature to a silent class of boys; I was told that he was one of the most distinguished of contemporary Flemish poets. Here was the sort of personality, the sort of influence, one ought to see in a schoolroom. Not, indeed, that every poet would make a good schoolmaster, or every schoolmaster a good poet. But how seldom here has the teacher any interest in literature at all; how seldom has he any horizon above his time-table, any soul larger than his results fees!

The fact is that, with rare exceptions, the men and women who are willing to work under the conditions as to personal dignity, freedom, tenure, and emolument which obtain in Irish schools are not the sort of men and women likely to make good educators. This part of the subject has been so much discussed in public that one need not dwell upon it. We are all alive to the truth that a teacher ought to be paid better than a policeman, and to the scandal of the fact that many an able and cultured man is working in Irish secondary schools at a salary less than that of the Viceroy's chauffeur.

IX

WHEN WE ARE FREE

In these chapters I have sufficiently indicated the general spirit in which I would have Irish education re-created. I say little of organisation, of mere machinery. That is the least important part of the subject. We can all foresee that the first task of a free Ireland must be destructive: that the lusty strokes of Gael and Gall, Ulster taking its manful part, will hew away and cast adrift the rotten and worm-eaten boards which support the grotesque fabric of the English education system. We can all see that, when an Irish Government is constituted, there will be an Irish Minister of Education responsible to the Irish Parliament; that under him Irish education will be drawn into a homogeneous whole — an organic unity will replace a composite freak in which the various members are not only not directed by a single intelligence but are often mutually antagonistic, and sometimes engaged in open warfare one with the other, like the preposterous donkey in the pantomime whose head is in perpetual strife with his heels because they belong to different individuals. The individual entities that compose the English-Irish educational donkey are four: the Commissioners of National Education, the Commissioners of Intermediate Education, the Commissioners of Education for certain Endowed Schools, and last, but not least, the Department of Agriculture and Technical Instruction — the modern Ioldánach which in this realm protects science, art, fishery, needlework, poultry, foods and drugs, horse-breeding, etc., etc., etc., etc., and whose versatile chiefs can at a moment's notice switch off their attention from archaeology in the Nile Valley to the Foot and Mouth Disease in Mullingar. I must admit that the educational work of the Department as far as it affects secondary schools is done efficiently; but one will naturally expect this branch of its activity to be brought into the general education scheme under the Minister of Education. In addition to the four Boards I have enumerated I need hardly say that Dublin Castle has its finger in the pie, as it has in every unsavoury pie in Ireland. And behind Dublin Castle looms the master of Dublin Castle, and the master of all the Boards, and the master of everything in Ireland — the British Treasury — arrogating claims over the veriest details of education in Ireland for which there is no parallel in any other adminsitration in the world and no sanction even in the British Constitution. My scheme, of course, presupposes the getting rid not only of the British Treasury, but of the British connection.

One perceives the need, too, of linking up the whole system and giving it a common impulse. Under the Minister there might well be chiefs of the various sub-divisions, elementary, secondary, higher and technical; but these should not be independent potentates, each entrenched in a different stronghold in a different part of the city. I do not see why they could not all occupy offices in the same corridor of the same building. The whole government of the free kingdom of Belgium was carried on in one small building. A Council of some sort, with sub-committees, would doubtless be associated with the Minister, but I think its function should be advisory rather than executive; that all acts should be the acts of the Minister. As to the local organisation of elementary schools, there will always be need of a local manager, and personally I see no reason why the local management should be given to a district council rather than left as it is at present to some individual in the locality interested in education, but a thousand reasons why it should not. I would, however, make the teachers, both primary and secondary, a national service, guaranteeing an adequate salary, adequate security of tenure, adequate promotion, and adequate pension: and all this means adequate endowment, and freedom from the control of parsimonious officials.

In the matter of language I would order things bilingually. But I would not apply the Belgium system exactly as I have described it in *An Claidheamh Soluis*. The status quo in Ireland is different from that in Belgium; the ideal to be aimed at in Ireland is different from that in

Belgium. Ireland is six-sevenths English-speaking with an Irish-speaking seventh. Belgium is divided into two nearly equal halves, one Flemish, the other French. Irish Nationalists would resote Irish as a vernacular to the English-speaking six-sevenths, and would establish Irish as the national language of a free Ireland: Belgian Nationalists would simply preserve their 'two national languages', according them equal rights and privileges. What then? Irish should be made the language of instruction in districts where it is the home language, and English the 'second language', taught as a school subject: I would not at any stage use English as a medium of instruction in such districts, anything that I have elsewhere said as to Belgian practice notwithstanding. Where English is the home language it must of necessity be the 'first language' in the schools, but I would have a compulsory 'second language', satisfied that this 'second language' in five-sixths of the schools would be Irish. And I would see that the 'second language' be utilised as a medium of instruction from the earliest stages. In this way, and in no other way that I can imagine, can Irish be restored as a vernacular to English-speaking Ireland.

But in all the details of their programmes the schools should have autonomy. The function of the central authority should be to co-ordinate, to maintain a standard, to advise, to inspire, to keep the teachers in touch with educational thought in other lands. I would transfer the centre of gravity of the system from the education office to the teachers; the teachers in fact would be the system. Teachers, and not clerks, would henceforth conduct the education of the country.

The inspectors, again, would be selected from the teachers, and the chiefs of departments from the inspectors. And promoted teachers would man the staffs of the training colleges, which, for the rest, would work in close touch with the universities.

I need hardly say that the present Intermediate system must be abolished. Good men will curse it in its passing. It is the most evil thing that Ireland has ever known. Dr. Hyde once finely described the National and Intermediate Boards as:

'Death and the nightmare Death-in-Life
That thicks men's blood with cold.'

Of the two Death-in-Life is the more hideous. It is sleeker than, but equally as obscene as, its fellow-fiend. The thing has damned more souls than the Drink Traffic or the White Slave Traffic. Down with it — down among the dead men! Let it promote competitive examinations in the under-world, if it will.

Well-trained and well-paid teachers, well-equipped and beautiful schools, and a fund at the disposal of each school to enable it to award prizes on its own tests based on its own programme — these would be among the characteristics of a new secondary system. Manual work both indoor and outdoor, would I hope, be part of the programme of every school. And the internal organisation might well follow the models of the little child-republics I have elsewhere described, with their own laws and leaders, their fostering of individualities yet never at the expense of the common wealth, their care for the body as well as for the mind, their nobly-ordered games, their spacious outdoor life, their intercourse with the wild things of the woods and wastes, their daily adventure face to face with elemental Life and Force, with its moral discipline, with its physical hardening.

And then, vivifying the whole, we need the divine breath that moves through free peoples, the breath that no man of Ireland has felt in his nostrils for so many centuries, the breath that once blew through the streets of Athens and that kindled, as wine kindles, the hearts of those who taught and learned in Clonmacnois.

Tabulated Bibliography

I. AN CLAIDHEAMH SOLUIS 1903-09

1. The Issue at Stake.   ACS 14.3.1903.
2. The University Commission Report.   ACS 28.3.1903.
3. Maynooth.   ACS 18.4.1903.
4. The New Coiste Gnótha: Its Work   ACS 9.5.1903.
5. The British University.   ACS 31.10.1903.
6. An Educational Programme.   ACS 7.11.1903.
7. Sham Teaching and Real Teaching.   ACS 14.11.1903.
8. The Function of Nationalism in Education.   ACS 5.12.1903.
9. An Educational Policy.   ACS 12.12.1903.
10. The 'Still Small Voice' Answered.   ACS 19.12.1903.
11. The Primary Schools.   ACS 26.12.1903.
12. Bilingual Education.   ACS 2.1.1904.
13. Bilingual Education.   ACS 9.1.1904.
14. Bilingual Education.   ACS 16.1.1904.
15. Bilingual Education.   ACS 23.1.1904.
16. The University Question.   ACS 30.1.1904.
17. The University Question.   ACS 6.2.1904.
18. Mr. Dale on the Irish Language.   ACS 26.3.1904.
19. A National Education.   ACS 16.4.1904.
20. Bilingual Education.   ACS 23.4.1904.
21. The Bilingual Programme.   ACS 30.4.1904.
22. The Bilingual Programme.   ACS 7.5.1904.
23. Ways and Means.   ACS 14.5.1904.
24. Irish Education.   ACS 28.5.1904.
25. The Training Colleges.   ACS 18.6.1904.
26. The Education Question.   ACS 13.8.1904.
27. Primary Schools.   ACS 20.8.1904.
28. The Bilingual Programme.   ACS 24.9.1904.
29. The Bilingual Programme in Practice.   ACS 1.10.1904.
30. The Bilingual Programme in an Irish-Speaking
    District.   ACS 8.10.1904.
31. The Bilingual Programme in Operation.   ACS 15.10.1904.
32. The Programme in a Bilingual District.   ACS 22.10.1904.

33. The Training Colleges.   ACS 22.10.1904.
34. The Inspection of Bilingual Schools.   ACS 29.10.1904.
35. Text-Books.   ACS 5.11.1904.
36. The Philosophy of Education.   ACS 12.11.1904.
37. The National Language in Maynooth.   ACS 12.11.1904.
38. The Children.   ACS 26.11.1904.
39. The University Question.   ACS 17.12.1904.
40. What is a National Language?   ACS 28.1.1905.
41. The University Question: Mr. Gwynn's Proposals.   ACS 28.1.1905.
42. Language and Nationality.   ACS 4.2.1905.
43. The British Treasury and Ireland.   ACS 25.2.1905.
44. The Training Colleges.   ACS 8.4.1905.
45. The Board, The Training Colleges and the National Language.   ACS 15.4.1905.
46. The Training Colleges and Irish.   ACS 22.4.1905.
47. A Welsh Syllabus.   ACS 10.6.1905.
48. More Points from Wales.   ACS 17.6.1905.
49. Reform of the National Board.   ACS 15.7.1905.
50. A National Board Minute.   ACS 26.8.1905.
51. What We Want.   ACS 9.9.1905.
52. How to Solve the Education Question.   ACS 16.9.1905.
53. Irish in Secondary Schools.   ACS 18.11.1905.
54. The Secondary School.   ACS 25.11.1905.
55. About the Intermediate.   ACS 9.12.1905.
56. The British Liberals and the Irish Language.   ACS 16.12.1905.
57. Live Teaching in the Secondary School.   ACS 6.1.1906.
58. The Secondary School. Thoughts and Suggestions.   ACS 13.1.1906.
59. The Secondary School: More Thoughts and Suggestions.   ACS 20.1.1906.
60. The Function of a Textbook.   ACS 27.1.1906.
61. The Secondary School: Conversation Teaching.   ACS 3.2.1906.
62. The Dublin Training College.   ACS 10.2.1906.
63. The Case for Bilingualism.   ACS 7.4.1906.
64. The Book Difficulty in Bilingual Schools.   ACS 21.4.1906.
65. The Schools.   ACS 23.6.1906.
66. An Educational Policy.   ACS 24.11.1906.
67. An Irish Education Board.   ACS 1.12.1906.
68. An Irish Education Authority.   ACS 8.12.1906.
69. The English-Speaking Tradition.   ACS 15.12.1906.
70. The Starvation Policy.   ACS 2.2.1907.
71. Trinity and the Gael.   ACS 9.2.1907.
72. Inspectors on the Language.   ACS 9.2.1907.
73. The Irish Fees.   ACS 23.3.1907.
74. The Teachers.   ACS 13.4.1907.
75. The Work of the Schools.   ACS 20.4.1907.
76. Educational Home Rule?   ACS 11.5.1907.
77. The Bill.   ACS 18.5.1907.
78. The Dead Bill and Ourselves.   ACS 25.5.1907.
79. A Forward Move.   ACS 29.6.1907.
80. The Duty of the Schools.   ACS 7.9.1907.

133. The Bishops' Statement.	ACS 7.8.1909.
134. Agriculture in Schools and the Training of Teachers.	ACS 16.10.1909.
135. Coláiste Laighean.	ACS 23.10.1909.
136. Irish in the Intermediate.	ACS 13.11.1909.
137. The Meaning of Bishop Day's Attack.	ACS 27.11.1909.
138. Teaching and its Results.	ACS 4.12.1909.
139. The School and the Nation.	ACS 1.1.1910.

II. BELGIUM AND ITS SCHOOLS 1905-1907

First Series

1. The Germ of things.	ACS 5.8.1905.
2. The Making of Belgium.	ACS 12.8.1905.
3. A Revolution and its Aftermath.	ACS 19.8.1905.
4. The Call To Arms.	ACS 16.9.1905.
5. Conscience.	ACS 23.9.1905.
6. The Revival.	ACS 30.9.1905.
7. 'In Flanders, Flemish'.	ACS 1905.
8. The Fight for the Schools.	ACS 21.10.1905.
11. A Circular from the Belgian Education Department.	ACS 25.11.1905.
12. The Direct Method.	ACS 2.12.1905.
13. A Summing-up and some Acknowledgements.	ACS 23.12.1905.
14. A Belgian Kindergarten.	ACS 30.12.1905.
15. A Belgian Kindergarten (continued).	ACS 6.1.1906.
16. A Belgian Kindergarten (continued).	ACS 13.1.1906.
17. A Belgian Kindergarten (continued).	ACS 20.1.1906.
18. A Belgian Kindergarten (continued).	ACS 27.1.1906.
19. The Primary School: The 'Series'.	ACS 3.2.1906.
20. The Primary School: The 'Series' (continued).	17.2.1906.
21. The Bilingual Principle in Practice.	ACS 3.3.1906.

*Second Series**

1. A Direct Method Lesson.	ACS 29.9.1906.
2. Comparison. Comparison − L'Image Animée.	ACS 13.10.1906.
3. Qualities: Colour.	ACS 27.10.1906.
4. Qualities: (continued): Comparison.	ACS 17.11.1906.
5. Position.	ACS 24.11.1906.
6. Action Teaching.	ACS 1.12.1906.
7. L'Image Animée in Action Teaching.	ACS 5.1.1907.
8. How to Teach Children.	ACS 26.1.1907.
9. How to Teach Children (continued).	ACS 2.2.1907
10. The Teaching of Composition.	ACS 16.2.1907.
11. Reading: Grammar.	ACS 2.3.1907.
12. The Teaching of Geography.	ACS 9.13.1907.

* The original numeration of the articles in the Second Series, is incorrect and has been corrected here.

III. EDUCATION IN THE GAELTACHT 1900-1905

1. Irish in the Schools. *Gaelic League Pamphlet,* no. 3, 1900.
2. Education in the West of Ireland. *Guth na Bliadhna,*
   11, 4, 1905, 375-380.

IV. ST. ENDA'S 1909-1913

1. From the Prospectus of Scoil Éanna. ACS 28.8.1909.
2. By Way of Comment. *An Macaomh,* I, 1,
   Cullenswood House. June 1909. 1909, 7-16.
3. By Way of Comment. *An Macaomh,* I, 2,
   Cullenswood House. Christmas 1909. 1909, 11-18.
4. By Way of Comment. *An Macaomh,* II, 3,
   The Hermitage. Christmas 1910. 1910, 9-19.
5. By Way of Comment. *An Macaomh,* II, 2,
   The Hermitage. May 1913. 1913, 5-10.
6. St. Enda's. *An Craobh Ruadh,* I, 1,
   May 1913, 79-81.

V. ANALYSIS CRITICISM AND AN IDEAL 1912-1914

1. Education under Home Rule. ACS 4.1.1913, 11.1.1913,
   (A Lecture Delivered at the Mansion 18.1.1913, 15.2.1913,
   House, Dublin, December 11th 1912). 22.2.1913, 1.3.1913.
2. The Education Problem in the *Irish Review,* II, 24,
   Home Rule Parliament. Feb. 1913, 617-620.
3. Irish Education. I, II, III. *Irish Freedom,*
   February, March,
   April 1913.
4. An Ideal in Education. *Irish Review,* IV, 40,
   June 1914, 171-173.

VI. THE MURDER MACHINE

This pamphlet which incorporates many of the topics from the articles listed in section V above was published early in 1916, and was later incorporated in the volume of the Collected Works entitled *Political Writings and Speeches.*

390